Communications
in Computer and Information Science　　2173

Editorial Board Members

Joaquim Filipe , *Polytechnic Institute of Setúbal, Setúbal, Portugal*
Ashish Ghosh, *Indian Statistical Institute, Kolkata, India*
Lizhu Zhou, *Tsinghua University, Beijing, China*

Rationale

The CCIS series is devoted to the publication of proceedings of computer science conferences. Its aim is to efficiently disseminate original research results in informatics in printed and electronic form. While the focus is on publication of peer-reviewed full papers presenting mature work, inclusion of reviewed short papers reporting on work in progress is welcome, too. Besides globally relevant meetings with internationally representative program committees guaranteeing a strict peer-reviewing and paper selection process, conferences run by societies or of high regional or national relevance are also considered for publication.

Topics

The topical scope of CCIS spans the entire spectrum of informatics ranging from foundational topics in the theory of computing to information and communications science and technology and a broad variety of interdisciplinary application fields.

Information for Volume Editors and Authors

Publication in CCIS is free of charge. No royalties are paid, however, we offer registered conference participants temporary free access to the online version of the conference proceedings on SpringerLink http://link.springer.comby means of an http referrer from the conference website and/or a number of complimentary printed copies, as specified in the official acceptance email of the event.

CCIS proceedings can be published in time for distribution at conferences or as postproceedings, and delivered in the form of printed books and/or electronically as USBs and/or e-content licenses for accessing proceedings at SpringerLink. Furthermore, CCIS proceedings are included in the CCIS electronic book series hosted in the SpringerLink digital library at http://link.springer.com/bookseries/7899. Conferences publishing in CCIS are allowed to use Online Conference Service (OCS) for managing the whole proceedings lifecycle (from submission and reviewing to preparing for publication) free of charge.

Publication process

The language of publication is exclusively English. Authors publishing in CCIS have to sign the Springer CCIS copyright transfer form, however, they are free to use their material published in CCIS for substantially changed, more elaborate subsequent publications elsewhere. For the preparation of the camera-ready papers/files, authors have to strictly adhere to the Springer CCIS Authors' Instructions and are strongly encouraged to use the CCIS LaTeX style files or templates.

Abstracting/Indexing

CCIS is abstracted/indexed in DBLP, Google Scholar, EI-Compendex, Mathematical Reviews, SCImago, Scopus. CCIS volumes are also submitted for the inclusion in ISI Proceedings.

How to start

To start the evaluation of your proposal for inclusion in the CCIS series, please send an e-mail to ccis@springer.com.

Knut Hinkelmann · Hanlie Smuts
Editors

Society 5.0

4th International Conference, Society 5.0 2024
Moka, Mauritius, June 26–28, 2024
Revised Selected Papers

Editors
Knut Hinkelmann ⓘD
FHNW University of Applied Sciences
and Arts Northwestern Switzerland
Olten, Switzerland

Hanlie Smuts ⓘD
University of Pretoria
Pretoria, Gauteng, South Africa

ISSN 1865-0929   ISSN 1865-0937 (electronic)
Communications in Computer and Information Science
ISBN 978-3-031-71411-5   ISBN 978-3-031-71412-2 (eBook)
https://doi.org/10.1007/978-3-031-71412-2

© The Editor(s) (if applicable) and The Author(s), under exclusive license
to Springer Nature Switzerland AG 2025

This work is subject to copyright. All rights are solely and exclusively licensed by the Publisher, whether the whole or part of the material is concerned, specifically the rights of translation, reprinting, reuse of illustrations, recitation, broadcasting, reproduction on microfilms or in any other physical way, and transmission or information storage and retrieval, electronic adaptation, computer software, or by similar or dissimilar methodology now known or hereafter developed.
The use of general descriptive names, registered names, trademarks, service marks, etc. in this publication does not imply, even in the absence of a specific statement, that such names are exempt from the relevant protective laws and regulations and therefore free for general use.
The publisher, the authors and the editors are safe to assume that the advice and information in this book are believed to be true and accurate at the date of publication. Neither the publisher nor the authors or the editors give a warranty, expressed or implied, with respect to the material contained herein or for any errors or omissions that may have been made. The publisher remains neutral with regard to jurisdictional claims in published maps and institutional affiliations.

This Springer imprint is published by the registered company Springer Nature Switzerland AG
The registered company address is: Gewerbestrasse 11, 6330 Cham, Switzerland

If disposing of this product, please recycle the paper.

Preface

It is with great pleasure that we write this foreword to the Proceedings of the 4th International Conference on Society 5.0, held from 26 to 28 June 2024 in Mauritius. The Society 5.0 Conference 2024 was hosted by the University of Technology in Mauritius, supported by the University of Pretoria, South Africa. This multi- and interdisciplinary conference is continuing to grow into a premier international conference series and is jointly organized by the University of Pretoria (South Africa), the FHNW University of Applied Sciences and Arts Northwestern Switzerland, the University of Camerino (Italy), the Universidad EAFIT (Colombia), the Business School of the Shenzhen Technology University (China), the Universiti Malaysia Kelantan (Malaysia) and Putra Business School (Malaysia).

We are living in an era with technologies available for software, hardware and data interconnectedness that do, and will, dictate the agenda for the future creating both challenges and opportunities for a Society 5.0. No doubt, words echoed in the New Delhi G20 Summit like the need for Creating a more Inclusive World, Driving Gender Inclusive Climate Action, Bridging the Gender Digital Divide, and Harnessing Artificial Intelligence responsibly for the Good and for all have set the agenda rolling. We are at a juncture in history where the decisions we make now will determine the future of our people and our planet. Together we have an opportunity to build a better future. We have to pursue development models that implement sustainable, inclusive and just transitions globally, while leaving no one behind. Improving access to digital services and digital public infrastructure and leveraging digital transformation opportunities to boost sustainable and inclusive growth may have to dictate the agenda for innovation so that we can promote sustainable, quality, healthy, safe and gainful employment. Innovations for sustainable and inclusive Social Good are essential for addressing the complex challenges facing our world and building a more equitable and environmentally responsible future. This conference provides an opportunity to make a meaningful contribution to a Society 5.0 in the making.

For the 2024 Society 5.0 conference we encouraged contributions from experienced and young researchers and practitioners from industry and looked forward to meeting old and new friends in June 2024.

We sincerely thank all organizers, partners, authors and reviewers without whom this conference would not have been realised.

Technical Information

We received 76 submissions, which were sent out for review to our Society 5.0 programme committee. 29 full research papers were selected for the proceedings of the Society 5.0 Conference 2024 which are published in this Springer CCIS volume (which translates to an acceptance rate of 38%) after a rigorous, single-blind review process. A further 18 submissions were invited for presentation at the conference; these papers are published as a separate report.

The programme committee comprised 59 members from 12 different countries across the world. Each paper was reviewed by three members of the programme committee in a rigorous review process. The review was organized using EasyChair, avoiding potential conflicts of interest when assigning the reviewers. Criteria such as the following were taken into consideration: Relevance to Society 5.0, Significance, Technical Quality, Scholarship and Presentation, which that included quality and clarity of writing.

Thank you to all the authors and programme committee members, and congratulations to the authors whose research was accepted for publication in these proceedings.

June 2024

Hanlie Smuts
Knut Hinkelmann

Organization

General Chair

Kesseven Padachi   University of Technology, Mauritius

Organization Committee

Aleesha Boolaky	University of Technology, Mauritius
Hemant B. Chittoo	University of Technology, Mauritius
Leenshya Gunnoo	University of Technology, Mauritius
Bhavna Mahadew	University of Technology, Mauritius
Diroubinee Narrainen	University of Technology, Mauritius
Kiran Odit-Dookhan	University of Technology, Mauritius
Needesh Ramphul	University of Technology, Mauritius
Prabha Ramseook-Munhurrun	University of Technology, Mauritius
Thakoor Sharma Geerawo	University of Technology, Mauritius
Hanlie Smuts	University of Pretoria, South Africa
Yuvraj Sunecher	University of Technology, Mauritius
Havisha Vaghjee	University of Technology, Mauritius

Steering Committee Chair

Knut Hinkelmann   FHNW University of Applied Sciences and Arts Northwestern Switzerland, Switzerland

Steering Committee

Hanlie Smuts	University of Pretoria, South Africa
Ahmad Shaharudin Abdul Latiff	Putra Business School, Malaysia
Marc Aeschbacher	FHNW University of Applied Sciences and Arts Northwestern Switzerland, Switzerland
Sara Aguilar-Barrientos	Universidad EAFIT, Colombia
Roselina Ahmad Saufi	Universiti Malaysia Kelantan, Malaysia
Flavio Corradini	University of Camerino, Italy
Noorshella Che Nawi	Universiti Malaysia Kelantan, Malaysia

Zhuoqi Ding	Shenzhen Technology University, China
Natalia Escobar Pemberthy	Universidad EAFIT, Colombia
Aurona Gerber	University of Western Cape, South Africa
Stephan Jüngling	FHNW University of Applied Sciences and Arts Northwestern Switzerland, Switzerland
Gordana Kierans	Shenzhen Technology University, China
Kesseven Padachi	University of Technology, Mauritius
Arie Hans Verkuil	FHNW University of Applied Sciences and Arts Northwestern Switzerland, Switzerland
Wan Fadzilah Wan Yusoff	Putra Business School, Malaysia

Program Committee Chairs

Hanlie Smuts	University of Pretoria, South Africa
Knut Hinkelmann	FHNW University of Applied Sciences and Arts Northwestern Switzerland, Switzerland

Program Committee

Ahmad Shaharudin Abdul Latiff	Putra Business School, Malaysia
Funmi Adebesin	University of Pretoria, South Africa
Timothy Adeliyi	University of Pretoria, South Africa
Marc Aeschbacher	FHNW University of Applied Sciences and Arts Northwestern Switzerland, Switzerland
Sara Aguilar-Barrientos	Universidad EAFIT, Colombia
Roselina Ahmad Saufi	Universiti Malaysia Kelantan, Malaysia
Luis Alvarez Sabucedo	Universidade de Vigo, Spain
Luis Anido Rifon	Universidade de Vigo, Spain
Dimitris Apostolou	University of Piraeus, Greece
Carolina Ardila-López	Universidad EAFIT, Colombia
Aleesha Boolaky	University of Technology Mauritius
Dominik Bork	Technical University of Vienna, Austria
Diletta Romana Cacciagrano	University of Camerino, Italy
Noorshella Che Nawi	Universiti Malaysia Kelantan, Malaysia
Hemant Chittoo	University of Technology, Mauritius
Flavio Corradini	University of Camerino, Italy
Zhuoqi Ding	Shenzhen Technology University, China
Sunet Eybers	University of South Africa, South Africa
Hans-Georg Fill	University of Fribourg, Switzerland
Aurona Gerber	University of the Western Cape, South Africa

Marie Hattingh	University of Pretoria, South Africa
Dikky Indrawan	IPB University, Indonesia
Mohammad Ismail	Universiti Malaysia Kelantan, Malaysia
Stephan Jüngling	FHNW University of Applied Sciences and Arts Northwestern Switzerland, Switzerland
Gordana Kierans	Shenzhen Technology University, China
Emanuele Laurenzi	FHNW University of Applied Sciences and Arts Northwestern Switzerland
George Maramba	University of Pretoria, South Africa
Andreas Martin	FHNW University of Applied Sciences and Arts Northwestern Switzerland, Switzerland
Machdel Matthee	University of Pretoria, South Africa
Heiko Maus	German Research Center for Artificial Intelligence DFKI, Germany
Siti Zaiton Mohd Hashim	Universiti Malaysia Kelantan, Malaysia
Andrea Morichetta	University of Camerino, Italy
Mohd Zulkifli Muhammad	Universiti Malaysia Kelantan, Malaysia
Uri Nahum	FHNW University of Applied Sciences and Arts Northwestern Switzerland, Switzerland
Deborah Oluwadele	University of Pretoria, South Africa
Kesseven Padachi	University of Technology, Mauritius
Yukthamarani Permarupan	Universiti Malaysia Kelantan, Malaysia
Erik Schkommodau	FHNW University of Applied Sciences and Arts Northwestern Switzerland, Switzerland
Sandra Schlick	FHNW University of Applied Sciences and Arts Northwestern Switzerland, Switzerland
Rainer Telesko	FHNW University of Applied Sciences and Arts Northwestern Switzerland, Switzerland
Marita Turpin	University of Pretoria, South Africa
Alta van der Merwe	University of Pretoria, South Africa
Phil van Deventer	University of Pretoria, South Africa
Ludger van Elst	German Research Center for Artificial Intelligence DFKI, Germany
Arie Hans Verkuil	FHNW University of Applied Sciences and Arts Northwestern Switzerland, Switzerland
Holger Wache	FHNW University of Applied Sciences and Arts Northwestern Switzerland, Switzerland
Wan Fadzilah Wan Yusoff	Putra Business School, Malaysia
Silke Waterstraat	FHNW University of Applied Sciences and Arts Northwestern Switzerland, Switzerland
Lizette Weilbach	University of Pretoria, South Africa
Hans Friedrich Witschel	FHNW University of Applied Sciences and Arts Northwestern Switzerland, Switzerland

| Mohd Fathi Yaziz | Universiti Malaysia Kelantan, Malaysia |
| Noor Raihani Zainol | Universiti Malaysia Kelantan, Malaysia |

Additional Reviewers

Krishnee Adnarain Appadoo	University of Technology, Mauritius
Petra Maria Asprion	FHNW University of Applied Sciences and Arts Northwestern Switzerland, Switzerland
Rosalina Babo	Porto Accounting and Business School, Portugal
Sheereen Banon Fauzel	University of Technology, Mauritius
Franz Barjak	FHNW University of Applied Sciences and Arts Northwestern Switzerland, Switzerland
Meera Bhugowandeen	University of Technology, Mauritius
Eric Bindah	University of Buraimi, Oman
Mathias Binswanger	FHNW University of Applied Sciences and Arts Northwestern Switzerland, Switzerland
Reinhard Botha	Noroff University College & Nelson Mandela University, South Africa
Rouma Bucktowar	University of Technology, Mauritius
Laurie Butgereit	Nelson Mandela Metropolitan University, South Africa
Robert M. Davison	City University of Hong Kong, China
Andre de la Harpe	Cape Peninsula University of Technology, South Africa
Joachim Ehrenthal	FHNW University of Applied Sciences and Arts Northwestern Switzerland, Switzerland
Barbara Eisenbart	FHNW University of Applied Sciences and Arts Northwestern Switzerland, Switzerland
Deepika Faugoo	University of Technology, Mauritius
Fabrizio Fornari	University of Camerino, Italy
Rouxan Colin Fouché	University of the Free State, South Africa
Stella Gatziu-Grivas	FHNW University of Applied Sciences and Arts Northwestern Switzerland, Switzerland
Claudio Giovanoli	FHNW University of Applied Sciences and Arts Northwestern Switzerland, Switzerland
Bertram Haskins	Nelson Mandela University, South Africa
Kevin Kativu	Nelson Mandela University, South Africa
Sean Kruger	University of Pretoria, South Africa
Josef Langerman	University of Johannesburg, South Africa
Wai Sze Leung	University of Johannesburg, South Africa
Soolakshna Lukea Bhiwajee	University of Technology, Mauritius
Bhavna Mahadew	University of Technology, Mauritius

Diroubinee Mauree-Narrainen	University of Technology, Mauritius
Tendani Mawela	University of Pretoria, South Africa
Neeta Mennega	University of Pretoria, South Africa
Rolf Meyer	FHNW University of Applied Sciences and Arts Northwestern Switzerland, Switzerland
Pascal Moriggl	FHNW University of Applied Sciences and Arts Northwestern Switzerland, Switzerland
Wynand Nel	University of the Free State, South Africa
Sue Petratos	Nelson Mandela University, South Africa
Delancia Pottas	Nelson Mandela University, South Africa
Tania Prinsloo	University of Pretoria, South Africa
Christopher Scherb	FHNW University of Applied Sciences and Arts Northwestern Switzerland, Switzerland
Bettina Schneider	FHNW University of Applied Sciences and Arts Northwestern Switzerland, Switzerland
Boopen Seetanah	University of Technology, Mauritius
Shawren Singh	University of South Africa, South Africa
Maja Spahic Bogdanovic	FHNW University of Applied Sciences and Arts Northwestern Switzerland, Switzerland
Riana Steyn	University of Pretoria, South Africa
Balakrishnen Tandarayen	Open University of Mauritius, Mauritius
Viraiyan Teeroovengadum	University of Mauritius, Mauritius
Ronald Tombe	Kisii University, Kenya
Christo Van der Westhuizen	University of Johannesburg, South Africa
Ilze Vermaak	University of Pretoria, South Africa
Christophe Viguerie	City University of Hong Kong, China

Contents

Ethical Implications of Precision Medicine for Society 5.0: A Systematic
Review 1
   Funmi Adebesin and Deborah Oluwadele

A Systematic Literature Review on How Conversational Agents are
Transforming Healthcare 14
   Nawaaz Antulay and Funmi Adebesin

Student-Mediated Knowledge Exchange in Switzerland 25
   Franz Barjak and Fabian Heimsch

Unveiling the *"Vulnerability Cycle"* of Migrant Workers in Mauritius:
Applying a Grounded Theory Approach to Health and Wellbeing
of Migrant Workers 41
   *Sanjayduth Bhundhoo, Preeya Vijayalakshmee Coolen,
   and Roslyn S. Fraser*

More Bureaucracy Instead of More Security or More Fairness: The Effects
of AI Regulation 57
   Mathias Binswanger

The Impact of Generative AI on Creative Professionals in Marketing:
A Systematic Review and Practical Framework 68
   Adriaan Coetzer, Lizette Weilbach, Marié Hattingh, and Shireen Panchoo

Towards a Smart City Sustainability Tracker for Achieving SDG 11 in Cities ... 84
   Miriam Mei Yi Dall'Agnolo, Stephan Jüngling, and Hanlie Smuts

Enhancing Cross-Cultural Teaching and Learning: An Instructor's View
on Africanization 98
   Sunet Eybers, Jan H. Kroeze, and Corne J. van Staden

Closing the Gap: Leveraging Recorded Video Lessons for Digital
Inclusion in Rural South Africa 111
   Rouxan Colin Fouché and Wynand Nel

Examining Smart Contracts Within Mauritian Contract Law: Assessing
Their Compatibility with Existing Legal Frameworks 123
   Viraj Fulena

The Influence of Board Characteristics on Environmental Sustainability
in Northern Europe 136
   Thakoor Sharma Geerawo and Bhavna Mahadew

Collaborative Online International Learning COIL: Trends, Definition &
Typology 152
   Susan Goeldi and Oscar Thees

Towards a Sustainable Future: Understanding Green Consumerism
in Mauritius 173
   Leenshya Gunnoo, Eric Bindah, and Nousrat Banu Emambocus

Assessing the Impact of Decent Work on the Mental Health of Female
Carers in Mauritius Through the Psychology of Working Theory 187
   Dayalutchmee Kodye-Domah, Leena Devi Sobha,
   and Soolakshna Desai Lukea-Bhiwajee

Transcultural Leadership and Sustainable Development in the Digital Era:
Navigating the 4IR in South Africa 207
   Sean Kruger

A Decision-Support Approach for University Incubators 218
   Emanuele Laurenzi, Dario Meyer, and Patrick Moesch

Advancing Financial Inclusion and Data Ethics: The Role of Alternative
Credit Scoring 229
   Keoitshepile Machikape and Deborah Oluwadele

Short Duration, Lasting Impression: The Role of Short-Term Study Trips
in Cross-Cultural Learning 242
   Dario Meyer, Alice Frey, and Rolf Meyer

The Influence of Tribal Leaders in the Adoption of e-Banking Products
in the Kingdom of eSwatini: Using Social Influence Theory 254
   Sandile Thamie Mhlanga and Josef Langerman

The Benefits and Challenges of Using Datathons as a Method of Learning
Data Analytics 269
   Nkosikhona Theoren Msweli and Tendani Mawela

Exploring the Innovation Capabilities of Mauritian SMEs: A Factor
Analysis Approach 282
   Kesseven Padachi, Diroubinee Mauree-Narrainen, Aleesha Boolaky,
   Hemant Chittoo, Needesh Ramphul, and Lizette Weilbach

CyMed: A Framework for Testing Connected Medical Devices 293
  Christopher Scherb, Adrian Hadayah, Luc Bryan Heitz,
  Hermann Grieder, and Petra Maria Asprion

Checklist for Effective Knowledge Visualization 305
  Iddo-Imri Scholtz and Hanlie Smuts

Business Agility to Cope with the Increasing National Minimum Wage
After the Covid-19 Pandemic: A Case of SMEs in Mauritius 320
  Trisheeta Sewdin, Hemant B. Chittoo, and Needesh Ramphul

Harnessing Technology for Mangrove Research in the Western Indian
Ocean to Enhance Climate Change Resilience 334
  Reshma Sunkur, Komali Kantamaneni, Chandradeo Bokhoree,
  Upaka Rathnayake, and Michael Fernando

Unveiling the Power of Apomediation: Perspectives from Individuals
Living with Autoimmune Disease 348
  Eldridge van der Westhuizen, Dalenca Pottas, and Sue Petratos

A Conceptual Framework for Digitalized Payment Systems in South Africa 366
  Mvelo Walaza and Sunet Eybers

Exploring the Innovation Capabilities of South African SMEs: A Principal
Component Analysis Approach 378
  Lizette Weilbach, Hanlie Smuts, Aleesha Boolaky, Hemant Chittoo,
  Diroubinee Mauree-Narrainen, Kesseven Padachi, and Needesh Ramphul

Predictors of Workplace Satisfaction: Working Onsite Versus Working
from Home 391
  Xinhua Wittmann and Daria Klyushina

Author Index 403

Ethical Implications of Precision Medicine for Society 5.0: A Systematic Review

Funmi Adebesin[✉] and Deborah Oluwadele

Department of Informatics, University of Pretoria, Pretoria, South Africa
{funmi.adebesin,deborah.oluwadele}@up.ac.za

Abstract. Genomic medicine, which entails the use of an individual's genomic data to guide healthcare, has the potential to revolutionize healthcare delivery through precision medicine (PM). PM is an innovative healthcare approach that goes beyond the traditional one-size-fits-all practice. PM integrates a diverse range of individualized data to provide targeted medical interventions. This approach is intricately linked to the United Nations Sustainable Development Goal 3 and a human-centered society, as envisioned by Society 5.0. Recent advancements in technological innovations, including artificial intelligence (AI) and big data, are becoming the catalyst for the integration of extensive datasets to formulate predictive models that enable individualized care. However, along with the promise of PM are several ethical issues that threaten health equity. This paper presents the result of a systematic literature review which investigated the dimensions of ethical issues in PM. We retrieved 355 peer-reviewed papers published between 2019 and 2023 from three databases using author-defined search phrases and three quality assessment criteria. Thirty-one papers were analyzed using qualitative content analysis. An important outcome of our analysis is a visual representation of the landscape of ethical concerns in PM through the mapping of the context of PM ethical concerns (e.g., genomic analysis and medical specialization), their dimensions (e.g., discrimination, privacy, and informed consent) and the implications of the ethical issues reported within these contexts. Given the potential of PM as an enabler of individualized healthcare, policymakers, healthcare providers, and researchers must address the ethical issues associated with PM to ensure equity in healthcare delivery.

Keywords: Artificial Intelligence · Big Data · Ethical Concerns · Genomics · Precision Medicine · Predictive Medicine

1 Introduction

In recent years, the field of genomic medicine has significantly advanced, offering unprecedented personalized healthcare and disease management opportunities. Genomic medicine, which involves the use of an individual's genetic information to guide medical decisions, has the potential to revolutionize healthcare delivery and outcomes (Roth, 2019). One of the main advances of genomic medicine is Precision Medicine - an innovative approach to healthcare that goes beyond traditional diagnostic methods based solely

© The Author(s), under exclusive license to Springer Nature Switzerland AG 2025
K. Hinkelmann and H. Smuts (Eds.): Society 5.0 2024, CCIS 2173, pp. 1–13, 2025.
https://doi.org/10.1007/978-3-031-71412-2_1

on observable signs and symptoms, to the integration of a diverse range of individualized data, including clinical, lifestyle, genetic, and other biomarker information, to provide more targeted and personalized medical interventions (König et al., 2017). One of the benefits of precision medicine is exemplified by the frequent reference to the successful determination of the human epidermal growth factor receptor (HER2) status in breast cancer patients (Hingorani et al., 2013), the identification of fibroblast growth factor receptors gene aberrations and rearrangements, and the treatment of allergic rhinitis (Licari et al., 2019), to mention a few.

Precision medicine has been widely adopted in various medical fields and disease management. In cancer treatment, specific biomarkers like BCR-ABL in chronic myeloid leukemia and EML4-ALK in lung cancer are targeted with drugs like Imatinib and Crizotinib, respectively. Other applications include using genetic information to guide interventions, such as avoiding prothrombotic drugs in thrombosis patients with Factor V Leiden mutation and using highly active antiretroviral therapy based on CD4+ T cell count and HIV viral load in HIV/AIDS. Precision medicine also extends to cardiovascular diseases, where genetic variants like CYP2C19 in coronary artery disease influence drug choices like Clopidogrel. This approach is similarly applied in pulmonary diseases like cystic fibrosis with the G551D mutation, as well as in renal diseases, infectious diseases, endocrine diseases, metabolic diseases, neurology, psychiatry, pharmacogenomics, and ophthalmology, showcasing the breadth of its impact across diverse medical conditions (Jameson & Longo, 2015).

In 2016, the Japanese government introduced the concept of Society 5.0 in its 5th basic plan for Science and Technology. Society 5.0 envisions an advanced and sustainable society driven by technological innovations like artificial intelligence (AI), cloud computing, and the Internet of Things (IoT). These technologies enable the collection and analysis of vast amounts of data, enhancing various societal functions. Society 5.0 aims to achieve sustainable development and align with the United Nations (UN) sustainable development goals (SDGs) (Fukuyama, 2018). In Society 5.0, achieving SDG-3, ensuring healthy lives and promoting well-being for all ages, can be facilitated through the incorporation and integration of novel technologies into healthcare practices (Dlamini et al., 2023). This concept emphasizes the use of modern technology solutions to ensure health equity, social upliftment, and equality (Marima et al., 2023). Society 5.0 envisions a human-centered society that leverages technological advancements, including genomics, to enhance the quality of life and address societal challenges.

In precision medicine, the future trajectory appears poised toward the integration of extensive datasets to formulate predictive models that can significantly enhance individualized patient care. This evolution suggests a paradigm shift towards tailored treatments based on comprehensive data analytics. A pivotal role is anticipated for AI in this context, given its potential to process and interpret the vast and complex datasets essential for developing these predictive models. The utilization of AI in precision medicine holds promise for unlocking valuable insights and solutions, thus ushering in a new era of healthcare customization and optimization (Verstegen & Ito, 2019). However, along with its promises, precision medicine also brings forth a myriad of concerns and considerations that must be carefully examined and addressed (Dlamini, 2023).

In the pursuit of precision medicine, two key frameworks have emerged: innovation policy and data-driven medicine. However, challenges have arisen simultaneously. Firstly, precision medicine is increasingly seen as a source of economic gain rather than improved health outcomes, leading to a focus on business opportunities over medical advancements. Secondly, the focus has shifted from molecular biology and tissue samples to managing diverse health-related data, indicating the complexity of modern precision medicine (Tarkkala et al., 2019). Furthermore, given that precision medicine requires a vast amount of information, the threats to data privacy especially in the context of ubiquitous computing and the Internet of Things where information can be gathered without patient permission and commercialized or used for other activities such as criminal investigation (Dlamini, 2023) is significantly amplified. Problems such as legal and ethical issues surrounding the privacy and protection of information, safety and trust in these new technologies pose barriers to leveraging precision medicine (Brothers & Rothstein, 2015), and in the context of society 5.0, must be resolved to realize the benefits of smart technologies in healthcare for the futurist society.

As a first step to solving these problems, this paper presents a systematic review of the literature (SLR) to identify the ethical concerns and dimensions of precision medicine. Conducting an SLR of the ethical implications of precision medicine for Society 5.0 provides a comprehensive understanding of the issues and concerns in the domain by identifying trends and context in the ethical discourse surrounding the subject and evidence-based insights by evaluating available evidence.

By examining existing literature, this paper seeks to provide a comprehensive mapping and overview of the ethical landscape surrounding precision medicine and stimulate further discussion and research in this crucial area. The findings of this review will not only contribute to the ethical discourse on precision medicine but also provide valuable insights for policymakers, healthcare providers, researchers, and other stakeholders involved in the implementation of precision medicine.

The remaining sections of the paper include the research method in Sect. 2, the results in Sect. 3, and the discussions and conclusion in Sect. 4.

2   Research Method

This study was based on the Preferred Reporting Items for Systematic Reviews and Meta-Analyses (PRISMA) guideline by Page et al. (2021). The research questions that we addressed in the paper were the following:

- What are the different dimensions of ethical concerns associated with precision medicine?
- What are the implications of the identified ethical concerns on precision medicine?

We sourced peer-reviewed papers from three databases (Web of Science (WOS), Scopus, and PubMed) using the search string ("Ethical considerations" OR "Ethical issues" OR "Ethical concerns") AND ("personalised medicine" OR "personalized medicine" OR "Precision medicine"). The databases were filtered to retrieve only papers that were published between 2019 and 2023, to ensure that we retrieve recent research papers that were published in the preceding five years. A total of 355 sources were retrieved from the three databases on 5 December 2023.

Following an initial screening, we deleted 77 duplicate sources that were published across the three databases. Thereafter, we screened the remaining 278 sources to ensure that they met our inclusion criteria. This process resulted in the exclusion of five non-English sources, nine editorials, one position paper, and 124 reviews. Three additional sources published before 2019 passed through the databases' filters and were subsequently excluded. An additional 77 research papers that were not aligned with the research objectives were excluded. Thereafter, the remaining 59 papers were assessed for quality using the following quality assessment (QA) criteria:

1. Does the paper adequately discuss ethical issues, considerations, or concerns related to precision medicine?
2. Does the paper discuss the different dimensions or components of ethical issues, considerations, or concerns related to precision medicine?
3. Does the paper discuss how ethical issues, considerations, or concerns could impact the potential transformational role of precision medicine?

For QA 1, papers that only mentioned ethical issues associated with precision medicine were awarded a score of 0, those that provided a limited explanation were awarded 0.5, while those that provided adequate explanation were awarded 1. For QA2, sources that did not have any ethical concern or issue were awarded a score of 0, those that provided at least one ethical concern or issue were awarded 0.5, while those that provided two or more concerns or issues were awarded 1. For QA3, sources that did not discuss the impact of ethical issues on precision medicine were awarded a score of 0, those that provided at least one impact were awarded 0.5, while those that provided two or more impacts were awarded 1. Thus, a paper could have a maximum score of 3. Only sources that obtained at least 1.5 were considered for inclusion in the SLR. Following the QA process, a total of 31 papers were included in the final set of papers that were analyzed. Figure 1 provides a graphical illustration of the source selection process.

We analyzed the 31 papers using descriptive statistics to count paper distributions by the year of publications and document type. Qualitative content analysis was used to extract concepts that were used to map the dimensions of ethical concerns with their contexts. The results of our analysis are presented in Sect. 3.

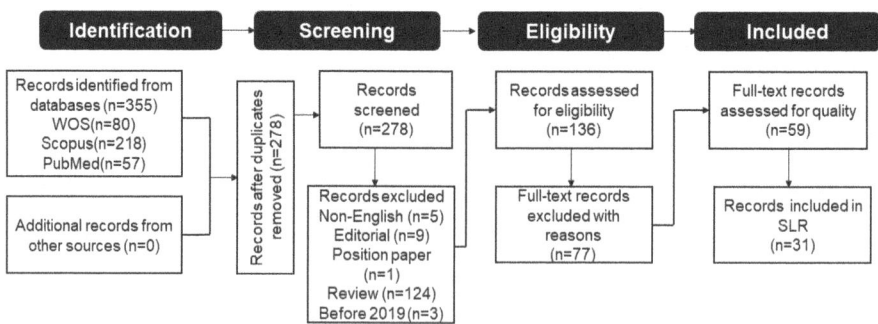

Fig. 1. Source selection process

3   Result

3.1   Basic Quantitative Analysis Results

The outcome of a descriptive statistics analysis of the 31 papers included in the SLR by their publication year showed that four papers were published in 2019 and 2022, respectively. There were five papers published in 2020, with nine in 2021 and 2023, respectively (see Fig. 2a). As illustrated in Fig. 2b, most of the papers included in the SLR were articles (20), followed by book chapters (8), and conference papers (3).

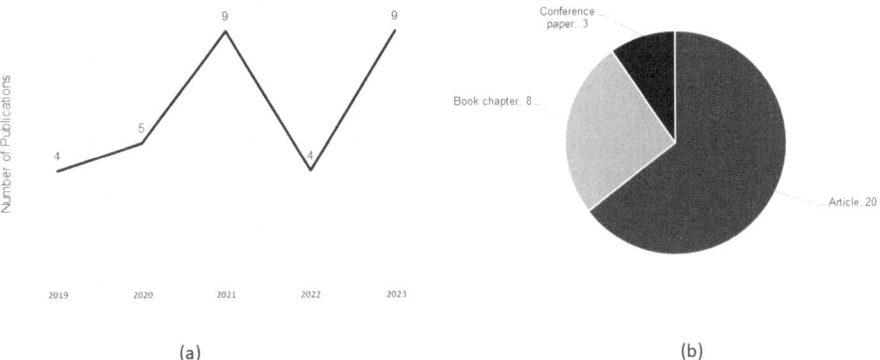

(a)   (b)

Fig. 2. (a) Number of publications by year (b) Paper distribution by document type

3.2   Qualitative Content Analysis Results

3.2.1   Dimensions of Ethical Concerns

Our qualitative content analysis of the 31 papers in the SLR revealed 16 dimensions of ethical concerns related to PM (see Fig. 3). One of the important dimensions of ethical concerns that we identified was *Equity/Access*. Equity and access are related concepts that entail ensuring fair access to healthcare by different population groups irrespective of their position in society or geographical location. This dimension was identified from 14 sources in the SLR (Bhayat et al., 2023; Grizzle, 2019; Housholder, 2021; Morgan, 2019; Ogamba et al., 2023; Ong et al., 2021; Pichini et al., 2022; Rauter et al., 2021; Riddle et al., 2023; Sarwar, 2023a; Schaefer et al., 2019; Toh et al., 2021; Vogt & Hofmann, 2022; Yadav & Thelma, 2021) and is one of the two ethical concerns with the highest number of occurrences. Another dimension of ethical concern that we identified centered around *Discrimination*. In the context of PM, discrimination is the unfair treatment of an individual or a population group based on their disease profile or genetic composition (Dennison et al., 2023; Ong et al., 2021; Sarwar, 2023a). The discrimination dimension was extracted from 14 of the papers included in the SLR (Carter et al., 2020; Dennison et al., 2023; Grizzle, 2019; Lysaght et al., 2020; McGuire et al., 2020; Mehlman & Parasidis, 2021; Ogamba et al., 2023; Ong et al., 2021; Pichini et al., 2022; Rawat et al., 2023; Riddle et al., 2023; Sarwar, 2023a; Schaefer et al., 2019; Sravani et al., 2023).

Privacy concern, identified in 13 papers (Brault & Aucouturier, 2022; Clasen et al., 2021; Far, 2023; McGuire et al., 2020; Mehlman & Parasidis, 2021; Moore, 2020; Morgan, 2019; Ogamba et al., 2023; Ong et al., 2021; Rawat et al., 2023; Sarwar, 2023a, b; Sravani et al., 2023), is another ethical issue that surrounds PM. Privacy breaches of genetic data have the potential to cause discrimination. Privacy is closely linked to *Data Security and Confidentiality*, a dimension of PM ethical concern with 10 occurrences (Carter et al., 2020; Clasen et al., 2021; Grizzle, 2019; Lysaght et al., 2020; Ogamba et al., 2023; Ong et al., 2021; Rawat et al., 2023; Sarwar, 2023a, b; Sravani et al., 2023). Because genomic data contains personally identifiable information (PII) (Sarwar, 2023a; Sravani et al., 2023), unauthorized access could result in *Data misuse*, another ethical concern extracted from two papers (Lysaght et al., 2020; Ong et al., 2021).

From the 31 papers included in the SLR, *Informed Consent* featured as a PM ethical issue of concern in 10 papers (Brault & Aucouturier, 2022; Carter et al., 2020; Dennison et al., 2023; Lysaght et al., 2020; McGuire et al., 2020; Pichini et al., 2022; Rawat et al., 2023; Sarwar, 2023a, b; Sravani et al., 2023). Another ethical issue closely linked to informed consent is *Patient Autonomy and Freedom*, identified in six of the sources included in the SLR (de Wert & Dondorp, 2019; Dennison et al., 2023; Far, 2023; Ó Cathaoir, 2021; Sarwar, 2023b; Toh et al., 2021). Autonomy and freedom deal with patients' right to decide on their treatment or participation in genomic research. Ethical concerns around *Transparency and Trust* are featured in eight of the sources included in the SLR (Bhayat et al., 2023; Housholder, 2021; Lysaght et al., 2020; Rawat et al., 2023; Sarwar, 2023a, b; Schaefer et al., 2019; Vogt & Hofmann, 2022). A corollary of transparency is trust. This requires openness regarding the storage of genetic data and how it will be used (Rawat et al., 2023; Sarwar, 2023a).

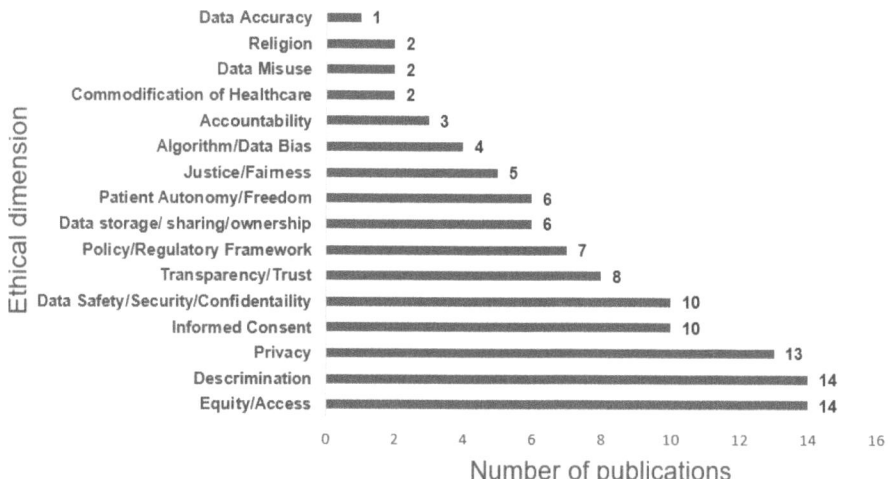

Fig. 3. Number of publications by dimensions of ethical concerns

We also identified concerns around *Data Storage, Sharing and Ownership* from six of the sources included in the SLR (Carter et al., 2020; McGuire et al., 2020; Ó Cathaoir,

2021; Ong et al., 2021; Sarwar, 2023a, b). The requirement to access large amounts of biomedical data in the context of genetics and AI creates concern over the potential for data breaches and the need for secure data storage. *Justice/Fairness* is related to equity/access, a concern extracted from five papers (Brault & Aucouturier, 2022; de Wert & Dondorp, 2019; Dennison et al., 2023; Housholder, 2021; Vogt & Hofmann, 2022), reflecting the need to ensure that PM benefits the population at large, not just a selected few. Two sources (Toh et al., 2021; Vogt & Hofmann, 2022) mentioned concerns around the *Commodification of Healthcare*, which could arise when only the rich in society can access specialized genomic treatment. Ethical concerns around *Algorithm/Data Bias* were extracted from four sources (Far, 2023; Moore, 2020; Rawat et al., 2023; Sarwar, 2023a), epitomizing genuine worry that minority groups may be underrepresented in biomedical/genomic research. We extracted ethical issues of *Accountability* from three papers (Bhayat et al., 2023; Carter et al., 2020; Vogt & Hofmann, 2022). This relates to concerns over who should be held accountable for incorrect decisions in the context of AI genomics. *Religion,* as a PM ethical dimension, was extracted from two papers (Shabana, 2022; Toh et al., 2021) and centers around the concern of different faith groups on genetic modification, seen as 'playing God'. Concerns over the lack of, or limited *Policy/Regulatory Framework* to govern the practice of PM was extracted from seven papers (Brunak et al., 2020; Carter et al., 2020; Lysaght et al., 2020; Ó Cathaoir, 2021; Pichini et al., 2022; Rawat et al., 2023; Toh et al., 2021). Finally, the potential for *Data Accuracy* being compromised, especially if genetic data is not correctly coded, was extracted from one source (Sarwar, 2023a).

3.2.2   Contexts of Ethical Concerns

We analyzed the contexts within which ethical concerns were reported in the papers included in the SLR. The 14 contexts of ethical concerns in PM were grouped into seven clusters (see Fig. 4). This enabled us to organize the terms based on their thematic similarities, making it easier to understand the different contexts.

The *Medical Specialization* context cluster includes Dermatology (Housholder, 2021), Oncology (Bhayat et al., 2023; Carter et al., 2020; Far, 2023; McGuire et al., 2020; Morgan, 2019), and Paediatric (Ó Cathaoir, 2021). These terms are clustered together as they represent specific medical specializations where PM is often applied, raising ethical concerns related to patient care and treatment outcomes. The *Genomic Analysis* cluster includes Human Genomic Editing (Yadav & Thelma, 2021), Genomic Screening (de Wert & Dondorp, 2019; Dennison et al., 2023; Grizzle, 2019; Pichini et al., 2022), Genomic Testing (Clasen et al., 2021; Mehlman & Parasidis, 2021), and the Biobanking contexts (Brault & Aucouturier, 2022). These terms are grouped because they all involve genetic analysis and manipulation, raising ethical concerns around privacy, consent, and potential misuse of genetic information. The *Technological* context cluster includes studies that represent the technological tools and methods such as AI, Big data and Machine Learning (ML) used in precision medicine, raising ethical concerns related to data security, algorithms bias, and the need for transparency in decision-making (Brunak et al., 2020; Sarwar, 2023b; Schaefer et al., 2019; Sravani et al., 2023; Willems et al., 2021). The *Healthcare Practices* cluster consists of the General (Sarwar, 2023a) and Personalized Nutrition contexts (Moore, 2020), which were clustered together as they represent general healthcare practices and the application of personalized approaches to nutrition, raising ethical concerns related to access to care, equity, and informed decision-making.

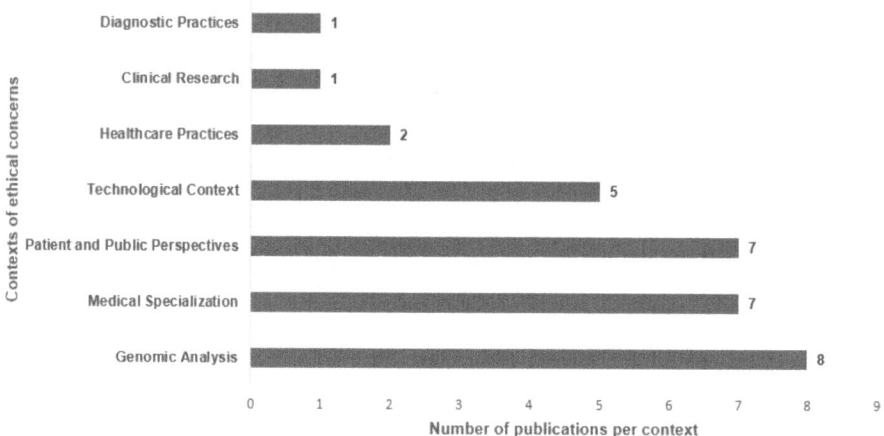

Fig. 4. Contexts of ethical concerns in precision medicine

The *Patient and Public Perspectives* cluster consists of Religious Perspective (Shabana, 2022; Toh et al., 2021) and Citizen/Public Perspective contexts (Lysaght et al., 2020; Ogamba et al., 2023; Ong et al., 2021; Rauter et al., 2021; Riddle et al., 2023), representing different perspectives on PM, raising ethical concerns related to cultural beliefs, values, and societal impacts of precision medicine. The *Clinical Research* cluster consists of the study expressing ethical concerns in the Clinical Trial context (Vogt & Hofmann, 2022). This term is grouped separately because it represents the conduct of clinical trials in PM, raising ethical concerns related to patient safety, informed consent, and the ethical conduct of research. Finally, the *Diagnostic Practices* context consists of the study that explores ethical concerns in Disease Diagnostics (Rawat et al., 2023). This term is grouped separately because it represents the diagnostic practices used in precision medicine, raising ethical concerns related to the accuracy of diagnoses, patient privacy, and the appropriate use of diagnostic tests.

3.2.3 The Landscape of Ethical Concerns

The ethical concerns raised in the different contexts of PM highlight various ethical implications, particularly concerning the use of AI and genetic testing. It raises concerns about accountability for incorrect AI judgments and the potential economic barriers for minority groups or under-resourced countries to access and maintain AI devices (Bhayat et al., 2023; Brault & Aucouturier, 2022). Far (2023) stressed the potential of AI in oncology to revolutionize cancer care. However, there is a need for clear guidelines and regulations to ensure the ethical use of AI to balance technological advancements with ethical considerations (Sravani et al., 2023). Scholars have also emphasized the ethical considerations in genetic testing, such as privacy, consent, and the potential misuse of genetic information by insurance companies (Clasen et al., 2021; Dennison et al., 2023; Grizzle, 2019; Lysaght et al., 2020; Ogamba et al., 2023; Ong et al., 2021). Figure 5 highlights the ethical landscape of precision medicine by mapping the contexts in precision medicine to the dimensions of ethical concerns expressed in the domain, revealing the importance of addressing these ethical challenges identified by scholars to ensure the responsible and beneficial use of AI and genetic testing in precision medicine.

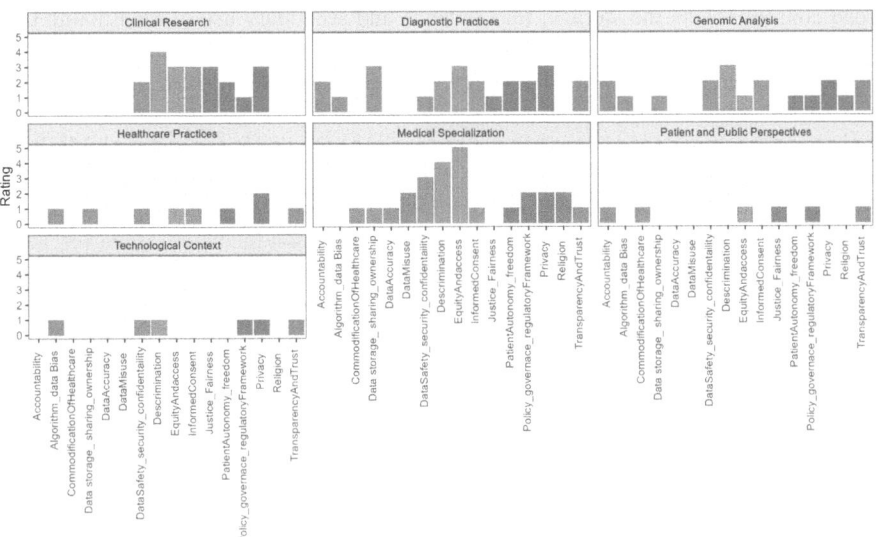

Fig. 5. The landscape of ethical concerns in precision medicine

4   Discussions and Conclusion

The primary goal of this paper was to investigate the ethical concerns associated with PM from extant literature and their implications on precision medicine, using an SLR. Our analysis showed that the Top-3 ethical dimensions were (i) equity/access, (ii) discrimination, and privacy. Extant literature emphasized the need to balance individual rights to treatment without infringing on the rights of minority groups or even discriminating against them by not offering them similar opportunities (Dennison et al., 2023; Housholder, 2021; Morgan, 2019). There is concern that low-resourced countries may not be able to take advantage of PM due to financial constraints (Bhayat et al., 2023). Within the context of the adoption of AI to support PM, discrimination and bias could arise from the underrepresentation of marginalized subgroups in the data used to train ML systems (Carter et al., 2020; Sarwar, 2023a). The potential for the violation of privacy is an important ethical concern from the perspective of patients. Citizens are rightly worried that unauthorized access to genetic data through security breaches could infringe on their privacy, which could result in discrimination by insurance companies, employers, or even society at large (Lysaght et al., 2020; McGuire et al., 2020; Ogamba et al., 2023; Ong et al., 2021; Sarwar, 2023a).

An important aspect of ethical concern is informed consent. Individuals involved in studies that require the collection of biomedical data, e.g., cancer screening, should be informed of the purpose and use of the data collected (Brault & Aucouturier, 2022; Dennison et al., 2023; Sarwar, 2023a). While consent is typically sought when an individual enrols in genetic screening studies (Lysaght et al., 2020), information about, and the implication of giving 'broad consent' should be provided and obtained from those who participate in genomic research (Brault & Aucouturier, 2022; Lysaght et al., 2020). Broad consent covers the storage, maintenance and secondary use of identifiable bio-data (Brault & Aucouturier, 2022). Where children are involved in genomic research, informed consent becomes a challenge and will necessitate resorting to assent (i.e., the child's agreement to participate in a study) (McGuire et al., 2020). McGuire et al. (2020) emphasized the importance of modifying information provided based on the child's level of comprehension when obtaining their assent. Vitally, religious groups are also concerned about the potential of PM to delve into the realm of the divine. In essence, faith groups are not necessarily averse to the promise of precision medicine. However, there may be pushback when medicine encroaches on the Power of God to fashion an individual as He pleases. Although developed countries from the Global North have laws that protect health data (Carter et al., 2020; Ó Cathaoir, 2021), there is also a need for policies and regulations by countries from the Global South, that govern areas like the application of AI in PM, the misuse of biomedical data for commercial purposes and discrimination based on an individual's predisposition to a specific disease (Carter et al., 2020; Lysaght et al., 2020; Pichini et al., 2022).

This paper has implications for researchers, medical professionals, and policymakers. Given the potential of precision medicine as an enabler of the vision of Society 5.0, ethical concerns that may impede the full realization of the benefits of PM must be addressed through collaborations between researchers and medical professionals, working together with policymakers to ensure that regulations are aligned with the technological advancements that enable precision medicine.

Acknowledgement. This study was partially funded by the South African National Research Foundation under the Incentive Funding for Rated Researchers.

References

Bhayat, A., Hull, R., Chauke-Malinga, N., Dlamini, Z.: Artificial intelligence-based medical devices revolution in cancer screening: impact into clinical practice. In: Dlamini, Z. (ed.) Artificial Intelligence and Precision Oncology: Bridging Cancer Research and Clinical Decision Support, pp. 195–215. Springer, Cham (2023). https://doi.org/10.1007/978-3-031-21506-3_10

Brault, N., Aucouturier, E.: Ethical horizons of biobank-based artificial intelligence in biomedical research. Artif. Intell. Comput. Dyn. Biomed. Res. **8**, 265 (2022)

Brothers, K.B., Rothstein, M.A.: Ethical, legal and social implications of incorporating personalized medicine into healthcare. Per Med. **12**(1), 43–51 (2015). https://doi.org/10.2217/pme.14.65

Brunak, S., et al.: Towards standardization guidelines for in silico approaches in personalized medicine. J. Integrative Bioinform. **17**(2–3) (2020). https://doi.org/10.1515/jib-2020-0006

Carter, S.M., Rogers, W., Win, K.T., Frazer, H., Richards, B., Houssami, N.: The ethical, legal and social implications of using artificial intelligence systems in breast cancer care. Breast **49**, 25–32 (2020). https://doi.org/10.1016/j.breast.2019.10.001

Clasen, K., Gani, C., Schroeder, C., Riess, O., Zips, D., Schöffski, O., Clasen, S.: Patient views on genetics and functional imaging for precision medicine: a willingness-to-pay analysis. Personalized Med. **19**(2), 103–112 (2021). https://doi.org/10.2217/pme-2021-0067

de Wert, G., Dondorp, W.: Opportunistic genomic screening: ethical exploration. In: Tibben, A., Biesecker, B.B. (eds.) Clinical Genome Sequencing, pp. 203–224. Academic Press (2019). https://doi.org/10.1016/B978-0-12-813335-4.00012-X

Dennison, R.A., Usher-Smith, J.A., John, S.D.: The ethics of risk-stratified cancer screening. Eur. J. Cancer **187**, 1–6 (2023). https://doi.org/10.1016/j.ejca.2023.03.023

Dlamini, Z.: Society 5.0 and Next Generation Healthcare: Patient-Focused and Technology-Assisted Precision Therapies. Springer, Cham (2023)

Dlamini, Z., Miya, T.V., Hull, R., Molefi, T., Khanyile, R., de Vasconcellos, J.F.: Society 5.0: realizing next-generation healthcare. In: Dlamini, Z. (ed.) Society 5.0 and Next Generation Healthcare: Patient-Focused and Technology-Assisted Precision Therapies, pp. 1–30. Springer, Cham (2023). https://doi.org/10.1007/978-3-031-36461-7_1

Far, F.B.: Artificial intelligence ethics in precision oncology: Balancing advancements in technology with patient privacy and autonomy. Explor Target Antitumor Ther **4**(4), 685–689 (2023). https://doi.org/10.37349/etat.2023.00160

Fukuyama, M.: Society 5.0: aiming for a new human-centered society. Jpn. Spotlight **27**(5), 47–50 (2018)

Grizzle, W.E.: Ethical and regulatory issues in the use of human tissues to support precision medicine. J. Health Care Poor Underserved **30**(4 Suppl.), 66 (2019). https://doi.org/10.1353/hpu.2019.0117

Hingorani, A.D., et al.: Prognosis research strategy (PROGRESS) 4: stratified medicine research. BMJ: Br. Med. J. **346**, e5793 (2013). https://doi.org/10.1136/bmj.e5793

Housholder, A.L.: Genetic medicine arrives in the outpatient clinic: Ethical concerns for dermatologists. In: Bercovitch, L., Perlis, C.S., Stoff, B.K., Grant-Kels, J.M. (eds.) Dermatoethics: Contemporary Ethics and Professionalism in Dermatology, pp. 25–38. Springer, Cham (2021). https://doi.org/10.1007/978-3-030-56861-0_3

König, I.R., Fuchs, O., Hansen, G., Mutius, E., Kopp, M.V.: What is precision medicine? Eur. Respir. J. **50**(4), 1700391 (2017). https://doi.org/10.1183/13993003.00391-2017

Larry Jameson, J., Longo, D.L.: Precision medicine-Personalized, problematic, and promising. Obstet. Gynecol. Surv. **70**(10), 612–614 (2015). https://doi.org/10.1097/01.ogx.0000472121.21647.38

Licari, A., Castagnoli, R., Tosca, M.A., Marseglia, G., Ciprandi, G.: Personalized therapies for the treatment of allergic rhinitis. Expert Rev. Precis. Med. Drug Dev. **4**(5), 275–281 (2019). https://doi.org/10.1080/23808993.2019.1681896

Lysaght, T., et al.: "Who is watching the watchdog?": ethical perspectives of sharing health-related data for precision medicine in Singapore. BMC Med. Ethics **21**(1), 118 (2020). https://doi.org/10.1186/s12910-020-00561-8

Marima, R., et al.: Health informatics applications in healthcare and society 5.0. In: Dlamini, Z. (ed.) Society 5.0 and Next Generation Healthcare: Patient-Focused and Technology-Assisted Precision Therapies, pp. 31–49. Springer, Cham (2023). https://doi.org/10.1007/978-3-031-36461-7_2

McGuire, A.L., Pereira, S., Gutierrez, A.M., Majumder, M.A.: Ethics in genetic and genomic research. In: Mazur, K.A., Berg, S.L. (eds.) Ethical Issues in Pediatric Hematology/Oncology, pp. 91–110. Springer, Cham (2020). https://doi.org/10.1007/978-3-030-22684-8_6

Mehlman, M.J., Parasidis, E.: Predictive genetic testing by the U.S. military: legal and ethical issues. Mil. Med. **186**(7–8), 726–732 (2021). https://doi.org/10.1093/milmed/usab011

Moore, J.B.: From personalised nutrition to precision medicine: the rise of consumer genomics and digital health. In: Proceedings of the Nutrition Society (2020)

Morgan, G.: Issues and ethical considerations in pharmaco-oncogenomics. In: Ruiz-Garcia, E., Astudillo-de la Vega, H. (eds.) Translational Research and Onco-Omics Applications in the Era of Cancer Personal Genomics, pp. 91–101. Springer, Cham (2019). https://doi.org/10.1007/978-3-030-24100-1_6

Ó Cathaoir, K.: The invisible child of personalized medicine. J. Law Biosci. **8**(2), 1–21 (2021). https://doi.org/10.1093/jlb/lsab029

Ogamba, C.F., et al.: Perceptions of Nigerian medical students regarding their preparedness for precision medicine: a cross-sectional survey in Lagos, Nigeria. BMC Med. Educ. **23**(879) (2023). https://doi.org/10.1186/s12909-023-04841-w

Ong, S., Ling, J., Ballantyne, A., Lysaght, T., Xafis, V.: Perceptions of 'precision' and 'personalised' medicine in Singapore and associated ethical issues. Asian Bioethics Rev. **13**(2), 179–194 (2021). https://doi.org/10.1007/s41649-021-00165-3

Page, M.J., et al.: The PRISMA 2020 statement: an updated guideline for reporting systematic reviews. Int. J. Surg. **88**, 105906 (2021). https://doi.org/10.1016/j.ijsu.2021.105906

Pichini, A., et al.: Developing a national newborn genomes program: an approach driven by ethics, engagement and co-design. Front. Genet. **13**, 866168 (2022). https://doi.org/10.3389/fgene.2022.866168

Rauter, C.M., Wöhlke, S., Schicktanz, S.: My Data, My Choice? – German patient organizations' attitudes towards big data-driven approaches in personalized medicine. An empirical-ethical study. J. Med. Syst. **45**(4), 43 (2021). https://doi.org/10.1007/s10916-020-01702-7

Rawat, B., Joshi, Y., Kumar, A.: AI in healthcare: opportunities and challenges for personalized medicine and disease diagnosis. In: 2023 5th International Conference on Inventive Research in Computing Applications (ICIRCA) (2023)

Riddle, L., Joseph, G., Caruncho, M., Koenig, B.A., James, J.E.: The role of polygenic risk scores in breast cancer risk perception and decision-making. J. Community Genet. **14**(5), 489–501 (2023). https://doi.org/10.1007/s12687-023-00655-x

Roth, S.C.: What is genomic medicine? J. Med. Libr. Assoc. **107**(3), 442–448 (2019). https://doi.org/10.5195/jmla.2019.604

Sarwar, E.: The emerging field of precision medicine–the new paradigm for healthcare. In: Sarwar, E. (ed.) Global Perspectives on Precision Medicine: Ethical, Social and Public Health Implications, vol. 19, pp. 9–32. Springer, Cham (2023a). https://doi.org/10.1007/978-3-031-28593-6_2

Sarwar, E.: Laying an ethical foundation in healthcare in the era of PM. In: Sarwar, E. (ed.) Global Perspectives on Precision Medicine: Ethical, Social and Public Health Implications, pp. 157–188. Springer, Cham (2023b). https://doi.org/10.1007/978-3-031-28593-6_7

Schaefer, G.O., Tai, E.S., Sun, S.: Precision medicine and big data. Asian Bioethics Rev. **11**(3), 275–288 (2019). https://doi.org/10.1007/s41649-019-00094-2

Shabana, A.: Between treatment and enhancement: Islamic discourses on the boundaries of human genetic modification. J. Religious Ethics **50**(3), 386–411 (2022)

Sravani, C., Pavani, P., Vybhavi, G., Ramesh, G., Farman, A.: Decoding the HumanGenome: machine learning techniques for DNA sequencing analysis. In: E3S Web of Conferences (2023)

Tarkkala, H., Helén, I., Snell, K.: From health to wealth: the future of personalized medicine in the making. Futures **109**, 142–152 (2019). https://doi.org/10.1016/j.futures.2018.06.004

Toh, H.J., et al.: Religious perspectives on precision medicine in Singapore. Asian Bioethics Rev. **13**(4), 473–483 (2021). https://doi.org/10.1007/s41649-021-00180-4

Verstegen, R.H.J., Ito, S.: The future of precision medicine. Clin. Pharmacol. Ther. **106**(5), 903–906 (2019). https://doi.org/10.1002/cpt.1622

Vogt, H., Hofmann, B.: How precision medicine changes medical epistemology: a formative case from Norway. J. Eval. Clin. Pract. **28**(6), 1205–1212 (2022). https://doi.org/10.1111/jep.13649

Willems, D., et al.: Ethical issues in two parallel trials of personalised criteria for implantation of implantable cardioverter defibrillators for primary prevention: the PROFID project-a position paper. Open Heart **8**(e001686) (2021). https://doi.org/10.1136/openhrt-2021-001686

Yadav, N., Thelma, B.: Human heritable genome editing-potential and current status for clinical use. Asian Biotechnol. Dev. Rev. **23**(1), 5–22 (2021)

A Systematic Literature Review on How Conversational Agents are Transforming Healthcare

Nawaaz Antulay and Funmi Adebesin[✉]

Department of Informatics, University of Pretoria, Pretoria, South Africa
u19008717@tuks.co.za, funmi.adebesin@up.ac.za

Abstract. Recent advancements in new technologies, including Artificial Intelligence (AI) and Machine Learning (ML) are revolutionizing healthcare. The healthcare sector has historically lagged in the adoption of digital technologies. However, the COVID-19 pandemic accelerated the pace of their adoption. AI-powered conversational agents like chatbots and virtual assistants, which are computer programs capable of mimicking human conversations, are increasingly being adopted to improve the quality of healthcare services. Conversational agents can increase access to healthcare and improve communications between patients and healthcare professionals. In this paper, we present the result of a systematic literature review that investigated the potential of conversational agents for transforming the healthcare sector. A total of 9,654 papers published between 2019 and 2023 were retrieved from three databases using author-defined search phrases and inclusion/exclusion criteria. Following the screening process, 35 peer-reviewed papers were analyzed using qualitative content analysis. We identified two main categories and eight sub-subcategories as areas where conversational agents could transform healthcare. The two main categories were 'augmentation of patient care and engagement', and 'optimization of clinical workflow and decision support'. The sub-categories include the dissemination of personalized information, chronic disease management and lifestyle integration, automated symptom triage, as well as telemedicine and remote consultation. The results showed that conversational agents have the potential to transform the healthcare sector and enhance the quality of healthcare service delivery.

Keywords: AI-Powered Chatbots · Conversational Agents · Healthcare Transformation · Virtual Assistants

1 Introduction

Advancements in new technologies, especially Artificial Intelligence (AI) and Machine Learning (ML) have the potential to transform healthcare (Lin et al., 2019; Poalelungi et al., 2023). Although the healthcare sector has historically lagged in the adoption of digital technologies (Pérez Sust et al., 2020), the COVID-19 pandemic accelerated the pace of integration of AI into different areas of healthcare, including clinical decision support

© The Author(s), under exclusive license to Springer Nature Switzerland AG 2025
K. Hinkelmann and H. Smuts (Eds.): Society 5.0 2024, CCIS 2173, pp. 14–24, 2025.
https://doi.org/10.1007/978-3-031-71412-2_2

of diagnosis and treatment options (Amann et al., 2020), remote patient monitoring, medical device automation, robotic-assisted surgical procedures (Bohr & Memarzadeh, 2020), and the automation of radiology reports (Jeyaraj & Narayanan, 2023). AI-powered technologies have several benefits, including improved clinical decisions, automation of routine tasks to reduce workload, as well as enabling individualized healthcare (Ellahham et al., 2020; Schwalbe & Wahl, 2020). Despite their benefits, AI-powered technologies are intended to augment, not replace the expertise of healthcare professionals (Bohr & Memarzadeh, 2020; Lee & Yoon, 2021).

One of the application areas of AI is conversational agents (Dingler et al., 2021). Conversational agents are computer programs that emulate human conversations and range from text-based chatbots to sophisticated AI-powered virtual assistants that can interpret natural language and engage in dynamic dialogues (Pernencar et al., 2022). Conversational agents can facilitate remote consultations, screening for disease conditions, patient triage during emergencies, access to health information, and support for self-management of chronic conditions (Dingler et al., 2021). The COVID-19 pandemic has heralded a paradigm shift for the healthcare sector as exemplified by the integration of conversational agents, AI-powered chatbots and virtual assistants into healthcare processes (Javaid et al., 2023; Jeyaraj & Narayanan, 2023). These digital companions are seen as transformative tools that hold the potential to revolutionize the way healthcare is experienced and delivered to patients and practitioners (Javaid et al., 2023). This paper reports on a systematic literature review (SLR) that investigated the potential of conversational agents in transforming the healthcare sector. Due to the restriction on the length of this paper, a discussion of the challenges associated with the integration of conversational agents into healthcare technologies is outside the scope of this paper. The remaining sections of the paper are structured as follows: the research methodology is explained in Sect. 2, followed by the SLR results in Sect. 3. A detailed discussion of the synthesis of the papers included in the SLR is provided in Sect. 4, while Sect. 5 concludes the paper.

2   Methodology

The research method adopted for the study was the Preferred Reporting Items for Systematic Reviews and Meta-Analyses (PRISMA) guideline by Page et al. (2021). The primary research question that we focused on was: *"How can conversational agents transform the healthcare sector"?* Peer-reviewed research papers were retrieved from three electronic databases (i) ScienceDirect, (ii) Web of Science (WOS), and (iii) Scopus. These databases were chosen based on their reputation for publishing high-quality research papers in e-health research. The following search phrases were used to retrieve research papers that could assist in answering the research question ("Artificial Intelligence" OR "Chatbot" OR "Virtual Assistant" OR "Conversational agents") AND ("Healthcare" OR "Health care" OR "health") AND ("Transformation" OR "transform*"). The inclusion and exclusion criteria listed in Table 1 were used to complement the search phrases.

A total of 9,654 papers were retried from the three databases (WOS = 4316; ScienceDirect = 2901; Scopus = 2437). Initial screening involved the removal of 11 duplicate sources. Thereafter, a combined total of 8,789 sources were excluded. These include

168 non-English sources, 718 with no abstracts available, 2,816 sources that were published before 2019, and 4,378 sources that were not related to the use of conversational agents in the healthcare context. An additional 819 papers that were not relevant to answering the research question were also removed. Thus, a total of 35 research papers were retained for inclusion in the SLR. The screening process is illustrated in Fig. 1.

Table 1. Inclusion and exclusion criteria

Inclusion criteria	Exclusion criteria
Papers published between 2019 and 2023	Papers published in non-English language
Peer-reviewed conference or journal papers	Duplicate papers from different databases
Papers that focused on the transformational role of conversational agents in healthcare	Papers with full text unavailable through open-access

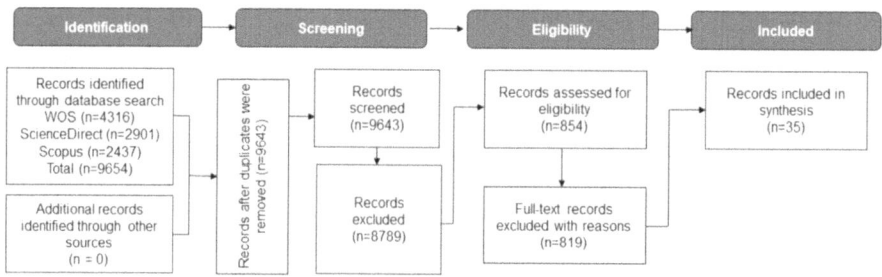

Fig. 1. SLR screening process

The 35 papers included in the SLR were analyzed using quantitative descriptive statistics and qualitative content analysis. Content analysis can be described as a methodical inspection and interpretation of specific texts or concepts in qualitative data. It entails coding and classifying textual material obtained from studies to find themes, patterns, or connections that are pertinent to the study's goals or research questions (Neuendorf, 2017). This process resulted in the identification of two categories and eight sub-categories, which are presented in Sects. 3 and 4.

3   Results

In this section, we present our findings from analysis of the 35 papers included in the SLR. The quantitative descriptive analysis revealed that almost half of the papers included in the SLR (16) were published in 2023, followed by 10 in 2022. There were five publications in 2021, three were published in 2019 and only one in 2020 (see Fig. 2). Analysis by document type showed that most of the papers (32) were journals while the remaining three were conference proceedings.

The 35 papers included in the SLR were analyzed using qualitative content analysis. This process resulted in two broad categories and four sub-categories per category of areas where conversational agents can transform the healthcare sector. Table 2 summarizes the potential transformational role of conversational agents in healthcare. Detailed discussions of the two categories and sub-categories are presented in Sect. 4.

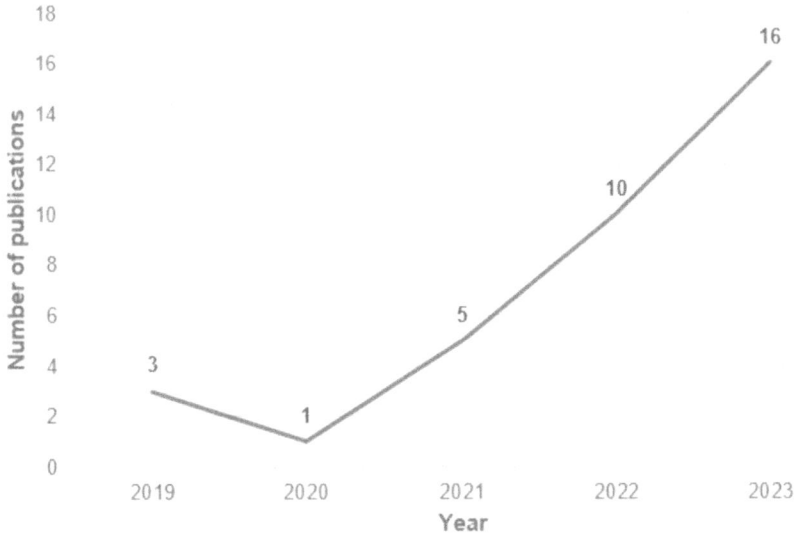

Fig. 2. Number of publications per year

Table 2. Summary of the potential transformational role of conversation agents in healthcare

Augmentation of patient care and engagement	Optimization of clinical workflow and decision support
Dissemination of personalized information	Automated symptom triage and severity ranking
Chronic disease management and lifestyle integration	Telemedicine and remote consultation
Real-time monitoring and alerts	AI-assisted diagnosis and treatment
Medication management and compliance	AI-assisted precision medicine

4   Discussion

This section provides a synthesis of the different areas where conversational agents can transform the healthcare sector.

4.1   Augmentation of Patient Care and Engagement

The adoption of conversational agents for healthcare purposes can enhance patient care processes in different ways, including the provision of personalized information, support of chronic disease self-management, remote monitoring of patients, early warning for critical conditions, as well as to support adherence to treatment regimens. The following sub-sections provide a synthesis of the different ways that conversational agents are being used to augment patient care.

4.1.1 Dissemination of Personalized Information

Conversational agents, powered by AI and chatbot technology serve as dynamic channels for the dissemination of personalized health information to support healthcare (Wang et al., 2021; Xiao et al., 2023). Chatbots are computer programs that are capable of mimicking human-like conversations using natural language (Athavale et al., 2023). Based on the understanding of individual patient's profiles, medical history, preferences, and current health status, conversational agents can deliver tailored health information to patients. This targeted approach transcends the limitations of a one-size-fits-all health information pamphlet and brochure (Vasileiou & Maglogiannis, 2022). This would enable patients to receive information that aligns with their unique health needs and circumstances. For instance, a patient diagnosed with diabetes may receive specialized advice on blood sugar management, while a patient with hypertension may be guided towards effective strategies for blood pressure control. By harnessing the power of conversational agents, healthcare providers can effectively bridge the information gap and empower patients with the knowledge they need to make informed decisions about their health (Pernencar et al., 2022).

4.1.2 Chronic Disease Management and Lifestyle Integration

For individuals grappling with chronic conditions, the fusion of effective disease management and seamless lifestyle change integration is paramount. Conversational agents can facilitate this integration by acting as a continuous companion in the patient's healthcare journey (Athavale et al., 2023). Conversational agents can transform the healthcare sector by supporting real-time guidance on the management of chronic conditions, offering insights on symptom recognition, medication adjustments, and the required lifestyle changes (Athavale et al., 2023). By seamlessly blending into the patient's daily routine, conversational agents can be used to ensure that healthcare is not an isolated event but an intrinsic part of everyday life (Dingler et al., 2021; Gong et al., 2020). This integration fosters a holistic approach to care, where the management of chronic conditions becomes a natural extension of the patient's lifestyle. Through this comprehensive support system, conversational agents can contribute to enhanced disease control, improved quality of life, and a sense of empowerment for patients navigating the complexities of chronic conditions (Liu et al., 2022). Lifestyle changes are an important element of chronic disease management. Conversational agents can play a supportive role in partnering with patients as they embark on the necessary lifestyle modifications by engaging patients in constructive dialogues about lifestyle choices, such as dietary habits, physical activities, and stress management techniques. These agents can provide personalized recommendations and evidence-based strategies to support healthier living (Liu et al., 2022). Through ongoing interactions, conversational agents can track patients' progress and provide positive reinforcement, motivating them to sustain positive behavioural changes (Dhinagaran et al., 2021; Fadhil et al., 2019).

4.1.3   Real-Time Monitoring and Alerts

A patient-centric healthcare environment requires real-time monitoring of patient's conditions and the generation of notifications to alert healthcare professionals in emergencies. Conversational agents equipped with AI capabilities can serve as vigilant guards, continuously monitoring and recording patients' conditions (Adikari et al., 2022; Mavropoulos et al., 2019). This proactive approach enables swift intervention, thereby preventing potential complications and ensuring that patients receive the timely care they need. By harnessing the power of remote monitoring, conversational agents can improve patient safety and serve as a vital bridge between patients and healthcare professionals, particularly in cases where immediate intervention is crucial (Suharwardy et al., 2023). Timely identification of critical health events is paramount in preventing adverse outcomes. Conversational agents equipped with AI capabilities can serve as vigilant monitors, constantly analyzing patient's data for signs of impending critical conditions and sending notifications to healthcare professionals so they can take the necessary actions (Humayun et al., 2022). This early warning system is particularly crucial for patients with complex or chronic conditions, where timely intervention can mean the difference between stabilization and deterioration of a patient's condition.

4.1.4   Medication Management and Compliance

Optimal medication management is an important cornerstone of effective healthcare, particularly for individuals with chronic conditions. Conversational agents are capable of sending medication reminders to patients to ensure that they comply with their treatment regimen (Dingler et al., 2021; Kowatsch et al., 2021). Through built-in reminders and notifications, conversational agents can ensure that patients adhere to their prescribed regimens (Fenza et al., 2023). In instances where medication is missed, a conversational agent can promptly alert the patient, offering guidance on corrective actions (Dworkin et al., 2019; Rodríguez et al., 2021). Additionally, the conversational agent can compile adherence data, providing both patients and healthcare providers with valuable insights into medication compliance (Dworkin et al., 2019). This approach not only fosters patient accountability but also empowers healthcare providers to make informed adjustments to treatment plans, ultimately leading to improved health outcomes.

4.2   Optimization of Clinical Workflow and Decision Support

Conversational agents can significantly enhance clinical workflows by automating processes, providing real-time support, and integrating with clinical decision-support systems. These advancements have the potential to result in more efficient and effective patient care, ultimately leading to improved health outcomes. The following subsections provide a synthesis of the different ways that conversational agents can be used to optimize clinical workflow and clinical decision support.

4.2.1 Automated Symptom Triage and Severity Ranking

The integration of conversational agents into clinical workflow has the potential to improve clinical operational efficiencies. Conversational agents with built-in advanced algorithms and medical knowledge can autonomously triage patients based on reported symptoms, thereby reducing patients' waiting time and improving clinical outcomes (Li, 2023). By engaging patients in intuitive dialogues, a conversational agent can systematically collect pertinent information about a patient's condition, which will then be used for triaging (Dingler et al., 2021). By leveraging natural language processing, conversational agents can swiftly analyze data to discern the urgency and severity of the situation. This automated triage process assigns a priority level to each case, ensuring that patients with critical needs receive immediate attention (Morse et al., 2020). In their study, Morse et al. (2020), found that the triage recommendations by a symptom checker chatbot were comparable with the ones made by nursing professionals in telephonic triage lines. By expediting the assessment process, conversational agents alleviate the burden on frontline healthcare staff, allowing them to allocate their expertise where it is needed most. This systematic approach not only accelerates response times but also enhances the overall efficiency of clinical operations.

4.2.2 Telemedicine and Remote Consultation

One of the ways that conversational agents can be used to transform the healthcare sector is in their application in telemedicine. Although the history of telemedicine can be traced back to the 19th century (Jagarapu & Savani, 2021), the COVID-19 pandemic saw a marked increase in its use by patients and healthcare professionals (Mann et al., 2020). With advancements in technologies, conversational agents equipped with telemedicine capabilities put healthcare services within the reach of hard-to-reach communities where geographical constraints often hinder access to healthcare services (Vasileiou & Maglogiannis, 2022). Conversational agents can facilitate remote consultations between healthcare providers and patients. Patients can engage in meaningful dialogues with their healthcare providers, discuss symptoms, receive medical advice, and participate in follow-up appointments, all from the comfort of their homes (Nadarzynski et al., 2019). Conversational agents can act as a seamless bridge, ensuring that vital healthcare services are delivered without the need for arduous travel. By leveraging telemedicine, conversational agents can play a pivotal role in dismantling geographical barriers to healthcare, particularly benefiting those in remote or underserved areas.

4.2.3 AI-Assisted Diagnosis and Treatment

The integration of AI-driven clinical decision support systems with built-in predictive models can support healthcare practitioners in diagnosing disease conditions and reduce diagnosis errors (Simegn et al., 2022). Conversational agents are increasingly being used to support automated disease diagnosis (Fan et al., 2021; Tiwari et al., 2022; Xu et al., 2019). With the global shortage of healthcare professionals (Tiwari et al., 2022), conversational agents have the potential to boost the doctor-to-patient ratio. Despite the potential of conversational agents to support the diagnosis of disease conditions, researchers have cautioned that they should not be seen as a replacement for healthcare professionals, many of whom have years of experience. Rather, conversational agents should be used to complement the work of healthcare professionals (Williams & Shambrook, 2023).

4.2.4 AI-Assisted Precision Medicine

Precision medicine entails tailoring medical interventions to an individual or subgroup's unique characteristics based on knowledge of their genetic formation, environment and lifestyle (Naithani et al., 2021; Yuan, 2022). AI-powered conversational agents are capable of engaging in dynamic dialogues with patients to collect a wealth of health data, including medical history and lifestyle factors. By leveraging this comprehensive patient profile, conversational agents can be integrated into healthcare processes to generate personalized treatment plans based on a patient's unique attributes (Goktas et al., 2023). These plans encompass a spectrum of interventions, including medication regimens, lifestyle modifications, and targeted interventions. By customizing treatment approaches based on individual patient data, conversational agents can contribute to improved treatment efficacy and patient outcomes. This personalized approach not only enhances the patient experience but also maximizes the likelihood of successful treatment outcomes (Fenza et al., 2023).

5   Conclusion

This paper reports on the outcome of an SLR that investigated the potential of conversational agents in transforming the healthcare sector. Advances in technologies and the COVID-19 pandemic have significantly changed the healthcare landscape. One of these changes can be seen in the adoption of AI-powered conversational agents to complement healthcare service delivery.

The majority of the papers analyzed in this SLR were journal papers, with only three being conference proceedings. The qualitative content analysis of the 35 papers resulted in two main categories and four sub-categories per category where conversational agents can transform the healthcare sector. The findings presented across the categories and sub-categories highlight the potential impacts of conversational agents on patient care, provider workflows, and the overall healthcare landscape. Augmentation of patient care emerged as a prominent category, showcasing how conversational agents can empower patients with personalized health information, which could improve their health literacy, and support them in the lifestyle changes that are necessary for the management of their chronic condition. Furthermore, by optimizing clinical workflows and decision support, conversational agents can assist in streamlining healthcare processes by expediting patient triage. The integration of AI-driven decision support systems amplifies the capabilities of healthcare providers, potentially leading to more accurate diagnoses and individually tailored treatment plans. This advancement stands as a testament to the potential of AI-powered conversational agents in clinical practice. Remote monitoring and timely interventions also emerged as an important aspect, illustrating how conversational agents can serve as vigilant monitors, providing real-time support and facilitating early interventions. The ability to track symptoms, ensure medication adherence, and identify critical conditions remotely can lead to a shift towards proactive and personalized healthcare delivery.

The results of the SLR underscore the potential transformative role of conversational agents and AI-powered Chatbots in healthcare. The synthesis of diverse studies presents a compelling case for the integration of these technologies into mainstream healthcare practices. Conversational agents have the potential to enhance patient engagement and optimize clinical workflows. Despite their potential benefits, conversational agents should not be seen as a replacement for healthcare professionals.

Further research is required to investigate the long-term impact of conversational agents on patient outcomes and healthcare service efficiencies. In addition, investigation into the ethical and legal implications of integrating conversational agents into existing healthcare applications is required to fully realize their potential transformative power.

References

Adikari, A., et al.: Empathic conversational agents for real-time monitoring and co-facilitation of patient-centered healthcare. Future Gener. Comput. Syst. **126**, 318–329 (2022). https://doi.org/10.1016/j.future.2021.08.015

Amann, J., Blasimme, A., Vayena, E., Frey, D., Madai, V.I., et al.: Explainability for artificial intelligence in healthcare: a multidisciplinary perspective. BMC Med. Inform. Decis. Mak. **20**(1), 310 (2020). https://doi.org/10.1186/s12911-020-01332-6

Athavale, A., Baier, J., Ross, E., Fukaya, E.: The potential of chatbots in chronic venous disease patient management. JVS-Vascular Insights **1**, 100019 (2023). https://doi.org/10.1016/j.jvsvi.2023.100019

Bohr, A., Memarzadeh, K.: The rise of artificial intelligence in healthcare applications. In: Artificial Intelligence in Healthcare, pp. 25–60. Elsevier (2020). https://doi.org/10.1016/B978-0-12-818438-7.00002-2

Dhinagaran, D.A., Sathish, T., Soong, A., Theng, Y.-L., Best, J., Tudor Car, L.: Conversational agent for healthy lifestyle behavior change: web-based feasibility study [Original Paper]. JMIR Form Res. **5**(12), e27956 (2021). https://doi.org/10.2196/27956

Dingler, T., Kwasnicka, D., Wei, J., Gong, E., Oldenburg, B.: The use and promise of conversational agents in digital health. Yearb. Med. Inform. **30**(01), 191–199 (2021). https://doi.org/10.1055/s-0041-1726510

Dworkin, M.S., et al.: Acceptability, feasibility, and preliminary efficacy of a theory-based relational embodied conversational agent mobile phone intervention to promote HIV medication adherence in young HIV-positive African American MSM. AIDS Educ. Prev. **31**(1), 17–37 (2019). https://doi.org/10.1521/aeap.2019.31.1.17

Ellahham, S., Ellahham, N., Simsekler, M.C.E.: Application of artificial intelligence in the health care safety context: opportunities and challenges. Am. J. Med. Qual. **35**(4), 341–348 (2020). https://doi.org/10.1177/1062860619878515

Fadhil, A., Wang, Y., Reiterer, H.: Assistive conversational agent for health coaching: a validation study. Methods Inf. Med. **58**(01), 009–023 (2019). https://doi.org/10.1055/s-0039-1688757

Fan, X., Chao, D., Zhang, Z., Wang, D., Li, X., Tian, F.: Utilization of self-diagnosis health chatbots in real-world settings: case study. J. Med. Internet Res. **23**(1), e19928 (2021). https://doi.org/10.2196/19928

Fenza, G., Orciuoli, F., Peduto, A., Postiglione, A.: Healthcare conversational agents: chatbot for improving patient-reported outcomes. In: Barolli, L. (ed.) Advanced Information Networking and Applications, pp. 137–148. Springer, Cham (2023). https://doi.org/10.1007/978-3-031-29056-5_14

Goktas, P., Karakaya, G., Kalyoncu, A.F., Damadoglu, E.: Artificial intelligence chatbots in allergy and immunology practice: where have we been and where are we going? J. Allergy Clin. Immunol. Pract. **11**(9), 2697–2700 (2023). https://doi.org/10.1016/j.jaip.2023.05.042

Gong, E., et al.: My diabetes coach, a mobile app–based interactive conversational agent to support type 2 diabetes self-management: randomized effectiveness-implementation trial [Original Paper]. J. Med. Internet Res. **22**(11), e20322 (2020). https://doi.org/10.2196/20322

Humayun, M., Jhanjhi, N.Z., Almotilag, A., Almufareh, M.F.: Agent-based medical health monitoring system. Sensors **22**(8), 2820 (2022). https://doi.org/10.3390/s22082820

Jagarapu, J., Savani, R.C.: A brief history of telemedicine and the evolution of teleneonatology. Seminars Perinatol. **45**(5), 151416 (2021). https://doi.org/10.1016/j.semperi.2021.151416

Javaid, M., Haleem, A., Singh, R.P.: ChatGPT for healthcare services: an emerging stage for an innovative perspective. BenchCouncil Trans. Benchmarks Stan. Eval. **3**(1), 100105 (2023). https://doi.org/10.1016/j.tbench.2023.100105

Jeyaraj, P., Narayanan, T.: Role of artificial intelligence in enhancing healthcare delivery. Int. J. Innov. Sci. Mod. Eng. **11**(12) (2023). https://doi.org/10.35940/ijisme.A1310.12111223

Kowatsch, T., et al.: Conversational agents as mediating social actors in chronic disease management involving health care professionals, patients, and family members: multisite single-arm feasibility study [Original Paper]. J. Med. Internet Res. **23**(2), e25060 (2021). https://doi.org/10.2196/25060

Lee, D., Yoon, S.N.: Application of artificial intelligence-based technologies in the healthcare industry: opportunities and challenges. Int. J. Environ. Res. Public Health **18**(1), 271 (2021). https://doi.org/10.3390/ijerph18010271

Li, L.: Role of chatbots on gastroenterology: let's chat about the future. Gastroenterol. Endosc. **1**(3), 144–149 (2023). https://doi.org/10.1016/j.gande.2023.06.002

Lin, S.Y., Mahoney, M.R., Sinsky, C.A.: Ten ways artificial intelligence will transform primary care. J. Gen. Intern. Med. **34**(8), 1626–1630 (2019). https://doi.org/10.1007/s11606-019-05035-1

Liu, H., Peng, H., Song, X., Xu, C., Zhang, M.: Using AI chatbots to provide self-help depression interventions for university students: a randomized trial of effectiveness. Internet Interv. **27**, 100495 (2022). https://doi.org/10.1016/j.invent.2022.100495

Mann, D.M., Chen, J., Chunara, R., Testa, P.A., Nov, O.: COVID-19 transforms health care through telemedicine: evidence from the field. J. Am. Med. Inform. Assoc. **27**(7), 1132–1135 (2020). https://doi.org/10.1093/jamia/ocaa072

Mavropoulos, T., et al.: A context-aware conversational agent in the rehabilitation domain. Future Internet **11**(11), 231 (2019). https://doi.org/10.3390/fi11110231

Morse, K.E., Ostberg, N.P., Jones, V.G., Chan, A.S.: Use characteristics and triage acuity of a digital symptom checker in a large integrated health system: population-based descriptive study [Original Paper]. J. Med. Internet Res. **22**(11), e20549 (2020). https://doi.org/10.2196/20549

Nadarzynski, T., Miles, O., Cowie, A., Ridge, D.: Acceptability of artificial intelligence (AI)-led chatbot services in healthcare: a mixed-methods study. Digit. Health **5**, 2055207619871808 (2019). https://doi.org/10.1177/2055207619871808

Naithani, N., et al.: Precision medicine: Uses and challenges. Med. J. Armed Forces India **77**(3), 258–265 (2021). https://doi.org/10.1016/j.mjafi.2021.06.020

Neuendorf, K.A.: The Content Analysis Guidebook, 2nd edn. (2017). https://doi.org/10.4135/9781071802878

Page, M.J., et al.: The PRISMA 2020 statement: an updated guideline for reporting systematic reviews. Int. J. Surg. **88**, 105906 (2021). https://doi.org/10.1016/j.ijsu.2021.105906

Pérez Sust, P., et al.: Turning the crisis into an opportunity: digital health strategies deployed during the COVID-19 outbreak [Viewpoint]. JMIR Public Health Surveill. **6**(2), e19106 (2020). https://doi.org/10.2196/19106

Pernencar, C., Saboia, I., Dias, J.C.: How far can conversational agents contribute to IBD patient health care-a review of the literature [Systematic Review]. Front. Public Health **10**, 862432 (2022). https://doi.org/10.3389/fpubh.2022.862432

Poalelungi, D.G., et al.: Advancing patient care: how artificial intelligence is transforming healthcare. J. Personalized Med. **13**(8), 1214 (2023). https://www.mdpi.com/2075-4426/13/8/1214

Rodríguez, M.D., Beltrán, J., Valenzuela-Beltrán, M., Cruz-Sandoval, D., Favela, J.: Assisting older adults with medication reminders through an audio-based activity recognition system. Pers. Ubiquit. Comput. **25**(2), 337–351 (2021). https://doi.org/10.1007/s00779-020-01420-4

Schwalbe, N., Wahl, B.: Artificial intelligence and the future of global health. Lancet **395**(10236), 1579–1586 (2020). https://doi.org/10.1016/S0140-6736(20)30226-9

Simegn, G.L., Gebeyehu, W.B., Degu, M.Z.: Computer-aided decision support system for diagnosis of heart diseases. Res. Rep. Clin. Cardiol. **13**, 39–54 (2022). https://doi.org/10.2147/RRCC.S366380

Suharwardy, S., et al.: Feasibility and impact of a mental health chatbot on postpartum mental health: a randomized controlled trial. AJOG Glob. Rep. **3**(3), 100165 (2023). https://doi.org/10.1016/j.xagr.2023.100165

Tiwari, A., Manthena, M., Saha, S., Bhattacharyya, P., Dhar, M., Tiwari, S.: Dr. can see: towards a multi-modal disease diagnosis virtual assistant. In: Proceedings of the 31st ACM International Conference on Information & Knowledge Management (2022)

Vasileiou, M.V., Maglogiannis, I.G.: The health chatbots in telemedicine: intelligent dialog system for remote support. J. Healthcare Eng. **2022**, 4876512 (2022). https://doi.org/10.1155/2022/4876512

Wang, X., et al.: Artificial intelligence-empowered chatbot for effective COVID-19 information delivery to older adults. Int. J. E-Health Med. Commun. (IJEHMC) **12**(6), 1–18 (2021). https://doi.org/10.4018/IJEHMC.293285

Williams, M.C., Shambrook, J.: How will artificial intelligence transform cardiovascular computed tomography? A conversation with an AI model. J. Cardiovasc. Computed Tomogr. **17**(4), 281–283 (2023). https://doi.org/10.1016/j.jcct.2023.03.010

Xiao, Z., Liao, Q.V., Zhou, M., Grandison, T., Li, Y.: Powering an AI chatbot with expert sourcing to support credible health information access. In: Proceedings of the 28th International Conference on Intelligent User Interfaces (2023)

Xu, L., Zhou, Q., Gong, K., Liang, X., Tang, J., Lin, L.: End-to-end knowledge-routed relational dialogue system for automatic diagnosis. In: Proceedings of the AAAI Conference on Artificial Intelligence (2019)

Yuan, B.: Hat personalized medicine humans need and way to it - also on the practical significance and scientific limitations of precision medicine. Pharmacogenomics Personalized Med. **15**, 927–942 (2022). https://doi.org/10.2147/PGPM.S380767

Student-Mediated Knowledge Exchange in Switzerland

Franz Barjak[✉] [iD] and Fabian Heimsch[iD]

School of Business, University of Applied Sciences and Arts Northwestern Switzerland FHNW, Riggenbachstrasse 16, 4600 Olten, Switzerland
franz.barjak@fhnw.ch

Abstract. The majority of the academic work on knowledge and technology transfer has been on two types, knowledge commercialization and academic engagement. Mechanisms which involve students have been neglected though they are as common and potentially as beneficial. This neglect harbors several risks with regard to the economic and social valorization of research results. We define and typify the construct of student-mediated knowledge exchange and review the literature which has reported multiple benefits for the involved parties, students, universities and companies, but also some costs. We then use survey data on two selected measures generated in a survey of the institutes of 18 Swiss higher education institutions (HEIs) for multivariate regression analyses at institute level to explain the differences for the student-mediated knowledge exchange metrics with structural characteristics of the institutes (university type, size, academic discipline) and variables on their activities (teaching focus, cooperation and commercialization orientation). The results show that student-mediated transfers capture knowledge exchange with companies that is not covered by the common metrics for knowledge commercialization and academic engagement. In sum, we argue that the scope of knowledge and technology transfer metrics should be expanded to include measures that capture student-mediated forms.

Keywords: Student-mediated knowledge exchange · university-industry cooperation · knowledge transfer metrics · teaching-oriented universities

1 Introduction

Research on the knowledge exchange between universities and their faculty and staff and non-academic organizations, above all private businesses, has predominantly focused on two institutionalized types, knowledge commercialization (via patenting, licensing, spin-off formation) and academic engagement (via research and consulting, Perkmann et al., 2013). Other knowledge exchange mechanisms are not institutionalized, more heterogeneous, in part difficult to measure and it has been suggested that "there is scant evidence in the literature on how to deal with them or the real necessity to institutionalize their management" (Geuna & Muscio, 2009, p. 96). Still, surveys have frequently obtained the result that the non-institutionalized mechanisms of knowledge exchange which involve

© The Author(s), under exclusive license to Springer Nature Switzerland AG 2025
K. Hinkelmann and H. Smuts (Eds.): Society 5.0 2024, CCIS 2173, pp. 25–40, 2025.
https://doi.org/10.1007/978-3-031-71412-2_3

students, such as joint theses with companies, employing graduates, participation in university education and training activities, are as common as the institutionalized mechanisms, e.g. in Austria (Schartinger, Schibany, & Gassler, 2001), the UK (D'Este & Patel, 2007; Hughes & Kitson, 2012), or Switzerland (Barjak & Heimsch, 2021).

Neglecting a large and important part of the knowledge exchange between universities and companies conceptually, empirically and in practice is not really satisfactory and creates risks. Decision-makers in universities and policy makers in the fields of higher education and innovation might put a too strong focus on mechanisms related to knowledge commercialization and academic engagement and create corresponding incentives, making policies dysfunctional and actually reducing the amount of knowledge exchanged (Arundel & Es-Sadki, 2021; Hayter, Rasmussen, & Rooksby, 2020; Rossi & Rosli, 2015). The strong focus on knowledge commercialization might also create the impression that universities with a teaching focus do not transfer knowledge and technologies to society (Rossi & Rosli, 2015; Sánchez-Barrioluengo, 2014), underrepresenting the scope of knowledge exchange activities outside research universities (Hewitt-Dundas, 2012; Kitagawa, Sánchez Barrioluengo, & Uyarra, 2016; Rossi, 2018). This would negatively affect the image and reputation of these universities and limit their abilities to contribute to economic development, e.g., because of a reduction of funds, partners, staff, and students.

This paper addresses this knowledge gap and first summarizes the literature on a set of mechanisms that it subsumes under the construct of "student-mediated knowledge exchange". It defines the construct, distinguishes it from knowledge commercialization and academic engagement, and presents a typology of student-mediated knowledge exchange mechanisms. We also include an overview of the benefits and costs for the involved parties, universities, students and firms, of student-based knowledge exchange as described in the literature. Last but not least, we report data from a survey of almost 800 institutes at 18 Swiss universities for two measures of student-based knowledge exchange. We use this data to explain the institutes' performance in student-based knowledge exchange in multiple regressions. The paper focusses on the following questions:

1. How has student-mediated knowledge exchange been distinguished from other types of knowledge exchange?
2. What types of student-mediated knowledge exchange have been described in the literature?
3. What characterizes university institutes focusing on student-mediated knowledge exchange?
4. Is student-mediated knowledge exchange a substitute or a complement of other knowledge exchange mechanisms?

2 Student-Mediated Knowledge Exchange as a Separate Type of Knowledge Exchange

2.1 Student-Mediated Knowledge Exchange, Knowledge Commercialization and Academic Engagement

Most work on university-industry knowledge exchange has focused either on knowledge commercialization or academic engagement. The knowledge commercialization activities of universities have received more attention after the passing of the Bayh-Dole Act in the US in 1980 that permitted universities to commercialize the results from their federally funded research as they now belonged to them (and not anymore the US federal government). Since then, universities have professionalized their patenting, licensing and spin-off activities and established the processes and offices that organized this (Henderson, Jaffe, & Trajtenberg, 1998, Mowery & Sampat, 2005). The trend was widely emulated, above all in Europe and Asia (Geuna & Rossi, 2011; Gores & Link, 2021; Mowery & Sampat, 2005). Academic engagement has focused on the knowledge-related interactions of individual faculty and researchers with non-academic organizations and their employees (Perkmann et al., 2013, 2021). It has been centered on the contribution of university staff to the production of commercially and socially valuable knowledge. For academic engagement research-related motives have been found to dominate, i.e. researchers want to do better and more relevant research by involving companies and non-academic organizations and the funding of research also matters (Perkmann et al., 2021).

Table 1 gives an overview of both types, and of a third type on which much less has been written: student-mediated knowledge exchange sometimes also discussed as educational collaboration (Kunttu, 2017) or teaching-based knowledge sharing (Barjak & Heimsch, 2021). Student-mediated knowledge exchange is understood in this contribution as any type of interaction between a university and a company or other organization in which knowledge is exchanged and which involves students and/or student work as main carriers of knowledge. It differs in many regards from academic engagement and commercialization (Table 1). The motivational set is different: raising students' employability and contributing to the third mission of the university are key for student-mediated knowledge exchange, while research-related motivations are largely absent (Orazbayeva, Davey, Plewa, & Galán-Muros, 2020). The decision to take up such collaborative work involving students may be taken at all levels: by the individual professor, research group, institute, department, school or entire organization. Whenever student-mediated knowledge exchange includes the movement of students between the university and the company, even if only temporarily as in student mobility and lifelong learning, it facilitates the transmission of tacit knowledge to companies (Thune, 2009).

2.2 Forms of Student Mediated Knowledge Exchange

Different forms of such student-mediated knowledge exchange have been described. They often relate to universities' teaching activities and involve different types of student groups. This contribution differentiates these transfer mechanisms by two criteria: a)

Table 1. Types of interactions between academia and private companies

	Knowledge commercialization	Academic engagement	Student mediated knowledge exchange
Knowledge carrier	Patent, artefact	Faculty	Students
Typical forms	Academic spin-offs, licensing of academic inventions	Collaborative and contract research, consulting	Joint theses, lifelong learning, student mobility, student start-ups, employing graduates
Benefit for the non-academic partner	Access to use rights for a (patented) academic invention	Research results, proof-of-concepts, problem solutions, knowledge, ideas, etc.	Access to tacit knowledge, academic networks, low-threshold (and partly low-cost) cooperation
Economic value	Direct, monetarized, e.g., through license fees, options and similar	Direct, monetarized, e.g., through research and consulting fees	Indirect, only partially monetarized, e.g., through course fees, wages
Incentives for the academic partner	Financial compensation for academic inventions, use of research in practice	Research funding, access to problems, knowledge, technology for research	Employability of students, contribution to 3rd mission
Responsible structures inside the university	Technology transfer offices	Research offices, industry liaison offices	Education departments/programs, lifelong learning programs, career centers, entrepreneurship centers

locus of control and b) type of knowledge that is transferred. The locus of control distinguishes mechanisms over which the university and its faculty have some authority from mechanisms over which primarily the student has control. The former are for instance university decisions to offer education programs, to request certain activities from students (e.g., internships) or to permit or even endorse collaboration with non-academic entities. Universities can decide strategically to engage in such transfer mechanisms and deepen their relationships with the private sector. This is less possible with regard to mechanisms where the students themselves make the decision, e. g., where to work after graduating or whether to start a new company. As the publishing of student work illustrates, the boundaries are not always clear-cut, and it might well be that universities make the publication of student work mandatory or at least push it. However, as authors students have the final word on the content of any publication they write. Therefore, we consider this mechanism as being largely under student control as well. Type of knowledge distinguishes mechanisms that contain tacit knowledge which is literally contained in students' minds from mechanisms that contain predominantly codified knowledge, especially the results of student work. Tacit knowledge can be know-how, knowledge that is too new and not enough understood or too expensive to be fully codified and therefore taught via "learning-by-doing" in the lab (Cowan, David, & Foray, 2000). Most importantly, it needs the mobility of students for being transferred. The properties of knowledge, including its tacitness and systemic character, have been found to influence the importance of channels of knowledge transfer for university and industry researchers (Bekkers & Bodas Freitas, 2008).

Table 2 gives an overview of the different mechanisms which can be subsumed under each of the four types of student-mediated exchange. The length restrictions of this paper do not permit a detailed discussion. For each type, several costs and benefits have been discussed in the literature. For instance, it has been found that students engaged in cooperative graduate work with firms might lose (part of) their autonomy and be expected to prioritize consulting work over PhD research, causing delays and even jeopardizing the success of a partnership (Bienkowska & Klofsten, 2012; Zalewska-Kurek & Harms, 2020), and that scientific creativity and out-of-the box thinking might be reduced (Borrell-Damian, 2009). Moreover, an industrial focus in the PhD might affect negatively the academic career possibilities (Lee & Miozzo, 2015). However, commonly more benefits than downsides have been found.

Table 2. Forms of student-mediated knowledge exchange

Type of knowledge exchanged	Controlled by the university	Controlled by the student
Codified knowledge, included in student work results (e.g., theses)	• Joint supervision and/or financing of doctoral theses • Joint supervision and/or financing of master's and bachelor's theses • Student projects • Student consulting	• Publication of student work
Tacit knowledge, embodied in students	• Lifelong learning • Temporary student mobility • Cooperative education program	• Employment of graduates • Student entrepreneurship

3 Student-Mediated Knowledge Exchange in Swiss Higher Education Institutions

This section attempts to illustrate the collection of student-mediated knowledge exchange measures by providing corresponding data from a survey of Swiss higher education institutions (HEIs). We first introduce the survey and report descriptive statistics on student-mediated knowledge exchange of Swiss HEIs. Second, we conduct regression analyses to explore the covariates of student-mediated knowledge exchange. In the process we show that depending on the metric student-mediated knowledge exchange can be either a complement or substitute to other mechanisms.

3.1 Data and Methods

The empirical basis of this example is a cross-sectional dataset of 18 Swiss HEIs: nine cantonal universities, two federal universities and seven universities of applied sciences UAS. A survey of these institutions was conducted between June and August 2018 to monitor knowledge exchange with private companies. The survey population comprised all institutes in these HEIs in 28 fields, including the natural sciences, engineering & technology, medical and health sciences, agricultural and veterinary sciences, and selected social sciences (psychology & cognitive sciences, economics & business). Institutes from the humanities (according to the OECD Frascati Manual, 2015) and the majority of social sciences were excluded, as business enterprises were not perceived as their primary partners. Institutes were understood to be scientific organizational units that carry out R&D projects and whose heads have project and personnel responsibility for a manageable number of projects and for 10 to 50 persons. Depending on the internal structure of the HEI, these may be institutes, laboratories, departments, groups, or other units. In the included HEIs and fields, we identified 1694 institutes (see Appendix Table 1), which were then invited to participate in the online survey. The data from 791 institutes (47% of the population) could be included in the present analysis. However, not all questions were answered by the 791 respondents included, and the proportion of missing values differs between the questionnaire items.

We used two dependent variables to operationalize student-mediated knowledge exchange: 1) the number of bachelor and master's (B/M) theses in cooperation with companies and 2) the number of doctoral theses in cooperation with companies. The dependent variables in the data analyses exhibit some important econometric barriers towards a straightforward application of ordinary least squares (OLS): They are non-negative count data and subject to zero inflation. Out of 716 valid observations for the number of B/M theses, 374 institutes (52%) indicated zero B/M theses; 560 institutes (78%) out of 716 valid observations indicated zero dissertations. Furthermore, the variables are strongly right skewed and affected by overdispersion, which occurs when the variance of the observed count data is larger than it would be expected based on a Poisson distribution.

Therefore, the analysis uses OLS regressions as a baseline, but draws on Tweedie regressions to overcome the estimation problems.

1. Count data and non-negative values: The Tweedie distribution is versatile and includes a wide range of distributions, including the Poisson distribution that is commonly used for count data. It allows for modelling non-negative, integer-valued data.
2. Zero inflation: The Tweedie distribution has a parameter (referred to as the index parameter) that can be adjusted to handle zero inflation. By selecting an appropriate index parameter, we can model the variance of the count data, which is beneficial in constellations with excess zeros.
3. Skewness: The Tweedie distribution is a generalized distribution that includes both the Poisson and Gamma distributions. This flexibility allows it to handle skewed data. By adjusting the power parameter of the Tweedie distribution, we can model different degrees of skewness. This makes it well-suited for situations where the data is not symmetrically distributed, as indicated by our right-skewed variables.
4. Overdispersion: The Tweedie distribution naturally accommodates overdispersion. It includes the Poisson distribution as a special case but also extends to handle variance greater than the mean, which is characteristic of over-dispersed count data. This makes it a suitable choice for count data where the observed variance is higher than expected under a Poisson distribution.

In addition, Tweedie regressions are generally robust to mild or moderate outliers. The flexibility of the Tweedie distribution, which includes both the Poisson and Gamma distributions, allows it to handle a range of data distributions, making it more resilient to outliers compared to some other regression models. Additionally, we performed sensitivity analyses and removed 1% of the strongest outliers and 1% of the most influential observations. The reported results are robust (in terms of sign and significance of the coefficients).

3.2 Measures of Student-Mediated Knowledge Exchange of Swiss Universities

Table 3 shows data from the survey on student-mediated knowledge exchange with companies. With regard to cooperative B/M theses we find higher values for all teaching oriented UAS except SUPSI, and for UNISG and UNIFR (but at a lower level than in the UAS). Moreover, we find that two of the UAS, namely FHNW and HSLU, place a particular focus on exchanging knowledge with companies by means of B/M theses, as in both cases external cooperation partners were involved in more than 70% of all theses. Doctoral education in cooperation with companies is above all found at UNISG, EPFL, ETHZ, and UNIFR. For the UAS this is not relevant, as they cannot offer PhD programs of their own.

3.3 Multivariate Analyses of Student-Mediated Knowledge Exchange

We conducted a series of regression analyses with two measures for student-mediated knowledge exchange to understand the extent to which this reflects a mechanism that is not yet captured by the existing measures (see Appendix 2 on descriptive statistics for the included variables).

The estimations consist of baseline OLS regressions and more robust Tweedie regressions plus two extensions, adding in three knowledge commercialization measures and

Table 3. B/M theses and doctoral theses in cooperation with companies and professional education theses in Swiss universities (2015–17)

	FHNW knowledge exchange survey 2018				
	Obs.	Cooperative B/M theses per scientist		Cooperative doctoral theses per scientist	
		Theses	in % of all B/M theses	Theses	in % of all doctoral theses
Universities[a]					
ETHZ	78	0.067	14.3%	0.024	14.2%
EPFL	132	0.119	33.4%	0.023	16.5%
UNIBAS	93	0.021	6.2%	0.014	8.9%
UNIBE	50	0.040	12.4%	0.010	8.4%
UNISG	10	0.487	20.9%	0.060	18.6%
UZH	73	0.066	11.0%	0.012	8.2%
UNIFR	30	0.311	32.1%	0.019	10.7%
UNIGE	58	0.040	12.1%	0.009	7.5%
UNIL	53	0.108	22.2%	0.006	3.4%
UNINE	16	0.104	19.4%	0.014	8.4%
USI	14	0.051	15.0%	0.002	2.4%
all UNI	*607*	*0.076*	*16.6%*	*0.015*	*10.1%*
Universities of Applied Sciences UAS					
FHNW	18	0.759	82.5%	0.000	0.0%
OST	21	0.489	41.4%	0.000	0.0%
HSLU	11	0.674	72.3%	0.003	40.0%
BFH	13	0.679	52.6%	0.004	13.6%
SUPSI	11	0.167	50.6%	0.004	20.0%
ZFH	21	0.850	43.8%	0.009	9.6%
HES-SO	35	0.573	47.8%	0.006	27.9%
all UAS	*130*	*0.646*	*53.1%*	*0.005*	*13.1%*
All	*737*	*0.195*	*31.7%*	*0.013*	*10.3%*

[a] See appendix for the meaning of the university abbreviations.

four indices (importance of informal, research-based and teaching-based knowledge exchange, and for knowledge commercialization). The intercept contains the results for the reference groups of institutes from the ETH domain, institute heads with work experience outside academia and the field of engineering.

B/M Theses in Cooperation with Companies. According to the baseline models, institutes in the ETH domain, institutes led by an institute head with working experience outside academia and institutes from engineering had a higher number of cooperative

Bachelor/Master theses with companies (Table 4). The numbers are even higher for institutes from universities of applied sciences (UAS) and social sciences institutes, but lower for institutes from the biomedical sciences and natural sciences. Moreover, institute size (no. of scientists) and overall teaching focus (no. of non-cooperative B/M theses) as well as the number of cooperative doctoral work with companies also show positive coefficients. These results are confirmed, if we add in the variables for knowledge commercialization (numbers of patent applications, license contracts and start-ups) in extension 1, except that the intercept loses significance. The coefficients for all three commercialization measures are close to zero and insignificant, i.e., they do not correlate with this mechanism of student-mediated transfer. The same applies to the indices used in extension 2, except for the teaching-based knowledge exchange mechanism which summarizes how important different teaching-related mechanisms were rated.

Table 4. Estimations on B/M theses in cooperation with companies

Variable/Model type	Baseline Model		Extension 1	Extension 2
	OLS	Tweedie	Tweedie	Tweedie
Intercept	+2.589***	+0.595**	+0.408	−0.295
Type:UAS	+7.937***	+1.610***	+1.735***	+1.358***
Type:University	−0.311	−0.192	−0.126	−0.293
No work exp outside academia	−1.078	−0.591**	−0.505**	−0.242
Field:Biomedical	−1.722**	−0.789***	−0.813***	−0.652***
Field:Social	−0.471	+0.618***	+0.668***	+0.745***
Field:Natural	−1.556**	−0.424**	−0.367*	−0.285
No. of scientists	+0.064***	+0.010***	+0.010***	+0.008***
No. of coop. B/M theses	–	–	–	–
No. of non-coop. B/M theses	+0.033	+0.009**	+0.008**	+0.011***
No. of coop. doctoral theses	+0.905*	+0.346***	+0.315***	–
No. of non-coop. doct. theses	−0.359***	−0.045*	−0.031	−0.032
No. of professional edu. theses	+0.533***	+0.004	+0.022	–
No. of patent applications	–	–	+0.018	–
No. of license contracts	–	–	−0.031	–
No. of start-up companies	–	–	+0.058	–
Index for informal KE	–	–	–	−0.134
Index for research-based KE	–	–	–	−0.176
Index for teaching-based KE	–	–	–	+0.658***
Index for knowledge and techn. commercialization	–	–	–	+0.127

(continued)

Table 4. (*continued*)

Variable/Model type	Baseline Model		Extension 1	Extension 2
	OLS	Tweedie	Tweedie	Tweedie
Observations	686	686	637	524
Adj./Pseudo R2	Adj. R2 45%	Ps. R2 51.4%	Ps. R2 48.8%	Ps. R2 42.9%
AIC	AIC 4934	AIC 2512	AIC 2401	AIC 1864

*** p < 0.01, ** p < 0.05, * p < 0.1

Doctoral Thesis in Cooperation with Companies. A large share of the institutes did not report any cooperation with companies within their doctoral work at all and the baseline models reports negative coefficients for the majority of variables (Table 5). A slight positive effect can be seen for the importance of doctoral education (no. of non-cooperative doctoral theses) and of B/M theses with companies, reflecting the importance of student-mediated knowledge exchange mechanisms within an institute. UAS cannot issue doctoral degrees themselves and their involvement in doctoral education is not institutional but largely based on the contacts and affiliations of individual professors, hence the strong negative coefficient. In both extensions we see that cooperative doctoral work with companies is a lot more closely linked to knowledge commercialization than cooperative work at undergraduate and Master level: both the coefficients for patent applications and start-ups of an institute are significantly positive. Moreover, informal knowledge exchange seems to contribute to some extent to explaining the number of cooperative doctoral theses.

Table 5. Estimations on doctoral theses in cooperation with companies

Variable/Model type	Baseline Model		Extension 1	Extension 2
	OLS	Tweedie	Tweedie	Tweedie
Intercept	+0.379***	−0.814***	−1.202***	−3.997***
Type:UAS	−0.330***	−2.023***	−1.985***	−2.134***
Type:University	−0.225***	−0.693***	−0.704***	−0.562***
No work exp outside academia	−0.140**	−0.542**	−0.429**	−0.084
Field:Biomedical	+0.054	+0.328	+0.392*	+0.440**
Field:Social	−0.138*	−0.476	−0.347	−0.166
Field:Natural	−0.083	−0.305	−0.120	−0.169
No. of scientists	−0.000	+0.002	+0.001	+0.001
No. of coop. B/M theses	+0.005*	+0.021**	+0.012	–
No. of non-coop. B/M theses	+0.002	+0.002	−0.002	+0.004

(continued)

Table 5. (*continued*)

Variable/Model type	Baseline Model		Extension 1	Extension 2
	OLS	Tweedie	Tweedie	Tweedie
No. of coop. doctoral theses	–	–	–	–
No. of non-coop. doct. theses	+0.067***	+0.073***	+0.079***	+0.062***
No. of professional edu. theses	−0.000	−0.002	+0.026*	–
No. of patent applications	–	–	+0.046**	–
No. of license contracts	–	–	+0.082	–
No. of start-up companies	–	–	+0.192**	–
Index for informal KE	–	–	–	+0.312*
Index for research-based KE	–	–	–	+0.166
Index for teaching-based KE	–	–	–	+0.439***
Index for knowledge and techn. commercialization	–	–	–	+0.269***
Observations	686	686	637	524
Adj./Pseudo R2 AIC	Adj. R2 19.7% AIC 1429	Ps.R2 24.1% AIC 747	Ps.R2 18.5% AIC 676	Ps.R2 22.2% AIC 527

*** $p < 0.01$, ** $p < 0.05$, * $p < 0.1$

In sum, the estimations show different patterns for the two different measures of student-mediated knowledge commercialization: whereas cooperative doctoral theses do indeed relate also to patent-applications and start-up companies and reflect the importance of knowledge commercialization in general and in the biomedical fields in particular, the results are different for cooperative B/M theses which are common in teaching-oriented universities of applied sciences and in social sciences institutes. Using such metrics helps with measuring better the knowledge exchange of institutions with these backgrounds.

4   Conclusion

Student-mediated knowledge exchange can be clearly differentiated from knowledge commercialization and academic engagement. It combines several different mechanisms, controlled either by the universities or by the students, that provide explicit or tacit knowledge. Even though several benefits for universities, firms, and students have been found, our knowledge of this mechanism and how students and recent graduates contribute their knowledge to innovation processes in industry is rather superficial. Clearly, mechanisms of knowledge exchange which involve students remain a neglected type of knowledge exchange that few universities seem to approach strategically.

A major obstacle to greater consideration of this type in higher education knowledge exchange strategies and in higher education and innovation policy is the lack of data and of tools for collecting such data. Studies on measuring knowledge exchange and third mission activities of HEIs have often included measures on some mechanisms of student-mediated knowledge exchange (European Commission Directorate-General for Education, Youth, Sport and Culture et al., 2017; Marhl & Pausits, 2013; Molas-Gallart et al., 2002; de la Torre et al., 2021), but they have not yet been taken up widely, for instance in national surveys of higher education institutions, knowledge transfer offices, or graduates. Even recent initiatives stress that knowledge transfer metrics should include teaching-mediated transfers, but exclude them as well from their suggested set of core indicators (Campbell et al., 2020). This is above all due to the difficulty of collecting reliable data which rarely exists at the level of the organization.

The present study demonstrates that it is possible to collect such data by surveying university sub-units. It uses self-assessed data on cooperative bachelor and master's theses (with companies), cooperative doctoral theses, and professional education theses supervised by the faculty of institutes of Swiss HEIs. We find that student-mediated knowledge exchange is a preferred mechanism for teaching-oriented universities. Furthermore, it either substitutes or complements other mechanisms of knowledge exchange and contributes to generating a more comprehensive picture of the knowledge exchange activities of universities. Similar results might be obtained by surveying individual faculty. Higher education institutions themselves as well as their sponsors would be in a good position to request the data from their faculty, opening up the possibility of comparisons and benchmarking and creating incentives for managing this type of knowledge exchange more strategically.

The current study is a first attempt at conceptualizing the phenomenon and providing and evaluating data for a small sample of HEIs, going beyond existing work. Still, further pilot studies and surveys are needed to better integrate student-mediated transfers into knowledge exchange and third mission activities and broaden the understanding of its antecedents and consequences.

Appendix

Appendix 1. Population and realized sample of Swiss HEI institutes

Abbreviation	Name	Population	Realised sample	
		Obs	Obs	in %
Universities				
ETHZ	Swiss Federal Institute of Technology Zurich	183	80	44%
EPFL	Swiss Federal Institute of Technology Lausanne	344	136	40%
UNIBAS	University of Basel	216	97	45%
UNIBE	University of Bern	123	56	46%
UNISG	University of St. Gallen	29	11	38%
UZH	University of Zurich	183	77	42%
UNIFR	University of Fribourg	71	32	45%

(*continued*)

(continued)

Abbreviation	Name	Population	Realised sample	
		Obs	Obs	in %
UNIGE	University of Geneva	134	63	47%
UNIL	University of Lausanne	131	62	47%
UNINE	University of Neuchâtel	27	16	59%
USI	University of Lugano	31	14	45%
All UNI		*1'472*	*644*	*44%*
Universities of Applied Sciences				
FHNW	University of Applied Sciences and Arts Northwestern Switzerland	29	20	69%
OST	Eastern Switzerland University of Applied Sciences	39	24	62%
HSLU	Lucerne University of Applied Sciences and Arts	17	12	71%
BFH	Bern University of Applied Sciences	20	13	65%
SUPSI	University of Applied Sciences and Arts of Southern Switzerland	15	11	73%
ZFH	Zurich University of Applied Sciences	48	27	56%
HES-SO	University of Applied Sciences and Arts Western Switzerland	54	40	74%
All UAS		*222*	*147*	*66%*
All		*1'694*	*791*	*47%*

Appendix 2. Arithmetic means per institute for the regression variables

Variable	Arithmetic Mean
Type:ETH domain (0/1 coded)	0.273
Type:UAS (0/1 coded)	0.186
Type:University (0/1 coded)	0.540
No work experience outside academia (0/1 coded)	0.365
Field:Biomedical (0/1 coded)[a]	0.314
Field:Social (0/1 coded)[a]	0.205
Field:Natural (0/1 coded)[a]	0.655

(continued)

(*continued*)

Variable	Arithmetic Mean
Field:Engineering (0/1 coded)[a]	0.408
No. of scientists	24.9
No. of non-cooperative B/M theses	9.19
No. of cooperative B/M theses	4.30
No. of non-cooperative doctoral theses	2.72
No. of cooperative doctoral theses	0.312
No. of professional education theses	2.25
No. of patent applications	0.891
No. of license contracts	0.386
No. of start-up companies	0.391
Index for informal knowledge and tech transfer (scale 1–5)	2.87
Index for research-based knowledge and tech transfer (scale 1–5)	2.72
Index for teaching-based knowledge and tech transfer (scale 1–5)	2.34
Index for knowledge and technology commercialization (scale 1–5)	1.89

References

Arundel, A., Es-Sadki, N.: Toward a comprehensive set of metrics for knowledge transfer. In: Arundel, A., Athreye, S., Wunsch-Vincent, S. (eds.) Harnessing Public Research for Innovation in the 21st Century, 1st edn., pp. 425–451. Cambridge University Press (2021)

Barjak, F., Heimsch, F.: Organisational mission and the involvement of academic research units in knowledge sharing with private companies. Ind. Innov. **28**(4), 395–423 (2021)

Bekkers, R., Bodas Freitas, I.M.: Analysing knowledge transfer channels between universities and industry: to what degree do sectors also matter? Res. Policy **37**(10), 1837–1853 (2008)

Bienkowska, D., Klofsten, M.: Creating entrepreneurial networks: academic entrepreneurship, mobility and collaboration during PhD education. High. Educ. **64**(2), 207–222 (2012)

Borrell-Damian, L.: Collaborative Doctoral Education: University-Industry Partnerships for Enhancing Knowledge Exchange; Doc-Careers Project. European University Association, Brussels (2009)

Campbell, A., Cavalade, C., Haunold, C., Karanikic, P., Karlsson Dinnetz, M., Piccaluga, A.: Knowledge Transfer Metrics—Towards a European-wide set of harmonised indicators (2020). https://ec.europa.eu/jrc/en/publication/knowledge-transfer-metrics-towards-european-wide-set-harmonised-indicators. Accessed 29 Oct 2020

Cowan, R., David, P.A., Foray, D.: The explicit economics of knowledge codification and tacitness. Ind. Corp. Chang. **9**(2), 211–253 (2000)

D'Este, P., Patel, P.: University-industry linkages in the UK: what are the factors underlying the variety of interactions with industry? Res. Policy **36**(9), 1295–1313 (2007)

European Commission Directorate-General for Education, Youth, Sport and Culture, Ingenio, Q-Plan International, University of Manchester, University of Rome, & University of Twente. Measuring the contribution of higher education to innovation capacity in the EU: Study. LU: Publications Office of the European Union (2017). https://data.europa.eu/doi/10.2766/802127. Accessed 26 Apr 2022

Geuna, A., Muscio, A.: The governance of university knowledge transfer: a critical review of the literature. Minerva **47**(1), 93–114 (2009)

Geuna, A., Rossi, F.: Changes to university IPR regulations in Europe and the impact on academic patenting. Res. Policy **40**(8), 1068–1076 (2011)

Gores, T., Link, A.N.: The globalization of the Bayh-Dole act. Ann. Sci. Technol. Policy **5**(1), 1–90 (2021)

Hayter, C.S., Rasmussen, E., Rooksby, J.H.: Beyond formal university technology transfer: innovative pathways for knowledge exchange. J. Technol. Transf. **45**(1), 1–8 (2020)

Henderson, R., Jaffe, A., Trajtenberg, M.: Universities as a source of commercial technology: a detailed analysis of university patenting, 1965–1988. Rev. Econ. Stat. **80**, 119–127 (1998)

Hewitt-Dundas, N.: Research intensity and knowledge transfer activity in UK universities. Res. Policy **41**(2), 262–275 (2012)

Hughes, A., Kitson, M.: Pathways to impact and the strategic role of universities: new evidence on the breadth and depth of university knowledge exchange in the UK and the factors constraining its development. Camb. J. Econ. **36**(3), 723–750 (2012)

Kitagawa, F., Sánchez Barrioluengo, M., Uyarra, E.: Third mission as institutional strategies: between isomorphic forces and heterogeneous pathways. Sci. Public Policy **43**(6), 736–750 (2016)

Kunttu, L.: Educational involvement in innovative university-industry collaboration. Technol. Innov. Manag. Rev. **7**(12), 14–22 (2017)

Lee, H., Miozzo, M.: How does working on university–industry collaborative projects affect science and engineering doctorates' careers? Evidence from a UK research-based university. J. Technol. Transf. **40**(2), 293–317 (2015)

Marhl, M., Pausits, A.: Third mission indicators for new ranking methodologies. Eval. High. Educ. **5**(1), 43–64 (2013)

Molas-Gallart, J., Salter, A., Patel, P., Scott, A., Duran, X.: Measuring Third Stream Activities. Final Report to the Russell Group of Universities. SPRU, University of Sussex, Brighton (2002)

Mowery, D.C., Sampat, B.N.: The Bayh-Dole act of 1980 and university-industry technology transfer: a model for other OECD governments? J. Technol. Transf. **30**(1), 115–127 (2005)

Orazbayeva, B., Davey, T., Plewa, C., Galán-Muros, V.: Engagement of academics in education-driven university-business cooperation: a motivation-based perspective. Stud. High. Educ. **45**(8), 1723–1736 (2020)

Perkmann, M., Salandra, R., Tartari, V., McKelvey, M., Hughes, A.: Academic engagement: a review of the literature 2011–2019. Res. Policy **50**(1), 104114 (2021)

Perkmann, M., et al.: Academic engagement and commercialisation: a review of the literature on university–industry relations. Res. Policy **42**(2), 423–442 (2013)

Rossi, F.: The drivers of efficient knowledge transfer performance: evidence from British universities. Camb. J. Econ. **42**(3), 729–755 (2018)

Rossi, F., Rosli, A.: Indicators of university–industry knowledge transfer performance and their implications for universities: Evidence from the United Kingdom. Stud. High. Educ. **40**(10), 1970–1991 (2015)

Sánchez-Barrioluengo, M.: Articulating the 'three-missions' in Spanish universities. Res. Policy **43**(10), 1760–1773 (2014)

Schartinger, D., Schibany, A., Gassler, H.: Interactive relations between universities and firms: empirical evidence for Austria. J. Technol. Transfer. **26**, 255–268 (2001)

Thune, T.: Doctoral students on the university–industry interface: a review of the literature. High. Educ. **58**(5), 637 (2009) de la Torre, E.M., Casani, F., Perez-Esparrells, C.: Measuring universities' engagement: a revision of the European research projects and the actual use of the so-called 'third mission' indicators. Revista de Estudios Regionales **120**, 97–128 (2021)

Zalewska-Kurek, K., Harms, R.: Managing autonomy in university-industry research: a case of collaborative Ph.D. projects in the Netherlands. Rev. Manag. Sci. **14**(2, SI), 393–416 (2020)

Unveiling the *"Vulnerability Cycle"* of Migrant Workers in Mauritius: Applying a Grounded Theory Approach to Health and Wellbeing of Migrant Workers

Sanjayduth Bhundhoo[1]([✉]) [iD], Preeya Vijayalakshmee Coolen[1] [iD], and Roslyn S. Fraser[2] [iD]

[1] Department of Environment, Science and Social Sustainability, University of Technology Mauritius, Port Louis, Mauritius
sanjayduth.bhundhoo@utm.ac.mu
[2] Stephen F. Austin State University, Nacogdoches, USA

Abstract. The welfare of migrant workers in Mauritius in terms of their health and wellbeing is the main topic of this research. The aim of this study is to understand the health and wellbeing of migrant workers from a social work perspective through the application of the grounded theory. A qualitative approach was used to gather the data. Semi-structured interviews were carried out with twenty-two migrant workers from Bangladesh, Madagascar, Nepal, South Africa and India who have been employed and reside in Mauritius for more than one year. The respondents are employed in a variety of industries, including vegetable plantations, supermarkets, hotels, building sites, ICT & BPO, Communication and textile factories. This study adds to the body of knowledge on migrant workers' well-being by utilizing the Grounded Theory in Mauritius. The main findings of this research emanate from the application of the Grounded Theory and through the application of the Theoretical Coding which is a qualitative research approach. The findings were presented in terms of initial coding then identifying relationship between the different codes that have been generated and finally developing a re-fined theoretical concept as follows: "The Vulnerability Cycle of Migrant workers": This refined code was generated from the findings of this research by application of the Grounded Theory. It comprises of the different elements such as precarious employment, substandard living conditions, and inadequate healthcare that affect negatively the health and wellbeing of migrant workers working in Mauritius.

Keywords: Grounded Theory · Migrant Workers · Social Work · Vulnerability Cycle · Wellbeing

1 Introduction

It is commonly known that the phenomenon of migration is intricate and multidimensional, influenced by a wide range of factors such as environmental, psychological, political, demographic, and sociological dimensions. Eventually, there is a lot of focus

© The Author(s), under exclusive license to Springer Nature Switzerland AG 2025
K. Hinkelmann and H. Smuts (Eds.): Society 5.0 2024, CCIS 2173, pp. 41–56, 2025.
https://doi.org/10.1007/978-3-031-71412-2_4

on "sustainable migration" these days. According to Erdal, et al. (2018), "sustainable migration" is defined as movement that has positive impacts on the environment, the economy, and society. Furthermore, "sustainable migration" was defined by the United Nations (1998) as the advantages and costs of migration with regard to its effects on politics, society, and culture. The welfare of migrant workers in Mauritius is the main topic of this research, as it is the contribution that social work makes in improving their well-being on both a social and environmental level. People have always migrated across human history in search of work opportunities elsewhere. History shows that social work has often helped migrant workers to overcome challenges and reintegrate into society. Tukkoch et al. (2022) assert that social workers are in a better position to advocate for their well-being in the host nation and to encourage sustainable labour mobility. Labour migration is seen as a moving activity rather than a notion in this quickly growing world. In terms of better living circumstances, employment opportunities, access to hygienic facilities, and ensuring that these foreign workers are effectively incorporated into the Mauritius society. Therefore, social work plays a significant role in promoting welfare (Arango, 2000). Given that the vast majority of the island's ancestors were international migrant labourers, Mauritius's history suggests that the country has always been one of migration. There were about 35768 registered migrant workers in Mauritius as of September 2023 (30902 men and 4866 women). They are mainly from India, Bangladesh, China, Madagascar, and Nepal (Ministry of Labour, Human Resource Development and Training, 2023).

1.1 Problem Statement

With the acceleration of economic globalization, there is a record number of migrant workers. Due to high unemployment and growing levels of poverty, many people in emerging nations are searching for work elsewhere. In industrialized countries, there is a growing need for labour, especially unskilled labour (International Labour Organization, 2024). Millions of workers and their families have therefore fled their own countries in quest of work abroad. It should be highlighted that significant efforts have been undertaken over the years to gather trustworthy and comparable data about labour migration worldwide. Due to unreported cases of migrant workers splitting up in different countries and working and living as illegal workers, there are still significant differences in estimating the precise number of migrant workers that have shifted in other countries, as the ILO and the international community have pointed out. In response, the ILO released global and regional estimates of migrant workers. These estimates suggest that there are currently 244 million migrants globally, or 3.3% of the world's population. Women make up over half of migrants. Migrant workers' remittances support the economic growth of both their home countries and the nations to which they relocate. However, migrant workers usually lack proper social protection and are vulnerable to human trafficking and exploitation.

1.2 Justification

Numerous studies have highlighted the disadvantaged and vulnerable position of migrant workers. Beijl (2000) found that many migrant workers never take a day off. In addition,

Moyce and Schenker (2018) reported that migrant labourers often work long hours in hazardous or isolated environments without access to social or legal services. Basey and Yeoh (2015) noted that migrant workers frequently incur debts and excessive placement fees, leading to long-term financial burdens. Additional challenges include unequal pay and benefits compared to local workers, racism and discrimination, limited citizenship rights, lack of social participation, and various forms of abuse (Syed, 2008). Despite numerous regulations in Mauritius designed to protect migrant workers, there are persistent complaints about migrant rights violations. The Integral Human Development report (2023) mentioned about forced and exploitative labour among migrant workers from Bangladesh, India, Madagascar, Sri Lanka, and Nepal. Trade unionists have highlighted issues of modern slavery, noting that migrant workers are underpaid, overworked, live in poor conditions, and may face deportation if they complain (Industrial Global Union, 2018). Nevertheless, there is a notable gap in research on the role of social work in enhancing the well-being of migrant workers in Mauritius. This study aims to fill that gap by conducting in-depth research and recommending strategies to improve health and well-being among migrant workers in Mauritius.

1.3   Research Gap

Numerous studies have been conducted on the economics, labour, immigration laws, and working conditions of migrant workers (Hatzigeorgiou & Lodefalk, 2021) (Doorn, et al., 2023). However, there is a significant study gap concerning the living conditions, health and general well-being of migrant workers. Despite, Mauritius is classified as a small island state there is a large number of migrant labour force working in Mauritius and the figures keep on increasing (Statistics Mauritius, 2023). However, little study has been done on the welfare of these workers. As a result, this research will contribute to the social work community's to better understand migrant workers' health and well-being.

1.4   Purpose of the Study

The aim of this study is to understand the health and wellbeing of migrant workers from a social work perspective through the application of the grounded theory.

1.5   Objective

- To determine factors that affect the health and wellbeing of migrant workers.
- To propose appropriate recommendations in improving the health and wellbeing of migrant workers in Mauritius
- To develop a theoretical concept towards health and wellbeing of migrant workers through the application of Grounded Theory.

2   Literature Review

2.1   Migrant Workers

Migrant workers are defined by the International Labour Organization (ILO) as people of working age who reside in the measurement country and who fit into one of the following categories: Regular inhabitants are foreign nationals who are either employed or unemployed in the labour force of their home countries. or uncommon citizens who were present in their country of origin and had a connection to the labour force. Employment performed by individuals who have migrated from another nation is referred to as migrant labour. In addition to the taxes that migrant workers pay in the host country and in terms of growth and development they contribute, the "host" country also gains from the talents that migrant workers already possess. (The 2020 United Nations Global Compact). ILO official figures indicate that there are around 169 million international migrant workers dispersed globally, accounting for 5% of the global labour force (International Labour Organization, 2024). This figure is segregated in terms of 41.5% of the population is female and 58.5% of the population is male. Migrant workers enable to fill shortages of labour in a range of industries, including construction, hospitality, agriculture, and domestic labour markets. Therefore, migrant workers are vital to the global labour market (International Labour Organization, 2024). Since the countries of origin and destination both gain significantly from the economic and social development of international migrant workers, migrant workers are vital to both nations.

2.2   Wellbeing of Migrants

According to studies, migrant workers frequently deal with a variety of challenges, such as limited access to services and facilities, employment exploitation, unsanitary housing conditions, lack of safety and healthy environment at work, inadequate health care, lack of settlement programs and services, difficulty in integrating into the local community, and a lack of social networks with inland residents (Shelley, 2007). Regrettably, these problems are not new and have significantly lowered the standard of living and wellbeing of migrants (Jackson, 2013). The following elements have been shown to have an impact on migrant worker's welfare in the literature that has been published on the topic: (i) the access to basic necessities like food, clothing, shelter, (ii) green space; (iii) social support; (iv) a sense of belonging and (v) living environment; (vi) job security; (vii) individual factors like health, employment, and finances; (viii) subjective wellbeing; (ix) civic engagement and (x) job security (Elroy, 2021). According to research, social capital also has an impact on migrants' well-being. It has to do with migrant workers' positive working relationships with their supervisors and co-workers. These connections are strengthened by mutuality and trust, which enhances worker wellbeing (Ngo, 2017). Nevertheless, some criticize the literature on subjective wellbeing, arguing that it provides a "eudemonic" notion of what makes a happy life and a limited concept of pleasure. That is, one that goes beyond "hedonic," which emphasizes pleasure, and is both functional and rewarding (Oles & Jankowski, 2018). However, keep in mind that the aforementioned healthiness differs based on the needs and preferences of different countries and people. The goals and mindset of migrant labourers are crucial in influencing their general well-being. Moreover, the extent to which the infrastructure of the receiving country has been altered to support the welfare of migrant workers (Singh & Vijila, 2024).

2.3 Migration Crisis and SDGs

Concerns about the health, welfare, and well-being of migrant workers are common (International Labour Organisation, 2024). United Nations stressed that the so-called "migrant crisis" is being exacerbated by the world's expanding labour migration, which includes Mauritius. This topic is increasingly well recognized because of its direct relationship to the complex difficulties being tackled by the United Nations Sustainable Development Goals (SDGs). The first mention of migration in the SDGs is found in Target 10.7, which is under Goal 10: eliminate inequality within and between nations. By implementing well-thought-out and well-managed migration policies, this objective, among other things, encourages human mobility and movement in an orderly, safe, regular, and responsible way (Global Migration Data Analysis Centre, 2023).

2.4 The Push and Pull Factors Explaining Migration

Globalization and the speed at which technology is developing have led to a rise in labour migration worldwide. The push and pull forces are the two basic theories that explain migration. The push factors are those that motivate people to leave their country of origin. The main causes of these problems are deplorable living conditions, political upheaval, corruption, racism, natural disasters, climate change, disputes between groups and religions, etc. Conversely, pull factors refer to the elements that attract migrant workers to a country or region. These elements include a high standard of living, low taxes, a reasonable employment opportunity, a stable political environment, access to modern medical care, acceptance of various religions and cultures, harmony and peace, and high income (Hear, et al., 2020).

2.5 Challenges of Migrant Workers in Accessing Their Health and Well Being

Research indicates that many migrant workers face challenges in obtaining certain types of wellbeing, like good health and favourable working conditions, due to low levels of education and literacy, as well as a lack of awareness about the laws pertaining to healthcare and equal rights in their new nation (Hasan, et al., 2021). Furthermore, despite the fact that migrant workers can get health insurance plans, they may still encounter barriers to accessing medical services due to social, cultural, and language marginalization (Ornek, et al., 2022). Research indicates that when migrant workers work in their host countries, they often face the lots of challenges and problems in terms of accessing to health care, language problem, marginalization, psychological and emotional problem, social isolation and poor access to leisure and entertainment (Bhundhoo, et al., 2024). Unfortunately, despite Mauritius's legislative structure being altered to provide fair access for foreign workers, the above-mentioned problems still exist among migrant workers (Caroll, 2000).

2.6 System Perspective Theory Explaining Migration

This theory posits that migration is a complex phenomenon encompassing various interconnected elements. It helps in comprehending the motivations, triggers, and repercussions of migration processes. The systemic approach encompasses factors like social, environmental, cultural, political, and global contexts concerning migration (Schluter et al., 2019). Adopting a systemic perspective facilitates a deeper understanding of the origins, effects, and potential remedies for migration challenges. Viewing migration through a systemic lens underscores its intricate nature, influenced by an array of inter-dependent factors such as push and pull forces (stemming from political, social, and environmental conditions) and migrants' backgrounds, including their socioeconomic status, educational attainment, and skill sets. The systemic perspective theory addition-ally assists host countries in understanding the ramifications that migration might bring in terms of demographic shifts, labour market dynamics, and demands on public ser-vices. Adopting a systemic perspective on migration enables policymakers, academics, and stakeholders to grasp its multifaceted dynamics fully, leading to the formulation of more comprehensive and effective solutions to migration related challenges. Recogniz-ing that migration issues cannot be tackled in isolation, this approach emphasizes the necessity for collabouration among all stakeholders (Tan et al., 2016).

2.7 Migration and Health

Migrant workers are required to undergo a comprehensive medical assessment as part of the work permit application process. Only individuals deemed free from major illnesses, infectious diseases, and pregnancy are permitted entry into the country. Subsequently, to assess their ongoing eligibility to remain in the country and to mitigate deportation risks, workers must undergo a follow-up medical examination within a month of their arrival. Additionally, they are subject to annual health assessments administered by a private entity contracted by the government, known as the Foreign Workers Medical Examination Agency (FOMEMA) (Loganathan, et al., 2019) (Abusuulah & Nooriah, 2002). Health is impacted by a complex network of social, economic, cultural, and gendered factors in addition to the existence or absence of disease. Only individuals who are deemed physically fit are permitted to enter the nation as migrant domestic workers thanks to pre-depature medical screening; yet, the stress of the job and potential for abuse and exploitation pose a threat to their mental and physical health (Human Rights Watch, 2005). Low socioeconomic status and the demanding nature of the work, which requires employees to live and work in their employer's private residence, can exacerbate stress and its related conditions, which include a lack of control over the workplace and restricted access to health determinants like social support, enough financial resources, and access to healthcare (Spitzer, 2016).

3 Methodology

3.1 Qualitative Approach - Classic Grounded Theory Approach

To develop a theory on the well-being of migrant workers in Mauritius, a qualitative approach using classic grounded theory was employed. Data was collected through in-depth, semi-structured interviews, which aligned with the objectives of grounded theory by allowing respondents to express their perspectives freely. Grounded theory aims to identify primary concerns of participants and how they address these issues (Charmaz &

Belgrave, 2012). It is particularly useful for exploring previously unexamined phenomena (Corbin & Strauss, 2014). Grounded theory's focus on marginalized populations makes it suitable for social work research (Holman, 1996). Its emphasis on participant knowledge and avoidance of preconceived notions helps cross-cultural research (Corbett, 2021). Unlike constructivist grounded theory, which seeks a broad range of information, classic grounded theory aims to identify a key variable to generate a precise theory (Glaser, 2002). The prescriptive data analysis method of Strauss' grounded theory was deemed incompatible with this study's focus on participant concerns (Azulai, 2020). Conventional grounded theory uses an inductive methodology, determining the study subject from participants' perspectives to generate theory. A full literature review is delayed until open and theoretical coding are nearly complete to avoid preconceived notions. Literature is then integrated as supplementary data (Dunne, 2011). The validity of a grounded theory is based on its application, relevance, workability, and modifiability, rather than verification. A theory is suitable if its categories align with observed events, meaningful if it captures participants' main concerns, and workable if it can explain, predict, and understand substantive facts (Heath, 2006).

Sampling and Eligibility Criteria
A purposeful convenience sample was employed, targeting migrant workers who had been in Mauritius for at least a year, originating primarily from Bangladesh, India, Madagascar, Nepal, and various African countries. These respondents were employed across diverse industries, including textiles, construction, supermarkets, hotels, ICT, BPO, and vegetable plantations.

Justification of Selected Audience
The selected migrant workers represent a diverse range of geographic, cultural, and socio-economic backgrounds similar to Mauritius, enriching the analysis by capturing varied perspectives. These countries are significant sources of migrant labour, providing insights into international labour migration dynamics. Studying both commonalities and differences among workers from these regions helps understand migration decision-making, integration experiences, and socio-economic outcomes.

Target Audience
The study interviewed 22 people, aged 21 to 45 (12 men and 10 women), all of whom had at least a basic education. Interviews lasted between 120 to 180 min. Casual discussions with other migrant workers in various sectors were also conducted to understand their living conditions and perceptions of well-being.

Procedure
Interviews were conducted with participant consent over three months (January to March 2024). Participants were informed about the study's aim, their right to withdraw, and confidentiality measures. Interviews focused on living conditions, well-being, and working conditions, with probing questions to elicit in-depth responses.

Interview Design and Process
The Grounded Theory approach was used, allowing flexibility in questioning to explore

emergent themes. Interviews were primarily conducted at participants' residences, involving respondents from different island regions. Cultural sensitivity, religious beliefs, and privacy were carefully respected, enhancing participant comfort and response validity. Data saturation was achieved when no new information emerged, indicating an appropriate sample size.

Ethical Considerations
Ethical considerations included participant consent, confidentiality, and voluntary participation. Participants were informed about the study's purpose, and their consents were obtained before recording interviews. Confidentiality was strictly maintained, with interpreters signing confidentiality agreements.

Problems Encountered
Language barriers required interpreters, and accessing participants' quarters often needed prior permission. Safety and security were managed by involving local guides. Some interviews were interrupted by participants' phone calls, and some workers were initially reluctant due to fear of repercussions.

Sample Size
While the study's findings cannot be generalized to the larger migrant worker population in Mauritius, it reflects significant insights into their health and well-being. The small sample size was due to resource and time constraints.

Limitations of the Research
Bias was a potential issue, as participants might have downplayed their struggles due to fear of employer retaliation. To mitigate this, confidentiality was emphasized, and probing techniques were used to ensure the accuracy and genuineness of responses.

4 Data Analysis

The main findings of this research emanate from the application of the Grounded Theory and through the application of the Theoretical Coding which is a qualitative research approach. Theoretical coding involves the process, as outlined by Glaser (1997), of initially dissecting data and subsequently organizing it into conceptual codes, which ultimately form the framework for explaining the underlying phenomena within the data. In this study, constant comparative method was employed, entailing meticulous line-by-line scrutiny of data gathered from interviews, focus group discussions, and observations (Hernandez, 2009). The data collected throughout this research was analysed by applying the thematic analysis. This process enables to determine patterns, themes, sub-themes, codes and theoretical codes. This process is explained as follows:

Diagram 1: Process of data coding and developing theoretical coding

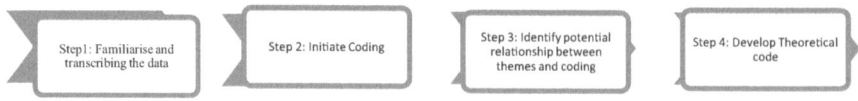

Step 1: Familiarise and transcribing the data

This step is the first phase of the process, it is about writing down a plethora of notes, annotating transcripts, underlining, highlighting and grouping all the data gathered from interviews of the migrant workers. The recorded interviews were listened at several times, review my interview transcripts and filter only the required information. MAXQDA software was used in grouping different data and transcribed audio files of participants easily.

Step 2: Initiating coding process

The second phase was to convert the filtered data into themes and then coding started. According to Braun & Clarke (2023) codes are considered as "the building blocks of analysis" that helps researchers to interpret data in relation to the research aim and objectives. Therefore, after filtering the data into themes, different codes were assigned to each theme. Coding involves systematically labelling or categorizing different parts of the data according to themes or concepts. The themes created in the previous steps were examined and cross-checked against coded segments, documents, and the full code system in this phase. The research questions, data, and topics must all be pertinent and consistent.

Step 3: Identify potential relationship between themes and coding

The themes and codes created were examined and cross-checked against the research aim and objectives. It is important to take into consideration the consistency of the data and themes. At this stage after taking into consideration the consistency of the data, themes and coding, the process of establishing potential relationship between themes and coding were done. This involved comparing different coded segments or looking for patterns across the data. This enable readers to better understand the correlation between the initial themes and coding (Braun & Clarke, 2023).

Step 4: Develop Theoretical code

This step is the most crucial step as it enables to summarise and bring together all the data into a single theoretical code. This allows to develop appropriate framework or theory (Byrne, 2022). The theoretical code design under each theme provides meaningful interpretations and implications for theory, practice and policy.

5   Results and Findings

Initial Coding and Theoretical Codes for Key Themes

Key theme	Initial Code	Identifying Relationship	Theoretical Code
Conditions of work	Working conditions	Negative impact on health and work	Precarious work conditions and health

Summary: Long hours, low pay, and safety hazards at work adversely affect migrant workers' physical and mental health. Overwork leads to fatigue, insomnia, and other health problems, reflecting a direct correlation between work hours and health consequences. Migrant workers often accept long working hours (12–16 h) to earn additional pay. However, this practice negatively impacts their long-term health and well-being, leading to various physical and mental health issues.

Key theme	Initial Code	Identifying Relationship	Theoretical Code
Mode of living and accommodation	Accommodation	Poor living conditions and illness	Poor living environment and health risk

Summary: Overcrowded and unhygienic living conditions increase the risk of infectious diseases. Poor ventilation, lack of privacy, and inadequate sanitation contribute to health vulnerabilities among migrant workers. Poor living conditions, such as overcrowding, inadequate sanitation, and poor ventilation, increase health risks for migrant workers. These conditions contribute to the spread of transmittable diseases and respiratory problems. Improving living standards and implementing preventive health measures are essential to safeguard their health.

Key theme	Initial Code	Identifying Relationship	Theoretical Code
Socialisation among community	Social Isolation	Psychological stress and feeling of marginalisation	Marginalisation and wellbeing

Summary: Language barriers and cultural differences lead to social isolation, causing psychological stress and feelings of marginalisation. Lack of integration with local communities exacerbates these issues. Systemic discrimination, social exclusion, and economic disadvantage reduce the physical, psychological, and social well-being of migrant workers. Addressing these issues requires inclusive policies, social support systems, and empowerment initiatives to overcome structural barriers and promote holistic well-being.

Key theme	Initial Code	Identifying Relationship	Theoretical Code
Healthcare facilities and services	Healthcare access and delayed in treatment	Limited choice in healthcare access and delayed treatment	Healthcare accessibility barriers and treatment delay

Summary: Migrant workers face significant barriers to accessing healthcare, including language problems and lack of health insurance, leading to delayed treatment and worsened health outcomes. Migrant workers face significant challenges in accessing healthcare due to financial constraints, language barriers, and lack of culturally sensitive healthcare facilities. These barriers lead to delays in seeking and receiving medical care, resulting in worsened health outcomes. Targeted interventions are necessary to ensure equitable healthcare access.

Key theme	Initial Code	Identifying Relationship	Theoretical Code
Leisure and entertainment facilities	Leisure and Entertainment	Lack of interest in leisure and entertainment facilities	Leisure deprivation and social disconnection

Summary: Limited access to recreational activities contributes to stress, burnout, and health issues. Lack of participation in cultural activities deepens the gap between migrant and local workers, increasing social disconnection. Limited access to leisure activities impacts the social integration and well-being of migrant workers. Lack of opportunities for recreation and cultural participation leads to isolation and alienation, exacerbating social inequalities. Promoting inclusive recreational initiatives and fostering cultural exchange are crucial for enhancing social cohesion and well-being.

Key theme	Initial Code	Identifying Relationship	Theoretical Code
Security and safety	Security	Safety and security concern	Safe living environment and tolerance

Summary: Migrant workers generally feel safe, but complaints from neighbors about noise pollution create tension. A safe and secure environment is crucial for their well-being, emphasizing the need for community tolerance. Providing safe accommodations for migrant workers ensures their physical safety and promotes an inclusive and accepting community environment. Safe living conditions foster tolerance and harmonious coexistence between migrant workers and local residents, enhancing the well-being and integration of migrant populations.

Key theme	Initial Code	Identifying Relationship	Theoretical Code
Sending money back to their family	Remittance	Remittance as subjective well-being	Remittance as subjective wellbeing

Summary: Sending money home is crucial for migrant workers' well-being. However, difficulties in remitting funds due to banking hurdles cause psychological stress. Remittances are vital for supporting families' basic needs and education. Sending remittances contributes to the subjective well-being of migrant workers and their families. The act of financially supporting family members provides fulfillment and satisfaction, positively impacting the mental and emotional health of migrant workers.

Key theme	Initial Code	Identifying Relationship	Theoretical Code
Social and psychological support in under distress situation	Social and psychological support	Absence of social and psychological help	Social support deficiency and mental strain

Summary: Lack of pre-departure and post-arrival counselling, coupled with unaware-ness of rights, leads to social deprivation and mental strain. Migrant workers experience loneliness and anxiety, highlighting the need for comprehensive support systems. Send-ing remittances contributes to the subjective well-being of migrant workers and their families. The act of financially supporting family members provides fulfillment and satisfaction, positively impacting the mental and emotional health of migrant workers.

6 Discussion

This study corroborates the findings of Shelley (2007) by confirming that migrant work-ers face numerous challenges, such as limited access to services, employment exploita-tion, unsanitary housing, inadequate healthcare, lack of settlement programs, and dif-ficulties in socializing with local communities. However, unlike Shelley's findings, the study found that in Mauritius, migrant workers do not suffer from lack of safety and poor working environments. The research aligns with Elroy (2021), demonstrating that living conditions, access to basic needs, social support, job security, health, and remit-tance directly impact the health and well-being of migrant workers. This study also supports Beijl (2000), who highlighted the disadvantaged and vulnerable positions of migrant workers, often requiring them to work long hours. It resonates with Moyce and Schenker (2018), emphasizing the lack of access to social or legal services for these workers. Consistent with Hasan et al. (2021), it reveals that language barriers hinder migrant workers from accessing healthcare facilities in host countries. Additionally, the research matches the findings of Ornek et al. (2022), showing that migrant workers struggle to socialize with local communities and often feel marginalised. The study fol-lows the system perspective theory, which advocates for a comprehensive approach from policymakers and stakeholders to address the challenges faced by migrant workers, as suggested by Tan et al. (2016). However, it contradicts Spitzer (2016), who associated low socioeconomic status and demanding work conditions with stress and poor living conditions. This research found that low socioeconomic background does not necessar-ily lead to poor living conditions and stress. Key findings highlight that difficulties in sending remittances, lack of leisure and entertainment facilities, poor socialization, lack of moral and emotional support, low self-esteem, isolation, low living standards, and job insecurity significantly impact migrant workers' health and well-being, reaffirming Jackson (2013). Utilizing the Grounded Theory and theoretical coding under a quali-tative research approach, the study develops a refined theoretical concept called **"The Vulnerability Cycle of Migrant Workers," illustrating the intricate relationships between various factors affecting their lives**.

7 Recommendations and Conclusion

7.1 Improvement in the Living Condition

There should be regular inspections of migrant housing premises, conduct by sanitary officers and labour officers. This will help in improving housing standards for migrant workers by enforcing regulations on overcrowding rooms, sanitation, and ventilation in living accommodations. In addition, employers should provide access to affordable and decent housing options that prioritize the health and safety of migrant workers.

7.2 Migrant Social Workers

Research indicates that social workers have the capacity to assist migrants in their integration into cultural and social contexts, thereby contributing to their overall well-being. Consequently, migrant social workers are positioned to play a pivotal role in enhancing the welfare of migrant workers. It is recommended that the government consider the recruitment of migrant social workers to provide essential social services and address the needs of migrant workers. This initiative would ensure that migrant workers have a dependable individual to turn to for guidance, assistance, and support as needed. Additionally, migrant social workers would actively engage in disseminating information on migrant rights, thereby facilitating access to various resources tailored to their specific needs.

7.3 Policies and Programs

Develop inclusive policies and programs that address systemic discrimination and promote social integration and economic empowerment for migrant workers. Provide culturally sensitive support services, including language assistance and mental health resources, to address the unique needs of migrant communities. Develop partnerships between government agencies, NGOs, and community organizations to advocate for the rights and well-being of migrant workers.

7.4 Access to Health Care Facilities

Expand access to healthcare services for migrant workers by providing affordable healthcare options and eliminating language barriers. Train healthcare providers on cultural competency and sensitivity to better serve migrant populations. Establish outreach programs to educate migrant workers about their healthcare rights and facilitate timely access to medical care.

7.5 Community Engagement and Cross-Cultural Interaction

Create recreational programs and cultural events that cater to the diverse interests and backgrounds of migrant workers. Promote community engagement and cross-cultural interactions through initiatives such as language exchange programs and cultural festivals. Encourage collaboration between migrant communities and local organizations to develop inclusive leisure opportunities.

7.6 Remittance Facilities

Facilitate access to affordable remittance services and financial literacy programs for migrant workers to maximize the positive impact of remittances sending to their families. Promote economic empowerment initiatives that enable migrant workers to invest in education, healthcare, and entrepreneurship in their home countries. Recognize the contributions of migrant workers to their families and communities through public awareness campaigns and policy advocacy efforts.

7.7 Social and Psychological Support Programme

Establish support networks and peer mentoring programs for migrant workers to provide emotional and practical assistance. Offer counselling services and mental health resources tailored to the needs of migrant populations, including trauma-informed care and stress management techniques. Strengthen collaboration between government agencies, NGOs, and community-based organizations to address social isolation and promote social connectedness among migrant communities.

7.8 Conclusion

In conclusion, this study shed light on the vulnerability experienced by migrant workers, which is perpetuated by interconnected factors across various domains of their lives. It illustrates how adverse working conditions, substandard living arrangements, social isolation, healthcare barriers, leisure deprivation, remittance challenges, and lack of social and psychological support collectively contribute to a continuous cycle of vulnerability. The different codes generated from this research emphasizes the dynamic interplay between these factors, highlighting how each element reinforces and exacerbates the vulnerabilities faced by migrant workers, leading to adverse outcomes in their physical, mental, health and social well-being. This research emphasises the potential roles of migrant social workers in facilitating the integration and promoting the well-being of migrant workers in Mauritius. Through their expertise and culturally sensitive approach, migrant social workers can address the multifaceted challenges faced by migrant populations, thereby enhancing their social and cultural adaptation and overall quality of life. The proposition of recruiting migrant social workers by the government emerges as a promising strategy to provide tailored social services and support, fostering trust and empowerment among migrant communities. By equipping migrant workers with essential information about their rights and available resources, migrant social workers can play a crucial role in bridging gaps and facilitating access to opportunities for migrant workers. In addition, concerted efforts from policymakers, social service agencies, and community stakeholders are essential to harness the full potential of migrant social workers in promoting inclusivity, social cohesion, and well-being for all members of society.

Disclosure of Interests. The authors have no competing interests to declare that are relevant to the content of this article.

References

Abusuulah, K.A., Nooriah, M.: Pre-employment screening and monitoring of the health of foreign workers. J. Health Transl. Med. (JUMMEC) **7**(1), 82–84 (2002)

Arango, J.: Explaining migration: a critical view. Int. Soc. Sci. J. **52**(165), 283–296 (2000)

Azulai, A.: Are grounded theory and action research compatible? Considerations for methodological triangulation. Can. J. Action Res. **21**(2), 4–24 (2020)

Basey, G., Yeoh, B.S.: Migration and precarious work: national debt, employment and livelihood strategies amongst Bangladeshi migrant men working in Singapore's construction industry. Migrating Out Poverty Working Paper **26**, 26–65 (2015)

Beijl, R.Z.: Documenting discrimination against migrant workers in the labour market: a comparative study of four European countries. International Labour Organisation (2000)

Bhundhoo, S., Coolen, V.L., Fraser, R.: Understanding the wellbeing of migrant workers using the Grounded Theory within the Small Island States-a case study of Mauritius, Milan. In: International Academic Conference on Humanities and Social Science (2024)

Braun, V., Clarke, V.: Towards good practice in thematic analysis: avoiding common problems and becoming a knowing researcher. Int. J. Transgender Health **24**(1), 1–6 (2023)

Byrne, D.: A worked example of Baun and Clarke's approach to reflexive thematic analysis. Qual. Quant. **56**(3), 1391–1412 (2022)

Caroll, B.W.: Accommodating ethnic diversity in a modernizing democratic state: theory and practive in the case of Mauritius. Ethnic Racial Stud. **23**(1), 120–142 (2000)

Charmaz, K., Belgrave, L.: Qualitative interviewing and Grounded Theory analysis. SAGE Handb. Interview Res. Complexity Craft **2**, 347–365 (2012)

Corbett, F.C.: Emergence of the Conncetivist Leadership Paradigm: A Grounded Theory Study in the Asia Region. Pepperdine University (2021)

Corbin, J., Strauss, A.: Basics of Qualitative Research: Techniques and Procedures for Developing Grounded Theory. Sage Publications (2014)

Doorn, V., Ferrari, N., Graham, M.: Migration and migrant labour in the gig economy: an intervention work. Employ. Soc. **37**(4), 1099–1111 (2023)

Dunne, C.: The place of the literature review in grounded theory research. Int. J. Soc. Res. Methodol. **14**(2), 111–124 (2011)

Elroy, E.: The individual, place and wellbeing-a network analysis. MBC Public Health **21**(1), 1621 (2021)

Erdal, M.B., Carling, J., Horst, C., Talleraas, C.: Defining sustainable migration. EMN Norway occassional papers. PRIO, Oslo (2018)

Glaser, B.G.: The Discovery of Grounded Theory. Strategies for Qualitative Research. 1st edn. Routledge, New York (1997)

Glaser, B.G.: Constructive grounded theory. Qual. Soc. Res. **3**(3) (2002)

Global Migration Data Analysis Centre (2023). www.migrationdataportal.org. Accessed 17 Mar 2024

Hasan, S.I., et al.: Prevalence of common mental health issues among migrant workers: a systematic review and meta-analysis. PLoS ONE **16**(12), 0260221 (2021)

Hatzigeorgiou, A., Lodefalk, M.: A literature review of the nexus between migration and internationalisation. J. Int. Trade Econ. **30**(3), 319–340 (2021)

Hear, N.V., Bakewell, O., Long, K.: Push-pull: reconsidering the drivers of migration. In: Aspiration. Desire and the Drivers of Migration, pp. 19–36 (2020)

Heath, H.: Exploring the influences and use of the literature during a grounded theory study. J. Res. Nurs. **11**(6), 519–528 (2006)

Hennink, M., Kaiser, B.N.: Sample sizes for saturation in qualitative research: a systematic review of empirical tests. Soc Sci Med **292**, 114523 (2022)

Hernandez, C.A.: Theoretical coding in grounded theory methodology. Grounded Theory Rev. **8**(3), 51–59 (2009)

Holman, W.D.: In their words: Mainland Puerto Rican poetry, grounded theory and the generation of culturally sensitive social work knowledge. J. Multicultural Soc. Work **4**(3), 69–79 (1996)

Human Rights Watch. Maid to Order: Ending Abuses Against Migrant Domestic Workers in Singapore, Human Rights Watch, New York (2005)

Industrial Global Union. Ending migrant workers' rights violations in Mauritius, Port Louis: Industrial Global Union (2018)

Integral Human Development. Migrants refugees: Mauritius profile, Palazzo san Calisto: Vatican (2023)

International Labour Organisation (2024). https://www.ilo.org/global/standards/subjects-covered-by-international-labour-standards/migrant-workers/lang--en/index.htm. Accessed 17 Mar 2024

International Organisation for Migration. Migration Governance Indicators. IOM, Geneva, Switzerland (2021)

Jackson, M.: The Wherewithal of Life: Ethics, Migration and the Question of Wellbeing. University of California Press, California (2013)

Loganathan, T., Rui, D., Ng, C.-W., Pocock, N.: Breaking down the barriers: understanding migrant workers' access to healthcare in Malaysia. Plos One (2019)

Ministry of Labour, Human Resource Development and Training. National Employment monthly bulletin, Port Louis: Ministry pf Labour, National Employment Department (2023)

Moyce, S.C., Schenker, M.: Migrant workers and their occupational health and safety. Ann. Rev. Public Health 351–365 (2018)

Ngo, H.Y.: Sociocultural adaptation, perceived workplace discrimination and psychological wellbeing of immigrant workers, pp. 76–99. Routledge (2017)

Oles, P., Jankowski, T.: Positive orientation- A common base for hedonistic and eudemonistic happiness? Appl. Res. Qual. Life **13**, 105–117 (2018)

Ornek, O.K., Waibel, J., Wulinger, P., Weinmann, T.: Precarious employment and migrant workers' mental health: a systematic review of qualitative and quantitative studies. Scand. J. Work Environ. Health **48**(5), 327 (2022)

Schluter, M., et al.: Capturing emergent phenomena in social ecological systems. Ecol. Soc. **24**(3) (2019)

Shelley, T.: Exploited: Migrant labour in the new global economy. Zed books (2007)

Singh, A., Vijila, Y.: Role of the protective factors in the resilience of the migrant workers in Tamil Nadu. Migr. Lett. **21**(5), 533–554 (2024)

Spitzer, D.L.: Engendered Movements: Migration, Gender and Health in a Globalised World. Edward Elgar Publishing, Cheltenham (2016)

Statistics Mauritius (2023). https://statsmauritius.govmu.org/Documents/Statistics/ESI/2022/EI1 649/LF_Emp_Unemp_Yr21_180522.pdf. Accessed 09 May 2024

Syed, J.: Employment prospects for skilled migrants: a relational perspective. Hum. Resour. Manag. Rev. **18**(1), 28–45 (2008)

Tan, Y., Xu, H., Zhang, X.: Sustainable urbanisation in China: a comprehensive literature review. Cities **55**, 82–93 (2016)

Tukkoch, O., Machingura, F., Melamed, C.: Health, migration and the 20230 Agenda for Sustainable Development. Overseas Development Institute (2022)

United Nations Global Compact. UN World Migrant Report, New York: United Nations (2020)

United Nations. Recommendations on statistics of international Migration, New York: United Nations, Department of Economic and Social Affairs (1998)

More Bureaucracy Instead of More Security or More Fairness: The Effects of AI Regulation

Mathias Binswanger[✉]

University of Applied Sciences and Arts Northwestern Switzerland, 4600 Olten, Switzerland
mathias.binswanger@fhnw.ch

Abstract. The paper poses the question whether regulation of AI applications can guarantee data sovereignty and fair treatment of individuals. A closer look at already existing regulations reveals that these lofty goals can hardly be achieved. Regulations mostly increase bureaucracy instead of increasing security or fairness. There are several reasons for this failure, which are highlighted in this paper.

Keywords: Artificial Intelligence · Regulation · Black Box · Bureaucracy

1 Introduction

AI applications offer enormous possibilities to make life more comfortable, more interesting and they promise to increase public security. But at the same time there is increasing concern about surveillance, data security and a loss of privacy. Moreover, AI is also expected to replace many traditional jobs, which causes fear of increased unemployment.

Such concerns were also the subject of an open letter written in 2023 by a group of scientists and entrepreneurs led by historian Yuval Noah Harari, Tesla CEO Elon Musk and Apple co-founder Steve Wozniak (Future of Life Institute, 2023). The letter asks the following questions: Should we let machines flood our information channels with propaganda and untruth? Should we automate away all the jobs, including the fulfilling ones? Should we develop nonhuman minds that might eventually outnumber, outsmart, obsolete and replace us? Should we risk loss of control of our civilization? Such decisions must not be delegated to unelected tech leaders. Nevertheless, the letter concludes on an optimistic note. According to the authors, humanity can enjoy a prosperous future with AI if it is used purposefully and responsibly. But how can this be guaranteed?

The usual answer to this question is: we have to regulate the use of AI. For example, the Digital Society, an association for the defense of fundamental rights in a digitally connected world in Switzerland, states in a position paper on the regulation of automated decision-making systems (Digital Society, 2023, p. 9) that human beings should have the authority over automated decision-making systems and not the other way round. However, as this paper will show, such an aspiration for 'digital sovereignty' turns out to be wishful thinking. With regulations introduced in the EU like the GDPR (General Data Protection Regulation) or the AI Act, which will become effective in 2024, it is not possible to guarantee that AI-based algorithms will turn into benign agents, who only

© The Author(s), under exclusive license to Springer Nature Switzerland AG 2025
K. Hinkelmann and H. Smuts (Eds.): Society 5.0 2024, CCIS 2173, pp. 57–67, 2025.
https://doi.org/10.1007/978-3-031-71412-2_5

act in the best interest of their users. Governments are not in a position to regulate a system effectively unless they are able to control whether providers of the system indeed comply to the regulations. But AI-systems are a black box to users as well as to the authorities, who are supposed to regulate them.

Decisions or predictions coming from AI systems are based on the identification of highly complex, multidimensional temporal and spatial patterns in large data sets. These patterns allow for decisions or predictions, which become increasingly accurate. Because algorithms are self-learning, responsibility for decisions or predictions cannot be shifted to inventors or developers of AI solutions. Even if algorithms have been trained with data, which has been selected according to criteria, which are supposed to guarantee fairness (e.g. no racial bias), there is uncertainty, whether algorithms will subsequently make fair decisions. The outcome of AI systems remains fundamentally unpredictable (Binswanger, 2024, p. 230).

Moreover, AI applications are developed for making money and to serve the economic interests of their developers, which often are Big-Tech companies such as Alphabet, Amazon, Apple or Meta. These companies possess considerable global market power, which also allows them to control and manipulate users of their applications. AI solutions are a powerful tool to gain control over consumers' demand, which makes it easier to maximize profits. But such claims of manipulation are difficult to "prove" by empirical evidence. This is due to the black box character of AI solutions. It is impossible to explain decisions made by self-learning algorithms by causal inference from data inputs to outputs (decisions, predictions) of AI applications (e.g. Pasquale, 2015).

In this paper, we will have a closer look at two important topics regarding regulations of AI applications. Section 2 highlights the challenge of ensuring data security and looks at regulations, which are supposed to fulfill this goal. The most prominent example of such a regulation is the GDPR, which became effective in the EU in 2018. Section 3 looks at another important challenge regarding AI applications. Predictions and decisions based on AI are supposed to be fair and regulations are supposed to guarantee such fairness. However, it turns out that this is a difficult task, as it is not clear what fairness means inv specific situations and how fairness can be enforced by regulations. Sections 4 draws important conclusions from the findings, which cast doubt on the claim that regulations can ensure digital sovereignty as well as responsible and fair use of AI applications.

2 Ensuring Data Security by Regulation?

Ensuring data security and maintaining privacy have turned out to be major issues of the digital transformation. The use of AI-based algorithms leads to an enormous demand for personal data, which can only be collected if people and processes are constantly monitored in real time. The digital world requires transparent citizens, who are ready to provide data about current location, current activities, current state of mind and current state of the body. As a result, surveillance is becoming ubiquitous and increasingly difficult to escape (Zuboff, 2019). This development poses a dilemma for governments in democratic political systems. On the one hand, governments are responsible for protecting people's privacy and guaranteeing sovereignty over their personal data. On the other hand, governments too, promote surveillance activities as they are interested in controlling people and in keeping them from misbehaving.

This dilemma is supposed to be solved by more regulation without imposing general restrictions on the access to data. Progress in AI systems crucially depends on the availability of a growing amount of data. Therefore, easy access to data is essential, but regulations should make sure that data collection only takes place, if people are willing to share their data and agree to its use by AI applications. Such regulation attempts are most advanced in the EU, where the General Data Protection Regulation (GDPR) has been in place since 2018. The regulation includes rules for the processing of personal data by private and public users. But at the same time the regulation is also supposed to guarantee free movement of data within the European market,

Art. 5 of the GDPR states that personal data may only be "processed lawfully, fairly and in a transparent way in relation to the data subject" meaning that the collection and processing of data about a specific person will still be possible but not without the person's consent. Whenever personal data is processed, the person, whose data is processed (data subject), must be informed about the legal basis, purpose and duration of storage in accordance with Art. 13 of the GDPR. And the data subject has the right to be informed about the use of personal data, the right to request access to personal data or the right to restriction of processing concerning the data subject or to object to processing. Moreover, data portability is guaranteed as well as the right to demand rectification and to withdraw consent at any time.

Especially profiling and the automated decisions based on profiling are strictly regulated. The GDPR defines profiling as "any form of automated processing of personal data consisting of the use of personal data to evaluate certain personal aspects relating to a natural person, in particular to analyze or predict aspects concerning that natural person's performance at work, economic situation, health, personal preferences, interests, reliability, behavior, location or movements". (Art. 4 No. 4 GDPR). According to the GDPR, a decision is automated if it is made "without any human intervention" (Recital 71 GDPR). An example of an automated decision would be the conclusion of a contract based solely on a pattern in a user's personal data, which is recognized by an algorithm.

In principle, automated decisions are not permitted under the GDPR if they have a legal effect or significantly affect the data subject in a similar way (Art. 22 para. 1 GDPR). For example, acceptance or denial of an online loan application or choosing a candidate following an online recruitment process should not be based exclusively on an automated decision-making process. But it is controversial, whether this restriction only applies to unfavorable decisions (Thouvenin et al. 2018). There are also various exceptions and special regulations regarding this restriction. For example, an automated decision may be permitted with consent of the data subject (Art. 22 para. 2 lit. c GDPR). But informed consent in the decision-making processes of complex AI systems seems utopian. The exceptions are also associated with further requirements: For example, the responsible AI controller must take appropriate measures to safeguard the legitimate interests of the data subject (Art. 22 para. 3 GDPR).

This short overview of the GDPR may suggest that the regulatory framework of the GDPR is indeed a major step forward, guaranteeing people a considerable amount of data protection and privacy within the EU. But in real life the average internet user has not benefited from the lofty goals of the GDPR. Instead, the GDPR annoys users on a daily basis, as they constantly have to give consent to cookie requests, which are popping up, whenever they visit a new webpage. The cookie banners serve the purpose of obtaining consent from users to process their data. By this procedure, users should be able to accept or reject cookies in a customized manner. However, if users are constantly asked to give consent, whenever they visit a new website, cookie banners quickly become a nuisance without offering a recognizable benefit. This is shown, for example, by a survey conducted in 2022 by the opinion research institute YouGov on behalf of the online services GMX and Web.de (see Süddeutsche Zeitung, 2022). According to the survey, 53% of people in Germany feel annoyed by cookie banners. Only 12% believe that cookie banners give them a "feeling of security". Obviously, the regulation failed in this respect.

In spite of this experience, website operators and app providers are forced to continue annoying users by cookie requests. If personal data is collected or stored and passed on to third parties, users must be informed about it. According to Article 6 of the GDPR, active consent is required, which must be obtained via a cookie banner or a pop-up. Failure to do so can result in high fines, which is why hardly any website operator wants to take this risk. The whole process of consenting to the use of data thus turns into a useless routine that makes life more difficult to operators of websites as well as to their visitors. It is no coincidence that the GDPR is repeatedly referred to as a "monster of bureaucracy" (Deutschlandfunk, 2019). Instead of guaranteeing data protection, it promoted bureaucracy even though fighting bureaucracy is one of the main goals of the EU (Haedke, 2018).

Additional bureaucratic measures are also enforced by national law. Larger companies that process personal data must hire a data protection officer. This is the case, if at least twenty people in an organization are permanently involved in the automated processing of personal data, as stipulated in the Federal Data Protection Act (BDSG, Article 38) in Germany, which complements the GDPR. Research conducted in 2019 indicated that already back then an estimated 500,000 organizations had registered data protection officers across Europe under the GDPR. (IAPP, 2019). Therefore, data protection offices at public and private organizations become larger, as more detailed regulations regarding data protection are introduced.

In addition, Big-Tech companies are able to exploit complex regulations such as the GDPR in their favor. Facebook CEO Mark Zuckerberg, for example, has praised the GDPR (Deutschlandfunk, 2019), as he (probably correctly) assumed that the GDPR does not pose a serious threat to Meta's business activities. For Big- Tech companies it is no big deal to hire data protection officers and to come up with user-friendly cookie banners. As long as Big-Tech companies are allowed to continue collecting data on a large scale and processing it with the help of AI, they can easily cope with regulations such as the GDPR. Such regulations also allow them to promote the illusion of data security, while being able to continue collecting and using personal data. And most users do not care much about data security issues anyway (e.g. Sahota, 2020). They are mainly interested in getting great services "for free" such as using Google's search engine or communicating on Facebook as their social media channel.

Regulations such as the GDPR primarily result in data protection bureaucracy rather than data protection. By regulating largely irrelevant details, regulations are distracting us from real problems of data protection. At the same time, data collection continues at a large scale, and data sovereignty remains an illusion. Governments are unable to resolve a fundamental contradiction. On the one hand, private and governmental organizations have a strong desire to collect an increasing amount of personal data in order to gain more control over people's behavior. On the other hand, governments are obliged to guarantee data protection and privacy. But both goals cannot be achieved simultaneously.

3   Ensuring Fairness by Regulations?

Whenever relevant decisions are delegated to AI-based algorithms, the goal is to ensure that those decisions are fair and transparent (see Bartoletti and Xenidis, 2023). Moreover, AI systems are even supposed to increase fairness and transparency if they are regulated appropriately (see, for example, Lopez, 2021). Such intentions are also included in the AI act, which will become effective in the EU in 2024. According to the act, AI systems should be designed in a way that respects the rule of law, human rights, democratic values and diversity, and should include appropriate safeguards to ensure a fair and just society. More concretely, Article 4 of the AI Act states that diversity, non-discrimination and fairness imply that AI systems are used in a way that promotes equal access, gender equality and cultural diversity, while avoiding discriminatory impacts and unfair biases.

But what do we really mean when we talk about fairness? Nowadays, fairness is primarily associated with the idea of guaranteeing equal opportunities for all people. Fairness suggests that people are treated equally, unless unequal treatment is objectively justified (Cremers et al., 2019). Individuals must therefore not be discriminated because they belong to a marginalized or socially disadvantaged group. This means, for example, that facial recognition software must not make mistakes more often about people with dark skin color or other phenotypic characteristics than about people with white skin color.

Especially data, which is used to train AI systems, is assumed to play an essential role for guaranteeing fair behavior of AI applications. There is consensus that the quality of the training data not only improves the functioning of a self-learning algorithm, but also has a strong influence on possible biases and thus on the fairness of an algorithm's decisions (Bartoletti and Xenidis, 2023). Because many AI applications are trained on pre-existing historical data, they can easily inherit a distorted view of the world from the past. For example, AI used for evaluating candidates for a vacant job position will usually be trained with historical data sets in order to identify the best candidates. If the historical data set only contains data from white candidates, it will only identify those individuals as suitable candidates, who fit the profile of an 'excellent Caucasian candidate'. But it is likely that people from different ethnic background would also make great candidates. However, they fit a different profile of excellency, which is not recognized by the AI application due to the racial bias in the training data.

Such biases in AI-based decision-making and the resulting lack of fairness are widely discussed in the literature (see for example, Deutscher Ethikrat, 2023; Ferrara, 2023; Kadiresan et al., 2022). Therefore, rules and regulations should ensure that algorithms are trained on the "right data". But this task turns out to be a complex issue. The more regulators try to guarantee fairness by detailed regulations, the less obvious it gets, what terms such as 'fairness', 'bias' or 'discrimination' exactly mean in specific circumstances. This is illustrated by the case of COMPAS (Correctional Offender Management Profiling for Alternative Sanctions). This AI application is used by judges in the United States in the states of New York, California and Wisconsin in order to assess the likelihood of recidivism. This is a crucial issue because judges must decide whether prison inmates should be released before the official end of their prison sentences (Chouldechova 2016). In 2016, the organization ProPublica published an analysis of COMPAS, stating that its predictions are biased with respect to race.

ProPublica claimed that COMPAS makes racist predictions, even though a prisoner's ethnicity is not included in the assessment. But evidence was provided that recidivism rates estimated for African-Americans, who did not relapse after release, were almost twice as high as those estimated for white prisoners. According to ProPublica, the algorithm thus violates the principle of fairness. People who do not relapse should be treated equally irrespective of their ethnicity by facing the same probability of being granted parole. How, can it be that people, who are equal according to the relevant criterion – not relapsing –, are treated differently by the algorithm? ProPublica suspected discrimination based on the fact, that white software developers preferred their own ethnicity (knowingly or unknowingly) when programming the algorithm. In this case, there would be a distortion with serious consequences for African Americans, as in many cases they are denied parole because of a racial bias.

But the real cause of the problem is more complicated and can hardly be explained by racist programmers. The specialists, who analyzed the problem after the claims made by ProPublica, concluded that discrimination cannot be avoided, even if there is no racial bias in programming algorithms or in the data set used for training algorithms (Chouldechova, 2016). Fairness cannot be evaluated by exclusively concentrating on the question, whether estimated recidivism rates are the same for prisoners of different ethnicities, who were released before the official end of their prison sentences. Fairness can also be assessed from a different point of view. For example, if the algorithm estimates a recidivism rate of 0.3 for a certain prisoner, the expectation is, that on average, 30% of those for whom the algorithm calculated this rate, will relapse irrespective of their ethnicities. But, if in reality, we will observe that indeed 30% of all white offenders relapse after being granted parole, but 50% of African-Americans relapse, it would be unfair to white prisoners and favor African-American offenders. In this case, it seems reasonable to calculate specific probabilities for each ethnicity. But calculating specific rates for different ethnicities is likely to be considered racist again. An AI system can be fair according to one criterion, but unfair according to another criterion (Angwin and Larson 2016).

The case of COMPAS provides an example for the fundamental difficulty of implementing requirements such as fairness and non-discrimination in AI systems. Such ethical values are complex and can be interpreted in a variety of ways. Even after lengthy and detailed discussions it will be impossible to come up with a definite answer about what is fair and what is not. Ethical challenges quickly lead to dilemmas that can be described by the simple folk wisdom that we cannot satisfy everybody. If algorithms are supposed to make "fair decisions" they cannot avoid making value judgments, which, however, usually are not stated explicitly. This inevitably leads to decisions that some individuals or entire population groups perceive as unfair.

Such reasoning raises the fundamental question about how people form implicit value judgments, which determine the decisions of algorithms. How should it be decided which of the above-mentioned ways of estimating and applying recidivism rates are "truly fair" when using COMPAS? Or should AI be banned from ethically challenging decisions, leaving such decisions to humans, as it was the case in the past? This question is especially important when judicial decisions relate to predicted – and thus not yet executed and perhaps not even planned – actions of individuals. The focus here is on predictive policing or profiling, which is also extensively discussed in the literature. These methods estimate probabilities of criminal activity for individuals or whole groups of individuals or, alternatively, for specified areas of a city or a country. In the first case, predictive policing asks who might become a criminal in the future. In the second case, it asks where a particular danger might arise (Leese 2018). AI-based personal predictive policing is mainly used in the US, but it is also increasingly applied in other countries (Som et al., 2020, p. 202).

No matter how you regulate or 'ethically optimize' predictive policing, the results will be unfair for certain groups of people or individuals. But if predictive policing is prohibited because of these unresolved issues, it can be unfair as well. If indeed you can prevent crime by predictive policing, and you do not prevent a crime because predictive policing is not allowed any more, it would be highly unfair to potential victims of the crime. For example, we could ask the questions, whether is it discriminatory to use a person's place of residence or his or her socio-economic status to predict his or her propensity to engage in criminal acts, if indeed we know that these criteria have a significant effect on the likelihood of a criminal act. Such questions are open to lengthy debates. At the end it depends on how we value the utility of the prevention of a potential crime compared to the disutility of potential discrimination. And such discussions also raise questions about surveillance and privacy. To what extent should people be monitored to increase potential security? With the argument of increasing security more surveillance and restriction of private freedom can easily be justified. But is the increase in security worth the sacrifice in privacy?

Another example may illustrate this point. On the internet, children and adolescents are exposed to the risk of online grooming, where adults form an emotional relationship with minors with the intention of establishing sexual contacts (see Wachs et al, 2012). In 2022, the Commission of the European Union therefore presented a draft regulation on preventing and combating sexual abuse of children. It envisages the systematic identification of conversations in chat rooms that may lead to sexual abuse as a preventive measure to protect minors from sexual offences in good time (Vogt et al., 2021). To do this, online chats are analyzed using automated AI algorithms trained specifically for this issue. But in many cases, people will be wrongly suspected of planning sexual offenses although they just engage in normal chats. Therefore, we may ask once more: Is this fair? And we also should take care of the chilling effect (Deutscher Ethikrat, 2023, p. 270). Worrying about possible surveillance may result in people censoring themselves. Adults may decide to refrain from friendly communication with minors, because this could be (wrongly) interpreted as initiation of a sexual offence.

In real life the notion of fairness is often treated rather selectively. Regulators look closely at issues, which feature prominently in current public debates, but neglect other, less popular issues. There are always arguments provided in favor of more data collection and monitoring, as this is supposed to increase security and guarantee more justice and more fairness. Government authorities typically also press for more supervision as they want to be on the safe side. They do not want to be blamed for a crime, if (theoretically or in reality) it could have been prevented. Therefore, there is a constant tendency to downplay privacy and personal freedom and to highlight security and convenience associated with more data collection, which is used for feeding AI applications.

AI-based algorithms also offer more and more opportunities to control individuals and organizations, whether they indeed comply with alleged principles of fairness such as equal treatment or non-discrimination. As almost everything what we write or say can be found online nowadays, all the online material can constantly be checked for potentially racist, sexist, anti-gay, or conspiratorial content. As a result, people become increasingly careful, whenever they are writing or talking. They constantly feel obliged to prove that they have the right attitude. These efforts result in a culture, which is often associated with the term wokeism. Large companies or public organizations not only employ an increasing number of data protection officers, but also anti-discrimination officers, equality and diversity officers, or gender officers, which are all part of an emerging controlling bureaucracy.

Therefore, attempts to establish a fair society also promote censorship and encourage denouncement of potential misbehaving (Gujer, 2022). There is an increasing number of hotlines where people can and should report discrimination as well as sexist or racist practices. The German Minister for Family Affairs started a 'hotline for anti-feminism' in 2023. A foundation supported by her office (Amadeu-Antonio foundation) has set up a webpage, where anyone can report 'sexist, misogynistic or misanthropic messages, attacks on equality or political strategies against emancipation'. And professors and researchers at universities or colleges feel increasingly controlled and monitored, which is why some of them have founded the Scientific Freedom Network. The website states: 'University members are subjected to considerable pressure to submit to moral, political and ideological constraints in exercising their freedom of research and teaching.

4 Conclusion

The paper started with the question whether regulation of AI applications can guarantee data sovereignty and fair treatment of individuals. A closer look at already existing regulations reveals that these lofty goals can hardly be achieved. Regulations mostly increase bureaucracy instead of increasing security or fairness. There are several reasons for this failure.

1. Many AI applications represent virtual black boxes to their users as well as to regulators (Bathaee, 2018). Regulatory authorities are unable to control whether providers of AI applications indeed comply to regulations. Of course, it could be argued that, for

example, aviation security can indeed be guaranteed by regulations. But in case of aviation security, it can be controlled, whether airports or airlines follow the procedures, which are required by regulations. In case of data security, we face a fundamentally different situation. Regulatory authorities claim to guarantee data security by requiring consent of the data subject, who's personal data is processed by AI applications. But it is impossible to control the exact use of data in virtual black boxes.

2. AI applications are typically based on self-learning algorithms by relying on methods such as deep learning or reinforcement learning. These algorithms can improve their performance over time without the need for explicit programming or supervision. Therefore, after some time, even programmers, who originally developed these algorithms, cannot explain, why these algorithms make specific predictions or decisions and even reverse engineering does not work in this case (Drexl and Hilty, 2019, p. 10). There is a lack of interpretability and explainability. The more powerful AI applications become, the less we understand how they function exactly. Therefore, it is not possible to guarantee a certain behavior of an AI application by regulating for example the choice of the data set, which is used for training algorithms. Even if the data does not show any racial or other bias, it cannot be guaranteed that algorithms indeed will make predictions, which do not discriminate some group of people. This could only be guaranteed if learning processes were prohibited.

3. Many companies, which provide AI applications, and which collect personal data, possess considerable global market power (e.g. Brühl, 2023). We usually refer to them as Big-Tech companies such as Alphabet, Amazon, Apple or Meta. These companies are difficult to regulate because they are much better informed about the exact functioning and use of data by AI applications than regulatory authorities. Typically, regulatory authorities have difficulties of proving that specific AI applications violate regulations such as the GDPR. Big-Tech companies hire a host of specialized lawyers, who can delay the progress of legal proceedings or to propose settlements in or outside of court. Such settlements often result in payments, which do not cause serious financial harm to Big-Tech companies. To mitigate this problem, it becomes essential to combat the abuse of market power of Big-Tech companies more vigorously.

For all of these reasons, we should not put too much faith in regulation of AI applications. Instead of benefitting people, the growing flood of regulations creates additional complexity and challenges, which necessitate further bureaucratic measures such as the creation of specialized bodies, guidelines, regulations, laws, contracts, expert opinions or expertise. As a result, employment is increasingly shifting away from production towards bureaucracy. Instead of traditional workers, modern companies hire an increasing number of people, who work, for example, as regulatory compliance managers, data security officers, quality auditors or gender equality officers.

Acknowledgments. The author would like to thank three anonymous referees for helpful suggestions and comments.

Disclosure of Interests. The author has no competing interests to declare that are relevant to the content of this article.

References

Angwin, J., Larson, J.: Bias in Criminal Risk Scores is Mathematically Inevitable, Researchers Say. ProPublica (2016). www.propublica.org/article/bias-in-criminal-risk-scores-is-mathematically-inevitable-researchers-say

Bartoletti, I., Xenidis, R.: Study on the impact of artificial intelligence systems, their potential for promoting equality, including gender equality, and the risks they may cause in relation to non-discrimination. Council of Europe. Strasbourg (2023)

Bathaee, Y.: The artificial intelligence black box and the failure of intent and causation. Harvard J. Law Technol. **31**(2), 889–938 (2018)

Binswanger, M.: Die Verselbständigung des Kapitalismus – Wie KI Menschen und Wirtschaft steuert und für mehr Bürokratie sorgt. Wiley Verlag, Weinheim (2024)

Brühl, V.: Big tech, the platform economy and the European digital markets. Intereconomics – Rev. Eur. Econ. Policy **58**(5), 274–282 (2023)

Chouldechova, A.: Fair Prediction with Disparate Impact: A Study of Bias in Recidivism Prediction Instruments (2016). http://arxiv.org/abs/1610.07524

Cremers, A., et al.: Vertrauenswürdiger Einsatz von Künstlicher Intelligenz. Handlungsfelder aus philosophischer, ethischer, rechtlicher und technologischer Sicht als Grundlage für eine Zertifizierung von Künstlicher Intelligenz. Fraunhofer IAIS (2019)

Deutscher Ethikrat. Mensch und Maschine – Herausforderungen durch Künstliche Intelligenz. Stellungnahme. Berlin (2023)

Deutschlandfunk. "Aus sinnvollem Gesetz ein Bürokratiemonster gemacht". Gespräch mit Thilo Weichert, 25. Mai, 2019 (2019)

Digital Society. Position of the Digital Society on the Regulation of Automated Decision-Making Systems. Digital Society, Basel (2023)

Drexl, J., Hilty, R.M., et al.: Technical aspects of artificial intelligence: an understanding from an intellectual property law perspective. In: Max Planck Institute for Innovation & Competition, Research Papers 19–13, University of Zurich/Max Planck Institute for Innovation & Competition München (2019)

Ferrara, E.: Fairness and Bias in Artificial Intelligence: A Brief Survey of Sources, Impacts, and Mitigation Strategies (2023). SSRN https://ssrn.com/abstract=4615421 or https://doi.org/10.2139/ssrn.4615421

Future of Life Institute. Pause Giant AI Experiments: An Open Letter (2023)

Gujer, E.: Cancel Culture ist kein Studentenulk. Es ist eine neue Form des Extremismus. Neue Zürcher Zeitung (2022)

IAPP. An estimated 500K organizations have registered DPOs across (2019). https://iapp.org/news/a/study-an-estimated-500k-organizations-have-registered-dpos-across-europe/

Haedke, J.: EU paradox: Bürokratie soll abgebaut werden - und dann kommt die DSGVO. Focus (2018)

Kadiresan, A., Baweja, Y., Ogbanufe, O.: Bias in AI-based decision-making. In: Albert, M.V., Lin, L., Spector, M.J., Dunn, L.S. (eds.) Bridging Human Intelligence and Artificial Intelligence, pp. 275–285. Springer, Cham (2022). https://doi.org/10.1007/978-3-030-84729-6_19

Leese, M.: Predictive Policing in der Schweiz: Chancen, Herausforderungen, Risiken. In: Nünlist, C. (Hrsg.). Bulletin 2018 zur schweizerischen Sicherheitspolitik, pp. 57–71 (2018)

Lopez, P.: Artificial Intelligence und die normative Kraft des Faktischen. In Merkur #863 (2021). https://www.merkur-zeitschrift.de/2021/03/25/artificial-intelligence-und-die-normative-kraft-des-faktischen/

Pasquale, F.: The Black Box Society: The Secret Algorithms that Control Money and Information. Harvard University Press, Cambridge (2015)

Sahota, N.: Privacy is Dead and Most People Really Don't Care. Forbes Magazine, October, 14th, 2020 (2020)

Som, C., Sutter, P., Thouvenin, F.: Wenn Algorithmen für uns entscheiden: Chancen und Risiken der künstlichen Intelligenz. In TA-SWISS Publikationsreihe (Hrsg.): TA 72/2020. Zürich: vdf (2020)

Süddeutsche Zeitung. Vier Jahre DSGVO: Monster oder Datenschutzvorbild?, 24. Mai, 2022 (2022)

Thouvenin, F., Früh, A., George, D.: Datenschutz und automatisierte Entscheidungen, Newsletter vom 26. November 2018 (2018)

Vogt, M., Leser, U., Akbik, A.: Early detection of sexual predators in chats. In: Zong, C., et al. (Hg.): Proceedings of the 59th Annual Meeting of the Association for Computational Linguistics and the 11th International Joint Conference on Natural Language Processing, pp. 4985–4999 (2021)

Wachs, S., Wolf, K.D., Pan, C.-C.: Cybergrooming: risk factors, coping strategies and associations with cyberbullying. Psicothema **24**(4), 628–633 (2012)

Zuboff, S.: The Age of Surveillance Capitalism: The Fight for a Human Future at the New Frontier of Power. Public Affairs, New York (2019)

The Impact of Generative AI on Creative Professionals in Marketing: A Systematic Review and Practical Framework

Adriaan Coetzer[1], Lizette Weilbach[1]([✉]) [iD], Marié Hattingh[1] [iD],
and Shireen Panchoo[2] [iD]

[1] University of Pretoria, Pretoria, South Africa
u17031690@tuks.co.za, {lizette.weilbach,marie.hattingh}@up.ac.za
[2] University of Technology Mauritius, Port Louis, Mauritius
s.panchoo@utm.ac.mu

Abstract. This paper examines the transformative impact of generative AI on creative professionals in the marketing sector. A systematic literature review was conducted to clarify the opportunities and challenges associated with the integration of generative AI into marketing strategies. Through inductive analysis, two main themes emerged: generative AI opportunities and drawbacks. The opportunities include enhanced marketing effectiveness, amplified creative capabilities, streamlined automation, increased productivity, user-friendly interfaces, and synergistic human-AI collaboration. Conversely, the drawbacks include concerns such as fear of job displacement, skepticism over AI-generated content, security and privacy risks, ethical considerations, and the potential for overreliance on AI. A comprehensive framework was developed to synthesize these findings, providing a structured understanding of generative AI's impact on creative professionals in marketing. This framework serves as a foundation for further research and offers practical insights for the responsible integration of generative AI into marketing workflows.

Keywords: Generative Artificial Intelligence (GAI) · Marketing · Creative Professionals · Systematic Literature Review · Practical Framework

1 Introduction

Technological innovation, particularly in Artificial Intelligence (AI), has emerged as a focal point for organizations seeking to enhance their competitive edge [1]. AI, encompassing various applications and subsets such as Generative AI models like ChatGPT, holds immense potential to transform business practices across diverse sectors. Notably, Generative AI has garnered significant attention in creative domains like marketing [2], where its ability to automate tasks and generate novel content has sparked considerable interest among professionals, offering new avenues for creativity and efficiency [3]. Generative AI, considered a relatively new field within AI, has attracted substantial public interest, particularly following the release of prominent models like ChatGPT

© The Author(s), under exclusive license to Springer Nature Switzerland AG 2025
K. Hinkelmann and H. Smuts (Eds.): Society 5.0 2024, CCIS 2173, pp. 68–83, 2025.
https://doi.org/10.1007/978-3-031-71412-2_6

[4]. These models boast capabilities such as generating videos, text, images, and even software design code, with some describing the output as remarkably human-like [5]. Generative AI has found applications across various business functions, including marketing, risk management, human resources, finance, and IT [6]. Despite its widespread adoption in professional settings, there remains a significant knowledge gap regarding its influence on creative professionals in marketing [5].

While marketing managers and creative professionals are increasingly embracing Generative AI, comprehensive studies addressing its impact on the marketing industry are lacking. This gap in understanding has implications for how professionals perceive and interact with AI technologies, potentially leading to misconceptions and mistrust [7]. To address this gap, this paper aims to explore the influence of Generative AI on creative professionals in marketing through a systematic literature review. The primary research question guiding this study is: *In what way does generative artificial intelligence influence creative professionals in marketing, and how can these insights be practically applied?*

Section 2 provides background information on Generative AI and its relevance to the field of marketing, setting the stage for the subsequent analysis. Section 3 outlines the research methodology, including criteria for the review process and data extraction and analysis. Section 4 presents the findings of the review, followed by a discussion in Sect. 5. Finally, the paper concludes with recommendations for future research in Sect. 6.

2 Background

Information technologies (ITs) have become pervasive in modern organizations, significantly impacting their operations and processes [8]. Among these technologies, AI has emerged as one of the most influential and rapidly evolving applications. AI, including Generative AI models like ChatGPT, has undergone substantial development, transitioning from theoretical concepts to practical applications [1].

Generative AI is a branch of AI that focuses on creating original content autonomously. Generative AI algorithms, such as Variational Autoencoders (VAEs) and Generative Adversarial Networks (GANs), learn from existing data patterns to generate new and diverse outputs, including text, images, and music. This capability enables machines to exhibit creativity and imagination, producing content that resembles human-generated work [9].

Within the domain of marketing, where creativity and innovation are paramount, Generative AI has gained significant traction. Creative professionals responsible for tasks such as content creation, brand management, and market segmentation have begun incorporating Generative AI tools into their workflows. These tools streamline the content generation process, allowing marketers to produce diverse and engaging materials more efficiently [5]. However, despite its potential benefits, the widespread adoption of Generative AI has raised concerns and uncertainties among organizations regarding its impact on business processes. Some professionals fear that AI technologies will replace human jobs, while others remain skeptical about the reliability and ethical implications of AI-generated content. As Generative AI tools continue to proliferate in the marketing sector, it becomes imperative to explore their influence on creative professionals and anticipate future implications [10].

Table 1 below provides an overview of some of the most popular Generative AI tools currently utilized in the marketing sector, showcasing their diverse applications and functionalities.

Table 1. Generative AI tools used in the marketing sector.

Generative AI Tools	Use in Marketing Sector
postwise.ai	Utilized for social media management, including platforms like Twitter. Capable of composing tweet threads and scheduling tweets [2]
compose.ai	An AI-powered text generator designed to enhance the quality of written content [2]
simplified.com	An all-in-one AI tool for content creation and design, covering image generation, presentation creation, social media quotes, reels and TikTok scripts, color palettes, and tweet-to-image conversion. Perfect for managing marketing strategies efficiently [2]
sembly.ai	Used to transcribe meetings, record minutes, and generate insights for professional marketing meetings [2]
clickable.so	Used to create superb visuals and adverts instantly [2]
ChatGPT	Used for content creation, audience research, customer surveys, chatbot support, personalized experiences, product info generation, and Search Engine Optimization (SEO) [11]
DALL-E	Used to generate marketing images for specific tailored products and/or services [4]
Artbreeder	An online platform that uses AI to create visual contents [12]

3 Research Method

This paper employs a systematic literature review methodology to examine the impact of generative AI on creative professionals in marketing. Drawing on established principles and guided by the work of Boland et al. [13], academic papers were sourced primarily through the Google Scholar Search Engine across various databases.

The following search terms were selected to capture relevant literature on generative AI and marketing.: ("generative artificial intelligence" OR "generative AI" OR "GenAI") AND ("marketing" OR "advertising").

Criteria applied to select papers for analysis are as follows: 1) Research aligning with the study's objectives, 2) Papers focusing on business individuals, 3) Publications in English, 4) Articles from conference proceedings or journals related to IT, or those containing relevant keywords, 5) Accessible full-text studies, 6) Primary research contributions.

Figure 1 depicts the PRISMA flowchart detailing the research methodology [14], consisting of four stages: identification, screening, eligibility, and inclusion. Utilizing

Google Scholar, 3050 papers were initially identified, with seven additional papers found through manual searching. After removing 874 duplicates, the remaining 2183 papers underwent title and abstract screening, leading to the exclusion of 2097 irrelevant papers. Full-text assessment of the remaining 86 papers was conducted, applying the criteria stated above. 19 Papers were excluded for lacking discussion on the influence of generative AI on creative professionals, while 16 were excluded due to ambiguous findings. Additionally, five papers were excluded for lack of accessibility. Finally, 40 papers were retained for the SLR following the completion of the PRISMA process.

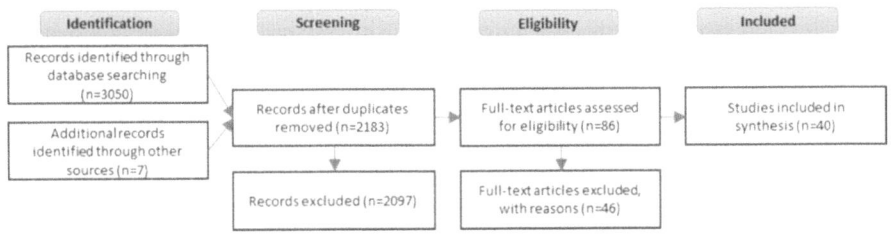

Fig. 1. PRISMA Flowchart

All 40 papers selected through the PRISMA process were included in the data extraction phase. Each paper's citation, title, type, name, codes, criteria, concepts, dimensions, main themes, and notes were recorded in an MS Excel workbook.

4   Data Analysis and Findings

The data analysis method employed is inductive thematic analysis, as described by Braun and Clarke [15]. This method involves identifying, analyzing, and reporting on themes or patterns within the dataset, which is systematically organized and described. It includes exploring the data for meaning, identifying relationships, clarifying similarities and differences, using coding and indexing, and ultimately identifying themes and categories. Among the 40 selected papers relevant to the research question, it was noted that publications spanned the past four years, with an increasing number of publications per year indicating growing interest in generative AI's influence. Specifically, 78% of the selected papers were published in 2023, highlighting the emerging nature of generative AI within the broader field of AI. Through the inductive thematic analysis process, multiple themes emerged and were grouped into two main categories: generative AI opportunities and drawbacks.

4.1   Generative AI Opportunities

Generative AI opportunities encompass various factors that positively influence creative professionals in marketing. These factors are categorized into multiple themes, which are now considered subthemes contributing to generative AI opportunities.

Generative AI Effectiveness. Generative AI Effectiveness, as extracted from 14 of the 40 included papers, pertains to its role in sustaining customer satisfaction and enhancing marketing effectiveness. It empowers creative professionals to craft personalized advertisements, thereby improving marketing outcomes [5, 6, 12, 16–21]. To ensure customer satisfaction, chatbots must accurately address consumer needs without infringing on privacy boundaries [22]. Adjustments to generative AI are necessary to prevent overly intrusive data collection [23]. Generative AI's capability to identify deepfakes preserves marketing credibility, thus maintaining customer trust [24, 25]. Additionally, when integrated into crowd-sourcing, generative AI allows professionals to leverage positive customer feedback for more effective marketing strategies [26]. Overall, the studies unanimously highlight generative AI's positive impact on marketing effectiveness, emphasizing its efficacy in ensuring customer satisfaction and driving successful marketing campaign.

Creative Capabilities Enhancements. The creative capabilities enhancements subtheme, covered in nine of the 40 papers, highlights generative AI's role in boosting creativity among professionals. It surpasses human limitations, aids in idea generation, and helps in creating standout content [17, 24, 27, 28]. By allowing synthetic endorsers, it offers novel creative opportunities, reducing reliance on conventional celebrities and animated characters [21, 24]. Generative AI enhances marketing platforms, fostering engaging customer experiences and improving effectiveness [5, 12, 29]. Overall, studies concur on generative AI's positive impact on creative professionals' capabilities, fostering innovation and enabling the creation of compelling content that broadens customer engagement and enhances marketing effectiveness.

Automation and Efficiency. The automation and efficiency subtheme, addressed in ten of the 40 papers, explores how generative AI streamlines marketing tasks, and enhances productivity. By automating routine tasks, it frees up creative professionals to focus on more complex work, ultimately boosting productivity [17, 19, 28–30]. Automation also improves decision-making abilities and responsiveness to innovative demands [12, 28]. Moreover, it leads to cost savings and enhances marketing analytics and campaign management [19]. Generative AI's ability to automate various marketing content creation processes, such as writing sales emails and social media posts, is noted [31]. Importantly, studies emphasize that generative AI enhances rather than replaces creative professionals' roles, offering them opportunities to become more effective and productive in marketing tasks [5]. Thus, generative AI empowers creative professionals to excel and make a significant impact in their field.

Generative AI Enhance Productivity. The generative AI productivity enhancement subtheme, discussed in seven papers, focuses on how generative AI improves the efficiency of marketing tasks. By generating multiple versions of marketing content quickly, creative professionals can select and utilize novel material rapidly, boosting productivity and task completion quality [6, 16, 18, 20, 27, 32, 33]. This efficiency allows professionals to dedicate more time to complex tasks and reach broader customer segments. Notably, all studies concur that generative AI enhances productivity in marketing tasks. A key takeaway is that productivity gains from generative AI intersect with automation and efficiency, underscoring the benefits of incorporating generative AI into marketing workflows. Moreover, embracing generative AI promises further productivity enhancements in marketing endeavors.

Generative AI Ease of Use. The generative AI ease of use subtheme, identified in two papers, assesses how quickly creative professionals can integrate and utilize generative AI in their marketing tasks. Abdel-kader [22] found that individuals with prior AI knowledge adapted more easily to generative AI, while Bankins et al. [32] noted that company policies promoting generative AI eased apprehensions among creative professionals, making its implementation smoother. Overall, the studies suggest that familiarity with AI facilitates seamless adoption of generative AI in marketing tasks, with training recommended for those less experienced.

Human-AI Collaboration. The Human-AI collaboration subtheme, identified in 30 papers, constitutes a significant aspect of generative AI opportunities, as 8 papers directly link it to the main theme [34]. It underpins various subthemes, accounting for 83.68% of all subthemes within the main theme. Despite initial concerns, creative professionals are willing to collaborate with generative AI, enhancing innovative work behavior through planning sessions [28]. Generative AI's medium-independence facilitates its broad applicability in marketing [17], with an inverse relationship observed between AI augmentation and marketing layoff rates [35]. Managerial views on generative AI are influenced by performance expectations and supportive conditions [36], addressing ethical concerns and boosting confidence among professionals [37]. This collaboration extends to improving deep fake identification [6] and maximizing generative AI's effectiveness [5, 18–24]. It enables automation of routine tasks, enhancing productivity [12], and fosters creativity by freeing professionals from mundane tasks. Utilizing generative AI to its full potential allows for personalized advertisements [5, 18–24], with ease of use requiring collaboration for effective implementation [25, 35]. In essence, human-AI collaboration is foundational to leveraging generative AI's potential in marketing, emphasizing the necessity of collaboration for realizing its opportunities.

4.2 Drawbacks of Generative AI

The drawbacks of generative AI refer to the factors that contribute to the negative influence of generative AI on creative individuals in marketing. Each of the subthemes will be discussed below.

Fear of Generative AI. Fear of generative AI, identified in two of the 40 papers analyzed, pertains to the apprehension among creative professionals regarding potential job displacement or replacement by AI systems. This fear has been associated with heightened job engagement, as noted in a study [34]. The evolution of generative AI alters the landscape of job requirements in marketing, further exacerbating the concerns of creative professionals regarding job security and potential replacement by ai-driven solutions. Consequently, an increasing number of creative professionals experience insecurity in their roles. However, it's noteworthy that in one study, job and task engagement showed a decline [32].

Skepticism Over Generative AI. Skepticism regarding generative AI emerged as a significant subtheme in four of the 40 papers examined. This skepticism primarily revolves around the lack of trust among marketing creative professionals in the capabilities of generative AI. For instance, Lanz, Briker, and Gerpott [38] noted that creative professionals exhibit reluctance in relying on the suggestions provided by generative AI for generating new content. There is a prevailing sentiment among creative individuals questioning the fairness of decisions or suggestions generated by AI systems, with many asserting the continued necessity of human intervention [34, 39]. Additionally, it was observed that creative professionals tend to trust generative AI solutions integrated into their tasks only when prioritizing task efficiency [23].

Risks of Generative AI. The exploration of risks associated with generative AI, encompassing 24 of the 40 analyzed papers, unveils multifaceted challenges inherent in its integration into marketing practices by creative professionals. Foremost among these risks is the potential compromise of marketing strategies, including the leakage of trade secrets or sensitive information, exposing organizations to the threat of ransom or misuse [9, 20, 26, 40, 41]. Moreover, the public accessibility of generative AI heightens susceptibility to malware attacks, posing risks even for non-technical individuals involved in illicit activities [9, 20, 26, 40, 41]. Training generative AI with biased or unauthorized data amplifies the risk of generating inaccurate content, jeopardizing customer trust in marketing endeavors [16, 17, 29, 30, 42–45]. Additionally, there's a concern regarding the potential production of patented derivative content [9, 31]. Despite its capacity to enhance creative capabilities, generative AI solutions may inadvertently lead to a decline in critical thinking skills among professionals, diminishing their reliance on personal ingenuity [6, 24, 37]. Furthermore, the misuse of deepfake technology presents ethical dilemmas, necessitating responsible usage to avoid blurring the lines between authentic and fabricated content [7, 21, 24, 40]. Absence of proper frameworks for generative AI deployment heightens the risk of ethical misconduct, underscoring the importance of organizational oversight [12]. Diminished job and task engagement in the absence of organizational policies to manage generative AI usage can lead to burnout and resistance among creative professionals [23, 32]. While generative AI may alleviate stress, its simplification of tasks may inadvertently reduce job satisfaction by diminishing the sense of challenge and fulfillment [46].

Ethical Considerations. Ethical considerations surrounding the integration of generative AI into marketing practices were explored across 22 of the 40 analyzed papers, shedding light on the ethical implications faced by creative professionals. These considerations are deeply intertwined with the risks associated with generative AI usage, necessitating a cohesive approach to risk management rooted in ethical standards [38]. Interviews revealed that creative professionals perceive generative AI as misleading due to its perceived lack of human-like cognition, raising ethical questions regarding its usage [39]. Concerns also arise regarding the potential exploitation of sensitive information, particularly when generative AI is trained on biased data, which could perpetuate discrimination or disseminate inappropriate content [6, 7, 17, 29, 30, 44]. Privacy violations pose another ethical dilemma, as some creative professionals may unethically leverage generative AI for targeted marketing using private customer information, highlighting the importance of transparency in AI interactions [16, 24, 26, 31, 40, 44, 45]. Additionally, generative AI's capacity to produce deceptive content raises ethical concerns, underscoring the need for creative professionals to exercise caution and critical awareness [16, 24, 26, 31, 40, 44, 45]. Moreover, ethical concerns extend to the potential falsification of metrics, such as video advertisement views on social media platforms [9, 20], and the misuse of deepfake technology to spread misinformation or create deceptive endorsements [21, 24, 25, 42, 43]. Effective frameworks for marketing management play a pivotal role in mitigating ethical misconduct associated with generative AI usage, emphasizing the importance of establishing robust ethical guidelines and oversight mechanisms [12].

Automation and Efficiency. The subtheme of automation and efficiency drawbacks emerged from a single paper out of the 40 analyzed. This subtheme underscores the interconnectedness between the risks associated with generative AI and its drawbacks, particularly concerning automation. creative professionals exposed to the risk of automation may experience reduced stress levels but are susceptible to health issues stemming from job dissatisfaction [46]. This finding highlights the adverse impact of automation on the well-being of creative professionals, underscoring the prevalence of job insecurities within this context.

Human-AI Collaboration. In eight of the 40 papers examined, Human-AI Collaboration emerged as a significant contributor to the overarching theme of drawbacks associated with generative AI. This subtheme intertwines with other subthemes, such as the risks of generative AI, automation and efficiency, and ethical considerations, within the broader context of generative AI drawbacks. Notably, 85.45% of all subthemes under the main theme of drawbacks of generative AI were influenced by human-AI collaboration. Human-AI collaboration encompasses the integration of generative AI into the workflow of creative professionals in marketing. Studies emphasize the importance of maintaining a balanced approach, cautioning against complete reliance on generative AI, as it has inherent limitations that must be acknowledged [24, 39, 40]. Additionally, human intervention is essential during the use of generative AI, as it lacks subjective judgment and critical thinking abilities [29, 44]. It is imperative for creative professionals to discern the tasks best suited for generative AI assistance and evaluate its actual efficacy to mitigate potential risks that could impact the core functioning of the company [23]. Contrary to expectations, studies indicate that job satisfaction does not necessarily increase with human-AI collaboration, often remaining neutral or decreasing [46].

Furthermore, all studies examining the risks of generative AI and ethical considerations are rooted in the concept of human-AI collaboration, as risks and ethical dilemmas arise from the collaborative interaction between humans and AI systems. However, human-AI collaboration comprises only 14.55% of the drawbacks of generative AI and does not directly inform other subthemes. Nonetheless, human-AI collaboration remains a central theme, permeating various aspects of generative AI's impact on creative professionals in marketing. In summary, human-AI collaboration not only serves as a standalone subtheme but also underpins several other subthemes, underscoring its pivotal role in shaping the landscape of generative AI integration in marketing practices.

4.3   A Practical Matrix for Marketing Professionals

The integration of generative artificial intelligence (AI) in the contemporary landscape of marketing, holds significant implications for creative professionals in marketing. To provide a comprehensive understanding of the opportunities and drawbacks associated with this integration, the findings from the SLR were synthesized into a practical framework. This framework delineates the main themes of generative AI opportunities and drawbacks identified in the literature, accompanied by specific subthemes and the corresponding number of papers that contributed to each. However, beyond merely elucidating these theoretical constructs, our aim is to offer practical insights for creative professional in the marketing industry. This framework serves as a valuable resource for creative professionals seeking to navigate the complexities of incorporating generative AI into their strategies, providing actionable guidance derived from the synthesis of existing literature (Table 2).

Table 2. A framework synthesizing the opportunities, drawbacks, and practical applications of Generative AI in Marketing.

Subtheme	Nr of Papers	Main Concepts/Criteria	Practical Application for creative professionals in Marketing
Main Theme: AI Opportunities			
Generative AI Effectiveness	14	Role in sustaining customer satisfaction; Enhancing marketing effectiveness; Personalized advertisements; Prevention of deepfakes; Utilization in crowd-sourcing	Creative professionals can leverage generative AI to enhance customer satisfaction through personalized marketing campaigns tailored to individual preferences
Creative Capabilities Enhancements	9	Boosting creativity; Idea generation; Use of synthetic endorsers; Improvement of marketing platforms; Production of engaging content	Creative professionals can foster a culture of innovation by providing employees with access to generative AI tools that facilitate idea generation and content creation

(*continued*)

Table 2. (*continued*)

Subtheme	Nr of Papers	Main Concepts/Criteria	Practical Application for creative professionals in Marketing
Automation and Efficiency	10	Automation of routine tasks; Increased productivity; Cost savings; Enhanced decision-making; Enhanced decision-making; Improved marketing analytics; Content creation automation	Creative professionals can streamline marketing workflows by automating repetitive tasks, thereby freeing up employees' time to focus on more strategic initiatives
Generative AI Enhance Productivity	7	Rapid content generation; Improved task completion; Increased efficiency; Focus on complex tasks; Reach broader customer segments	Creative professionals can empower their marketing teams to achieve greater productivity by integrating generative AI tools that facilitate rapid content generation and task completion
Generative AI Ease of Use	2	Adoption ease for knowledgeable users; Company policy influence; Prior AI knowledge facilitation	Creative professionals can promote the adoption of generative AI by providing comprehensive training programs and fostering a supportive organizational culture
Human-AI Collaboration	30	Collaboration with AI in marketing tasks; Innovative work behaviour; Medium-independent applicability; Influence on managerial views	Creative professionals can encourage collaboration between employees and AI systems to harness the collective strengths of human creativity and machine intelligence

(*continued*)

Table 2. (*continued*)

Subtheme	Nr of Papers	Main Concepts/Criteria	Practical Application for creative professionals in Marketing
		Addressing privacy and ethics	Training programs on AI ethics and privacy can equip employees with the knowledge and skills needed to navigate ethical considerations effectively and maintain transparency in AI-driven initiatives
Main Theme: AI Drawbacks			
Fear of Generative AI	2	Job security concerns: Increased job/task engagement; Fear of job replacement	Creative professionals can address employees' fears by providing reassurance about the role of AI as a complement to human creativity rather than a replacement
Scepticism over Generative AI	4	Lack of trust in AI suggestions; Perceived lack of mind; Fairness of decisions; Task efficiency reliance	Creative professionals can build trust in AI systems by demonstrating their reliability and transparency in decision-making processes
Risks of Generative AI	24	Leaked marketing strategies; Malware susceptibility; Biased or inaccurate content; Patent infringement risk; Overreliance on AI; Deepfake misuse; Ethical misconduct	Creative professionals can mitigate risks associated with generative AI by implementing robust security measures, such as encryption and access controls, to safeguard sensitive information

(*continued*)

Table 2. (*continued*)

Subtheme	Nr of Papers	Main Concepts/Criteria	Practical Application for creative professionals in Marketing
Ethical Considerations	22	Misleading content; Exploitation of sensitive information; Bias in training data; Privacy violations; Deceiving content; Misuse for fake news	Creative professionals can prioritize ethical considerations by establishing clear guidelines for AI usage and content creation
Automation and Efficiency	1	Stress reduction; Job dissatisfaction; Health concerns	Creative professionals can proactively address potential negative impacts on employee well-being by implementing measures to mitigate stress and job dissatisfaction associated with AI adoption
Human-AI Collaboration	8	Overreliance avoidance; Need for human intervention; Task assessment; Job satisfaction effects	Creative professionals can foster a culture of balanced collaboration between humans and AI by encouraging employees to take an active role in task assessment and decision-making processes

The next section will delve into a discussion of the findings.

5 Discussion

Generative AI presents a plethora of opportunities for creative professionals in marketing, offering a range of potential benefits. These advantages include heightened marketing effectiveness, amplified creative capabilities, streamlined automation of routine tasks, increased productivity, ease of use, and fruitful human-AI collaboration. By harnessing the power of generative AI, creative professionals can elevate their marketing strategies, enhance customer satisfaction, and unlock new avenues for creativity and innovation. However, alongside its potential benefits, generative AI also introduces several challenges and concerns for creative professionals. These include fears of job displacement, scepticism about AI-generated content, security and privacy risks, ethical considerations, and the possibility of overreliance on AI. Without proper guidance and support, organizations may encounter resistance during the implementation phase. Therefore, it becomes imperative to underscore the importance of human oversight in monitoring AI-generated outcomes, mitigating potential risks, and maintaining overall job satisfaction among team members. Clear communication regarding the capabilities and limitations of generative AI is essential to foster transparency and trust among all stakeholders.

Resistance to the adoption of generative AI may stem from concerns about inefficient workplace structures, privacy violations, and ethical dilemmas. However, it is crucial to emphasize that many of these challenges can be effectively managed through responsible AI deployment. By prioritizing human oversight, ethical standards, and ongoing training, organizations can ensure that generative AI enhances, rather than replaces, human creativity. Ultimately, the successful integration of generative AI into marketing strategies hinges on fostering a collaborative ecosystem where human creativity and AI capabilities complement each other synergistically. This requires a balanced approach that acknowledges both the opportunities and challenges posed by generative AI, while also emphasizing the importance of responsible implementation and ongoing support for creative professionals.

In addition, it is crucial to consider the practical implications for creative professionals in marketing. The last column of the synthesized findings practical highlights key aspects that could be practically implemented to navigate the integration of generative AI into marketing strategies. This includes developing clear frameworks and guidelines for AI utilization, providing comprehensive training programs for employees, and fostering a culture of collaboration and innovation. Furthermore, organizations must prioritize transparency and communication to ensure that creative professionals understand the capabilities and limitations of generative AI, thereby fostering trust and confidence in its use. By embracing these practical applications, creative professionals in marketing can effectively harness the power of generative AI to drive innovation, enhance productivity, and ultimately achieve marketing success in the digital age.

6   Conclusion

This study reported on an exploration of generative AI's impact on creative marketing professionals, guided by the framework of Boland et al. [13]. Two overarching themes emerged: the diverse opportunities presented by generative AI and the corresponding challenges inherent in its adoption. The identified opportunities encompass a range of benefits, including enhanced marketing effectiveness, strengthened creative capabilities, streamlined automation, increased productivity, user-friendly interfaces, and synergistic human-AI collaboration. These findings underscore generative AI's transformative potential in revolutionizing marketing practices, enabling professionals to craft more impactful campaigns and deepen customer engagement. Conversely, the study also highlighted potential drawbacks and challenges, such as fear of job displacement, skepticism over AI-generated content, security and privacy risks, ethical considerations, and the risk of overreliance on AI. Addressing these challenges is crucial for ensuring responsible integration into marketing workflows.

The study contribution is the proposed synthesized framework capturing generative AI's influence on creative professionals in marketing. This framework provides a structured understanding and serves as a springboard for future research, enabling deeper exploration of specific subthemes and evolving dynamics within the field. Moreover, the implications extend beyond academia to practical applications in the marketing industry.

By equipping professionals with informed insights, organizations can navigate generative AI implementation with greater confidence and foresight, ensuring ethical and responsible use through appropriate frameworks and guidelines.

In conclusion, this study offers a comprehensive understanding of generative AI's influence on creative professionals in marketing, clarifying both opportunities and challenges. Informed decision-making and responsible innovation are vital as the landscape of AI-driven marketing continues to evolve, shaping the future of marketing practices.

References

1. Mariani, M.M., Perez-Vega, R., Wirtz, J.: AI in marketing, consumer research and psychology: A systematic literature review and research agenda. Psychol. Mark. **39**, 755–776 (2022). https://doi.org/10.1002/mar.21619
2. Mondal, S., Das, S., Vrana, V.G.: How to bell the cat? a theoretical review of generative artificial intelligence towards digital disruption in all walks of life. Technologies. **11**, 44 (2023). https://doi.org/10.3390/technologies11020044
3. Sako, M.: Artificial Intelligence and the Future of Professional Work. Communications of the ACM, 63 (2020). https://doi.org/10.1145/3382743
4. Brühl, V.: Generative Artificial Intelligence (GAI) Foundations, Use Cases and Economic Potential. SSRN Electronic Journal (2023)
5. Dadman, S.: Boosting Creativity with AI: Exploring Advanced Models, Multi-Agent Systems, and Design Grammar. Department of Computer Science (2023). https://doi.org/10.13140/RG.2.2.24877.67041
6. Fui-Hoon Nah, F., Zheng, R., Cai, J., Siau, K., Chen, L.: Generative AI and ChatGPT: Applications, challenges, and AI-human collaboration. J. Info. Technol. Case and Appl. Res. (2023). https://doi.org/10.1080/15228053.2023.2233814
7. Wach, K., et al.: The dark side of generative artificial intelligence: a critical analysis of controversies and risks of ChatGPT. Entrepren. Bus. Econ. Rev. **11**, 7–24 (2023). https://doi.org/10.15678/EBER.2023.110201
8. Devaraj, S., Rajiv, K.: Performance impacts of information technology: is actual usage the missing link? Manage. Sci. **49**, 273–289 (2003)
9. Garon, J.M.: A practical introduction to generative AI, synthetic media, and the messages found in the latest medium. SSRN Electronic J. (2023)
10. Buzzell, R.D.: Market functions and market evolution. J. Mark. **63**, 61–63 (1999). https://doi.org/10.1177/00222429990634s107
11. Chui, M., Roberts, R., Yee, L.: Generative AI is here: How tools like ChatGPT could change your business. Quantum Black AI by McKinsey (2022)
12. Ramdurai, B.: The Impact. Technology in Society, Advancements and Applications of Generative AI (2023)
13. Boland, A., Cherry, M.G., Dickson, R.: Doing a systematic review : a student's guide. SAGE, Los Angeles (2017)
14. Moher, D., Liberati, A., Tetzlaff, J., Altman, D.G.: Preferred reporting items for systematic reviews and meta-analyses: the PRISMA statement. BMJ **339**, b2535 (2009). https://doi.org/10.1136/bmj.b2535
15. Braun, V., Clarke, V.: Thematic analysis. Presented at the January 1 (2012)
16. Fredriksson, D., Eriksson, M.: Can Generative AI Replace Human Communication Professionals? (2023)
17. Kowalczyk, P., Röder, M., Thiese, F.: Nudging Creativity in Digital Marketing with Generative Artificial Intelligence: Opportunities and Limitations (2023)

18. Mayahi, S., Vidrih, M.: The Impact of Generative AI on the Future of Visual Content Marketing (2022)
19. Petrescu, M., Krishen, A.S.: Hybrid intelligence: human–AI collaboration in marketing analytics. Journal of Marketing Analytics, 1–12 (2023)
20. Vice, J., Akhtar, N., Hartley, R., Mian, A.: BAGM: A Backdoor Attack for Manipulating Text-to-Image Generative Models (2023). arxiv:2307.16489
21. Whittaker, L., Letheren, K., Mulcahy, R.: The rise of deepfakes: a conceptual framework and research agenda for marketing. Australas. Mark. J. **29**, 204–214 (2021)
22. Abdelkader, O.A.: ChatGPT's influence on customer experience in digital marketing: Investigating the moderating roles. Heliyon. **9**, 18770 (2023). https://doi.org/10.1016/j.heliyon. 2023.e18770
23. Baek, T.H., Kim, M.: Is ChatGPT scary good? how user motivations affect creepiness and trust in generative artificial intelligence. Telematics and Informatics, 102030 (2023)
24. Campbell, C., Plangger, K., Sands, S., Kietzmann, J.: Preparing for an era of deepfakes and AI-generated ads: a framework for understanding responses to manipulated advertising. J. Advert. **51**, 22–38 (2022)
25. Roy, M., Raval, M.S.: Unmasking deepfake visual content with generative AI. J. Advert. Res. (2020)
26. Peres, R., Schreier, M., Schweidel, D., Sorescu, A.: On ChatGPT and beyond: How generative artificial intelligence may affect research, teaching, and practice. Int. J. Res. Market. (2023)
27. Cardon, P.W., Getchell, K., Carradini, S., Fleischmann, C., Stapp, J.: Generative AI in the workplace: employee perspectives of ChatGPT benefits and organizational policies. J. Market. Analy. (2023)
28. Verma, S., Singh, V.: Impact of artificial intelligence-enabled job characteristics and perceived substitution crisis on innovative work behavior of employees from high-tech firms. Comput. Hum. Behav. **131**, 107215 (2022)
29. Bi, Q.: Analysis of the application of generative ai in business management. Adv. Econ. Manage. Res. **6**, 36 (2023)
30. Suvanto, E.: Applications of Generative AI in Business (2023)
31. Davenport, T.H., Mittal, N.: How Generative AI Is Changing Creative Work. Harvard Business Review (2022)
32. Bankins, S., Ocampo, A.C., Marrone, M., Restubog, S.L.D., Woo, S.E.: A multilevel review of artificial intelligence in organizations: Implications for organizational behavior research and practice. Journal of Organizational Behavior (2023)
33. Eisfeldt, A.L., Schubert, G., Zhang, M.B.: Generative AI and firm values. NBER Working Paper Series (2023)
34. Koo, C., Chung, N., Kim, H.-W.: Examining explorative and exploitative uses of smartphones: a user competence perspective. Inf. Technol. People **1**, 133–162 (2015)
35. Huang, Q., Shen, Y., Sun, Y., Zhang, Q.: The Layoff Generation: How Generative Ai Will Reshape Employment and Labor Markets. SSRN Electron. J. (2023). https://doi.org/10.2139/ssrn.4534294
36. Cao, X., Sun, J.: Exploring the effect of overload on the discontinuous intention of social media users: An S-O-R perspective. Comput. Hum. Behav. **81**, 10–18 (2018). https://doi.org/10.1016/j.chb.2017.11.035
37. Shan, G., Qiu, L.: Examining the Impact of Generative AI on Users' Voluntary Knowledge Contribution: Evidence from A Natural Experiment on Stack Overflow (2023)
38. Lanz, L., Briker, R., Gerpott, F.H.: Employees adhere more to unethical instructions from human than AI supervisors: complementing experimental evidence with machine learning. J. Bus. Ethics (2023). https://doi.org/10.1007/s10551-023-05393-1

39. Heyder, T., Passlack, N., Posegga, O.: Ethical management of human-AI interaction: Theory development review. J. Strateg. Inf. Syst. **32**, 101772 (2023). https://doi.org/10.1016/j.jsis.2023.101772
40. Ray, P.P.: ChatGPT: A comprehensive review on background, applications, key challenges, bias, ethics, limitations and future scope. Internet of Things and Cyber-Physical Systems (2023)
41. Teichmann, F.: Ransomware attacks in the context of generative artificial intelligence—an experimental study. Int. Cybersecu. Law Rev. 1–16 (2023)
42. Dwivedi, Y.K., et al.: So what if ChatGPT wrote it?" Multidisciplinary perspectives on opportunities, challenges and implications of generative conversational AI for research, practice and policy. Int. J. Inf. Manage. **71**, 102642 (2023)
43. Ghosh, A., Lakshmi, D.: Dual Governance: The intersection of centralized regulation and crowdsourced safety mechanisms for Generative AI (2023)
44. Khowaja, S.A., Khuwaja, P., Dev, K.: ChatGPT Needs SPADE (Sustainability, PrivAcy, Digital divide, and Ethics) Evaluation: A Review (2023)
45. Lu, Z., et al.: Seeing is not always believing: Benchmarking Human and Model Perception of AI-Generated Images (2023)
46. Nazareno, L., Schiff, D.S.: The impact of automation and artificial intelligence on worker well-being. Technol. Soc. **67**, 101679 (2021)

Towards a Smart City Sustainability Tracker for Achieving SDG 11 in Cities

Miriam Mei Yi Dall'Agnolo[1]([✉]), Stephan Jüngling[1], and Hanlie Smuts[2]

[1] University of Applied Sciences and Arts Northwestern, Olten, Switzerland
`miriam.dall@alumni.fhnw.ch`, `stephan.juengling@fhnw.ch`
[2] University of Pretoria, Pretoria, South Africa
`hanlie.smuts@up.ac.za`

Abstract. Cities are considered one of the largest emitters of greenhouse gas emissions and consume vast amounts of energy. They, therefore, play a significant role in achieving the Sustainable Development Goals (SDGs). However, the SDG indicators are reported on a country level, and city-level assessments in Switzerland are voluntary, non-standardized, and only updated in larger time intervals.

The current paper focuses on applying SDG 11 as a metric for visualizing urban efforts toward achieving a broader set of SDGs. This involves a thorough assessment of each goal within SDG 11 to determine its measurability. With the Smart City Sustainability Tracker (SCST), we propose a platform based on KNIME, which can help monitor the progress in cases where sufficient data is available for doing a regression analysis. In cases where too little information is available, we propose to at least provide some process models, which can help to standardize at least the processes of collecting measurable KPIs to turn manual project work conducted in heterogeneous environments into reference processes, which can help to implement the necessary data collection more quickly.

The standardization and visualization of city-level reporting could support decision-makers in developing more adequate measures to follow the trajectories of successful implementations or to detect and correct failures quickly to ensure reaching the shared goals in time. Finally, we conclude with a short validation of the potential reuse and adaptability of the SCST from the application of the city of Zurich, to cities in totally different circumstances such as for the situation of SDG11 in Pretoria, South Africa.

Keywords: Society5.0 · smart cities · SDGs · sustainability tracker · reference processes

1 Introduction

In the transition from the era of Industry 4.0, the concept of Society 5.0 emerged placing human beings at the center of innovation. This new societal model prioritizes leveraging the benefits of data-driven innovation to ensure all people live comfortable and vigorous lives [18]. This transformation is marked by rapid technological advancement, particularly in information and communications technology (ICT) causing a significant increase in digital data and the expansion of cyberspace [18].

© The Author(s), under exclusive license to Springer Nature Switzerland AG 2025
K. Hinkelmann and H. Smuts (Eds.): Society 5.0 2024, CCIS 2173, pp. 84–97, 2025.
https://doi.org/10.1007/978-3-031-71412-2_7

At the same time, the phenomenon of increasing urbanization across the globe poses considerable challenges, including its significant contributions to climate change and biodiversity loss harming the quality of life for more than half of the world's population [22]. Urban settlements cover just 3% of the world's surface but consume 78% of the world's energy and emit more than 60% of the world's greenhouse gas emissions (GHG) [22, 27].

Policymakers, researchers and urban residents recognize that cities play an essential role in securing sustainable futures across a range of vital global issues and the relevance of the cities in achieving the SDGs of the 2030 Agenda was recognized and materialized in SDG 11: Make cities and human settlements inclusive, safe, resilient and sustainable [1, 27]. However, there is still little progress after five years of adopting the 2030 Agenda on a national, regional, or global scale [4].

Strong and resilient communities ultimately thrive by fostering partnerships and evolve through collaborative efforts facilitated by good governance [29]. To promote sustainable urban development, the information society emphasizes the importance of information resources [31]. Data gathered through smart systems can help decision-makers to make more informed decisions but can also help to facilitate better communication with different stakeholders [2, 20]. Besides, in a smaller city context, the responsibility of each individual is more relevant, enabling more direct and impactful contributions to sustainability efforts. This approach can foster a sense of ownership and accountability, aligning with Society 5.0's human-centric focus and ensuring that technological and data-driven innovations serve the specific needs of communities and their environments.

Industry and academia consider smart cities as a solution that can address these challenges [23]. Combining SDGs and smart cities could help cities overcome the denounced siloed approach and lead to synergies. A long-term objective to address today's challenges is the establishment of a "smart city brain" aimed at providing sustainable data insights to decision-makers. As a first step towards this vision, we propose the introduction of the Smart City Sustainability Tracker (SCST). The goal is to integrate diverse data streams and analytical capabilities to visualize the transition towards a more sustainable and efficiently managed urban environment of the city of Zurich, which could serve as a reference to other cities with similar interests to create feedback loops that not only report on the outcome of successful implementation of projects but also highlight the processes, innovations, and efforts of all stakeholders involved to create more transparency and encourage a culture of shared responsibility and recognition.

The challenges mentioned above led us to the following research questions, which were used as starting points for the development of the SCST:

- RQ 1: How accessible is data regarding SDG 11 on a city level in Switzerland?
- RQ 2: How can the collected data and efforts be represented in a model?
- RQ 3: How many indicators could be visualized, and do they represent the respective indicators?

2 Sustainable Development Strategy in Zurich

Switzerland has defined a sustainable development strategy including the 2030 Agenda, even though they are not legally binding [25]. It is important to understand that Switzerland is a federalist state, where the responsibility of implementing actions is mainly attributed to its cantons and communities [26]. Despite the relevance of cantons, no clear instructions were formulated on a sub-national level through the Sustainability Strategy, but the Confederation offers support in facilitating collaboration, knowledge sharing and financial support.

The City of Zurich has defined its own environmental strategy focusing on four goals: Climate-neutral city, healthy urban environment, networked urban nature, and intelligent use of resources. The strategy defines goals and corresponding environmental specifications, including dedicated indicators for their target. The progress on its targets is explained and made available in the City of Zurich's environmental report [5, 6]. The strategy further includes additional measures to become more sustainable, such as Circular Zurich and 2000-Watt Society [9, 11].

In addition to the environmental projects, the city is focused on its digitalization to become a smart city. In 2018 the City of Zurich started the project 'Smart City Zurich' to embrace the digital transformation and to maintain and further improve Zurich's high quality of life. They intend to promote sustainable development and strengthen Zurich as a site of business and innovation. Therefore, three focus areas were defined; integrated public mobility, digital city, and smart participation [24]. Another important aspect of the smart city project is the transparent communication about the collection and use of collected data. The City of Zurich considers public trust in the responsible use of data as central [5]. Citizens must understand how the data is collected and for what purposes. For example, the data gathered from sensors measuring water and air quality or traffic frequencies is made available and is freely accessible. Additionally, sensors in public spaces are clearly labeled using pictograms and are accessible through a Quick Response (QR) Code [8].

The selection of Zurich as a case study is inherently tied to the authors' background providing a strong understanding of the local political system and governance dynamics. Zurich's commitment to sustainability and smart city development broadens the context for exploring the fusion of environmental objectives and digital innovation in urban landscapes. This commitment is exemplified by Zurich's consistent top rankings in the International Institute for Management Development's (IMD) 'Smart City' index [17].

3 Creating Categories for the SCST

Data can be used to monitor progress toward the SDGs by transforming it into models, which can be used for forecasts, risk assessments, or implementation of strategies [2]. Data regarding the SDGs is collected and published in various forms and degrees, which makes progress difficult to track. In addition, the indicators are often presented in an aggregated form on a national level rather than on a city level. Integrating data from the City of Zurich with an open-source platform like KNIME, represents a critical part in the development of the SCST. The SCST aims to offer consistent and easily accessible data to track progress towards SDG 11 and our study emphasizes establishing replicable practices for the scalability and adaptability of successful measures. The overarching goal is to contribute to Switzerland's advancement in achieving SDG 11 by providing targeted and data-driven insights.

First, SMART (specific, measurable, achievable, relevant, and time-related) targets need to be identified to track the progress and to systematically show the tangible impacts of implemented strategies. Second, the measurability of data related to the SMART target needs to be evaluated. Hence, a decision process as shown in Fig. 1 determines four possible categories of assessments. First, it must be reviewed whether the indicator is suitable for the particular SDG target and can be evaluated. In case a measurable target cannot be derived, it will be marked as "grey" (not suitable), which means the SDG target itself requires further research. If a suitable indicator can be derived, it needs to be reviewed whether the data is also available on a city level. If data is unavailable on a city level, the responsible department is identified and contacted to confirm that this data is unavailable. Subsequently, a process model should be created on how the data is currently being gathered and how it might be improved. Further, data that is accessible through reports or homepages but is not in a processible file format will also be considered and added manually. Based on both criteria, the following rule applies. If no data is available to directly visualize the progress in the SCST, it still can be shown as a process model. If open data is available on a cantonal level, the goal

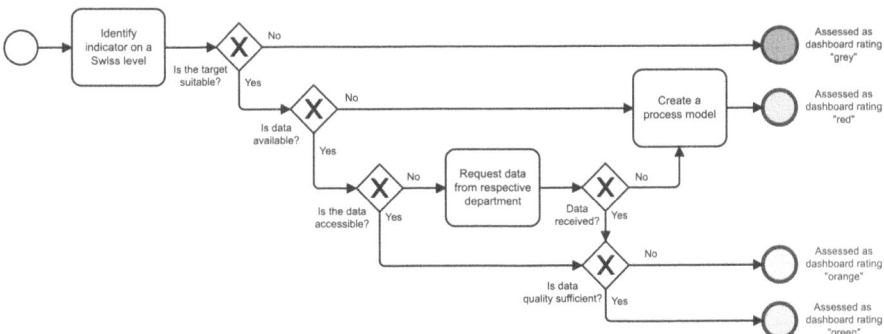

Fig. 1. Decision process for assessment categorization based on data availability, accessibility, and quality. The color-coded ratings in the figure are determined by the number of criteria that apply.

is to implement a data processing pipeline to measure the target on a city level. If the data is available on the city level but only upon request, there might be a chance to make it publicly available. The data quality can be measured by the frequency of its collection and its actuality. If data is not updated yearly, it would still be considered as shown by example for each of the categories.

Finally, the availability and accessibility lead to the final rating as visualized with different color codes in Table 1.

Table 1. Category evaluation criteria and rating

Assessment Criteria	Evaluation	Rating
Target can be derived from the indicator	No	0
	Yes	3
Data Availability	No data	0
	Available Country Level	1
	Available Canton Level	2
	Available City Level	3
Data Accessibility	No data	0
	No access / No response	1
	Access upon request	2
	Access available/open source	3
Data History	No data	0
	1 year of data	1
	< 5 years of data	2
	> 5 years of data	3
Data Collection Frequency	No data	0
	< Every 2 years	1
	Every 2 years	2
	Every year	3

In the upcoming sub-chapters, we delve into the various categories, highlighting specific SDGs that serve as typical examples for each assessment category. We begin with the most demanding grey category.

3.1 Assessment Category Grey – SDG 11.A and 11.C

SDG 11.a focuses on strengthening national and regional development planning and SDG 11.c focuses on supporting least developed countries in building sustainable and resilient buildings [28]. Process-oriented targets of SDG 11, specifically targets 11.a and 11.c, exemplify the challenges associated with identifying suitable targets for tracking the progress. The absence of academic research on this topic is highlighted by Berisha et al. [3], underscoring the complexities involved in this topic. They propose an approach focusing on formal, functional, and goal-oriented coordination and cooperation, which primarily evaluates the effectiveness through quantitative measures such as the number of policies, the involvement of municipalities, the engagement of populations, or the allocation of funds. Even though there are policies defined, it is difficult to measure their effectiveness due to the absence of a universally accepted policy measurement methodology. Since no general policy measurement methodology for SDG 11.a and 11.c exist, a new method needs to be elaborated. The category rating for SDG 11 a and c is therefore rated as *grey*.

3.2 Assessment Category Red and Orange – SDG 11.2

The modal split, which determines the mode of transport for passengers and freight volumes, serves as an indicator in both of Switzerland SDG reporting tools, MONET2030 and SDGital2030. Additionally, it is part of the urban transport strategy of the City of Zurich [8]. It was therefore simple to derive a measurable target: *Increase the modal split of public transport, pedestrian and bicycle traffic in the total traffic volume in the City of Zurich by 10% points by 2025 compared to 2020.* As it is typical for this category, a process model could be compiled, which is shown in Fig. 2.

Notably, the city-level representation of this indicator is more granular, encompassing additional data on pedestrians and bicycles. The modal split figures are formed based on the nationwide survey conducted every five years. Additionally, these surveys occur throughout Switzerland, enabling comparisons with other cities [14]. The data is not readily available on a homepage in its raw format. Detailed information on the survey can be requested through the homepage of the ARE or, with little effort, copied from the homepage of the City of Zurich [15, 21]. The City of Zurich mentions that it is relevant to additionally consider the frequency of transport usage as well as the regular use of transport to be able to assess the traffic development [14]. While the frequency is already measured through sensors and updated every 15 min, the usage of transport is collected in a survey every two years [21]. The nationwide survey remains relevant, as it also considers information from people not living in Zurich but traveling through Zurich.

The classification of this indicator as "orange" is attributed to the availability of data that is not readily accessible. This requires the development of a process model to better understand and visualize which parties are involved and potential areas for improvement. The existing process, as depicted in Fig. 2, reveals that most data collection efforts rely on manual processes, primarily through the use of surveys. The process model shows that data comes from three different data sources: a nationwide survey, a local survey and automatically gathered data. The representation highlights the reliance on manual labor and the various origins of the data, which collectively contribute to the indicator's *orange* status. The data for the modal split was transferred from the homepage to an Excel sheet. Therefore, no data cleaning was necessary. The data was then processed using a Python script. Figure 3 represents a simple workflow adopted for most of the process where data was not readily accessible.

No red category indicators where there is a complete absence of data was identified in this study. For all indicators examined, it was possible to either collect some form of data through requests at the respective departments or to locate relevant data online.

3.3   Assessment Category Green – SDG 11.6

PM10, or particulate matter, also known as airborne dust, is a mixture of tiny particles less than 10 μm in diameter [10]. It is a complex mixture of primary particles originating from combustion processes like diesel engines, mechanical abrasion from tires, brakes, and road surfacing, and secondary particles formed in the atmosphere by interacting with gaseous precursors [16]. The World Health (WHO) Organization estimates that exposure to air pollution causes millions of deaths and lost years of healthy life, annually [30]. They set four interim targets for PM10 values. The City of Zurich has set its limits at PM10, which are equivalent to the fourth interim target level [10]. These targets only slightly differ from the ultimate air quality guideline levels of the WHO [30].

- Switzerland's long-term limit value: 20 μg/m3 annual average
- Switzerland's short-term limit value: 50 μg/m3 24-h average (maximum three exceedances per year)
- WHO long-term limit value: 15 μg/m3 annual average

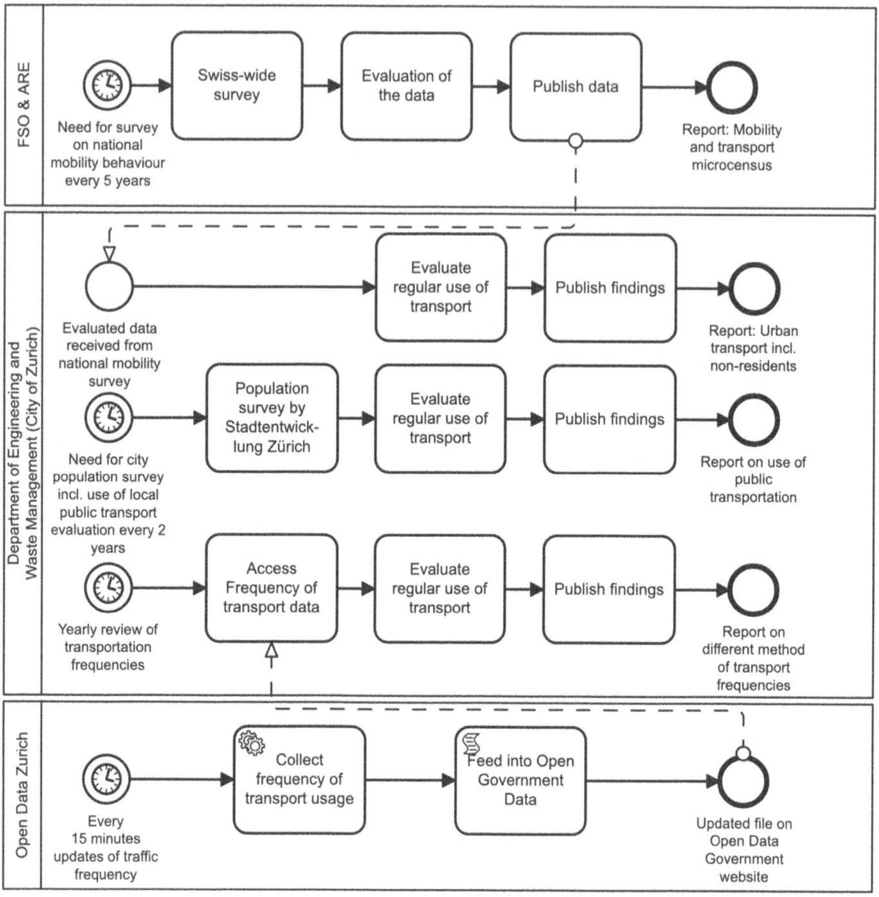

Fig. 2. Process model of data collection for the modal split includes all stakeholders, including the Federal Statistical Office (FSO) and the Federal Office for Spatial Development (ARE), conducting a nationwide survey every five years. This data is complemented by more frequent data collection efforts by the city and information from sensors distributed throughout the urban area, enriching the dataset.

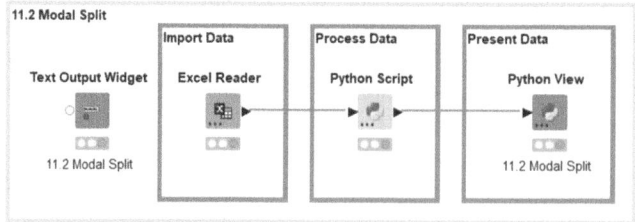

Fig. 3. KNIME Workflow Modal Split Traffic Usage

- WHO short-term limit value: 45 μg/m3 24-h average (maximum three exceedances per year)

The SCST focuses on the 2030 Agenda and will therefore focus on the interim target and limit values defined by the City of Zurich. The target is therefore defined as follows: *The PM10 annual mean must not exceed 20 μg per cubic meter ($μg/m^3$), while the PM10 daily mean must not exceed the 50 $μg/m^3$ limit more than three times per year.* Figure 4 shows the analysis of PM10 as the result of an almost fully automated process within the KNIME analytics platform [19].

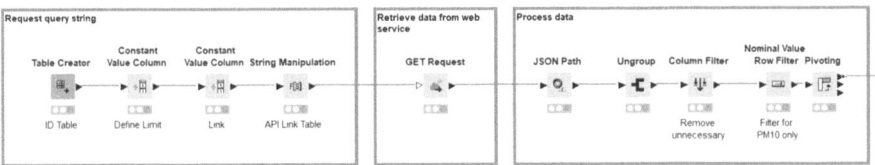

Fig. 4. Accessing PM10 data through application programming interfaces in a KNIME workflow

It can access the information through an application programming interface (API) on the Open Government Data Platform of the city of Zurich [12]. Subsequent stages involve the refinement and processing of this data which can use Python nodes for the execution of regression analysis in the end, such as shown in Fig. 5.

The visualization facilitates the interpretation that the existing measures implemented by the city of Zurich have contributed to a decrease in PM10 concentrations, suggesting that the objectives regarding air quality improvement are being met and that progress is aligned with the established SDG targets.

The dashboard creation using KNIME for evaluating the efforts of the City of Zurich toward achieving SDG 11 revealed that data was available for most targets. Six out of ten targets met the criteria for measurability, while data issues complicated the evaluation of four others. Process targets were notably challenging to quantify due to a lack of suitable definitions of objectives. The assessment detailed in Table 2 underscores issues with data accessibility and collection frequency, particularly highlighting that health-related targets like noise pollution and particulate matter concentration received higher scores.

4 Findings

The SCST can effectively provide insights into the specific targets from cities and can automate the reporting of accessible data. Nevertheless, some major issues need to be mentioned with respect to the availability and quality of the data.

- **Data Availability**: A significant finding was that readily available online data for the city's targets under SDG 11 is limited, with only two out of the ten being directly accessible through the Open Government Data platform. Other necessary data was obtained through requests to relevant departments or manual collecting from websites and reports, indicating availability but not accessibility for automated reporting processes like the Smart City Sustainability Tracker (SCST).

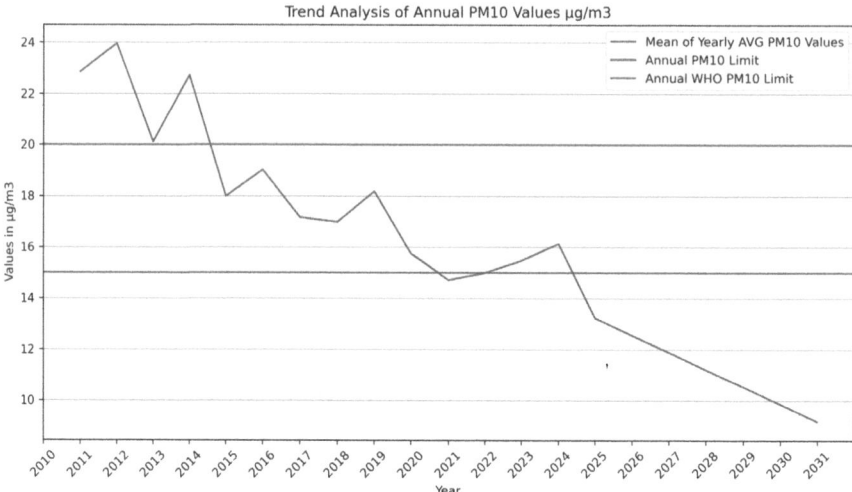

Fig. 5. Visualization and Regression Analysis of Annual PM10 Values

Table 2. Final criteria ratings for indicators

SDG	Indicator	Indicator driveable	Data Availability	Data Accessibility	Data History	Data Collection Frequency	Overall Measurability	Overall Rating
11.1	Housing Costs	3	1	2	3	2	11	Target measurable with data issues
11.2	Modal Split	3	3	2	3	1	12	Target measurable with data issues
11.2	Independent use of Public Transport	3	3	2	1	3	12	Target measurable with data issues
11.3	Building Zones	3	3	3	3	3	15	Target and data available
11.4	Ecologically Valuable Spaces	3	3	2	3	1	12	Target measurable with data issues
11.5	Natural Disaster Damage	3	3	2	3	3	14	Target and data available
11.6	PM10 Concentration	3	3	3	3	3	15	Target and data available
11.6	Noise Pollution	3	3	2	3	3	14	Target and data available
11.7	Min. Recreational Space	3	3	2	3	2	13	Target and data available
11.a	-	0	0	0	0	0	0	Target currently not measurable
11.b	Natural Disaster Damage	3	3	2	3	3	14	Target and data available
11.c	-	0	0	0	0	0	0	Target currently not measurable
		30	28	22	28	24		

- **Data Quality**: The analysis showed that when data is available, usually a data history can be found. However, the frequency with which this data is collected and updated depends on the collection method. Data from surveys or methods requiring significant manual labor generally have update frequencies of less than two years, making ongoing monitoring and precise forecasting challenging.
- **Target Evaluation**: Targets were found to be specific but not always comprehensive, and therefore, potentially misleading. However, the assessed targets provided insights into the city's efforts, with a noticeable emphasis on spatial issues related to urban planning. Spatial topics related to SDG 11, such as transport renovation and zoning, emphasized the importance of spatial development in achieving urban sustainability. A critical aspect in this context is whether the targets are closely monitored and

evaluated. The net-zero target, for example, just recently published a monitoring cockpit dedicated to measuring its progress and providing information to the broader mass [7]. This reinforces the importance of a dashboard providing information about progress and measures.

The SDGs are designed with a degree of flexibility that allows every country or city to derive targets according to its specific needs. It is, therefore, challenging to understand which efforts different cities took and their contributions to the SDGs. The exploration of Sustainable Development Goal (SDG) 11, specifically within the context of Swiss cities, reveals significant insights into the accessibility of data, the representation of collected efforts, and the visualization of indicators. The accessibility of city-level data in Switzerland regarding SDG 11 poses a challenge, as it is fragmented across various departments, each bearing different responsibilities. This fragmentation complicates the consolidation and reporting processes, underscoring the necessity for a versatile platform that can accommodate and visualize diverse data formats for different stakeholders. The research questions can be answered as follows:

- RQ 1: How accessible is data regarding SDG 11 on a city level in Switzerland?

The integration of the SDGs into Switzerland's sustainability strategy emphasizes the supporting alignment among diverse stakeholders. Additionally, the analysis reveals that the same or similar information is shared across different channels such as SDGital2030 or MONET2030. This overlap complicates the process of understanding which indicator is relevant for which goal and what should be used to compare the data. Further, the sustainability targets of the city are not directly connected to SDG 11 and therefore difficult to map.

- RQ 2: How can the collected data and efforts be represented in a model?

Analyzing the different indicators has demonstrated the relevance of available and reliable data for advancing the SDGs. Although an open government data platform exists, only some required data is available. Sometimes, the data must be manually copied from existing reports or directly from the homepage into an Excel file. This situation illustrates that, despite adopting a shared data approach, comprehensive data accessibility has not been fully achieved. Ideally, relevant data should be easily accessible online in a CSV format, which simplifies the processes of data cleaning and formatting, thus facilitating data forecasting. The data shouldn't be pre-calculated if possible, allowing for the analysis of potential input factors and enabling more accurate forecasting.

- RQ 3: How many indicators could be visualized, and do they represent the respective indicators?

The study confirms the feasibility of mapping ten out of twelve city targets with SDG 11, enhancing the visual representation of progress towards these targets. It was also found that the data collection type should be considered in the future as it signif-icantly influences the measurability of a target. Apart from the assessment of targets, the replicability of processes and monitoring must be kept in mind. The incorporation of charts to illustrate progress emphasizes the importance of setting SMART targets, alongside acknowledging the critical roles of data availability and quality. This type of data collection significantly impacts target measurability, suggesting a future focus on refining data collection methodologies to ensure accurate and meaningful assessments.

The City of Zurich has created a good foundation with its smart city project, as its data is accessible to everyone. Providing such information comprehensively and showing how it has been collected could help other cities to use a similar approach. Nonetheless, an advanced digital structure provides a significant advantage in environmental monitoring and strategic planning. Knowledge creation and sharing and the involvement of all relevant stakeholders have been proven to be crucial for the implementation of sustainability measures. Greater collaboration between cities is therefore desirable to avoid isolated approaches and to ensure a more comprehensive and cohesive approach. This highlights not only the need for replicable measuring methodologies but also the need for a replicable measuring process. The insights from this research offer valuable directions for enhancing the replicability of processes and the strategic planning of urban sustainability initiatives. This effort not only contributes to the collective understanding of SDG 11's implementation challenges but also illustrates pathways toward more sustainable, resilient and smarter urban environments.

5 Scalability, Local and Global Reuse

Our current state of research revealed valuable insights into the efforts of the city of Zurich toward reaching the defined targets of SDG11. However, the purpose of the SCST is not only the visualization of progress towards the given targets but also to show at least the processes, which on one hand should be further automated and on the other hand could be reused by other cities and cantons of Switzerland. The insights from the city of Zurich can be used to further enhance the replicability of processes and to share the rationale for selecting appropriate targets and methodologies used for their evaluation within the shared legal frameworks in Switzerland. This includes how the departments and organizations collect and process the available data. Replicability is not only considered at the process level but also at the reporting level and serves as a blueprint for other cities on a lower technological level than the City of Zurich.

Such a city is the administrative capital of South Africa (SA), Pretoria, located in the City of Tshwane (CoT Precinct) in the Gauteng Province. Gauteng is one of the nine provinces of SA, and although it accounts for only 1.5% of SA's land area, it is home to more than a quarter of SA's population of 59 million. The SA Constitution established local government as a fully developed component within the cooperative government system. Hence, the constitution assigns local governments, such as CoT, the responsibility for fostering the social and economic development of communities. In the context of CoT, SDG11 proposes critical dimensions of the urban challenge in Tshwane: housing and basic services, informal settlement upgrading, transport, participatory planning, the safeguarding of cultural and natural heritage, disaster prevention and resilience, the environmental impact of cities, green and public spaces, and urban-rural links. Furthermore, the CoT faces sustainability challenges as far as migrant workers and high unemployment numbers are concerned. According to the SA SDG goal tracker (https://south-afr ica.goaltracker.org/platform/south-africa/goals/11), SDG11 is tracked through the data availability for SA, as shown in Table 3.

Table 3. SDG Indicators and Data Availability for CoT

SDG	Description	Indicator	Data Availability
11.1	Housing costs	3	3
11.2	Modal split	1	0
11.3	Independent use of public transport	2	1
11.4	Building zones	1	0
11.5	Ecologically valuable spaces	2	0
11.6	Natural disaster damage	2	2
11.7	Min. recreational space	2	0
11.a	Strong national and regional development planning	1	0
11.b	Natural disaster risk reduction	2	1
11.c	Support least developed countries in sustainable and resilient building	0	0
	Total	16	7

When considering global reuse, clear differences are observed between the City of Zurich (CoZ) and the CoT with 30 SDG11 indicators for the CoZ (tracked at the city level) as opposed to 10 indicators for CoT (tracked at the country level). The key differences between the two cities are primarily driven by two key factors: the context of the two cities and the prioritization of efforts to achieve SDG11. In terms of the context of the two cities, CoZ is a financial hub and economic center of Switzerland, while CoT faces urbanization challenges. Therefore, SDG11 prioritization in CoZ focuses on environmental impact aligned with its reputation as a green city, while CoT prioritizes an inclusive economy, quality infrastructure development that supports liveable communities, and social equity.

In summary, both Pretoria and Zurich are committed to SDG11, but their approaches are tailored to their distinct contexts and challenges. The common thread is creating resilient, inclusive, and sustainable cities for present and future generations.

6 Limitations and Outlook

SDG 11 covers a broad range of topics relevant to a city. Getting familiar with each topic and the relevant data type takes time. It requires analytical skills and the ability to understand and process different data formats. Spatial data was not extracted and processed for this study and is, therefore, limited to non-spatial data. Furthermore, the study is limited to one or two targets per indicator, which might not sufficiently represent the efforts taken by the city [13].

The development of the SCST demonstrates that a more comprehensive view of the efforts taken by the City of Zurich's initiatives can be achieved by mapping specific targets with their respective indicators. Finally, establishing a collaborative platform could enhance the development, measurement, and replicability of the SDGs, in addition to just providing data through an open government platform. A platform that supports this level of collaboration and transparency could be instrumental in fostering a more cohesive and comprehensive approach to achieving the SDGs.

References

1. Al-Zu'bi, M., Radovic, V.: Sustainable Cities and Communities: Towards Inclusive, Safe, and Resilient Settlements, First Edition. Emerald Publishing Limited (2018). https://doi.org/10.1108/9781787569218
2. Bachmann, N., Tripathi, S., Brunner, M., Jodlbauer, H.: The Contribution of Data-Driven Technologies in Achieving the Sustainable Development Goals. Sustainability **14**(5), Article 5 (2022). https://doi.org/10.3390/su14052497
3. Berisha, E., Caprioli, C., Cotella, G.: Unpacking SDG target 11.a: What is it about and how to measure its progress? City and Environment Interactions **14**, 100080 (2022). https://doi.org/10.1016/j.cacint.2022.100080
4. Breu, T., et al.: Where to begin? Defining national strategies for implementing the 2030 Agenda: the case of Switzerland. Sustain. Sci. **16**(1), 183–201 (2021). https://doi.org/10.1007/s11625-020-00856-0
5. City of Zurich: Digitale Transparenz im öffentlichen Raum—Stadt Zürich (2023a). https://www.stadt-zuerich.ch/portal/de/index/ogd/anwendungen/2021/dtoer.html
6. City of Zurich: Environmental Strategy (2023b). https://www.stadt-zuerich.ch/portal/en/index/portraet_der_stadt_zuerich/environmental-strategy.html
7. City of Zurich: Netto-Null-Cockpit | Treibhausgasemissionen. Netto-Null-Cockpit (2023c). https://netto-null-cockpit.stadt-zuerich.ch/
8. City of Zurich: Stadtverkehr2025 Bericht 2022 (2023d). https://www.stadt-zuerich.ch/content/dam/stzh/ted/Deutsch/stadtverkehr2025/Publikationen_und_Broschueren/Stadtverkehr2025_Bericht_2022.pdf
9. City of Zurich, DHE, D. of H. and E.: 2000-Watt-Gesellschaft (2023a). https://www.stadt-zuerich.ch/gud/de/index/umwelt_energie/2000-watt-gesellschaft.html
10. City of Zurich, DHE, D. of H. and E.: Feinstaub PM10—Stadt Zürich (2023b). https://www.stadt-zuerich.ch/gud/de/index/umwelt_energie/luftqualitaet/schadstoffe/feinstaub.html
11. City of Zurich, DHE, D. of H. and E.: Strategy «Circular Zurich» (2023c). https://www.stadt-zuerich.ch/gud/de/index/departement/strategie_politik/umweltstrategie/klw_en/klw-strategie-en.html
12. City of Zurich Open Data: Täglich aktualisierte Luftqualitätsmessungen, seit 1983 (2023). https://data.stadt-zuerich.ch/dataset/ugz_luftschadstoffmessung_tageswerte
13. Dall'Agnolo, M.M.Y.: Visualising the impact of Swiss cities' efforts towards SDG 11 using KNIME: Overcoming barriers and promoting replicability for achieving the SDGs (Master's Thesis) (2023). Retrieved from https://studierendenprojekte.wirtschaft.fhnw.ch/en/view/3356
14. Dorbritz, R.: Kennzahlen der Verkehrsentwicklung. Stadt Zürich (2020). https://www.stadt-zuerich.ch/ted/de/index/taz/verkehr/webartikel/webartikel_kennzahlen_verkehrsentwicklung.html
15. Federal Office for Spatial Development [ARE]: Entwicklungen Personenverkehr (n.d.). Retrieved 1 March 2024, from https://www.are.admin.ch/are/de/home/verkehr-und-infrastruktur/grundlagen-und-daten/verkehrsperspektiven2050/entwicklungen-personenverkehr.html
16. Federal Office for the Environment [FOEN]: Fine particles (2023). https://www.bafu.admin.ch/bafu/en/home/themen/thema-luft/luft--fachinformationen/luftqualitaet-in-der-schweiz/feinstaub.html
17. IMD - International Institute for Management Development: City summary Zurich (2024). https://www.imd.org/entity-profile/zurich/
18. Kayano, F.: Science, technology and innovation ecosystem transformation toward society 5.0. Int. J. Product. Econ. **220**, 107460 (2020). https://doi.org/10.1016/j.ijpe.2019.07.033
19. KNIME: KNIME Analytics Platform. KNIME (2023). https://www.knime.com/knime-analytics-platform

20. Kloss, P.: The interaction between resilience and intelligence of cities. In: Minaei, N. (ed.) Smart Cities, 1st ed. CRC Press (2022). https://doi.org/10.1201/9781003272199-3
21. Nübold, N.: Indikatoren «Stadtverkehr 2025» (Jahresbericht 2022)—Stadt Zürich (2023). https://www.stadt-zuerich.ch/ted/de/index/taz/verkehr/webartikel/webartikel_stadtverkehr2 025_2023.html
22. Saiu, V., Blečić, I., Meloni, I.: Making sustainability development goals (SDGs) operational at suburban level: Potentials and limitations of neighbourhood sustainability assessment tools. Environ. Impact Assess. Rev. **96**, 106845 (2022). https://doi.org/10.1016/j.eiar.2022.106845
23. Silva, B.N., Khan, M., Han, K.: Towards sustainable smart cities: A review of trends, architectures, components, and open challenges in smart cities. Sustain. Cities Soc. **38**, 697–713 (2018). https://doi.org/10.1016/j.scs.2018.01.053
24. Stadtrat Stadt Zürich: Strategie Smart City Zürich—Stadt Zürich (2018). https://www.stadt-zuerich.ch/portal/de/index/politik_u_recht/stadtrat/weitere-politikfelder/smartcity/strategie/publikationstrategie.html
25. Swiss Federal Council: Sustainable Development Strategy 2016–2019 (812.101.e) (2016). https://www.are.admin.ch/dam/are/en/dokumente/nachhaltige_entwicklung/publikationen/strategie_nachhaltigeentwicklung2016-2019.pdf.download.pdf/sustainable_developments trategy2016-2019.pdf
26. Thier, A., et al.: Introduction to Swiss Law In: Thommen, M. (ed.) sui generis Verlag (2022). https://doi.org/10.38107/026
27. UN-Habitat: World Cities Report 2022: Envisaging the Future of Cities, p. 422. United Nations Human Settlements Programme (UN-Habitat) (2022). https://unhabitat.org/world-cities-rep ort-2022-envisaging-the-future-of-cities
28. United Nations: Goal 11 | Department of Economic and Social Affairs (n.d.). Retrieved 28 May 2023, from https://sdgs.un.org/goals/goal11
29. Ween, C.: Sustainable Urbanization: Why We Have to ChangeToward Justice and Lifestyles That Respect the Planet and Its Inhabitants. In: Minaei, N. (ed.) Smart Cities, 1st ed. CRC Press (2022). https://doi.org/10.1201/9781003272199-2
30. WHO: WHO global air quality guidelines. Particulate matter (PM 2.5 and PM 10), ozone, nitrogen dioxide, sulfur dioxide and carbon monoxide. Licence: CC BY-NC-SA 3.0 IGO (2021)
31. Zheng, C., Yuan, J., Zhu, L., Zhang, Y., Shao, Q.: From digital to sustainable: A scientometric review of smart city literature between 1990 and 2019. J. Clean. Prod. **258**, 120689 (2020). https://doi.org/10.1016/j.jclepro.2020.120689

Enhancing Cross-Cultural Teaching and Learning: An Instructor's View on Africanization

Sunet Eybers[(✉)] [ID], Jan H. Kroeze [ID], and Corne J. van Staden [ID]

University of South Africa, Johannesburg, South Africa
`eeyberss@unisa.ac.za`

Abstract. Research has indicated that learners who receive education in a context they can relate to are more successful in acquiring knowledge and skills. For this reason, educators in Africa often explore the concept of Africanization as part of cross-cultural teaching and learning efforts. Africanization includes local and indigenous cultural considerations to instill African culture and identity in teaching and learning environments. This qualitative study investigates the perceptions of academic staff, focusing on the effectiveness of using an African case study to explain important theoretical constructs in an undergraduate Business Analysis and a Human-Computer Interaction course at a higher-educational institution. Thematic analysis performed on the results of in-depth semi-structured interviews involving academic instructors reveals seven main themes, with the theme on the relevance and interpretation of practical examples occurring most frequently. The findings suggest that the Africanization of content, using local and Afrocentric examples, can assist learners in acquiring relevant knowledge and skills and be useful in cross-cultural teaching and learning, as learners can relate the theory to their local context. However, the concept should be presented to learners before introducing new academic content.

Keywords: cross-cultural · Africanization · decolonization · teaching and learning · case study · business analysis · human-computer interaction

1 Introduction

Although some African scholars have produced scholarly work about Africanization and the meaning of the term, only a little has been written about the concept by international scholars from other continents. This is evident when searching for the key term "Africanization", with fewer than 400 published academic articles returned from Web of Science and African Journals Online (an Africa-focused online platform for searching Africa-based content). This is not surprising, as the term is continent-specific and implies the inclusion of local, indigenous cultural considerations as part of instilling African culture and identity within tertiary environments [10]. This is particularly important, as academic contextualization is an integral part of the learning process, fostering the understanding

© The Author(s), under exclusive license to Springer Nature Switzerland AG 2025
K. Hinkelmann and H. Smuts (Eds.): Society 5.0 2024, CCIS 2173, pp. 98–110, 2025.
https://doi.org/10.1007/978-3-031-71412-2_8

and application of concepts. Currently, academic content is often explained using Western terminology [10]. Also, Africanization is important as the indigenous knowledge of ancestors needs to be instilled into the thinking and continuation of a rich cultural heritage, without compromising on quality education. Furthermore, in the bigger context of cross-cultural teaching and learning, understanding the diverse cultures of learners, and in particular African cultures, sensitizes instructors to the need for different teaching and learning approaches and contextualization.

Not surprisingly, the call of African scholars for Africanization (in particular in South Africa) as part of curriculum transformation is nothing new in higher educational institutions [3, 7, 8, 10, 12]. While some academic scholars argue in favor of the Africanization of curricula [10], others oppose the idea due to the so-called incompatibility of indigenous knowledge systems with global contexts and the subsequent lowering of standards to accommodate these local contexts [8]; or even the possibility of introducing "cognitive conflict" during the learning process among learners [7]. However, there remains a high demand to investigate the effect of Africanization in higher educational institutions [3], as indigenous knowledge can be applied to more extraordinary global phenomena and enhance the learners' understanding of often foreign theoretical Western-based constructs.

From a theoretical perspective, Spencer [12] expresses the need for an indigenous information theory (IIT). Decolonization attempts have driven a growing demand for information services and systems to fulfill the needs of indigenous communities. Such services should include the cultural values of the communities to be served. While indigenous people should be included in the leadership of such projects, other members of the development teams should also be committed to the ideal, upskilled, and educated. According to Spencer [12], IIT recognizes that there are multiple, unique indigenous knowledge systems. Indigenous groups should be the primary beneficiaries of indigenous information systems and should have the right to decide who has access to the knowledge to prevent exploitation. They should be allowed to assess whether the information has been rendered correctly and grow the knowledge system using modern tools.

In favor of cross-cultural teaching and learning, Spencer [12] indicates the need for Information Systems curricula to be adjusted to increase mindfulness about indigenous values and beliefs: "Indigenous examples should be included amongst case studies used and opportunities provided to complete assessment tasks on Indigenous topics." [12]. This will equip graduates to effectively design and build software with and for indigenous groups.

Based on a critical and transformative epistemological paradigm, Thambinathan and Kinsella [13] propose four methods to create space for the transformation of qualitative research, namely (1) critical reflexivity, i.e., considering one's philosophical assumptions; (2) reciprocity, i.e., ensuring that participant communities benefit equally (3) embracing diverse bodies of knowledge, i.e., including indigenous knowledge and rethinking how knowledge is constructed; and (4) transformative praxis, i.e., creating space for decolonizing perspectives in scholarly work.

We believe that Spencer's proposed IIT and Thambinathan and Kinsella's [13] four methods provide a solid theoretical basis to achieve the main objective of this study, namely, to investigate the perceptions of instructors after attempts to Africanize the syllabi of two undergraduate modules, Human-Computer Interaction (HCI) and Business Analysis (BA), at an open distance education institution in Africa. This is important, as the authors believe that the bigger Information Systems discipline can benefit immensely from integrating African knowledge constructs and ways of knowing into mainstream academia and practice. We believe that the ideal way to do this is by listening to the voices of indigenous scholars, learners, and research participants. We hope to have made a small but noteworthy contribution by introducing localized case studies to equip our graduates to prepare for their careers in the Information Technology (IT) industry and for postgraduate research. While the attempt forced us to reflect critically on the domination of Western paradigms in Information Systems (IS), we trust that we have created an awareness of diverse epistemologies among lecturing staff and learners in our attempts to introduce cross-cultural teaching and learning.

This study focuses on the qualitative feedback received from academics (primary and secondary lecturers, internal and external moderators, e-tutors, and assignment markers) after implementing Africanization-related constructs, for example, case studies and practical assignments, into the syllabi of both an undergraduate HCI and BA module. The research approach and methodology are discussed in the following section. The data analysis section explains the thematic analysis process. After the discussion of the results, a conclusion winds up the study.

2   Research Approach and Methodology

The study assumed a qualitative research approach with an interpretive paradigm to understand better academics' perceptions about the utilization of Africanization in the context of teaching and learning in HCI and BA undergraduate modules at an open distance learning institution in a developing African country. To Africanize the content of the modules, African case studies were developed and used to explain theoretical concepts. Additional reading was included in the learners' study material, presenting the idea of Africanization. After consulting the material, the learners were expected to complete a practical assignment. Semi-structured interviews were conducted with members of the lecturing staff at the end of the two modules.

The study participants were pre-selected based on the prerequisite of historical involvement in an academic teaching capacity in the undergraduate modules HCI at the third-year level (NQF-level 7) and Business Analysis at the second-year level (NQF-level 6). Therefore, purposive sampling was applied to invite 12 possible participants via e-mail. Of these, 7 participants declined the invitation to participate in the research project or did not react to the invitation. The 5 remaining participants were available via some electronic platform for online, semi-structured interviews. The interview questions were asked using a pre-developed semi-structured interview protocol containing 20 questions. The questions were categorized into the following themes: Academic Staff (feedback and support); Academic Content (syllabus and practical examples); Assessments (case study assignment, practical assignment, tools, feedback to learners, and assessment level based on Bloom's taxonomy). This research focuses on formative assessment, not summative assessment.

The online interviews, conducted using MS Teams, took part from December 2021 to April 2022. A total of 5 in-depth interviews were conducted and transcribed by an external party. Once the transcription process was complete, the text files produced anonymous participant feedback, which an external qualitative research consultant used as the basis for analysis.

3 Data Analysis

Following the coding process of Braun and Clarke [4, 6], thematic analysis was used to analyze the unstructured data from the five transcribed documents. ATLAS.ti v23 generated codes through an inductive process, during which the participants' perceptions were examined. Based on these perceptions, open codes were assigned. Furthermore, selective coding generated additional open codes to match similar perceptions and experiences. After all the codes were established and applied, the qualitative research consultant grouped the codes with similar meanings. This grouping facilitated the identification of themes that represented shared experiences and perspectives. The themes furthermore aligned with the study's research objectives.

4 Discussion of Results

Seven main themes were identified during the data analysis phase and included: (1) the application of Bloom's taxonomy to academic material; (2) the assessment and application of the theory presented as part of the course; (3) issues experienced when the concept of Africanization was applied to the existing course context; (4) the preparation of materials and assessment processes; (5) the relevance and interpretation of practical examples; (6) learners' inquiries around Africanization tasks; and (7) learners' support processes during assessment. Lower-level coding identified sub-themes for each of the seven main themes. A frequency indicator depicted the number of occurrences of the sub-themes: the higher the frequency or number of occurrences, the more critical the sub-themes were to the respondents. This article discusses only the top three sub-themes based on the highest frequency numbers.

4.1 Main Theme 1: Application of Bloom's Taxonomy

In 1956, the educational psychologist Benjamin Bloom, together with fellow collaborators Englehart, Furst, Hill, and Krathwohl, published the first version of a hierarchical model known as Bloom's Taxonomy [2]. The proposed taxonomy assists educators in identifying instructional goals and a plan, using objectives, on how to achieve the instructional goals. A need to simplify and set clear educational instruction goals led to an updated, revised version of the taxonomy in 2001 [1, 2]. The revised version made provision for six learning stages, with various cognitive processes progressing from lower to higher levels, namely: remember, understand, apply, analyze, evaluate, and create [2]. The taxonomy is of particular importance to educators, as clear instructional objectives ensure that learners are prepared to remember facts and understand constructs and, as a result, apply them to practical examples. Once a level of understanding is mastered, learners should be able to analyze constructs further to evaluate and subsequently create new constructs. Bloom's taxonomy is, therefore, an instructive framework in academic environments.

In this study, the modules were presented at NQF levels 6 and 7, which require learners to apply what they have learned practically. Therefore, one would expect that the concept of Africanization could assist learners in understanding and applying constructs beyond the level of "remembering". As a result, the instructors were asked if they got *"the impression that the assignments on the African case study fostered the learners' higher-order or critical thinking skills"*. The top three sub-themes that emerged are the application and evaluation, understanding, and knowledge components.

Although the participants believed that the course content and assessment should be set using Bloom's taxonomy as a foundation, the African context case study did not enhance learners' *understanding* and engagement with the different levels of Bloom's taxonomy. Instead, the case study frustrated learners in achieving higher levels of Bloom's taxonomy as the case study, and not necessarily the content, required more preparation and higher-order thinking.

The instructors indicated that they had implemented various levels of Bloom's taxonomy within the assessment opportunities. As the modules focused on interactive design and required learners to explain concepts and provide illustrations and examples, the assessment questions prompted them to *apply* their *knowledge* rather than recite information from the textbook. Although the theoretical aspects of design are universal, the module aimed to make learners visualize or *understand* the concepts within an African context. The instructors felt that some learners rushed through the questions and gave superficial answers, therefore not achieving the goal of the module, namely critical thinking and higher-order thinking skills: *"There were other students, however, who just rushed through the questions and either paraphrased the textbook, or they gave surface-level information when the question wanted a detailed discussion."*

4.2 Main Theme 2: Assessment and Application of Theory

Theme 2 focused on the formative assessment process and the objective of enhancing learners' understanding and application of HCI constructs when given Africanized case studies. The interviewed participants were asked to reflect on whether they felt the learners had acquired the necessary subject-related knowledge to apply it to local case study scenarios. The focus here was on the practical application of theory.

As part of the *good foundational grasp* sub-theme, the participants were asked whether assignment memoranda and model examples provided to the learners were sufficient for preparing them to apply theory and concepts to the assignment case study. The responses could be grouped into two main categories:

(a) Clear instructions could have prepared the learners better for the assessment opportunities. At the same time, additional reading material could have provided valuable contextual background information, which could also have assisted them in applying the theory. It was, therefore, suggested that additional reading on both the theoretical constructs of HCI and the concept of Africanization and practical examples of Africanization may benefit learners.

(b) The memoranda and model answers provided were sufficient and helped the learners to understand the concepts. The examples in the textbook were also relevant to the learners and easily understandable. Overall, the Africanization of the curriculum entailed identifying problems and challenges in different contexts portrayed in the case studies. The learners improved their understanding, and the pass rate on the exam was good. Furthermore, it was felt that the examples and case studies used were adequately contextualized to relate to the lives of the learners. Since the theoretical concepts of design are universal and can be applied within any context, including the African context [it should be stressed that this was the opinion of the lecturing staff interviewed and not necessarily that of the researchers], the African case studies helped stimulate the learners to think about developing applications for their people, within their environment:

"Some students also did say they appreciated the challenge and felt like they were able to understand the coursework better thanks to how the questions were structured."

As part of the *difficulty with the application of the theory sub-theme, the interviewees identified issues in the learners' attempts to answer assignment questions* when applying theoretical aspects to the assignment cases presented to them. The feedback indicated that it was not that the learners did not understand the theory but that the application of the theory in context was not fully understood. It was also mentioned that it was difficult for the learners to implement the theory of Africanization in their studies, as they were not necessarily familiar with the theory of Africanization within their context. Therefore, the problem was not a lack of understanding of the theory but rather how the theory had to be applied practically. Overall, the learners had a mixed understanding of the theory and struggled to use it in practical examples. Half of the learners understood well, while the other half were lost and had difficulty translating theory into practice. The addition of the African context further frustrated the learners, as they felt like they were *"fighting a war on two fronts"*. Some learners went overboard in focusing on the African aspect, while others failed to address the application of this aspect in the questions. The learners did not show much interest or appetite for the African context, and they were more focused on understanding what was expected of them, than on questioning the theory from an African perspective. Overall, the learners struggled immensely with the application of the theory.

"I ... Feel bad to say this but I think, in general, the students felt more frustrated with the African context being brought in. So, I ... Didn't really encounter that students were ... They had an appetite for having African context there."

The third sub-theme extended the previous sub-theme and referred to *sufficient understanding and application of the theory*. The participants indicated that some learners grasped the theory and its concepts in this sub-theme. They subsequently sufficiently answered the theoretical assignment questions and completed the tasks as expected. However, although learners understood what was expected of them, it wasn't easy to apply their understanding. The learners felt that they gained much information from the theory in their textbooks and the e-tutoring sessions, which helped them understand the concept of Africanization. As the assignment questions became more demanding, a higher level of critical thinking skills was acquired. Compared to previous assignment results, a significant improvement in marks was noticed, which indicated that the learners grasped the concepts. This was also supported by the in-depth questions posed by the learners during assignment discussions.

Practically orientated assignment questions require the learners to apply what they have learned. While some learners displayed a thorough understanding of theoretical design principles and made proper connections in their examples, a few got too focused on Africanization and needed to remember to apply the theory. The reason for this was not apparent: it was possibly due to a lack of understanding or poor learner time management in completing the assignment. From a marker's perspective, the learners had sufficient knowledge and the ability to apply the theoretical content.

4.3   Main Theme 3: Issues in Application of Africanization to Context

Theme 3 reported feedback from the instructors' interaction with learners while completing two assignments and from other learner inquiries. The top three sub-themes that emerged included technological issues, instructional design issues, and lack of focus on implementing the theoretical concepts.

Technological issues refer to the platforms available to the learners when completing their assignments and exclude instructional design and assignment material layout. In this instance, the platform was the social media platform the learners used to complete their assignment questions. The learners indicated that they experienced issues with the accessibility of the assignment platform, which was Telegram. Some learners were not familiar with the platform and felt that assignments should be designed with the greater learner population's access to and familiarity with platforms and technologies (in this instance, Telegram) in mind. Furthermore, because most of the student population resides in rural areas, more than one application should be made available for selection when completing assignments (for example, WhatsApp and WeChat). To keep up with the changing demands of the job market and increase learners' employability, the choice of technology should be regularly updated (examples mentioned were AWS, Azure, and Google Cloud).

Instructional design refers to the need indicated by the interviewed participants to consider preparing learners, from an instructional design perspective, to complete two tasks in one assignment. The instructions needed to be more apparent from a design point of view to implement the concepts of Africanization and HCI. The learners suggested including additional material and discussions to help them understand how Africanization can be applied before issuing a case study assignment. It was further mentioned that simply reading a question and comparing it to the model answer did not assist them in their understanding of the question.

The *lack of focus on the theoretical implementation* sub-theme indicates that the participants indicated a need for more theoretical implementation in their feedback on the assignments. The participants felt that the learners were so focused on implementing Africanization in the assignment that they lost track of the application of the theory. It was noted that theoretical aspects should also be considered when completing an assignment, especially when the practical implementation of the theory of Africanization is significant in a particular context. The overfocus on Africanization threw learners off the primary academic focus in completing their assignments. Furthermore, the requirement to submit a report, which is not a typical assignment, confused the learners and caused them to diverge from the leading academic concepts of HCI and interaction design. The instructors had to guide the learners to the modules' focus and emphasize the importance of understanding the academic concepts. In summary, introducing new educational concepts, combined with unfamiliar terms such as Africanization and the unusual assignment structure (report), making it challenging for the learners to grasp all at once.

4.4   Main Theme 4: Preparation of Materials and Assessment Processes

This theme focused on the adequate preparation of academic material to teach a particular concept to learners, thus contributing to the successful grasping of constructs and their implementation in real-life scenarios.

The top three sub-themes that emerged included communication issues, memoranda, and materials, and reading into the concept.

Communication issues refer to communication challenges that arose because of the structure of the teaching and learning teams. For example, additional information, such as clear teaching instructions and assignment instructions, was not communicated to the tutors by the module leaders and designers of the assignments. Therefore, the need for clear communication and instructions among the teaching and learning teams was mentioned. The release of memoranda took too long, which hindered learners' ability to review them. In addition, some tutors did not have access to the memoranda before the learners submitted their work. There was also a communication gap between the tutors and lecturers, leading to an incomplete dissemination of information. Access to additional resources was not readily available for all. Learners were not informed about how the assignments would be marked, making it challenging to provide helpful advice. Improved communication and accessible information are necessary in the future. However, these sub-theme issues were not restricted to cross-cultural Africanization attempts.

The *memoranda and materials* sub-theme refers to the lecturers' preparation of the learning material. The lecturers prepared for a course by considering the assignments and memoranda and then proposed additional reading. In this case, they used additional articles published by renowned authors in the field of Africanization to introduce learners to the concept of Africanization. This assisted the learners in understanding the fundamental aspects of Africanization. The idea was that this knowledge should then be used and applied to the practical case study to critically process the information and report on it as part of the formative assessment process. The interviewed participants indicated that, although they were familiar with the coursework, it was unclear how the assignments would be marked. The module answers, and memoranda provided sufficient information and were clear. However, it took long for the memoranda to be released. The memoranda and the additional articles offered in-depth information on Africanization, making understanding the concept and assignment requirements easier. It would nevertheless have been helpful to have additional articles on the topic. Overall, the memoranda provided adequate information and relevant points. Like the previous sub-theme, this is not an isolated issue related to cross-cultural teaching and learning but rather a general need across all academic modules.

The third sub-theme, namely *reading into the concept*, referred to the lecturers indicating that they prepared themselves by acquiring relevant subject-related knowledge before they prepared and sent assignment content to the learners. The lecturers further stated the importance of being well-informed about the concept of Africanization and applying it in an instructional design manner that would allow the teaching and learning process to unfold fully in the context of Africanization.

4.5   Main Theme 5: Relevance and Interpretation of Practical Examples

The most vital theme emerging from the thematic analysis was theme 5: relevance and interpretation of practical examples. This theme dealt with the significance of the practical case study scenarios that were presented and their relevancy and applicability to Africanization. The top three sub-themes that emerged were also the most prevalent sub-themes in the thematic analysis process, namely Africanization case application, more effective local examples, and preparation with practical examples.

Africanization case application: This sub-theme refers to the agreement among the teaching team members that using locally based, Africanized case studies is more helpful in assisting learners to understand and apply the concepts to real-life examples. This is because of the familiarity with their surroundings and upbringing within the African context. Therefore, the learners could use real-life examples they are exposed to daily in their application and critical understanding and reasoning of the concepts and theory for assessment purposes. Furthermore, the teaching team indicated that Africanization can be applied within the HCI and BA contexts, as the program has an Afrocentric approach using real-life examples. Applying this process to the curriculum assists learners in understanding the theory of HCI because of its grounding in Africanization.

Local examples are more effective: This sub-theme refers to the relevance of implementing Afrocentric or local examples in the assignments. It was indicated that the learners tended to understand and apply the theoretical aspects related to the theory of Africanization and HCI more easily when local cases are presented or something universally African is given, where they can relate to a context they are familiar with. Using case studies and long questions was an excellent way to engage learners in the coursework theory while applying it to real-life situations. However, some learners expressed frustration with the African contextualization and wanted to focus on completing the assignments quickly. Still, the participants believed that the African context made it easier for the learners to apply the concepts to design applications. The African case studies were seen as relevant in stimulating learners to think about developing applications for their communities. It was suggested that the case studies focus on identifying problems and providing solutions within the African context. The Africanization of the curriculum was seen as a means of finding solutions to challenges faced by African people. Familiarity with the examples and case studies was a critical aspect of fostering learner engagement. However, some learners struggled with the unfamiliarity of Africanization.

The learners focused on completing the assignments on time rather than fully engaging with the African context. Nevertheless, the African case studies provided guidelines and direction for learners and allowed them to feel a sense of ownership of their work.

Preparation with practical African examples: This sub-theme refers to the teaching team indicating that the use of local and Afrocentric examples seemed more effective than other examples, as they relate to the learners' local contexts and helped them grasp the theoretical aspects of the course. It seemed as if the learners were more satisfied with trying to understand and apply local Afrocentric examples than the textbook's Eurocentric practical examples. Additionally, it was mentioned that additional reading material was distributed to the learners and that this assisted them in grasping the theoretical constructs of Africanization. The African case studies made it easier for learners to understand and engage with the content as they aligned with their familiar cultural context. However, additional reading and resources would be beneficial to enhance understanding further.

4.6 Main Theme 6: Learner Inquiries Around Africanization Tasks

Theme 6 focused on learner inquiries received, specifically related to the tasks involving the contextualization of Africanization. The three sub-themes identified were *the format of the assignment, the Africanization concept, and the assignment structure.*

Format of the assignment: This sub-theme refers to the learners voicing their concerns about the format and structure of the assignment questions. The learners indicated that the assignment structure was difficult to understand and that the theory application questions based on the case studies were challenging. However, they received continuous support and assistance from the academic instructors. Most inquiries focused on how to approach the assignments and the level of detail required in the answers rather than the content itself. Many learners were frustrated and anxious about the assignment format and felt that the context of Africanization added additional complexity. Some non-academic inquiries were also made about the due dates and extensions.

Africanization concept: This sub-theme refers to the learners' questions about the concept of Africanization and how it fits into the framework of the assignment. Some learners indicated their unfamiliarity with the concept of Africanization. The academic instructors indicated that they provided the learners with additional Africanization material, which assisted the learners in understanding what was expected of them when implementing the concept of Africanization in the assignment. There were even instances where the learners indicated that they had no interest in the Africanization component and that it would not be relevant to them as individuals. In summary, some inquiries about Africanization were received from the learners, as many of them were unfamiliar with the concept. The academic instructors responded to these inquiries by providing additional explanations and directing the learners to draw from their cultural experiences when using examples. Some learners did not like incorporating an African background into their designs, while others included historical and political elements. Some learners performed well when applying the Africanization aspect, even if they did not do well in other parts of the assignment. Most learners understood the theoretical concept of Africanization, but some had reservations about it, probably due to the diverse cultural backgrounds in the participating groups.

Assignment structure: This sub-theme refers to the actual structure of the assignment. Three main inquiry categories were received, namely: (a) what should be included in the assignments (number of facts) to score high marks; (b) what the outline of a report should look like; (c) what the features and tools of the prescribed assignment platform (namely Telegram) were and how they worked. Although some learners complained about the difficulty level of the questions, most learners were excited to use Telegram in their assignments and showed interest in new technology.

4.7 Main Theme 7: Learner Support Processes During Assessment

The *learner support process during assessment* focused on the learner support processes implemented by the academic instructors to assist learners in understanding and applying the study material to complete the formative assignments. Three sub-themes were identified: teaching team support, additional reading on Africanization, and lack of preparedness.

Teaching team support: This sub-theme refers to the learners' requests to obtain more information about the assignment structure, concepts, theories, and the application thereof when completing assignments. Although the learners struggled with various components of the assignment, more questions seemed to arise from the concept of Africanization and its application in the cases provided. However, the academic instructors managed to assist the learners by guiding them to complete the assignments successfully. Overall, according to the lecturers, the learners were happy with the explanations provided by the academic instructors. Although some learners faced challenges with access to resources and data during the COVID-19 pandemic, no learners could complete the module. The module answers and memoranda were fair and clear, with no major issues or complaints reported by the learners.

Additional reading on Africanization: This sub-theme focused mainly on the provision of additional reading material on Africanization provided by the academic instructors to the learners when inquiries arose. There was a big need to provide learners with additional reading to gain an understanding of certain topics, mainly Africanization. Although in the minority, there was also a need to provide additional information about the technology used (Telegram) and technical information (such as the maximum capacity of groups). The learners had trouble understanding the academic research articles, which improved with experience. The sub-theme further emphasizes the applicability of good academic publications on Africanization to assist learners with understanding and augment the theory.

Lack of preparedness: This sub-theme refers to students not being prepared well enough for the concept of Africanization. Given that additional reading was provided, this might be attributed to learners' inability to grasp and apply the idea. The academic instructors' suggestions included simplifying and clarifying questions and more guidance. The interviewed participants also indicated a lack of material on Africanization pertaining to the context of the courses offered, which may contribute to the gap in understanding. They further believed that adding practical assignment activities could encourage the learners to apply their knowledge.

The authors acknowledge the limitation of the paper, namely that it discusses an early and cautious step towards Africanization by simply providing case studies as examples of African scenarios to be used in formative assessments. Much scholarly discourse is still needed to embed African values, bodies of knowledge, and ways of knowledge creation in scientific theorization [5]. A recent book on issues and approaches regarding the Africanization of Information Systems and other social sciences, edited by Okyere-Manu [9], provides valuable pointers to guide researchers. Furthermore, while the sub-Saharan philosophy of Ubuntu represents a widespread ethics of communalism that could serve as the foundation of an African epistemology, it has to be noted that there are many diverse cultures on the African continent [11] and that it was, therefore, not possible to generalize our findings.

5 Conclusion

This thematic analysis of semi-structured interviews with academic instructors indicated that the Africanization of content in the undergraduate BA and HCI modules, as part of cross-cultural teaching and learning, might benefit learners. The seven identified themes suggest that introducing Africanization into undergraduate curricula has a decolonizing potential, thus answering the call for transforming tertiary curricula, albeit to a limited extent. The essential sub-theme that emerged, namely the relevance and interpretation of practical examples, indicates that the introduction of Africanization was generally well accepted by the learners but that they struggled to deal with three unfamiliar concepts, namely Africanization, the report structure of the assignment (a non-typical assignment format) and the digital platform (Telegram). Although the instructors anticipated that the learners would achieve a higher level of understanding according to Bloom's taxonomy, they indicated frustration experienced by the learners who had to grasp the meaning of Africanization before engaging with the module-specific content. This is probably due to the cognitive conflict or even an experience of incompatibility between the mainstream textbooks' Eurocentric learning content and the African scenarios used in the formative assessments [7, 8]. Despite the learners showing a positive attitude toward the introduction of Africanization, they were primarily focused on completing the tasks of the modules and, therefore, experienced the introduction of a new concept as a barrier that extended the time it took them to complete their formative assessments. Future research could focus on the applicability of the introduction of the idea of Africanization in other undergraduate modules, as well as post-graduate modules, which the authors believe to be in line with Prinsloo's [10] finding that it has a rightful place in African educational spaces. Prinsloo [10] suggests various ways in which tertiary education can be Africanized, and this article especially contributes to "the manner in which the curriculum encourages students to apply their learning to the unique challenges they face in their local communities impacted by global changes" [10]. Using local case studies in formative assessment is but one way to start building an IIT [12]. The endeavor may be regarded as a cautious attempt toward transformative praxis and embracing indigenous epistemology and knowledge [13] While the students were challenged to reflect on the Eurocentric content of their study material, they also had an opportunity to inform the lecturing staff. Furthermore, the article presented the instructors' critical reflections on the intervention. In related work, the students' experiences will be reported on using both qualitative and quantitative research approaches.

Acknowledgments. The research was supported in part by the National Research Foundation (NRF) of South Africa (grant number 132180) and the Research Professor Support Programme of the University of South Africa (Unisa). The grant holder acknowledges that opinions, findings, conclusions, or recommendations expressed in the article are those of the authors and that neither the NRF nor Unisa accepts any liability whatsoever in this regard. We also acknowledge valuable feedback received from the peer reviewers and editors.

References

1. Anderson, L., et al.: A Taxonomy for Learning, Teaching, and Assessing: A Revision of Bloom's Taxonomy of Educational Objectives (2001)
2. Bloom, B., Krathwohl, D.R.: Taxonomy of educational objectives: the classification of educational goals, by a committee of college and university examiners. In: Handbook 1: Cognitive domain. Longmans, New York (1956)
3. Botha, A.J.M.: A learning management system based framework for higher education quality programme review. University of Pretoria (2020)
4. Braun, V., Clarke, V.: Successful Qualitative Research: A Practical Guide for Beginners. SAGE Publications Inc. (2013)
5. Chung, A., et al.: Decolonizing information technology design: A framework for integrating knowledge in design science research. In: Proceedings of the 57th Hawaii International Conference on System Sciences, pp. 6944–6953. Hawaoo (2024)
6. Clarke, V., Braun, V.: Thematic analysis. J. Posit. Psychol. **12**(3), 297–298 (2017). https://doi.org/10.1080/17439760.2016.1262613
7. Louw, W.: Africanisation: a rich environment for active learning on a global platform. Progressio **32**(1), 42–54 (2010)
8. Msila, V.: Africanisation of education and the search for relevance and context. Edu. Res. Rev. **4**(6), 310–315 (2009). https://doi.org/10.5897/ERR.9000029
9. Okyere-Manu, B.D. (ed.) African Values, Ethics, and Technology: Questions, Issues, and Approaches. Springer International Publishing, Cham (2021). https://doi.org/10.1007/978-3-030-70550-3
10. Prinsloo, P.: Some reflections on the africanisation of higher education curricula: a south african case study. Africanus **40**(1), 19–31 (2010)
11. Sadiki, L., Steyn, F.: Decolonising the criminology curriculum in South Africa: views and experiences of lecturers and postgraduate students. Transform. High. Edu. **7** (2022). https://doi.org/10.4102/the.v7i0.150
12. Spencer, L.: The future is in the past: creating an indigenous information theory. In: ACIS 2021 Proceedings, pp. 1–7 (2021)
13. Thambinathan, V., Kinsella, E.A.: Decolonizing methodologies in qualitative research: creating spaces for transformative praxis. Int. J. Qual. Methods **20**, 1–9 (2021). https://doi.org/10.1177/16094069211014766

Closing the Gap: Leveraging Recorded Video Lessons for Digital Inclusion in Rural South Africa

Rouxan Colin Fouché[(✉)] [iD] and Wynand Nel [iD]

Department of Computer Science and Informatics, University of the Free State, Bloemfontein, South Africa
{foucherc,nelw}@ufs.ac.za

Abstract. Access to digital technology and computer literacy skills is crucial in bridging the digital divide, particularly in rural areas where resources are often scarce. This study investigates the feasibility of implementing university service-learning projects in distant rural areas by delivering computer literacy training through recorded video lessons. The project aims to address the South African digital divide by providing essential skills training to community members who lack access to traditional face-to-face educational opportunities. Due to logistical constraints preventing direct student involvement in remote areas, the study explores the effectiveness of utilising recorded video lessons as an alternative delivery method.

The findings reveal that face-to-face and recorded video implementations of computer literacy training led to significant improvements for participating community members. Analysis of the data showed that there was no significant difference in the level of improvement between the two methods. These results underscore the potential of recorded video lessons to effectively deliver educational content to remote communities, thereby extending the reach and impact of university service-learning initiatives. The study contributes to efforts to bridge the digital divide in South Africa and offers insights into scalable and sustainable solutions for empowering underserved populations with essential digital skills.

This research highlights the importance of innovative approaches to address the challenges of delivering education to remote areas where traditional methods may be impractical or inaccessible. By leveraging technology to disseminate educational content, universities can promote digital inclusion and empower communities to thrive in an increasingly digitised world.

Keywords: Access to Education · Content Delivery Strategies · Community Empowerment · Computer Literacy · Digital Divide · Rural Communities · Service-Learning

© The Author(s), under exclusive license to Springer Nature Switzerland AG 2025
K. Hinkelmann and H. Smuts (Eds.): Society 5.0 2024, CCIS 2173, pp. 111–122, 2025.
https://doi.org/10.1007/978-3-031-71412-2_9

1 Introduction

In today's digitally driven world, access to digital technology and proficiency in computer literacy are increasingly recognised as essential components for socioeconomic development and individual empowerment [1]. However, the digital divide persists as a significant barrier, particularly in rural areas where resources and opportunities for technological advancement are often limited. Bridging this gap requires innovative approaches that transcend traditional educational boundaries and embrace the potential of technology to deliver learning experiences effectively [2].

This article explores the utilisation of recorded video lessons as a means to enhance computer literacy and address the digital divide in rural South Africa through university service-learning projects. By leveraging the expertise and resources of higher education institutions, this study seeks to extend the reach of essential skills training to communities that lack access to conventional face-to-face educational opportunities. Through the lens of engaged scholarship and service-learning principles, the research investigates the feasibility and effectiveness of implementing such projects in remote areas where logistical constraints may hinder direct student involvement.

In the remainder of this paper, the background is presented in Sect. 2. The aims and problem statement follow this in Sect. 3. Section 4 discusses the methodology. The findings of this study are presented in Sect. 5, followed by the conclusion in Sect. 6.

2 Background

The University of the Free State (UFS) stands as a beacon of engaged scholarship, committed to responding to community needs with scholarly expertise and a public intent for social benefit [3]. Grounded in principles of social justice and compassion, the institution has continually adapted to meet the challenges of an evolving higher education landscape in South Africa.

Central to UFS's mission of engaged scholarship is the concept of service-learning (SL), which integrates academic learning with community service to address identified needs. Through initiatives such as the CSIS2642 module, second-year undergraduate students engage in practical projects aimed at improving the computer literacy levels of communities near the university [4]. This module exemplifies the university's commitment to bridging the digital divide by empowering local communities with essential digital skills.

Originally designed as a face-to-face intervention, the Information Technology Service-Learning (ITSL) project faced challenges during the COVID-19 pandemic, necessitating a shift to virtual delivery methods [5]. Despite the success of the virtual approach, concerns arose regarding the diminished interaction between SL students and community members, prompting a return to face-to-face implementation. This transition underscores the importance of evaluating and comparing the effectiveness of different delivery methods in achieving desired learning outcomes.

In light of these developments, this study aims to assess the impact of both face-to-face and recorded video implementations of the ITSL project on the computer literacy levels of participating community members [6]. By examining these dimensions, the research endeavours to provide insights into scalable and sustainable solutions for empowering underserved populations with essential digital skills, thereby contributing to the ongoing efforts to bridge the digital divide in South Africa.

2.1 Information Technology Service-Learning (ITSL) Project

The ITSL project, conducted annually by the Department of Computer Science and Informatics (CSI) at UFS, aims to boost computer literacy among rural community members. Second-year students enrolled in the SL module, under the guidance of their lecturer, serve as presenters of the project on campus.

A total of 50 community members participated in the ITSL project at UFS, while 100 took part in Botshabelo. Recruitment was facilitated by three community partner organisations: Mangaung Concerned Residents, the South African Red Cross Society, and the loveLive organisation. Communication and coordination were facilitated through a WhatsApp group, providing essential project details to participants.

Training sessions for Bloemfontein (BFN) community members were conducted in a computer laboratory on the UFS campus (see Fig. 1), while a laboratory at the loveLife Y-Center in Botshabelo (see Fig. 2) was utilised for rural participants.

Fig. 1. Computer laboratory on the UFS Bloemfontein Campus

Fourteen second-year students enrolled in the CSIS2642 module served as presenters on the UFS campus. Despite limited training, they delivered comprehensive computer literacy training covering MS Word and MS Excel over a 10-week period. Each student presenter led sessions in English to ensure clarity, while in Botshabelo, facilitators showed video recordings to participants.

Training covered various aspects of computer literacy, starting with basic computer components and operations. Face-to-face lectures were supplemented by hands-on assistance from non-presenting students acting as tutors, and participants received hard copy instructional materials.

Fig. 2. Computer venue on the Botshabelo loveLife Y-Center

3   Aims and Problem Statement

Despite the increasing recognition of the importance of digital technology and computer literacy skills in today's society, significant disparities persist in access to these resources, particularly in rural areas of South Africa [7]. The digital divide presents a formidable barrier to socioeconomic development and individual empowerment, hindering opportunities for education, employment, and civic engagement [1]. In response to this challenge, universities have increasingly turned to service-learning projects as a means to extend essential skills training to underserved communities [8].

However, the effectiveness of traditional face-to-face service-learning interventions in remote areas is often limited by logistical constraints and resource scarcity. The COVID-19 pandemic further exacerbated these challenges, necessitating a shift to virtual delivery methods, which, while successful in maintaining continuity, may have implications for the quality and depth of community engagement.

Amidst these complexities, there is a pressing need to evaluate alternative approaches to service-learning implementation that can effectively bridge the digital divide and enhance computer literacy in rural South Africa. This study seeks to address this gap by investigating the feasibility and effectiveness of leveraging recorded video lessons as a delivery mechanism for computer literacy training in university service-learning projects. By comparing the outcomes of face-to-face and recorded video implementations, the research aims to provide insights into the potential of technology-mediated learning to overcome barriers of distance and resource scarcity, thereby contributing to efforts to empower marginalised communities and foster digital inclusion.

Research Question: What is the comparative effectiveness of recorded video lessons versus traditional face-to-face delivery methods in enhancing computer literacy skills and bridging the digital divide in rural South Africa through university service-learning projects?

4   Methodology

In order to best answer the stated research question, a survey method [9] was the most suitable. This method allowed for data collection regarding the participants' level of computer literacy before and after their attendance of the 2023 ITSL project.

4.1   Population and Sampling Decisions

The research population comprised the 150 community members who participated in the 2023 ITSL project. Of the 150 participants, 50 participated in the face-to-face (FTF) presentation on the BFN UFS campus and 100 in the video-recorded presentation at the loveLife Youth Development Centre in Botshabelo. Both purposive and convenience sampling strategies were utilised to select the research sample [10–12]. The eventual research sample included 45 FTF and 64 Recorded session respondents who participated in both the pre-test and post-test data collection activities.

4.2   Data Collection Method

It was necessary to measure the difference between the participants' computer literacy levels before and after attending the ITSL project to answer the research question. Therefore, pre-test and post-test self-assessment questionnaires were selected as the most appropriate data-collection method [9, 11]. The respondents were asked to assess their computer literacy skills by completing the questionnaire before and after attending the ITSL project [12]. Self-assessment of their computer literacy skills (instead of task completion) allowed the respondents to rate their abilities without fearing failure or humiliation [9].

4.3   Questionnaire Design

The questionnaire was designed by purposefully selecting, adapting, and combining questions from different computer literacy self-assessment questionnaires used in previous studies [13–17]. All these studies focused on the self-assessment of basic computer literacy skills. While most of the questions were selected from the source questionnaires, some had to be adapted to fit the context of this study. It was also deemed necessary to include additional questions to fully answer the stated research question and to cover the advanced computer literacy skills included in the project content. The questionnaire was divided into two sections. Section A, which contained 50 close-ended questions, was grouped into four categories: attitude towards the use of computers, basic computer use, self-assessment of MS Word proficiency and self-assessment of MS Excel proficiency.

The sequence of the different categories in the questionnaire was carefully chosen since it could affect the responses to questions in the following categories. For the self-assessment section, easy questions were included that could be comprehended by most, balanced with computer literacy questions that were more complex to answer. Five-point ranked Likert-scale questions and dichotomous (yes/no) questions were utilised in the questionnaire [9].

Section B of the questionnaire focused on gathering basic demographic information (regarding gender, age, home language, and employment status) from the respondents.

4.4 Data Analysis

All the data collected through the pre-test and post-test questionnaires were manually captured and numerically coded in an MS Excel spreadsheet. The data was exported to SPSS Statistics for Windows, version 28.0. The means of the responses to the five-point Likert-scale items were reported using the weighted mean intervals suggested by Pimentel [18]. The Wilcoxon signed-rank test was used to compare two sets of scores from the same respondents. In order to analyse the dichotomous data collected from the basic computer use category in the questionnaire, the McNemar test was employed [19]. A confidence level of 95% was employed for the calculation of confidence intervals, with statistical significance set at a p-value of 0.05.

5 Results

This sub-section discusses the results of the data collected from the pre-test and post-test questionnaires. The discussion is grouped according to the demographic data and the four main computer literacy self-assessment categories.

5.1 Demographic Data

Of the 45 participants who attended and completed the BFN (F2F) ITSL project, 16 (35.6%) were male, and 29 (64.4%) were female. In comparison, of the 64 participants who attended and completed the Botshabelo (Recorded) ITSL project, 15 (23.4%) were male, and 49 (76.6%) were female. The participants' ages in the BFN (F2F) group ranged from 18 to 48. The largest proportion of participants (60%) was in the age group of 17 to 25 years old, with 16% in the age group 26 to 35, 18% in the age group of 36 to 45, and only 7% were older than 46 years. The Botshabelo (Recorded) group participants' ages ranged from 18 to 29. The largest proportion of participants (94%) was in the age group of 17 to 25 years old, while only 6% were older than 26 years.

In the BFN (F2F) group, the majority (51%) of the participants indicated Sesotho as their home language, followed by isiXhosa (16%), Setswana (16%), and English (13%). In the Botshabelo (Recorded) group, the majority (75%) of the participants indicated Sesotho as their home language, followed by Setswana (11%) and isiXhosa (6%).

The participants were requested to indicate their employment status at the time of the ITSL project. The participants could select from the following options: unemployed, employed part-time or employed full-time. The BFN (F2F) group reported that 85% of the participants were unemployed, while 15% were employed either part-time or full-time.

The Botshabelo (Recorded) group reported similarly that 95% of the participants were unemployed, while 5% were employed either part-time or full-time. This response indicates that a relatively large percentage of the community members who attended the ITSL project were unemployed, which further necessitates the need for skills development in both the campus and rural areas.

5.2 Participants' Attitudes Towards the Use of Computers

The first section of the questionnaire related to the participants' feelings and beliefs about using computers. The inspection of the means values for these questions indicates a shift to a more positive attitude towards computers for both groups of participants.

Individual analysis of the Wilcoxon test results (both groups) for Question 1 (*I feel comfortable using computers.*) and Question 3 (*I think that computers are difficult to use.*) shows significant changes between the pre-test and post-test responses. These results indicate that the participants felt more comfortable using computers after attending the ITSL project. Additionally, the participants felt that computers were less challenging to use than before the project.

Although no significant difference is indicated for Question 2 (*I am willing to learn more about computers.*), mentioning the participants' responses to the pre-test question-naire is essential. The initial mean for Question 2 was 4.8 (BFN F2F group) and 4.7 (Botshabelo Recorded group), which falls within the 4.20 to 5.00 interval suggested by Pimentel [18], which indicates that the participants strongly agreed that they were willing to improve their computer literacy levels from the very beginning of the project, leaving little room for further improvement. It is also noteworthy that the participants' need to use computers (Question 6 - *I would like to use computers at home or work.*) (4.7 – BFN F2F group and 4.7 – Botshabelo Recorded group), as well as realising the importance of computer literacy related to finding employment (Question 7 – *I believe that com-puter literacy can improve my chances to find employment.*) (4.8 – BFN F2F group and 4.7 – Botshabelo Recorded group), was already very high in the pre-test responses. This suggests that the participants from both groups were aware of the importance of computer literacy before the project commenced.

Most importantly, the results revealed no significant differences in improvement between the campus and rural groups. This indicated that the content delivery strategy had no impact on the improvement of participants' attitudes towards computers. Even before the project was initiated, the BFN F2F and Botshabelo Recorded groups showed a positive attitude towards computers and computer use.

The results revealed an improvement in both groups relating to their comfort in using computers and their perceived difficulty. Although no significant change was seen for the other questions in this category, it became clear that the participants initially had a very optimistic outlook at the start of the project. Therefore, most participants were already aware of the benefits of computer use and had a positive view of computers and computer use. This result reveals the need for computer literacy skills development in the community since the participants' need for development is prevalent even without intervention from the ITSL project to inform the community of its benefits.

5.3 Basic Computer Use

The second questionnaire category related to the participants' self-assessment of their basic computer use. Both Lickert Scale Questions 8 (*Overall, how would you rate your own computer literacy skills?*) and 9 (*How would you rate your own typing skills?*) show significant differences in responses between the first and last session for both groups. When inspecting the means, it becomes evident that the mean for both questions increased from 2.9 to 3.7 for the BFN F2F group and from 2.4 to 3.3 for the Botshabelo Recorded group. According to Pimentel's [18] classification, the mean response changed from *good* to *very good* for the BFN F2F group's computer literacy and typing skills self-assessment. Meanwhile, the mean response for the Botshabelo Recorded group changed from *fair* to *good*. Although not the purpose of the inquiry, the analysis reveals that both post-test means for both groups were less than 4, which indicates that there is still potential for considerable improvements in the participants' computer literacy and typing skills. This could indicate a need for additional computer literacy content, such as MS Access or MS PowerPoint, to be introduced through the ITSL project.

Individual question analysis of the dichotomous questions reveals that 6 of the ten questions show significant differences in the responses between the first and last sessions for both groups. After inspecting the means and percentages for the questions in this category, it became evident that there was a positive shift in basic computer use aptitude for both groups. These results indicate that both groups' basic computer use knowledge improved after participating in the ITSL project. Consequently, it can be reasoned that repeated exposure to computer literacy training sessions through the ITSL project significantly impacted the participants' basic computer use aptitude.

Regarding the difference in improvement between the two groups, only Questions 13 (*Can you identify the basic parts of a computer system?*) and 16 (*Can you use a computer mouse?*) showed significant differences. When inspecting the means, it was evident that participants from the rural group had less experience with using computers and, therefore, had increased improvement in these two basic computer use questions compared to their campus counterparts. Nevertheless, most questions did not show any statistically significant difference in improvement between the two groups, indicating that the Botshabelo Recorded group showed basic computer use improvements that mirrored the BFN F2F group.

5.4 Participant Self-assessment of MS Word Proficiency

The proficiency of participants in using MS Word was assessed, and upon examining the means for these questions, it is evident that both groups demonstrated improved proficiency in MS Word. This shift in means indicates a significant enhancement in self-assessed MS Word proficiency for both groups.

In terms of the discrepancy in improvement between the groups, significant differences were observed in five questions. Upon closer examination of the means, it became apparent that the Botshabelo Recorded group exhibited greater improvement compared to the BFN F2F group. Notably, the Botshabelo Recorded group initially had lower scores on the pre-test, suggesting more room for improvement. Despite these five questions showing increased improvement in the Botshabelo Recorded group, there was no difference in improvement between the groups for the remaining 13 questions.

Further analysis reveals that the pre-test means for all questions in the rural group were relatively low, indicating lower initial competency in MS Word for this group. This underscores the need for additional MS Word training opportunities in Botshabelo and other rural communities to address the low proficiency.

Although significant improvements were observed in post-test means for both groups (ranging between 3.1 and 4.3 for the BFN F2F group and 2.9 and 4.3 for the Botshabelo

Recorded group), there is still considerable room for further enhancement. This suggests that participants' competency could potentially be improved further by allocating more time or implementing additional assistance and training.

An individual question analysis indicates significant differences in responses between the first and last sessions for all 18 MS Word questions for both groups. This implies substantial improvement in both basic and advanced MS Word functionalities. Comparing the difference in improvement between the groups revealed that the Botshabelo Recorded group reported larger enhancements in five of the 18 questions, possibly due to their lower initial proficiency in MS Word.

Although both groups had low pre-test scores, the Botshabelo Recorded group had the lowest scores, indicating that the content delivery method had a limited impact on improving MS Word proficiency between the two groups. Interestingly, recorded videos led to larger increases in improvements compared to face-to-face strategies. However, there was no difference in improvement between the groups for 13 out of the 18 questions.

Overall, these results suggest that participation in the ITSL project significantly improved the MS Word proficiency of both groups. Repeated exposure to computer literacy training sessions through the ITSL project significantly enhanced participants' skills in using MS Word functionalities.

5.5   Participant Self-assessment of MS Excel Proficiency

In the fourth category, participants evaluated their own proficiency in using MS Excel. Upon analysing the mean scores, there's a noticeable increase in self-assessed proficiency in MS Excel for all questions across both groups. This suggests a significant shift in how participants perceive their ability to use MS Excel, indicating substantial improvement in the skills of both groups.

A closer look at the mean scores highlights significant improvements noted by participants in both groups. Following the intervals recommended by Pimentel [18], participants rated themselves as having no proficiency in four MS Excel questions (BFN F2F group) versus 12 (Botshabelo Recorded group) during the pre-test. Additionally, the BFN F2F group reported fair proficiency in eight questions. However, in the post-test questionnaire, participants rated themselves as *very good* in 11 questions for the BFN F2F group and eight for the Botshabelo Recorded group.

The pre-test mean scores for all questions were remarkably low, indicating a starting point of low competency in MS Excel. These scores were even lower than those reported for MS Word, suggesting that participants in both groups were less familiar with MS Excel than with MS Word. Considering the lower initial proficiency with MS Excel, allocating more time and resources to MS Excel training during computer literacy sessions is essential. The low pre-test scores highlight the need for additional learning opportunities in both BFN F2F and Botshabelo Recorded communities. Although there was significant improvement in all areas based on post-test scores, most scores remained below 4 for both groups, indicating room for further enhancement in participants' MS Excel skills.

An individual question analysis using the Wilcoxon signed-rank test revealed significant differences between the first and last sessions for all 12 questions in both groups.

This suggests that participants' MS Excel proficiency improved significantly after attending the revised ITSL project. Initially, most participants felt they couldn't use MS Excel, but after the ITSL project, they believed their proficiency in MS Excel was very good. Thus, repeated exposure to computer literacy training sessions through the ITSL project significantly enhanced the MS Excel skills of both BFN F2F and Botshabelo Recorded participants. Although significant improvement was seen in all questions, there was no significant difference in improvement between the two groups. This suggests that participants in the Botshabelo Recorded implementation using recorded lessons showed similar levels of improvement to those who attended the face-to-face ITSL project on the university campus.

6   Conclusion

This study investigated the feasibility of utilising recorded video lessons to improve computer literacy and bridge the digital divide in rural South Africa. The significant interest in the project, combined with the low initial levels of computer literacy among participants, underscores the scarcity of computer literacy training opportunities in rural communities like Botshabelo. This scarcity aligns with Sikhakhane and Lubbe's [20] observation that educational opportunities are challenging to access in isolated rural areas of the country.

The findings from the four categories of inquiry provide valuable insights into the impact of this approach. Participants demonstrated significant improvements across various aspects, including attitudes towards computer use, basic computer skills, and proficiency in MS Word and MS Excel. Notably, both groups exhibited positive shifts in their attitudes towards computers, indicating increased comfort and reduced perceived difficulty in using them. Moreover, participants reported notable enhancements in their basic computer skills, MS Word proficiency, and MS Excel proficiency, highlighting the effectiveness of the recorded video lessons in improving computer literacy. This emphasises the importance of the continued implementation of the ITSL project in communities with low levels of computer literacy.

Furthermore, the study revealed no significant differences in improvement between the BFN F2F and Botshabelo Recorded groups across multiple categories, suggesting that the delivery method (recorded video lessons versus face-to-face instruction) had comparable impacts on participants' skill development. This underscores the potential of recorded video lessons to effectively deliver educational content to remote communities, extending the reach and impact of university service-learning initiatives.

The findings emphasise the urgency of addressing this gap to empower rural residents with essential digital skills. With limited access to traditional face-to-face educational opportunities, innovative approaches such as recorded video lessons offer a promising solution to extend computer literacy training to remote areas. The significant improvements observed in participants' skills highlight the effectiveness of such approaches in bridging the digital divide and promoting digital inclusion.

Upon examining the means, it's evident that although there was significant improvement in participants' computer literacy levels, there is still ample room for further growth. Increasing the project duration and session time could further improve participants' computer literacy levels. To continue addressing computer literacy in campus and rural communities, additional service-learning projects focusing on MS PowerPoint and MS Access could be developed and implemented as part of the ITSL project. Due to the effectiveness of recorded sessions for rural implementation, in the future, more time should be spent training the SL students to improve their ability to produce high-quality training videos that could further improve the project's impact.

Following the success of the project implementation at the loveLife centre in Botshabelo and the fact that many more community members are eager to participate in the project to improve their computer literacy, it was decided that the ITSL project will be presented at least once a year at this venue. This research project has ensured a lasting partnership between the university and the loveLife organisation.

Overall, the study contributes to efforts to bridge the digital divide in South Africa and offers insights into scalable and sustainable solutions for empowering underserved populations with essential digital skills. Moving forward, policymakers, educators, and community leaders must prioritise initiatives enhancing rural computer literacy. By leveraging technology to disseminate educational content, universities can promote digital inclusion and empower communities to thrive in an increasingly digitised world. Further research on the impact of the ITSL project on the participant's lived experiences and the implementation of similar initiatives are warranted to continue bridging the gap and promoting equitable access to technology and education.

References

1. Reddy, P., Sharma, B., Chaudhary, K.: Digital literacy: a review of literature. Int. J. Technoeth. **11**(2), 65–94 (2020). https://doi.org/10.4018/IJT.20200701.oa1
2. Afzal, A., Khan, S., Daud, S., Ahmad, Z., Butt, A.: Addressing the digital divide: access and use of technology in education. J. Soc. Sci. Rev. **3**, 883–895 (2023). https://doi.org/10.54183/jssr.v3i2.326
3. UFS: About the UFS. https://www.ufs.ac.za/about-the-ufs. Last accessed 13Mar 2024
4. Martin, R.: Dr Rouxan Fouché's research helps improve computer literacy in Mangaung. https://www.ufs.ac.za/templates/news-archive-item/campus-news/2023/april/dr-rouxan-fouch%C3%A9-s-research-helps-improve-computer-literacy-in-mangaung. Last accessed 7 Aug 2023
5. Fouché, R.C.: Addressing the South African digital divide through a community-informed strategy for service-learning: a Critical Utopian Action Research (CUAR) approach (2022)
6. Snell, R.S., Lau, K.H.: The development of a service-learning outcomes measurement scale (S-LOMS). Metrop. Univ. **31**, 44–77 (2020). https://doi.org/10.18060/23258
7. Faloye, S.T., Ajayi, N.: Understanding the impact of the digital divide on South African students in higher educational institutions. Afr. J. Sci. Technol. Innov. Dev. **14**, 1734–1744 (2022). https://doi.org/10.1080/20421338.2021.1983118
8. Ramahlele, B.: Community Engagement Model Transformation at the UFS. https://www.ufs.ac.za/supportservices/departments/community-engagement-home/new-approach-to-ce/engaged-scholarship. Last accessed 14 Mar 2024
9. Stausberg, M.: Surveys and questionnaires. In: Stausberg, M., Engler, S. (eds.) The Routledge Handbook of Research Methods in the Study of Religion, pp. 461–482. Routledge, New York (2022)
10. Plowright, D.: Using Mixed Methods: Frameworks for an Integrated Methodology. SAGE Publications, Inc. (2011). https://doi.org/10.4135/9781526485090

11. Trochim, W.M., Donnelly, J.P., Arora, K.: Research Methods: The Essential Knowledge Base. Cengage, Boston (2016)
12. Cohen, L., Manion, L., Morrison, K.: Research Methods in Education. Routledge, London (2017). https://doi.org/10.4324/9781315456539
13. Bandy, J.: What is Service Learning or Community Engagement? https://cft.vanderbilt.edu/guides-sub-pages/teaching-through-community-engagement/. Last accessed 7 May 2020
14. Isaac, J.P.: Comparing Basic Computer Literacy Self-Assessment Test and Actual Skills Test in Hospital Employees (2015)
15. Markose, M.P.: An investigative study of computer literacy skills of public library users in Thiruvananthapuram District, Kerala an investigative study of computer literacy skills. ILIS J. Librarianship Inform. **2**, 79–85 (2019)
16. Son, J., Robb, T., Charismiadji, I.: Computer literacy and competency: a survey of Indonesian teachers of English as a foreign language. Comput.-Assist. Lang. Learn. Electr. J. **12**, 26–42 (2011)
17. Spicer-Sutton, J., Lampley, J., Good, D.W.: Self-Assessment and student improvement in an introductory computer course at the Community College Level. J. Learn. High. Educ. **10**, 59–65 (2014)
18. Pimentel, J.L.: Some biases in Likert scaling usage and its correction. Int. J. Sci. Basic Appl. Res. **45**, 183–191 (2019)
19. Pallant, J.: SPSS Survival Manual: A Step by Step Guide to Data Analysis Using IBM SPSS. Routledge (2020)
20. Sikhakhane, B., Lubbe, S.: Preliminaries into problems to access information – the digital divide and rural communities. SA J. Inform. Manage. **7**, 20–27 (2005). https://doi.org/10.4102/sajim.v7i3.273

Examining Smart Contracts Within Mauritian Contract Law: Assessing Their Compatibility with Existing Legal Frameworks

Viraj Fulena[✉] [ID]

University of Technology, Port Louis, Mauritius
vfulena@utm.ac.mu

Abstract. This research paper explores the complexities surrounding smart contracts, computer code designed to automate contractual processes, thus bypassing the need for intermediary enforcement. As smart contracts gain traction, jurisdictions worldwide grapple with regulating them. Challenges arise from the novel nature of these contracts, as their enforcement poses unique dilemmas within legal frameworks. While some believe regulation is feasible, others question the enforceability of code-based agreements. Mauritius, aspiring to be Africa's Fintech hub, is addressing these issues through the Virtual Asset and Initial Token Offering Services Act 2021. However, uncertainties persist regarding the enforceability of smart contracts. This research examines smart contracts comprehensively, exploring technical and legal dimensions to unravel their complexity. It scrutinises Mauritius' legal landscape to ascertain the compatibility of smart contracts with existing contract laws and the effectiveness of the 2021 Act in regulating them.

Keywords: Smart Contract · Contract Law · Civil Code · CCM · VAITOS

1 Introduction

The aftermath of the 2008 global financial crisis marked the onset of a transformative era, ushering in a novel trading system that brought cryptographically produced currency into tangible existence (Nakamoto, 2008). This transformative shift, epitomized by the ascent of Bitcoin and other cryptocurrencies, introduced an alternative avenue for financial transactions, diverging from the conventional fiat currency system and reshaping the global financial landscape (Swan, 2015). The rapid evolution of the cryptocurrency ecosystem underscores the direct influence of technology in restructuring financial sectors worldwide, signifying a paradigmatic shift in transactional modalities and economic frameworks.

Despite recognising the potential benefits of technological innovations in enhancing the financial sector, regulators are confronted with the imperative to institute comprehensive regulations to govern these advancements (Financial Stability Board, 2019). While blockchain technology, for instance, has garnered global recognition and widespread

© The Author(s), under exclusive license to Springer Nature Switzerland AG 2025
K. Hinkelmann and H. Smuts (Eds.): Society 5.0 2024, CCIS 2173, pp. 123–135, 2025.
https://doi.org/10.1007/978-3-031-71412-2_10

adoption within the financial realm, the absence of established regulatory frameworks and oversight renders it susceptible to being dubbed the "wild west of the finance industry" (Arner et al., 2017). Scholars underscore the critical importance of implementing robust regulations, highlighting the potential catastrophic consequences of failed technological innovations within financial systems, ranging from infringements upon consumer protection rights to systemic institutional failures, thereby imperiling the fundamental financial stability of economies (Böhme et al., 2015). Incidents such as the 2016 Decentralised Autonomous Organisation (DAO) hack, resulting in the theft of $60 million in crowdsourced funds, and the collapse of the Bahamas-based cryptocurrency exchange platform FTX, once valued at approximately $40 billion, underscore the imperative for stringent regulatory frameworks to safeguard investors and uphold the financial stability of economies (Möser et al., 2018). Furthermore, effective regulation of financial activities necessitates a multifaceted approach encompassing not only basic commercial laws but also comprehensive regulatory supervision to uphold the integrity of financial systems (G20, 2018).

1.1 Regulatory Mechanisms for Blockchain Technologies

Various jurisdictions globally have implemented diverse approaches to regulate the FinTech sector. While certain nations have embraced innovation through the establishment of sandbox environments and regulatory sandboxes aimed at testing blockchain technologies within the financial sphere, others have opted for regulatory measures prohibiting the use of such technologies due to their disruptive potential. An illustrative example is the Central Bank of Nigeria's issuance of regulatory notices, which prohibit regulated institutions from engaging in cryptocurrency transactions or exchanges.

1.2 The Virtual Asset and Initial Token Offering Services Act 2021("VAITOS")

Mauritius has embraced blockchain technologies as a means of advancing its financial system, aiming to position itself as the leading FinTech hub in Africa. In line with Recommendation 15 of the Financial Action Task Force, the Virtual Asset and Initial Token Offering Services Act 2021 (VAITOS) was enacted to regulate the sector. This legislation provides a controlled environment for virtual asset providers to operate in Mauritius. Section 2 of VAITOS introduces smart contracts within the Mauritian legislative framework, defining them as the protocols necessary for executing transactions involving virtual assets on digital platforms operating on blockchain technologies.

1.3 Smart Contracts

Nick Szabo, a computer lawyer and scientist, first introduced the term "smart contract" in the early 1990s, defining it as digital promises governed by protocols within which parties perform (Szabo, 1997). Essentially, a smart contract comprises code and data deployed on a blockchain network to facilitate transactions, functioning similarly to traditional contracts but with automated execution based on predefined conditions. Szabo emphasizes that smart contracts aim to ensure fulfillment of contractual obligations while minimizing risks and eliminating the need for trusted intermediaries (Szabo, 1997). They offer advantages such as reduced reliance on intermediaries, lower transactional costs, and faster transactions, informing participants instantly about outcomes without delays. Additionally, smart contracts can automate workflows within organizations.

Although smart contracts are not a novel concept, their widespread adoption has surged with the rise of blockchain technology, leading governmental, financial, and commercial entities to integrate them into their operations. Recognizing their significance, legal scholars, regulatory bodies, and legislators advocate for the development of legal frameworks to govern smart contracts, given their potential for both beneficial and detrimental applications. While smart contracts are inherent to blockchain ecosystems and not considered virtual assets themselves, the Virtual Asset and Initial Token Offering Services Act 2021 (VAITOS) in Mauritius accommodates them within the legal framework, reflecting the recognition of their importance in modern financial systems.

Due to the novelty of smart contracts, there is a scarcity of case law in this domain. Consequently, a descriptive secondary data analysis approach has been employed to explore the functionality of smart contracts and their legal treatment. This method offers insights into the technical intricacies and challenges inherent in smart contracts, enhancing our comprehension of their operation within legal frameworks.

2 Literature Review

The term "smart contract," originally coined by Nick Szabo, represents a multifaceted concept with legal and technological dimensions. Legally, smart contracts are considered legal contracts, designed to self-execute when predefined conditions are met, while in the realm of computer science, they are essentially computer scripts capable of autonomous execution. They can be deployed on both distributed and non-distributed ledger technologies. However, there is ongoing debate regarding the extent to which smart contracts should be subject to traditional contract law, primarily due to their nature as pieces of computer code.

Smart contracts possess distinctive characteristics that differentiate them from traditional contracts. Firstly, they operate autonomously, executing without human intervention once predefined conditions are satisfied. Secondly, they are immutable, meaning their terms and code cannot be altered after execution, ensuring contract integrity. Additionally, smart contracts are digital in form and reduce reliance on intermediaries, facilitating streamlined and efficient transactions.

Comparing the formation of traditional contracts with smart contracts reveals significant differences in the process. Traditional contracts involve a series of steps including offer and acceptance, formalities such as written documentation, involvement of third parties like lawyers or notaries, and execution of obligations once the contract becomes legally binding. In contrast, the formation of smart contracts begins with agreement between parties, followed by the creation of digital code containing all terms and conditions, and automatic execution when predefined conditions are met.

The dichotomy between traditional and smart contracts underscores the evolving landscape of contract law in response to technological advancements. While traditional contracts rely on established legal procedures and intermediaries for enforcement, smart contracts leverage automation and cryptographic technology to execute agreements efficiently. Understanding these distinctions is crucial for navigating the intersection of law and technology in the realm of contract formation and enforcement.

2.1 J.G Allen Contract Stack Theory

J.G. Allen's model employs a stack analogy to illustrate the comparison between traditional contracts and smart contracts. In traditional contracts, the layers consist of spoken words, written text, and legal rules, with the legal rules layer often disregarding "off-contract" materials. Conversely, in smart contracts, the written intention is predominantly or entirely represented by machine-executable code, often encapsulating the entire contract. Despite this digital simplification, J.G. Allen's Contract Stack Theory underscores that smart contracts still adhere to the traditional contractual framework. Their formation hinges on the parties' intent to contract, and they must adhere to specific rules aligned with the contract's terms.

2.2 Technical Aspects of Smart Contracts

Human language, or natural language, serves as the primary medium for formulating traditional contracts. However, computers operate on their own set of programming languages, rendering natural language ineffective for smart contract formulation. The process of creating a smart contract involves several layers: at the High-Level Programming Layer, developers utilize user-friendly languages like Solidity to define the contract's logic. This code is then compiled into assembly language at the Compilation/Interpretation Layer, which computers can understand. Subsequently, the Assembly Layer converts this human-readable assembly code into non-readable binary instructions, forming the Machine Code Layer, which comprises instructions executed by the computer's CPU.

Smart contracts can manifest in various forms, with three main categories serving as broad classifications. Firstly, Natural Language contracts entail automatic execution of contractual obligations by computer code, falling outside the parties' legally binding agreement. This form presents no unique legal challenges and is commonly encountered. Secondly, Hybrid Contracts combine contractual obligations defined in both natural language and computer code. Finally, Contracts recorded solely in code define all terms and performance exclusively through computer code, presenting significant legal challenges. While all forms of smart contracts rely on computer code, the distinction lies in the role played by the code. For instance, in the first form, the code merely executes obligations defined by the natural language contract, whereas in the latter forms, the code formulates contractual obligations and executes them.

2.3 Behaviour of Smart Contracts Under the Principles of Traditional Contracts

For a smart contract to possess legal enforceability akin to traditional contracts, it must exhibit analogous characteristics, adhering to fundamental principles such as offer, acceptance, consideration, and intention to enter into a legal agreement. An offer within the context of smart contracts entails a party's willingness to commit to specific terms, which is accepted upon execution rather than through verbal affirmation. This operational difference stems from the unique nature of smart contracts, where acceptance is realized through their automated execution, as illustrated in the legal precedent set by *Thornton v Shoe Lane Parking*, where the automated process of a parking machine was deemed a contractual offer accepted upon payment.

Consideration, a cornerstone of contract law, necessitates a promise or performance exchange between contracting parties for an agreement to be valid. In the realm of smart contracts, consideration manifests through actions such as the sale of digital assets at agreed prices between parties. Despite the challenge of interpreting the intention to enter into a legal agreement from unreadable code inherent in smart contracts, parties' agreement to utilize smart contracts for executing their agreements serves as an indication of intent. However, complexities arise when parties may not have intended to enter into a legal agreement through the use of smart contracts but merely sought to automate transactional processes, underscoring the nuanced considerations surrounding the legal implications of smart contract utilisation.

2.4 Real Life Case Scenarios of the Interpretation of Smart Contracts Under the Law

Singapore. The *Quoine Pte Ltd v B2C2 Ltd* case, commonly known as the Quoine Case, stands as a significant legal precedent in Singapore, addressing a dispute arising from a cryptocurrency trading platform utilizing algorithms for automated transactions. A glitch in Quoine's algorithm resulted in trades being executed at highly unfavourable market rates, causing substantial losses for Quoine Pte Ltd and gains for B2C2 Ltd. In its ruling, the Singapore International Commercial Court found Quoine in breach of contract and trust, offering insight into how smart contracts and automated trading platforms may be treated within the framework of traditional contract law. Additionally, the Court acknowledged the adaptability of existing laws to effectively address issues related to algorithmic trading and smart contracts, signaling a willingness to accommodate technological advancements within legal frameworks.

In the Quoine Case, the Doctrine of Unilateral Mistake under Singaporean law was examined regarding the voidability of contracts. It was established that a contract could be voided if one party is mistaken about a fundamental term, and the other party has knowledge of this mistake, whether actual or constructive. However, Quoine Pte Ltd's argument that B2C2 Ltd had knowledge of traders' mistaken beliefs about trade prices was refuted by Singapore's highest court. The court determined that the mistake wasn't about the fundamental term of price, but rather an assumption about the trading platform's operation.

Critics of the Quoine Case raised concerns regarding the court's focus solely on the programmer's state of mind who set up B2C2 Ltd's trading platform, neglecting Quoine Pte Ltd's intentions in controlling the computer system. The separation between the intentions of Quoine Pte Ltd and the programmer was likened to a court considering a lawyer's intention rather than their client's, potentially leading to absurd outcomes. Moreover, critics noted that the court primarily highlighted deficiencies in Quoine's system, such as lacking alert messages and circuit breakers, without thoroughly exploring the concept of what constitutes a reasonable coder. Instead, the court suggested that these omissions could be interpreted as Quoine knowingly assuming risks associated with algorithm behavior. However, critics argue that courts should apply a reasonable standard based on prevailing risk limitation practices rather than expecting parties to foresee every outcome when using contracts.

United Kingdom. In 2021, the Law Commission of England and Wales (LCEW) conducted an evaluation of the legal framework in the UK, concluding that it is robust and adaptable enough to accommodate the utilization of smart legal contracts. The assessment revealed that smart contracts have the capacity to establish binding obligations enforceable according to their terms. Notably, the study underscored two critical aspects concerning contracts: firstly, the importance of understanding how the terms of a smart legal contract are defined, impacting available remedies and requiring an assessment of whether the code defines or implements the parties' obligations. Secondly, in cases of inconsistencies between terms within a contract, the court should consider the contract as a whole, irrespective of whether those terms are contained in one document or multiple documents. Additionally, the study acknowledged the concept of a "reasonable coder test," which serves as a benchmark for assessing the expectations of a coder in the context of creating smart contracts.

2.5   Additional Concepts that May Be Applicable to Smart Contracts

The Reasonable Coder Test, as proposed by the Law Commission of England and Wales (LCEW), suggests that when courts interpret the coded terms of a smart legal contract, they should consider what those terms would mean to a "reasonable coder" - someone proficient in understanding and interpreting the programming language used in the contract's creation. This approach acknowledges that contractual rights and obligations in smart contracts are typically embedded in human-readable source code. However, if the contract terms are encoded in machine code or a lower-level code that is not human-readable, the "reasonable coder" test may not be applicable, and the code's meaning should be inferred through its execution.

Green proposed a two-step approach for applying the reasonable coder test. In the first step, a traditional reasonable observer test is utilized to understand the agreement between humans and how the smart contract code is expected to function. In the second step, the reasonable coder test is then applied to determine if the smart contract code aligns with the human agreement. It is crucial that the coder's interpretation of the code remains consistent with the initial human agreement established during programming. Any discrepancies between the code and the human agreement must be addressed effectively, considering that computers do not recognize court judgments.

The introduction of the US Securities and Exchange Commission's ("SEC") Rule 15c3-5 aimed to mitigate risks associated with automatic and electronic trading on US stock exchanges. This rule requires brokers-dealers' platforms to implement specific controls to ensure regulatory compliance before order entry and to restrict unauthorized trading to prevent erroneous orders. Instances such as Knight Capital Americas LLC being fined \$12 million for violating the SEC market access rule highlight the importance of such regulatory measures.

In conclusion, while smart contracts present ground-breaking opportunities by merging technology and law, they also pose significant challenges compared to traditional contract law. These challenges include interpreting code, establishing consensus or a "meeting of minds," and ensuring a comprehensive legal framework that acknowledges the distinctive characteristics of smart contracts while ensuring fair resolution of contractual obligations and disputes. There is a growing need for universal standards and methodologies, as well as potential incorporation of existing regulatory controls, to effectively address the complexities surrounding smart contracts in legal contexts.

3 Research Methodology

3.1 Application of Secondary Data Analysis

The literature review embarks on an exploration of contracts, tracing their origin from Nick Szabo and delving into their multifaceted aspects. It grapples with the complexities associated with these contracts, especially focusing on the emergence and implications of smart contracts. Given the relative novelty of smart contracts and the scarcity of case law, the review adopts a descriptive secondary data analysis method to gain insights into their functioning and legal treatment. This approach provides a deep understanding of the technical intricacies and challenges inherent in smart contracts.

Within the literature review, a comprehensive examination of contracts unfolds, bridging the realms of law and computer science. It elucidates key features such as automation, immutability, and reduced reliance on intermediaries, while thoroughly analysing their technical aspects to discern their compatibility with legal frameworks. The primary distinction between traditional contracts and smart contracts lies in the interpretation and enforcement of computer code under the law, prompting various analytical techniques within the secondary data analysis methodology.

Utilising secondary data sources, the literature review relies on existing frameworks, theoretical foundations, and legal principles to construct its narrative. By evaluating, synthesizing, and presenting existing literature, it offers readers a holistic perspective on the evolution of smart contracts within traditional legal frameworks and the technical complexities surrounding them. Moreover, employing a comparative analysis approach allows for insightful comparisons between contracts and smart contracts, shedding light on their formation, execution, and legal implications.

Additionally, the literature review delves into case studies and legal analyses to comprehend how traditional contracts are interpreted legally and how these interpretations can be applied to smart contracts. By grounding concepts in real-life scenarios, such as the *Quoine Pte Ltd v B2C2 Ltd* case in Singapore and the exploration of smart contracts by the Law Commission of England and Wales, the review elucidates the challenges, consequences, and interpretations associated with the integration of smart contracts within legal frameworks.

The realm of contracts is intricate, blending elements from both computer science and traditional legal systems. These contracts, known as smart contracts, operate with automation, immutability, and reduced reliance on intermediaries, presenting challenges in interpretation and enforcement within legal frameworks. To elucidate this complex subject, a literature review was undertaken, employing a secondary data analysis approach. By analyzing existing literature, drawing comparisons, and examining case studies, the review offers insights into smart contracts, exploring their distinctions from traditional contracts, technical complexities, and the challenges they pose to established legal norms.

Utilising the comparative method, the review identifies similarities and differences between smart contracts and traditional ones, revealing nuances in their formation, execution, and legal implications. Real-life examples, such as the Quoine Pte Ltd v B2C2 Ltd case, are incorporated to ground theoretical concepts in practical scenarios, enabling readers to comprehend the ramifications of integrating smart contracts into legal systems. Through this comprehensive approach, the literature review aims to shed light on the complexities and implications of smart contracts, providing a deeper understanding of their integration into legal frameworks and the challenges they present to traditional contractual norms.

4   Data Analysis

This part will employ insights gleaned from the literature review to address the following research inquiries:

1. Should the designation of "contracts" be conferred upon smart contracts solely due to the inclusion of the term "contract"?
2. To what extent do smart contracts adhere to traditional contract laws in Mauritius?
3. Does the Virtual Asset and Initial Token Offering Services Act (VAITOS) accommodate the diverse manifestations of smart contracts?
4. What approach will the Mauritian Court take in interpreting smart contracts within the framework of Mauritian laws?

4.1   Should the Designation of "Contracts" Be Conferred upon Smart Contracts Solely Due to the Inclusion of the Term "Contract"?

Various sources suggest that despite fundamental differences, smart contracts can indeed be treated as traditional contracts. The J.G. Allen Contract Stack Theory illustrates this by demonstrating how the layers of smart contracts align with traditional contractual frameworks. Similarly, the Law Commission of England and Wales's study highlights that smart contracts can be subject to existing contract laws within the UK legal system. Even in cases of full automation, such as in *Thornton v Shoe Lane Parking*, where the offer and acceptance principle were automated, courts recognized it as a contractual offer. Additionally, in the Quoine case in Singapore, which involved smart contracts, the courts concluded that existing contractual laws could be adapted to address issues related to algorithmic trading and smart contracts. These instances collectively suggest that existing contract laws can be modified to accommodate smart contracts.

However, despite their potential compatibility with existing laws, the primary legal challenge lies in the interpretation of smart contracts. While they may fit within the existing legal framework, the intricacies of interpreting automated processes and code present significant hurdles. This highlights the need for careful consideration and adaptation of legal principles to effectively address the complexities introduced by smart contracts.

4.2 To What Extent Do Smart Contracts Adhere to Traditional Contract Laws in Mauritius?

Article 1101 of the Mauritian Civil Code defines a contract as an agreement between parties to do or not do something, while Article 1108 outlines four fundamental conditions for a valid contract: consent, capacity to contract, a certain object, and a lawful cause. Consent, as established in *Pougnet Raymond v The Medine Sugar Estate Co Ltd*, is realized through acceptance of a proposal, which can be applicable to smart contracts where parties must agree before terms are coded. However, challenges arise in cases where smart contracts deviate from parties' intentions during execution, as seen in the Quoine Case, where adverse effects occurred despite initial consent.

Capacity to contract, per Article 1123 of the Mauritian Civil Code, involves ensuring individuals are legally capable, categorizing minors, adults under "tutelle" or "curatelle," and those prohibited by law. In the context of smart contracts, determining capacity becomes challenging without third-party involvement, potentially enabling individuals without legal capacity to enter contracts unnoticed.

The object of the contract, according to Articles 1126 to 1130, must be specific and legal. However, in smart contracts, legality can be compromised due to automation, with computers executing contracts regardless of legality, presenting potential misuse and legal complexities unaddressed by programmers.

A lawful cause, outlined in Article 1131, mandates contracts have a legitimate purpose. However, challenges emerge in smart contracts' execution, as they may proceed despite illegitimate causes due to their immutable nature. Additionally, vices of consent, such as errors, violence, or deceit, may render traditional contracts null, but in smart contracts, execution occurs regardless, posing challenges in remedying invalid contracts.

Ultimately, while Mauritian contract law provides a framework, challenges persist in adapting it to smart contracts, particularly in addressing deviations from parties' intentions, determining capacity, ensuring legality, and remedying vices of consent. These complexities underscore the need for comprehensive legal frameworks and considerations specific to smart contracts within Mauritius.

4.3 Does the Virtual Asset and Initial Token Offering Services Act (VAITOS) Accommodate the Diverse Manifestations of Smart Contracts?

Section 2 of VAITOS defines a smart contract as a technological arrangement that can be fully or partly electronic, automatable, and enforceable by computer code, with provisions for human input and control. This definition underscores the acknowledgment that smart contracts rely on technology and can exist in various forms, including those that integrate traditional contract elements. It highlights the automated nature of smart contracts, while also recognizing the potential for human intervention in their execution, as well as the enforceability of their terms through legal methods.

The interpretation of the definition reveals several key points. Firstly, it emphasizes that smart contracts are not mere digital representations of traditional contracts but are fundamentally reliant on technology. Secondly, it recognizes the flexibility of smart contracts, which can be fully automated or hybrid in nature, combining elements of both traditional and digital contracts. Thirdly, it underscores the automatic enforcement of smart contract terms by computer code, reducing the need for human intervention in execution. However, it also acknowledges the possibility of human involvement in certain aspects of smart contract execution, providing a balance between automation and human control.

Moreover, the definition allows for the enforcement of smart contracts through traditional legal methods or a combination of both traditional and digital enforcement mechanisms. This ensures that smart contracts are recognized within existing legal frameworks while also accommodating their unique features. Additionally, the definition encompasses the three main forms of smart contracts identified in the literature: natural language contracts, hybrid smart contracts, and solely code smart contracts.

Overall, Section 2 of VAITOS provides a comprehensive framework for interpreting and understanding smart contracts, allowing for their implementation in various forms and facilitating their enforcement through legal mechanisms. This observation suggests that VASP can offer non-financial services in Mauritius using smart contracts across a spectrum of forms, ranging from those with human-readable elements to fully automated code-based contracts.

4.4   What Approach Will the Mauritian Court Take in Interpreting Smart Contracts Within the Framework of Mauritian Laws?

In the significant case of *Bahemia MH & Partner Ltd v Production Menuiseries Industrielles Ltd*, the Supreme Court of Mauritius underscored the importance of discerning the common intention or "volonté commune" of contracting parties rather than rigidly adhering to a literal interpretation of the contract. The Court emphasized the relevance of considering the context "le contexte de l'acte" and surrounding circumstances "les circonstances de la cause" in understanding the agreement's true meaning.

When it comes to traditional contracts, the Courts, drawing principles from cases like *Chartbrook Ltd v Persimmon Homes Ltd* and *Arnold v Britton*, typically examine the terms and conditions of the written agreement to ensure that the mutual intentions, obligations, and expectations of the parties are upheld, consistent with the guidance provided in *Bahemia MH & Partner Ltd v Production Menuiseries Industrielles Ltd*.

However, interpreting solely code-based smart contracts presents a more nuanced challenge. Given the complexity of the code and its potential to elude human comprehension, including that of the judiciary, Courts may need to look beyond the literal expressions of the contract. In such cases, they may rely on pre-contractual communications such as emails or oral discussions to ascertain the shared intentions "volonté commune" of the parties.

On the other hand, natural language smart contracts, where the agreement is expressed in human-readable form with code serving as an executor, allow for a more straightforward interpretation akin to traditional contracts. Courts can refer to precedents like Chartbrook Ltd v Persimmon Homes Ltd and Arnold v Britton while considering the overarching principle from Bahemia MH & Partner Ltd to interpret based on context and circumstances.

Hybrid smart contracts, combining natural language and code, offer a dual avenue for interpretation. While the code executes specific provisions, the natural language sheds light on the parties' shared intentions. In these cases, Courts must balance the standards of traditional contract interpretation with an understanding of the contract's broader context, as guided by the Supreme Court of Mauritius. However, a challenge arises from the lack of technical competency among judges to interpret smart contracts effectively. Drawing parallels from Baldwin & Francis Ltd v Patents Appeal Tribunal, judges may rely heavily on programmers to decipher the terms of smart contracts, potentially leading to ambiguity and dilution of the contracting parties' original intentions during interpretation.

Upon analysis, smart contracts in Mauritius present a mix of opportunities and challenges within the legal landscape. While they differ from traditional contracts in their execution, there are notable similarities in their foundational principles, as evidenced by the J.G Allen Contract Stack Theory and research by the Law Commission of England and Wales. The Supreme Court of Mauritius, in Bahemia MH & Partner Ltd v Production Menuiseries Industrielles Ltd, underscores the importance of understanding the broader context and shared intentions in contract interpretation.

However, navigating smart contracts in legal contexts demands a nuanced approach, acknowledging their technical intricacies while upholding the integrity and intention of the agreement. Despite these challenges, it is reasonable to consider smart contracts as subject to existing laws in Mauritius. Nonetheless, the primary hurdle lies in the interpretation of smart contracts by the Courts, given the potential complexity of their technical aspects and the need for judges to grasp their nuances effectively.

5   Recommendations and Conclusion

5.1   Challenge 1: Deviation from Parties' Intention in the Execution of Smart Contracts

In addressing the challenge of smart contracts potentially deviating from the parties' original intentions during execution, it is suggested that the Court adopt a different approach than it would for traditional contracts. Instead of solely analysing the terms of the contract, the Court should assess the performance of the smart contract to ensure it aligns with the mutual consent of the parties. By focusing on the actual execution of the contract and its adherence to the parties' intentions, the Court can better uphold the integrity of the agreement.

5.2   Challenge 2: Determining the Capacity of Parties in Smart Contracts

To tackle the challenge of determining the capacity of parties in smart contracts, Virtual Asset Service Providers (VASPs) could implement Know Your Customer (KYC) protocols. These protocols would require parties to verify their identities before accepting the terms of the smart contract, ensuring that only legally capable individuals participate in the agreement. By verifying the identities of the parties involved, VASPs can help mitigate risks associated with capacity issues in smart contracts.

5.3 Challenge 3: Execution of Smart Contracts Against the Intention of the Parties

A potential solution to the challenge of smart contracts being executed against the parties' intentions is for the Financial Services Commission (FSC) to develop guidelines for the formulation of smart contracts. These guidelines could outline activities that are not legal under the law, providing programmers with clear parameters to follow when creating smart contracts. Additionally, the FSC could issue guidelines similar to the SEC Rule 15c3–5, offering a checklist for smart contract providers to mitigate associated risks effectively.

5.4 Challenge 4: Lack of Judges' Competency to Interpret Smart Contracts

In response to the challenge of judges lacking the technical expertise to interpret smart contracts, one potential solution is for judges to apply the Reasonable Coder's test when interpreting smart contract terms. However, without adequate training for judges, the strict interpretation of computer code may still pose challenges. Judges would need to adopt a dynamic approach, discerning between acceptable coding mistakes and intentional alterations aimed at changing the contract's outcome. Through continuous education and training, judges can enhance their competency in interpreting smart contracts effectively within the legal framework.

Conclusion

The advent of smart contracts in the digital era has fundamentally altered the landscape of agreement formulation and execution. While rooted in technology, these contracts retain key elements of traditional contracts. Through insights gleaned from existing literature and legal interpretations, it's apparent that Mauritius' legal framework is adaptable to incorporate these innovative digital agreements. However, applying traditional methods to navigate the automated and immutable nature of smart contracts poses challenges for the courts, necessitating a revised approach within the judicial system.

Various challenges, from issues of consent to the technical proficiency required to understand code, underscore the need for an updated approach. While the Virtual Asset and Initial Token Offering Services Act (VAITOS) can accommodate different types of smart contracts, and existing contract laws can encompass them, the dynamic nature of this technology demands ongoing legal adaptation and guidance.

As we progress further into the digital age, a balanced approach is crucial—one that upholds the foundational principles of contracts, acknowledges the technical complexities of smart contracts, and ensures accessibility and equity in justice. Implementing measures such as the Reasonable Coder's test, providing clear guidelines, and emphasizing pre-contractual communications can facilitate a smoother integration of technology and jurisprudence in Mauritius.

The path forward will be characterized by collaboration among legal experts, coders, and policymakers to ensure that as technology evolves, principles of fairness, clarity, and justice remain paramount in all contractual engagements.

Disclosure of Interests. The author has no competing interests to declare that are relevant to the content of this article.

References

Arnold v Britton [2015] UKSC 36

Arner, D.W., Barberis, J., Buckley, R.P.: FinTech, RegTech and the Reconceptualization of Financial Regulation. Northwest. J. Int. Law Bus. **37**(3), 371–413 (2017)

Bahemia MH & Partner Ltd v Production Menuiseries Industrielles Ltd [2016] SCJ 66

Baldwin & Francis Ltd v Patents Appeal Tribunal [1959] AC 663, 684

Böhme, R., Christin, N., Edelman, B., Moore, T.: Bitcoin: Economics, technology, and governance. J. Econo. Perspect. **29**(2), 213–238 (2015)

Central Bank of Nigeria: Cryptocurrency trading: CBN orders banks to close operating accounts. CBN UPDATE **3**(1), 2 (2021)

Chartbrook Ltd v Persimmon Homes Ltd [2009] UKHL 38

FATF: Updated Guidance for a Risk-Based Approach to Virtual Assets and Virtual Asset Service Providers. FATF, Paris (2021)

Financial Stability Board: Crypto-assets: Report to the G20 on work by the FSB and standard-setting bodies, https://www.fsb.org. Accessed May 2024

Green, S.: Smart contracts: interpretation and rectification. Lloyd's Maritime Commercial Law Quart **2**, 234–251 (2018)

G20: G20 Leaders Declaration, Buenos Aires (2018). https://www.g20.org. Accessed May 2024

Möser, M., Böhme, R., Breuker, D.: An inquiry into money laundering tools in the Bitcoin ecosystem. In: 2013 APWG eCrime Researchers Summit, San Francisco, CA, USA, pp. 1–14. IEEE (2018)

Nakamoto, S.: Bitcoin: A Peer-to-Peer Electronic Cash System (2008). https://bitcoin.org/bitcoin.pdf. Accessed May 2024

Pougnet Raymond v The Medine Sugar Estate Co. Ltd. [1966] SCJ 222

Quoine Pte Ltd v B2C2 Ltd [2020] SGCA(I) 02

Szabo, N.: Smart Contracts Glossary. Phonetic Sciences, Amsterdam (1995)

Swan, M.: Blockchain: Blueprint for a New Economy. O'Reilly Media (2015).

Thornton v Shoe Lane Parking [1971] 2 QB 163

The Influence of Board Characteristics on Environmental Sustainability in Northern Europe

Thakoor Sharma Geerawo$^{(\boxtimes)}$ [ID] and Bhavna Mahadew [ID]

University of Technology, Port Louis, Mauritius
thakoor.geerawo@utm.ac.mu

Abstract. This paper empirically analyses the influence of board characteristics on the environmental sustainability of listed companies in the United Kingdom, France and Germany. This quantitative study spans from 2013 to 2023, utilising a dataset comprising 2,726 firm-year observations. Employing robust panel data regression with multiple fixed effects, the analysis reveals that board gender diversity, board cultural diversity, the presence of a corporate governance committee and larger firms tend to exhibit higher environmental sustainability performance. The findings of this paper advance the understanding of two key theories: the agency theory and the stakeholder theory. This study thus contributes to the growing literature on corporate governance and sustainability by providing empirical evidence of the role of board characteristics in shaping environmental sustainability outcomes.

Keywords: Environmental Sustainability · Gender Diversity · Cultural Diversity · Corporate Governance · Firm Size

1 Introduction

One of the most often used terms in talks about climate change is environmental sustainability. The fight against climatic catastrophes can be greatly impacted by the significance of environmental sustainability. Yet, a broad cross-section of the population does not know exactly what it is or what actionable activities each person or business should take. Environmentally sustainable development is the conventional concept of environmental sustainability, but what does that actually mean in real life? It implies that the amount of natural resources we have access to and the amount of those resources that humans use must be in balance [26]. The rate of harvesting should not outpace the rate of regeneration for renewable resources, such as timber or crops. This is referred to as "sustainable yield" which is the rate at which renewable alternatives, such as solar or wind power, are developed should not outpace the rate at which non-renewable resources, such as fossil fuels, are depleted [26]. When it comes to pollution, the pace of waste output should not be higher than the rate at which the environment can absorb that waste. This is called: "sustainable waste disposal" [26].

© The Author(s), under exclusive license to Springer Nature Switzerland AG 2025
K. Hinkelmann and H. Smuts (Eds.): Society 5.0 2024, CCIS 2173, pp. 136–151, 2025.
https://doi.org/10.1007/978-3-031-71412-2_11

Environmental sustainability, put simply, is the idea that naturally occurring processes may sustainably extract renewable resources, deplete non-renewable resources, and assimilate pollution at endless rates. In addition, the United Nations World Commission on Environment and Development defines environmental sustainability as acting in a way that guarantees the availability of natural resources for future generations to maintain a standard of living that is at least as high as that of the present generation [33]. Achieving a balance between human consumption and natural resources is crucial for climate change. Unchecked resource depletion can lead to food and energy shortages, and a spike in greenhouse gas emissions that trigger global warming. Policy experts, scientists, philosophers, and politicians have focused on sustainability, the environment, and society for years.

Business and environmental sustainability are interconnected with sustainability referring to a company's approach to reducing environmental and social impacts. Environment, Social and Governance (ESG) criteria evaluate sustainability practices and climate change threats are too severe to ignore, causing alarm over global natural systems and societies. If they haven't already, businesses are under pressure to set sustainable goals as well as opportunities to do so [21]. Businesses have continued to support the United Nations General Assembly's Sustainable Development Goals (SDGs) despite the COVID-19 pandemic. These goals aim to address poverty, inequality, environmental degradation, and climate change. Examples include reducing greenhouse gas (GHG) emissions, conserving water resources, and promoting sustainable consumption, waste design, and risk management.

The unpredictable world of business influenced by natural resource depletion, climate change, and rising energy and food prices necessitates a revaluation of both public and private organisations. Successful transformation into sustainable firms requires adaptability, resilience and ethical environmental practices. Employees increasingly seek mission-driven, purpose-led companies. Companies that practise environmental sustainability are viewed as more desirable employers by 71% of workers and job seekers [20]. Customers are prepared to spend more on products from companies that practise environmental responsibility. According to 80% of consumers, sustainability is significant to them [19]. Businesses are under pressure to address climate change with corporate disclosure laws, which are being developed by several of the world's leading economies [15]. A sustainable business is intrinsically more appealing to the growing number of responsible investors due to the emergence of ESG investment criteria to which by 2025, investments in ESG assets could amount to USD 53 trillion, accounting for more than one-third of all assets worldwide [11].

COP26 highlights 2022 as a year for businesses to take action, develop plans, and collaborate with governments. They must prepare for climate action, measuring and accountability, and adapt to shifting regulatory and market environments. Prioritizing adaptation is crucial for businesses to ensure survival and convergence of sustainability requirements [1]. Everyone has business when it comes to climate change, and businesses need to listen to a variety of viewpoints. The board of directors of corporations have an essential role to play towards environmental sustainability [43]. The board of directors is responsible for an organisation's sustainability and ESG issues, ensuring long-term success. They integrate sustainability into growth strategies and decision-making processes, requiring robust board leadership and sustainability knowledge. They also integrate ESG issues into purpose, governance, strategy, risk management, and accountability reporting ensuring targets and metrics align with financial data.

This study examines the impact of board characteristics on environmental sustainability in Germany, France, and the UK using 2,726 firm-year observations from 2013–2023, providing existing literature, methodology and recommendations.

2 Literature Review

2.1 Theoretical Framework

2.1.1 Agency Theory

An agency relationship involves a principal hiring an agent to perform a service on their behalf, with the agent having decision-making authority. As per Brennan, agency issues arise from contracting for actions that impact the principal's welfare [13]. Managers often face inefficiency when they choose not to pursue their objectives. Managerial incentives to maximize value can reduce this inefficiency. Agency costs, which include monitoring expenses, bonding costs, and residual loss, are a result of conflicts of interest between managers and shareholders as per Jensen and Meckling [23]. Corporate governance affects a company's performance, but opinions vary on what constitutes a good system [12]. Roberts [39] has argued that agency theory has influenced the conception and reform of corporate governance, but it may not provide enough insight due to its influence on institutional elements and local contexts. Strategies like strong ownership control, managerial ownership, independent board members, and committees can help reduce agency conflict and associated costs [36].

2.1.2 Stakeholder Theory

Diverging from the agency theory whereby management is the agent of the shareholder, the stakeholder theory's basic premise involves the needs of various stakeholders. This theory is involved in the recognition of the stakeholders' diverse needs [16]. According to stakeholder theory, the board is in charge of protecting and balancing the interests of each stakeholder. Thus, information may be shared to accomplish meeting such needs [17]. As per Liao et al. [27], stakeholder theory is in fact regarded as an explainable theory for corporate environmental accounting. It recognises and identifies the connection between the actions of the business and how those actions affect its stakeholders. Stakeholder theory states that for businesses to have a competitive edge, they must be able to adapt to complicated rules and establish a relationship of mutual trust, engagement, and constructive communication with their stakeholders [6].

2.2 Empirical Review

The level of corporate environmental disclosure in the annual report of a firm is positively correlated with board composition, but there is a significant negative correlation between board size and this level of disclosure, according to empirical findings from a study by Uwuigbe et al. [42]. Regression analysis results in a study by Akbas [3] show that the only factor that positively and statistically significantly correlates with the level of environmental disclosure is board size. According to this finding, companies with bigger boards tend to release more environmental data than companies with smaller boards. According to the results of another study conducted by Tarus [40], firm size had a considerable and beneficial impact on environmental accounting disclosure, whereas board size had a significant and negative impact. This suggests that while large corporations have high levels of environmental information reporting, firms with larger boards are less likely to reveal environmental accounting information. Nguyen and Thanh also show that an increase in the percentage of independent directors on a manufacturing company's board is associated with improved environmental performance. On the other hand, the environmental performance is unaffected by the CEO and board chair functions being separate [34]. Thus, this leads to the expectation that:

H1: Board Size influence positively environmental sustainability.

A study by Adeniyi and Fadipe [2] revealed that board gender diversity does not significantly affect sustainability reporting. Al-Shaer and Zaman [4], however, discover that gender-diverse boards are linked to sustainability reports of better calibre and that independent female directors have a stronger influence on the calibre of sustainability reporting than do female directors. Using a comparatively large dataset (10,334 firm-year observations) of publicly traded companies in the United States, Nadeem et al. [31]. Discover a strong positive correlation between BGD and environmental innovation. Additionally, it was discovered that this association is stronger in industries that are sensitive to environmental issues. According to Kassinis et al. [25], a firm's environmental sustainability initiatives are significantly predicted by both "demographic" and "structural" gender diversity. Their research demonstrates that gender diversity also affects sustainability. Gender diversity, according to Lu and Herremans [28], is positively correlated with companies' environmental performance scores, especially in the more ecologically sensitive industries.

Ben-Amar et al. [9] found that the presence of women on boards improves the chance of voluntary climate change disclosure based on a sample of publicly listed Canadian corporations over the period 2008–2014, validating the critical mass idea [9]. In a study on boardroom gender diversity and corporate sustainable practices, Nadeem et al. [32] examined the effect of boardroom gender diversity on corporate sustainability practices on a sample of all Australian Securities Exchange (ASX) listed firms from 2010 to 2014. They did this by using a sophisticated dynamic panel generalised method of moments (GMM) estimator to account for endogeneity. The results of the study show a strong correlation between corporate sustainability initiatives and the representation of women on boards. Drawing from the upper echelon and value belief theories, as well as substantial empirical studies conducted in research by Bazel-Shoham et al. [8], the results provide compelling evidence that the inclusion of women on boards fosters innovation directed towards environmental sustainability. According to the findings of another study conducted by Carvajal et al. [14] utilising data from 2400 US enterprises, BGD is essential for creating strategies related to biodiversity and ecosystem restoration, protection, and impact reduction. Thus, it would be expected that:

H2: Board Gender Diversity influence positively environmental sustainability.

Biswas et al. [10] have argued that sustainability committees tend to have better social and environmental performance. Barnard [7] has suggested that a board-level sustainability committee has several advantages and should be considered by firms. Peters and Romi [37] find that the likelihood of adopting sustainability assurance is only influenced by environmental committees that contain directors with relevant expertise, thereby supporting the argument that some firms establish sustainability-related governance merely to conform to socially desired behaviour. According to Orazalin [35], having a sustainability committee enhances the potency of CSR initiatives. The findings also show that companies with strong CSR programmes perform better in terms of the environment and society. Additionally, the empirical findings complement the study's theoretical framework by demonstrating how well CSR strategy explains the positive correlation between board sustainability committees and business environmental and social performance. Thus, we expect that:

H3: The presence of a Corporate Governance Committee improves the environmental sustainability score.

Biswas et al. [10] have also suggested that the independence of board members allows companies to have greater and better social and environmental performance. De Villiers and van Staden [44] specifically find evidence of improved environmental performance in firms with higher board independence and a smaller concentration of directors appointed after the CEO on the board of directors, which is consistent with their agency theory-driven assumptions. Post et al. [38] assert that a company's likelihood of forming alliances with a sustainability theme increases with the proportion of independent directors on the board. In turn, these partnerships improve the environmental performance of corporations. Higher board independence, according to Jizi [24], makes it easier for businesses to project a positive image of good citizenship by raising social conscience. Thus, it is expected that:

H4: Independence of board members improves environmental sustainability.

According to Martinez-Ferrero et al. [29], a company's commitment to sustainability concerns is strengthened and its social and environmental performance is improved by having a diverse board of directors. According to Mohy-ud-Din [30], Australian directors are more likely than US directors to support sustainable development in their companies due to their varied cultural backgrounds. But unlike their Australian counterparts, cultural diversity on US boards strongly supports CSR initiatives. Amiri et al. [5] also found a good and significant correlation between the workforce, community, and product responsibility—the three aspects of social sustainability—and cultural diversity. The human rights dimension, however, have been found to have a negligible and unfavourable link. Thus, this creates an expectation of:

H5: The cultural diversity of board members positively influences the environmental sustainability score of a firm.

3 Methodology

The sample dataset utilised in this study is downloaded from the London Stock Exchange Group (LSEG, previously known as Refinitiv Eikon). The United Kingdom, France and Germany were chosen as they are among the largest economies in the world. They also are compliant on the environmental sustainability and are members of the action teams of COP26, thus it would be expected that they would set up environment-conscious rules and regulations for their listed companies. The requirements for the data were that each firm should have an environmental pillar score as measured independently by LSEG (Refinitiv Eikon) and readings in all other variables. This Environmental pillar score is a relative score based on the weight on "Emissions, Waste, Biodiversity, Environmental management systems, Innovation, Green revenues, research and development and capital expenditures, Resource use Water, Energy, Sustainable packaging, and Environmental supply chain." This score is utilised as a proxy for Environmental sustainability as the dependent variable. The independent and control variables were also downloaded from the LSEG software based on the literature review [18, 44]. Thus, the equation to be analysed in this study is as follows (Table 1):

$$ENV_{l,t} = BSIZE_{l,t} + GEND_{l,t} + CGC_{l,t} + IND_{l,t} + CDIV_{l,t} + CV_{l,t} + FE_{l,t} + u_{l,t} \tag{1}$$

Table 1. Variable measurement description

Variable	Code	Definition
Dependent Variable:		
Environment Sustainability	ENV	Environmental pillar score as provided by the LSEG software
Independent Variables:		
Board Size	BSIZE	Number of directors on the board of directors
Board Gender Diversity	GEND	gender diversity ratio within the board of directors
Corporate Governance Committee	CGC	Dichotomous variable representing the presence of a Corporate Governance Committee within the firm
Independent Directors on BOD	IND	Ratio of independent directors within the board of directors
Board Cultural Diversity	CDIV	Ratio of culturally diverse directors within the board of directors
Control Variables:		

(continued)

Table 1. (*continued*)

Variable	Code	Definition
Attendance policy	ATTP	Dichotomous variable confirming the presence of a board attendance policy
Board Attendance Percent	ATT	Percentage of Attendance during Board of Directors
Board Member Skills	SK	Percentage of Board Members having skills related to the firm or to finance
Board Term	TERM	The number of years for a board term
Independence in Audit Committee	INDA	Percentage of independent directors in the Audit Committee
CEO Chairman Duality	CEOC	Dichotomous variable confirming the presence of the Chief Executive Officer being the Chairman at the same time
Chairman Ex CEO	CEXC	Dichotomous variable confirming that the chairperson was an ex-CEO of the firm
Average Member Compensation	lnCOMP	The natural logarithmic of the average board member compensation
Firm Size	FSIZE	The natural logarithmic of the total assets of the firm
Leverage	LEV	Ratio calculated from total liabilities divided by Total Assets
Return on Assets	ROA	Ratio calculated from Net Income after tax over Total Assets

In order to choose the Fixed Effects (FE) model, the Hausman test was run, which rejected the Random Effects regression model (p-value = 0.000). This is consistent with literature which studied EU countries and adopted the panel data regression with multiple fixed effects [18]. Thus, three fixed effects are employed: the industry, year and country to control for endogeneity. The Breusch-Pagan test will be employed to test for heteroskedasticity. Furthermore, the Pearson Correlation coefficients and Variance Inflation Factor (VIF) will be calculated to identify any possible multicollinearity.

4 Analysis and Discussion of Findings

4.1 Descriptive Statistics

The number of firm-year observations from each country is presented in Table 2. The UK makes up about 53% of the sample whereas France takes up 31% of the sample and 16% of the sample data relates to Germany.

For each of the variables, whether dependent, independent or control, the summary statistics are presented in Table 3. Interestingly, on average, the listed firms have a 61%

Table 2. Firm-year observations per country

Country	Freq	Percent	Cum
France	858	31	31
Germany	435	16	47
UK	1,433	53	100
Total	2,726	100	

score which deviates much from this mean. The number of board members on average is around 12. Most companies do have an attendance policy (60.5%), but not necessarily in line with the attendance policy presence, the attendance of board members remained high at 96%. Despite high attendance, the board member skills were only 44% related to the firm's area or had expertise in finance. Also, the female ratio was 31% among the tested data, with a lower 26% of board members coming from diverse cultural backgrounds. The board member term was on average 2.5 years. Independent board members constituted 60% of the composition, whereas independent members on the audit committee were around 83%.

Table 3. Summary Statistics of each variable

Variable	Obs	Mean	Std. Dev
ENV	2,726	61.137	24.409
BSIZE	2,726	11.512	3.838
ATTP	2,726	0.605	0.489
ATT	2,726	95.669	5.720
SK	2,726	43.790	20.987
GEND	2,726	31.072	13.013
CDIV	2,726	26.347	20.074
TERM	2,726	2.492	1.507
INDA	2,726	82.750	24.449
IND	2,726	60.428	19.705
CGC	2,726	0.365	0.482
CEOC	2,726	0.242	0.429
CEXC	2,726	0.225	0.417
COMP	2,726	13.851	0.961
FSIZE	2,726	23.105	1.908
LEV	2,726	0.618	0.251
ROA	2,726	0.039	0.104

36.5% of companies reported having a separate corporate governance committee. In terms of interaction between CEO and Chairman, 24% of companies reported CEO-Chairman duality whereas 22.5% reported that the Chairperson is an ex-CEO of the company. For board member compensation, there was not much standard deviation noted. Firm characteristics such as leverage reveal that firms on average have a 61.8% indebtedness, while they generate around 3.9% of their total assets as net income after taxes, with a large deviation between companies. Prior to running the full panel regression model, it is essential to check for multi-collinearity within the independent variables so that the model produces reliable and statistically relevant insights. Thus, Table 4 shows the pairwise Pearson correlation coefficients which revealed an important issue. After running the Pearson Correlation tests, the chairman-CEO duality and the chairman being an ex-CEO had a 90% correlation coefficient. This was verified through the Variance Inflation factor (VIF) test as well. Thus, the ex-CEO variable was dropped since there was a substantial overlap between the mentioned two variables. Table 4 shows the Pearson correlation coefficients following the mentioned adjustment.

Table 4. Pairwise **Pearson correlations**

VAR	(1)	(2)	(3)	(4)	(5)	(6)	(7)	(8)	(9)	(10)	(11)	(12)	(13)	(14)
BSIZE	1.00													
ATTP	(0.30)	1.00												
ATT	(0.19)	0.23	1.00											
SK	(0.29)	0.31	0.13	1.00										
GEND	0.20	(0.04)	0.06	(0.21)	1.00									
CDIV	(0.17)	0.10	0.03	0.05	(0.01)	1.00								
TERM	0.35	(0.41)	(0.24)	(0.49)	0.13	(0.08)	1.00							
INDA	(0.25)	0.33	0.18	0.39	(0.02)	0.17	(0.51)	1.00						
IND	(0.20)	0.25	0.14	0.08	0.11	0.18	(0.25)	0.68	1.00					
CGC	0.25	(0.08)	(0.07)	0.02	0.15	0.10	0.07	0.07	0.05	1.00				
CEOC	0.20	(0.25)	(0.19)	(0.09)	0.16	(0.00)	0.29	(0.11)	(0.17)	0.20	1.00			
COMP	0.50	(0.04)	(0.01)	(0.08)	0.05	0.02	0.06	(0.02)	0.04	0.19	(0.06)	1.00		
FSIZE	0.60	(0.17)	(0.10)	(0.21)	0.21	0.05	0.25	(0.05)	0.09	0.33	0.11	0.54	1.00	
LEV	0.32	(0.12)	(0.07)	(0.11)	0.05	(0.07)	0.14	(0.11)	(0.14)	0.16	0.07	0.23	0.37	1.00
ROA	(0.07)	0.03	0.04	0.06	0.01	(0.00)	(0.08)	0.07	0.03	(0.10)	(0.02)	(0.04)	(0.15)	(0.17)

After the correction, both tables show acceptable ranges of correlation coefficients. The highest correlation coefficient is between firm size and board size. Yet this is not worrisome as the maximum variance inflation factor (VIF) was below three (3). Altogether, the mean VIF after the deletion of the variable step was 1.66 as reported in Table 5 which is well below the rules of thumb for multicollinearity [22]. Table 6 thus presents the panel data regression with multiple fixed effects model utilised in this paper as suggested from the Hausman test.

The fixed effects panel regression model comprised robust standard errors corrected for heteroskedasticity using the White/Huber sandwich method. The key results are

Table 5. Variance Inflation Factor (VIF)

Variable	VIF	1/VIF
INDA	2.74	0.36
BSIZE	2.60	0.38
IND	2.29	0.44
FSIZE	2.23	0.45
TERM	1.98	0.50
SK	1.70	0.59
COMP	1.52	0.66
CEOC	1.37	0.73
ATTP	1.35	0.74
LEV	1.27	0.79
CGC	1.24	0.81
GEND	1.23	0.81
ATT	1.16	0.87
CDIV	1.10	0.91
ROA	1.08	0.92
Mean VIF	1.66	

identified using the p-values which are less than 5%. The coefficients of each variable with respect to the Environment Sustainability Score. Board Size was not significant in the model. This provides limited evidence towards H1; thus, we reject H1; referring that board size does not influence environmental sustainability. Gender diversity on the board of directors is positively associated with a higher environmental sustainability score (0.18), providing concrete evidence for accepting H2. The higher number of female directors in a board of directors provides a higher probability of environmental sustainability. The dichotomous variable regarding corporate governance committee registered a positive significant association thus accepting H3, suggesting that a separate corporate governance committee does not only benefit shareholders but also the environment. However, the ratio of independent board directors to the total directors did not register any significance, rejecting H4, inferring that, additional independent directors do not necessarily improve environmental sustainability. The cultural diversity in the board of directors is also associated with a better environmental sustainability score (0.06), thus providing evidence towards accepting H5. Having a diverse cultural board thus implies a higher probability of environmental sustainability. Within the model, it was revealed that a larger firm is significantly associated with a better Environmental Sustainability score. Robustness tests carried out using the two-stage least squares instrumental variable regression method following Tingbani et al. [41] confirmed the initial findings of the study.

Table 6. Panel Data Regressions with multiple fixed effects model

Dependent Variable: ENV score		
Independent and Control Variables	Coeff	p-value
BSIZE	−0.168	0.930
ATTP	−1.093*	0.022
ATT	0.021	0.568
SK	−0.026	0.165
GEND	0.184***	0.000
CDIV	0.061***	0.002
TERM	−0.306	0.601
INDA	0.026	0.216
IND	0.026	0.249
CGC	2.472*	0.024
CEOC	−0.264	0.766
COMP	0.277	0.237
FSIZE	3.416***	0.000
LEV	0.975	0.677
ROA	−3.582	0.239
Cons	−33.022	0.084
N	2726	
F	6.416	
p-value	0.000	
Industry FE	Yes	
Country FE	Yes	
Year FE	Yes	
R2adj	0.880	

4.2 Discussion of Findings

Consistent with Nadeem et al. [31] and Lu and Herremans [28], gender diversity on the board of directors is strongly correlated with environmental sustainability scores. Such positive association was present in other developed economies as well in the instances of USA, Canada and Australia [9, 14, 32]. Gender diversity therefore could be classified as a global phenomenon within corporate governance which may improve satisfaction of the different stakeholders' needs based on the stakeholder theory especially since the environment influences a myriad of stakeholders including society, local organisations, government, and health institutions among others. Thus, this paper contributes to the Northern European literature on gender diversity and environmental sustainability performance.

Cultural diversity in the board of directors is often overlooked in studies on listed companies. We find that a culturally diverse board reflects on the environmental sustainability agenda as demonstrated above. This is consistent with Martinez-Ferrero et al. [29] and Amiri et al. [5] who suggested that cultural diversity works closely with sustainability. This is an addition to understanding the stakeholder theory as we thus extend cultural diversity to improve environmental sustainability. In terms of agency theory, extrapolating the positive effects of both gender and cultural diversity on the board of directors could suggest more vigilance from diversity, in line with the idea of more vigilance from independent directors help in decreasing agency issues as suggested by de Villiers et al. [43].

Surprisingly, the ratio of independent board directors did not register a significant coefficient with environmental sustainability within any of the models. This is contrary to Post et al. [38] who suggested that sustainability partnerships within independent directors improve the environmental performance of that organisation. Thus, directors, whether independent or not, are concerned with the environmental sustainability of the firm, showing the impact of global climate change awareness and other systemic issues in the environment. Furthermore, board size is not significantly associated with environmental sustainability scores in this study. The result is not consistent with Akbas [3]. This draws novel insights in the sense that larger boards may not necessarily improve the environmental sustainability impact of the firm.

The presence of a corporate governance committee typically is associated with better social and environmental performance and the results in this study support the findings of Biswas et al. [10]. There is a statistically significant connection between the presence of a corporate governance committee and environmental sustainability, whereby a separate corporate governance committee improves the environmental sustainability of the company. Typically, the corporate governance committee was introduced to control agency issues related to managers acting in their self-interests [12, 23]. In addition, the findings here support that the corporate governance committee also contributes to the fulfilment of the stakeholder theory through transparency, accountability, ethical conduct and via this study environmental sustainability.

5   Conclusion and Recommendations

In the discussion of corporate governance and environmental sustainability, understanding the factors influencing environmental sustainability performance has garnered significant attention. This study delves into this crucial area by empirically investigating the impact of board characteristics on environmental sustainability across three prominent European nations: Germany, France, and the United Kingdom. This study uses empirical research to examine how board characteristics affect environmental sustainability in listed companies of the above-mentioned countries. This quantitative analysis uses a dataset with 2,726 firm-year observations from 2013 to 2023. Higher levels of board gender diversity, board cultural diversity, the presence of a corporate governance committee, and larger firm size are associated with superior environmental sustainability performance, according to the analysis, which makes use of fixed effects regressions with robust standard error correction. The key findings of this paper refer to the impact of diversity on the board of directors in improving the transparency, accountability and ethical conduct of companies in terms of environmental sustainability. Furthermore, in addition to decreasing agency issues, a separate corporate governance committee helps improve meeting the environmental needs of stakeholders.

5.1 Recommendations

Based on the findings of this study complemented by a critical review of the literature, several recommendations can be made to encourage higher environmental sustainability of firms through corporate governance. First, it is important to encourage higher gender and cultural diversity on the board of directors. Diversity typically improves the environmental sustainability score of firms since the knowledge and skills from different cultural segments enhance environmentally conscious actions. Furthermore, bundled with the above, the setting up of a corporate governance committee in listed firms could be achieved through the inclusion of such advice into the best practices of the code of corporate governance, if not embedded within legal frameworks.

5.2 Limitations and Future Research

As with all research, this study is not exempt from limitations. First, the dependent variable could be construed by some academics as a crude way to assess sustainability. However, this study argues only from the view of the environmental sustainability score calculated by LSEG, which offers an objective metric to assess a firm's commitment towards saving the environment. In addition, despite being backed by a multitude of research papers and having several control and independent variables, the study depends on one particular equation. Future research could thus include other sets of equations to complement the existing findings. Furthermore, the study is limited to only three European countries. So, caution is warranted when interpreting the results, especially for other areas within Europe or any other continent. Therefore, future research could be extended towards other European countries and other areas around the world.

Acknowledgements. The authors thank the peer reviewers for their constructive feedback.

Disclosure of Interests. The authors have no competing interests to declare that are relevant to the content of this article.

References

1. Abhayawansa, S., Adams, C.: Towards a conceptual framework for non-financial reporting inclusive of pandemic and climate risk reporting. Meditari Account. Res. **30**(3), 710–738 (2021). https://doi.org/10.1108/medar-11-2020-1097
2. Adeniyi, S.I., Fadipe, A.O.: Effect of board diversity on sustainability reporting in Nigeria: a study of beverage manufacturing firms. Indonesian J. Corp. Soc. Responsib. Environ. Manage. **1**(1), 43–50 (2018). https://doi.org/10.32456/IJCSREM.V1I1.12

3. Akbas, H.E.: The relationship between board characteristics and environmental disclosure: evidence from Turkish listed companies. South East Eur. J. Econ. Bus. **11**(2), 7 (2016). https://doi.org/10.1515/jeb-2016-0007

4. Al-Shaer, H., Zaman, M.: Board gender diversity and sustainability reporting quality. J. Contemp. Account. Econ. **12**(3), 210–222 (2016). https://doi.org/10.1016/j.jcae.2016.09.001

5. Amiri, M.H., et al.: Diversity in the board of directors and the social sustainability pillar of the firm: evidence from countries with high environmental, Social, and Governance scores. Int. J. Organ. Diversity **22**, 1, (2022). https://doi.org/10.18848/2328-6261/cgp/v22i01/63-83

6. Baalouch, F., et al.: A study of the determinants of environmental disclosure quality: evidence from French listed companies. J. Manag. Gov. **23**(4), 939–971 (2019). https://doi.org/10.1007/s10997-019-09474-0

7. Barnard, J.W.: At the intersection of corporate governance and environmental sustainability. Wm. & Mary Bus. L. Rev. **2**, 207 (2011)

8. Bazel-Shoham, O., et al.: Board gender diversity, feminine culture, and innovation for environmental sustainability. J. Prod. Innov. Manag. (2023). https://doi.org/10.1111/jpim.12672

9. Ben-Amar, W., et al.: Board gender diversity and corporate response to sustainability initiatives: evidence from the carbon disclosure project. J. Bus. Ethics **142**(2), 369–383 (2017). https://doi.org/10.1007/s10551-015-2759-1

10. Biswas, P.K., et al.: Board composition, sustainability committee and corporate social and environmental performance in Australia. Pac. Account. Rev. **30**(4), 517–540 (2018). https://doi.org/10.1108/par-12-2017-0107

11. Bloomberg: ESG assets may hit $53 trillion by 2025, a third of global AUM. https://www.bloomberg.com/professional/blog/esg-assets-may-hit-53-trillion-by-2025-a-third-of-global-aum/ (2021)

12. Bonazzi, L., Islam, S.M.: Agency theory and corporate governance: a study of the effectiveness of board in their monitoring of the CEO. J. Model. Manag. **2**(1), 7–23 (2007). https://doi.org/10.1108/17465660710733022

13. Brennan, M.J.: Corporate finance over the past 25 years'. Financ. Manage. **24**, 9–22 (1995). https://doi.org/10.2307/3665531

14. Carvajal, M., et al.: Biodiversity disclosure, sustainable development and environmental initiatives: does board gender diversity matter? Bus. Strateg. Environ. **31**(3), 969–987 (2022). https://doi.org/10.1002/bse.2929

15. Ernst, Young: the future of sustainability reporting standards, https://assets.ey.com/content/dam/ey-sites/ey-com/en_gl/topics/sustainability/ey-the-future-of-sustainability-reporting-standards-june-2021.pdf (2021)

16. Freeman, R.E., et al.: Stakeholder theory and The Corporate Objective Revisited. Organ. Sci. **15**(3), 364–369 (2004). https://doi.org/10.1287/orsc.1040.0066

17. Frias-Aceituno, J.V., et al.: The role of the board in the dissemination of integrated corporate social reporting. Corp. Soc. Responsib. Environ. Manag. **20**(4), 219–233 (2012). https://doi.org/10.1002/csr.1294

18. García Martín, C.J., Herrero, B.: Do board characteristics affect environmental performance? A study of EU firms. Corp Soc Responsib. Env. **27**(1), 74–94 (2020). https://doi.org/10.1002/csr.1775

19. I.B.M.: Meet the 2020 consumers driving change (2020). https://www.ibm.com/downloads/cas/EXK4XKX8

20. I.B.M.: Sustainability at a turning point (2023). https://www.ibm.com/downloads/cas/WLJ7LVP4

21. I.B.M.: What Is Sustainability in Business?, https://www.ibm.com/topics/business-sustainability, (2024)

22. Inekwe, M., et al.: CSR in developing countries–the importance of good governance and economic growth: evidence from Africa. Soc. Responsib. J. **17**(2), 226–242 (2021). https://doi.org/10.1108/srj-10-2019-0336

23. Jensen, M.C., Meckling, W.H.: Theory of the firm: Managerial behavior, agency costs and ownership structure. J. Financ. Econ. **3**(4), 305–360 (1976). https://doi.org/10.1016/0304-405x(76)90026-x

24. Jizi, M.: The influence of board composition on sustainable development disclosure. Bus. Strateg. Environ. **26**(5), 640–655 (2017). https://doi.org/10.1002/bse.1943

25. Kassinis, G., et al.: Gender and environmental sustainability: a longitudinal analysis. Corp. Soc. Responsib. Environ. Manag. **23**(6), 399–412 (2016). https://doi.org/10.1002/CSR.1386

26. Lawrence, B.: The Importance of Environmental Sustainability, https://www.cooleffect.org/the-importance-of-environmental-sustainability, (2020)

27. Liao, L., et al.: Gender diversity, board independence, environmental committee and greenhouse gas disclosure. Br. Account. Rev. **47**(4), 409–424 (2015). https://doi.org/10.1016/j.bar.2014.01.002

28. Lu, J., Herremans, I.M.: Board gender diversity and environmental performance: an industries perspective. Bus. Strateg. Environ. **28**(7), 1449–1464 (2019). https://doi.org/10.1002/bse.2326

29. Martínez-Ferrero, J., et al.: The impact of board cultural diversity on a firm's commitment toward the sustainability issues of emerging countries: the mediating effect of a CSR committee. Corp. Soc. Responsib. Environ. Manag. **28**(2), 675–685 (2021). https://doi.org/10.1002/csr.2080

30. Mohy-ud-Din, K.: Board diversity and corporate social responsibility versus sustainability development: evidence from US and Australia. J. Clean. Prod. **417**, 138030 (2023). https://doi.org/10.1016/j.jclepro.2023.138030

31. Nadeem, M., et al.: Are women eco-friendly? Board gender diversity and environmental innovation. Bus. Strateg. Environ. **29**(8), 3146–3161 (2020). https://doi.org/10.1002/bse.2563

32. Nadeem, M., et al.: Boardroom gender diversity and corporate sustainability practices: evidence from Australian securities exchange listed firms. J. Clean. Prod. **149**, 874–885 (2017). https://doi.org/10.1016/j.jclepro.2017.02.141

33. Nations, U.: Sustainability, United Nations WWW Document (2024). https://www.un.org/en/academic-impact/sustainability

34. Nguyen, L.T., Thanh, C.L.: The influence of board characteristics on environmental performance: evidence from East Asian manufacturing industries. Int. J. Emerg. Mark. **17**(10), 2702–2720 (2022). https://doi.org/10.1108/IJOEM-07-2020-0744

35. Orazalin, N.: Do board sustainability committees contribute to corporate environmental and social performance? The mediating role of corporate social responsibility strategy. Bus. Strateg. Environ. **29**(1), 140–153 (2020). https://doi.org/10.1002/bse.2354

36. Panda, B., Leepsa, N.M.: Agency theory: review of theory and evidence on problems and perspectives. Indian J. Corp. Governance. **10**(1), 74–95 (2017). https://doi.org/10.1177/0974686217701467

37. Peters, G.F., Romi, A.M.: The association between sustainability governance characteristics and the assurance of corporate sustainability reports. Audit. J. Pract. Theor. **34**(1), 163–198 (2015)

38. Post, C., et al.: From board composition to corporate environmental performance through sustainability-themed alliances. J. Bus. Ethics **130**, 423–435 (2015). https://doi.org/10.1007/s10551-014-2231-7

39. Roberts, J.: Agency theory, ethics and corporate governance. In: Corporate governance: does any size fit? pp. 249–269. Emerald Group Publishing Limited (2005)

40. Tarus, J.K.: Do board size and firm size affect environmental accounting disclosure? Evidence from selected listed firms in kenya. Econ. Res. **4**, 1 (2020). https://doi.org/10.29226/tr1001. 2020.181

41. Tingbani, I., et al.: Board gender diversity, environmental committee and greenhouse gas voluntary disclosures. Bus Strat Env. **29**(6), 2194–2210 (2020). https://doi.org/10.1002/bse. 2495

42. Uwuigbe, U.N., et al.: The effect of board size and board composition on firms corporate environmental disclosure: a study of selected firms in Nigeria. Acta Universitatis Danubius. Œconomica. **7**, 5 (2011)

43. de Villiers, C., et al.: The effect of board characteristics on firm environmental performance. J. Manag. **37**(6), 1636–1663 (2011). https://doi.org/10.1177/0149206311411506

44. de Villiers, C., van Staden, C.J.: Where firms choose to disclose voluntary environmental information. J. Account. Public Policy **30**(6), 504–525 (2011). https://doi.org/10.1016/j.jac cpubpol.2011.03.005

Collaborative Online International Learning COIL: Trends, Definition & Typology

Susan Goeldi[ID] and Oscar Thees[(✉)][ID]

School of Business, University of Applied Sciences Northwestern Switzerland FHNW,
Riggenbachstrasse 16, 4600 Olten, Switzerland
`oscar.thees@fhnw.ch`

Abstract. Collaborative Online International Learning (COIL) is an increasingly popular element of a modern university's internationalization strategy and an important measure for internationalization at home. COIL directly contributes to more sustainability and fairness at tertiary educational institutions, while participating students are equipped with relevant future skills in international competency. The School of Business of the University of Applied Sciences Northwestern Switzerland FHNW started to develop a COIL-program in 2023, to scale-up the preexisting COIL-courses at the school. This initiative revealed that the definition of COIL is still not fully agreed upon and that no typology of COIL has been established. To address these gaps a systematic literature review, using Swisscovery, an extensive database that includes access to databases such as ERIC, OECD library, Psyndex, Teacher Reference Center, WISO and Web of Science was conducted. Based on the findings of the review, a definition and a typology of COIL were developed. This definition and typology were then validated with a series of interviews with COIL experts, including COIL-researchers, COIL-service providers and COIL-champions, meaning COIL-coordinators with experience in setting up dozens of COIL-courses. Based on the findings from the eight interviews the definition and typology were revised. The article shows the increase in the literature on COIL and most frequently addressed themes, such as case studies, assessment, effectiveness, and efficiency. In addition, it presents the synopsis of the experts' feedback together with a definition of COIL based on characteristics relating to collaborators, blending with physical exchange and facilitation.

Keywords: COILtrends · COILdefinition · COILtypology · COILbenefits · internationalization at home · virtual exchange

1 Introduction

Collaborative Online International Learning (COIL) is becoming increasingly popular as part of a modern university's internationalization strategy, particularly as an internationalization at home measure. Internationalization at home is seen as a complement to traditional student exchanges. The latter has been an integral part of university life for more than three decades and its European label, Erasmus, is well known. Internationalization at home, on the other hand, only gained momentum during the Covid-19

© The Author(s), under exclusive license to Springer Nature Switzerland AG 2025
K. Hinkelmann and H. Smuts (Eds.): Society 5.0 2024, CCIS 2173, pp. 152–172, 2025.
https://doi.org/10.1007/978-3-031-71412-2_12

pandemic due to travel restrictions and the accelerated digital transformation of the education sector. Increasingly, it is driven by efforts to bring more sustainability and equity to participation in education. Both are related to internationalization at home in general and COIL in particular, as not all students can study abroad for sustainability and personal reasons, but all students should be given the opportunity to acquire intercultural competences.

Intercultural competences are seen as an important part of study success, personal development to become a member of the globalized society and relevant for the labor market. Oberhelman & Dunn [1] claim that first-generation and minoritized students in particular benefit from COIL achieving better grades and increasing their chances of graduation. The DAAD study [2], which examines the impact of international experience on the career success of university graduates in the German labor market, finds an increase in opportunities that can promote career success. The annual report of the Swiss Mobility Agency [3. p. 14] states that approximately 15% of tertiary students in Switzerland study abroad for an extended period. Switzerland ranks fourth place in the OECD ranking of international student mobility [4], with an average percentage much higher than the OECD average of around 10% (over the period from 2013–2020). It is undeniable that there is a significant gap between the "mobile few and the grounded many" [5] (p. 354), highlighting the urgent need for innovative approaches to the internationalization of higher education.

With this in mind, the School of Business at the University of Applied Sciences FHNW started to set up a COIL program in 2023 to expand the few existing COIL. A grant from the Swiss Mobility Agency, Movetia, was awarded to support this project. It is a work in progress that will continue until the end of 2025. In this paper we present the results of the first stage of the project: a comprehensive literature review and results of a series of interviews with COIL experts. Both aimed to provide a well-supported definition of COIL and a typology to categorize COIL. We had hoped to find typologies or classifications or models of COIL-types (hereinafter referred to as typologies) in the literature but didn't. So, we constructed one and asked COIL experts to comment on it. The main desired benefits of the typology are to help lecturers develop a COIL and to communicate the type of COIL to students and the interested public. While the COIL definition answers the question: What are the main features of a COIL in general, the typology should help to answer the question: What are the specific features of a particular COIL?

2 Methodology

The systematic literature review was conducted between July 2023 and February 2024 and focused on finding the main topics discussed in relation to COIL and the main characteristics of COIL, to define and categorize COIL. We were specifically looking for typologies to categorize COIL and/or to describe different types of COIL. Aware of the comprehensive "Virtual Exchange Typology", which provides a glossary and a framework for describing virtual exchange courses [6], we were looking for a lean model specifically for COIL to identify distinguishing features in order to quickly capture and communicate course characteristics. In a systematic search of databases with particular relevance to the field of education and educational management, we focused on the following databases: OECD Library, ERIC, Psyindex, Teacher Reference Center, Web of Science, FISBildung and WISO – the latter two providing articles in German. We limited the search to papers published in 2018 and later, with an overlap of two years with the meta-analysis by Barbosa & Ferreira [7] to cover the period before, during and after the Covid19 pandemic.

Approach to Literature Review

As well as searching for the key phrase "collaborative online international learning" and combinations of variations such as international AND student AND learning AND online, we also searched for the abbreviation COIL. As this is often related to chemistry, biology, medicine, and technology using so-called peptides, a "coiled" molecular structure, we searched for the abbreviation COIL combined with NOT e.g. physics. Lastly, the search included combinations of "virtual exchange" AND collaboration, also AND co-teaching, as virtual exchange has been established as the umbrella term that includes COIL [8]. We clustered the results using the time of publication and keywords to identify trend peaks and trending topics. Therefore, we have adopted an approach that first defines a population of COIL-related literature and then clusters this literature into groups in order to understand the different emphases in the COIL literature.

The literature population was defined by filtering the collected literature from the literature review (N = 144) according to specific criteria, i.e. COIL describing words that are used interchangeably to describe COIL (cf. [7, p. 575]). Thus, the literature sample included papers that contained the words "COIL", "collaborative online learning", "collaborative online international learning", "international collaborative learning", "virtual exchange", "telecollaboration", "global virtual team" and "virtual collaborative learning" either in the title or in the abstract. After this filtering, we ended up with a sample of n = 85 articles published 2018 to 2023. Chapter 3 summarizes the key findings of the literature review, identifies characteristics of study designs and clusters, and the benefits and challenges of COIL. To cluster topics, we used a tagging system developed for knowledge interests and implemented it in the reference management software "Zotero". Based on the literature and our previous experience with COIL we drafted a general definition and developed a COIL typology. This process has been guided less by analysis and more by intuition but is certainly inspired by the various sources included.

The sample of n = 85 articles was classified into four non-exclusive groups using a tagging system. In the group *COIL conceptual approaches* we tagged articles about COIL typologies, including different COIL model approaches and frameworks, as well as different ways of representing COIL patterns. Tagged with *COIL research* were articles containing scientific assessments and evaluations of case studies on COIL be it in quantitative or qualitative nature, as well as articles containing of concepts and approaches to the assessment and the evaluation of COIL. *COIL cases description* was used as a tag for more anecdotal reviews of COIL cases, e.g. the process of how the COIL was defined and set up, what structures were chosen to conduct what type of COIL, what technologies were used, what key roles and facilitators were needed to make the COIL a success or were lacking which made the COIL a failure or led to the abortion of the COIL. The tag *COIL benefits* was used for articles that emphasized the plethora of advantages and benefits of COIL, mostly related to the growth of students' intercultural awareness and skills.

Interview-based Validation of COIL Definition and Typology

The process of drafting the definition and typology relied on a close reading of the sample of COIL papers, to allow the fundamental characteristics of COIL to be identified, as well as the explicit or implicit themes associated with different forms of COIL to be linked to emerging COIL categories. To test and, where possible, validate our definition and typology drafts we conducted interviews with COIL experts. In eight interviews, conducted online in February 2023 we asked experts to comment on the two drafts. The expert sample was structured into three groups of experts: experts with a strong research background regarding COIL (4); COIL service providers (2); COIL champions (3). The three segments overlap, but the process promised to get feedback from key figures. Experts with a strong research background were identified via their numerous, continuous, and widely referenced contributions to this specific research area. By COIL-service providers, we refer to COIL Connect, which provides guidance on setting up COIL, monitor COIL developments of affiliated institutions and enable them to connect and share news. With COIL champions we refer to COIL coordinators or COIL developers at universities with over a hundred COIL courses according to the public member list of the COIL Connect initiative of the COIL Virtual Exchange Foundation [9]. The three segments overlap, as highly active COIL coordinators are likely to be part of a COIL services network and/or active in research and vice versa. We used a structured interview guide and shared with interviewees the drafted COIL definition and the drafted COIL typology and asked to comment on both. As evaluation criteria we used the categories "agreement" and "completeness" for the COIL definition and "acceptability" and "usefulness" for the COIL typology. In Chapter 4 we focus on the synopsis where there is agreement and discuss characteristics and aspects of disagreement in the Result and Discussion section. The final chapter provides an optimized definition and suggestions for continuing work on the typology.

3   Findings of the Literature Review

3.1   Increasing Interest in the Topic

As expected, a search on Google Scholar (compare Fig. 1, top picture) shows an increase in publication activity on COIL over the observed period. We take this as an indicator of the spread of the new concept in educational institutions. Interestingly, the first two Google search hits on the topic in 2006 refer to the CVs of scholars, suggesting that a professionalization of this field of expertise has begun. According to the Google Scholar search, the first academic papers on the topic appeared in the *Journal of Studies in Intercultural Education* in 2006 and 2007. One of them points out that internationalization is a consequence of economic and academic globalization and as such a challenge for higher education [10]. The other aims to identify elements of intercultural competence and methods of assessment [11]. In 2009, Rubin's contribution to the *3rd International Technology, Education and Development Conference,* held in March of that year in Spain

(Valencia), is listed. He presented several COIL courses he had co-developed as director of SUNY's Center for Collaborative Online International Learning[1]. Since then, the topic has grown in popularity, with publications in educational journals such as *Curriculum, Instruction and Pedagogy* [12] or *Education + Training* [13], as well as in various journals such as *The Journal for Nurse Practitioners* [14] or *Food, Culture and Society* [15]. The latter two are examples of its gaining of "mass appeal" [12].

Barbosa & Ferreira-Lopes [7] conducted a meta-analysis of research trends in the field of "telecollaboration and virtual exchange", analyzing 254 articles from the Web of Science and Scopus databases over the period of 2008 to 2020. They show that COIL is one of the terms often used interchangeably with terms such as "online intercultural exchange", "intercultural virtual collaboration" and "virtual exchange". The latter is the most used, due to an Erasmus + program to promote virtual mobility. An EU-funded large scale project, the Evolve[2] project, frames VE (for virtual exchange) as a "collaborative international form" in higher education [16, p. 20]. However, although there are contributions on the subject related to European universities and projects, the vast majority of the articles found are (still) associated with authors from US-universities, as already noted by Barbosa & Ferreira-Lopes [7]. Their presentation of the "evolutionary trend in the number of publications covering telecollaboration" during this period shows a slow start with four papers in 2008, a first peak in 2013 with just over 20 papers and then a steady increase in publication activity on the topic with more than 30 papers in the last two years of the period examined.

Notes: The Google Scholar search (top picture) for "collaborative online international learning" and "COIL", was carried out on 28 February 2024 and shows annual results from 2018 to 2023. Google Scholar is a rough indicator of increasing interest in the topic, as Google results are neither stable nor is Google's search algorithms fully known. The middle graphic shows the number of articles from the article's sample (n = 85) by year. As with the Google Scholar plot above, the increasing number of publications over the years can be seen as an indicator of growing interest in the topic, which has received a lot of attention, particularly during the global Covid19 pandemic. The bottom plot divides the middle plot into four topic clusters, demonstrating that while conceptual works are experiencing a gradual increase, other categories such as case descriptions and COIL benefits have experienced a significant surge during the pandemic.

3.2 Trending Topics

Most of the papers included in the review (2018–2023) were published in journals and conference proceedings, some as research papers related to projects in international education such as Erasmus + projects. The previous impression that many papers related to COIL describe cases and/or report experiences with COIL (42) could be verified, cf. Figure 1 (lower plot) and Fig. 2. A considerable number of papers (40) address the benefits of COIL and research (33) towards the assessment of COIL-related learnings

---

[1] SUNY is an acronym that stands for the State University of New York.

[2] The acronym EVOLVE stands for Evidence Validated Online Learning through Virtual Exchange. It is a research initiative that investigates the impact of virtual exchange (VE) in higher education, involving several research groups.

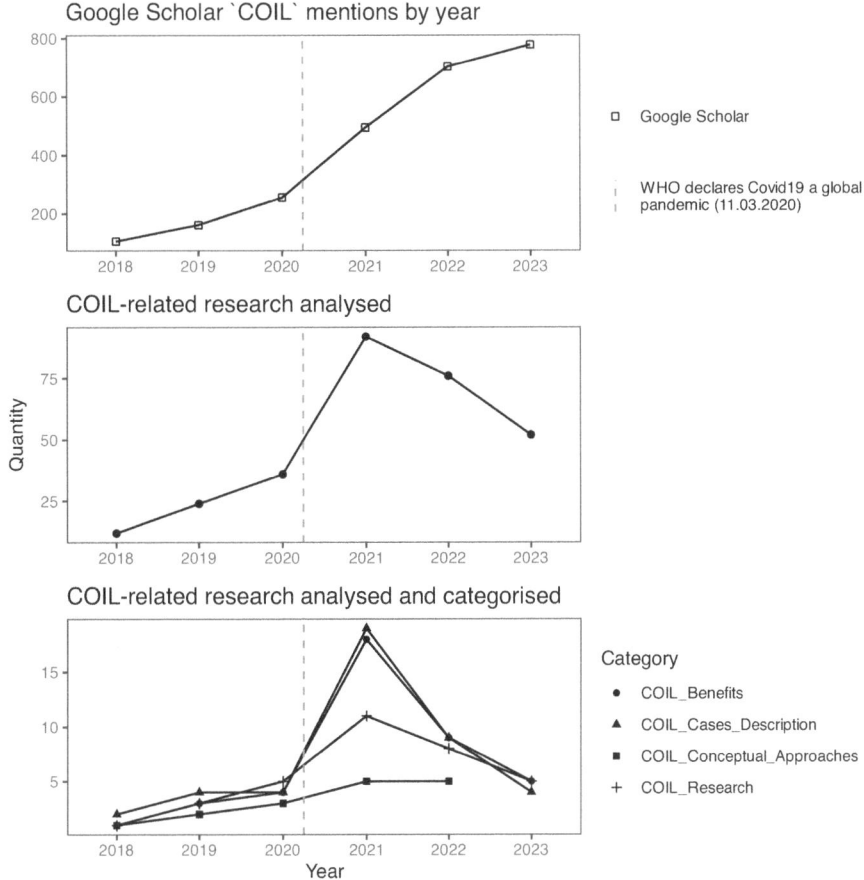

Fig. 1. COIL-related publications in the years 2018 till 2023.

often in combination with case descriptions. Fewer papers (16) deal with conceptual aspects of COIL, cf. Figure 2.

Notes: 85 articles were analyzed, and central topics were clustered. The four categories are not distinct as for example case description is sometimes combined with case research or research is focused on finding specific benefits. Therefore, the sum in the plot is higher than 85.

3.3   Case Studies and COIL Research

COIL studies often involve class size samples, and the research is primarily concerned with assessing the impact on learners. Accordingly, research is often driven by lecturers at universities and based on their experiments, course developments and their learnings. Sample sizes are mostly n = 10 to approx. 40 (e.g. [17], n = 10; [18], n = 14/n = 21; [19], n = 17; [14], n = 29; [20], n = 30; [21], n = 33; [14], n = 34; [22], n = 35; [23], n = 35; [24], n = 39; [25], n = 43). Larger sample sizes can span COIL iterations

Distribution of the tagged Categories

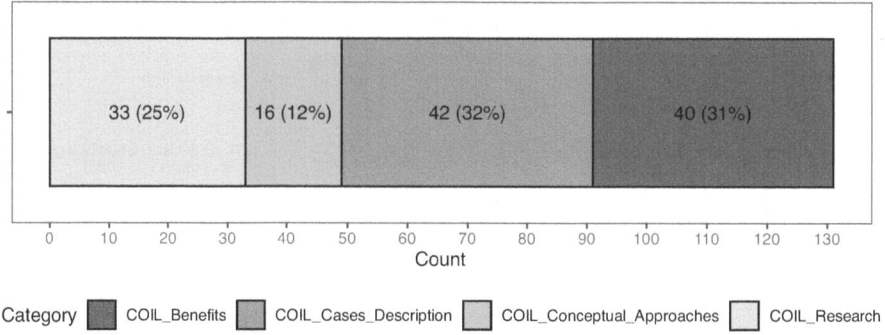

Fig. 2. Main topics in papers about COIL.

(e.g. [26], n = 64), multiple virtual exchanges (e.g. [27], n = 167) and control groups (e.g. [28], n = 106) and are often conducted by researchers. An example of the latter is the EVOLVE Project Team [16], which was conducting a study on 16 virtual exchange courses in a collaborative setting between 23 universities with data from 248 students.

Many authors use narration to share their experiences and learnings (e.g. [12, 29–32]; examples in whitepapers by Kansai Universities COIL-network[3]). Many contributions are descriptive, some with detailed descriptions of learning sequences, objectives, and activities (e.g. [14, 33, 34]). Student assessment is often based on a mixed-methods approach, using survey data from student groups, often with a pre- and post-COIL questionnaire in written or oral form, and data from written assessments or written reflections, data from observations, data from discussion boards, group discussions or interviews, mostly collected by lecturers (e.g. [27, 35, 36] or in larger studies by researchers such as the EVOLVE Project Team [16], which conducted a pre- and post-test survey, post-hoc interviews and analyzed student portfolios. Hackett et al. [28] use an elaborate setting with control groups and two established scales, the Cultural Intelligence (CQ) scale and Multicultural Personality Questionnaire (MPQ), as well as focus groups and reflection reports. Also, the Impact of Event scale (IES) has been used to measure the impact of COIL [37]. Romero-Rodríguez et al. [13] present a small study showing that the Creativity Self-efficacy scale shows that participants improved scores on creativity competence in a pre/post-COIL-test comparison. Kumi-Yeboah [38] presents a rare study on teacher experience (n = 40). The study focuses on identifying instructional strategies to facilitate COIL and on challenging factors. The study is based on interviews with the participants and summarizes results in a framework structured in design stages: planning; pedagogical strategies; inclusion of multicultural learning content; facilitation of technology and interaction.

---

[3] https://www.kansai-u.ac.jp/Kokusai/IIGE/resources/whitepaper.php.

3.4 Benefits Connected to COIL

Benefits could be clustered in several ways. We have chosen a simple way with two clusters around effectiveness (educational effects) and efficiency (costs in relation to educational effects). These two clusters may be particularly relevant to university management and strategic decisions about whether to include COIL in their internationalization at home strategy.

Effectiveness: Language Skills and Intercultural Competencies
Language teachers have been among the language skills [7]. One example is the "Cultura" project between French teachers at an American university and English teachers at a French university in 1997 which focused on intercultural aspects, inspired by the philosopher Marcel Proust "to look at the universe through the eyes of others" [39, p. 58]. Nishio et al. [40, p. 28] list sources in the introduction to their case study, that support the more than plausible assumption that foreign language skills are developed by increasing motivation to communicate with peers abroad. Although COIL has its roots in language learning [41], this seems to be a declining topic, while emerging topics are intercultural exchange and intercultural competences, as shown in a meta-analyses by Barbosa & Ferreira-Lopes [7, p. 579]. Nevertheless, the range of topics has increased over the last two decades, improving language skills remains an important benefit for students. This seems justified: when employers or graduates are asked whether they consider foreign language skills as important, they agree that they are important in the context of global business and global teams and a booster for successful carriers [2]. One of the few larger scaled studies [16, p. 104] finds "significant improvement in … communication ability, building confidence, vocabulary control, interaction, propositional precision and thematic development, goal-oriented collaboration, spoken fluency, and grammatical range and control"

Overall, the study indicates that "significant progress in most of the items [were] measured. These include use and appropriate choice of text, audio and video communication tools … strong evidence that students managed to establish a connection with others, and that they helped others establish presence and a voice and that they engaged critically with computer mediated communication…. Participants demonstrated high levels of reflexivity and empathy" [16, p. 103-106].

Anderson & Or [22, p. 8] in a recent small sample study claim a significant effect of a COIL on gains in intercultural competencies, namely: intercultural awareness, ability to understand peers with a different cultural background, overcoming biases and interacting with a culturally diverse group. This is in line with previous findings e.g. in the field of engineering or nursing (see references on this specific aspect in Anderson & Or [22]). Some researchers also refer to these general skills as employability skills (see e.g. [7, p. 562]. That makes sense not only because many societies are multicultural and therefore the work force is too, but also because international companies may prefer culturally literate employees to reduce conflict and improve performance. Hackett et al. [28, p. 4] define as intercultural competence "the ability to communicate effectively and appropriately in intercultural situations based on one's intercultural knowledge, skills and attitudes" and could measure positive effects in the intercultural intelligence.

Efficiency: Bridging the Global South-North Divide and Curriculum Development
Ben Malek [26, p. 26] claims that the newly developed interactive and collaborative
two courses proved to be an "efficient tool" for developing intercultural competencies.
Ben Malek, who works at a Tunisian university, bases this assessment on the unequal
conditions for physical mobility in the Global South e.g. with severe restrictions on visa
procedures. COIL is often associated with the issue of the South-North divide. Naicker
[42] suggests using COIL for "pluralistic internationalizations" and a means to "advance
equity, inclusion, and social justice". DeWinter & Klamer [43] present results of an
EU-funded project between five South African and five European universities (IKudu-
Project) to promote equality and decolonialization through COIL. They draw attention
to the criticisms of traditional student mobility, seen as elitist, especially because of
the necessary travel budget and travel privileges many students don't have. COIL and
internationalization at home in general is seen as a way for universities in the Global
South to develop higher education and address the hegemony of universities in the Global
North. De Wit [44, p. 15] calls on the education community to strive for a "more inclusive
and less elitist approach to internationalization", which can be achieved by focusing on
internationalization at home.

Another aspect of efficiency is the observation that through collaborative virtual
exchange, faculty can innovate their content and improve their teaching methods [45].
Thus, COIL provides a lean solution for curriculum and faculty development. Nissen &
Kurek [46, p. 44] find in their research part of the EVOLVE study focused on faculty
strong evidence that collaborative virtual exchange "has a positive impact on the development of teacher's general pedagogical competences" as well as on specific skills, such
as digital competence, collaborative virtual exchange task design and assessment. They
conclude that collaborative virtual exchange "is a powerful learning environment" for
students and teachers; it allows teachers to improve their course design skills towards
student-centered approaches, contributing to "quality teaching" [46, p. 5].

3.5 Challenges Connected to COIL

While most research is benefit-centered, several also document challenges. These can be
roughly categorized into coil-specific challenges such as collaboration across different
time zones, and coil-unspecified challenges such as digital learning or intercultural collaboration in general. Challenges include different language skills [7]. Hackett et al. [28]
also mention this in a collaboration between students from the USA and the Netherlands.
They report that Dutch students were concerned about their language proficiency. At the
same time, the fact that the Dutch students – not the students form the USA – were studying in an international program and in a foreign language seems to have had an impact on
the research results. The program in the Netherlands may have attracted more interculturally competent students and/or the program itself may have produced a higher level of
intercultural competence. Therefore, this challenge also applies to the COIL-research.
Naicker [42] identifies several major challenges, some of which are connected to the
global North-South divide. In the three COIL courses she analyzed, universities in the
Netherlands and Germany collaborated with a university in South Africa. Students from
South Africa faced technological barriers (devices, internet connectivity, digital literacy,
access to data) as well as high cultural barriers and unequal power dynamics. On the one

hand, different conflict management and student engagement in two different learning cultures are mentioned, which can widen the gap between students from different backgrounds instead of bridging it. On the other hand, COIL can provide an environment for bridging the gap due to specific COIL features such as anticipating challenges, preparing students in advance, reflecting with students on experiencing intercultural phenomena and facilitating collaborative learning. COIL therefore seems well suited to address these challenges, which exist independently of COIL. The same is true for challenges related to student motivation or student engagement. Regarding the latter there is evidence that COIL can increase student engagement [35]. COIL can therefore be seen as a cure rather than a cause of problems.

Other challenges associated with COIL are not specific to COIL either, such as the reluctance of students to asynchronous-focused learning or the flipped classroom (discussed e.g. in [17] and [47]). Whether a learning design is implemented through a traditional course or a COIL, it needs to be professional in order to engage students and facilitate learning. The EVOLVE Project Team [16, p. 105] points out that the relevant aspects of a socio-constructivist learning paradigm apply to both traditional learning and coiling: sufficient time, support, informal interaction. The study by McCollum et al. [48] focuses on finding barriers to coiling from the students' perspective. As theirs is a pre-Covid19 study, some of the barriers, particularly in the cluster technology, may be outdated, while others remain relevant. The Evolve team's large-scale study also identifies technology as a source of barriers. For example, they note that videoconferencing is very important for building collaborative relationships, but it is also the most vulnerable tool [16, p. 105]. This may remain the case for the time being, especially in regions with weekly infrastructure, but may improve over the years. McCollum et al. [48] identify a challenge due to different time zones. The challenge of time zones is often addressed in case studies (e.g. [49, 50, 51]). A successful strategy in this particular area is to address it early and to include it in the didactic framework and provide support [17]. Medina & Hestler [50] identify many more challenges – such as differences in academic culture or team building – all of which can lead to solutions and opportunities for both learners and teachers. As soon as the first teachers began to collaborate online, it became clear that lecturers needed "the same level of commitment and involvement" [39, p. 95]. A recurring challenge is that the online environment requires creativity and new ways of building and maintaining relationships between teachers and students [52]. Many challenges in COIL are therefore inherent in the concept of intercultural communication based on building relationships and trust across borders, with the added challenges of online communication.

All of these challenges require committed faculty and, at best, strategic implementation of internationalization at home to ensure that individuals and institutions go the extra mile to meet the challenges and turn them into opportunities. O'Dowd [8] notes that faculty need to be trained and incentivized to enable online intercultural exchange projects, and that such projects need to be incorporated into the university curriculum to provide appropriate incentives for students. In this context, an interesting approach is described by Suarez & Michalska Haduch [53]. They look back on a COIL with ten iterations between 2003 and 2019 with changing faculty, supporting the claim that COIL can be seen as an implementable pedagogical model that can be institutionalized.

Apart from the benefits for students, including intercultural competence in addition to enhanced critical thinking skills, learning agility and many other desired effects, they emphasize the international and professional development of faculty and staff through COIL. A similar approach with comparable effects is taken by Titarenko & Little [54] with a COIL running for 15 consecutive years.

3.6 Conceptual Approaches

One early, broad and partly conceptual approach is the book "Globally Networked Teaching in the Humanities" [55], published in 2015 providing "an overview and concrete examples of globally networked learning environments across the humanities from the perspective of all their stakeholders". Many contributions stem from the fifth COIL conference, organized by SUNY COIL center, in 2013. Conceptual approaches work with learning theories and theories from specific disciplines. A certainly comprehensive collection of practical and conceptual approaches is offered by "The Guide to COIL Virtual Exchange", edited by Rubin & Guth [56]. It contains mostly case studies, identifies and addresses relevant aspects of COIL from different perspectives in an informative and guiding way. In chapter 20, Prior & Jager [57] refer to a five-level policy model by Casanova & Price [58], published in 2018, for implementing COIL in higher education. The model starts with basic needs (financial and technical support), continues with institutional motivation, and is concluded with personal motivation of stakeholders. It was tested in a large case study with six universities that have achieved, or are trying to achieve, the institutionalization of COIL. Rubin [59, p.16] raises the question of whether COIL is a method, a model, a format or even a pedagogy. While the latter encompasses much more, the term *format* may be too strict to allow for the necessary flexibility. It could be called a *pedagogical model* or a *teaching method*. Mostly Rubin and the co-authors of "The Guide to COIL Virtual Exchange" use the term *model* with COIL. As COIL is considered a work in progress, it does not seem to lend itself to working with a template [59, p.71]. In Chapter 8, Rubin [60] describes different methods for establishing partnerships for COIL universities, developing models such as the profile outreach or request model, where COIL coordinators approach potential COIL partners to provide or request interested COIL instructors to get the process started.

A conceptual approach towards COIL is presented by Adefila et al. [61] with the introduction of EcoCOIL for "Ecologized Collaborative Online International Learning". They offer EcoCOIL- and COIL definitions, an EcoCOIL model with essential tools and principles, guidelines and a process flow when it comes to organizing an effective COIL that focuses on key competences for sustainability. Another conceptual approach in the COIL context with the ultimate goal of a more sustainable world is taken by Guimarães & Finardi [62]. They argue that the United Nations goal of global citizenship through education could be achieved through a global-national-local ('glonacal') pathway provided by COIL. Iyamu & Adelakun [63] provide a model to help build Global Virtual Teams (GVT), often linked to COIL with a problem-based approach. The model is based on literature and a COIL project that has been running for several iterations. The model includes human factors, collaborative activities and technology artefacts. Jacobs et al. [5] explored aspects of managing a COIL network (IKudu, see above in "Efficiency: Bridging the global South-North divide and curriculum") during the pandemic. Based on feedback from 15 university partners they visualize in the form of a kudu (antelope) the key elements of adapting COIL, including five clusters: strong conceptualization (e.g. building on existing networks and previous experience); enabling collective leadership (e.g. flexibility and reflectivity); thorough management and administration (e.g. dedicated project management); values (e.g. trust and openness); validating and encouraging relationships (e.g. fun and inclusivity). Salmon et al. [64] construct and test a 'map' for implementing COIL using a project management approach. They identify six model factors: common goals, actor motivation and readiness, communication routines, relationship building and organization. For each of the six factors, they define two tasks for setting up a COIL. They also identify four output elements: actor outcomes, impact, satisfaction and commitment. They rightly emphasize the importance of the triadic nature of COIL: learning course material, dealing with different cultural contexts and digital communication, and thus engaging in multifaceted personal development.

4 COIL Definition and Typology Evaluation

4.1 Results for the Definition Statement

With regard to the first evaluation criterion, "agreement," all eight respondents expressed unreserved agreement with all five definition statements. However, they did provide comments:

Statement 1: "Teachers AND students collaborate in a COIL."
    On the first statement, one respondent elaborates on the need for teachers to work together beforehand to align objectives and content.

Statement 2: "A COIL does not involve any physical exchange. It is entirely online. It may be followed by a physical exchange of teachers and/or students."
    For the second statement, there are comments about the exclusivity of online exchanges. Two respondents mention that a COIL can be preceded and not only followed by physical exchange, one of them mentions that it could also involve physical exchange. Another respondent estimates that the latter may be only true for a few percent of COIL, but it is not excluded. One respondent mentions events that could be related to COIL and inviting students for face-to-face meetings.

Statement 3: "A COIL involves teachers and students from at least two different educational institutions, which may be in different countries (international) or in different parts of one country (intercultural). The "I" in COIL can therefore stand for both international and intercultural."
    At the third statement, half of the interviewees (4) elaborate on the I for *intercultural* in the sense that it is not correct for their university's policy, not usual, not included or even should be extended to also stand for *interdisciplinary*.

Statement 4: "In COILs lecturers moderate the international collaboration and provide cultural education to facilitate collaborative learning. Collaborative learning needs to be moderated and facilitated. It does not happen naturally in an international classroom in an online setting."

For the fourth statement, one respondent would only use the term facilitate (not moderate). One respondent does not agree with the part that teachers "provide cultural education" because they are not necessarily experts in it.

Statement 5:"Lecturers moderate or initiate students' reflection on the international collaboration. They encourage reflection on students' expectations and perceptions; they conceptualize learnings, and they may add context. This process can be part of the COIL or part of the preparation beforehand or a follow-up."

For the fifth statement, one respondent tends to a possible but not necessary feature or has not yet experienced this feature.

Final comments range from "spot on" to "tons to add to it". With regard to the second evaluation criterion "completeness", the feedback focuses mainly on two aspects of COIL that are missing from the definitional statements: Half of the respondents (4) mention that the multicultural collaborative task is crucial for COIL, indicating the idea of coursework culminating in a final outcome such as a solution to a problem, a creative outcome, and/or a skill related to e.g. global citizenship. Two respondents mention that it should be explicitly stated that COIL is an integral part of the curriculum or integrated as part of a university's internationalization program at home. Finally, one comment mentions that COIL is a spectrum of activities. Another comment mentions that the facilitation to collaborate through technology is missing in the definition.

4.2   Results for the Draft Typology (See Appendix 1)

With regard to the first evaluation criterion "acceptability", half of the respondents (4) think that the draft is suitable for describing and sorting COIL. One respondent agrees with the draft, with the caveat that terms (such as "global virtual teams") need to be very clearly defined and that although small COIL are possible, they are not usually the case, but COIL tend to last 6 to 8 weeks. Two respondents think that the draft applies to a virtual exchange typology, not a COIL typology. It is also mentioned that e.g. e-tandems belong to virtual exchange in general. One respondent also mentions that COIL is more complex than the draft suggests. One of the interviewees would have to study it in depth before agreeing or disagreeing with it, mentioning that the categories overlap in terms of modes of collaboration. The four respondents who partially or completely disagree with the draft suggest different ways forward or, in one case, reject the concept. One of the participants suggests using the length (4–8) weeks to distinguish COIL from other approaches under the umbrella term "virtual exchange". It is added that the number of synchronous and asynchronous student meetings could also play a role. One comment is that a typology should focus less on tools and more on collaboration and tasks. A general comment is that it needs more thought and should be connected to existing virtual exchange frameworks.

With regard to the second evaluation criterion "usefulness", i.e. whether the typology would be considered helpful for lecturers in setting up COIL, the same respondents agreed that the typology would be useful (4). Two respondents partially agree that a typology would be helpful, implying that the draft needs to be improved. One respondent is generally skeptical about developing something useful to meet everyone's needs because of the didactic diversity in general and in terms of disciplines in particular.

One respondent rejects the usefulness of a typology as it would limit the possibilities of designing COIL instead of opening them up to innovation. The feeling of being constrained rather than empowered by a typology is shared by one respondent who partially agrees with its usefulness. This already summarizes the answers to the follow-up question "what typology would be helpful" by three experts who share a general skepticism about the acceptabilty and/or usefulness of the concept of a typology. The last question, if a typology would be helpful in communicating about COIL is supported by the five respondents who fully or partially agree with the first question. From the perspective of the skeptical experts, one of them points out that a typology would have to be tool-neutral (not referring to e.g. jam boards, padlets) as tools tend to change quickly. It is also mentioned again that it should be about student collaboration as this is the most differentiating feature of COIL.

5   Discussion

5.1   COIL Definition

The proposed definition of COIL is not controversial. It is based on the introductions in many case studies, a few conceptual approaches and the ideas developed over the years by its initiators, especially John Rubin – director of the SUNY COIL center, which was first established in 2004[4]. The COIL experts, including authors of comprehensive books on the subject, experienced coilers and researchers, supported the five defining statements and suggested few changes and additions. Especially, the first statement works very well.

As COIL are placed under the umbrella term virtual exchange according to O'Dowd [65], it is clear to the community that COIL are part of the cross-border collaboration between universities as well as completely virtual. However, experiences and examples of COIL show an openness to beneficial combinations. The second statement should therefore be formulated more openly when it comes to the combination of COIL with physical exchanges.

Regarding the suggestion to interpret the I in COIL as well as interculturally, the experts are open to the idea. It is also mentioned by Beelen & Jones [66] with their attempt to redefine "internationalization at home". They cite several sources that combine international and intercultural, or international and multicultural. In the context of developing intercultural communicative competencies (ICC), the term international is not part of the label, but of the setting when combined with virtual collaboration (e.g. [26]). Schultheis Moore & Simon [55] list different settings for Globally Networked Teaching (GNT) and conclude: "Across these different forms, the courses we feature share a commitment to combining intercultural understanding with content knowledge". One consideration in integrating intercultural was to explicitly include intra-national collaboration in a multicultural society such as Switzerland with its four national languages. Therefore, we propose to keep *intercultural* in statement 3.

Regarding the one comment on the fourth and fifth statements we found many case studies (e.g. [18, 67]) that agree that students need to be prepared and supported for successful COIL, especially when it comes to intercultural awareness and open exchange

---

[4] https://coil.suny.edu/

across borders. Ben Malek [26, p. 81] plans as the first two stages in the development of collaborative and interactive virtual exchange courses, a preparation phase in which students are assisted in becoming aware of their own cultural preconditions and a reflection phase in which students are encouraged to accept differences and to view them as an enrichment. Accordingly, lecturers act as "cultural mediators" (p.83). Gutiérrez et al. [27] refer to O'Dowd's three stages of mentoring: pre-virtual exchange, during and post-virtual exchange. They also provide guidance in their "Mentoring Handbook for Virtual Exchange Teachers" based on research. Therefore, even though specialist lectures may lack expertise in intercultural or international education, we consider it as an important and accepted feature of COIL that faculty should provide cultural education. When it comes to institutionalizing internationalization at home this has to be considered and the seriousness of an institution to implement it in the curriculum could be measured by the expertise of lecturers in this specific field. This expertise can be recruited and be part of the employment policy and/or trained as part of personal development of the faculty.

Regarding missing features, we can understand the experts' impression that the collaborative task or outcome should be a defining characteristic. However, from reading many case studies we can see that collaborative tasks can take on many forms and do not necessarily have to be output oriented or part of a problem-based learning scenario. As representatives of a university that is first and foremost dedicated to "Bildung" in the sense of personal development we suggest excluding goal orientation or rather to stick to a general orientation towards intercultural competences. Also, the experts' remarks that COIL should be institutionalized is important as it is more sustainable to develop intracurricular innovation than extracurricular events. Nevertheless, it is more of a should than a must for the time being.

5.2 COIL Typology

With half of the experts fully agreeing with the suitability of the proposed typology and its usefulness, while the other half shared general or specific skepticism, the typology is much more controversial than the definition. The experts shared conflicting desires for a suitable and useful typology: a more suitable typology might turn out to be more complex, but to be useful a typology must be simple. It certainly seems to be a good idea to link it more to existing categories of virtual exchange in general [65] and to look for characteristics of different types of virtual exchange in terms of instructional design. The latter could focus on specific outcomes or a key outcome such as intercultural competencies and be linked to the overview by Kolm et al. [68, p. 7f].

6 Conclusion

The SUNY COIL Center and its many collaborations especially between US and South American universities, as well as the Stevens initiative launched in 2015, contributed to the network building and promotion of virtual exchange and shed light on its potential to bridge the global South-North divide. An Erasmus + program fostering virtual exchange and initiatives such as in Japan (IIGE), have additionally spread the idea of COIL around the globe. With the digitalization push and the travel restrictions during Covid19, the idea of virtual exchange in general and COIL in particular has taken hold. Many lecturers who had already coiled or started to coil during the pandemic published case studies and shared their experience. Experiences are presented both in scientific as well as descriptive ways, highlighting the benefits and challenges of coiling.

In terms of conceptualizing COIL, there are few and varied approaches that are barely connected. However, there is much agreement on the benefits of COIL, such as improving language skills, intercultural competence, and inclusiveness. There is also an awareness of the challenges, including technological barriers. The challenges are mostly seen as learning opportunities, such as learning to work successfully in global teams, dealing with new technologies and overcoming prejudices, and as inherent to COIL.

While the definition of COIL has solidified over the past twenty years it is too early to present a typology. By definition, we can present the following summary:

Lecturers AND students collaborate in a COIL. A COIL is usually conducted entirely online. It may be preceded, accompanied, or followed by a physical exchange of faculty and/or students. A COIL involves teachers and students from at least two different educational institutions, which may be in different countries (international) or in different parts of one country (intercultural). In COIL lecturers moderate the international collaboration and provide cultural mediation to facilitate collaborative learning. Lecturers moderate or initiate students' reflection on the international collaboration: they encourage reflection on students' expectations and perceptions, they conceptualize learnings, and they may add context. This process can be part of the COIL or part of the preparation beforehand or a follow-up.

More work is needed on the typology. As a first step, we will simplify our draft by abandoning the size (x axis) and instead stating that a COIL can last several weeks or a whole semester. In terms of improving and clarifying modes of collaboration (y axis), one way of categorizing could be to analyze the many case studies and cluster modes of collaboration. For this to be successful, it would be necessary to have case studies from different cultural contexts and disciplines. As this is a work in progress, we will certainly be looking more closely at the implementation and evaluation of COIL in the next phase of the ongoing project.

Acknowledgments. This study is funded by the Swiss European Mobility Program, Movetia.

Disclosure of Interests. The authors have no competing interests to declare that are relevant to the content of this article.

Appendix 1: Interview Guide Regarding the COIL Typology

The interviewees were asked to comment on the matrix shown on the slide. As an introduction to the matrix the following was offered:

The x-axis shows either-or-categories: small, medium or large. A large COIL requires a lot of collaboration and learning in an international setting. A small COIL can take many forms from a single interactive lesson/discussion in a shared classroom to a shared Padlet by two coiling lectures. Medium COIL covers the middle ground.

The y-axis shows different modes of collaboration that are common in online learning and teaching such as the virtual classroom, the use of collaborative tools or working in intercultural pairs or teams. The modes/modalities of collaboration can stand alone or be combined.

COIL-Typology / Collaboration mode (AND)	Size (OR) Small part of a course covering one or two interactive lessons or small assignments	Medium part of a course e.g. covering 3-7 weeks or up to half of the lessons/workload in a course	Large part of a course covering half of the lessons/workload of a course up to whole courses
Interactive lesson/s in an international/intercultural virtual classroom (synchronous)			
Assignments for international/intercultural pairs (E-tandems) (synchronous/asynchronous)			
Assignments for Global virtual teams (GVTs) (synchronous/asynchronous)			
Working with collaborative tool/s such as Padlet, whiteboard, Miro, jam board etc. as an asynchronous extension of the international virtual classroom			

As follow up questions interviewees were asked:

a) Do you think the typology shown is suitable for describing and sorting COIL?
   If no, how do you/would you systematically describe and sort COIL?
b) Do you think that **this** typology would be helpful to support lecturers in developing COIL?
   If no, what would be helpful?
c) Do you think that **this** typology would be helpful in communicating about COIL?
   If no, what would be helpful?

References

1. Oberhelman, S.M., Dunn, C.A.: Globally networked learning in a university classroom: a pilot program. Athens J. Educ. **6**(1), 1–12 (2019)
2. Konegen-Grenier, C.: Geifes, S., Steinmann, M.: Die Bedeutung von Auslandserfahrung für den Karriereerfolg von Hochschulabsolventen auf dem deutschen Arbeitsmarkt, DAAD-Wirkungsstudie (2020)

3. Movetia, Movetia - Jahresbericht 2022, 2023. Zugegriffen: 13. März 2024. Verfügbar unter. https://www.movetia.ch/news-events/grosse-unterschiede-bei-mobilitaetschancen-fuer-studierende-schweizer-hochschulen

4. OECD, International student mobility (indicator) 2013–2020 (2024). https://doi.org/10.1787/4bcf6fc3-en

5. Jacobs, L., et al.: Adapting a capacity-development-in-higher-education project: doing, being and becoming virtual collaboration. Perspect. Educ. **39**(1), 353–371 (2021). https://doi.org/10.18820/2519593X/pie.v39.i1.22

6. The Stevens initiative, Virtual exchange typology, Virtual exchange program framework (2021). https://www.stevensinitiative.org/wp-content/uploads/2021/09/Stevens-Initiative-Virtual-Exchange-Typology_090121_singlepages.pdf

7. Barbosa, M.W., Ferreira-Lopes, L.: Emerging trends in telecollaboration and virtual exchange: a bibliometric study. Educ. Rev. **75**(3), 558–586 (2021). https://doi.org/10.1080/00131911.2021.1907314

8. O'Dowd, R.: Introducing virtual student exchange in international university education, Deutscher Akademischer Austauschdienst (DAAD), Juli 2022. https://doi.org/10.46685/DAADStudien.2022.09

9. COIL Virtual Exchange Foundation, Inc., Virtual Exchange Directory (2024). Zugegriffen: 13. März 2024. https://coilconnect.org/

10. Altbach, P.G., Knight, J.: The internationalization of higher education: motivations and realities. J. Stud. Int. Educ. **11**(3–4), 290–305 (2007). https://doi.org/10.1177/1028315307303542

11. Deardorff, D.K.: Identification and assessment of intercultural competence as a student outcome of internationalization. J. Stud. Int. Educ. **10**(3), 241–266 (2006). https://doi.org/10.1177/1028315306287002

12. Ingram, L.A.: Fostering distance education: lessons from a united states-england partnered collaborative online international learning approach, Frontiers in Education, Bd. 6 (2021). Zugegriffen: 26. July 2023. https://www.frontiersin.org/articles/10.3389/feduc.2021.782674

13. Romero-Rodríguez, J.-M., Ramirez-Montoya, M.S., Glasserman-Morales, L.D., Ramos, N.-P.M.: Collaborative online international learning between Spain and Mexico: a microlearning experience to enhance creativity in complexity. Education + Training **65**(2), 340–354 (2022). https://doi.org/10.1108/ET-07-2022-0259

14. Davis, L.L., Bhatarasakoon, P., Chaiard, J., Walters, E.M., Nance, J., Mittal, M.: Use of collaborative online international learning to teach evidence-based practice. J. Nurse Practitioners **19**(5), 104498 (2023). https://doi.org/10.1016/j.nurpra.2022.11.008

15. West, H., Goto, K., Alonso, S., Trechter, S., Klobodu, S.: Evaluation of a collaborative online international learning (COIL): a food product analysis and development project. Food Culture Society, May, 2022. https://doi.org/10.1080/15528014.2022.2069441

16. EVOLVE Project Team, the impact of virtual exchange on student learning in higher education, EVOLVE Project publication (2020)

17. Kučerová, K.: Benefits and challenges of conducting a collaborative online international learning class (COIL). Int. J. Stud. Educ. **5**(2), 193–212 (2023)

18. Vahed, A.: Factors enabling and constraining students' collaborative online international learning experiences. Learn. Environ. Res. **25**(3), 895–915 (2022). https://doi.org/10.1007/s10984-021-09390-x

19. Vahed, A., Rodriguez, K.: Enriching students' engaged learning experiences through the collaborative online international learning project. Innov. Educ. Teach. Int. **58**(5), 596–605 (2021). https://doi.org/10.1080/14703297.2020.1792331

20. Asojo, A.O., Kartoshkina, Y., Amole, D., Jaiyeoba, B.: Multicultural learning and experiences in design through the collaborative online international learning (COIL) framework. J. Teach. Learn. Technol. **8**, 5–16 (2019)

21. Inada, Y.: Collaborative online international learning classes to enhance co-creation in Canada and Japan. J. Educ. Learn. **11**(4), 15–30 (2022)
22. Anderson, A., Or, J.: Fostering intercultural effectiveness and cultural humility in adult learners through collaborative online international learning. Adult Learn. June 2023. https://doi.org/10.1177/10451595231182447
23. Harris, J.M., Seo, M., McKeown, J.S.: Global competency through collaborative online international learning (COIL). In: 7th International Conference on Higher Education Advances (HEAd 2021). Domenech, J., Merello, P., DeLaPoza, E. Hrsg., Valencia: Univ Politecnica Valencia, pp. 1351–1358 (2021). Zugegriffen: 26. Juli 2023. http://ocs.editorial.upv.es/index.php/HEAD/HEAd21/paper/view/13080
24. Marzetti, M.: Cross-cultural perspectives on privacy law: reflections after a Franco-American virtual education-collaborative online international learning experience. Southern Illinois Univ. Law J. **46**, 113 (2021)
25. Kuzmina, S.A., Foo Sue, F., Matviienko Olha, V., Glazunova, T.V.: Advancing internationalization agenda amidst the war in Ukraine: kindness and trauma-informed teaching project in teacher education. In: gehalten auf der 9th International Conference on Higher Education Advances (HEAd 2023) Universitat Politecnica de Valencia, Valencia, vol. 2023, (2023). https://headconf.org/head23book/head23book.pdf
26. Ben Malek, D.: Internationalisation at home through virtual collaborative learning. In: IJMKL, Bd. 12, Juli 2023. https://doi.org/10.53615/2232-5697.12.S79-87
27. Gutiérrez, B.F., Glimäng, M.R., Sauro, S., O'Dowd, R.: Preparing students for successful online intercultural communication and collaboration in virtual exchange. J. Int. Stud. **12**(S3), Art. Nr. S3, (2022). https://doi.org/10.32674/jis.v12iS3.4630
28. Hackett, S., Janssen, J., Beach, P., Perreault, M., Beelen, J., van Tartwijk, J.: The effectiveness of collaborative online international learning (COIL) on intercultural competence development in higher education. Int. J. Educ. Technol. High. Educ. **20**(5) (2023). https://doi.org/10.1186/s41239-022-00373-3
29. Anderson, A.: Reflecting on training to facilitate collaborative online international learning courses. JSE **5**(2), 6–13 (2022). https://doi.org/10.9743/JSE.2022.5.2.2
30. Callahan, C.: Adding international elements to a social studies teacher education program. Soc. Stud. **113**(6), 271–282 (2022). https://doi.org/10.1080/00377996.2022.2053831
31. Forward, M.L.: Virtual engagement--real-world impact: how students are working with communities across the globe despite the pandemic. Liber. Educ. **107**(3) (2021). https://www.aacu.org/liberaleducation/articles/virtual-engagement-real-world-impact
32. Hautala, J., Schmidt, S.: Learning across distances: an international collaborative learning project between Berlin and Turku. J. Geogr. High. Educ. **43**(2), 181–200 (2019). https://doi.org/10.1080/03098265.2019.1599331
33. Mackey, T.P., Aird, S.M.: Integrating metaliteracy into the design of a collaborative online international learning (COIL) course in digital storytelling. Open Praxis **13**(4), 397–403 (2021)
34. Jie, Z., Pearlman, A.M.G.: Expanding access to international education through technology enhanced collaborative online international learning (COIL) courses. Int. J. Technol. Teach. Learn. **14**(1), 1–11 (2018)
35. Miller, B.T., Goeldi, S., Lin, M.H.: Increasing student engagement with COIL Padlet. In: In: 9th International Conference on Higher Education Advances, Valencia, Spain (2023)
36. King Ramírez, C.: Influences of academic culture in collaborative online international learning (COIL): differences in Mexican and U.S. students' reported experiences. Foreign Lang. Ann. **53**(3), 438–457 (2020). https://doi.org/10.1111/flan.12485
37. Liu, Y., Shirley, T.: Without crossing a border: exploring the impact of shifting study abroad online on students learning and intercultural competence development during the COVID-19 Pandemic. Online Learn. **25**(1), 182–194 (2021)

38. Kumi-Yeboah, A.: Designing cross-cultural collaborative online learning framework for online instructors. Online Learn. **22**(4), 4 (2018). https://doi.org/10.24059/olj.v22i4.1520

39. Furstenberg, G., Levet, S., English, K., Maillet, K.: Giving a virtual voice to the silent language of culture: the cultura project. Lang. Learn. (2001). https://www.lltjournal.org/item/10125-25113/

40. Nishio, T., Fujikake, C., Osawa, M.: Language learning motivation in collaborative online international learning: an activity theory analysis. J. Virt. Exchange **3**, 27–47 (2020). https://doi.org/10.21827/jve.3.35780

41. O'Dowd, R.: Emerging trends and new directions in telecollaborative learning. CALICO **33**(3) (2016). https://doi.org/10.1558/cj.v33i3.30747

42. Naicker, A.: Sustaining opportunities and mutual partiality through collaborative online international learning in South Africa. Policy Futures Educ. 14782103231176359 (2023). https://doi.org/10.1177/14782103231176359

43. DeWinter, A., Klamer, R.: Can COIL be effective in using diversity to contribute to Equality? Experiences of iKudu, a European-South African consortium operating via a decolonised approach to project delivery. Research-publishing.net. La Grange des Noyes, 25110 Voillans, France. e-mail: info@research-publishing.net. http://research-publishing.net (2021)

44. De Wit, H.: Internationalization in higher education. A critical review. Boston College, Center for International Higher Education, Dez. 2019. https://journals.lib.sfu.ca/index.php/sfuer/article/view/1036/696

45. Baroni, A.: Evaluating the impact of virtual exchange on initial teacher education: a European policy experiment. Research-publishing.net, Voillans, France, März 2019. https://doi.org/10.14705/rpnet.2019.29.9782490057337

46. Nissen, E., Kurek, M.: The impact of virtual exchange on teachers' pedagogical competences and pedagogical approach in higher education, Evolve Project Publication (2020). http://hdl.handle.net/11370/bb89998b-c08b-41f4-aee6-08faf1208433

47. Chaudhury, P.: Asynchronous learning design—lessons for the post-pandemic world of higher education. J. Econ. Educ. **54**(2), 214–233 (2023). https://doi.org/10.1080/00220485.2023.2174233

48. McCollum, B., Morsch, L., Shokoples, B., Skagen, D.: Overcoming barriers for implementing international online collaborative assignments in chemistry. Can. J. Scholarship Teach. Learn. **10**(1) (2019). Zugegriffen: 24. Juli 2023. https://eric.ed.gov/?id=EJ1218782

49. Miller, E., Ceballos, H., Engelmann, B., Schiffler, A., Batres, R., Schmitt, J.: Industry 4.0 and international collaborative online learning in a higher education course on machine learning. In: 2021 Machine Learning-Driven Digital Technologies for Educational Innovation Workshop, pp. 1–8, Dez. 2021. https://doi.org/10.1109/IEEECONF53024.2021.9733776

50. Medina, A.L., Hestler, C.: How a challenge is also a chance: shaping teacher education through collaborative online international learning. Ludwigsburger Beiträge zur Medienpädagogik **21**, 1–16 (2021). https://doi.org/10.21240/lbzm/21/08

51. Mundel, J.: International virtual collaboration in advertising courses: building international and intercultural skills from home. J. Advert. Educ. **24**(2), 112–132 (2020). https://doi.org/10.1177/1098048220948522

52. Murdoch-Kitt, K.M., Emans, D.J.: Making the virtual tangible: using visual thinking to enhance online transnational learning. In: Virtual Exchange: Towards Digital Equity in Internationalisation, 1. Aufl., M. Satar, Hrsg., Research-publishing.net, pp. 85–100 (2021). https://doi.org/10.14705/rpnet.2021.53.1292

53. Suarez, E.D., Michalska Haduch, A.: Teaching business with internationally built teams. J. Teach. Int. Bus **31**(4), 312–336 (2020). https://doi.org/10.1080/08975930.2020.1851625

54. Titarenko, Л.Г., Little, К.Б.: An asynchronous university distance course as a possible model for international online collaboration. Мир России **30**(1), 1 (2021). https://doi.org/10.17323/1811-038X-2021-30-1-134-150

55. Schultheis Moore, A., Simon, S.: Globally Networked Teaching in the Humanities Theories and Practices. Routledge, London (2015). https://www.routledge.com/Globally-Networked-Teaching-in-the-Humanities-Theories-and-Practices/Moore-Simon/p/book/9781138084650

56. Rubin, J., Guth, S.: The Guide to Coil Virtual Exchange. Routledge, London (2022)

57. Prior, C., Jager, S.: The implementation and sustainability of coil at research and research-aspiring universities. In: The Guide to Coil Virtual Exchange (2022)

58. Casanova, D., Price, L.: Moving towards sustainable policy and practice – a five level framework for online learning sustainability | progresser vers des politiques et des pratiques durables : un cadre à cinq niveaux pour un apprentissage en ligne durable. In: CJLT/RCAT, Bd. 44, Nr. 3, Dez. 2018. https://doi.org/10.21432/cjlt27835

59. Rubin, J.: Collaboration. In: The Guide to Coil Virtual Exchange (2022)

60. Rubin, J.: Developing effective international institutional partnerships for coil virtual exchange. In: The Guide to Coil Virtual Exchange (2022)

61. Adefila, A.: Ecologized collaborative online international learning: tackling wicked sustainability problems through education for sustainable development. J. Teach. Educ. Sustain. **23**(1), 41–57 (2021)

62. Guimarães, F.F., Finardi, K.R.: Global citizenship education (GCE) in internationalisation: COIL as alternative Thirdspace. Globalisation, Soc. Edu. **19**(5), 641–657 (2021). https://doi.org/10.1080/14767724.2021.1875808

63. Iyamu, T., Adelakun, O.: A global virtual team model to improve software development collaboration project. Inf. Syst. E-Bus Manage. **19**(3), 937–956 (2021). https://doi.org/10.1007/s10257-021-00530-7

64. Salmon, J., Satoğlu, E.B., Ogutu, V., Thurston, P.: Teaching international business skills across US and Kenya: a model for international collaboration. J. Teach. Int. Bus. **33**(2–3), 127–148 (2022). https://doi.org/10.1080/08975930.2022.2123427

65. O'Dowd, R.: From telecollaboration to virtual exchange: state-of-the-art and the role of UNI-Collaboration in moving forward. J. Virt. Exchange **1**(1), 1–23 (2018). https://doi.org/10.14705/rpnet.2018.jve.1

66. Beelen, J., Jones, E.: Redefining internationalization at home. In: Curaj, A., Matei, L., Pricopie, R., Salmi, J., Scott, P. (eds.) The European Higher Education Area. Springer, Cham, pp. 59–72, January 2015. https://doi.org/10.1007/978-3-319-20877-0_5

67. Singh, E., Naicker, A., van Genugten, T.: Collaborative online international learning (COIL): preparedness and experiences of South African students. Innov. Educ. Teach. Int. **59**(5), 499–510 (2021). https://doi.org/10.1080/14703297.2021.1895867

68. Kolm, A.: International online collaboration competencies in higher education students: a systematic review. J. Stud. Int. Educ. **26**(2), 1–19 (2021). https://doi.org/10.1177/102831532110162

Towards a Sustainable Future: Understanding Green Consumerism in Mauritius

Leenshya Gunnoo[1]([✉]) [iD], Eric Bindah[2] [iD], and Nousrat Banu Emambocus[2]

[1] University of Technology Mauritius, Port Louis, Mauritius
leenshya.gunnoo@utm.ac.mu
[2] University of Mauritius, Port Louis, Mauritius

Abstract. The global energy landscape is undergoing significant transformation, spurred by factors such as the Russian invasion of Ukraine and the imperative for sustainability. Mauritius, a small island nation, faces the challenge of transitioning to renewable energy sources amidst limited conventional energy options. While governmental initiatives aim to promote renewable energy adoption, individual household contributions to this endeavor remain understudied. This research addresses this gap by evaluating Mauritian consumer purchasing behavior regarding green home energy solutions and their utilization of government incentives. The study aims to determine the level of knowledge, beliefs, and understanding of green energy products among Mauritians, along with their buying habits and socio-demographic influences. Additionally, it seeks to identify factors influencing purchasing behavior towards greener energy habits at home and pinpoint the most influential factor promoting green consumerism in this context. Through surveys conducted among Mauritian individuals, the research intends to sensitively promote the importance of transitioning to sustainable lifestyles and green energy consumption. Ultimately, this endeavor aims to contribute to Mauritius' renewable energy mix, supporting the government's objectives for sustainable development and a greener future. By fostering a culture of green consumerism, the research endeavors to enhance Mauritius' standard of living and quality of life while mitigating environmental degradation and energy dependency on polluting sources.

Keywords: Purchasing behaviour · Renewable energy · green home energy · Mauritius

1 Introduction

With the energy demand increasing at an unprecedented rate, irreplaceable energy sources are also being depleted rapidly resulting in an alarming situation whereby alternative sustainable energy sources have to be explored and energy saving practices and habits have to be adopted so as to transform lives and economies while at the same time leave a cleaner planet Earth for the future generations [1–3].

In the case of Mauritius, it is a primary concern to become self-sufficient in terms of energy needs by developing independent sources of renewable energy [4]. With regards to

© The Author(s), under exclusive license to Springer Nature Switzerland AG 2025
K. Hinkelmann and H. Smuts (Eds.): Society 5.0 2024, CCIS 2173, pp. 173–186, 2025.
https://doi.org/10.1007/978-3-031-71412-2_13

the use of renewable energies in households, the Government of Mauritius has announced various projects like the installation of solar panels on low-income families' houses, provision for individuals and companies to sell the excess green electricity straight to the Central Electricity Board (CEB) [5, 6]. Furthermore, long-term measures and targets as well as motivations for Mauritius to put at the forefront environmental, social and corporate governance have been announced which will result into future sustainable development and economic strategy [7].

The aim of this research is to evaluate the consumer's purchasing behavior of Mauritians, especially with regards to green home energy solutions while benefitting from the government incentives. Furthermore, several elements that affect the purchasing behavior of Mauritians towards green home energy solutions despite the high initial investment accompanying the green energy option for households instead of electricity or gas for energy production at home will also be studied. This study's objectives are to examine green consumer behavior in Mauritius with regards to green home energy solutions. By studying the green consumer behavior in Mauritius while bearing in mind to build on the factors contributing the most to promote green purchasing behavior among Mauritians, inhabitants will be sensitized about the importance of shifting to a more sustainable and greener lifestyle instead of investing in polluting sources of energies at home. As a result of endorsing Mauritians to shift to REs, this study will contribute to the RE mix of the country which will help the government to achieve its set objectives and targets in terms of green non-polluting energy consumption across the island. Ultimately, the objective of this research is to make Mauritius a greener and more sustainable island with not only a better standard of living but also an improved quality of life.

2 Review of Literature

2.1 Factors Affecting Consumer Purchasing Behavior Towards Green Products

Green consumer behavior involves actions undertaken by a person, either individually or in a collective scenario, in favor of the conservation of natural resources and with the intention to obtain a better environmental quality [7]. Numerous environmental issues that consumers encounter have caused a shift in purchasing behavior from traditional to more environmentally friendly habits [8–10].

Koger [11], and Brewer & Stern [12] have all used the theory of planned behavior (TPB), which makes the assumption that people behave rationally based on their attitudes, subjective norms, and perceived behavioral control [13]. To investigate environmental problems, TPB has been applied in distinct studies. Since the theory encourages the investigation of attitudes, cultural and personal components, and conscious behavior control, Kalafatis et al., [14] investigated the TPB to find potential implications on consumers' intentions to purchase environmentally friendly items.

In addition, one of the primary theoretical approaches in marketing is the theory of consumer behavior, which postulates that three things influence customers' decisions to buy [11]. Individual traits, societal circumstances, and psychological considerations are some of them. Since consumer behavior theory explains consumer behavior, green purchase intention may be understood as a form of embodiment of consumer purchase behavior [11, 15]. Other than psychological and sociocultural factors, product-related factors were also a factor driving consumers' desire to participate in the green consumption culture [15–18].

2.1.1 Green Product Orientation

Green product orientation (GPO) is the term used to describe an individual's strong sympathies for natural or eco-friendly items that pose no health risks. According to a study by Sony and Ferguson [19], customers' attitudes about purchasing green products are influenced by their GPO. Furthermore, additional studies discovered that GPO acknowledges a person's personal attitude toward consuming green products [14, 20]. Similarly, Amin et al., [21] found a strong correlation between GPO and pro environmental behavior, and Danso et al., [22] and Wickramasinghe [23] observed that GPO had a significant influence on consumers' attitudes toward buying green products. Yu and Huo [24] also found a positive correlation between GPO and green management mindset. Buying ecologically friendly products is another outcome of having a positive attitude toward the environment [25–27]. Therefore, those who truly care about the environment are likely to take the required actions to stop further environmental degradation. There is a strong correlation between green product attitudes and consumption [28]. Therefore, the following hypothesis is proposed: H1: GPO has a positive effect on Consumer Green Purchasing Behavior (CGPB).

2.1.2 Social Influence

When people alter their beliefs to satisfy the expectations of product consumption, this is known as social influence (SI). While people's cultural and traditional trends as well as commercial media have a significant impact on society, SI can also come from obedience, conformity, peer pressure, sales, or marketing. People may develop attitudes toward consuming green products and behavioral intentions as a result of these variables [28]. In reality, as customers live in a social environment and are surrounded by one another, this could affect one another's decision to choose environmentally friendly goods and services [29]. Before deciding to buy a green product, customers who are purchasing a new product from the market consult with friends and family [30].

Also, peer influence and parental influence are the two categories into which social influence can be subdivided, according to earlier research by Lee [31]. Nonetheless, given that families are seen as among the most significant origins according to personal standards and beliefs, family is categorized as an external element that directly influences the products that are bought [32]. Consequently, there is a clear correlation between family and environmental knowledge and purchasing behavior [32, 33]. The popularity of a product in society is also significantly influenced by SI [24, 34].

Social impact directly affects a consumer's attitudes and developed from the perceived social pressure that shapes an individual's views [13, 35–37]. According to some earlier research, SI has a favorable effect on people's attitudes [28, 38]. Furthermore, according to Choshaly [39], SI has a big impact on consumers' intentions to make green purchases. In contrast, Rimadias [40] found no evidence of a significant relationship between SI and customers' intentions to purchase environmentally friendly items because consumers continue to place a higher value on the benefits of using these products than on the SI they receive [41]. Similarly, studies conducted Achchuthan et al., [42] respectively did not find a substantial correlation between social impact and intentions to make green purchases. Hence, H2: SI has a positive effect on CGPB.

2.1.3 Green Product Pricing

Price can play a significant role in the formation of brand perceptions, particularly with regard to value and prestige [16, 29]. Although many consumers are generally concerned about environmental safety and even their health; they are also extremely price sensitive towards green product pricing (GPP) [25, 43]. Product cost is a vital factor considered when willing to pay more for green products especially when there is lesser brand awareness of eco-friendly [44]. In some cases, customers who are concerned about ecological problems, are agreeable to pay more to be eco-responsible but businesses have to improve their products' performance and environment friendliness, even though the price has to be increased [25]. However, some customers do not agree to pay more for green products [45].

Sena [46] conducted a survey and discovered that 55% of consumers in 60 countries are willing to pay more for products made by environmentally responsible businesses. Normally, consumers will only pay more for a product that is of higher quality. Furthermore, Purohit's [16] study found that consumers were willing to spend even more for environmentally friendly items because they pollute the environment less than conventional ones. It's also important to remember that, depending on the item's value, customers' readiness to pay more for forest products with eco-labels ranges from 4.4% to 18.7% [31]. However, Miller [47] and Gan et al. [25] observed that buyers are willing to spend an additional 5% for products classified as ecologically friendly. Furthermore, D'Souza et al. [48] report an inverse link between the price premium and the likelihood of purchasing a green product.

When it comes to GPP, unfair pricing which is defined as charging either a fake price or an exorbitant price in comparison to the original price is also a significant problem [49–51]. Additionally, numerous additional researches have revealed that, frequently, marketers' overcharge for environmentally friendly goods in an irrational and opaque manner, discouraging and demotivating consumers to switch to green buying practices [52]. Therefore, H3: Higher GPP is associated with a decrease in CGPB.

2.1.4 Green Product Marketing

Green marketing, which is described as marketing operations that entail manufacturing, distinguishing, pricing, and promoting goods or services that are environmentally safe and that meet consumers' environmental needs, is a growing concern for businesses and society at large [53]. According to [54], green marketing is a set of actions that include changing the way products are produced, modifying product lines, making packaging advancements, and changing advertising through the use of green marketing tools like eco-brands, eco-labels, and environmental advertisements. These tools are crucial for improving perception and raising consumer awareness of the qualities and attributes of green products. As a result, consumers are encouraged to buy ecologically friendly goods, which lessens the harm that synthetic goods cause to the environment [55].

Marketing uses environmental labels, often known as eco-labelling, to help consumers identify green products [56]. According to study by Nik Abdul Rashid [38], consumers' willingness to buy and their understanding of green products are both positively impacted by eco-label awareness. Numerous studies that demonstrated the value of using ecological production techniques to promote and incentivize the purchasing of ecofriendly products supported this study [57, 58]. In a similar vein, Jarvi [59] discovered that eco-labeling had a major influence on customer purchasing decisions in Finland. On the other hand, additional research revealed that even if some customers understand the purpose of labelling, this does not always translate into green buying decisions [60]. Furthermore, as noted by Cherian and Jacob [61], eco-labelling is not always trusted by consumers.

Green positioning, which can be either functional or emotional, is the primary strategy used for green branding. While the emotional approach concentrates on the emotional demands of customers, the functional strategy speaks to rational minds by offering comprehensive information about the environmental benefits of products [62]. Green marketing enhances a brand's image. Suki [63] examined the effect of green brand positioning on consumer intentions in Malaysia based on earlier research and came to the conclusion that green brand positioning techniques had a major positive impact on consumer purchasing behavior. In Taiwan, too, green branding has a significant influence on consumers' intentions to make green purchases [64]. Nevertheless, Raska and Shaw [65] cast doubt on a green brand positioning strategy's efficacy. According to a US consumer study, customers may have doubts about companies' green initiatives, which could have a negative impact on their decision to buy. Finally, Cherian and Jacob [61] came to the conclusion that while consumers' perceptions of green brands are influenced, there is little proof that this view has an effect on their purchase behavior.

Advertising is an effective mean of increasing consumers' knowledge about the environment and green products allowing them to make informed decisions about the consumed products and their environmental impact; thus, an important factor to convert their purchase decisions [66]. Tariq et al., [67] came to the conclusion that, in the context of Pakistan, green advertising has a direct impact on Pakistanis' purchasing behavior and level of satisfaction after a number of previous research in other nations were carried out to ascertain the impact of green advertising on customer buying behavior. According to [68], individuals in Malaysia began to consider environmentally friendly items as a result of increased awareness of eco-labels and green advertising. Additionally, a study conducted in by Govender and Govender [69] revealed that 78% of respondents agreed that advertisements for green products are effective in raising awareness of environmental issues, and 76% agreed that such advertisements influence consumers to buy green products in order to support the environment. Accordingly, the following hypothesis is proposed: H4: GPM has a positive effect on CGPB.

3   Methodology

Since this study's main purpose is to evaluate the different factors that affects consumer's purchasing behavior towards green home energy products, the targeted population is Mauritian households. As per the available survey conducted by the Mauritius Statistics Bureau in 2022, there are currently 448,000 households in Mauritius. A sample size of 400 was obtained for this study considering a confidence level of 95% and sampling error of 5%.

Questionnaires were employed as the quantitative research approach in this study to collect data. The respondents for the online data collection were selected using a non-probability quota sampling method. The researcher established quotas to ensure representation from each of the 9 districts on the island of Mauritius. To achieve this, the researcher set a quota with an average of 45 respondents per district. An online survey strategy was used to share the questionnaire with participants once it was produced using Google Form. A total of 328 people answered the survey. All study ethics guidelines were adhered to, and questionnaires were kept private. The statistical software IBM Statistical Package for Social Sciences (SPSS) V 23.0 was used for statistical analysis. There were twenty-nine questions altogether across the seven sections of the poll. All portions of the questionnaire used a 5-point Likert scale.

Nevertheless, this research method also has a few drawbacks which may affects the results of this study. For instance, using questionnaires yields limited answers that offer less nuanced interpretations of human vision in general and more numerical descriptions than complex narratives of behavior and views. Moreover, correlations between variables and trends in the data can be shown by quantitative data, but the reason for the link cannot be explained by the data. Since the research itself doesn't offer a justification for the study's conclusion, the researcher must infer explanations for the findings from the data gathered.

4   Analysis and Discussion

In all, 328 replies were received, with about equal numbers of men and women expressing interest in participating in the poll. From the poll, 48% of respondents were women and 52% of respondents were men. Furthermore, the age range of the respondents ranged from under 25 to over 60. Nonetheless, the largest proportion of respondents, about 38.3%, were between the ages of 25 and 35, suggesting that these were young adults who were probably familiar with the idea of being green by consuming less energy in order to protect the environment for coming generations. In terms of educational attainment, around 43.4% of the sample size held an undergraduate degree. As a result, the data demonstrated the quality and accessibility of education in Mauritius, and it also suggests that 43.4% of the respondents must have learned the fundamentals of green RE sources and their significance for preventing the destruction of our current ecology at home. It has been noted that the highest percentage recorded for the Income level group is between Rs 15 001 and Rs 30 000. Even though this could be a quite decent earning, they may still find some of the green home energy products expensive to invest into without proper support from the Government. Around 61% of the respondents confirm that Mauritians are not green consumers with regards to green home energy products, and this makes the purpose of this research successful such that the most determining factor which encourage green purchasing behavior towards green home energy products is known.

When assessing the reliability of a Likert scale used in survey questionnaires with several questions, Cronbach's alpha is the most commonly used metric for internal consistency or reliability [70, 71, 72]. As a result, the Cronbach's Alpha coefficient was determined and reported for each variable as indicated in Table 1 below.

Table 1. Reliability Statistics Table

		Cronbach 's Alpha Value
Dependent Variable	CGPB	0.752
Independent Variables	GPO	0.720
	SI	0.769
	GPP	0.730
	GPM	0.826

Referring to the 'Reliability Statistics' Table 1 shown above, all Cronbach's Alpha values for all the variables indicate a high level of internal consistency for the scale selected as all the values are greater than 0.7. In addition, for the independent variable GPM, the value is above 0.8 which indicates a better level of reliability for the scale used to measure this particular variable in the survey questionnaire. Thus, the scale used to measure each variable was consistent and the items for each variable were highly interrelated with the one another whereby the items for each variable were measuring the same characteristic of that particular variable. Therefore, the data obtained through this questionnaire could be used to perform further tests to determine the relationship between the variables.

Next, a multiple linear regression analysis was performed. By fitting a line to the observed data, regression models enable researchers to determine the relationships between variables. The Model Summary for the Multiple Regression Test conducted in SPSS is displayed in Table 2 below.

Table 2. Model Summary for Multiple Regression Test

Model	R	R Square	Adjusted R Square	Std. Error of the Estimate	Durbin-Watson
1	0.710[a]	0.504	0.499	0.75823	1.969

[a]Predictors: (Constant), GPM, GPP, SI, GPO. [b]Dependent Variable: CGPB

The degree of correlation is determined by taking into account the R and R2 values displayed in Table 2. The statistical indicator of how strongly two variables is linearly related is the r value correlation, which is always between + 1 and –1. According to Rumsey et al., [74], a score close to 1 indicates a strong correlation and a value close to zero indicates a poor correlation. The R value for this study is 0.710, which indicates a high degree of association because it is closer to 1 than 0. However, in a regression model, the R2 value, also known as the coefficient of determination, is a statistical measure that establishes the percentage of variance in the dependent variable that can be accounted for by the independent variable [75]. The dependent variable CGPB of this study, has an R2 value of 0.504, which represents the amount of variance that the model (which includes the variables of GPM, GPP, SI, and GPO) explains. When expressed as a percentage, the R2 value is 50.4%, indicating that 50.4% of the variation in consumers' green buying habits can be explained by the model. In order to determine the relationship between the variables, the linear regression model looks for the best fit line. But as a perfect linear relationship can only be achieved with a correlation of 1 or -1, a value of R of 0.701 indicates that the line is not perfect. In order to establish the reliability of the linear regression line of best fit, it is necessary to analyze the residuals. Reliable findings can only be obtained under the premise that the error term for each pair of data is uncorrelated, meaning that the residual lacks any pattern. Analyzing the Durbin Watson statistic, checks for autocorrelation. A test statistic that looks for autocorrelation in the residuals returns a value between 0 and 4, with a value of 2 denoting no autocorrelation. The Durbin-Watson statistic for this study is 1.969 (approximately 2), which means that there is no autocorrelation. The analysis of the variance was also done by performing the ANOVA for Multiple Regression. The result is shown in the Table 3 below.

Table 3. ANOVA for Multiple Regression Analysis

Model	Sum of squares	df	Mean square	F	Sig
1 Regression	207.693	4	51.923	90.314	<.001[b]
Residual	204.096	355	0.575		
Total	411.789	359			

[a]Dependent Variable: CGPB. [b]Predictors (Constant): GPM, GPP, SI, GPO

The dependent variable is accurately predicted by the regression model, as demonstrated by the findings in Table 3. With an F-Statistics of 90.314 and a significance value less than 0.001, the data pointed to a significant model. Our finding is significant at the 1% significance level based on the commonly used reference point, indicating 99% confidence. The error margin is therefore small. Thus, we may say that the model as a whole contributes significantly to the explanation of changes in the dependent variable (CGPB). Out of 411.789 total sum of squares, this model with four predictors can explain 207.693 regression sum of squares. Therefore, 50.4% of the variability in the explained variables can be explained by the regression model. Additionally, since this study is comparing the contributions of each independent variable, the Beta values under the title standardized coefficients as stated in Table 4 below were taken into consideration in order to find which of the model's elements contributed to the prediction of the dependent variable.

Table 4. Coefficients for Multiple Regression Analysis

| | Unstandardized Coefficients Collinearity Statistics | | | | | | |
Model	B	Std. Error	Standardised Coefficients Beta	t	Sig	Tolerance	VIF
1 (Constant)	1.872	0.378		4.948	0.00		
GPO	0.267	0.064	0.231	3.291	0.002	0.567	1.764
SI	0.119	0.059	0.089	5.197	0.032	0.477	2.097
GPP	−0.447	0.077	−0.344	−0.24	0.008	0.555	1.803
GPM	0.326	0.053	0.279	9.213	0.023	0.680	1.470

To start with, the highest value (ignoring any negative sign) is considered. The biggest beta coefficient in this study is 0.447, which is for GPP. This suggests that when the variation described by all other variables in this model is adjusted for, this variable has the strongest unique contribution to explaining the dependent variable. Secondly, the variable GPM has a beta value of 0.326 indicating that it contributes less to explaining the dependent variable compared to GPP. SI made the lowest contribution (b = 0.119) to explaining the dependent variable while GPO has a beta value of 0.267 implying that GPO contributes to explaining the dependent variable CGPB more that SI. The VIF Statistics for all the independent variables are under the value of 10 which means that there is no problem of multicollinearity. We use the significant value to ascertain whether this number makes a unique, statistically significant contribution to the equation. Every independent variable in this study has a statistically significant unique contribution to explaining the dependent variable, as demonstrated by the significant value being less than the significant level. Additionally, to know the degree of importance each predictor has on the independent variable the regression coefficient B was analyzed. It can be seen that GPP has a negative value which means that if the independent variable increases by 1 unit, consumer's green purchasing habit will decrease by 0.447 units. For GPO, SI and GPM an increase of 1 unit in the independent variable will increase the dependent variable by 0.267, 0.119 and 0.326 respectively.

5   Conclusion and Recommendation

The research findings highlight key insights for marketers and businesses regarding consumer behavior towards eco-friendly products and environmental sustainability. The study provides guidance on involving consumers in sustainability efforts through the purchase of green home energy products, which can promote green energy and reduce fossil fuel dependency. The study identified several factors affecting green purchase behavior. The main factors are Green Product Price (GPP), Green Product Marketing (GPM), Green Product Opportunity (GPO), and Social Influence (SI). GPP had the most significant negative impact, indicating that high prices deter consumers from buying green products. GPM was the second most influential factor, suggesting that effective marketing can encourage green purchases, but current advertising in Mauritius is insufficient. GPO also positively influenced green purchases but was less significant compared to other factors. Respondents recognized the importance of protecting the environment but prioritized price due to income constraints. SI had the least impact in this study, contrasting with findings from other countries, possibly due to limited accessibility and awareness of green products in Mauritius. In fact, looking back at earlier research, it was discovered in many of them that consumers' green purchasing behavior was positively impacted by low price sensitivity, whereas consumers' green buy behavior was negatively impacted by high price sensitivity [76, 77].

The study provides a comprehensive understanding of factors influencing green purchase behavior, highlighting incentives and obstacles. It offers valuable insights for marketers and policymakers on consumer purchasing patterns for green home energy products in Mauritius. The key implications include the need for marketers to understand elements driving and impeding green purchases to develop effective strategies and for policymakers to promote green products through financial assistance and environmental education to address the main obstacle—price.

It is recommended that policy makers should promote affordable green products and encourage environmental sustainability, developing innovative and practical eco-friendly products, and increasing consumer awareness through education and advertising. Trust can be built by ensuring sellers also use green products, and subsidies can reduce prices, facilitating economies of scale. Retailers should ensure a variety of eco-friendly products are conveniently available, and regulations should prevent the import of low energy-efficient appliances while monitoring eco-labeling credibility.

The study has limitations, such as potential bias in online surveys, the broad scope covering various products, the dynamic nature of consumer behavior requiring longitudinal studies, and the consideration of only four predictors due to resource constraints. Future research should use more representative samples, validate findings with additional factors, explore situational effects, and further analyze how price affects different age groups. Empirical studies on identified drivers and obstacles are also recommended to develop new frameworks and models.

In conclusion, the study identifies factors influencing green purchases in Mauritius, offering insights for marketers and green firms to promote eco-friendly products effectively. It underscores the need for government intervention to make green products more accessible. Overall, the findings support strategies to increase green purchasing habits, contributing to a sustainable and green Mauritius and improving residents' quality of life.

Disclosure of Interests. The authors have no competing interests to declare that are relevant to the content of this article.

References

1. Kirsch, R.E.: Limits to Terrestrial Extraction. Routledge, Milton Park (2020)
2. Kayaalp, E., Arslan, O.: Earth in practice: uncertainty, expertise and the expected Istanbul earthquake. Environ. Plann. E. Nat. Space. **5**, 1579–1596 (2022). https://doi.org/10.1177/251 48486211022451
3. Net zero by 2050 – analysis – IEA. https://www.iea.org/reports/net-zero-by-2050
4. Khadoo-Jeetah, P.D.: Investigating the appropriate renewable energy technologies in the mauritian context (2011). https://www.diva-portal.org/smash/record.jsf?pid=diva2:481081
5. Government information service. https://gis.govmu.org/SitePages/Index.aspx, https://www. bing.com/search?pglt=41&q=+Government+Information+Service+%3A+https%3A%2F% 2Fgis.govmu.org%2FSitePages%2FIndex.aspx&cvid=939da37bce84469886561d20d45 15bc7&gs_lcrp=EgZjaHJvbWUyBggAEEUYOTIG-CAEQRRg80gEHNTg5ajBqMagC ALACAA&FORM=ANNTA1&PC=HCTS
6. PricewaterhouseCoopers: National Budget 2023 – 2024, Legal Landscape, PwC Mauritius. https://www.pwc.com/mu/en/events/budget/Sustainability.html
7. Ken Poonoosamy editorial for budget newsletter 2023/24 - EDB Mauritius. https://edbmau ritius.org/newsroom/ken-poonoosamy-editorial-for-budget-newsletter-2023-24
8. Vermillion, L.J., Peart, J.: Green marketing: making sense of the situation. In: Allied Academies International Conference. Academy of Marketing Studies. Proceedings, p. 68. Jordan Whitney Enterprises, Inc (2010)
9. Wahid, N.A., Rahbar, E., Shyan, T.S.: Factors influencing the green purchase behavior of Penang environmental volunteers. Int. Bus. Manag. **5**, 38–49 (2011)
10. Dagher, G.K., Itani, O.: Factors influencing green purchasing behaviour: empirical evidence from the Lebanese consumers. J. Consum. Behav. **13**, 188–195 (2014). https://doi.org/10. 1002/cb.1482
11. Koger, S.: Coping with the deepwater horizon disaster: an ecopsychology interview with Deborah Du Nann Winter. Ecopsychology. **2**, 205–209 (2010). https://doi.org/10.1089/eco. 2010.0059
12. Stern, P.C., Brewer, G.D.: Decision making for the environment: Social and behavioral science research priorities. National Academies Press, Washington (2005)
13. Ajzen, I.: The theory of planned behavior. Organ. Behav. Hum. Decis. Process. **50**, 179–211 (1991)
14. Kalafatis, S.P., Pollard, M., East, R., Tsogas, M.H.: Green marketing and Ajzen's theory of planned behaviour: a cross-market examination. J. Consum. Mark. **16**, 441–460 (1999)
15. Lee, S.Y., Gregg, A.P., Park, S.H.: The person in the purchase: narcissistic consumers prefer products that positively distinguish them. J. Pers. Soc. Psychol. **105**, 335 (2013)
16. Purohit, H.C.: Consumer buying behaviour of green products. Int. J. Res. Comm. Econ. Manage. **1**, 94–97 (2011)
17. Boztepe, A.: Green marketing and its impact on consumer buying behavior. Eur. J. Econ. Polit. Stud. **5** (2012)
18. Gungaphul, M., Heeroo, S.: Green buying behavior among mauritian consumers: Extending the TPB model. PEOPLE: Int. J. Soc. Sci. 7, 189–207 (2022)
19. Sony, A., Ferguson, D.: Unlocking consumers' environmental value orientations and green lifestyle behaviors: a key for developing green offerings in Thailand. Asia-Pacific J. Bus. Admin. **9**, 37–53 (2017)
20. Paswan, A., Guzmán, F., Lewin, J.: Attitudinal determinants of environmentally sustainable behavior. J. Consum. Mark. **34**, 414–426 (2017)
21. Amin, I., Zailani, S., Rahman, M.K.: Predicting employees' engagement in environmental behaviours with supply chain firms. Manag. Res. Rev. **44**, 825–848 (2021)

22. Danso, A., Adomako, S., Amankwah-Amoah, J., Owusu-Agyei, S., Konadu, R.: Environmental sustainability orientation, competitive strategy and financial performance. Bus Strat Env. **28**, 885–895 (2019). https://doi.org/10.1002/bse.2291

23. Wickramasinghe, K.: Measuring environmental orientation in hotels: empirical evidence from Sri Lanka. Anatolia. **30**, 420–430 (2019). https://doi.org/10.1080/13032917.2019.1613667

24. Yu, Y., Zhang, M., Huo, B.: The impact of supply chain quality integration on green supply chain management and environmental performance. Total Qual. Manag. Bus. Excell. **30**, 1110–1125 (2019). https://doi.org/10.1080/14783363.2017.1356684

25. Gan, C., Wee, H.Y., Ozanne, L., Kao, T.-H.: Consumers' purchasing behavior towards green products in New Zealand. Innov. Mark. **4** (2008)

26. Balderjahn, I.: Personality variables and environmental attitudes as predictors of ecologically responsible consumption patterns. J. Bus. Res. **17**, 51–56 (1988)

27. Crosby, L.A., Gill, J.D., Taylor, J.R.: Consumer/voter behavior in the passage of the Michigan container law. J. Mark. **45**, 19–32 (1981). https://doi.org/10.1177/002224298104500203

28. Chen, X., Rahman, M.K., Rana, M.S., Gazi, M.A.I., Rahaman, M.A.: Predicting consumer green product purchase attitudes and behavioral intention during COVID-19 pandemic. Front. Psychol. **12**, 760051 (2022)

29. Maram, H.K., Kongsompong, K.: The power of social influence: east-west comparison on purchasing behavior (2007)

30. Young, W., Hwang, K., McDonald, S., Oates, C.J.: Sustainable consumption: green consumer behaviour when purchasing products. Sustain. Dev. **18**, 20–31 (2010). https://doi.org/10.1002/sd.394

31. Lee, K.: Predictors of sustainable consumption among young educated consumers in Hong Kong. J. Int. Consum. Mark. **26**, 217–238 (2014). https://doi.org/10.1080/08961530.2014.900249

32. H'Mida, S.: Factors contributing in the formation of consumers' environmental consciousness and shaping green purchasing decisions. In: 2009 International Conference on Computers & Industrial Engineering, pp. 957–962. IEEE (2009)

33. Imamović, I., Azevedo, A.J.A., de Sousa, B.M.B.: The urban sensescapes and sensory destination branding. In: New governance and Management in Touristic Destinations, pp. 276–293. IGI Global (2022)

34. Dewi, C.S., Annas, M.: Consumption Value dimension of green purchase intention with green trust as mediating variable. Dinasti Int. J. Econ. Finan. Account. **3**, 315–325 (2022)

35. Ojo, A.O., Fauzi, M.A.: Environmental awareness and leadership commitment as determinants of IT professionals engagement in Green IT practices for environmental performance. Sustain. Prod. Consum. **24**, 298–307 (2020)

36. Bratu, S.: Can social media influencers shape corporate brand reputation? Online followers' trust, value creation, and purchase intentions. Rev. Contemp. Philos. **18**, 157–163 (2019)

37. Koo, C., Chung, N.: Examining the eco-technological knowledge of smart green IT adoption behavior: a self-determination perspective. Technol. Forecast. Soc. Chang. **88**, 140–155 (2014)

38. Yılmaz, Y., Anasori, E.: Environmentally responsible behavior of residents: impact of mindfulness, enjoyment of nature and sustainable attitude. J. Hospitality Tourism Insights. **5**, 1–14 (2022)

39. Choshaly, S.H.: Consumer perception of green issues and intention to purchase green products. Int. J. Manage. Account. Econ. **4** (2017)

40. Rimadias, S., Faradila, L.: The role of attitudinal loyalty, behavioral loyalty, sponsor awareness, and attitude toward sponsorship in creating purchase intention on specs. Jurnal Ilmu Manajemen & Ekonomika. **11**, 71–80 (2019)

41. Firmansyah, M.A., Artanti, Y.: The driver of green purchase intention: environmental responsibility, spirituality, and social influence. J. Bus. Manage. Rev. **3**, 386–398 (2022)

42. Achchuthan, S., Thirunavukkarasu, V.: Enhancing purchase intentions towards sustainability: the influence of environmental attitude, perceived consumer effectiveness, health consciousness and social influence. Health Consciousness and Social Influence (2016)
43. Mainieri, T., Barnett, E.G., Valdero, T.R., Unipan, J.B., Oskamp, S.: Green buying: the influence of environmental concern on consumer behavior. J. Soc. Psychol. **137**, 189–204 (1997). https://doi.org/10.1080/00224549709595430
44. Shukla, J.: Predictability in the midst of chaos: a scientific basis for climate forecasting. Science **282**, 728–731 (1998). https://doi.org/10.1126/science.282.5389.728
45. Ottman, J.: The New Rules of Green Marketing: Strategies, Tools, and Inspiration for Sustainable Branding. Routledge, Milton Park (2017)
46. Percie Du Sert, N., et al.: The ARRIVE guidelines 2.0: updated guidelines for reporting animal research*. J. Cereb. Blood Flow Metab. **40**, 1769–1777 (2020). https://doi.org/10.1177/0271678X20943823
47. Miller, C.: Sustainable marketing and the green consumer. In: Contemporary Issues in Marketing and Consumer Behaviour, pp. 153–172. Routledge (2009)
48. D'Souza, C., Taghian, M., Lamb, P., Peretiatkos, R.: Green products and corporate strategy: an empirical investigation. Soc. Bus. Rev. **1**, 144–157 (2006)
49. French, W.A., Barksdale, H.C., Perreault, W.D.: Consumer attitudes towards marketing in England and the United States. Eur. J. Mark. **16**, 20–30 (1982)
50. Kaynak, E.: Some thoughts on consumerism in developed and less developed countries. Int. Mark. Rev. **2**, 15–30 (1985)
51. Lisa, A.: Is it unfair pricing. Tire Bus. **22**, 15 (2004)
52. Kaufmann, H.R., Panni, M.F.A.K., Orphanidou, Y.: Factors affecting consumers' green purchasing behavior: An integrated conceptual framework. Amfiteatru Econ. J. **14**, 50–69 (2012)
53. Ansar, N.: Impact of green marketing on consumer purchase intention. Mediterr. J. Soc. Sci. **4**, 650–655 (2013)
54. Diglel, A., Yazdanifard, R.: Green marketing: it's influence on buying behavior and attitudes of the purchasers towards eco-friendly products. Global J. Manage. Bus. Res. **14**, 10–17 (2014)
55. Delafrooz, N., Taleghani, M., Nouri, B.: Effect of green marketing on consumer purchase behavior. QScience Connect. **2014** (2014). https://doi.org/10.5339/connect.2014.5
56. Rahbar, E., Wahid, N.A.: Investigation of green marketing tools' effect on consumers' purchase behavior. Bus. Strat. Ser. **12**, 73–83 (2011)
57. Kwok, L., Huang, Y.-K., Hu, L.: Green attributes of restaurants: what really matters to consumers? Int. J. Hosp. Manag. **55**, 107–117 (2016)
58. Chkanikova, O., Lehner, M.: Private eco-brands and green market development: towards new forms of sustainability governance in the food retailing. J. Clean. Prod. **107**, 74–84 (2015)
59. Järvi, J.: The behaviour of finnish consumers towards eco-labelled products; Case: S-Group Oyj (2010)
60. Leire, C., Thidell, Å.: Product-related environmental information to guide consumer purchases–a review and analysis of research on perceptions, understanding and use among Nordic consumers. J. Clean. Prod. **13**, 1061–1070 (2005)
61. Cherian, J., Jacob, J.: Green marketing: A study of consumers' attitude towards environment friendly products (2012)
62. Hartmann, P., Apaolaza Ibáñez, V., Forcada Sainz, F.J.: Green branding effects on attitude: functional versus emotional positioning strategies. Mark. Intell. Plan. **23**, 9–29 (2005)
63. Suki, N.M.: Consumer environmental concern and green product purchase in Malaysia: structural effects of consumption values. J. Clean. Prod. **132**, 204–214 (2016)
64. Huang, Y.-C., Yang, M., Wang, Y.-C.: Effects of green brand on green purchase intention. Mark. Intell. Plan. **32**, 250–268 (2014)

65. Raska, D., Shaw, D.: When is going green good for company image? Manag. Res. Rev. **35**, 326–347 (2012)
66. Maheshwari, A., Malhotra, G.: Green marketing: a study on Indian youth. Int. J. Manage. Strategy. **2**, 1–15 (2011)
67. Tariq, A., Tabasam, N., Bakhsh, K., Ashfaq, M., Hassan, S.: Food security in the context of climate change in Pakistan. Pakistan J. Comm. Soc. Sci. (PJCSS). **8**, 540–550 (2014)
68. Rashid, N.: Awareness of eco-label in Malaysia's green marketing initiative. Int. J. Bus. Manage. **4**, 132–141 (2009)
69. Govender, J.P., Govender, T.L.: The influence of green marketing on consumer purchase behavior. Environ. Econ. **7**, 77–85 (2016)
70. Gliem, J.A., Gliem, R.R.: Calculating, interpreting, and reporting Cronbach's alpha reliability coefficient for Likert-type scales. In: Midwest Research-to-Practice Conference in Adult, Continuing, and Community Education, pp. 82–87. Columbus, OH (2003)
71. George, D., Mallery, P.: SPSS for windows step by step: a simple guide and reference. Contemp. Psychol. **44**, 100 (1999)
72. Hair, J.F., Anderson, R.E., Babin, B.J., Black, W.C.: Multivariate data analysis: a global perspective, vol. 7, (2010)
73. Samo, Y.-L.K., Hendricks, D.: What makes an asset useful? (2018). http://arxiv.org/abs/1806.08444
74. Ruffman, T., Slade, L., Rowlandson, K., Rumsey, C., Garnham, A.: How language relates to belief, desire, and emotion understanding. Cogn. Dev. **18**, 139–158 (2003)
75. Taylor, C.: Interpretation and the sciences of man. In: The Philosophy of Society, pp. 156–200. Routledge (2023)
76. Eze, U.C., Ndubisi, N.O.: Green buyer behavior: evidence from Asia consumers. J. Asian Afr. Stud. **48**, 413–426 (2013). https://doi.org/10.1177/0021909613493602
77. Ma, Y., Wang, N., Che, A., Huang, Y., Xu, J.: The bullwhip effect under different information-sharing settings: a perspective on price-sensitive demand that incorporates price dynamics. Int. J. Prod. Res. **51**, 3085–3116 (2013). https://doi.org/10.1080/00207543.2012.754551

Assessing the Impact of Decent Work on the Mental Health of Female Carers in Mauritius Through the Psychology of Working Theory

Dayalutchmee Kodye-Domah[✉], Leena Devi Sobha,
and Soolakshna Desai Lukea-Bhiwajee

School of Sustainable Development and Tourism, University of Technology, Port Louis,
Mauritius
dkodye@utm.ac.mu

Abstract. Using the Psychology of Working Theory as a pillar, this study has aimed to examine the impact of decent work (subscales: interpersonal and physical safe working conditions, adequate health care, adequate compensation, hours that allow for free time and rest, and lastly, organisational values) directly and indirectly through the use of mediators namely, survival needs, social contribution needs, and self-determination needs. Moreover, the study also assessed the influence of the subscales of decent work on the mental health of female carers in Mauritius. Quantitative data was collected from 136 working women working in care homes or acting as carers for individual households through a questionnaire adopted from previous studies. The data analysis was done by use of SPSS 26.0. The findings showed that there were a positive and significant relationship between physical and interpersonal safe working conditions, access to adequate health care, and organisational and family values and mental health of female carers. In addition, the result could imply that there was a positive relationship related to survival needs, satisfaction needs and self-determination needs among individual carers and their mental health. The influence of the subscales of decent work on mental health showed a strong positive correlation but two factors namely, adequate compensation and hours that allow for free time and rest had low correlations. Overall, the findings suggested that decent work indeed contributed positively to the mental health of the female carers. Decent work promotes good psychological well-being of female workers because work is pivotal in the attainment of individual needs such as survival, social contribution, and self-determination. Implications for practice and future research are discussed.

Keywords: Decent Work · Mental Health · Psychology of Working Theory

© The Author(s), under exclusive license to Springer Nature Switzerland AG 2025
K. Hinkelmann and H. Smuts (Eds.): Society 5.0 2024, CCIS 2173, pp. 187–206, 2025.
https://doi.org/10.1007/978-3-031-71412-2_14

1   Introduction

Over the last few years, there has been a disruption in the normal running of people's lives, not only due to the pandemic but also because of the current VUCA (Volatility, Uncertainity, Complexity and Ambiguous context). Goal 8 of the Sustainable Development Goals (SDG), named Decent Work (DW) and Economic Growth, has as its objective to "promote inclusive and sustainable economic growth, employment and DW for all," where workers have access to "safe and secure working environments" (United Nations 2023). The main thrust of DW is to ensure that both men and women have access to respectable and productive jobs whereby dignity and access to a safe, equitable, and free workplace and environment are of paramount importance (Khairy and Ghoneim 2023). According to Strandh et al. (2013), inequality still exists in the labour market and households contributing to a ripple gendered effect in the realm of work and ultimately on the Mental Health (MH) of both men and women. It has also been recorded that women experience greater feelings of burnout at work compared to men thus affecting their MH in the long term (Mucharraz et al. 2023). DW is interrelated to the fifth goal of the SDGs (Achieve Gender Equality and Empower all Women and Girls) which is centered on the promotion of gender equality furthering the elimination of gender biases and empowering women (Souza 2022). Following the same line of thought, research has shown that women are exposed to and subjected to poor working conditions and a restrictive career path compared to their male counterparts (Mehta 2016). Studies indicate that working conditions and the environment can have a big impact on MH. Full-time working women are nearly twice as likely to have MH problems as full-time working men (Stansfeld 2016). The former UN Women Executive Director emphasised that women are particularly vulnerable because of the burden of their crucial obligations as parents and carers to other family members (United Nations 2020).

Over the last years, numerous studies have been conducted concerning DW parameters across different country settings (Çolakoğlu and Toygar 2021; Dodd and Burke 2022; Kashyap et al. 2022; Gallo et al. 2020; Khairy and Hebatallah Ghoneim 2023). These studies have utilised the Psychology of Working Theory (PWT) as the theoretical framework to investigate the different predictors of DW (Douglass et al. 2017; Duffy et al. 2018; Tokar and Kaut 2018) and this framework has proven its applicability in different contexts. However, scant, if any, research to date has studied how DW can impact on MH of workers except the studies of Amponsah-Tawiah et al. (2023) and Duffy et al. (2019). The former study was mainly focused on the Ghanian mining industry where the relationship between the different parameters of DW was analysed onto the MH of workers in general. On the other hand, the main thrust of Duffy et al. (2019) was on linking the impact of DW on both mental and physical health which concluded that satisfaction of the needs of individuals leads to greater mental well-being. This study will therefore address this gap by testing the relationships and effects of DW on the MH of female caregivers/carers working in Mauritius.

2   Literature Review

This section highlights the existing literature related to the key concepts of DW and MH, including the theoretical framework utilised in the field of DW.

2.1 The Concept of Decent Work

Work forms an integral part of an individual's life as the latter spends many resources in ensuring that work is manageable and meaningful to them (Kashyap et al. 2022). However, the changing patterns and trends in the world of work call for constant and rigorous probe for a fulfilled and accomplished professional life (Gibb and Ishaq 2018). Coined as a panacea to maintaining social justice and respecting human rights at work, the concept of DW emerged as a saviour (Podvorica and Murati 2023) for many working individuals. DW is defined as "productive work in which rights are protected, which generates an adequate income, with adequate social protection" (ILO 1999, pp.3). According to Duffy et al. (2016), DW is any work whereby the working environment is safe physically and psychologically; good compensation is provided; there is free time and sufficient time to relax; there is access to adequate health care settings and finally organisational values that correspond with familial and social values.

According to Wei et al. (2022), in the actual business context, individuals hold high expectations for their future jobs and expect them to be decent and in line with the same, the perception of future DW includes good working conditions, a balance between work and life, good wages, values and access to health care. Moreover, the concept of DW has reinforced with the introduction of laws pertaining to human rights, labour and welfare (Duffy et al. 2022). Nonetheless, the occurrence of Covid-19 has significantly plagued the sustainability pathway weakening the achievement of the SDG 8 targets across the world (Anholon et al. 2021). Following the same line of thought, the pandemic has been a threat to the socio-economic pillars of SDGs, namely, SDG 1 (no poverty) and SDG 8 (DW and economic growth) (Hörisch 2021). With organisations thriving for social sustainability through accountability and disclosure reports, COVID-19 influenced same and threatened to derail existing efforts (Caruana et al. 2021).

2.2 Linking Decent Work and Mental Health

In recent years, a lot of concerns about the relationship between experiences at work and their impinged impact on a person's MH and well-being have become a subject of interest for many researchers (Amponsah-Tawiah et al. 2023; Blustein et al. 2023; Chinyamurindi et al. 2023). PWT postulates that having a decent job is essential to enhancing one's welfare since it allows one to meet their most fundamental demands (Duffy et al. 2016). These fundamental demands, also known as the basic needs, englobe the social contribution or connection needs (that is, the capacity to utilise one's job to improve the lives of others) and survival needs (the availability and ability to pay for food and shelter) as well as the urge for self-determination (fulfilling emotions like competence, autonomy, and relatedness through employment) (Duffy et al. 2016).

MH is the ability to manage life's stressors, reach one's full potential, learn and work effectively, give back to one's community, make decisions, form relationships, and influence the world around us is a fundamental aspect of health and well-being on both an individual and a societal level (World Health Organisation (WHO 2022). MH encompasses psychological, social, and emotional well-being and greatly influences the ability to manage stress, mingle with others, and make decisions. Previous research has demonstrated that unfavorable workplace experiences such as job insecurity, pressures, inconsistent hours, and inadequate workplace support have a deleterious effect on employees' MH and welfare concerning a physically and psychologically secure working environment (Maggiori et al. 2013; Costa 2010; Hellgren and Sverke 2003; Sverke et al. 2002). Although, the literature on the effects of DW on employee MH is either scarce or still developing, Nizami and Prasad (2017) further contended that the absence of decent employment contributed to work-life imbalance and, as a result, harmed employees' MH.

It was also known that employer relations and work circumstances were important avenues to pursue in resolving health disparities, as stated by the Commission on Social Determinants of Health (2007) and as reported to the World Health Organisation (2007). Much research has focused on elements like occupational hazards, job security, job stress, job control, and the imbalance between job demands and remunerations (Landsbergis et al. 2014). Moreover, several studies have demonstrated in-depth insight into people working in perilous environments, anxious, challenging, low-paid, momentary, or unstable jobs who were more prone to suffer detrimental effects on their physical and MH (Baron et al. 2014; Martens et al. 1999). Simultaneously, there was evidence that the awareness of healthcare professionals' MH and suicide has also grown in recent years, partly due to the numerous stressors they faced on the job in addition to a plethora of other factors (New 2023). Investigation into the relationship between the essential elements of DW and health outcomes would be beneficial, as the cumulative impacts of the elements included in the concept of DW have not been studied as much.

2.3 Theoretical Framework: The Psychology of Working Theory

Over the last years, numerous scholars provided due attention to the concept of DW from a wide range of perspectives (Di Ruggiero et al. 2015; Allan et al. 2019; Buyukgoze-Kavas and Autin 2019; Vignoli et al. 2020). Numerous studies in developed countries investigated the different factors affecting DW (Douglass et al. 2017; Duffy et al. 2017; Tokar and Kaut 2018). However, scant research focused on the effect of DW conditions on mental and physical health (Amponsah-Tawaiah et al., 2023; Duffy et al. 2019). Over the past years, Duffy et al. (2016; 2017) discussed the need to introduce a psychometrically-self report tool to help and guide researchers on the determining factors and influences of DW and under the same line of thought, a panoply of scholars adopted this tool to demonstrate that there was an intrinsic link between DW and other factors such as psychological dimensions, job/ life satisfaction, MH, and wellbeing (Duffy et al. 2017, 2019) and emotional exhaustion (Ferreira et al. 2019). PWT has widely been utilised in Turkey, Italy, U.S and China (Buyukgoze-Kavas and Autin 2019; Di Fabio and Kenny 2019; Dodd et al. 2019; Ribeiro et al. 2019) and in different contexts (Tokar and Kaut 2018; Wang et al. 2019) to elucidate these relationships.

2.3.1 Psychology of Working Theory and Decent Work Variables

Duffy et al. (2016) have captured the variables of DW under PWT and these included safe and healthy working conditions, access to healthcare settings, adequate compensation, a balance between working hours and relaxation time, and positive organisational values.

It posits that contextual barriers, such as economic constraints and marginalisation, are negatively associated with individuals' access to DW. Instead of directly assessing individuals' economic constraints and marginalisation, studies have empirically tested PWT through various variables to measure economic constraints (such as annual income and financial strain) and marginalisation with particular emphasis on discrimination and stigma (Smith et al. 2020). In addition, a burgeoning literature has focused on the influence of different factors on securing DW conditions with different groups of workers such as ethnic minorities (Duffy et al. 2018), employees receiving beyond-average salaries (Kozan et al. 2019a), and gender and sexual minority workers (Smith et al. 2020). Furthermore, according to Kozan et al. (2019b), most studies conducted in favour of DW were done in developed countries, specifically, the United States. It thus remains necessary to test the various parameters influencing PWT in different cultural and socio-economic settings. Likewise, sparse research has been conducted with regard to the antecedents and outcomes of DW and only a few studies have tested the mediation hypothesis in PWT (Wang et al. 2019).

2.4 The Association between Decent Work, Need Satisfaction and Health

Survival Needs

Studies that have utilised the DW Scale have recognised the fact that there was a correlation between DW and life satisfaction needs (Autin et al. 2019; Kozan and Işık 2018). According to Blustein et al. (2016), with DW, workers can fulfill their survival needs such as access to food, shelter, medical expenditures, and any other resources through their wages. Blustein (2006) first suggested the significance of survival needs and their relationship to both DW and well-being within PWT in the original Psychology of Working Framework (PWF) taxonomy. This theory is based on earlier research, conducted both inside and outside of the psychology community, which showed how crucial survival needs and DW were in fostering well-being. Likewise, a handful of research conducted on needs satisfaction, and the mental and physical health of workers demonstrated a significant relationship (González et al. 2016; Kim et al. 2018) between these two. Additionally, the study of Duffy et al. (2019) showed that DW was strongly predicted by the three needs satisfaction namely, survival needs, social contribution needs, and self-determination needs which further impacted the mental and physical health of workers.

Self-determination Needs

PWT's self-determination requires the fulfillment of feelings associated with relatedness through work, independence or autonomy at work, and competence (Duffy et al. 2016). Accessibility to the three basic needs contributes to the commitment and motivation of workers toward their work. The need for autonomy was the deepest desire to have control of one's life (Ryan and Deci 2002), having control of one's own life triggered self-motivation. Human beings have a basic psychological need for autonomy, which was described as "the need to self-organise experience and behaviour, and to have activity be concordant with one's integrated sense of self" (Deci and Ryan 2000, p. 231). On the other hand, competence implies the need for the acquisition of required skills to be able to perform optimally at work (Autin et al. 2019; Ryan and Deci 2002), the need to seek learning skills enhances the satisfaction and competence in work. Another basic need related to PWT is relatedness, which explains the struggle of human beings to bond with people in their surroundings and have the feeling of being cared for and showing care to other people (Autin et al. 2019; Ryan and Deci 2002). Relatedness at work forms an integral part of the human need which makes them a social entity and part of the group.

Social Contribution Needs

The term 'social contribution needs' has also been referred to as the capacity to make a difference in other's lives at the workplace (Duffy et al. 2016), resulting in the contribution toward the satisfaction of being connected with people. Autin et al. (2019) postulated that life satisfaction was the consequence of the culmination of the fulfillment of survival needs, social contribution needs, and self-determination needs, the three needs were interrelated when optimal life satisfaction was concerned. Social contribution needs were vital elements in completing the paramount of one's basic needs satisfaction and made it plausible for the construction of DW (AmponsahTawiah et al. 2023). Literature exposed the harmful impact on workers' well-being and health caused by tight working timetables, uneven work programs, and extensive working hours. Posner (2010) concluded that the influencing factors for workers' motivation, satisfaction, arousal of anxiety, and stress are determined by the consonance of the organisational values and self-concept of the workers. Social contribution and connection in one's working environment were a human need to achieve the sense of contentment to feel complete and fulfilled.

2.5   Specificities of Caregivers/Carers

Carers, also referred to as caregivers, help residents with daily activities as specified in their care plans, including clothing, grooming, bathing, going to and from meals, and moving around. They also gave out prescriptions, made sure that they were followed, and helped the residents assume as much personal care as they could. Despite playing such a vital role, caregivers were confronted numerous difficulties which might impact their well-being. Hado and Feinberg (2021) highlighted that carers frequently worked long shifts (12 hours or more), which may physically and psychologically exhaust them in turn impacting both their physical and mental tiredness (Aldridge 2022). As a result, carers might also experience a decrease in job satisfaction and burnout (Hado and Feinberg 2021). Carers in the healthcare industry faced a great deal of difficulty when working shifts. It could be difficult for carers to maintain a healthy work-life balance because many of them were obliged to work irregular hours, which can include weekends and late shifts (Hado and Komisar 2019). It could also be difficult for carers to arrange their personal lives and participate in activities outside of work due to inconsistent work schedules, which could exacerbate feelings of social disconnection and loneliness.

Carers were also known to respond rapidly to changing conditions and maintain cool under pressure because their work environments are frequently fast-paced, high-pressure, and emotionally exhausting (Bauer and Sousa-Poza 2015). The caregivers encounter resource constraints, such as a lack of manpower and insufficient training and assistance in numerous healthcare environments, resulting in increased stress levels and a lower standard of care they deliver, intensifying the difficulties encountered by carers causing them to experience dissatisfaction and powerlessness (Hado and Komisar 2019; Duggleby et al. 2016). The stress level of the carer was influenced by several factors, including age, gender, occupation, and family (Ramachandran et al. 2020). It could be challenging for carers to effectively aid patients with chronic illnesses or impairments due to their mood swings, agitation, or resistance to care (Twigg and Martin 2015). On the other hand, carers' mental and emotional health might suffer from ongoing exposure to difficult circumstances, which could raise stress levels and cause discontent with their jobs.

2.6 The Context of the Study

Mauritius (MRU), a Small Island Developing State (SIDS), has a working population of 49.7%. MRU became a signatory of the DW Country Programme in 2012 to improve working conditions for employees. Women are employed in the caregiving sector mostly in caregiving homes or as individual carers providing the necessary care to those in need. However, with the recent economic downturn, new challenges have emerged in the world of work. The current VUCA context has made businesses revamp their processes and strategies to take into account such a competitive and changing environment (Valamede and Akkari 2020). It is crucial that an empirical understanding of the impact of DW on employees' mental health is needed. Following the same line of thought, the present study will attempt to understand the impact of DW variables on need satisfaction to demonstrate the outcome on the mental health of carers.

The indicators for DW at the macro-level were based on the ILO's definition of DW which aimed to measure the performance of a country or region in terms of economic growth, demographic changes, expansion of the labour market, and societal development to the four dimensions of DW including human rights, employment, social dialogue, and social protection. These four parameters also served as the foundation for DW (Yan et al. 2023). Additionally, corporations in the 21st century were now operating in an environment that was characterised by VUCA (Bennis and Nannus 1985). Another contributor to the VUCA environment was the emergence of Industry 4.0. Both the VUCA environment and Industry 4.0 were now generating various challenges which they were interfering with ways of managing and leading a business (Ahmed et al. 2022).

Based on the literature review, the following hypotheses have been formulated:

H_1: There was a positive relationship between decent work and survival needs.

H_2: There was a positive relationship between decent work and contribution needs.

H_3: There was a positive relationship between decent work and self-determination needs.

H_4: There was a positive relationship between survival needs and mental health.

H_5: There was a positive relationship between contribution needs and mental health.

H_6: There was a positive relationship between self-determination needs and mental health.

H_7: There was a direct and positive relationship between decent work and mental health.

3 Methodology

This section indicates the research method used for this study as well as the use of different studies whereby the scales were adopted.

3.1 Sample and Procedures

The present study collected data from 136 respondents from care homes or individuals employed as household carers. Given the practice that carers are not registered in Mauritius, no statistics were available hence, the recruitment of carers was done randomly. Participants had to have worked as carers for a minimum of two years to be eligible for this survey. This was done to make sure that participants understood the work-related laws and regulations surrounding DW. To control common method bias, the participants were instructed to provide honest responses to the questions in the questionnaires. Questionnaires in English language were distributed to the respondents and the questions and its meaning were explained. The respondents were assisted with data collection. Before answering any questions, participants were fully informed of the purpose of the study, and their consent was obtained. Confidentiality and anonymity were also considered during the phases of data processing and gathering. The data from respondents was only handled by researchers involved in the study.

3.2 Instrument

To evaluate DW, Duffy et al. (2016) created the DW Scale (DWS). The DWS is a 15-item scale with five subscales that evaluate the following: (a) safe working conditions, both physically and interpersonally; (b) access to health care; (c) adequate compensation; (d) hours that allow free time and rest; and lastly, (e) organisational values that align with social and family values. The DWS was scored using a seven-point Likert scale, where one (1) represented strongly Disagree and seven (7) represented Strongly Agree.

Three (3) questions were used to measure MH of female carers which were retrieved from the Health-Related Quality of Life (HRQOL– 4; Centers for Disease Control and Prevention, 2000). Additionally, 5 questions related to satisfaction with Life Scale (SWLS) which had widely been used in previous studies were employed to assess MH of female workers (Headey et al. 1993; Lombardo et al. 2018). The questions for MH were taken from these two mentioned sources as they were relevant to this study and its context. The respondents had to rate their responses on a 7-point Likert Scale ranging from Strongly Disagree to Strongly Agree. The SWLS is a scale that has proven its reliability (Duffy et al. 2019).

For Work Need Satisfaction, a 20-item question was utilised to measure fulfillment of needs satisfaction. This scale consisted of five subscales which measured the variables such as survival needs, social contribution needs, and competence, relatedness, and autonomy needs were re-grouped under the self-determination needs. Participants were instructed to rate each of the items based on a 7-point Likert-type scale ranging from Strongly disagree to Strongly agree.

3.3 Pilot Testing

An initial set of 20 questionnaires were provided to respondents who were conversant with the English language. After receiving feedback from these individuals, the questionnaire was amended for a few statements and they were written in simple terms ensuring that the nature of the questions has not been altered. The internal consistency of the whole questionnaire was run and a value of 0.903 was obtained further to the Cronbach Alpha test indicating that the scales had good reliability.

4 Results

The statistical analysis of data was made using IBM SPSS, version 26.0. The focus was particularly on female carers as they are still considered the most vulnerable and negligible to some extent in the labour market. A structured questionnaire was provided to respondents and they were interviewed based on the items highlighted in the questionnaires. 136 valid responses were collected from the target population. The sample included solely 136 female carers and they were mainly found in the age group of 3140. The majority of respondents (44.9%) had secondary educational qualifications and most of them (39.7%) have 2–7 years of experience as carers. The data also showed that most of the respondents earned a salary of USD 357.95 but 18.4% still having a salary below the national minimum wages (USD 357.95) as stipulated in the labour laws in Mauritius. Only 28% of the respondents have a salary of USD 650.82 or USD 759.30 The work schedule of respondents was also captured suggesting that most of the carers were regular workers (72%) meaning they have full-time employment mainly from 9 am to 5 pm. In addition, 31% and 33% of carers were working on a part-time basis and shift system (night and day) respectively.

Moreover, the five variables of the questionnaire showed good reliability and validity with the value being greater than 0.70 as indicated in Table 2. The data collected was examined for univariate and multivariate outliers, skewness, and kurtosis. No outliers with a score greater than 3.29 were found on the study constructs. According to Osborne and Overbay (2019), a level of 1% is acceptable regarding data containing extreme values. However, in this study, no cases of extreme values were noted. Skewness and kurtosis were also assessed for this study using the guidelines of Weston and Gore Jr (2006). It is worthy to note that the variables did not approach the thresholds as set for skewness $|>3|$ and kurtosis $|>10|$ (Table 1).

This study also aimed at examining the influence of different variables (interpersonal and physical safe working conditions, adequate health care, adequate compensation, free time and rest, and organisational and family values) of DW on the MH of female carers. As shown in Table 2, Pearson's correlation examining the interrelationship between each variable of DW and MH showed that there was a positive and significant relationship between physical and interpersonal safe working conditions, access to adequate health care, and organisational and family values and MH. However, a low positive correlation was exhibited between the variables such as adequate compensation and free time and rest when associated with MH. The variable physical and interpersonal safe working conditions emerged as the most significant factor when linked with the MH of female carers.

The second objective of the present study examined the influence of components of DW on employees' MH (Table 3). The results in Table 3 show a positive significant and high relationship between physical and interpersonal safe working conditions (b = 0.475, t = 6.254, p < 0.05), access to health care (b =0.389, t = 4.885, p < 0.05), and organisational and family values (b = 0.375, t =4.688, p< 0.05) on employee MH. The

Table 1. Demographics profile of respondents

Variables		Frequency	Percentage (%)
Age	Under 30	30	22.1
	31–40	44	32.0
	41–50	32	23.8
	Above 50	30	22.1
Education	Primary	8	5.9
	Secondary	61	44.9
	Technical	12	8.8
	Tertiary	55	40.4
Number of years as carers	8–13	38	27.9
	2–7	54	39.7
	14 +	44	32.4
Marital Status	Divorced	21	15.4
	Married	74	54.4
	Single	27	19.9
	Widowed	14	10.3
Employment Type	On-Contract	20	14.7
	Permanent	98	72.1
	Temporary	18	13.2
Average Net Basic Salary	Less than USD 357.95	25	18.4
	USD 357.95	35	25.7
	USD 542.35	20	14.7
	USD 650.82	28	20.6
	USD 759.30	28	20.6
Work Schedule	Shift worker	33	24.2
	Regular worker	72	52.9
	Part-time worker	31	22.7

results further indicated a significantly low effect of adequate compensation ($b = 0.114$, $t = 1.330$, $p < 0.05$) and hours that allow for free time and rest ($b = 0.191$, $t = 2.247$, $p < 0.05$) on employees' MH, respectively. The beta coefficient of the sub-scales is positive showing statistical significance.

Regression analysis was run to check the hypothesis testing of the variables in the conceptual framework. Hypothesis H_1 laid out that there was a positive relationship between DW and MH of female carers. From the findings of Table 4, it could be deduced that there was indeed a positive relationship between DW and the survival needs of individual female carers ($\beta = 0.622$, $t = 7.635$, $p < 0.001$). Concerning the link between DW and the

Table 2. Results of preliminary analysis and Pearson's Correlation (N = 136)

	Skew ness	Kur- tosis	Cronbach Alpha	1	2	3	4	5	6
DW _1	−.432	−1.063	0.7 43						
DW _2	−.077	−1.099		0.5 66					
DW _3	.1 24	−.733		0.0 96	0.0 35				
DW _4	−.011	−.664		0.2 13	0.0 31	0.6 34			
DW _5	.0 91	−1.211		0.6 64	0.6 68	0.1 58	0.1 41		
MH	−.291	.8 53		0.4 75	0.3 89	0.1 14	0.1 91	0.3 75	

** DW_1: Interpersonal and physical safe working conditions; DW_2: Adequate health care; DW_3: Adequate compensation; DW_4: Hours that allow for free time and rest; DW_5: Organisational values; MH: MH

Table 3. Relationship between DW sub-scales and MH

Sub-Scales	Mean Score	Beta	T-value	p
Physical and interpersonal safe working conditions	4.16	0.475	6.254	0.000
Adequate health care	3.91	0.389	4.885	0.000
Adequate compensation	3.75	0.114	1.330	0.000
Hours that allow free time and rest	3.75	0.191	2.247	0.000
Organisational and family values	3.77	0.375	4.688	0.000

second satisfaction needs, that is, contribution needs, a statically significant relationship was also demonstrated with the values being $\beta = 0.703$, t = 8.001, p<0.001 confirming hypothesis, H_2. The third hypothesis, H3, proposed that DW positively influenced the self-determination needs of female individual carers and their MH. The empirical findings provided sufficient evidence that indeed a positive relationship existed between these two variables as exhibited by the individual female worker. This finding was supported by $\beta = 0.686$, t-value = 8.475, p<0.001. The high values of the t-value suggested that a significant relationship did exist between the variables mentioned above. Concerning the relationship between survival needs and MH, significant bearing was shown as well confirming the hypothesis, H_4, $\beta = 0.495$, t-value = 6.601, p<0.001. However, it can be seen that the regression relationship between these two variables was low as per its standardized beta coefficient. For contribution needs and MH, the regression results indicated a positive low relationship as well $\beta = 0.569$, tvalue $= 8.006$, p<0.001. With regard to self-determination needs, the values $\beta = 0.591$, tvalue $= 8.475$, p<0.001, were obtained indicating a significant positive relationship. Nevertheless, the association was noted to be low.

Table 4. Summary of regression analysis

Hypothesis	Pathways	b-value	t-value	p-value	Remarks
H_1	DW- > Survival Needs	0.662	7.635	0.000	Supported
H_2	DW- > Contribution Needs	0.703	8.001	0.000	Supported
H_3	DW- > Selfdetermination Needs	0.686	8.475	0.000	Supported
H_5	Survival Needs > MH	0.495	6.601	0.000	Supported
H_6	Contribution Needs - > MH	0.569	8.006	0.000	Supported
H_7	Self-determination Needs - > MH	0.591	8.475	0.000	Supported
H_8	DW - > MH	0.468	6.124	0.000	Supported

Table 5. Relationship between DW and MH

Model	1	F	Mean Square	P
Regression	134 135	37.503	21.886	0.000

Table 6. Effect of variables

Independent variable	Mediating Variable	Dependent Variable	Effect of influence	Total Effect
DW	Survival Needs	MH	$= 0.662 \times 0.495$	0.327
	Contribution Needs		$= 0.703 \times 0.569$	0.400
	Self-determination Needs		$= 0.686 \times 0.591$	**0.405**
DW		MH		**0.468**

Further to the results of the simple linear regression analysis as indicated in Table 4, a positive relationship existed between DW and MH. The variables accounted for 37.5% of the variance in DW. In accordance with Table 5, there is a significant and direct positive relationship between DW and MH [F $(1, 134) = 37.503$, p< 0.001] with $\beta = 0.468$, t-value $= 6.124$, however, the results predicted a low association between DW and MH.

In a nutshell, we can conclude that there was a strong and direct positive relationship between DW and MH without the mediation of survival needs, contribution needs, and self-determination needs ($\beta = 0.468$). From Table 6, there was a high influence of self-determination needs on the effect between DW and MH of female carers as the total effect of $\beta = 0.405$ suggested which is further followed by contribution needs ($\beta = 0.400$) (Fig. 1).

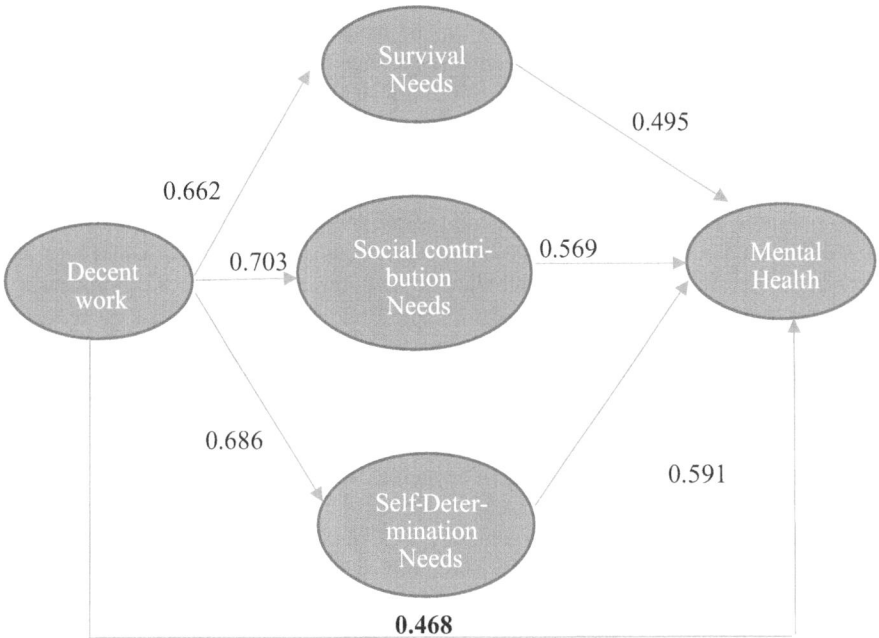

Fig. 1. Conceptual model with standardised coefficients

5 Discussion

The first objective of the study was to examine the mediating roles of survival needs, social contribution needs and self-determination needs over DW and MH of female carers within a PWT framework. Secondly, the study also aimed at verifying the influences of DW sub scales onto MH of these female workers within the Mauritian context. It was noted that all the hypotheses were supported providing insight on how DW related to MH and the mediators played a role in that effect.

As predicted, DW was a strong predictor of survival, social contribution, and self-determination needs, supporting earlier research made by Autin et al. (2019). These needs were viewed as having large and significant effects (Cohen 1988) and offer evidence that people are more likely to address their needs when they have DW. In furtherance to the study of (Amponsah-Tawiah et al. 2023), employees who have DW are more likely to be in a good state of mind and MH since their needs are being fulfilled through their jobs. The findings of this study were also aligned with the study of Duffy et al. (2019) which mirrored that there is a positive association between DW and MH through the satisfaction of an individual's needs. It is understood that in Mauritius, the legislative norms regarding employment are well established and there are Government enforcement agencies that ensures that these laws are complied with. Earlier research on needs satisfaction indicated that critical components influencing psychological well-being include social connection need satisfaction (Autin et al. 2019), survival need satisfaction (Sirgy et al. 2001), and SDT need satisfaction (Deci et al. 2017). The results contribute to the literature by demonstrating the relationship between MH and needs that are specifically measured within a PWT framework. In general, this study supported the link between DW and MH. Female carers with good and decent jobs were more likely to experience good MH because their survival needs, social contribution needs, and self-determination needs were met in Mauritius.

Concerning the influence of the different variables of DW on MH, this study demonstrated that interpersonal and physical safe working conditions, adequate health care, and organisational values had a higher influence when compared to adequate compensation and hours that allow for free time and rest. The finding pertaining to adequate health care was consistent with the study of Ayanian et al. (2000). Physical and interpersonal safe work conditions can affect an individual's MH and, in this study, the finding on this association demonstrated that the individuals had safe and sound working conditions as well as a conducive environment. For access to health care, same is provided on a free basis by the Government of Mauritius to the public. However, there are certain arrangements which need to be made in case of work accident or injury. In view of this, the respondents feel that these arrangements are well made by their employer. Moreover, a few benefited from medical insurance schemes which are partly contributed by the employers. Furthermore, family is the most important non-work domain for the respondents and has significant impact on them, including their work behaviors and well-being (Ford et al. 2007; Liu et al. 2013; Zhu et al. 2019; Ye et al. 2021). Compared to the other variables, adequate compensation and hours that allow for free time and rest had moderate associations in relation to past studies (Baron et al. 2014; Duffy et al. 2019; Harris et al. 2011; Martens et al. 1999). Overall, the findings are consistent with PWT highlighting that when work fulfills an individual's needs for survival and social connection, the well-being and MH of these female workers will improve eventually. The findings of the difference in correlations between the different sub-scales of decent work and mental health showed that Mauritian women had different perspectives of decent work as they were subjected to different work conditions.

6   Implications of Study

Employment plays a leading role in shaping an individual's physical and MH (Modini et al. 2016). In every organisation, MH has become a burning issue and various strategies are now being implemented by them to understand the effect of organisational pressure onto workers and to improve their MH (Amponsah-Tawiah et al. 2023). This study provides insight into how the different variables of DW could hinder/improve the MH of female workers, specifically, carers. These findings provide experts in the field with substantial information on how and why the MH of women may be affected at work. They will thus be able to formulate specific strategies to deal with the MH issues at the workplace.

From a DW perspective, the five subscales (interpersonal and physical conditions, adequate health care, adequate compensation, hours that allow for free time and rest, and organisational values) were interrelated even though the correlation was low for two of the subscales. This implies that female workers possess varying degrees of understanding concerning DW. The needs of female carers also follow a similar reasoning, showing uniqueness despite their tendency to be moderately connected. Having a clear picture of the gaps can help counsellors work on these to eliminate issues hindering the MH of female workers. Likewise, this study adds to the literature in the sense that it examines the general effect of DW on the MH as well as the distinct effect of each subscale on MH of female carers in Mauritius whereby studies on same were limited as well as policies on MH still at a nascent stage.

7   Limitations and Recommendations for Future Studies

It is important to note that the study presented a few limitations after evaluation of findings was made. Firstly, the data used was collected at a one-time point. This indicates the inability of authors to make causal inferences about the present findings. It is therefore recommended that there is use of a wide range of different techniques for future studies such as longitudinal design to overcome this limitation. The use of longitudinal data will be much richer compared to cross-sectional studies allowing future research to take a wide array of background characteristics and to have full control over the variables into account. This will definitely reduce the risk of issues such as unobserved heterogeneity or confounding. Causal inferences about DW and MH can be predicted using data that has been collected over a period of time. Moreover, data collected was only from female carers, that is, from only one occupation in Mauritius, hence, this is not a full representation of the situation across the island. Future studies should collect data from different occupations in Mauritius as well as from both males and females to have a more accurate representation of DW on MH of female and male workers across different regions in Mauritius. Therefore, it remains important to find other studies that can account for this residual variance. It is crucial to incorporate DW, needs satisfaction, and well-being into the structural model along with work fulfillment components (such as job satisfaction and work meaning) from the PWT framework. It will be possible to draw more certain conclusions regarding the significance of work in people's lives by looking at how need satisfaction, which is a prerequisite for good employment, affects work fulfillment and, in turn, the well-being of female workers.

8   Conclusion

Concerns for DW have grown in Mauritius after organisations have been impacted from Covid-19 and the VUCA context but fortunately, we have the required legislation to overcome this (The Workers' Rights Act 2019). However, it is a matter of concern when employees are not informed of the labour laws and let their rights just go away, hence DW gets compromised. In addition, factors related to the job tend to affect the MH of workers as depicted in the literature of this study. Looking at the importance of the subscales of DW and how it exerts an influence on the MH of female workers, there is no doubt that employers as well as the Government should understand and study all the factors that can impede achievement of DW and assess as well how the needs satisfaction elements can be attained by individual female workers.

References

Aldridge, Z., Harrison Dening, K.: Family and other unpaid carers supporting people with dementia. J. Commun. Nursing **36**(1), 47–51 (2022)

Allan, B.A., Tebbe, E.A., Bouchard, L.M., Duffy, R.D.: Access to decent and meaningful work in a sexual minority population. J. Career Assess. **27**(3), 408–421 (2019)

Amponsah-Tawiah, K., Mensah, J., Boakyewaa, R., Asare, G.: From muddiness to madness: an examination of decent work and mental health in the Ghanaian mining industry. Int. J. Law Manage. **65**(4), 289–299 (2023)

Anholon, R., Rampasso, I.S., Martins, V.W., Serafim, M.P., Leal Filho, W., Quelhas, O.L.: COVID-19 and the targets of SDG 8: Reflections on Brazilian scenario. Kybernetes **50**(5), 1679–1686 (2021)

Autin, K.L., et al.: The development and initial validation of the work needs satisfaction scale: Measuring basic needs within the psychology of working theory. J. Couns. Psychol. **66**(2), 195–209 (2019). https://doi.org/10.1037/cou0000323

Ayanian, J.Z., Weissman, J.S., Schneider, E.C., Ginsburg, J.A., Zaslavsky, A.M.: Unmet health needs of uninsured adults in the United States. JAMA **284**(16), 2061–2069 (2000)

Baron, S. L., e t al.: Promoting integrated approaches to reducing health inequalities among lowincome workers: applying a social ecological framework. J. Ind. Med. **57**, 539–556 (2014). https://doi.org/10.1002/ajim.22174

Bauer, J.M., Sousa-Poza, A.: Impacts of informal caregiving on caregiver employment, health, and family. J. Popul. Ageing **8**, 113–145 (2015)

Duggleby, W., et al.: Factors influencing changes in health related quality of life of caregivers of persons with multiple chronic conditions. Health Qual. Life Outcomes **14**, 1–9 (2016)

Bennis, W., Nanus, B.: Leaders: the strategies for Taking Charge. Harper & Row, New York (1985)

Blustein, D.L.: The Psychology of Working: a New Perspective for Career Development, Counseling, and Public Policy. Routledge, NY (2006)

Blustein, D.L., et al.: Profiles of decent work and precarious work: exploring macro-level predictors and mental health outcomes. J. Career Assess. **31**(3), 423–441 (2023)

Buyukgoze-Kavas, A., Autin, K.L.: Decent work in Turkey: context, conceptualization, and assessment. J. Vocat. Behav. **112**, 64–76 (2019)

Caruana, R., Crane, A., Gold, S., LeBaron, G.: Modern slavery in business: the sad and sorry state of a non-field. Bus. Soc. **60**(2), 251–287 (2021)

Chinyamurindi, W., Mathibe, M., Marange, C.S.: Promoting talent through managing mental health: the role of decent work and organisational citizenship behaviour. SA J. Ind. Psychol. **49**(1), 1–10 (2023)

Cohen, J.: Statistical Power Analysis for the Behavioral Sciences, 2nd edn. Lawrence Erlbaum Associates, Publishers, Hillsdale, NJ (1988)

Çolakoğlu, C., Toygar, A.: The psychological effect of compensation on decent work dimensions: a research on public and private school teachers in Turkey. Int. J. Soc. Econ. **48**(8), 1191–1212 (2021)

World Health Organisation. Commission on Social Determinants of Health, Employment conditions and health inequalities: final report to the World Health Organisation (2007). www.who.int/social_determinants/resources/articles/emconet_who_report.pdf

Costa, G.: Shift work and health: current problems and preventive actions. Saf. Health Work 1(2), 112–123 (2010)

Deci, E.L., Olafsen, A.H., Ryan, R.M.: Self-determination theory in work organizations: the state of a science. Annu. Rev. Organ. Psychol. Organ. Behav. 4(1), 19–43 (2017)

Di Fabio, A., Kenny, M.E.: Decent work in Italy: context, conceptualization, and assessment. J. Vocat. Behav. 110, 131–143 (2019)

Di Ruggiero, E., Cohen, J.E., Cole, D.C., Forman, L.: Competing conceptualizations of decent work at the intersection of health, social and economic discourses. Soc Sci Med 133, 120–127 (2015)

Dodd, V., Hooley, T., Burke, C.: Decent work in the UK: context, conceptualization, and assessment. J. Vocat. Behav. 112, 270–281 (2019)

Douglass, R.P., Velez, B.L., Conlin, S.E., Duffy, R.D., England, J.W.: Examining the psychology of working theory: decent work among sexual minorities. J. Couns. Psychol. 64(5), 550 (2017)

Duffy, R.D., et al.: The development and initial validation of the decent work scale. J. Couns. Psychol. 64(2), 206 (2017)

Duffy, R.D., et al.: Developing, validating, and testing improved measures (2019)

Duffy, R.D., Blustein, D.L., Diemer, M.A., Autin, K.L.: The psychology of working theory. J. Couns. Psychol. 63(2), 127 (2016)

Duffy, R.D., Kim, H.J., Perez, G., Prieto, C.G., Torgal, C., Kenny, M.E.: Decent education as a precursor to decent work: an overview and construct conceptualization. J. Vocat. Behav. 138, 103771 (2022)

Duffy, R.D., et al.: An examination of the psychology of working theory with racially and ethnically diverse employed adults. J. Couns. Psychol. 65(3), 280 (2018)

Ferreira, A.I., da Costa Ferreira, P., Cooper, C.L., Oliveira, D.: How daily negative affect and emotional exhaustion correlates with work engagement and presenteeism-constrained productivity. Int. J. Stress. Manag. 26(3), 261–271 (2019)

Ford, M.T., Heinen, B.A., Langkamer, K.L.: Work and family satisfaction and conflict: a meta-analysis of cross-domain relations. J. Appl. Psychol. 92(1), 57 (2007)

Gallo, Ó., Gonzales-Miranda, D.R., Roman-Calderon, J.P., García, G.A.: Decent work and healthy employment: a qualitative case study about Colombian millennials. Int. J. Workplace Health Manage. 13(5), 477–495 (2020)

Gibb, S., Ishaq, M.: Decent work: what matters the most and who can make a difference? Employee Relat. Int. J. 42(4), 845–861 (2018)

González, M.G., Swanson, D.P., Lynch, M., Williams, G.C.: Testing satisfaction of basic psychological needs as a mediator of the relationship between socioeconomic status and physical and mental health. J. Health Psychol. 21(6), 972–982 (2016)

Hado, E., Feinberg, L.F.: Amid the COVID-19 pandemic, meaningful communication between family caregivers and residents of long-term care facilities is imperative. In: Older Adults and COVID-19, pp. 128–133. Routledge (2021)

Hado, E., Komisar, H.: Fact sheet: long-term services and supports. AARP Public Policy Institute (2019). https://www.aarp.org/content/dam/aarp/ppi/2019/08/long-termservices-and supports.doi.10.26419-2Fppi.00079.001.pdf

Harris, J.R., Huang, Y., Hannon, P.A., Williams, B.: Low–socioeconomic status workers: their health risks and how to reach them. J. Occup. Environ. Med. 53(2), 132–138 (2011)

Headey, B., Kelley, J., Wearing, A.: Dimensions of mental health: life satisfaction, positive affect, anxiety and depression. Soc. Indic. Res. 29, 63–82 (1993)

Hellgren, J., Sverke, M.: Does job insecurity lead to impaired well-being or vice versa? Estimation of cross-lagged effects using latent variable modelling. J. Organ. Behav. Int. J. Ind. Occup. Organ. Psychol. Behav. **24**(2), 215–236 (2003)

Hörisch, J.: The relation of COVID-19 to the UN sustainable development goals: Implications for sustainability accounting, management and policy research. Sustain. Account. Manage. Policy J. **12**(5), 877888 (2021)

International Labour Organization (ILO). Decent work. Report of the director general [Internet]. 87 Session. Geneva (Switzerland): International Labour Conference. [cited 2022 July 20], J. Couns. Psychol. **64**(206), (2017) (1999). https://www.ilo.org/public/english/standards/relm/ilc/ilc87/rep-i.htm

Kashyap, V., Nakra, N., Arora, R.: Do, decent work dimensions lead to work engagement? Empirical evidence from higher education institutions in India. Eur. J. Training Dev. **46**(1/2), 158–177 (2022)

Khairy, Y.H., Ghoneim, H.: Women's access and perception of decent work: a case study on Egypt. Manage. Sustain. Arab Rev. **2**(2), 177–202 (2023)

Kim, S.Y., Fouad, N., Maeda, H., Xie, H., Nazan, N.: Midlife work and psychological well-being: a test of the psychology of working theory. J. Career Assess. **26**(3), 413–424 (2018)

Kozan, S., Işık, E., Blustein, D.L.: Decent work and well-being among lowincome Turkish employees: testing the psychology of working theory. J. Couns. Psychol. **66**(3), 317 (2019)

Kozan, S., Işık, E. and Blustein, D.L.: Decent work and well-being among low-income Turkish employees: testing the psychology of working theory. J. Couns. Psychol. **66**(3), 317 (2019)

Landsbergis, P.A., Grzywacz, J.G., LaMontagne, A.D.: Work organization, job insecurity, and occupational health disparities. Am. J. Ind. Med. **57**, 495–515 (2014). https://doi.org/10.1002/ajim.22126

Liu, J., Kwan, H.K., Lee, C., Hui, C.: Work-to-family spillover effects of workplace ostracism: the role of work-home segmentation preferences. Hum. Resour. Manage. **52**(1), 75–93 (2013)

Lombardo, P., Jones, W., Wang, L., Shen, X., Goldner, E.M.: The fundamental association between mental health and life satisfaction: results from successive waves of a Canadian national survey. BMC Public Health **18**, 1–9 (2018)

Maggiori, C., Johnston, C.S., Krings, F., Massoudi, K., Rossier, J.: The role of career adaptability and work conditions on general and professional well-being. J. Vocat. Behav. **83**(3), 437–449 (2013)

Martens, M.F.J., Nijhuis, F.J.N., Van Boxtel, M.P.J., Knottnerus, J.A.: Flexible work schedules and mental and physical health: A study of a working population with non-traditional working hours. J. Organ. Behav. **20**, 35–46 (1999). https://doi.org/10.1002/(sici)1099-1379(199901)20:1%3c35::aid-job879%3e3.0.co;2-z

Martens, M.F.J., Nijhuis, F.J.N., Van Boxtel, M.P.J., Knottnerus, J.A.: Flexible work schedules and mental and physical health: a study of a working population with non-traditional working hours. J. Organ. Behav. **20**(1), 35 (1999)

Mehta, B.S.: A decent work framework: women in the ICT sector in India. Inf. Dev. **32**(5), 1718–1729 (2016)

Mental Health, World Health Organisation (2022). https://www.who.int/news-room/fact-sheets/detail/mental-health-strengtheningour-response/?gclid=CjwKCAiAtt2tBhBDEiwALZuhANFt_5-Uwi1O3dXEUrHWXez6X4B9aSoDL-5DvVIVid49WcMY4Q0xERoC5cIQAvD_BwE

Modini, M., et al.: The mental health benefits of employment: results of a systematic meta-review. Australas. Psychiatry **24**(4), 331–336 (2016)

Mrugalska, B., Ahmed, J.: Organizational agility in industry 4.0: a systematic literature review. Sustainability **13**(15), 8272 (2021)

Mucharraz y Cano, Y., Davila Ruiz, D. and Cuilty Esquivel, K. Burnout effect on working mothers in leadership positions during the COVID-19 lockdown. Gender Manage. Int. J. **38**(7), 962–977 (2023)

New, L.L.: How workplace challenges affect the risk of substance use disorders in a health care environment. Nurs. Clin. **58**(2), 183–195 (2023)

Nizami, N., Prasad, N.: Decent work. Springer, Singapore, (2017)

Osborne, J.W., Overbay, A.: The power of outliers (and why researchers should always check for them). Pract. Assess. Res. Eval. **9**(1), 612 (2019)

Podvorica, G., Murati, V.: Promotion, public policies and decent work: how to foster community cohesion and common vision?. J. Enterp. Commun. People Places Global Econ. **18**(4), 728-745(2023)

Posner, B.Z.: Another look at the impact of personal and organizational values congruency. J. Bus. Ethics **97**(4), 535–541 (2010). www.jstor.org/stable/40929512

Ramachandran, A., Vyas, N., Pothiyil, D.I.: Stress among the caregivers of mentally disabled children visiting a rehabilitation centre in Chennai, Tamil Nadu–a cross-sectional study. Clin. Epidemiol. Global Health **8**(4), 11551157 (2020)

Ribeiro, M.A., Teixeira, M.A.P., Ambiel, R.A.M.: Decent work in Brazil: context, conceptualization, and assessment. J. Vocat. Behav. **112**, 229240 (2019)

Ryan, R.M., Deci, E.L.: Overview of self-determination theory: An organismic dialectical perspective. Handbook Self-determination Res. **2**(333), 36 (2002)

Sirgy, M.J., Efraty, D., Siegel, P., Lee, D.J.: A new measure of quality of work life (QWL) based on need satisfaction and spillover theories. Soc. Indic. Res. **55**, 241–302 (2001)

Smith, R.W., Baranik, L.E., Duffy, R.D.: Psychological ownership within psychology of working theory: a three-wave study of gender and sexual minority employees. J. Vocat. Behav. **118**, 103374 (2020)

Souza, T.F.: Gender equality and decent work: Japan. In The Sustainable Development Goals, pp. 113–126. Routledge (2022)

Stansfeld, S., Clark, C., Bebbington, P.E., King, M., Jenkins, R., Hinchliffe, S.: Common mental disorders. In: NHS Digital (2016)

Strandh, M., Hammarström, A., Nilsson, K., Nordenmark, M., Russel, H.: Unemployment, gender and mental health: the role of the gender regime. Sociol. Health Illn. **35**(5), 649–665 (2013)

Sverke, M., Hellgren, J., Näswall, K.: No security: a meta-analysis and review of job insecurity and its consequences. J. Occup. Health Psychol. **7**(3), 242 (2002)

The Workers' Rights Act 2019. https://labour.govmu.org/Documents/Legislations/THE%20W ORKERS%20RIGHTS%20Act%202019/A%20Consolidated%20Version%20of%20the% 20Workers%27%20Rights%20Act%202019%20as%20at%202%20August%202023.pdf, Gazetted on 23 May 2020

Tokar, D.M., Kaut, K.P.: Predictors of decent work among workers with Chiari malformation: an empirical test of the psychology of working theory. J. Vocat. Behav. **106**, 126–137 (2018)

Twigg, J., Martin, W.: The challenge of cultural gerontology. Gerontologist **55**(3), 353–359 (2015)

United Nations leads call to protect most vulnerable from mental health crisis during and after COVID-19. https://news.un.org/en/story/2020/05/1063882. May 2020, Accessed 1 December 2022, (2020)

United Nations. The Sustainable Development Goals Report 2023: Special edition Towards a Rescue Plan for People and Planet. [online] UNITED NATIONS, United States of America: United Nations, pp. 1–80 (2023). https://www.un.org/sustainabledevelopment/economic%20g rowth/#:~:text=Goal%208%20is%20about%20promoting,global%20economy%20under% 20serious%20threat. Accessed 20 May 2024

Vignoli, E., et al.: Decent work in France: context, conceptualization, and assessment. J. Vocat. Behav. **116**, 103345 (2020)

Wang, D., Jia, Y., Hou, Z.J., Xu, H., Zhang, H., Guo, X.L.: A test of psychology of working theory among Chinese urban workers: examining predictors and outcomes of decent work. J. Vocat. Behav. **115**, 103325 (2019)

Wei, J., Chan, S.H.J., Autin, K.: Assessing perceived future decent work securement among Chinese impoverished college students. J. Career Assess. **30**(1), 3–22 (2022)

Weston, R., Gore Jr, P.A.: A brief guide to structural equation modeling. Couns. Psychol. **34**(5), 719–751 (2006)

Yan, Y., Geng, Y., Gao, J.: Measuring the decent work of knowledge workers: constructing and validating a new scale. Heliyon **9**(7) (2023)

Ye, Y., Zhu, H., Chen, Y., Kwan, H.K., Lyu, Y.: Family ostracism and proactive customer service performance: an explanation from conservation of resources theory. Asia Pacific J. Manage. **38**, 645–667 (2021)

Zhu, H., Lyu, Y., Ye, Y.: Workplace sexual harassment, workplace deviance, and family undermining. Int. J. Contemp. Hosp. Manag. **31**(2), 594–614 (2019)

Transcultural Leadership and Sustainable Development in the Digital Era: Navigating the 4IR in South Africa

Sean Kruger[✉] [iD]

Centre for the Future of Work, University of Pretoria, Pretoria 0002, GT, South Africa
sean.kruger@up.ac.za

Abstract. This study investigates transcultural leadership's role in navigating organisations through the Fourth Industrial Revolution (4IR) towards sustainable development, with a focus on the South African context. It examines the intersection of digital transformation with key sectors like energy transition, circular economy, and sustainability, advocating for leaders to blend global sustainability aims with local cultural insights. Through a mixed-methods approach, combining qualitative focus group discussions with a meta-analysis of literature, the research captures the nuanced interplay between digital maturity and sustainable practices. The findings highlight transcultural leadership as vital for fostering transparency, reform, and digital progress, essential for aligning with Society 5.0 goals. This approach offers strategic insights into digital transformation that promotes sustainable and equitable growth. By engaging a diverse group of participants from various sectors, the study complements its empirical data, ensuring a comprehensive exploration of strategies for achieving sustainability in the 4IR era. This synthesis of leadership strategies and stakeholder insights provides valuable guidance for policymakers, business leaders, and scholars in addressing the 4IR's challenges and leveraging its opportunities for sustainable development.

Keywords: Transcultural leadership · Digital transformation · Sustainable development · Fourth Industrial Revolution (4IR) · Future of Work

1 Introduction

In an era where the pace of technological advancement is unprecedented, organisations worldwide are grappling with the necessity to adapt to a rapidly evolving business landscape. This urgency is primarily driven by the advancements across industries introduced by the Fourth Industrial Revolution (4IR), pushing organisations to either innovate or face obsolescence. The scholarly work of several authors [1–3] underlines the critical pressure on organisations to stay competitive through the adoption of digital transformation processes. These processes are not mere options but imperatives for achieving digital maturity, a state where organisations can thrive amidst technological disruptions [4].

© The Author(s), under exclusive license to Springer Nature Switzerland AG 2025
K. Hinkelmann and H. Smuts (Eds.): Society 5.0 2024, CCIS 2173, pp. 207–217, 2025.
https://doi.org/10.1007/978-3-031-71412-2_15

However, the journey towards digital transformation and maturity presents a multi-faceted challenge, especially when considered within the African context. Despite South Africa's relative progress, the region faces profound challenges, including pervasive corruption, as detailed by Transparency International's Corruption Perceptions Index (CPI) for 2022 [5]. These challenges underscore the indispensable role of new leadership in fostering an environment conducive to transparency, reform, and digital advancement.

To navigate these complexities, a comprehensive digital strategy that aligns with the organisation's overarching objectives is essential. Several works have looked to develop this, where an overarching model was presented for organisational readiness [6]. This overarching strategy serves as a bridge from current operations to future digital aspirations, leveraging emerging technologies as key resources for competitive advantage [7]. Such a strategic approach is vital in cultivating innovative business models adaptable to the dynamic digital ecosystem [8, 9].

Recognising the specific hurdles faced by South Africa and the broader Sub-Saharan region, such as underdeveloped digital infrastructure and significant technological capability gap, it becomes evident that digital transformation can act as a catalyst for overcoming these barriers. Enhanced access to markets, improved public service delivery, and strengthened economic resilience are among the myriad of benefits digital transformation can offer, driving toward sustainable development goals [10].

This study aims to further dichotomise the implications of digital transformation within the South African context, focusing on leadership. The study employs a methodological framework that assesses focus group sessions across four pivotal themes, each of which addresses essential facets of the global transition towards resilience and equity through digital transformation. The methodology not only captures the thematic intricacies but also embodies a novel approach in examining leadership's expertise. The themes for this study includes the energy transition and the future of work, as the energy sector, particularly renewable energy, plays a pivotal role in job creation and drives the need for skills (competency) development, particularly among youth [11–13]. Secondly, the transition to a circular economy that underscores the necessity for innovative financial mechanisms, robust regulatory frameworks, and targeted educational initiatives to foster sustainability and minimise waste, particularly within critical sectors such as agriculture and construction [14, 15]. The third theme, sustainability, and futures literacy, emphasises the significance of equipping individuals and organisations with the tools to forecast and navigate future challenges [6]. This includes scenario planning and the adoption of inclusive infrastructure and conservation strategies to mitigate impending environmental and societal challenges. Finally, integrating sustainability into business strategy examines how embedding sustainable practices within corporate operations can serve as a competitive advantage [16].

By integrating these considerations, the paper seeks to contribute both theoretical insights and practical guidance for policymakers, business leaders, and scholars. It underscores the importance of digital maturity and transformation as mechanisms not only for navigating the challenges presented by the 4IR but also for driving sustainable practices within an inclusive Society 5.0. Through this exploration, the study endeavours to highlight the role of transcultural leadership in steering organisations towards resilience, equity, and environmental stewardship in an increasingly digital world.

The paper is structured as follows. Section 2 briefly reviews leadership in the digital age. Section 3 presents the methodology followed by the findings section, that provides grouped insights per the four themes. Discussion around the findings is then presented, ending with conclusions drawn, acknowledgements and limitations.

2   Background

In the wake of escalating economic and geopolitical challenges, leaders worldwide are navigating an increasingly complex and unpredictable landscape. The convergence of global disruptions, such as the COVID-19 pandemic and geopolitical tensions, has precipitated a series of economic shocks, underscoring the urgency for adept leadership in steering organisations through these turbulent times [17, 18]. The 4IR further compounds these challenges, introducing rapid technological changes that disrupt traditional business models and necessitate agile responses to consumer demands and supply chain pressures [19, 20].

As organisations integrate emerging technologies of the 4IR like the Internet of Things (IoT) and Artificial Intelligence (AI), the landscape of operations and the future of work undergo significant transformations. These technologies not only optimise operational efficiencies but also usher in new business models and strategies for competitive advantage [6, 21]. Amidst this technological disturbance, the role of leadership evolves, emphasising the need for leaders to adapt across cultures, reviewing their strategies and competencies to navigate the intricacies of digital transformation and the future of work effectively.

2.1   Digital Maturity, Transformation and Strategic Implementation

Digital maturity represents an organisation's adaptability and responsiveness to digital changes, encapsulating the integration of digital processes across all organisational levels [7]. This study adopts a nuanced definition of digital maturity, viewing it as a gradual but comprehensive embedding of digital practices within an organisation's fabric, from employee engagement to overarching strategic aims.

Digital transformation, albeit without a universally accepted definition, is broadly understood as the process through which organisations embrace digital strategies. This transformation transcends the mere adoption of new technologies; it entails a profound reshaping of business structures, cultures, leadership approaches, and personnel dynamics [4]. It can be argued as a holistic socio-technical endeavour, necessitating a shift towards a digital mindset that permeates the entire organisational culture and strategy.

The formulation and execution of an effective digital strategy hinge on aligning technological initiatives with the core business strategy, ensuring organisational agility, and fostering an environment conducive to digital innovation [6]. This approach requires a commitment from all organisational levels, from leadership to frontline staff, necessitating skills development and knowledge enhancement to drive the digital agenda forward [22].

2.2   Transcultural Leadership in Navigating Digital Transformation

Transcultural leadership emerges as a pivotal force in guiding organisations through the complexities of digital transformation. This "new" leadership style, characterised by its ability to transcend cultural boundaries and adapt to global digital trends, is crucial for driving transformational efforts across diverse and geographically dispersed teams. By fostering inclusivity, innovation, and adaptability, transcultural leaders play a crucial role in ensuring their organisations are not only digitally mature but also equipped to leverage digital transformation for sustainable competitive advantage [23].

3   Methodology

The research design of this study encompasses a mixed-methods approach, predominantly qualitative, through the execution of structured focus group sessions. This methodological choice reflects the study's commitment to capturing the complexities and nuances of sustainability, renewable energy transitions, circular economies, futures literacy, and the integration of sustainability into business strategies. By incorporating both focus group discussions and a meta-analysis of existing literature and case studies, the research offers a multifaceted exploration of these critical themes. This dual approach not only enriches the empirical data gathered through direct stakeholder engagement but also situates these insights within a broader scholarly and practical context, ensuring a comprehensive understanding of the subjects at hand [24, 25].

For the focus group sessions, the study prioritised diversity in participant selection, encompassing industry experts, academics, practitioners, and policymakers. This strategic composition facilitated multidimensional dialogues, capturing a wide array of perspectives on the transition to renewable energy, the circular economy, and other related themes. The sessions were designed to promote open and in-depth discussions, utilising interactive methodologies such as group brainstorming and role-play exercises. This engagement strategy was aimed at stimulating creative thinking and encouraging the sharing of experiences and insights, thereby enriching the qualitative data collected. The meticulous recording of thought leadership of these sessions underscored the commitment to thorough qualitative analysis, ensuring the depth and reliability of the data [25]. It must be noted that the participants were completely anonymised, allowing for free speech and minimal risk in any form of discrimination where insights were tracked on a project management tool, Miro.

The thematic structure of the focus group discussions was curated to address objectives related to the study's overarching themes. Each theme was explored through targeted discussion points and activities designed to elicit detailed insights and strategies from participants. For instance, discussions on the shift towards renewable energy examined its implications for job markets and skill requirements, while dialogues on the circular economy focused on its potential for sustainable development, particularly within the South African context. Futures literacy was investigated for its role in enhancing sustainability planning, and the integration of sustainability into business strategies was scrutinized for its capacity to drive competitive advantage and sustainable growth.

Complementing the focus group sessions, a meta-analysis of relevant literature and case studies was conducted. This review aimed to contextualise the insights from the discussions, drawing on peer-reviewed articles, industry reports, and case studies to identify trends, gaps, and opportunities in the fields under investigation. The synthesis of this literature with the empirical data from the focus groups provided a comprehensive understanding of the challenges and potential solutions in advancing sustainability [26].

The qualitative data derived from the focus group sessions were analysed through thematic analysis. This involved coding the data logged to identify emergent patterns and themes, guided by the objectives of the study. The integration of findings from the meta-analysis further enriched this analysis, enabling the research to draw on a broad spectrum of sources. This comprehensive approach facilitated the identification of actionable insights and strategies for promoting sustainable development.

4 Findings

The research delves into the role of leadership across four key sectors, offering insights into the leadership strategies deemed critical for navigating the challenges and opportunities presented by the 4IR, such as digital transformation. It particularly focuses on areas where leadership can drive significant change, particularly in South Africa. Transcultural leadership, with its emphasis on cross-cultural understanding and global inclusivity, emerges as a critical facilitator in this transition. This leadership is now assessed across four themes.

4.1 Theme 1: The Energy Transition and the Future of Work

The energy transition from fossil fuels to renewable sources represents a critical juncture in both global and national economic landscapes, with far-reaching implications for job creation, workforce development, and leadership strategies [11]. This transition, driven by the urgent need for environmental sustainability, is also emerging as a vital engine for economic growth and employment opportunities. Notably, the renewable energy sector is projected to generate 42 million jobs worldwide by 2050, as highlighted by the International Renewable Energy Agency (IRENA). In the South African context, initiatives such as the Renewable Energy Independent Power Producer Procurement Programme (REIPPPP) are pivotal, aiming not only to mitigate the country's energy crisis but also to foster job creation and industrial advancement. This underscores the critical role of leadership in spearheading skills development and educational reforms, especially in technical and vocational areas, to align the workforce with the demands of the burgeoning green economy. The group noted that this growth presents several opportunities across diverse roles across manufacturing, installation, maintenance, and support services within various technologies such as solar, wind, hydro, and bioenergy. The resulting job opportunities across these technologies highlights the sector's capacity to drive economic benefits across various regions and skill sets, thus presenting a critical focus area for policymakers and leaders worldwide [11, 27].

In South Africa, the group noted the need for strategic initiatives to leverage renewable energy for not only addressing energy challenges but also for catalysing job creation and industrial development. However, it was argued that leadership in this transformative period demands a multifaceted approach, focusing on skills development, educational reform, supportive policy and regulatory frameworks, and comprehensive stakeholder engagement. There is a pressing need for initiatives that equip the workforce with relevant skills for the green economy, fostering innovation, critical thinking, and adaptability. Moreover, the development and implementation of policies that encourage investment in renewable energy, ensure fair labour practices, and promote sustainable development are essential. Engaging a broad spectrum of stakeholders, including industry, academia, communities, and government, is crucial to ensuring an inclusive and beneficial transition. Furthermore, the specific skills required for the future in the renewable energy sector, such as installations, maintenance, and the development of new technologies, underscore the importance of basic education reform, the introduction of technical subjects, and a shift towards technical and vocational education and training (TVET) colleges with a focus on extensive skills development. Initiatives such as bursaries from the government, pilot plants for renewables by Eskom, and programs to engage young people in renewable energy from an early age are essential steps in building a workforce ready for the challenges and opportunities of the green economy.

4.2 Theme 2: Just Transition to a Circular Economy

Central to a circular economy, a model predicated on minimising waste and maximising the reuse of resources is the notion that economic growth can be uncoupled from increased resource consumption, thereby paving the way for sustainable development paradigms. The Ellen MacArthur Foundation's projections posit that by 2030, a circular economy could stimulate economic benefits amounting to US $4.5 trillion [15].

The group noted that within the South African context, the shift towards a circular economy is deemed imperative for fostering sustainable growth, addressing environmental demands, and mitigating economic disparities. The pivotal role of transcultural leaders in championing financial innovation, regulatory reforms, and educational endeavours to advance circular economy principles was underscored. Such a transition, especially within critical sectors like agriculture and construction, will necessitate a comprehensive strategy encompassing financial innovation, regulatory overhaul, and educational initiatives. This means that, based on feedback and literature, a departure from the conventional linear economy model ("take, make, dispose") will be needed. It needs to change towards a regenerative circular economy is pivotal in addressing global challenges such as climate change, resource scarcity, and social inequity. In South Africa, the circular economy transition must be viewed not just as an environmental imperative but also as a keystone for economic and social resilience, reflecting the nation's unique socio-economic fabric [28]. To do so, it was noted that financial innovation is paramount in facilitating a shift towards a circular economy. Emerging financing models, including green bonds and sustainability-linked loans, can be instrumental in incentivising circular practices adoption. In South Africa, channelling investments into sustainable ventures in agriculture and construction can benefit several stakeholders, particularly small and medium-sized enterprises (SMEs) that traditionally face hurdles in securing conventional financing. Interestingly, it was noted that policies that promote product longevity, recycling, and renewable materials usage are essential. The National Development Plan 2030 of South Africa underscores this. Nevertheless, the implementation of these policies demands robust governance and interdisciplinary collaboration, which was highlighted as severally lacking. Finally, education was considered the cornerstone of the circular economy, giving individuals with the requisite knowledge and skills for sustainable innovation and practice. Transcultural leadership can play a vital role in bridging circular principles across diverse cultural and social backgrounds, globally and within South Africa. This entails the integration of circular economy concepts into educational curricula and professional development initiatives, alongside augmenting public consciousness regarding sustainable consumption and production methodologies.

4.3   Theme 3: Sustainability and Futures Literacy

The integration of futures literacy and scenario planning emerges as indispensable tools in the realm of sustainable development, offering a strategic edge in navigating the complexities of future challenges [22]. The delegates noted the UNESCO Futures Literacy Framework as a good foundational perspective, emphasising the value of competencies in fostering informed decision-making processes. Such tools can be particularly relevant in both global and South African contexts, where transcultural leadership plays a pivotal role. This leadership style can weave futures literacy into the fabric of strategic planning, equipping organisations to confront the uncertainties brought on by the 4IR.

However, such leadership would necessitate a profound understanding and integration of diverse cultural perspectives and practices. It would need to extend the narrative beyond mere cultural navigation to a holistic approach that considers the long-term impacts of decisions on global sustainability. The global orientation intrinsic to transcultural leadership would then need to be adaptive, inclusive, and forward-looking.

Within South Africa, characterized, the group noted that futures literacy and scenario planning hold significant promise. The adoption of technologies by South African leaders can facilitate the development of resilient and inclusive strategies that address critical issues such as water scarcity, energy transition, and socio-economic disparities. Such strategies not only cater to the immediate needs of the diverse population but also contribute to the broader global sustainability agenda. The focus group sessions and expert insights highlighted that there are complex dynamics of water sustainability, emphasising the necessity for accessible clean water for every household. The discussions revealed a consensus on the need for a multifaceted approach that includes legislative measures, proactive water use, sustainable town planning, pollution management, and community education. The exploration of innovative solutions such as greywater systems, rainwater harvesting, and the redesign of water fixtures underscores the urgency of addressing water sustainability comprehensively. The dialogue further identifies several challenges, including water overconsumption across industries, the "brain drain" of graduates, and political and socio-economic obstacles. The proposed solutions encompass a broad spectrum of strategies, from enhancing water conservation education to implementing industry-specific key performance indicators for water usage. The emphasis on community engagement, sustainable urban planning, and improved farming practices reflects a collective aspiration towards a more sustainable and water-secure future.

4.4   Theme 4: Integrating Sustainability in Business Strategy

From focus group sessions and expert insights, there is transformative potential of integrating sustainability into business strategy, where competitive advantage must be grounded in the principles of environmental, social, and governance (ESG) considerations. This discussion reviewed that there is a strong need for sustainable practices across diverse industries, with an in-depth examination of the mining sector, renowned for its profound environmental and societal footprints, thereby underlining the imperative for sustainable operational paradigms. Specifically, it was argued that in the South African context, transcultural leadership is essential for integrating business strategies with sustainability goals, propelling the nation towards a more sustainable economic framework. The dialogue further highlighted the strategic benefits of sustainability, illustrating how incorporating ESGs into corporate strategies not only enhances brand reputation and fosters customer loyalty but also boosts financial and market performance in the long term. This was evidenced by the increasing assets under management by sustainable investment funds, which signal growing investor confidence in the principles of sustainability as noted by an expert.

Within the mining sector, attention was drawn to the necessity for companies to adopt sustainable practices, such as responsible mineral sourcing, carbon footprint reduction, and active community engagement. These measures are critical for mitigating environmental and social risks and securing operational legitimacy. The discussion wrapped up with practical suggestions for transcultural leaders to effectively weave sustainability into business strategies. These suggestions include developing transcultural competence to adeptly manage global sustainability standards within local contexts, strategically aligning business decisions with the ESGs, investing in sustainable practices to minimise environmental impact and enhance community relations, engaging stakeholders to ensure initiatives meet diverse needs, and implementing thorough monitoring and transparent reporting mechanisms to track sustainability progress and demonstrate accountability.

5   Discussion

This study considered the critical domains of the energy transition, circular economy, sustainability, and futures literacy, and their integration into business strategy. These themes were explored through the lens of transcultural leadership, underscoring the need for investigations into ways to navigate the digital transformation whilst fostering sustainable practices within the emerging Society 5.0 framework.

The discourse around the energy transition and the future of work within the renewable energy sector highlights a pressing need for upskilling and reskilling the workforce to meet the sector's evolving demands. This aligns with the Technology-Organisation-Environment (TOE) framework, suggesting that organisations must adapt to their changing environments or face obsolescence. A key component in the 4IR is leveraging the emerging technologies it brings with it. In this context, transcultural leadership emerges as a critical facilitator, bridging the gap between global best practices and local applicability. Such leadership underscores the importance of integrating diverse cultural perspectives and knowledge systems, enabling organisations to navigate the complexities of the energy transition effectively.

In the shift towards a circular economy, the discussion points to significant barriers such as regulatory hurdles and the necessity for substantial investment in new technologies. Yet, it also shows the potential for economic and environmental benefits that serve as pivotal motivators. This transition demonstrates the practical implications of transcultural leadership in steering organisations through diverse cultural, economic, and social landscapes, advocating for a collaborative approach that transcends national boundaries and sectors. It embodies the TOE by illustrating how adaptive strategies, rooted in sustainability, and leveraging technology can foster organisational resilience in this new age.

The emphasis on sustainability and futures literacy brings to light the indispensable role of scenario planning and systems thinking in anticipating and navigating future sustainability challenges. This necessitates a leadership style that is inclusive, forward-looking, and adept at integrating global sustainability goals with local realities. Such a leadership approach is vital for creating sustainable futures, emphasising the role of leaders in championing inclusive infrastructure and conservation practices. Integrating sustainability into business strategy, particularly through the alignment with ESGs, presents not only ethical imperatives but also avenues for competitive advantage. This finding reiterates the significance of transcultural leadership in the synthesis of global objectives and local cultural and socio-economic realities. It highlights the evolving role of leaders in ensuring that their organizations are not only participants in the global market but also contributors to a sustainable and equitable future.

In the context of Society 5.0, these discussions underscore the urgent need for leaders who can navigate the complexities of digital transformation while championing sustainable practices. Transcultural leadership, with its emphasis on inclusivity, adaptability, and a global-local synthesis, is identified as crucial for the successful implementation of sustainability initiatives that are coherent with global standards yet resonant with local nuances. Such leadership is pivotal in driving organisations towards resilience, equity, and environmental stewardship in an increasingly digital and interconnected world.

6   Conclusion

This study reviewed the interplay between digital transformation and sustainable development within the South African landscape, through the lens of transcultural leadership. Employing a methodological framework that integrated focus group discussions and expert insights across four pivotal themes—sustainable development, the future of work, circular economy, and futures literacy—this research aimed to uncover the strategic imperatives for leadership in the era of the 4IR. The findings show the indispensable role of transcultural leadership in navigating the multifaceted challenges and opportunities presented by digital transformation towards fostering sustainable and inclusive growth. It also showed a critical demand for upskilling the workforce to meet the needs of the renewable energy sector, overcoming regulatory and technological hurdles in the adoption of a circular economy, harnessing futures literacy for strategic sustainability planning, and embedding sustainability within business strategies for a competitive edge. It underscores the imperative for a new paradigm of leadership that champions educational reform, financial innovation, regulatory adaptation, and the strategic integration of sustainability principles. Such leadership is essential for guiding both global and local communities towards resilience, equity, and environmental stewardship.

Acknowledgments. The author would like to thank all participants and supporting agents during the TLS workshop.

Disclosure of Interests. The authors have no competing interests to declare that are relevant to the content of this article. No funding was received for this study.

References

1. Galindo-Martín, M.Á., Castaño-Martínez, M.S., Méndez-Picazo, M.T.: Digital transformation, digital dividends and entrepreneurship: a quantitative analysis. J. Bus. Res. **101**, 522–527 (2019). https://doi.org/10.1016/j.jbusres.2018.12.014
2. Bygstad, B., Aanby, H.P., Iden, J.: Leading digital transformation: the scandinavian way. In: Stigberg, S., Karlsen, J., Holone, H., Linnes, C. (eds.) Nordic Contributions in IS Research, SCIS 2017, LNBIP, vol. 294, pp. 1-14. Springer, Cham (2017). https://doi.org/10.1007/978-3-319-64695-4_1
3. Shaughnessy, H.: Creating digital transformation: strategies and steps. Strat. Leadersh. **46**, 19–25 (2018). https://doi.org/10.1108/SL-12-2017-0126
4. Pinto, M.R., Salume, P.K., Barbosa, M.W., de Sousa, P.R.: The path to digital maturity: A cluster analysis of the retail industry in an emerging economy. Technol Soc. **72** (2023). https://doi.org/10.1016/j.techsoc.2022.102191
5. Transparency International: Corruption Perception Index: 2022 (2022)
6. Kruger, S., Steyn, A.A.: Leveraging technology adoption to navigate the 4IR towards a future-ready business: a systematic literature review. Eng. Rep. (2023). https://doi.org/10.1002/eng2.12762
7. Salviotti, G., Gaur, A., Pennarola, F.: Strategic Factors Enabling Digital Maturity: An Extended Survey. Presented at the
8. Coskun-Setirek, A., Tanrikulu, Z.: Digital innovations-driven business model regeneration: a process model. Technol. Soc. **64**, 101461 (2021). https://doi.org/10.1016/j.techsoc.2020.101461
9. Kruger, S., Steyn, A.A.: Developing breakthrough innovation capabilities in university ecosystems: a case study from South Africa. Technol. Forecast Soc. Change. **198** (2024). https://doi.org/10.1016/j.techfore.2023.123002
10. Shubha, V.: Leading digital transformation with e-Governance competency framework. In: De', R., M, M.N., Baguma, R., Janowski, T. (eds.) ACM International Conference Proceeding Series, pp. 11–17. Association for Computing Machinery (2017). https://doi.org/10.1145/3055219.3055223
11. IRENA: renewable energy statistics: international renewable energy agency (2021)
12. McDowall, W.: Technology roadmaps for transition management: the case of hydrogen energy. Technol. Forecast Soc. Change. **79**, 530–542 (2012). https://doi.org/10.1016/j.techfore.2011.10.002
13. Rockefeller foundation: digital jobs in Africa: Catalyzing inclusive opportunities for Youth. (2013)
14. Walter, A., Finger, R., Huber, R., Buchmann, N.: Smart farming is key to developing sustainable agriculture. Proc. Natl. Acad. Sci. **114**, 6148–6150 (2017). https://doi.org/10.1073/pnas.1707462114

15. Nudurupati, S.S., et al.: Transforming sustainability of Indian small and medium-sized enterprises through circular economy adoption. J. Bus. Res. **149**, 250–269 (2022). https://doi.org/10.1016/j.jbusres.2022.05.036

16. Fan, Y.-J., Liu, S.-F., Luh, D.-B., Teng, P.-S.: Corporate sustainability: Impact factors on organizational innovation in the industrial area. Sustainability (Switzerland). **13**, 1–24 (2021). https://doi.org/10.3390/su13041979

17. Tripathi, S., Gupta, M.: Identification of challenges and their solution for smart supply chains in Industry 4.0 scenario: a neutrosophic DEMATEL approach. Int. J. Logist. Syst. Manage. **40**, 70–94 (2021). https://doi.org/10.1504/IJLSM.2021.117691

18. Vasilieva, E.V: Development of leadership institute and personnel landscape in conditions of digital transformation. In: Becker, J., Matveev, M., Taratukhin, V. (eds.) CEUR Workshop Proceedings. CEUR-WS (2020)

19. Frederico, G.F., Garza-Reyes, J.A., Anosike, A., Kumar, V.: Supply chain 4.0: concepts, maturity and research agenda. Supply Chain Manage. **25**, 262–282 (2020). https://doi.org/10.1108/SCM-09-2018-0339

20. Nasiri, M., Ukko, J., Saunila, M., Rantala, T.: Managing the digital supply chain: The role of smart technologies. Technovation. **102121** (2020). https://doi.org/10.1016/j.technovation.2020.102121

21. Sohn, K., Kwon, O.: Technology acceptance theories and factors influencing artificial Intelligence-based intelligent products. Telematics Inf. **47** (2020). https://doi.org/10.1016/j.tele.2019.101324

22. Kolade, O., Owoseni, A.: Employment 5.0: the work of the future and the future of work. Technol Soc. **71** (2022). https://doi.org/10.1016/j.techsoc.2022.102086

23. Gilli, K., Lettner, N., Guettel, W.: The future of leadership: new digital skills or old analog virtues? J. Bus. Strat. (2023). https://doi.org/10.1108/JBS-06-2022-0093

24. Saunders, M.N.K., Lewis, P., Thornhill, A.: Research Methods for Business Students. Pearson, London (2019)

25. Cassell, C., Cunliffee, A., Grandy, G., Cunliffe, A.L., Grandy, G.: Qualitative Business and Management Research Methods. SAGE Publications, London (2018)

26. Tashakkori, A., Teddlie, C., Teddlie, C.B.: Mixed Methodology: Combining Qualitative and Quantitative Approaches. SAGE, Thousand Oaks (1998)

27. Arias, K., et al.: Green transition and gender bias: An analysis of renewable energy generation companies in Latin America. Energy Res. Soc. Sci. **101** (2023). https://doi.org/10.1016/j.erss.2023.103151

28. Hoosain, M.S., Paul, B.S., Doorsamy, W., Ramakrishna, S.: Comparing South Africa's sustainability and circular economic roadmap to the rest of the world. Mater. Circ. Econ. **5** (2023). https://doi.org/10.1007/s42824-023-00073-x

A Decision-Support Approach for University Incubators

Emanuele Laurenzi[✉][iD], Dario Meyer[iD], and Patrick Moesch

FHNW - University of Applied Sciences and Arts Northwestern Switzerland,
Riggenbachstrasse 16, 4600 Olten, Switzerland
{emanuele.laurenzi,dario.meyer}@fhnw.ch

Abstract. University incubators support students in the creation of innovative startups and promise to play a crucial role in fostering economic growth in the Society 5.0 paradigm. However, most of these incubators are still in their infancy, making their success a trial-and-error practice. To foster the fast successful development of incubators by universities, this paper proposes a decision-support system (DSS). The latter has been built by following the Design Science Research methodology, where the design was driven by accommodating findings from both the literature and interviews with 7 Swiss university incubators. The approach has been instantiated in a web-based questionnaire, which outputs a radar chart containing an assessment of critical success factors. This provides awareness of and suggestions about what shall be improved, thus supporting decision-making. The evaluation was carried out to prove the system's correctness by showing that values of critical success factors were calculated correctly for each university incubator involved in the study. This work is the first attempt toward an open-source decision-support system that each university incubator can use and extend to increase its success ratio.

Keywords: Critical Success Factors · Decision Support System · Evaluation · University Incubator

1 Introduction

As a user-centric society, the Society 5.0 paradigm has the grand challenge of balancing economic development while resolving social problems and ensuring a high quality of life [10]. Universities incubators can contribute significantly to tackling this challenge by providing the right skills to the current and future workforce [16]. This type of incubator supports students in the creation of startups, thus offering a practical learning experience in innovation and entrepreneurship [8,11,13]. The subsequent creation of startups (1) have a positive impact on society as their products and services address human needs and (2) supports economic growth by creating new jobs. Despite their benefits, university incubators are still in their infancy.

© The Author(s), under exclusive license to Springer Nature Switzerland AG 2025
K. Hinkelmann and H. Smuts (Eds.): Society 5.0 2024, CCIS 2173, pp. 218–228, 2025.
https://doi.org/10.1007/978-3-031-71412-2_16

This also holds for Switzerland, despite being among the most innovative countries in the world [12]. Prestigious universities like the Swiss Federal Institute of Technology Zurich (ETH), Ecole Polytechnique Fédérale de Lausanne (EPFL), and the University of St. Gallen (HSG) established incubators around a decade ago. Other Swiss universities and universities of applied sciences have recognized the value of having incubators only more recently. For example, Impact-Lab[1] was launched just in 2020 as the first incubator of the FHNW - University of Applied And Arts Northwestern Switzerland.

The establishment of successful university incubators, however, is not a trivial task. It is still a trial-and-error activity with not yet solid best practices.

In this work, we propose a decision-support system for managers or heads of university incubators to support the successful establishment of university incubators. The paper is structured as follows. Section 2 presents the relevant literature. Section 3 describes the methodology. Section 4 describes the proposed approach while Sect. 5 elaborates on the evaluation. Finally, Sect. 6 concludes the paper.

2   Literature Review

Incubators have become an important tool for bringing startups and spin-offs to the market - at universities and in the economy in general. The primary goal of an incubator is to create jobs, revitalize economic development, support particular target groups or industries, and develop companies and clusters [2,15]. At the micro level, the aim is to increase the chances of its incubated companies to survive the initial stages by providing tailored services [3]. An incubator can be defined as follows: *"developmental assistance offered to client firms via the incubator management through in-tangible services such as coaching, mentoring, consulting, general advice, motivation and 'pep-talk', business introductions, technical appraisal and business network access"* [1]. The importance of incubators for university was demonstrated in a study with more than 60'000 students from more than 20 countries. The study discovered that 43% of participants planned to become self-employed within five years after graduation. This shows the close connection between higher education and entrepreneurship [18] and the importance of having offerings such as incubators to support students in their entrepreneurial endeavors. Additionally, universities can benefit from incubators by promoting and commercializing their academic research into tangible products, which in turn benefits the university by strengthening the interactions between the university research and the industry [21]. Thus, incubators are an essential part of any entrepreneurial university.

Studies have shown that it is unclear whether incubators benefit the firms involved and under what conditions. Some studies have found a positive impact [7,9,30], while others have questioned the service quality and the legal protection of the ideas in an incubator [22]. For an incubator to succeed, elements that directly or indirectly impact an organization's performance must be

---

[1] https://impactlab.fhnw.ch/.

managed and navigated [24]. These elements, also referred to as "critical success factors", are those that must be successfully carried out in order to accomplish the mission, objectives, or goals of an organization or project [24] and overcome the challenges. For university incubators CSFs have already been identified in previous research [14,20] and can be summarized with the below categories:

Innovation and Adaptability: incubators, much like users during the adoption phase [8], need to reinvent or modify innovations. To sustain success, incubators must remain at the forefront of innovation, adapting strategies, programmes and offerings to changing demands and technological advances [23].

Operational Factors: an integral role in shaping the business' operational aspects is determining the specific needs of entrepreneurs [13,20]. Those with a technical background may face challenges in understanding financial aspects. Therefore, beyond providing favorable conditions, incubators guide growth, set realistic targets, monitor progress, and enforce documentation and structure, serving as a manual for startups' operations and fostering long-term success [13].

Resource Provision: incubator networks are one of the critical resources provided to entrepreneurs [28]. There are internal and external networks and partnerships that can increase the perceived technological potential of companies through effective knowledge sharing and access to complementary resources [27]. Moreover, new businesses often require a large sum of funding to finance research and development, which they often struggle to obtain.

Legitimacy: the record of the financial success of their incubated firms, the development of robust networks, high-quality services, and a positive influence on the local economy and community are some of the factors that impact the reputation of an incubator [28]. A specialized focus of an incubator in a specific industry or technology may further bolster an incubator's legitimacy [26]. This can result in the incubator's better reputation within a particular industry and a better reputation amongst potential investors and clients.

Future Strategies: profit-oriented incubators' future success involves balancing industry expertise with diversification, prioritizing entrepreneurs' interests, and offering value-added services [29]. University-based incubators, per Yamockul et al. [31], should prioritize candidates based on education, early investments, financial capacity, and readiness to leverage university research and technology.

To support incubators in implementing these success factors, the goal of this research is to develop a DSS. DSS are information systems that assist and enhance managerial decision-making. Keen [19] narrowed the focus of DSS to semi-structured managerial choices, which is still the case today. The primary goal of DSS developers was to foster a collaborative environment where a human decision-maker and an IT-based system could work together to solve issues. While the information system automates the structured elements of the decision scenario, the human handles the complicated, unstructured portions of the problem [19]. The objective of this method is not to deliver a finished application software that effectively resolves the issue at hand [4]. The issues encountered are, by definition, either unsolvable or inappropriate for an IT-based solution. Instead, improving the decision-makers effectiveness is the aim of DSS development. Therefore, DSS can also be a crucial tool for an incubator in decreasing the failure rate of incubated startups by supporting various processes, such as selection, profitability and survivability.

3   Methodology

Given the design challenge posed in this research work, we followed the Design Science Research methodology [17], which consists of five phases: problem awareness, suggestion, development, evaluation, and conclusion.

The *problem awareness* was deepened by investigating literature review and by interviewing seven university incubators. In the *suggestion phase*, the approach was proposed with (1) a list of critical success factors (CSFs), (2) a questionnaire and formula for the calculation of CSFs values, and (3) recommendations for the given CSF values.

In the *development phase*, we implemented the approach in a web-based solution, in which, given the answers to the questionnaire, a radar chart is created, where each CSF gets a value. Based on these values, specific recommendations are given. Next, in the *evaluation phase*, the approach was evaluated with respect to its correctness. Namely, we filled out one questionnaire for each university incubator, with the data collected during the interviews. Next, the expected results (CSFs values and recommendations) were shown in the radar chart interface. Finally, the *conclusion* summarizes the research, identifies the limitations and suggests future research.

4   A Decision-Support Approach for University Incubators

The Decision Support System in this research is based on the literature and qualitative data collection from experts. It should help to effectively manage an incubator that assesses all the critical areas of a university incubator. For the collection of data in the problem phase, 7 expert interviews with incubator managers in Swiss universities were conducted, which have successful incubators. The interviews were structured against critical success factor categories from the literature review to gather knowledgeable insights in these categories. This helped to identify leaders and laggards in each of the separate areas. The chosen categories for the questionnaire with the key findings from the interviews were as follows:

– Organizational Structure & Strategy [20,29]: All incubators have different focus areas. While some focus more on technology, others have their expertise in biotechnology or medical technology (medtech). There are also incubators with no specific focus.

- Selection & Onboarding Process [25,29]: The key distinctions were in the way applicants are selected. Some have a very clear evaluation process while others require a link to research and IP and some prioritize soft skills over just their idea or research.
- Support & Resources [6,20]: There are many differences in this area including the amount of funding provided, from a large grant to no funding, from many networking events to almost none and from providing office space to no dedicated co-working space.
- Performance Measurement & Feedback [5,29]: Some universities track the engagement through their newsletter and blog while also keeping track of the number of startups, coaching sessions and events and others focus more on successful founding and amount of funding raised.
- Adaptability & Innovation [8,23]: All of the incubators had ways on how they ensure staying open for change. Either through their networks, attending conferences or some are part in global alliances that ensure staying connected and informed.
- Stakeholder Engagement & Networking [6,29]: Some have no formal mechanisms in place on how to stay engaged with their stakeholders, while other institutions place significant importance on maintaining solid relationships with their partners.

The key findings show, there are significant differences within the offerings and the management of the incubators. Based on the success and the comparison of the incubators, a best practice for each of these categories could be identified in the suggestion phase. Also the relevant areas of each CSF were identified. These factors allow for distinction, and therefore evaluation. Based on these, the DSS will provide an option for how university incubators in Switzerland, and globally, can assess their incubator against those categories. Based on the outcome, actions and decisions can be derived.

The first step of developing the DSS is the collection of data through its users. In this step, a form with a series of questions across the different success factors is created and answered based on the data collected from the interviews. For each of the CSF categories, at least four questions were asked to get an estimate of where the incubator stands in each of the mentioned categories. There were different types of scales: 1–10, True and False and likert scale questions. The questionnaire was implemented in a Google form and can be found on the following link: **Link to the survey**.

In a second step, the collected data were normalized to make the various scales comparable. The below transformation was performed.

1. Scale from 1–10 will remain as is
2. True or False: A true will result in 10 and a false in 1
3. To compare the Likert scale with the above values, the min-max normalization is used.

$$x_{scaled} = \frac{x - x_{min}}{x_{max} - x_{min}} \tag{1}$$

After applying the above formula, the below values are derived. Strongly disagree = 1
Disagree = 3.25
Neutral = 5.5
Agree = 7.75
Strongly Agree = 10

The below formula was applied to calculate the final score, from 0 (min) to 6 (excellent), where 4 is sufficient. This is consistent with the Swiss grading system and Swiss to which Swiss university incubators are familiar. figr

$$\text{Score} = \left(\frac{\sum \text{Answers}}{\text{Number of Questions}} \right) \times \frac{6}{10} \tag{2}$$

The normalization allows the data to be compared, also visually.

Each CSF's best practices identified from the interviews were considered to provide recommendations in a written format. Due to space limitation, Table 1 shows the recommendations for three of the six CSFs. The guidance intensifies if the score of a CSF is below 4.

Table 1. An excerpt of the recommendations for each CSF

Category	Rating 4–6	Rating below 4
Organizational Structure & Strategy	Your current structure is effective. Consider periodic strategy workshops to explore emerging trends and opportunities. Collaboration with international incubators could bring fresh perspectives	Develop a more streamlined organizational structure with clearly defined roles and responsibilities. Consider setting up an advisory board comprising industry experts and successful entrepreneurs to guide strategic decisions. Engaging with alumni can also provide valuable insights into improving incubator strategies. Consider expanding the incubator into other departments of the university
Selection & Onboarding Process	Your process is robust. You could enhance it by integrating advanced analytics for more nuanced applicant assessments and personalized mentorship strategies for new startups	Implement a mentor-matching program during onboarding to pair startups with mentors who have relevant industry experience. Consider workshops focused on pitch development and business model validation to assist new startups in their early stages. Try to find more options to promote the incubator inside the university and outside. Consider adding entrepreneurship as part of the curricula in some departments or programs to promote entrepreneurship
Support & Resources	You provide great support. Explore partnerships with leaders in their field for advanced resources and consider hosting industry-specific innovation labs. Also, if you think you are lacking support in an area, consider improving e.g. provide office space	Consider increasing the variety of support, like legal advice, marketing expertise, IP consulting, access to a cohort or office space, and access to investors. Regularly evaluate the needs of your startups and adapt your resources accordingly. Consider partnerships with local businesses for real-world exposure and potential pilot projects for startups

In the third step, the artifact was developed using R and allowed the visual-itazion of data. This step helps to show where the incubator stands in each field and in which fields it can improve or adapt. The visualization consists of a radar chart that can be interpreted and compared. Lastly, a report with potential rec-ommendations is created after the data is visualized using R. This should help incubator managers get advice on what they could do to improve in a specific CSF.

5   Evaluation of the Decision-Support System

In this section, the evaluation of the proposed decision-support system is dis-cussed. The evaluation focused on the correctness of the artifact, which in this work relates to whether the expected results of the decision-support system are met. For this, the aforementioned questionnaire was sent to the managers of the seven university incubators involved in this study. The answers were then used as input of system to create the radar chart for each university incubator.

Figure 1 shows the radar chart of a Swiss university incubator. This is followed by the recommendations presented in Fig. 2.

Fig. 1. Radar chart of a Swiss university incubator and respective score for each CSF

Figure 3 shows the result of a less-performing Swiss university incubator.

By incorporating a scoring matrix and generating tailored recommendations within the R environment, the radar goes beyond mere data presentation. It provides strategic insight and actionable guidance for improvement.

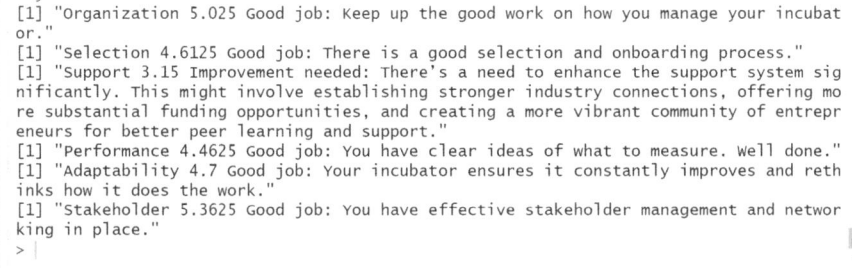

```
[1] "Organization 5.025 Good job: Keep up the good work on how you manage your incubat
or."
[1] "Selection 4.6125 Good job: There is a good selection and onboarding process."
[1] "Support 3.15 Improvement needed: There's a need to enhance the support system sig
nificantly. This might involve establishing stronger industry connections, offering mo
re substantial funding opportunities, and creating a more vibrant community of entrepr
eneurs for better peer learning and support."
[1] "Performance 4.4625 Good job: You have clear ideas of what to measure. Well done."
[1] "Adaptability 4.7 Good job: Your incubator ensures it constantly improves and reth
inks how it does the work."
[1] "Stakeholder 5.3625 Good job: You have effective stakeholder management and networ
king in place."
> |
```

Fig. 2. Recommendations for the given score in 1

Fig. 3. Radar chart of a less-performing Swiss university incubator

The values of each radar chart were previously calculated (incl. the recommendations) in an Excel sheet to document the expected results. These were then compared with the actual results from the radar charts. This proved the correctness of the DSS.

The DSS can be extended with the progress of the incubator just by updating the answers to the questionnaire. Results in the radar chart strictly depend on the answers given by the user, thus they can be quite subjective. However, we assume that managers answer fairly for their own benefits.

The DSS can be used by incubator managers to process and present the collected data in a way that facilitates decision-making. For example, it may visually evaluate performance across multiple crucial success factors, including the onboarding process, stakeholder involvement, and networking opportunities.

Moreover, the DSS aids as a benchmarking tool. If it is used by multiple universities, one can compare themselves to the best-in-class practices in the industry. The visualization and comparison helps to identify areas that need attention or development and offers a clear picture of the present performance. In addition, incubators are assisted in making decisions that align with their strategic objectives by the DSS's recommendation tool, which makes practical suggestions based on the data analysis. Therefore, the DSS serves as a holistic support system that facilitates strategic planning, improves decision-making, and ultimately aids in the successful management of incubation programs.

6   Conclusion

This paper presents a decision-support system (DSS) for university incubators. This first version is contextualized in Switzerland, which is witnessing an increased establishment of university incubators. Following the Design Science Research methodology, this study first deepened understanding of the phenomena of university incubators, their benefits, and their offerings from the literature. Seven Swiss university incubators were involved in this study, and the respective managers were interviewed. Findings from both the literature and the interviews converged into six main critical success factors (CSFs). The DSS was then conceptualized to calculate a score for each CSF based on a set of questions. Subsequently, the concept was implemented in an online questionnaire and a visual tool, where the scores for each CSF are displayed in a radar chart. Scores are accompanied by specific recommendations, which managers can turn into action to improve the respective university incubators. The approach was evaluated with respect to its correctness. Namely, the expected results for each university incubator were compared with the results outputted by the DSS.

The relevance of this research extends to the Society 5.0 paradigm, as it contributes to the advancement of university incubators, which hold the promise to play a central role in fostering innovation and entrepreneurship.

Future work centers on investigating extending the list of recommendations and their effective visualization.

References

1. Ahmad, A.J., Ingle, S.: Relationships matter: case study of a university campus incubator. Int. J. Entrep. Behav. Res. **17**(6), 626–644 (2011). https://doi.org/10.1108/13552551111174701
2. Al-Mubaraki, H.M., Busler, M.: Business incubators models of the USA and UK: a SWOT analysis. World J. Entrep. Manage. Sustain. Dev. **6**(4), 335–354 (2010). https://doi.org/10.1108/20425961201000025
3. Allen, D., Rahman, S.: Small business incubators: a positive environment for entrepreneurship. J. Small Bus. Manage. **23**, 12 (1985)
4. Arnott, D., Pervan, G.: A critical analysis of decision support systems research, pp. 127–168. Palgrave Macmillan, London (2015)

5. Becker, B., Gassmann, O.: Gaining leverage effects from knowledge modes within corporate incubators. R&D Manage. **36**(1), 1–16 (2006). https://doi.org/10.1111/j.1467-9310.2005.00411.x, https://onlinelibrary.wiley.com/doi/abs/10.1111/j.1467-9310.2005.00411.x

6. Bøllingtoft, A., Ulhøi, J.P.: The networked business incubator-leveraging entrepreneurial agency? J. Bus. Ventur. **20**(2), 265–290 (2005). https://doi.org/10.1016/j.jbusvent.2003.12.005

7. Bruneel, J., Ratinho, T., Clarysse, B., Groen, A.J.: The evolution of business incubators: comparing demand and supply of business incubation services across different incubator generations. Technovation **32**, 110–121 (2012). https://doi.org/10.1016/j.technovation.2011.11.003

8. Chandra, A., Chao, C.A.: Growth and evolution of high-technology business incubation in china. Hum. Syst. Manag. **30**(1–2), 55–69 (2011). https://doi.org/10.3233/HSM-2011-0739

9. Cohen, S., Fehder, D., Hochberg, Y., Murray, F.: The design of startup accelerators. Res. Policy **48**(4) (2019). https://doi.org/10.1016/j.respol.2019.04.003

10. Deguchi, A., et al.: What is society 5.0?. In: Hitachi-UTokyo Laboratory (ed.) Society 5.0, pp. 1–23. Springer, Singapore (2020). https://doi.org/10.1007/978-981-15-2989-4_1

11. Doga-Mirzac, M.: Methodological aspects oriented to structure the university incubators. Oblik finansi (2), 124–129 (2021).https://doi.org/10.33146/2307-9878-2021-2, https://ideas.repec.org/a/iaf/journl/y2021i2p124-129.html

12. Dutta, S., Lanvin, B., Rivera León, L., Wunsch-Vincent, S.: Global innovation index 2023: innovation in the face of uncertainty, pp. 1–250 (2023). https://doi.org/10.34667/tind.48220, http://tind.wipo.int/record/48220

13. Flanschger, A., Heinzelmann, R., Messner, M.: Between consultation and control: how incubators perform a governance function for entrepreneurial firms. Account. Audit. Account. J. **36**(9), 86–107 (2023). https://doi.org/10.1108/AAAJ-09-2020-4950

14. Gerlach, S., Brem, A.: What determines a successful business incubator? Introduction to an incubator guide. Int. J. Entrep. Ventu. **7**(3), 286–307 (2015)

15. Hackett, S., Dilts, D.: A systematic review of business incubation research. J. Technol. Transf. **29**, 55–82 (2004). https://doi.org/10.1023/B:JOTT.0000011181.11952.0f

16. Hassan, N.A.: University business incubators as a tool for accelerating entrepreneurship: theoretical perspective. Rev. Econ. Polit. Sci. (2020). https://doi.org/10.1108/REPS-10-2019-0142

17. Hevner, A., Chatterjee, S.: Design science research in information systems. In: Hevner, A., Chatterjee, S. (eds.) Design Research in Information Systems. Integrated Series in Information Systems, vol. 22, pp. 9–22. Springer, Boston (2010). https://doi.org/10.1007/978-1-4419-5653-8_2

18. Hofer, A.R., Potter, J.: Universities, innovation and entrepreneurship (2010). https://doi.org/10.1787/5km7rq0pq00q-en, https://www.oecd-ilibrary.org/content/paper/5km7rq0pq00q-en

19. Keen, P.G.: Decision support systems: the next decade. Decis. Support Syst. **3**(3), 253–265 (1987). https://doi.org/10.1016/0167-9236(87)90180-1

20. Lee, S.S., Osteryoung, J.S.: A comparison of critical success factors for effective operations of university business incubators in the united states and korea. J. Small Bus. Manage. **42**(4), 418–426 (2004)

21. Lewis, D.: Does technology incubation work? A critical review. Rev. Econ. Dev. Lit. Pract. (2001)

22. Lukosiute, K., Jensen, S., Tanev, S.: Is joining a business incubator or accelerator always a good thing? Technol. Innov. Manage. Rev. **7**(6), 5–15 (2019). https://doi.org/10.22215/timreview/1251

23. Maritz, A.: Illuminating the black box of entrepreneurship education programs: part 2. Educ. + Train. **59** (2017).https://doi.org/10.1108/ET-02-2017-0018

24. Rockart, J.F.: The changing role of the information systems executive: a critical success factors perspective. Sloan Manage. Rev. **24** (1980)

25. Soetanto, D., Geenhuizen, M.V.: Technology incubators as nodes in knowledge networks. In: ERSA Conference Papers ersa05p621. European Regional Science Association (2005). https://ideas.repec.org/p/wiw/wiwrsa/ersa05p621.html

26. Stokan, E., Thompson, L., Mahu, R.J.: Testing the differential effect of business incubators on firm growth. Econ. Dev. Q. **29**(4), 317–327 (2015). https://doi.org/10.1177/0891242415597065

27. Wang, J., Shapira, P.: Partnering with universities: a good choice for nanotechnology start-up firms? Small Bus. Econ. **38**(2), 197–215 (2012). https://doi.org/10.1007/s11187-009-9248-9

28. van Weele, M., Van Rijnsoever, F., Groen, M., Moors, E.: Gimme shelter? Heterogeneous preferences for tangible and intangible resources when choosing an incubator. J. Technol. Transf. **45** (2020). https://doi.org/10.1007/s10961-019-09724-1

29. Wiggins, J., Gibson, D.: Overview of us incubators and the case of the Austin technology incubator. Int. J. Entrep. Innov. Manage. **3**, 56–66 (2003). https://doi.org/10.1504/IJEIM.2003.002218

30. Woolley, J.L., MacGregor, N.: A comparison of critical success factors for effective operations of university business incubators in the united states and korea. Entrep. Theory Pract. **46**(6), 1717–1755 (2022). https://doi.org/10.1177/10422587211024510

31. Yamockul, S., Pichyangkura, R., Chandrachai, A.: University business incubators best practice: factors affecting Thailand UBI performance. Acad. Entrep. J. **25**, 1–14 (2019)

Advancing Financial Inclusion and Data Ethics: The Role of Alternative Credit Scoring

Keoitshepile Machikape and Deborah Oluwadele(✉) (iD)

Department of Informatics, University of Pretoria, Pretoria, South Africa
`deborah.oluwadele@up.ac.za`

Abstract. Alternative credit scoring plays a vital role in advancing the goals of balancing economic progress with resolving social issues by promoting financial inclusion, supporting data-driven decision-making, fostering innovation, enhancing risk management, and addressing ethical considerations. This research investigates alternative data sources and credit-scoring algorithms to evaluate the creditworthiness of individuals with limited credit histories. The study conducts a systematic literature review and meta-analysis to explore and evaluate alternative data sources and advanced credit scoring algorithms used in assessing the creditworthiness of individuals. Alternative data such as Online Behaviour and E-commerce, Social Networks and Relationships, Location, and Property Details were identified, while Machine Learning techniques such as Gradient-Boosted Decision Trees and Light Gradient-Boosting Machine demonstrate superior performance. However, ethical and privacy concerns regarding alternative data sources are paramount. The study's implications extend to financial institutions and credit-scoring agencies, offering insights to enhance credit assessment processes and stressing the importance of ethical data handling and privacy. This research contributes to understanding the dynamics between alternative data and credit-scoring algorithms, providing a roadmap for their responsible integration in credit assessments, thereby fostering financial inclusion and ethical data practices in the fut. Juristic society.

Keywords: alternative data · credit scoring · machine learning · financial inclusion · ethical data handling

1 Introduction

Numerous interventions have been proposed to address some of the most persistent challenges in global development, particularly in the context of poverty reduction [1]. In recent decades, efforts to reduce poverty and promote economic development have increasingly emphasized the potentially transformative impact of gaining entry into the financial system [1]. Credit has become prominent as a potent tool for combatting poverty and fostering socioeconomic empowerment [2]. Nobel Laureate Muhammad Yunus asserts that access to credit should be regarded as a fundamental human right [2]. A substantial body of evidence indicates that a significant proportion of adults, particularly in sub-Saharan Africa, lack access to accounts and fundamental financial services

© The Author(s), under exclusive license to Springer Nature Switzerland AG 2025
K. Hinkelmann and H. Smuts (Eds.): Society 5.0 2024, CCIS 2173, pp. 229–241, 2025.
https://doi.org/10.1007/978-3-031-71412-2_17

provided by the formal financial sector [3]. This issue affects a substantial portion of the population, with 31% of adults worldwide classified as unbanked [4]. The status of being unbanked or underbanked brings to the forefront the issue of individuals without a sufficient credit history, often termed thin-file borrowers [5]. Thin-file borrowers are customers for whom a creditworthiness assessment is uncertain due to their lack of credit history [6]. These individuals encounter difficulties in accessing loans, not due to poor payment behavior but because they lack the attributes typically evaluated by traditional credit scoring models [7]. Furthermore, such individuals are deemed too risky since financial institutions are reluctant to do business with them because they lack credit bureau data [8]. The global financial system has undergone significant transformation through the arrival of big data, machine learning, and alternative data [3]. With the emergence of big data, lenders can select the appropriate alternative data sources to service and score customers who have not been exposed to credit before [9]. Experiments are now conducted to profile and predict the behavior of customers by using non-bureau data [8]. Credit scoring the unbanked population by using alternative data could be a mechanism to create wealth and improve the economy if employed correctly [10]. Furthermore, credit-scoring individuals using alternative data can be an effective tool for growing businesses by maximizing existing customers and unlocking financial opportunities for low-income individuals and investors [11].

Credit scoring uses extensive datasets with machine-learning algorithms to construct scorecards that characterize a loan applicant's creditworthiness [12]. Furthermore, credit scoring using alternative data leads to the global effort for financial inclusion, intending to encompass unbanked or underbanked individuals within financial markets and facilitate their access to financial services, including credit, at fair and affordable rates [13]. Unbanked borrowers, devoid of bank accounts and established credit histories, coexist with underbanked borrowers who might possess bank accounts but have either no or incomplete credit histories [6]. However, It is important to note that customers not on the bureau are deemed high-risk and may cause profit loss if models and selection criteria are not modeled correctly [4]. These borrower categories present risks to credit institutions due to limited available data for evaluating creditworthiness [12].

This study aims to conduct a systematic literature review (SLR) and meta-analysis to investigate and evaluate the role of alternative data sources and advanced credit scoring algorithms in assessing the creditworthiness of individuals. Thus, the research question posed for this study is "What are the commonly used credit scoring algorithms and alternative data to evaluate individuals with limited credit bureau data?". By utilizing advanced credit-scoring algorithms and alternative data sources, such as transaction histories and online behavior, the research aims to present comprehensive and practical scoring techniques for the effective use of alternative data. The following section describes the methodology employed for this research, after which Sect. 3 presents the systematic review and meta-analysis results. Section 4 discusses the study's findings, and the study is concluded in Sect. 5.

2   Methods

This study utilized a Systematic Literature Review (SLR) process, which was guided by the methodologies outlined by Okoli [14] and Peters [15]—the review aimed to prioritize knowledge related to credit scoring algorithms and alternative data. An SLR aims to comprehensively locate and synthesize related research using organized, transparent, and replicable procedures at each step in the process. It is a valuable scientific tool to interpret a wealth of knowledge and gain insights by utilizing published materials on a particular research topic [14]. Researching credit scoring and creditworthiness for individuals with limited credit histories presents challenges. This is because existing literature often focuses solely on data analysis and statistical discourse, excluding the comprehensive perspective provided by traditional systematic literature reviews [16]. Meta-analysis offers a systematic approach to combining and synthesizing data from various quantitative studies [16]. In addressing this discordance, this study compares meta-analysis with descriptive analysis, providing a holistic understanding of the evolving landscape of alternative data and credit scoring algorithms. Various stages of meta-analysis, including data aggregation, scrutiny, and communicating findings, were explored. Best practices for each stage were identified to ensure rigor and transparency in the systematic literature review and meta-analysis.

2.1   Data Selection and Search Strategy

The search strategy began with Google Scholar to identify articles on systematic literature review, credit scoring, and alternative data. This initial step guided the selection of prominent academic databases such as ScienceDirect, Taylor and Francis Online, ProQuest, Wiley, IEEE Xplore, and Sage. These databases collectively cover a wide array of disciplines and offer access to various publication types, facilitating an in-depth exploration of the research landscape. The search terms were developed based on the study's research questions and title, aiming for a comprehensive review. Adjustments were made to streamline the search string, ensuring relevance and scholarly rigor until the final search string "("Alternative Data" OR "thin file") AND ("credit score" OR "credit scoring" OR "credit assessment" OR "Credit worthiness") AND ("methods" OR "techniques" OR "Algorithms")" was coined.

2.2   Inclusion, Exclusion, and Quality Assessment

During the systematic literature review process, relevant literature was sought through traditional data sources, supplemented by grey literature due to the novelty of alternative data. Grey literature, comprising non-peer-reviewed sources like reports, theses, and conference literature, augmented the search for information [14]. No specific time frame or geographic location was imposed as search criteria. In the eligibility and screening process, duplicates and scholarly works that did not address alternative credit scoring and data were removed. Exclusion criteria were defined to maintain accuracy: articles using alternative data for purposes other than credit scoring were excluded ("wrong outcome"). Similarly, inaccessible articles, non-English articles, and those employing unsuitable study designs were excluded to ensure rigor and relevance (Fig. 1).

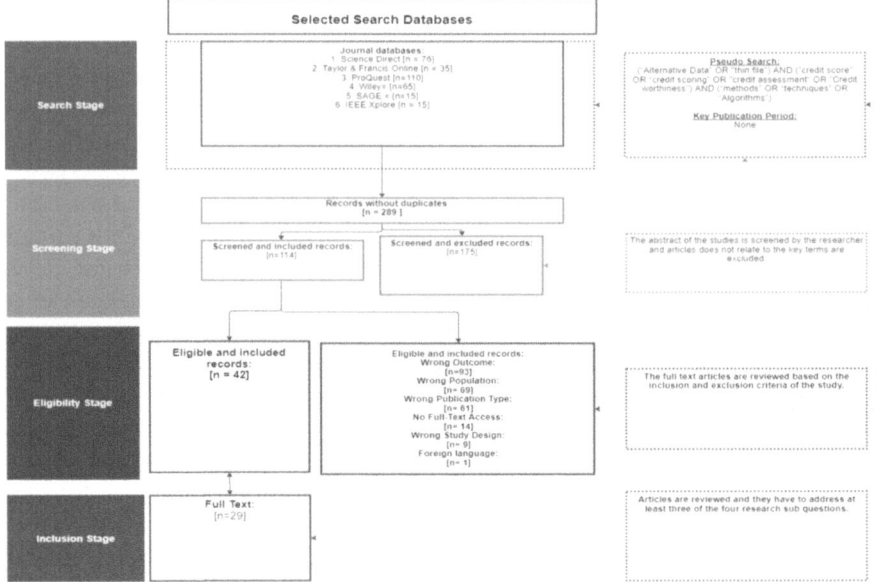

Fig. 1. SLR steps, pseudocode, and sources.

3 Result

Each publication underwent a thorough analysis to extract pertinent data relevant to the research question. The extracted metadata were organized into four categories and stored within an Excel spreadsheet: Demographic Data, Credit Scoring Algorithms Data, Alternative Data, and Impact of Using Alternative Data. Under Demographic Data, essential information such as author names, article titles, publication years, and an indication of whether the article originated from an academic journal was recorded. Additionally, details regarding the database sources were documented. For Credit Scoring Algorithms Data, the analysis encompassed the algorithm or method employed in the credit scoring process alongside metrics such as AUC for both test and training data. The computation of the GINI coefficient, using the formula (AUC*2) −1, was also included to provide further insights into the effectiveness of the scoring algorithms.

3.1 Alternative Credit Scoring Data

The Alternative Data category comprised details regarding the specific feature or data utilized, the type of data employed, and the total observations within the dataset. Valuable insights emerged regarding the use of alternative data through a thorough thematic analysis of 29 articles. The researcher identified distinct themes within the collected data, ultimately demonstrating the significant amount of information available to evaluate the creditworthiness of individuals. This alternative data encompassed personal attributes, online footprints, economic indicators, and unconventional identifiers, all of which have transformed the credit assessment process, as shown in Table 2.

Table 1. Types of alternative data

Theme	Features/Variables	References
Online Behavior and E-commerce	Frequency of online purchases, Amount spent on e-commerce platforms, Payment history for online subscriptions, Frequency of online bill payments, Devices used for online transactions, Website navigation patterns, Use of digital wallets and payment apps	[9, 10, 17–22]
Social Network and Relationships	Number of social media connections, Frequency and nature of social media interactions, Relationships with family members and close friends, Shared financial responsibilities within the network, Endorsements, and recommendations from network connections	[5, 7, 23–25]
Location and Property Details	Geographic coordinates of a property, Proximity to essential infrastructure (roads, rivers, public services), Property ownership details, Property value and historical price trends, Elevation and vulnerability to natural disasters, Property tax payment history	[4, 24–26]
Mobile App and Online Interaction	Mobile app usage patterns, Call and text message logs, Data usage, and traffic patterns, Types of apps installed (e.g., financial apps, gaming apps, productivity apps), Frequency of online banking transactions, Mobile device information (e.g., model, operating system)	[4, 23, 25–33]
Miscellaneous Data	Employment history, Salary transfers and pay stub records, Ownership of assets or businesses, Anonymized customer or user identifiers, Parent company information for businesses, Educational background and qualifications	[4, 5, 7, 25, 27, 34–36]

3.2 Impacts of Using Alternative Credit Scoring Data

Table 2 highlights the recurring themes, objectives, and concerns the researcher identified when analyzing either the conclusion or discussion section of the 29 selected articles. The analysis reveals several key themes that underscore the multifaceted impacts of using alternative credit scoring data (Table 1).

Table 2. Types of alternative data

Theme	Description
Enhanced Predictive Accuracy	Aimed at improving credit scoring models through alternative data for better risk assessment [9]
Financial Inclusion of Disadvantaged Groups	Focused on enabling credit scoring for individuals traditionally considered "credit invisible" [5]
Accessing New Economic Segments	Aims to unlock new markets or customer segments, potentially increasing lenders' profitability [34]
Optimization of Credit Risk Management	Concentrates on refining credit risk assessment processes to make informed lending decisions [27]
Privacy and Ethical Considerations	Addresses ethical and privacy concerns related to the collection and use of alternative data [30]
Provide more value compared to Traditional Data	Explores the value of alternative data sources compared to traditional credit scoring variables [28]
Regulatory and Compliance Impacts	Considers compliance with credit lending regulations and acts when using alternative data [35]
Machine Learning and Data Analytics	Utilizes machine learning and data analytics techniques to leverage alternative data for improved models [37]
Customer Retention and Management	Focuses on improving customer retention and customizing credit solutions for individual borrowers [28]

3.3 Alternative Credit Scoring Algorithms

Various machine learning algorithms and methods are employed to assess creditworthiness. Logistic regression emerges as the most frequently utilized technique, appearing 23 times in the dataset. This suggests that traditional statistical methods retain relevance in credit scoring due to their interpretability and reliability [38]. Ensemble methods such as Random Forests and Support Vector Machines are also commonly employed, each appearing 12 times. This underscores the significance of predictive accuracy and risk assessment in credit decisions. Extreme Gradient Boosting surfaced 11 times, revealing an interest in advanced ensemble techniques for refining credit risk models. Although relatively infrequent, deep learning methods such as Convolutional Neural Networks and Artificial Neural Networks were occasionally used, indicating an inclination towards experimenting with complex neural network architectures for credit scoring. The results of this study highlight the diverse array of methodologies applied in credit scoring, reflecting the researchers' commitment to utilizing various techniques to assess borrowers' creditworthiness accurately.

3.4 Alternative Credit Scoring Algorithms: Meta-Analysis

We conducted a comprehensive meta-analysis to identify optimal credit-scoring algorithms integrating alternative data, thereby informing credit risk assessment and decision-making processes. The process commenced with the systematic review of 29 academic articles. A stringent criterion was applied to ensure the reliability of the meta-analysis. This led to the exclusion of articles that lacked both AUC and Gini coefficient metrics. This process resulted in a refined dataset of 26 articles, which improved the quality of insights into algorithm performance. Further, articles that lacked data on the total number of observations were excluded. Finally, 21 articles that passed the screening process were analyzed using SPSS using the Random Effect and Meta-Regression Models.

3.5 Random Effect Model

Figure 2 presents the results of a meta-analysis conducted using a random-effects model, focusing on credit scoring algorithms that use alternative data reported across 21 studies. This study utilizes credit scoring algorithms to predict the creditworthiness of an individual by using alternative data. The following key findings have been observed:

Overall Estimated Pooled Effect Size: The effect size estimated from the random-effects model is −24.97%. This indicates that, on average, the credit scoring models using alternative data are associated with a reduction of approximately -24.97% in some outcome or effect compared to a reference value. The negative sign indicates that the overall effect is in the opposite direction of what might be considered a reference point (e.g., no effect or baseline).

Confidence Interval (95% CI): The 95% confidence interval provides a range within which the true population effect size resides. In this case, the confidence interval is (−31.22%, -18.71%). Thus, there is a 95% confidence that the true effect size falls within this range, which suggests that since the entire range is negative, the true effect is likely to be negative.

I2 (I-squared): I2 is a measure of heterogeneity in meta-analysis. It quantifies the percentage of variation in effect sizes due to real differences between studies rather than a sampling error. In this case, I2 is 96.31%, indicating a high heterogeneity among the studies. This suggested that the studies in the meta-analysis had inconsistent findings and substantial variability in effect sizes. As depicted in Fig. 3, the findings indicate that no single algorithm can be definitively recommended as the best for credit scoring. Therefore, the choice of the most suitable algorithm depends on the specific context of the alternative scoring data.

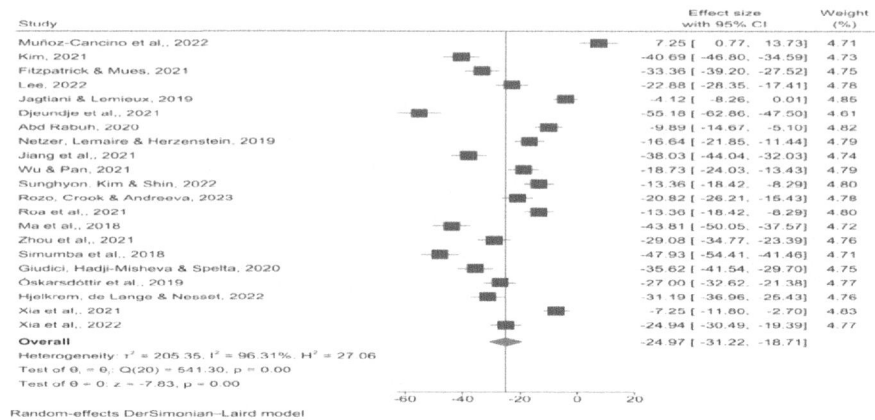

Fig. 2. Forest Plot of the Different Studies Using Credit Scoring Algorithms.

Table 3 presents the outcomes of a meta-regression analysis conducted to explore the factors contributing to the observed heterogeneity across studies. Two distinct models, Model 1 and Model 2, were evaluated using the DerSimonian–Laird method, with 21 observations considered in each case.

Table 3. Meta-regression Analysis Results

Model	Wald chi-square (Prob > chi^2)	Coefficients	Interpretation
Model 1	0.2003	Positive coefficient for "Year"	Non-significant influence on observed variability
		(2.374036)	Lack of statistical significance for "Year"
Model 2	0.0025	Positive coefficients for "Year,"	At least one predictor is statistically significant
		"AUCTraining," and "TotalObservationsDS1"	Contribution to model's explanatory power
		Negative coefficient for "GiniCoefficientTraining"	

The statistically significant coefficients in Model 2 provide meaningful insights into the factors influencing observed heterogeneity among studies. Positive coefficients for "Year," "AUCTraining," and "TotalObservationsDS1" suggest positive associations, while the negative coefficient for "GiniCoefficientTraining" indicates a potential adverse effect. Figure 5 highlights the subgroup analysis undertaken to evaluate potential heterogeneity among studies on credit scoring and alternative data.

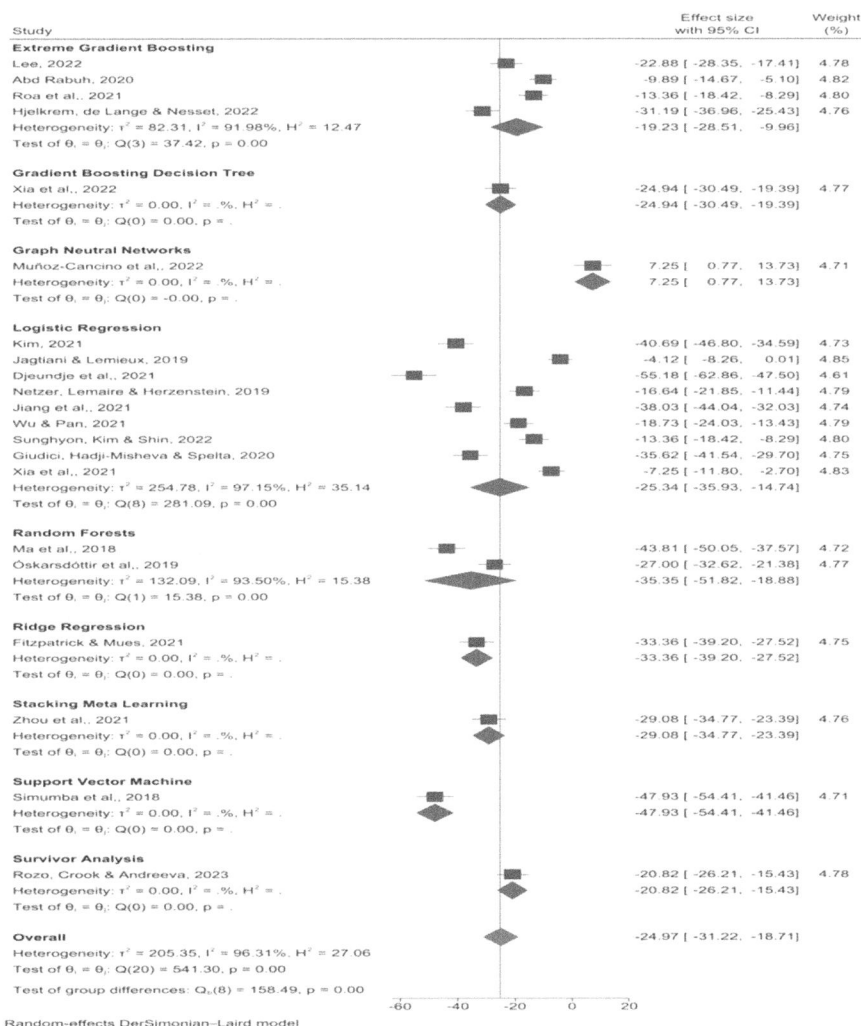

Fig. 3. Subgroup analysis by categorization of the credit scoring algorithms

3.6 Meta-regression Model

These findings enhance the understanding of factors influencing meta-analytic outcomes, emphasizing the superiority of Model 2 in explaining observed heterogeneity. Based on the meta-analysis of the studies, the following key findings have been observed:

Top-Performing Machine-Learning Algorithms: Gradient boosting decision tree and light gradient boosting machine, both machine learning methods, exhibit the highest performance with an average AUC and Gini of 0.974 and 0.948, respectively.

Consistent Performance in Machine Learning: Categorical gradient boosting, another machine learning technique, also performs well, with an average AUC of 0.9682 and an average Gini of 0.9364, supported by a frequency count of 2.

Widespread Use but Lower Performance: Random Forests, while widely utilized, exhibit slightly lower performance metrics, reporting an average AUC of 0.9498 and a Gini of 0.8996. However, the integrated approach of Random Forests places it within the machine-learning category, contributing to its predictive capabilities.

Challenges for Extreme Gradient Boosting: Despite frequent employment (frequency count of 11), extreme gradient boosting, a machine learning method, has an average AUC of 0.8019 and an average Gini of 0.6038, indicating challenges in credit scoring tasks.

Commonly Utilized but Moderate Performers: Logistic regression, another commonly used method, reports average AUC and Gini values of 0.8 and 0.6, respectively, with a high-frequency count of 23.

Challenges for Various Methods: Ridge Regression, Lasso Regression, Decision Trees, and K-Nearest Neighbors demonstrate lower performance metrics, indicating potential challenges in credit-scoring tasks. Compared to the top-performing ensemble methods, these traditional and machine-learning methods might face limitations.

4   Discussion

In credit assessment, evaluating the creditworthiness of individuals with limited credit histories is critical [39]. This study provides insights into alternative data and algorithms for credit-scoring individuals with limited credit data, shedding light on the debate between machine learning and traditional models. Lenders increasingly use alternative data sources, such as online behavior, social networks, and location details, to understand an individual's financial behaviors [4]. This shift recognizes the limitations of traditional credit-scoring models, which often exclude demographic segments with limited credit histories [8]. Online behavior and e-commerce data are valuable indicators of financial behavior, including e-commerce spending habits and payment records [9]. Social network data, like the number of social media connections and interactions, provides insights into an applicant's support and financial responsibilities [7]. Location data, such as proximity to essential infrastructure and property ownership details, offer insights into financial stability [26]. Mobile app and online interaction data, including mobile phone and app usage patterns, provide clues about an applicant's financial status [25], while miscellaneous data sources, such as payroll records and ownership information, add another layer of evaluation to an applicant's financial health [34].

Integrating alternative data opens new market segments and enhances risk management, allowing lenders to mitigate financial uncertainties more effectively [27]. However, ethical and privacy concerns must be addressed, and compliance with credit lending regulations is necessary [30]. Advanced machine learning and data analytics techniques are essential for utilizing alternative data effectively [37]. Customizing credit solutions based on alternative data improves customer retention and satisfaction [28]. The meta-regression analysis results provide insights into the efficacy of various credit-scoring algorithms incorporating alternative data ($I^2 = 96.30\%$). Subgroup analyses focusing on algorithms like extreme gradient boosting and gradient boosting decision tree revealed significant reductions in estimated pooled effect sizes, suggesting their enhanced effectiveness in capturing complex data relationships [5]. These findings inform the selection of algorithms for credit assessment, improving our understanding of their performance when incorporating alternative data.

5   Conclusion

The study highlights the critical role of credit scoring algorithms in incorporating alternative data into the credit assessment process. It provides insights into the effectiveness of various algorithms, emphasizing the need for tailored selection, ongoing optimization, and consideration of regulatory and ethical implications. Machine learning-based algorithms, like extreme gradient boosting and random forests, demonstrate substantial predictive accuracy in handling alternative data, particularly for individuals with limited credit histories. However, traditional algorithms such as logistic regression and decision trees can also become more inclusive by incorporating alternative data, albeit with sensitivity to context, bias, and discrimination. Integrating alternative data brings about a paradigm shift in the financial industry, enhancing predictive accuracy while raising concerns about data privacy, ethics, and regulatory compliance. Despite the challenges, alternative data offers opportunities for financial inclusion, economic segmentation, and optimized credit risk management.

Practical implications suggest a balance between predictive accuracy and fairness in credit assessment, with a need for further research to explore algorithm performance under different contextual factors. The future of credit scoring depends on the ethical use of alternative data and the development of refined models that leverage a broader array of data sources while maintaining transparency and fairness in the lending process.

Disclosure of Interests.   No conflict of interest was declared.

References

1. Azevedo, V., et al.: Credit cards issued by non-financial companies: an alternative tool for financial inclusion and economic development? J. Dev. Effect. **13**(1), 47–83 (2021)
2. Njuguna, R., Sowon, K.: Poster: a scoping review of alternative credit scoring literature. In: ACM SIGCAS Conference on Computing and Sustainable Societies, Cape Town (2021)

...

240   K. Machikape and D. Oluwadele

3. Bongomin, G.O.C., et al.: Agent liquidity: a catalyst for mobile money banking among the unbanked poor population in rural sub-Saharan Africa. Cogent Econ. Finan. **11**(1), 2203435 (2023)
4. Simumba, N., et al.: Multiple objective metaheuristics for feature selection based on stakeholder requirements in credit scoring. Decis. Support. Syst. **2022**(155), 113714 (2022)
5. Muñoz-Cancino, R., et al.: On the combination of graph data for assessing thin-file borrowers' creditworthiness (2022). Cornell University Library, arXiv.org: Ithaca
6. Agarwal, S., Qian, W., Tan, R.: Financial inclusion and financial technology. In: Household Finance. Palgrave Macmillan, Singapore, pp. 307–346 (2020). https://doi.org/10.1007/978-981-15-5526-8_9
7. Muñoz-Cancino, R., et al.: On the combination of graph data for assessing thin-file borrowers' creditworthiness. Expert Syst. Appl. **213**, 118809 (2023)
8. Aitken, R.: 'All data is credit data': Constituting the unbanked. Compet. Chang. **21**(4), 274–300 (2017)
9. Djeundje, V.B., et al.: Enhancing credit scoring with alternative data. Expert Syst. Appl. **2021**(163), 113766 (2021)
10. Xia, Y., et al.: Deep learning meets decision trees: an application of a heterogeneous deep forest approach in credit scoring for online consumer lending. J. Forecast. **41**(8), 1669–1690 (2022)
11. Patwardhan, A.: Chapter 4 - Financial inclusion in the digital age. In: Handbook of Blockchain, Digital Finance, and Inclusion, Volume 1, Lee Kuo Chuen, D., Deng, R. (eds.). Academic Press, pp. 57–89 (2018)
12. Lainez, N., Gardner, J.: Algorithmic credit scoring in Vietnam: a legal proposal for maximizing benefits and minimizing risks. Asian J. Law Soc. **1**(1), 1–32 (2023)
13. Baghdasaryan, V., et al.: Comparison of econometric and deep learning approaches for credit default classification. Strateg. Chang. **30**(3), 257–268 (2021)
14. Okoli, C.: A guide to conducting a standalone systematic literature review. Commun. Assoc. Inf. Syst. **37**(1), 43 (2015)
15. Peters, M.D.J.: Managing and coding references for systematic reviews and scoping reviews in endnote. Med. Ref. Serv. Q. **36**(1), 19–31 (2017)
16. Paul, J., Barari, M.: Meta-analysis and traditional systematic literature reviews—what, why, when, where, and how? Psychol. Mark. **39**(6), 1099–1115 (2022)
17. Rozo, B.J.G., Crook, J., Andreeva, G.: The role of web browsing in credit risk prediction. Decis. Support. Syst. **164**, 113879 (2023)
18. Lee, J.Y.: Essays on Alternative Data in the Consumer Credit Market. Northwestern University: United States – Illinois, p. 130 (2022)
19. Hjelkrem, L.O., de Lange, P.E., Nesset, E.: The value of open banking data for application credit scoring: case study of a Norwegian bank. J. Risk Finan. Manage. **15**(12), 597 (2022)
20. Jagtiani, J., Lemieux, C.: The roles of alternative data and machine learning in fintech lending: Evidence from the LendingClub consumer platform. Financ. Manage. **48**(4), 1009–1029 (2019)
21. Leo, M., Sharma, S., Maddulety, K.: Machine learning in banking risk management: a literature review. Risks **7**(1), 29 (2019)
22. Khandani, A.E., Kim, A.J., Lo, A.W.: Consumer credit-risk models via machine-learning algorithms. J. Bank. Finance **34**(11), 2767–2787 (2010)
23. Óskarsdóttir, M., et al.: The value of big data for credit scoring: enhancing financial inclusion using mobile phone data and social network analytics. Appl. Soft Comput. **2019**(74), 26–39 (2019)
24. Simumba, N., et al.: Alternative scoring factors using non-financial data for credit decisions in agricultural microfinance. In: 2018 IEEE International Systems Engineering Symposium (ISSE) (2018)

25. De Cnudde, S., et al.: What does your Facebook profile reveal about your creditworthiness? Using alternative data for microfinance. J. Oper. Res. Soc. **70**(3), 353–363 (2019)
26. Okami, S., Kodaka, A., Kohtake, N.: Spatiotemporal integration of mobile, satellite, and public geospatial data for enhanced credit scoring. Symmetry **13**(4), 575 (2021)
27. Zhou, J., et al.: Inferring multi-stage risk for online consumer credit services: an integrated scheme using data augmentation and model enhancement. Decis. Support. Syst. **149**(1), 113611 (2021)
28. Sunghyon, K., Kim, D., Shin, J.: Can system log data enhance the performance of credit scoring?—evidence from an internet bank in Korea. Sustainability **14**(1), 130 (2022)
29. Netzer, O., Lemaire, A., Herzenstein, M.: When words sweat: identifying signals for loan default in the text of loan applications. J. Mark. Res. **56**(6), 960–980 (2019)
30. Ma, L., et al.: A new aspect on P2P online lending default prediction using meta-level phone usage data in China. Decis. Support. Syst. **111**, 60–71 (2018)
31. Fitzpatrick, T., Mues, C.: How can lenders prosper? Comparing machine learning approaches to identify profitable peer-to-peer loan investments. Eur. J. Oper. Res. **294**(2), 711–722 (2021)
32. Jiang, J., et al.: Deciphering big data in consumer credit evaluation. J. Empir. Financ. **62**, 28–45 (2021)
33. Kim, D.: Empirical evidence of faulty credit scoring and business failure in P2P lending. Glob. Bus. Finan. Rev. **26**(2), 67–82 (2021)
34. Roa, L., et al.: Super-app behavioral patterns in credit risk models: financial, statistical and regulatory implications. Expert Syst. Appl. **169**, 114486 (2021)
35. Croux, C., et al.: Important factors determining Fintech loan default: evidence from a lendingclub consumer platform. J. Econ. Behav. Organ. **173**, 270–296 (2020)
36. Giudici, P., Hadji-Misheva, B., Spelta, A.: Network based credit risk models. Qual. Eng. **32**(2), 199–211 (2020)
37. Wu, Y., Pan, Y.: Application Analysis of Credit Scoring of Financial Institutions Based on Machine Learning Model. Complexity, vol. 2021 (2021)
38. Bellotti, T., Crook, J.: Support vector machines for credit scoring and discovery of significant features. Expert Syst. Appl. **36**(2), 3302–3308 (2009)
39. Gao, Y., et al.: CATE: Contrastive augmentation and tree-enhanced embedding for credit scoring. Inf. Sci. **651**, 119447 (2023)

Short Duration, Lasting Impression: The Role of Short-Term Study Trips in Cross-Cultural Learning

Dario Meyer[(✉)] ⓘ, Alice Frey, and Rolf Meyer

University of Applied Sciences and Arts Northwestern Switzerland, Bahnhofstrasse 6, 5210 Windisch, Switzerland
dario.meyer@fhnw.ch

Abstract. In the context of an increasingly globalized society, this paper investigates the effectiveness of short-term study trips in enhancing intercultural sensitivity among Swiss university postgraduate students. Recognizing the crucial role of intercultural competencies in navigating both personal and professional life, this study focuses on the pedagogical value of week-long immersive experiences abroad. Using a pre- and post-test survey, we assessed changes in intercultural sensitivity following participation in two different study tours: one to Colombia and one to Malaysia. The surveys examined changes in several dimensions of intercultural sensitivity, including engagement, enjoyment, confidence, respect for cultural differences, and awareness. Results indicate significant improvements in country-specific intercultural sensitivity, particularly in areas that were actively engaged during the trips. However, improvements in general intercultural sensitivity were less pronounced, suggesting that while short-term trips can strengthen specific facets of intercultural competence, its impact on broader competencies may be limited or are only visible in the long-term. To enhance the educational impact of short-term study programs abroad, we recommend several strategies, which aim to deepen students' intercultural understanding and ensure lasting benefits. This research contributes to the discourse on intercultural education by providing insights into designing effective short-term study programs abroad that foster globally competent and interculturally sensitive students.

Keywords: Intercultural Sensitivity · Cross-cultural Competence · Short-term Study Trip · Cultural Immersion

1 Introduction

One of the goals of a Society 5.0 is to build a people with mutual respect, while solving social problems and economic inequality [1]. In a globally connected society, intercultural skills are essential. Not only to achieve the goals of Society 5.0, but also for personal development and professional success [2]. As a result, educational institutions and organizations are continuously looking for effective ways to teach these competencies. Short-term study trips abroad, known for their intensity and immersion, offer a unique pedagogical approach [2, 3].

© The Author(s), under exclusive license to Springer Nature Switzerland AG 2025
K. Hinkelmann and H. Smuts (Eds.): Society 5.0 2024, CCIS 2173, pp. 242–253, 2025.
https://doi.org/10.1007/978-3-031-71412-2_18

The digital transformation and virtual exchange programs have led to new ways in organizing intercultural exchanges. While technology offers new opportunities for intercultural learning, the discussion on the effectiveness of virtual versus physical experiences in developing understanding among cultures is still there. Moreover, the logistical and financial accessibility of these programs cannot be overlooked [4]. Short-term trips may be a more feasible option for a broader group of students compared to longer programs, allowing more people access to international educational experiences. However, the shortness of these programs raises questions about the sustainability of skills learned and whether such experiences can instill a lasting awareness and understanding of cultural diversity [5].

This paper seeks to fill the gap in the literature by examining the effectiveness of one-week study trips in increasing intercultural sensitivity among participants. The study is focusing on a comparative analysis of two different cultural settings, Colombia and Malaysia. The following research questions will be addressed (adapted from [6]):

- Do participants report higher levels of intercultural sensitivity, by dimension, after exposure to a one-week study tour?
- How do these dimensional results vary by type of intercultural sensitivity (general sensitivity versus sensitivity toward the specific local culture)?

Additionally, this research will offer recommendations for program managers to improve the outcomes of short-term study abroad experiences. The study contributes to the discourse on intercultural teaching and learning methodologies in the age of Society 5.0, where the integration of technology is reshaping the education landscape.

This paper is organized as follows. Section 2 provides a review of the existing literature on short-term study programs. Section 3 presents the methodology and describes the questionnaire used for this study. The results are then presented, followed by a discussion and recommendations. The paper ends with a conclusion and future research.

2 Literature Review

To lay the basis for this study, the concepts of intercultural competence and sensitivity as well as intercultural dimensions are defined. Also, an overview of the research on short-term study abroad programs is given.

Intercultural competence can be defined as *"the ability to communicate effectively and appropriately in intercultural situations based on one's intercultural knowledge, skills, and attitudes"* [7]. This competence includes a wide range of skills, such as understanding and being aware of cultural differences, as well as managing perceptions, relationships, and oneself, both personally and professionally [8, 9]. It has three dimensions. The cognitive one, which refers to the knowledge about a culture, the conative one, which includes the skills and behaviors and lastly, the affective dimension with attitudes and traits [10]. Measuring intercultural competences has been proven to be difficult. On the one hand, its concept has been defined differently by different scholars. On the other hand, it is not only about measuring categories that are easier to measure, such as know-how, but also about soft factors, like awareness [3, 10].

It is believed that intercultural sensitivity precedes intercultural competence, often referred to as the affective dimension, as described above [10, 11]. Intercultural sensitivity refers to an individual's awareness, understanding, and appreciation of cultural differences and the capacity to adapt one's behavior accordingly in intercultural situations [6] or simply defined *"as a person's response to intercultural difference"* [12]. The Developmental Model of Intercultural Sensitivity by Bennett [13], shows how people go from ethnocentrism to ethnorelativism in developing sensitivity. Initially, individuals evaluate all cultures against their own, leading to denial, defense, and minimization of differences. Moving to ethnorelativism, they embrace cultural diversity through acceptance, adaptation, and integration, moving from a self-centered view to appreciating and incorporating diverse cultural perspectives [13]. Thus, understanding and developing intercultural sensitivity is a dynamic journey that involves continuous learning, reflection, and adaptation [14].

Measuring intercultural sensitivity is as difficult as measuring intercultural competence. Many frameworks have been developed and tested by various scholars [6]. It was decided to use Chen and Starosta's Intercultural Sensitivity Model, because it provides a general overview and does not focus on a single cultural dimension. Also, it has been adapted and validated to measure both, general and country-specific factors. The following section will therefore look in depth at the components of the model [15], as one way of measuring intercultural sensitivity.

2.1 Overview of Chen and Starosta's Intercultural Sensitivity Model

The Intercultural Sensitivity Scale (ISS) [15] is designed to assess the sensitivity of people to and awareness of cultural differences. It focuses on assessing an individual's capability to behave effectively and appropriately when interacting with different cultures using a scale with five key factors [15]:

Engagement: Measures "the feeling of participation in intercultural communication" of a person [15].
Respect for Cultural Differences: Determines how much a person values and accepts other cultures.
Confidence: Evaluates the self-assurance an individual has when interacting with people from different cultures.
Enjoyment: Measures the pleasure and positive regard an individual experiences during cross-cultural interactions.
Awareness: Measures the level of understanding an individual has of the complexity of cultural identities and the impact of culture on people's behavior, including one's own cultural biases and cultural influences on one's perceptions and behavior.

Together, these factors contribute to the understanding of intercultural sensitivity. In the context of this study, since short-term programs provide limited exposure to the respective cultural contexts, it is essential to efficiently assess participants' intercultural sensitivity. The ISS provides a structured and validated tool [6] to measure these effects.

2.2 Short-Term Study Trips and Intercultural Learning

Short-term study trips have emerged as a popular means of enhancing intercultural learning with a growing amount of research around them [17]. They can be defined as *"programs of higher education taking place outside the geographical boundaries of the student's country of origin"*, and range in duration from 1 to 8 weeks [2, 17]. These programs are designed to immerse participants in a foreign culture and provide first-hand experiences that are difficult to replicate in a traditional classroom setting [18]. Through the direct exposure to different cultural practices, languages, and ways of thinking, students gain a deeper understanding and appreciation of other cultures and an opportunity for personal and professional development [17, 18]. In addition to the cultural aspects, research on short-term study programs has also examined the pedagogical aspects, the development of language skills, and the professional and personal outcomes for students and participating teachers [17].

The majority of the research has focused on programs of 2 + weeks, leaving a gap in understanding the specific impact of shorter study trips [2]. A systematic literature review [16] on these study trips found mixed results on intercultural dimensions. While the interest in and awareness of other cultures has increased, the results for sensitivity are inconclusive, with some studies reporting positive impacts and others reporting no differences [16]. A short-term program in India with students from the United States, using the ISS as a measurement tool, showed no significant impact and even a decrease in the dimensions of confidence and enjoyment, which was attributed to too few interactions with locals and possibly a gap between the two cultures that was too big [20]. Goldstein [16] also mentions that participant characteristics, such as gender, race, cultural background or languages spoken, and program characteristics, such as length, location and teaching methods, can have a significant impact on the outcomes. It is therefore important that these are taken into account when analyzing the data.

Short-term study abroad programs provide valuable learning opportunities, but they also present a significant challenge. The limited duration of these programs appears to limit the depth of cultural immersion and understanding [21]. To maximize the impact of short-term trips, it is important for program managers to carefully plan activities that promote meaningful cultural engagement and reflection [19]. This includes pre-departure training, reflections during the trip, and post-trip debriefing sessions to help participants process their experiences and integrate their new knowledge into their personal and professional lives [19].

2.3 Cultural Dimensions

It is important to be aware of the different cultural dimensions when immersing oneself to different cultures, as they show how the culture of a society influences the values of its members and the connection between these values and their behavior [22]. One of the most popular models of cultural aspects in this context is that of Geert Hofstede, which provides insights into the differences between cultures and their possible effects on intercultural sensitivity [22].

Hofstede identified six key dimensions that can be used to describe cultural differences. The following description also includes the level for the three countries Switzerland, Malaysia and Colombia [23], as they were relevant for this study. The model uses a scale of 1 to 100. 1 is the lowest and 100 is the highest score for each dimension. The corresponding scores are shown in parentheses.

Power Distance: Measures how power is distributed and how a society deals with inequality. Switzerland (34) has a lower power distance, indicating a preference for equality and decentralization, while Malaysia (100) and Colombia (67) have higher power distances, indicating a more hierarchical society with an acceptance of unequal power distribution [23].

Individualism (100) vs. Collectivism (1): Switzerland (79) is more individualistic, valuing personal freedom and achievement. In contrast, Colombia (29) and Malaysia (27) are considered more collectivistic, where group loyalty and societal norms are emphasized [23].

Motivation Towards Achievement and Success: Switzerland (70) and Colombia (64) are considered more masculine, where achievement and material rewards are valued. Malaysia's score (50) is exactly in the middle, showing no preference for either side [23].

Uncertainty Avoidance: This dimension measures the degree to which a culture tolerates ambiguity. Malaysia (36) has the lowest uncertainty avoidance, while Switzerland has a moderate score (58). Colombia (80) has higher levels, showing a preference for structure and clear rules [23].

Long-Term Orientation: This dimension shows a society's approach to time management and planning. Switzerland (42) is balanced between long-term and short-term orientation. Malaysia (47) is slightly higher than Switzerland, and Colombia (6) in contrast has a strong short-term orientation, with less thought given to the future. [23].

Indulgence (100) vs. Restraint (0): This dimension evaluates how freely people can satisfy their desires. Switzerland (66) is considered more indulgent, whereas Malaysia (57) is seen as more restrained. Colombia (83) is the most indulgent of the three countries [23].

Cultural dimensions significantly influence intercultural sensitivity. For example, individuals from cultures with high uncertainty avoidance may experience more anxiety in unfamiliar cultural settings, which can affect their confidence and enjoyment in intercultural interactions. In contrast, those used to low uncertainty avoidance may approach new cultures with more openness and curiosity, potentially improving their intercultural sensitivity. Awareness of these cultural dimensions allows individuals to anticipate and manage cultural differences more effectively. It enables a deeper understanding of why people from different cultures behave in certain ways, fostering greater empathy and respect for cultural differences [22]. In the context of short-term study trips, understanding cultural dimensions can help participants prepare for and adapt to the cultural environments they will encounter.

2.4 Gaps in the Literature

Even though there is an increasing body of research on intercultural sensitivity and the effects of study programs abroad, several gaps remain in the literature. They are mainly regarding the impact of very short-term study trips (below one week) and comparative studies. Most existing studies focus on longer-term exchanges, leaving questions about the effectiveness of short intercultural experiences in fostering substantial changes in intercultural sensitivity. This study aims to fill this gap by examining the effects of one-week study trips on the development of intercultural sensitivity of participants. It compares the outcomes of trips to two Colombia and Malaysia. In addressing this gap, the research contributes to the academic field of intercultural education, but also offers recommendations for program managers, based on our experiences. The study aims to support the design of future programs, ensuring they are accessible and effective in preparing students for the opportunities of a society 5.0.

3   Methodology

3.1   Sample and Data

The MBA-programs of the University of Applied Sciences and Arts Northwestern Switzerland (FHNW) are organizing two study trips of one week (7 days) each once a year. The study trips usually have between 20 and 24 MBA-students participating. The students in the MBA-program have an average age of 35 years and typically hold a middle-management position in their company. All of them study part-time and are proficient in English. Due to the low number of women in the MBA-program, it was not possible to make an analysis based on gender. A review of similar studies has shown though that there are mostly no differences between gender in the cultural effects of short-term study tours [16]. Before going on the study trip, all students have to attend a module in international management, which includes cross-cultural management, international trade and globalization, as well as negotiations and sales in an international context.

The study tour always begins with an extensive introduction to the country, its economy, culture and social norms. This is followed by a variety of activities during the week including visits to companies, governmental and/or social organizations, the Swiss Embassy, as well as cultural activities. There are several opportunities to interact directly with local people. As an assignment, the participants choose an economic and/or cultural topic at the beginning of the tour. On the last afternoon, they present their findings and receive a grade for it. The study tour counts towards completing the MBA degree, if successfully completed.

We surveyed two study trip-groups (n = 20 and n = 21). The first study trip was in Malaysia, the second one in Colombia. The group completed the same questionnaire before and after the study trip.

3.2   Measures of Variables

The variables are based on the intercultural sensitivity scale by Chen & Starosta, as described in chapter 2. The scale has been deemed reliable with western study populations in mind [6]. We used the slightly adapted questionnaire by Coffey et al. [6]. While the questionnaire of Chen & Starosta looks at the general sensitivity, Coffey et al. [6]

added questions that particularly address a specific country context. The questionnaire includes 15 general questions, 15 country-specific questions and 15 foil questions. In addition, some of the questions were reverse-coded.

3.3 Data Analysis Procedure

Throughout the data analysis, several steps were undertaken to achieve a comprehensive understanding of the impacts of intercultural exchange programs. Initially, a descriptive statistical evaluation was conducted to summarize the overall survey results. Reverse coding was applied, and foil items were removed. Subsequently, a comprehensive ANOVA was performed to identify significant differences in participants' intercultural sensitivity before and after the study trip. The internal consistency of the questionnaires was assessed using Cronbach's Alpha, and effect size was calculated to evaluate the practical significance of the results. These methodological steps enable a thorough assessment of the effects of intercultural education programs. Significant interaction effects led to post-hoc analyses for a detailed examination of differences between groups. Finally, we compared the effect sizes of the intervention between countries to assess the impact strength in each context. These results were discussed in the context of intercultural education to identify implications for the design of future programs.

4 Results

This section provides the results of the statistical analysis. Tables 1 and 2 show the results for the two study trips. The category "General" refers to the overall cultural dimension, while the category with the country name shows the country-specific dimensions.

The statistical analysis results for the dimensions of intercultural competence in the studies from Colombia and Malaysia can be summarized as follows.

Engagement: For the general effect, there was only a significant effect for the group in Malaysia (P-value: 0.028). For the country-specific effect, both countries showed nearly significant results. Colombia showed an F-value of 3.467 with a P-value of 0.070 and an effect size of 0.084, indicating a nearly significant effect. Malaysia had an F-value of 3.72, a P-value of 0.061, and an effect size of 0.085, also showing a nearly significant improvement.

Enjoyment: No significant effects were found on the general cultural level. The Colombia study revealed an F-value of 5.345, a P-value of 0.026, and an effect size of 0.123, indicating a significant improvement on a country-specific level. In Malaysia, an F-value of 2.46, a P-value of 0.125, and an effect size of 0.058 were found, which did not reach statistical significance.

Confidence: The overall cultural effect was only significant for the Malaysia group (P-value: 0.0078). For the country-specific effects, an F-value of 5.626, a P-value of 0.023, and an effect size of 0.129 were observed in Colombia, indicating a significant improvement. Malaysia showed an exceptionally high F-value of 13.71, a P-value of 0.001, and an effect size of 0.255, indicating a very strong and significant improvement.

Table 1. Statistical analysis study trip Colombia

Category	Effect	F-value	Df between	Df within	Sig. (P-Value)	Partial Eta^2
General	Engagement	0.691	1	38	0.411	0.018
General	Enjoyment	0.858	1	38	0.360	0.022
General	Confidence	0.112	1	38	0.740	0.003
General	Respect for cultural differences	0.059	1	38	0.810	0.002
General	Awareness	0.739	1	38	0.395	0.019
Colombia	Engagement	3.467	1	38	0.070	0.084
Colombia	Enjoyment	5.345	1	38	**0.026**	0.123
Colombia	Confidence	5.626	1	38	**0.023**	0.129
Colombia	Respect for cultural differences	2.402	1	38	0.129	0.059
Colombia	Awareness	0.008	1	38	0.927	0.0002

Table 2. Statistical analysis study trip Malaysia

Category	Effect	F-value	Df between	Df within	Sig. (P-Value)	Partial Eta^2
General	Engagement	5.29	1	40	**0.0268**	0.117
General	Enjoyment	1.45	1	40	0.2351	0.035
General	Confidence	7.84	1	40	**0.0078**	0.164
General	Respect for cultural differences	2.84	1	40	0.0996	0.066
General	Awareness	4.37	1	40	**0.0429**	0.098
Malaysia	Engagement	3.72	1	40	0.0610	0.085
Malaysia	Enjoyment	2.46	1	40	0.1245	0.058
Malaysia	Confidence	13.71	1	40	**0.0006**	0.255
Malaysia	Respect for cultural differences	6.10	1	40	**0.0179**	0.132
Malaysia	Awareness	8.88	1	40	**0.0049**	0.182

Respect for Cultural Differences: There was no significant change on the overall level in neither context. In the country-specific analysis, mixed effects were found. Colombia achieved an F-value of 2.402, a P-value of 0.129, and an effect size of 0.059, which did not reach statistical significance. In Malaysia, an F-value of 6.10, a P-value of 0.018, and an effect size of 0.132 were found, indicating a significant improvement.

Awareness: The study trip in Malaysia again led to a significant improvement (P-value 0.0049 in the overall cultural sensitivity, while there was none for the group in Colombia. Looking at Colombia only, a very low F-value of 0.008, a P-value of 0.927, and an effect size of almost 0 were determined, showing no improvement. Malaysia demonstrated an F-value of 8.88, a P-value of 0.005, and an effect size of 0.182, indicating a significant improvement.

These results show the diverse impacts of short-term study programs on Swiss participants in Colombia and Malaysia, with specific improvements in certain areas of intercultural sensitivity that show country-specific differences. Malaysia demonstrated stronger effects in confidence, respect for cultural differences, and awareness, suggesting a higher impact on these aspects of intercultural interactions compared to Colombia. While Colombia showed a significant improvement in enjoyment, the overall data suggest that Malaysia's program had a stronger impact on developing key dimensions of intercultural sensitivity.

5   Discussion

Our study shows that the strongest impact of the one-week study program in both contexts was observed in the area of intercultural confidence among the participants. This significant increase in confidence may be attributed to the immersive nature of the short-term trip, which required rapid adaptation to a new cultural environment. The short time frame likely forced participants to engage in more direct and frequent intercultural interactions and pushing them out of their comfort zones. This might have accelerated their confidence in dealing with unfamiliar social and cultural contexts. Such intensive exposure can quickly build an individual's confidence in their ability to communicate and connect across cultural boundaries. This finding shows the potential of week-long programs.

The overall results are positive in all dimensions, but with larger differences between the two countries, especially in the significance. This result is also visible in existing research, which showed short-term programs with positive, but also with no effects [16]. This is one of the first studies on a short-term program that used the adapted ISS with a general and a country-specific part and might therefore be difficult to compare to the existing research. The low effect on general sensitivity is particularly interesting. It shows that within one week the participants focus on the country-specific culture and do not have the time to reflect on the larger intercultural context.

The differences in results between the trips to Colombia and Malaysia can be partially explained by Hofstede's cultural dimensions [23]. For instance, Colombia had a strong effect in the country-specific setting on enjoyment. This could be partially explained by the high score on indulgence in Colombia, which makes it easier to enjoy a culture. In contrast, enjoyment did not change significantly in Malaysia, which could be attributed to the low level in indulgence, but also to the high power distance, making it harder to get in contact with local people. Overall, the cultural differences according to the six dimensions between Colombia and Switzerland are smaller than between Malaysia and Switzerland. This may explain part of the lower impact of the Colombia trip, as participants did not have to adapt as much.

The culture of the Swiss students in terms of individualism and power distance may also limit a higher impact. In general, Switzerland has a very individualistic culture compared to Malaysia and Colombia. This may lead to more individual adventures during the study tour with peers from Switzerland than the desire to meet local people. The much lower power distance can make it difficult for Swiss students to interact meaningfully with people above or below them in the social structure.

Our study's emphasis on short-term study abroad as a pedagogical tool reflects a broader educational shift towards developing global competencies. The accessibility of short-term programs, as opposed to longer exchanges, addresses the need for opportunities that appeal to a wider range of students. To ensure a positive impact on intercultural sensitivity, the following recommendations can be made based on our experience and the literature (2;19; 26). First, pre-departure sessions should be conducted that include cultural awareness training, and an overview of the host country's social norms and expectations. This preparation can help to set realistic expectations and reduce culture shock. Second, students can be encouraged to regularly reflect on their experiences, challenges faced, and lessons learned, for example through debriefing sessions. We have found that by discussing their experiences, students are better able to process them and come up with their own conclusions. Third, use assignments that require students to apply what they have learned about the host culture. These may include essays, research projects, or presentations. Fourth, encourage interdisciplinary learning by including history or politics into the program to provide a holistic understanding of the culture. In this regard, inputs before departure, but also during the trip by locals, can provide a broad picture. Fifth, include collaboration with local organizations as part of the program. This can enable meaningful interactions and provide first-hand insights into the challenges and strengths of the host community. In addition, arrange cultural immersion activities that go beyond tourist sites, such as homestays, in-depth exchanges with local people in different contexts, workshops with artisans, or participation in local events. The participants of the study tours particularly benefited from these exchanges, as they not only interacted with each other outside of company visits. Lastly, ask for ongoing feedback from participants during and after the program to assess its effectiveness and identify areas for improvement.

Various factors play an important role in the success of a short-term study program. It is also worth mentioning that, even though the two programs were organized with very similar activities in both countries, the quality of each visit and interaction also influences the perception of a culture. In addition, while both study groups appear to be a homogenous group of students, groupthink and different personal characters have an impact as well. Thus, it is essential to keep these factors in mind, when discussing these results.

6 Conclusion

The research findings of the two trips of Swiss graduate-students to Malaysia and Colombia indicates some advancements in important areas of intercultural sensitivity, with the Malaysian group showing more improvements overall. Additionally, compared to a general cultural sensitivity, higher impacts in country-specific sensitivity have been demonstrated. The study's findings, taken together, demonstrate that a week-long study tour can bring significant, positive changes in the intercultural abilities needed for society 5.0 and that it can be a valuable pedagogical tool for cross-cultural learning.

This research has several limitations. Firstly, the limited sample size and homogeneity of the participant group restrict the generalizability of the results across varied populations. Additionally, the short follow-up period does not capture the long-term effects and the sustainability of the intercultural sensitivity developed during these experiences. Relying on self-reported data can lead to bias in the responses, affecting the accuracy of the reported changes. Adding qualitative interviews would bring stronger insights. The study's focus on only two destinations may also restrict the applicability of our conclusions to other cultural contexts.

Future research should focus on longer-term impacts and include a more diverse sample and possibly also a control group at home. Comparing a broader variety of cultural destinations can also lead to more nuanced results. In addition, a mixed methods research design will allow a better understanding of the findings and reduce the self-reporting bias.

Disclosure of Interests. The authors have no competing interests to declare that are relevant to the content of this article.

References

1. Cabinet Office: What is society 5.0? https://www8.cao.go.jp/cstp/english/society5_0/index.html. Last accessed 7 Feb 2024
2. Iskhakova, M., Bradly, A.: Short-term study abroad research: a systematic review 2000–2019. J. Manag. Educ. **46**(2), 383–427 (2022)
3. Behrnd, V., Porzelt, S.: Intercultural competence and training outcomes of students with experiences abroad. Int. J. Intercult. Relat. **36**(2), 213–223 (2012)
4. Roy, A., Newman, A., Lahiri-Roy, R.: Antecedents of short-term international mobility programs: a systematic review and agenda for future research. Globalisation, Soc. Educ. **22**, 226-239 (2022)
5. Roy, A., Newman, A., Ellenberger, T., Pyman, A.: Outcomes of international student mobility programs: a systematic review and agenda for future research. Stud. High. Educ. **44**(9), 1630–1644 (2019)
6. Coffey, A.J., Kamhawi, R., Fishwick, P., Henderson, J.: New media environments' comparative effects upon intercultural sensitivity: a five-dimensional analysis. Int. J. Intercult. Relat. **37**(5), 605–627 (2013)
7. Deardorff, D.K.: Intercultural competence: a definition, model, and implications for education abroad. In: Savicki, V. (ed.) Developing Intercultural Competence and Transformation: Theory, Research, and Application in International Education. Stylus, pp. 32–52 (2008)

8. Bird, A., Mendenhall, M., Stevens, M.J., Oddou, G.: Defining the content domain of intercultural competence for global leaders. J. Manag. Psychol. **25**(8), 810–828 (2010)
9. Paine, D.R., Jankowski, P.J., Sandage, S.J.: Humility as a predictor of intercultural competence. Fam. J. **24**(1), 15–22 (2015)
10. Hennings, J.: What is Intercultural Competence and Why is it Important to Business? In: 2018 Engaged Management Scholarship Conference (2018)
11. Moore-Jones, P.: Intercultural sensitivity, intercultural competence & intercultural intelligence: a review of the literature and a proposition of a linear relationship. J. Educ. Cult. Stud. **2**(2), 75–86 (2018)
12. Straffon, D.A.: Assessing the intercultural sensitivity of high school students attending an international school. Int. J. Intercult. Relat. **27**(4), 487–501 (2003)
13. Bennett, M.J.: A developmental approach to training for intercultural sensitivity. Int. J. Intercult. Relat. **10**(2), 179–195 (1986)
14. Bennett, M.J.: Becoming interculturally competent. Toward multiculturalism: a reader in multicultural education **2**(1), 62–77 (2004)
15. Chen, G.-M., Starosta, W.J.: The development and validation of the Intercultural Sensitivity Scale. In: Paper presented at the Annual Meeting of the National Communication Association (2000)
16. Goldstein, S.B.: A systematic review of short-term study abroad research methodology and intercultural competence outcomes. Int. J. Intercult. Relat. **87**, 26–36 (2022)
17. Bradly, A., Iskhakova, M.: Systematic review of short-term study abroad outcomes and an agenda for future research. J. Int. Educ. Bus. **16**(1), 70–90 (2022)
18. Doerr, N.: Modes of study abroad learning: Toward short-term study abroad program designs beyond the study abroad effect. Front.: The Interdisc. J. Study Abroad **34**(2), 112–132 (2022)
19. Nguyen, A.: Intercultural competence in short-term study abroad. Front. The Interdisc. J. Study Abroad **29**(2), 109–127 (2017)
20. Richards, C.A., Doorenbos, A.Z.: Intercultural competency development of health professions students during study abroad in India. J. Nurs. Educ. Pract. **6**(12), 89–98 (2016)
21. DeDee, L.S., Stewart, S.: The effect of student participation in international study. J. Prof. Nurs. **19**(4), 237–242 (2003)
22. Hofstede, G. Cultures and Organizations: Software of the Mind: Intercultural Cooperation and Its Importance for Survival. McGraw-Hill Publishing Co. (1991)
23. Hofstede Insights. Country comparison tool. https://www.hofstede-insights.com/country-comparison-tool. Last accessed 1 Mar 2024

The Influence of Tribal Leaders in the Adoption of e-Banking Products in the Kingdom of eSwatini: Using Social Influence Theory

Sandile Thamie Mhlanga and Josef Langerman[✉]

University of Johannesburg, Johannesburg, South Africa
{smhlanga,josefl}@uj.ac.za

Abstract. In eSwatini, traditional authority is essential for handling conflicts, making decisions, allocating land, and providing cultural activities for the people living in their chiefdom. In this study we examine the role of traditional chiefs in the acceptance of electronic banking (e-Banking) products in eSwatini. The aim was to look specifically at the tribal authority's influence. Therefore, Social Influence Theory as our theoretical lens was employed for this study with the purpose of understanding changes brought about in individual's attitude. A focus group discussion was embarked on to obtain a diverse and comprehensive view of factors that are associated with the adoption of electronic banking products. A qualitative data analysis software ATLAS.ti version 9 was used for qualitative analysis in this study. The study shows that even though there is a positive view around Identification with traditional leadership, Compliance and Internalization contradict the view that traditional leadership influences the adoption of e-Banking products. This leads us to conclude that leadership does not have a strong effect on the adoption of these e-Banking products.

Keywords: Tribal Leadership · e-Banking · eSwatini

1 Introduction

In this paper, we investigate the role of tribal leaders in the acceptance of electronic banking (e-Banking) products in the Kingdom of eSwatini (Swaziland). E-banking for the purposes of this paper implies the provision of banking products and services through electronic delivery channels [1]. Based on this definition, products typically include Internet banking, automated teller machines, mobile banking applications and also mobile money. Many see mobile banking as one of the most revolutionary mobile technology breakthroughs in the banking sector as it enables customers to independently initiate financial transactions at the time and place of their choosing [2–4]. In many cases, mobile banking services can enable mobile payments where a formal bank account is unnecessary, thereby improving financial inclusiveness [5].

Investigating the drivers of these e-Banking products in eSwatini is important for a couple of reasons. Firstly, in the post-Covid era, economic reactivation is necessary.

© The Author(s), under exclusive license to Springer Nature Switzerland AG 2025
K. Hinkelmann and H. Smuts (Eds.): Society 5.0 2024, CCIS 2173, pp. 254–268, 2025.
https://doi.org/10.1007/978-3-031-71412-2_19

Secondly, eSwatini is a developing country and the population is generally seen as poor compared to the developed world. Banking is a good example showing that the improvement of information technology infrastructure has played a significant role in the economic development of developing countries [6, 7].

2   Importance of e-Banking

One of the outcomes of e-banking is financial inclusion and it is a key mechanism for banks to reach more people [1]. In essence, financial inclusion relates to the access and availability of formal financial systems to all sections of society [2]. Financial inclusion benefits society by helping people to manage their resources better and improving their financial capabilities. Innovative financial ecosystems drive inclusive banking and include solutions around payment systems, M-bank, Internet banking, sustainable banking, remittance management and many other types of products and services [3]. The adoption of e-banking is therefore crucial to financial inclusion.

These results have been confirmed specifically for eSwatini by Hlophe [4] where it was confirmed that in line with the general trends in the outline previous paragraph, financial development causes financial inclusion. Policy recommendations from these results advise that financial inclusion strategies include policy decisions that are geared toward increased financial development in eSwatini [4]. The reality is that E-Banking services have not been fully adopted by the citizens of eSwatini. As an example only 44% of the adult population are formally banked, i.e. has access to a bank account [5]. In contrast, 88% of adults have access to at least one connected mobile phone [5]. With regard to economic progress, this is a concern as marginalized groups cannot fully participate in the country's financial systems. Lower-income segments of the population, especially rural communities and small-scale farmers continue to be excluded from possibly beneficial banking services [5].

E-banking services, like mobile money, are experiencing rapid growth in Africa and it is driven by improved access to technology, difficulties in accessing traditional financial services and an increase in contactless payments, especially after the Covid-19 pandemic. Mobile money is primarily provided by telecommunication companies and supported nu a network of licenses. Agents, mobile money services etc. These services allow users to deposit cash into virtual wallets and use those funds for payments and purchases including peer-to-peer payments [6]. Mobile money provides a pathway to financial inclusion for those without a bank account. This has led to a boom in the use of mobile money in Africa. In 2019, 200 million users made 24.46 billion mobile money transactions in Sub-Saharan Africa and the Middle East and Northern Africa, accounting for 64% of all transactions made worldwide. Of the 690.1 billion U.S. dollars in mobile money transactions made in 2019, 456.3 billion USD was exchanged in Sub-Saharan Africa [6].

The results show that mobile money does not seem to be accelerating the reach of financial services to those who are structurally excluded from the formal financial system and suggest the need for ongoing review of the financial inclusion strategies of the country to enhance access to financial services in underserved areas [7].

3   Role of Tribal Authorities

Goodfellow and Lindemann [8] note the widespread resurgence of traditional authorities in Africa since the 1990s. This can be seen in South Africa and eSwatini, which are neighbouring countries that recognize the traditional institution in their constitutions and promote its involvement in development. In South Africa, there are 8 241 chiefs and headmen responsible for the distribution of land under the chief's jurisdiction in the country, and approximately 400 chiefdoms cover more than 70% of eSwatini. [9]. Traditional authorities are integral part of the social, political and cultural establishments in swazi communities. Traditional authorities are regarded as custodians of the values of society and have immense influence. Chiefs are responsible for the welfare of communities through land distribution for areas on Swazi National Land (SNL) for subsistence and grazing purpose. Therefore, traditional authorities provide organic form of governance that is close to the people [9]. Most of the research on tribal authorities is focused on urban development [9], the management of land and gatekeepers of state bureaucracy [10], crop production ([11], etc. We found no literature of the tribal leadership's role in technology adoption. This is seen was a possible aspect of consider as the traditional authorities have engaged in local practices that reimagine and remake urban life, centred on the role of chieftaincy. These practices are made visible mostly on the urban peripheries, which have absorbed a large proportion of the poor since the end of the colonial era. [9].

4   Factors Affecting the Adoption of e-Banking Products

Most of the research on the adoption of e-Banking products relies on the Technology Acceptance Model (TAM) and the extended version of the Unified Theory of Acceptance and Use of Technology (UTAUT2) model [3]. Daka [12] established in a Zambian context that performance expectancy, effort expectancy, facilitating conditions and behavioural intention were the main drivers for the adoption of e-Banking services. The authors also concluded that Social Influence was not a major driver for the adoption of e-Banking services in Zambia. A paper to shed light on the roles of counter-conformity motivation, social influence, and trust in explaining customers' intention to adopt Internet banking services. Results show that the intention to adopt Internet banking is mainly influenced by trust in the Internet banking services, followed by customers' counter-conformity motivation and performance expectancy. Social influence and trust in the physical bank, however, have indirect impacts on customers' intention to adopt Internet banking [31].

In contrast to this, Samartha et al. [14] established using UTAUT that "Social Influence" has a great impact on "purchasing intention". According to this study, customers in India are influenced by their peer group or people around them to use mobile-banking applications. In their views, "social influence", "effort expectancy", and "trust" had a very strong influence on purchase intention, while "effort" and "risk" factors had a negligible impact. Correa et al. [3] has shown that Colombian low-income consumers' are mainly driven by technology. Disposition to adopt e-Banking services. A paper presented by Sitorus et al. [32] work that examines the role of usability, compatibility and social influence in explaining people's intention to continue using mobile banking in Indonesia.

Using an interaction perspective framework. The results show that all the hypotheses are supported, and it was found that people's intention to continue using mobile banking is significantly affected by satisfaction, compatibility, perceived usefulness, perceived learnability and social influence.

Works presented by Giovanis et al. [33] to identify the factors influencing the adoption of mobile self-service retail banking technologies, and the degree of influence of each factors leading their usage. Having mobile banking as the reference service and drawing on previous studies in the field, an extended Unified Theory of Acceptance and Use of Technology (UTAUT) model was proposed and empirically validated to investigate the impact of technology, social, channel and personal factors on potential customers' usage intentions. The results indicated that technology-related factors, expressing innovation expected performance, and social influence are the leading determinants of mobile banking adoption intentions. As can be seen, the models do not seem to be in agreement. Daka [12] and Chaouali et al. [31] notes that social influence is non-significant in the adoption of banking products, while Samartha et al. [14], Sitorus et al. [32], and Giovanis et al. [34] claims it is, both utilizing UTAUT. In none of these studies, there was a reference to tribal leadership, and the literature is also unclear on the role of Social Influence. This, therefore, creates a research opportunity to investigate this in more detail in eSwatini.

5   Research Problems

As shown in the previous paragraphs, E-banking is an important digitization strategy, and it is therefore important for banks to understand the mechanisms driving the adoption of it. Even though this topic has been investigated, there remains a significant gap in understanding the adoption mechanisms in the eSwatini and the tribal leadership's influence on the adoption. Most research in e-Banking follows a quantitative method using the Technology Adoption Model (TAM) or the Unified Theory of Acceptance and Use of Technology (UTAUT). There is, therefore, a need for a qualitative approach that investigates the nuanced social influences in a small developing country like eSwatini, where much of the decision-making is still driven by tribal authorities. In eSwatini, traditional authorities provide an organic form of governance that is close to the people and is part of their day-to-day activities [16]. Based on the dearth of literature on tribal leadership's effect on the adoption of e-Banking products and the importance of e-Banking in developing countries, we propose the following research question:

- What is the role of traditional authorities in the adoption of inclusive banking products in eSwatini?

6   The Social Influence Theory Theoretical Framework

For this research, we chose Social Influence Theory as our theoretical lens. Social Influence Theory attempts to understand changes brought about in an individual's attitude or behaviour by external stimuli such as information communicated to them. Kelman [21] proposed that individuals can accept influence through three processes of social influence:

- Compliance is when people appear to agree with others but actually keep their dissenting opinions private.
- Identification is when people are influenced by someone who is liked and respected, such as a famous celebrity.
- Internalization is when people accept a belief or behaviour and agree both publicly and privately.

The decision not to use the more established TAM and UTAUT theories as our aim was to look specifically at the tribal authority's influence, which is a social influence rather than the broader theories like TAM or UTAUT.

7 Methodology

Qualitative research is a broad term encompassing different data collection and analytical approaches with the aim of providing cultural and contextual descriptions and interpretations of social phenomenon [22]. In this study, focus group discussion was embarked on to obtain a diverse and comprehensive view of factors that are associated with the adoption of electronic banking products. Doing this thereby enables the achievement of the stated research questions. Thematic analysis was employed for analyzing qualitative data, this entailed searching across the data set to identify, analyze, and report repeated patterns [23]. A qualitative data analysis software ATLAS.ti version 9 was used for qualitative analysis in this study. The steps of the qualitative phase which was applied in this study are shown in below.

7.1 Participants

Our research questions drove our choices in composing the Focus group (FG) participants and also the ability and capacity of participants to provide relevant information. Therefore, purposive sampling approach was applied when selecting the FG participants [24]. A resident of Moneni community, in the Manzini Region of eSwatini who spoke both siSwati and English was selected. The focus group consisted of 10 participants, and all participants had a banking account with a bank in eSwatini.

7.2 Focus Group Execution

The Focus group (FG) was conducted in the boardroom of Swedish Free Church, situated in a town called Manzini. The FG consisted of a facilitator and a note-taker and 10 participants. However, one the day of the study, 4 participants cancelled their partaking due to the local government elections which was taking place on the same weekend in eSwatini. The FG took a duration of 1 h 40 min. The 1 h 40 min were spent as presented in Table 1. Directly after the meeting, the researcher wrote up a quick summary of his impressions.

Table 1. Presents the agenda of the FG session

Time	Researcher	Participants
0–15	The researcher greets the participants. The moderator explains purpose and context, explains what a FG is, and introduces the note-taker and her role. Explains that information is confidential and no names will be used. Instead, numbers were distributed to the participants. Then, lets the FG members make introductions. Last the moderator presents the goal of the study, the list of questions	Get participant number
16–90	Moderator probes and follows up questions to explore the key concepts more deeply. Moderator makes sure that each FG member expresses his/her opinion and gets a chance to participate in the FG conversation. The note-taking researchers make sure they collect observations	Participants express opinions, share experiences about the role of traditional authority in inclusive banking products
91–100	Researchers thank participants, give them contact information for further follow up if requested, explain how they will analyze and share the data	

7.3   Thematic Data Analysis

Thematic analysis (TA) is a popular qualitative data analysis technique utilized in a variety of fields including psychology [25] and health care [26]. The main advantage of thematic data analysis is its flexibility, which has positioned it as a beneficial tool for interpreting rich and extensive data [25, 27], thus the motivation of analyzing the research data thematically. The main aim of employing thematic data analysis in this study was to gain more insights into the factors that affect the adoption of electronic banking products from participants and understanding the role of traditional authorities in adoption of inclusive banking products. There are several techniques to thematic analysis in the literature [25, 28, 29]. However, [25] theme approach of qualitative analysis will be largely used in this study, with influences derived from other approaches as necessary. The following thematic steps were taken in this study to conduct thematic data analysis.

Phase 1: Familiarization with the Data.   The initial step in thematic analysis is becoming acquainted with the complete data set, which requires repeated and active reading of the data [17]. The focus group data gave the researchers with early knowledge of the at the preliminary stage of analysis prior to the real reading. Furthermore, for a better grasp of all data components, the researchers read through the data several times and actively noted meanings and patterns. Important concepts, meanings, and patterns that arose in the data were highlighted using Microsoft Word while actively looking through the data, and comments were made for informed coding in phase 2.

Phase 2: Generation of Initial Code. Phase 2 begins after you have studied and become acquainted with the data, as well as developed an initial list of ideas on what is in the data and what is intriguing about it. The data is then used to generate initial codes in this phase. The term "code" refers to "the most basic segment, or element, of the raw data or information that can be assessed in a meaningful way regarding the phenomenon [18] as cited by [17]. As previously stated, ATLAS.ti 9 was the software package used for qualitative data analysis in this study. After becoming acquainted with the raw data, the data files were imported into ATLAS.ti 9 for coding and theme categorization. There are numerous coding methods; however, open coding was employed in this study because it allowed the researcher to code freely as a deeper and more complete understanding of the phenomenon of the role of traditional authority in the adoption of electronic banking products was formed. During this phase, the researcher combed over the transcribed data in ATLAS.ti and generated open codes in a data-driven manner. This meant that the researcher intentionally coded the data by just observing the surface meaning of focus group data. As a result, the code names reflected a surface representation of respondents' statements about the data. The data was not approached with a predefined set of codes. A total of 29 open codes were generate from the data based on the initial code. Since the codes generated in this phase were still initial codes, the codes were prone to change either by deletion or merging them with other codes in the next two phases during code categorisation and themes creation as well as naming and defining codes.

Phase 3: Categorisation of Codes, Themes Creation and Network Diagrams. When all data has been initially coded and aggregated, and you have a big list of the various codes you have identified across your data collection, the third phase begins. This phase, which re-focuses the study on themes rather than codes, entails sorting the various codes into probable themes and combining all relevant coded data extracts within the identified themes [19–21]. The themes were initially compared to the recognized codes and data extracts for accuracy and to guarantee a coherent pattern, and then the themes were validated against the entire data set. New codes were generated as needed, codes were transferred across themes, and unneeded codes were eliminated.

8   Results

8.1   Compliance

Agreed on traditional authorities in general is associated with compliance. This implies that compliance is related to or linked with when individuals or entities concur with or accept the views, directives, or advice offered by established or acknowledged traditional authorities in a general context. In essence, people are more likely to adhere to rules, regulations, or standards when they follow the advice or directives of reputable individuals or institutions, hence exhibiting a higher level of compliance with accepted norms or practices.

Participant 8: "I listen and respect chiefs"

Participant 2: "When chiefs call a meeting we ensure we avail ourselves"

Participant 5: "letinye tikinga temmango ticatululwa tikhulu" which translate to, "some community disputes are resolved by chiefs"

Agreed on recommendations of traditional authorities in the inclusive banking products is associated with Compliance. This implies that acceptance and adherence to advice given by recognized authorities or personalities in the field of inclusive banking are related to upholding compliance. In plainer terms, it helps to ensure that inclusive banking's laws, regulations, and standards are upheld by agreeing with and following the guidance provided by recognized authorities in the field.

Participant 6: "Ngingawulalela ubono wetikhulu" which translates to "I would listen to advice given by traditional authorities"

Participant 7: "I do not know whether I would agree with traditional authority suggestion regarding electronic banking products"

Participant 3: "No"

Discussion on Compliance. In general, the Compliance Network diagram shows that tribal leadership does not affect Compliance regarding e-Banking Product? Fig. 1. Clearly shows by means of themes which contradict compliance such as "Do not feel compelled with their recommendation financial products", "Disagree on recommendation from traditional authorities in inclusive banking", and "Negative that traditional authority influence decision making in inclusive banking".

8.2 Identification

Alignment with traditional authorities who promote inclusive banking have a positive relationship with identification. This implies that when people or groups hold the same values as recognized authorities who support inclusive banking (banking services available to a wide variety of people), it has a positive effect on the identification process. "Identification" in this context could refer to a variety of things, like appreciating the value of inclusive banking, comprehending its advantages, or actively taking part in efforts related to it. The coordination between these agencies appears to be facilitate beneficial effects of identification in the area of inclusive banking.

Participant 6: "It would also depend on the particular person within the traditional authority that is promoting that product"

Participant 4: "If I like the person, I would be tempted to try that electronic banking product"

Participant 5: "Yes, but I might need be trained on how to use that electronic banking product"

Lack of confidence in identification contradicts with identification. This implies that the idea of identification as a whole is violated or contradicted when there is a lack of

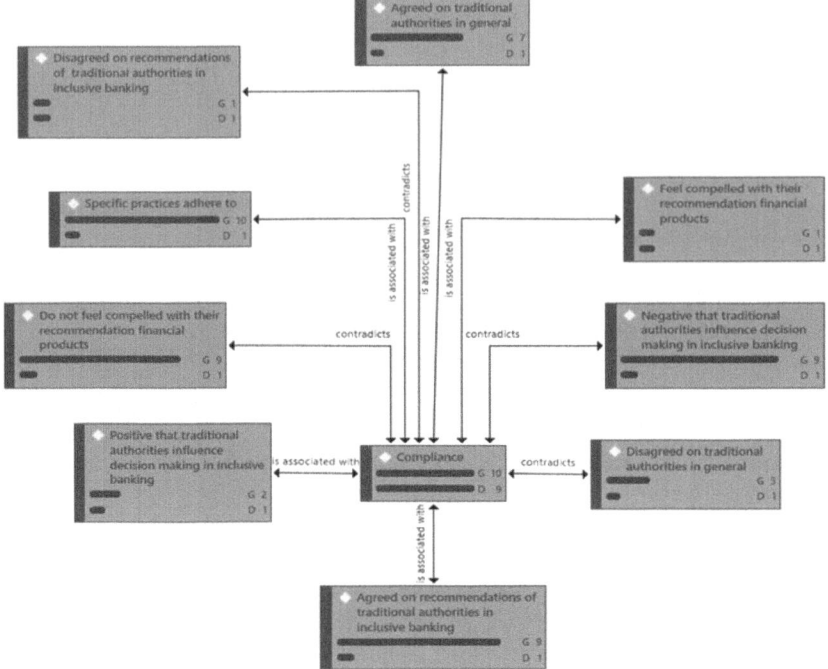

Fig. 1. Network diagram presents 8 themes identifying compliance

confidence in the identifying process. In other words, the fundamental concept or goal of identification is undermined if people or organizations do not trust or believe in the reliability, validity, or efficacy of identification methods or systems. For the identification process to be effective and meaningful, confidence in it is essential.

> *Participant 9: "Because we are in semi-urban area, some people in different chiefdoms have full confidence in traditional authority, we are closer to town.*

> *Participant 6: "In other area, chiefs, get a lots of audience and information is disseminated through traditional authority, therefore people in rural have full confidence in traditional authority, as oppose to Moneni, partly urban and partly rural."*

> *Participant 3: "The age also contributes; older people have confidence while young generate may differ"*

Discussion on Identification. In general, the Identification Network diagram shows that tribal leadership does affect Identification regarding e-Banking Product? Fig. 2. Illustrates by means of themes which associates with identification such as "Align with traditional authority who promote inclusive banking", "Confidence in identification", "Trust in identification", and "Security in identification". Participants mentioned that if the community trust the traditional authority of that chiefdom, associating with a banking products promoted by chiefs can be achieved. The integrity of the traditional

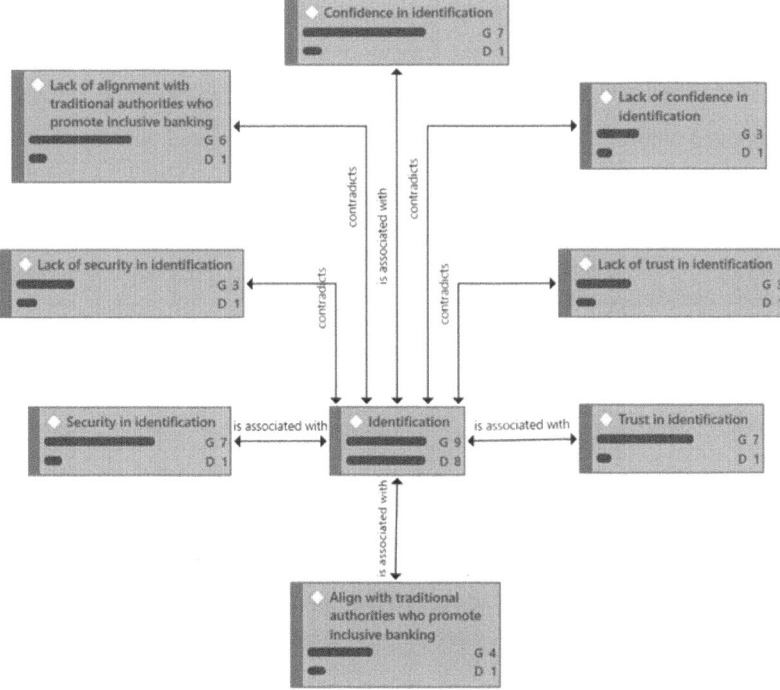

Fig. 2. Network diagram presents 8 themes identifying Identification

authority contributes immensely in identification, especially within most Swazi community where respect, honesty is of high value. In addition, participant mentioned that age was another contributing factor where older generation has confidence in traditional authority guidance, while the younger generation may differ.

8.3 Internalization

In line with shape overall financial decision making process and behaviors is associated with internalization. It implies that internalizing various external factors, such as societal norms, cultural values, economic conditions, financial education, and personal experiences, has an impact on how people make financial decisions and the behaviors they display in relation to their finances. Their perceptions of financial options, risk tolerance, investment strategies, and spending patterns may change as a result of this internalization process. Embraced and internalized the concepts of inclusive banking advocated by traditional authorities is associated with internalization. The idea is that when people or communities actively adopt and incorporate inclusive banking concepts—which aim to provide financial services to underserved and marginalized populations—they internalize these principles into their own financial decision-making processes and behaviors. A wider segment of the public may benefit from a more egalitarian and open financial environment as a result.

Participant 7: "You are most the questions involving traditional authority"

Participant 3: "With the unrest we have as a country, my heart is still not well, regarding traditional authority"

I adopt and embrace inclusive banking practices is associated with internalization. The themes in this case means that people internalize these ideas into their own financial behaviors and decision-making processes when they intentionally choose to include and fully support inclusive banking practices. This shows that people are actively incorporating the idea into their mentality and behavior in the area of banking and money, rather than merely passively accepting it.

Participant 1: "Some of the question feels like we have answered them"

Participant 10: "No, chiefs cannot influence my decision regarding electronic banking products"

Internalized the values and principles promoted by traditional authorities in the inclusive banking advocated by traditional authorities is associated with internalization. Argues that people are engaging in a process of internalization when they not only accept but also fully incorporate the values and ideals promoted by traditional authorities within the framework of inclusive banking. This indicates that, particularly in the area of inclusive banking practices, they are incorporating these values and principles into their own views, perspectives, and decision-making procedures.

Discussion on Internalization. In general, the Internalization Network diagram shows that tribal leadership does not affect Internalization regarding e-Banking Product? Fig. 3 presents 8 themes identifying Internalization which contradicts Internalization such as "Lack of internalized values and principle promoted by traditional authority", "Lack of embraced and internalized concept of inclusive banking advocated by traditional authority", and "Do not adopt and embrace banking practices" Some participants asked why most questions revolved around traditional authority and they were concerned that some responses may have differ if this discussion took place before the political unrest that engulfed the Kingdom of eSwatini.

9   Discussion of the Results

As can be seen from Fig. 4, the focus group felt that even though there is a positive view around Identification with Tribal leadership, Compliance and Internalization contradict the view that Tribal Leadership influences the adoption of e-Banking products. This leads us to conclude that Tribal Leadership does not have a strong effect on the adoption of these e-Banking products.

10   Opportunities for Further Research

The fact that the focus group was conducted with participants from a more urban setting limits the applicability of this research across all of eSwatini. Future research should be conducted to see if these findings will hold in a rural setting, as most of eSwatini

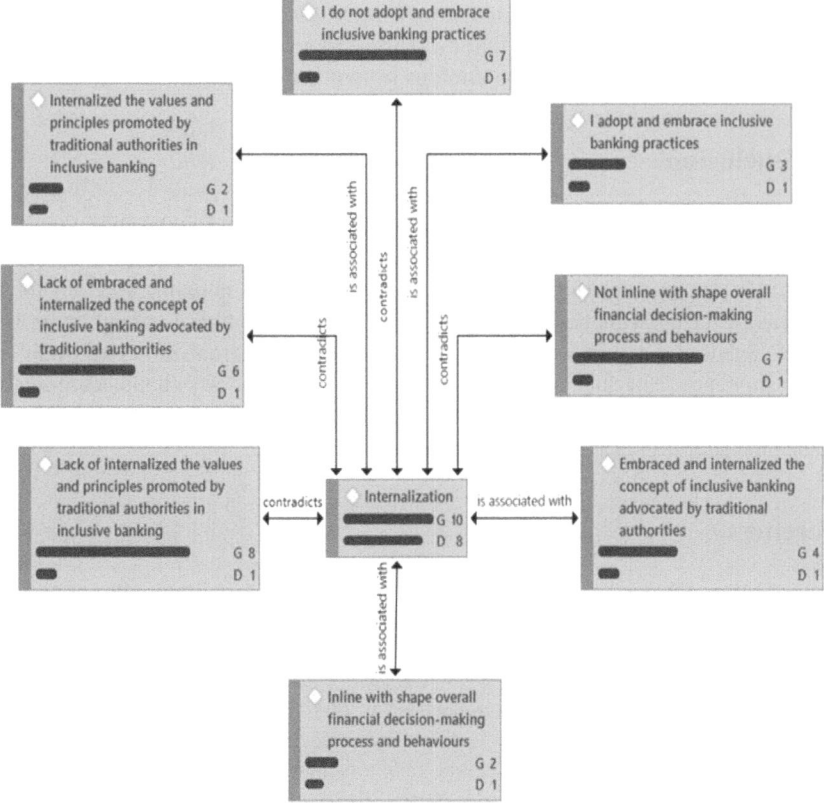

Fig. 3. Network diagram presents 8 themes identifying Internalization

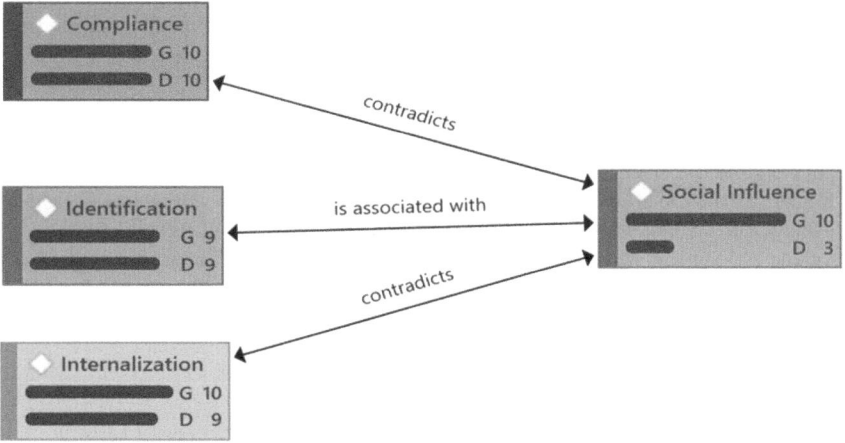

Fig. 4. Social Theory Network Diagram for this study

consists of a rural population. A second area of opportunity for research will be to expand the research to look at the factors that drive the adoption of e-Banking technology in eSwatini and compare this results to findings from other countries.

11   Conclusion

In eSwatini, Moneni community respect and accept traditional authorities' guidance. However, regarding e-Banking products, the traditional authority cannot influence the community's decision making. Figure 4 illustrates a social network diagram for the study showing the most contradicting factors which were compliance and internalization. The participants did not associate with compliance and internalization of traditional authority guidance regarding e-Banking products. While on the other hand, identification was positive, participants associated with identification. Traditional authority does not influence the adoption of e-Banking products.

References

1. Nitsure, R.R.: E-banking: challenges and opportunities. Econ. Polit. Wkly. **38**(51/52), 5377–5381 (2003)
2. Alalwan, A.A., Dwivedi, Y.K., Rana, N.P.: Factors influencing adoption of mobile banking by Jordanian bank customers: extending UTAUT2 with trust. Int. J. Inf. Manag. **37**(3), 99–110 (2017). https://doi.org/10.1016/j.ijinfomgt.2017.01.002
3. Laukkanen, T.: Consumer adoption versus rejection decisions in seemingly similar service innovations: the case of the Internet and mobile banking. J. Bus. Res. **69**(7), 2432–2439 (2016). https://doi.org/10.1016/j.jbusres.2016.01.013
4. Sharma, S.K., Sharma, M.: Examining the role of trust and quality dimensions in the actual usage of mobile banking services: an empirical investigation. Int. J. Inf. Manag. **44**, 65–75 (2019). https://doi.org/10.1016/j.ijinfomgt.2018.09.013
5. Donovan, K.: 'Mobile money for financial inclusion', in information and communications for development. The World Bank **2012**, 61–73 (2012). https://doi.org/10.1596/9780821389911_ch04
6. Cheng, C.-Y., Chien, M.-S., Lee, C.-C.: ICT diffusion, financial development, and economic growth: an international cross-country analysis. Econ. Model. **94**, 662–671 (2021). https://doi.org/10.1016/j.econmod.2020.02.008
7. Kamel, S.: The use of information technology to transform the banking sector in developing nations. Inf. Technol. Dev. **11**(4), 305–312 (2005). https://doi.org/10.1002/itdj.20023
8. Sithole, N., Sullivan Mort, G., D'Souza, C.: Building blocks of financial inclusion through customer experience value at financial touchpoints in Southern Africa. Int. J. Bank Mark. **39**(3), 360–380 (2021). https://doi.org/10.1108/IJBM-07-2020-0409
9. Rastogi, S., Goel, A., Doifode, A.: Open API in Indian banking and economic development of the poor: opportunities and challenges. Int. J. Electron. Bank. **2**(4), 321–348 (2020). https://doi.org/10.1504/IJEBANK.2020.114772
10. Correa, J.C., Dakduk, S., van der Woude, D., Sandoval-Escobar, M., Lopez-Llamas, R.: Low-income consumers' disposition to use automated banking services. Cogent Bus. Manag. **9**(1), 2071099 (2022). https://doi.org/10.1080/23311975.2022.2071099
11. Hlophe, N.: Does financial development mean financial inclusion? A causal analysis for Eswatini. Afr. Rev. Econ. Financ. **10**(2), 2 (2018)

12. Dlamini, T.L.: 'Factors affecting adoption of mobile money by farming households in Lomahasha Inkundla of the Lubombo Region, Eswatini'
13. Taylor, P.: Mobile Money in Africa – statistics & facts', Statista (2023). Accessed 18 Jul 2023. https://www.statista-com.eu1.proxy.openathens.net/topics/6770/mobile-money-in-africa/
14. Myeni, S., Makate, M., Mahonye, N.: Does mobile money promote financial inclusion in Eswatini? Int. J. Soc. Econ. **47**(6), 693–709 (2020). https://doi.org/10.1108/IJSE-05-2019-0310
15. Goodfellow, T., Lindemann, S.: The clash of institutions: traditional authority, conflict and the failure of "hybridity" in Buganda. Commonw. Comp. Polit. **51**(1), 3–26 (2013). https://doi.org/10.1080/14662043.2013.752175
16. Simelane, H.Y., Sihlongonyane, M.F.: A comparative analysis of the influence of traditional authority in urban development in South Africa and Eswatini. Afr. Stud. **80**(2), 153–171 (2021). https://doi.org/10.1080/00020184.2021.1932417
17. Tieleman, J., Uitermark, J.: Chiefs in the city: traditional authority in the modern state. Sociology **53**(4), 707–723 (2019). https://doi.org/10.1177/0038038518809325
18. Dlamini, S.I., Huang, W.-C.: A double hurdle estimation of sales decisions by smallholder beef cattle farmers in Eswatini. Sustainability **11**(19), 19 (2019). https://doi.org/10.3390/su111195185
19. Daka, G.C., Phiri, J., et al.: Factors driving the adoption of e-banking services based on the UTAUT model. Int. J. Bus. Manag. **14**(6), 43–52 (2019)
20. Samartha, V., Shenoy Basthikar, S., Hawaldar, I.T., Spulbar, C., Birau, R., Filip, R.D.: A study on the acceptance of mobile-banking applications in India—unified theory of acceptance and sustainable use of technology model (UTAUT). Sustainability **14**(21), 14506 (2022)
21. Kelman, H.C.: Further thoughts on the processes of compliance, identification, and internalization. In: Social Power and Political Influence, Routledge (1974)
22. M. Vaismoradi and S. Snelgrove, 'Theme in Qualitative Content Analysis and Thematic Analysis', 2019
23. Kiger, M.E., Varpio, L.: Thematic analysis of qualitative data: AMEE Guide No. 131. Med. Teach. **42**(8), 846–854 (2020). https://doi.org/10.1080/0142159X.2020.1755030
24. Daneva, M., Herrmann, A.: Understanding the Most In-demand Soft Skills in Requirements Engineering Practice: Insights from Two Focus Groups (2019)
25. Braun, V., Clarke, V.: Using thematic analysis in psychology. Qual. Res. Psychol. **3**(2), 77–101 (2006). https://doi.org/10.1191/1478088706qp063oa
26. Braun, V., Clarke, V.: What can "thematic analysis" offer health and wellbeing researchers? Int. J. Qual. Stud. Health Well-Being **9**(1), 26152 (2014). https://doi.org/10.3402/qhw.v9.26152
27. Braun, V., Clarke, V.: Reflecting on reflexive thematic analysis. Qual. Res. Sport Exerc. Health **11**(4), 589–597 (2019). https://doi.org/10.1080/2159676X.2019.1628806
28. Attride-Stirling, J.: Thematic networks: an analytic tool for qualitative research. Qual. Res. **1**(3), 385–405 (2001). https://doi.org/10.1177/146879410100100307
29. Cruzes, D.S., Dyba, T.: Recommended steps for thematic synthesis in software engineering. In: 2011 International Symposium on Empirical Software Engineering and Measurement, Banff, AB: IEEE, pp. 275–284 (2011). https://doi.org/10.1109/ESEM.2011.36
30. Boyatzis, R.E.: An overview of intentional change from a complexity perspective. J. Manag. Dev. **25**(7), 607–623 (2006). Accessed: 20 Oct 2023. https://doi.org/10.1108/02621710610678445/full/html
31. Chaouali, W., Ben Yahia, I., Souiden, N.: The interplay of counter-conformity motivation, social influence, and trust in customers' intention to adopt Internet banking services: The case of an emerging country. J. Retail. Consum. Serv. **28**, 209–218 (2016). https://doi.org/10.1016/j.jretconser.2015.10.007

32. Sitorus, H.M., Govindaraju, R., Wiratmadja, I.I., Sudirman, I.: Examining the role of usability, compatibility and social influence in mobile banking adoption in Indonesia. Int. J. Technol. **10**(2), 351 (2019). https://doi.org/10.14716/ijtech.v10i2.886
33. Giovanis, A., Assimakopoulos, C., Sarmaniotis, C.: Adoption of mobile self-service retail banking technologies: the role of technology, social, channel and personal factors. Int. J. Retail Distrib. Manag. **47**(9), 894–914 (2019). https://doi.org/10.1108/IJRDM-05-2018-0089

The Benefits and Challenges of Using Datathons as a Method of Learning Data Analytics

Nkosikhona Theoren Msweli$^{(\boxtimes)}$ ⓘ and Tendani Mawela ⓘ

Department of Informatics, University of Pretoria, Pretoria 0028, South Africa
u19401958@tuks.co.za

Abstract. The acquisition of data analytics skills is becoming increasingly crucial in today's data-driven world. At the same time datathons are gaining traction in the field of data science since these events enable participants to collaboratively solve practical problems and make decisions using real-world data sets. This study explored how datathons may support the learning of data analytics. The study, which was exploratory and qualitative, collected data via five focus group sessions that were conducted with datathon participants. The aim was to investigate participants' views on the perceived benefits, and challenges of using datathons to learn data analytics. The study results indicate that datathons provide a productive starting point for learning data analytics for individuals with no knowledge of data science. However, further learning opportunities and research are needed for an individual to fully grasp data analytics. For students in the field of technology, participating in datathons provides a unique opportunity to hone their data analytical skills in a competitive and collaborative environment. By working on real-world datasets and solving complex problems, participants indicated that they gained practical experience and learned valuable techniques for extracting insights from data. While datathons offer enriching experiences, there are some challenges with the intense, time-limited and competitive nature of these events. This study contributes to the understanding of the role of datathons in facilitating learning and skill development in data analytics and provides recommendations towards leveraging the potential of datathons as a learning tool in the field of data science.

Keywords: datathon · data analytics · data science · pedagogies · transdisciplinary

1 Introduction

Data analytics is the process of examining large sets of data to uncover patterns, trends, and valuable insights that can drive business strategies [1]. It entails various techniques, such as statistical analysis, data mining, building predictive models, and machine learning, to find meaningful information from data. Data analytics capabilities are widely used by organisations to improve efficiency and gain a competitive advantage. Consequently, data analytics skills have been listed as a requirement in many job listings by employers [2]. These skills encompass various competencies, including data visualisation, analysis,

© The Author(s), under exclusive license to Springer Nature Switzerland AG 2025

K. Hinkelmann and H. Smuts (Eds.): Society 5.0 2024, CCIS 2173, pp. 269–281, 2025.
https://doi.org/10.1007/978-3-031-71412-2_20

modeling, and interpretation. Persaud [3] further confirmed that employers are extensively recruiting employees with cognitive competencies in data analytics, business, and a wide range of 21st-century skills. Organisations are leveraging these skills to boost their businesses.

There is a growing skills gap among professionals with data analytics. This gap prevents organisations from transforming insights into valuable information, and this impacts various disciplines [3]. Learning institutions face challenges related to how they may incorporate data analytics within the curriculum to support the growing demand for these skills. Few studies have noted that only computer science students are taught data analytics [4–6]. It is difficult for learning institutions to support data analytics if there are no resources available. In particular, the social sciences have lagged in keeping up with more modern statistical methods [7]. Various tools have been developed and refined to support traditional learning of modern data analytics, such as incorporating GitHub, Matlab, and Azure ML into the classroom [8]. Limited resources such as competent faculty were noted as a challenge of integrating data analytics skills into non-science courses [9]. This further discourages the advancement of society 5.0 goals which aims to integrate technology, data, and human capabilities across diverse communities.

There is a need to explore alternative methods to support the acquisition of data analytics skills across different disciplines. This includes exploring how available resources can be maximized to grow the data analytics talent. The goal of this paper is to identify the challenges and benefits to students of using datathons as a method of acquiring data analytics skills. Therefore, the following research question was formulated:

What are the benefits and challenges of using datathons to learn data analytics?

The paper offers two contributions. Firstly, the paper provides an analysis of the benefits and challenges associated with using datathons for learning data analytics skills, and offering new insights into the topic. Secondly, the paper offers an evaluation of datathons as an alternative method of learning data analytics based on students perceptions.

Based on the analysis of benefits and challenges, the paper offers practical recommendations for individuals, learning institutions, and other organisations interested in leveraging datathons for learning data science effectively. The remainder of the paper is structured as follows: the next section presents the literature overview, which is then followed by the research methodology that was adopted. Thereafter, the data analysis, findings and discussion are presented. The final section presents the conclusions, limitations, and areas for further research.

2   Literature Review

2.1   Understanding Data Analytics

Conway [10] provided a summary of data analytics through a Venn diagram, which illustrates the intersection of Hacking Skills, Mathematical and Statistical Knowledge, and Substantive Expertise. The combination of these elements create a multidisciplinary nature out of data analytics. While these foundational elements remain crucial, the scope of data analytics has expanded to incorporate a broader range of skills, techniques, and technologies. The application of data analytics also differs across fields, for instance, for the detection of diseases in medicine [11], and forecasting in aviation [1]. It is important that individuals understand the importance of data and data analytics, and also the benefits and opportunities of its application [12]. Data analytics skills are in demand due to the need in organisations for the capability to effectively generate valuable patterns that can influence the way industry is doing business [11]. However, there are various technologies that need to be mastered in order to correctly and successfully apply data analytics [11]. This includes knowledge of machine learning, programming (both linear and non-linear), regression and business acumen among others [4, 13]. Universities are now looking for ways to embed data analytics to create a multidisciplinary curriculum [5].

2.2 Data Analytics in Developing Countries

The adoption and application of data analytics is growing globally including within various organisations across developing nations. For instance, Shereni and Chambwe [14] observed that data analytics in Zimbabwe is new and they highlight uptake specifically in the hospitality sector. Whereas, Motau and Kalema [15] highlighted various factors that affect the readiness for data analytics in South Africa, which included technological infrastructure, security, availability of finances, and competitors. Hermínio et al. [16] confirmed these factors as common in developing countries, and continued to add the shortage of skills as another impeding factor towards the use of data analytics in organisations. These limitations prohibit the acceleration of development initiatives which may result in delays in achieving the Sustainable Development Goals (SDGs) aimed at changing the world [17], and those of society 5.0. Therefore, the barriers need to be addressed to promote the adoption and use of data analytics and to uplift developing countries.

2.3 Datathons and Data Analytics

A datathon is an event similar to a hackathon where individuals, normally students, come together over a certain period of time to work on problems with a specific real-world dataset [18]. Engaging with real data in datathon events benefits students in terms of building their data related skills and also enables them to be part of an interdisciplinary team. Unlike before where only computer science students were interested in datathons [19], Msweli et al. [20] found that students from other disciplines are participating in datathons and other similar events. Based on their experiences of hosting datathon events, Anslow et al. [18] recommended that technical and non-technical teams work together focusing on problems they want to tackle at that particular time. This approach aims to balance skills development, and to promote creativity amongst team members. Longo et al. [21] highlighted the following factors as drivers of datathons:

- There is a growing need to enhance and modernize traditional data science education curricula, opening up new opportunities for the systematic integration of datathons into learning programs, and
- There is also a rising demand for adequate data literacy across disciplines.

Successful teams coming from datathons are associated with higher effective learning [22]. This was further supported by Salinas et al. [23], where they evaluated students after participating in a datathon. The students indicated that datathons made them understand data analysis better. Datathons are known for promoting student collaboration [18, 23], albeit an informal learning environment [18]. There is no doubt that such events are gaining popularity as valuable learning experiences, especially in fields like data science, machine learning, and analytics [18, 22, 24]. However, the formal recognition and endorsement of these events within traditional educational institutions vary and are often not extensively deliberated upon.

3 Methodology

3.1 Research Design

The study is underpinned by the interpretivist philosophical paradigm. The study is qualitative and exploratory and seeks to understand the perceptions, benefits, and challenges towards the use of datathons as a method of learning data analytics.

3.2 Participants and Data Collection

Focus groups were used as a method of data collection. Datathons are a novel addition in the learning environment [21]. It was considered important to spend time in the field and understand participants' perceptions on this new addition, so as to understand the benefits and challenges it introduces in the learning landscape. The development of the interview protocol used in this study was informed by a literature review. It was developed with an intent of understanding the perceptions, benefits and challenges of using datathon to learn data analytics. Ethical approval for the study was obtained from the applicable research ethics committee. Data was collected over a period of 1 month (February 2024), from students studying at various higher education institutions (HEIs) in South Africa. The students were briefed about the purpose of the study. The study sample included five focus group sessions with five datathon teams each comprising of five participants. Each session was approximately 1 h and 30 min long. The data was transcribed and coded using ATLAS.ti 8. The codes and themes were extracted and analysed using the thematic analysis method [25]. To maintain participant's anonymity, the quotes were anonymized using the team code and participant number.

4 Results and Discussion

4.1 Student's Perceptions on Datathon as a Tool for Learning Data Analytics

Scholars have previously suggested the use of datathons to augment data science curriculums to address the needs of students learning data analytics skills [18]. The majority of participants in these events are students from the STEM (Science, Technology, Engineering and Mathematics) field, however, it has been noted that datathons can also benefit students from the non-STEM fields [21, 22]. The reasons for datathon participation vary from one student to the next and their expectations will also differ. There is limited research on the effectiveness of datathons as a tool for learning data analytics. Therefore, participants were asked several questions on how they perceive datathons, and whether they believe such events have a place within HEIs. Table 1 provides the themes and codes that were extracted from transcriptions.

Based on the sentiments shared, datathons offer students more than just an opportunity to acquire data analytics skills. Datathons provide a platform for building connections, fostering collaboration, and expanding professional networks. Through their participation in datathons, students not only enhance technical expertise but also develop invaluable soft skills and establish relationships that can support their personal and professional growth in the field of data science. Project-based or hands-on learning was the popular learning style among students to learn data analytics. This finding confirms those of others scholars who cited this learning style as an effective method of learning data analytics [7, 26]. Participants find datathons as enriching in terms of learning new skills. For instance, teaching business understanding as part of data science curriculum is a challenge. Participants in this study indicated that they did not expect to learn business acumen. Previous studies have indicated that it is difficult to incorporate business programs into data science education [13]. Therefore, datathons may guide the curriculum development process and further augment classroom lessons. In addition, datathons accommodate students from many disciplines together with their varied expectations.

4.2 Benefits of Using Datathons to Learn Data Analytics

There are various benefits that have been shared by other scholars. The collaborative process, creative thinking, and networking opportunities are highlights of the datathon experience [23, 27]. The table below shows the benefits of using datathons to learn data analytics as shared by the participants during the focus group sessions (Table 2).

The growing demand for data analytics skills requires pedagogies that are flexible and responsive to industry demands. From the sentiments shared, datathons offer more than an opportunity to learn data analytics skills. The events also support career development by exposing participants to real world scenarios. Interdisciplinary collaborations among the peers, further prepare them for challenges they may encounter in the data science field [27]. By working with individuals from diverse backgrounds, each bringing unique perspectives and expertise to the table, participants in datathons gain invaluable experience in navigating complex problems and developing innovative solutions. Prior studies have reported that datathons help participants understand more about data analysis and visualisation [23]. Responses from participants confirmed these reports, for instance, one participant cited improvement in understanding data trends. Participants appreciated learning how to analyze trends and use data effectively in building innovative systems. Society 5.0 creates a human-centric society where technology serves the needs of individuals and communities. Not only do the learners gain skills by being part of the event, the datathons also contribute to the production of actionable insights and solutions that have a tangible impact on people's lives. Continued learning is a necessity in the evolving era of data science, for candidates to remain competitive in job market. Datathons provide the participants with an opportunity to interact with industry experts on the application of data analytics in real-world problems [24]. One of the key benefits

Table 1. Quotes from participants on datathon perceptions

Theme	Code	Sample Quote
Learning opportunities	Data exposure and literacy	*"They help you understand how data can be used to solve real world problems and are a really great way to connect with people who have industry experience."* **U2**
	Skills Development Industry connection	*"I strongly believe that datathons have a valuable place in institutions of higher learning. This is because datathons provide skill development, experiential learning, interdisciplinary learning and collaboration, and the ability to build your portfolio and network with like-minded people. Datathons also help promote data literacy."* **TT3** *"It is an accessible way to meet experts and sharpen my skills, especially quite rapidly"* **PA4**
	Hand-on Learning	*"I am certain that individuals can learn data analytics through datathons. Datathons are hands-on educational experiences in which participants are tasked with analyzing real-world datasets to solve specific challenges within a specific time frame."* **HT5**
Expectations	Business acumen	*"I hoped to learn the business side of building an application, and I've learned what makes an app appealing to investors. I believe most of my expectations were met, I still need to understand the marketing side of developing applications."* **U3**
		"I hoped to learn more about health data analysis. My expectations have been exceeded as I learnt far more, such as about developing a business model and securing the solution." **TT1**
Learning Style	Project- Based learning	*"I have found that the best way for me to learn something is by working on a project and, researching how to build and troubleshoot features that I need to complete my project."* **U2**

(continued)

Table 1. (*continued*)

Theme	Code	Sample Quote
	Hands-on Learning	*"I learn best when I have hands-on experience (practical). It's true what they say when they say that nothing beats experience."* **HT1**
Accessibility	Inclusivity	*"Make them more accessible to students and the general public. So that more people can be encouraged to join."* **U3**
	Institutional Support	*"Many institutions already have hackathons and datathons are similar so it could fit well.."* **HC1**
		"We are definitely encouraged to participate in events like these and I had lots of encouragement when I asked to take time off." **TT1**
Skills Development Soft skills	Leadership skills	*"I learnt a wide variety of information, as well as how to apply it, and deepened my leadership skills. It was an enjoyable experience."* **PA1**

of working with mentors from industry is their wealth of knowledge and experience, which they can share with mentees during the idea development process. HEIs can further capitalize on these collaborations by co-developing data analytics programmes with industry.

4.3 Challenges Faced by Students in Learning Data Analytics Using Datathons

While datathons prove to improve soft skills and experiential learning among participants [21], there are also challenges experienced. Working in a team can be frustrating along with challenges such as struggling to find suitable datasets, and technical difficulties among others. Table 3 below shares the challenges experienced by datathon participants in this study.

An important element of hosting datathons is the availability of data [18]. In addition, access to additional materials such as software tools and platforms is also important in learning data analytics [8]. The absence of these resources affects the learning process and delays the problem-solving process. Choosing data visualisation tools has also been previously noted as a challenge [23]. While many participants often choose the tools and platforms they will use, it is recommended that datathon organisers provide a set of resources that participants can use where necessary.

The significance of interdisciplinary skills among team members was underscored. This approach aims to offer support in areas where certain skills may be lacking, while also creating opportunities for team members to learn from each other. For example,

Table 2. Benefits of using datathons

Theme	Code	Sample Quote
Skills and career Development	Data Literacy	*"It gives you the skills to understand trends better and the best way of using raw data to build better systems"* **PA1**
	Employment opportunities	*"I am currently employed as data scientist and data analytics are a key part of my job. So, it helped prepare me for employment."* **TT4** *"Successfully completing a datathon project enables me to demonstrate my data science talents and accomplishments to potential employers. Including datathon projects in my portfolio highlights my ability to tackle real-world problems and provide meaningful insights using data analysis."* **TT5**
	Entrepreneurial opportunities	*"Datathons also allow institutions to assess where students' data skills are and what young entrepreneurs are envisioning."* **HC4** *"It's a great way to apply my skills, and a great way to learn to make your ideas appealing to investors."* **HC3**
	Continuous Learning	*"Students are very busy and often do not have the time to dedicate to continuously learning something every day. But a datathon is only one weekend to sacrifice and teaches data skills very rapidly."* **HT2**

(*continued*)

Table 2. (*continued*)

Theme	Code	Sample Quote
		"It upskills their learners and provides them with networking and business opportunities." **PA3**
Interdisciplinary Collaboration Soft Skills	Communication skills	*"Collaboration is a common aspect of datathons, forcing participants to work well with others who have varying backgrounds, abilities, and communication styles."* **U5**

difficulties with data visualisation were observed among participants, impacting the data analytics process. Collaborating across disciplines can help mitigate such challenges by leveraging diverse expertise within the team and fostering a culture of shared learning and skills development [27]. Datathons require skills in programming, data manipulation, machine learning, and data visualisation, which can be challenging for less experienced participants. The intense nature of datathons, including all-nighters and tight deadlines, may deter some students, but they offer valuable learning experiences in data science.

The concentrated, time-limited nature of datathons may also deter some students, especially those with busy schedules. For instance, strict timelines in datathons can be challenging for students who still need to cope with their formal academic responsibilities. Support from the institutions of learning is necessary in such situations, where students can be allowed time to participate in these events without missing out on any important lessons, disrupting their academic progress or compromising their assessment. It has been recommended that datathons should not extend to the night like the norm to accommodate participants' schedules and responsibilities outside of the event [18]. The majority of participants were not familiar with the problems faced by HEIs. This lack of awareness may indicate an issue of limited discussions pertaining to datathons among stakeholders within HEIs. To bridge this communication gap, it is essential to foster a culture of interdisciplinary collaboration and engagement within HEIs, where students, faculty, and other stakeholders participate in discussions and initiatives related to data-driven problem-solving and data related skills development. It is also crucial to understand the effectiveness of datathons in learning data analytics and preparing students for the workforce. Frameworks or other tools are necessary to support the evaluation of datathons and also document evidence on datathon effectiveness that can support or influence policy development. It can be argued that community groups and data enthusiasts are often the primary organisers of these events, rather than HEIs directly [18, 24]. Regardless, HEIs can still play a role in supporting these community-driven initiatives. They can encourage student participation in datathons by promoting awareness of these events, providing resources and support for student-led initiatives, and integrating experiential learning opportunities into the curriculum.

Table 3. Challenges of using datathons

Theme	Code	Sample Quote
Minimal resources	Absence of appropriate data set	*"Acquiring the right kind of data, how to fully process your data to get the most out of it and how to apply that data in your project"* **HT4**
	Lack of Resources	*"Access to resources was a bit of a challenge. Unfortunately, in order to learn data analytics, there are some resources that one needs to learn and practice."* **U2**
Lack of Soft skills	Critical Thinking	*"Coming up with an idea that can be solved using data alone was a challenge."* **HC1**
	Managing conflict	*"For students, managing team dynamics, settling disputes, and guaranteeing that each team member contributes equally can be difficult."* **TT5**
Lack of Data skills	Lack of data visualisation skill	*"Being able to turn data into valuable insights and use the data to tell a story (storytelling) was somehow hard."* **PA4**
Academic Stress	Fatigue	*"It is a very intensive experience that may discourage some students."* **U2**
	Time constraint	*"Staying up all night can be daunting when you have to go to classes the next day. Some students may also not have the time to dedicate to the datathon because of an intensive study schedule."* **PA3**
	Frustration	*"It's one thing to work solo but working in a team (while essential and extremely valuable) comes with lots of frustration and time spent arguing and discussing things."* **TT1**
	Student Diversity	*"Developing technical skills takes time and practice, and as students from different backgrounds, we encounter obstacles along the way."* **HT2**

5   Conclusions, Limitations, and Areas for Further Research

The purpose of the study was to investigate the use of datathons as a learning approach for developing data analytics skills. Participants shared their perceptions on the benefits and challenges posed by datathons in learning data analytics. The results indicated that datathons are valuable in learning data analytics, gaining practical experience, improving technical skills, building professional networks, and showcasing data science talent. They offer hands-on learning opportunities that are linked to real-life scenarios, interdisciplinary teamwork experiences, and exposure to industry professionals. Those who are already in the field gained an opportunity to improve their data analysis techniques and making data science solutions appealing to potential investors and industry experts. Datathons serve as a holistic learning experience that goes beyond technical data analytical skills to encompass the development of essential soft skills such as teamwork, critical thinking, problem-solving, communication, resilience, and adaptability. By participating in datathons, individuals not only enhance their technical proficiency but also cultivate the well-rounded skillsets needed to excel in the data science profession. Participants benefit from practical experience, collaboration, and building their professional portfolios through connections that are built during these events.

In addition to learning analytical skills, datathons offer participants opportunities to understand real-world problems by analysing data and engage with industry experts on the proposed solutions. Such exposure is not common in traditional learning environments. While some participants may prefer working independently, they acknowledge the benefits of being part of an interdisciplinary team. Collaborative problem-solving and creativity are the highlights of datathons, revealing the value of communication skills and networking opportunities benefiting both educational institutions and participants. It was a recommendation from the participants that clear criteria be shared on how the solutions are evaluated. While data analytics skills are important, it is also crucial to consider other data related skills in the process such as critical thinking, domain knowledge, and research [28]. Essentially, this presents an opportunity for HEIs to develop innovative assessment criteria that consider various skills and competencies [21]. This includes recording the evidence of skills attainment such as e-portfolios. Future studies may investigate how the identified challenges may be addressed to improve the acquisition of data analytics skills and datathon experiences.

Disclosure of Interests.   The authors have no competing interests to declare that are relevant to the content of this article.

References

1. Chung, S.H., Ma, H.L., Hansen, M., Choi, T.M.: Data science and analytics in aviation. Transport. Res. Part E: Logist. Transport. Rev. **134**, 101837 (2020). https://doi.org/10.1016/j.tre.2020.101837
2. Vaughan, R.J.: Examining the data analytics skill gap in mid-level marketing professionals, driven by the continuing exponential growth of big data. J. Bus. Theory Pract. (2017). https://doi.org/10.22158/jbtp.v5n3p267

3. Persaud, A.: Key competencies for big data analytics professions: a multimethod study. Inf. Technol. People **34**(1), 178–203 (2021). https://doi.org/10.1108/ITP-06-2019-0290

4. Chiang, R.H.L., Goes, P., Stohr, E.A.: Business Intelligence and Analytics education, and program development: a unique opportunity for the Information Systems discipline. ACM Trans. Manag. Inf. Syst. **3**(3), 1–13 (2012). https://doi.org/10.1145/2361256.2361257

5. Hassan, I.B., Liu, J.: Embedding data science into computer science education. IEEE Int. Conf. Electro Inf. Technol. **2019-May**, 367–372 (2019). https://doi.org/10.1109/EIT.2019.8833753

6. Garcia-Algarra, J.: Introductory Machine Learning for Non STEM Students (2020)

7. Aikat, J., et al.: Scientific training in the era of big data: a new pedagogy for graduate education. Big Data **5**(1), 12–18 (2017). https://doi.org/10.1089/BIG.2016.0014

8. Kim, B., Henke, G.: Easy-to-use cloud computing for teaching data science. J. Stat. Data Sci. Educ. **29**(S1), 103–111 (2021). https://doi.org/10.1080/10691898.2020.1860726

9. Andiola, L.M., Masters, E., Norman, C.: Integrating technology and data analytic skills into the accounting curriculum: accounting department leaders' experiences and insights. J. Account. Educ. (2020). https://doi.org/10.1016/j.jaccedu.2020.100655

10. Conway, D.: The Data Science Venn Diagram (2010(. http://drewconway.com/zia/2013/3/26/the-data-science-venn-diagram. Accessed 14 Aug 2022

11. Razzak, M.I., Imran, M., Xu, G.: Big data analytics for preventive medicine. Neural Comput. Appl. **32**(9), 4417–4451 (2020). https://doi.org/10.1007/s00521-019-04095-y

12. Biehler, R., Budde, L., Frischemeier, D., Heinemann, B., Podworny, S., Schulte, C.: Paderborn Symposium on Data Science Education at School Level 2017: The Collected Extended Abstracts (2018). https://doi.org/10.17619/UNIPB/1-374

13. Li, G., Yuan, C., Kamarthi, S., Moghaddam, M., Jin, X.: Data science skills and domain knowledge requirements in the manufacturing industry: a gap analysis. J. Manuf. Syst. **60**(June), 692–706 (2021). https://doi.org/10.1016/j.jmsy.2021.07.007

14. Shereni, N.C., Chambwe, M.: Hospitality big data analytics in developing countries. J. Qual. Assur. Hosp. Tour. **21**(2), 361–369 (2020). https://doi.org/10.1080/1528008X.2019.1672233

15. Motau, M., Kalema, B.M.: Big data analytics readiness: a South African public sector perspective. In: 2016 IEEE International Conference on Emerging Technology Innovation Business Practice Transformation Social Emerging Technologies 2016, no. August 2016, pp. 265–271 (2016). https://doi.org/10.1109/EmergiTech.2016.7737350

16. Hermínio, G., Marcondes De Moraes, S., Pelegrini, G.C., Porfírio De Marchi, L., Pinheiro, G.T.: Antecedents of big data analytics adoption: an analysis with future managers in a developing country. Bottom Line **35**(2/3), 73–89 (2021). https://doi.org/10.1108/BL-06-2021-0068

17. Orhan, C.C., Guajardo, M.: Analytics in developing countries: methods, applications, and the impact on the UN Sustainable Development Goals. Int. Trans. Oper. Res. **29**(4), 2041–2081 (2022). https://doi.org/10.1111/itor.13018

18. Anslow, C., Brosz, J., Maurer, F., Boyes, M.: Datathons: an experience report of data hackathons for data science education. In: Proceedings of the 47th ACM Technical Symposium on Computing Science Education, pp. 615–620 (2016). https://doi.org/10.1145/2839509.2844568

19. Olesen, F., Brodersen, N., Falk, J., Brodersen Hansen, N., Kannabiran, G.: What do hackathons do? understanding participation in hackathons through program theory analysis. In: Proceedings of 2021 CHI Conference on Human Factors in Computing Systems, pp. 1–16 (2021). https://doi.org/10.1145/3411764.3445198

20. Msweli, N.T., Mawela, T., Twinomurinzi, H.: Massifying data science education through immersive datathons. In: AMCIS 2023 Proceedings, p. 8 (2023)

21. Longo, A., Zappatore, M., Martella, A., Rucco, C.: Enhancing data education with datathons: an experience with open data on renewable energy systems. In: DataED, vol. 22 (2022). https://doi.org/10.1145/3531072.3535322
22. de Toledo Piza, F.M., et al.: Assessing team effectiveness and affective learning in a datathon. Int. J. Med. Inform. **112**(November 2017), 40–44 (2018)
23. Salinas, M.N., Emer, M.C.F.P., Neto, A.G.S.S.: Short datathon for the interdisciplinary development of data analysis and visualization skills. In: Proceedings of the – 2019 IEEE/ACM 12th International Working Cooperation Humanities Aspects of Software Engineering CHASE 2019, pp. 95–98 (2019). https://doi.org/10.1109/CHASE.2019.00031
24. Fritz, S., Milligan, I., Lin, J., Cheriton, D.R.: Fostering community engagement through datathon events: the archives unleashed experience. DHQ Digit. Humanit. Q. **15**(1) (2021)
25. Braun, V., Clarke, V.: Using thematic analysis in psychology. Qual. Res. Psychol. **3**(2), 77–101 (2006). https://doi.org/10.1191/1478088706qp063oa
26. Saltz, J., Heckman, R.: Big Data science education: a case study of a project-focused introductory course. Themes Sci. Technol. Educ. **8**(2), 85–94 (2015). Accessed 02 Jul 2021. https://www.learntechlib.org/p/171521/
27. Aboab, J., et al.: A 'datathon' model to support cross-disciplinary collaboration HHS Public Access. Sci. Transl. Med. **8**(333), 333–341 (2016). https://doi.org/10.1126/scitranslmed.aad9072
28. Demchenko, Y., Wiktorski, T., Cuadrado Gallego, J., Brewer, S.: EDISON data science framework (edsf) extension to address transversal skills required by emerging industry 4.0 Transformation. In: Proceedings – IEEE 15th International Conference on eScience, eScience 2019, pp. 553–559 (2019). https://doi.org/10.1109/eScience.2019.00076

Exploring the Innovation Capabilities of Mauritian SMEs: A Factor Analysis Approach

Kesseven Padachi[1]([⊠]) [iD], Diroubinee Mauree-Narrainen[1] [iD], Aleesha Boolaky[1] [iD], Hemant Chittoo[1] [iD], Needesh Ramphul[1] [iD], and Lizette Weilbach[2] [iD]

[1] University of Technology Mauritius, Port Louis, Mauritius
{kpadachi,d.mnarrainen,aboolaky,hchittoo,needesh.r}@utm.ac.mu
[2] University of Pretoria, Pretoria, South Africa
lizette.weilbach@up.ac.za

Abstract. Amidst a rapidly evolving business landscape, Small and Medium Enterprises (SMEs) face increasing pressure to innovate and adapt to remain competitive. However, despite the critical role of innovation in driving business growth and competitiveness, there exists a notable gap in understanding the innovation capabilities of SMEs in Mauritius. To address this gap, this paper undertakes a comprehensive exploration of the innovation landscape among Mauritian SMEs, drawing upon survey data collected from 280 SMEs across various sectors. The survey instrument, designed to capture key dimensions of innovation capability based on authoritative literature, delved into critical areas including knowledge exploitation, entrepreneurial acumen, risk management, networking proficiency, development capacity, and change management strategies. Utilizing factor analysis, the study identified four distinct factors shaping innovation capabilities within Mauritian SMEs: customer and market acquisition, radical innovation and knowledge management, risk management, and networking. These findings underscore the imperative for SMEs to embrace innovation as a strategic pathway for sustainable growth and competitive advantage. Notably, the study highlights the essential role of internalizing and leveraging external knowledge in driving innovation within organizations, fostering dynamic adaptation and resilience. By clarifying key drivers of innovation, this research offers actionable insights for policymakers, business leaders, and stakeholders seeking to cultivate a conducive innovation ecosystem in Mauritius. Ultimately, the study contributes to filling a critical knowledge gap and provides a foundation for informed decision-making aimed at enhancing innovation and driving economic prosperity in Mauritius' SME sector.

Keywords: Innovation capabilities · Innovation capacity · SME · Factor analysis

1 Introduction and Background

Research on the contribution of Small and Medium Enterprises (SMEs) to economic development and job creation is extensive worldwide, with Mauritius being no exception. In Mauritius, SMEs contributed to 37.5% Gross Value Added (GVA), 50% employment,

© The Author(s), under exclusive license to Springer Nature Switzerland AG 2025
K. Hinkelmann and H. Smuts (Eds.): Society 5.0 2024, CCIS 2173, pp. 282–292, 2025.
https://doi.org/10.1007/978-3-031-71412-2_21

and 12% of total exports in 2019, constituting 99% of all enterprises in the country [1]. However, nearly half of these firms, as classified by a government report, operate at subsistence levels, with fewer than 5 employees and limited growth prospects. Apart from these, the economy is populated by numerous micro, small and medium-sized enterprises [1, 2]. Encouraging innovation and enhancing efficiency in these enterprises has been proposed to lift Mauritius out of the middle-income trap [3].

Recognizing this, the government established SME Mauritius in 2018 to facilitate innovation and support the SME sector. Three main schemes provided by SME Mauritius include a Technology and Innovation Scheme, which supports digital solutions, robotics and artificial intelligence, and website development. This reflects consensus on importance of innovation for SMEs in Mauritius. In today's competitive business environment, innovation is crucial for SMEs to sustain growth and competitiveness. Mauritius, ranked 57th in the Global Innovation Index in 2023 (down from 45th in 2022), underscores the urgency for enhancing innovation in its SMEs [4].

Despite the consensus on the need for technology adoption and innovation in Mauritian SMEs, this has not been grounded in rigorous research but rather mimics international trends. Therefore, this research aims to fill this gap by investigating the innovation capabilities of Mauritian SMEs using a factor analysis approach. By analyzing interconnected variables, this study seeks to identify underlying patterns in the data to provide empirical evidence for recommended strategies.

This paper therefore addresses a critical gap by examining the innovation capabilities of Mauritian SMEs through survey data and factor analysis. By surveying a representative sample, it aims to identify and analyze key factors contributing to innovation capabilities, guiding the formulation of strategies to safeguard these capabilities amidst a dynamic global economic landscape.

Subsequent sections will delve into the literature review, research methodology, data analysis, and findings before drawing conclusions for an ecosystem favorable to enhancing the innovative capabilities of Mauritian SMEs for sustainable job creation.

2   Literature Review

2.1   SMEs and Economic Development

SMEs are essential for Africa's socio-economic advancement, contributing significantly to job creation, income generation (wealth), and poverty reduction [5]. Their impact extends across production, investment, and consumption, thereby fostering economic progress [6].

2.2   SMEs and Innovation Capacity

SMEs are recognized as drivers of innovation and competition across diverse economic sectors [7, 8]. However, they encounter challenges such as limited financial resources, time constraints, workforce shortages, and a lack of market knowledge and technological infrastructure [9]. These challenges impede their competitive advantage [9, 10]. Innovation plays a crucial role in distinguishing SMEs' products and services, enhancing agility, reducing costs, improving quality, and meeting evolving customer demands

[11]. Strategies such as fostering an innovation-friendly culture, establishing partnerships, and embracing digital technologies are recommended for SMEs [12]. Product innovation capability enables firms to swiftly respond to customer needs with new ideas, products, and services [13] thereby positively impacting SME performance [14].

2.3 SMEs and Innovation Capabilities

Research and Development (R&D). R&D are key components of SMEs' innovation endeavors [15], with cloud-based accounting, digital payments, and automated invoicing and settlement procedures playing significant roles [5]. Innovation encompasses the implementation of new or improved products, processes, marketing methods, or organizational practices, contributing strategically to societal growth [16]. It is essential to examine SMEs' attitudes toward R&D trends and common challenges to gain a better understanding of their positioning within the business R&D landscape [17]. Moreover, the IP protection framework facilitates investments in R&D for SMEs, ensuring the development of distinct and high-value products, proprietary technologies, and branding [15].

Capabilities for Knowledge Exploration. Organizations possess the ability to transform knowledge through both exploitation and exploration strategies, aiming to enhance incremental improvements and foster research, discovery, and experimentation [18, 19]. Maintaining a balance between exploration and exploitation is crucial for enhancing competitiveness [20, 21].

Entrepreneurial Capabilities. Entrepreneurial capability refers to the skills, experience, and knowledge necessary to identify and capitalize on business opportunities [22, 23]. Entrepreneurship embodies innovation and plays a crucial role in driving economic development by facilitating change and transformation in a discreet manner [24], considering that entrepreneurs transform their organization and build ecosystems through strategic actions outside routine or the need to create new routines [25]. Entrepreneurial orientation (EO) within organizations is characterized by innovation, risk-taking, proactiveness, autonomy, and competitive aggressiveness [23].

Change Management Capabilities. Effective change management involves identifying business objectives, strategies, and implementing programs to achieve desired outcomes [26]. Strategic management plays a key role in adapting, integrating and reconfiguring internal and external organizational skills, resources, and competencies in response to evolving environment dynamics [27].

Risk Management Capabilities. Proper risk management enhances organizations' competitiveness and sustainability by identifying, assessing, and mitigating risks [28, 29]. While SME owners often prioritize crisis management over comprehensive risk management practices, adherence to risk management standards is essential for ensuring sustainable growth [30, 31].

Networking Capabilities. Networking capabilities enable organizations to manage changing external relationships effectively [32–34]. These capabilities involve establishing and nurturing business connections at all stages, leveraging partnerships, collaborations, and interactions with various stakeholders, including suppliers, customers, and other organizations [32–34].

External Input. External assistance [35], for bridging information and knowledge gaps, is primarily observed in the newly established businesses, given their limited resources and skill sets. Conversely, SME owner-managers benefit from external support provided by a diverse array of service providers operating across various market landscapes and engaging with clients [36]. These 'outsiders' contribute to informal advice and decision-making processes, guiding owner-managers toward more formal sources [37]. The proposition presented in [38] underscores a positive correlation between growth orientation and the pursuit of external support. As businesses grow and undergo organizational changes, they face significant challenges due to limitations in internal resources and knowledge, particularly within small management teams. In Mauritius, SMEs are incentivized by schemes and initiatives aimed at fostering innovation among micro, small, and medium-sized enterprises (MSMEs) and entrepreneurs. For instance, the Innovation and Technology Fund [1], managed by the SME Equity Fund Ltd, offers financing to technology and innovation-oriented companies with at least 51% equity stake, ensuring the sustainability and commercial viability of proposed business models. Additionally, the Technology and Innovation Scheme (TINNS) [1] supports registered SMEs in continually investing in technology and automated production capabilities to enhance their sustainability.

3   Research Methodology

A quantitative research methodology was employed for this study. According to the SME e-Directory of the Ministry of Industrial Development, SMEs and Cooperatives (2024), there were 9313 registered SMEs in Mauritius, representing the population for this research. SMEs in Rodrigues were excluded from the study due to inaccessibility for data collection. A questionnaire was developed based on the literature on disruptive innovation capabilities within SMEs. Data were gathered from 280 SMEs operating in various sectors across Mauritius, selected from the Ministry's list. The survey included SMEs from different geographical areas, ensuring a representative sample that included both rural and urban regions.

A stratified sampling approach was used so ensure representation of SMEs of different sizes. This method was deemed appropriate as it accounts for potential variations in innovation perspectives among SMEs based on their size and location, thereby capturing diverse viewpoints across the Mauritian SME landscape.

The survey instrument was structured into sections, each addressing different aspects of innovation in Mauritian SMEs. The first section examined SMEs' capacity for investment in R&D, focusing on the amount allocated to innovation and the implementation of new processes and product enhancements. Subsequent sections evaluated various innovation capabilities using a 5-point Likert scale. These included knowledge exploitation capabilities (assessing the extent to which SMEs utilize new knowledge for business benefit); entrepreneurial capabilities (evaluating SMEs' ability to identify and seize opportunities and mitigate threats in their business environment); risk management capabilities (determining SMEs' risk-taking behavior and their ability to assess and manage risks effectively); networking capabilities (examining SMEs' engagement with external entities to enhance business operations); development capabilities (assessing SMEs' capacity to innovate by creating new products or improving existing ones); and change management capabilities (investigating SMEs' adaptability to market and customer needs through business adjustments).

To identify key factors influencing SME innovation, a factor analysis was conducted using principal component analysis. This method extracted maximum variance and categorized it into different factors. Varimax with Kaiser Normalization [39] was employed as the rotation method to ensure uncorrelated factors and simplify factor interpretation. The analysis aimed to identify up to four factors, converging in 6 iterations during rotation. The maximum number of iterations was set to 25.

Table 1 presents key demographic and operational characteristics of the surveyed SMEs, providing insights into their needs and behaviors within the business landscape. Analysis reveals that nearly two-thirds of respondents are male, reflecting the predominance of male management in SMEs. Additionally, over 65% of respondents fall within the 31–55 age group. Educational attainment among SME owners/managers varies, with approximately 47.8% possessing intermediate or advanced qualifications, while a similar proportion holds basic qualifications. Business-wise, nearly 90% of SMEs employ fewer than 20 people, and only one-third have operated for more than 10 years, aligning with global trends indicating a relatively short SME lifecycle. Furthermore, 77.5% of SMEs report annual turnovers of up to 10 MUR, with limited investment in R&D. Only 15% of SMEs invest more than 300 K MUR in R&D, while 15% report zero R&D investment. These statistics provide preliminary insights into Mauritian SMEs' innovation capacity and capabilities, which are further examined in the subsequent analysis.

4   Data Analysis and Findings

The survey instrument utilized in this study captured the main constructs through 19 item statements measured on a 5-point Likert scale, ranging from 'very low' to 'very high'. These constructs included knowledge exploitation, entrepreneurial capabilities, risk management, networking, R&D, and change management. Statistical analysis conducted with SPSS v29.0 encompassed descriptive analysis, reliability tests using Cronbach's alpha, and principal component analysis (PCA). The Cronbach's alpha reliability for the factors yielded a score of 0.921, indicating strong internal consistency among the 19 item statements measuring innovation capabilities [40]. This suggests a close association among the factors.

Principal component analysis, a data reduction technique, was employed to identify a concise number of factor groupings representing relationships among numerous interrelated variables. The Varimax rotation method was utilized to minimize the number of variables with high loadings [41]. The PCA revealed that the 19 statements could be grouped into four principal factors, as summarized in Table 2:

Table 1. Respondent Profile and Firms' Characteristics

Demographic Characteristic	Full Sample n=280		Demographic Characteristic	Full Sample n=280	
	f	%		f	%
Gender			**Turnover (MUR)**		
Female	109	38.9	Up to 10 M	217	77.5
Male	170	60.7	Above 10M-30M	37	13.2
			Above 30M- 100M	26	9.3
Age (years)			**Education**		
18-30	48	17.1	Basic	123	43.9
31-45	94	33.6	Technical	23	8.3
46-55	89	31.8	Intermediate	73	26.1
Above 55	49	17.6	Advanced	61	21.8
Employees			**R&D Investment**		
1-4	149	53.2	None	43	15.4
5-19	97	34.6	Less than 50K	81	28.9
20-49	22	7.9	50001-200k	72	25.7
50-199	9	3.2	201k-300k	42	15.0
200 and above	3	1.1	300k-1000k	25	8.9
			Above 1000k	17	6.1
Years of Operation					
<1 year	5	1.8			
1-2 years	47	16.8			
3-5 years	62	22.1			
6-10 years	70	25.0			
>10 years	96	34.3			

- Factor grouping 1 represents customer and market acquisition.
- Factor grouping 2 represents radical innovation and knowledge management.
- Factor grouping 3 represents risk management.
- Factor grouping 4 represents networking.

The statistical properties of the PCA, including eigenvalues and Cronbach's alpha for each factor, confirmed the retention of these four factors. Together, they accounted for 73% of the total variances among SME innovation capabilities. Following Varimax rotation, Factor Grouping 1 (Customer and Market Acquisition) explained 24.20% of the total variances, Factor Grouping 2 (Innovation and Knowledge Management) explained 22.12%, Factor Grouping 3 (Risk Management) explained 14.20%, and Factor Grouping 4 (Networking) explained 12.13% [42].

The analysis identified four key capability groupings essential for Mauritian SMEs to enhance their innovation capacity. These groupings encompass various aspects of innovation, facilitating a comprehensive understanding of innovation capabilities among

Table 2. Rotated factor matrix (loading) of Capabilities to undertake Innovation

FACTOR COMPONENTS	COMPONENT			
	1	2	3	4
Capabilities to expand to new markets	.769			
Capabilities to improve existing products and services	.760			
Capabilities to quickly implement change based on market and customer knowledge	.739			
Capabilities to exploit innovations developed by others	.728			
Capabilities to generate new innovations which differ from competitors' offerings	.714			
Capabilities to acquire new customers	.703			
Capabilities to increase sales to existing customers	.695			
Capabilities to exploit new knowledge for innovation		.821		
Capabilities to internalise new external knowledge		.815		
Capabilities to recognise relevant external knowledge		.810		
Capabilities to exploit opportunities for generating new profitable business		.721		
Capabilities to seize new opportunities for developing new solutions		.709		
Capabilities to recognise new opportunities		.689	.412	
Willingness to take risks			.833	
Abilities to take risk			.796	
Capabilities for risk assessment			.672	
Capabilities to create collaborative relationship				.761
Capabilities to exploit networks in business				.715
Always follow a networking orientation				.678
% Variance explained	24.20	22.12	14.20	12.13
Eigen Value	9.571	1.793	1.517	0.924
Cronbach Alpha	0.908	0.919	0.890	0.845

Note: Extraction Method: Principal Component Analysis.
Rotation Method: Varimax with Kaiser Normalization.
Rotation converged in 6 iterations.

Mauritian SMEs. Subsequent investigation into cross-loading for specific capabilities revealed minimal ambiguity in factor assignment, with no instances of cross-loading above 0.45.

Factor Grouping 1, customer and market acquisition, comprises 7 SME innovation capabilities. The factors showing the strongest associations (0.769, 0.760, 0.739, and 0.728, respectively) include the abilities required to expand into new markets, enhance existing products and services, swiftly implement changes based on market and customer insights, and capitalize on innovations. The willingness of SMEs to take risks and embrace capabilities in assessing and seizing opportunities is crucial for generating novel innovations that set them apart from competitors' offerings, attracting new customers, retaining existing ones, and fostering sustained business expansion. These factors exhibited factor loadings of 0.714, 0.703, and 0.695, respectively. The ability to seize emerging opportunities relies on effectively leveraging organizational expertise to develop innovative solutions. These capabilities synergize to drive sustainable growth by capitalizing on both market opportunities and internal resources, thereby gaining a competitive edge.

Factor Grouping 2, radical innovation and knowledge management, comprises 6 SME innovation capabilities. The three factors showing the strongest associations (0.821, 0.815, and 0.810, respectively) include the capability to exploit new knowledge for innovation, the capability to internalize new external knowledge, and the capability to recognize relevant external knowledge. The next three factors, with factor loadings of (0.721, 0.709, and 0.689), provide insights into the abilities of the owner-manager to exploit opportunities for generating new profitable business, seize new opportunities for developing new solutions, and recognize new opportunities, which also have cross-loadings with Factor Grouping 3, risk management. The capability of internalizing and acknowledging pertinent external knowledge enhances the organization's ability to capitalize on new opportunities for innovation, fostering dynamic adaptation and growth. These interconnected capabilities create a mutually beneficial relationship that fuels sustainable innovation and competitive advantage gain.

Factor Grouping 3, risk management, encompasses 3 SME innovation capabilities, all adequately loaded within this factor grouping [42]. The factors with the strongest associations (0.833, 0.796, and 0.672, respectively) include the willingness to take risks, the ability to take risks, and capabilities for risk assessment. The willingness to undertake risks directly impacts SMEs' capacity to evaluate risks and make well-informed decisions, thereby influencing their ability to identify new opportunities. Organizations with higher risk assessment capabilities are better equipped to appraise potential innovations, thereby enhancing their ability to create unique offerings. Ultimately, the interplay among risk-taking, risk assessment, opportunity recognition, and innovation capabilities determines an SME's competitive edge in the market.

Factor Grouping 4, networking, encompasses 3 SME innovation capabilities. These include the ability to create collaborative relationships (with a strong association of 0.761), the capability to exploit networks in business (with a factor loading of 0.715), and consistently following a networking orientation (with an association of 0.648). These capabilities describe the networking proficiency and collaborative capabilities of Mauritian SMEs. The ability to forge collaborative relationships nurtures a robust ecosystem for expanding networks conducive to business progress. These interconnected capabilities enable the efficient utilization of networks to enhance opportunities for innovation, share resources, and explore new markets, thereby boosting SME growth and competitiveness.

The above factor analysis provides valuable insights that have facilitated the understanding of the underlying dimensions of innovation capability among Mauritian SMEs. This would assist them and policymakers in identifying areas for improvement and strategic focus.

5   Conclusion

The primary focus of the study was to explore the innovation capabilities of Mauritian SMEs, aiming to understand the factors and their significance in driving innovation, which is increasingly vital for ensuring sustainable growth and competitive advantage.

This was accomplished through the analysis of 280 cases, representing a sample of SMEs in Mauritius. The survey instrument comprised 19 item statements derived from the literature review on SME innovation capacity, aiming to assess SMEs' capabilities to embrace innovation throughout the business life cycle.

The analysis revealed four distinct factor groupings that significantly influence the innovation capabilities of Mauritian SMEs: customer and market acquisition, radical innovation and knowledge management, risk management, and networking. These factors are expected to enhance product offerings, develop and capture new markets, enabling firms to remain competitive in a market dominated by large firms.

The findings highlight the interconnectedness of factors crucial for SMEs to develop and assimilate innovation capabilities. Consequently, SMEs should strategically prioritize business networking (Factor 4), manage business risks (Factor 3), and undertake radical innovation and knowledge management (Factor 2), which collectively would facilitate customer and market acquisition. These preliminary findings lay the groundwork for policymakers and industry support associations, such as the Ministry of Industry and Commerce, the Economic Development Board, SME Mauritius, and the Mauritius Research and Innovation Council, to collaboratively create an enabling ecosystem to enhance innovation capabilities among SMEs in Mauritius.

While this study offers robust insights specific to Mauritius, further validation through comparative studies in other developing countries is necessary to ascertain emerging common patterns in supportive factors and challenges, thereby informing potential solutions. Future research endeavours could also delve into longitudinal studies to track the evolution of SME innovation capabilities over time and evaluate the effectiveness of intervention programs, comparing emerging patterns with those of other African countries such as South Africa and successful small nations like Singapore, renowned for their high standing in the Global Innovation Index.

Disclosure of Interests. The authors have no competing interests to declare that are relevant to the content of this article.

References

1. Ministry of Finance, Economic Planning and Development: 'Handbook on Schemes & Incentives for MSMEs & Entrepreneurs – Building Resilience through SMEs and Entrepreneurship (2020). https://business-support-portal.edbmauritius.org/wp-content/uploads/2021/04/Final_Handbook.pdf
2. Dargah, A.: Use of Digital and Social Media Marketing among SMEs in Mauritius, Mauritius Research Council _ Ebene, Mauritius (2018)
3. Houlder, V.: Mauritius caught in middle-income trap, (Financial Times) (2016). https://www.ft.com/content/67e331d8-75b1-11e6-bf48-b372cdb1043a. Accessed on 17 Nov 2022
4. World Intellectual Property Organisation (WIPO): Global Innovation (2023). https://www.wipo.int/edocs/pubdocs/en/wipo-pub-2000-2023/mu.pdf
5. AUDA-NEPAD. Annual Report African Union Development Agency Nepad (2022). https://www.nepad.org/publication/auda-nepad-2022-annual-report
6. World Bank: World Bank Small and Medium Enterprises (SMEs) Finance (2018). https://www.worldbank.org/en/topic/smefinance

7. Bayarçelik, E.B., Taşel, F., Apak, S.: A Research on determining innovation factors for SMEs. Procedia – Soc. Behav. Sci. **150**, 202–211 (2014)
8. Kaua, C.K.: Influence of Innovation on the Financial Performance of Small and Medium Women-Owned Enterprises in Nairobi City County, in Agriculture and Technology. Jomo Kenyatta University of Agriculture and Technology: Juja, Kenya (2021)
9. Taneja, S., Pryor, M.G., Hayek, M.: Leaping innovation barriers to small business longevity. J. Bus. Strategy **37**(3), 44–51 (2016)
10. Lecerf, M.-A.: Internationalization and innovation: the effects of a strategy mix on the economic performance of French SMEs. Int. Bus. Res. **5**(6), 2 (2012)
11. Laforet, S.: A framework of organisational innovation and outcomes in SMEs. Int. J. Entrepreneurial Behav. Res. **17**(4), 380–408 (2011)
12. Binte Rajah, R., de Fauconberg, A., Woeffray, O.. Future Readiness of SMEs: Mobilizing the SME Sector to Drive Widespread Sustainability and Prosperity. World Economic Forum (2021)
13. Civelek, M., Ključnikov, A., Fialova, V., Folvarčná, A., Stoch, M.: How innovativeness of family-owned SMEs differ depending on their characteristics? Equilibrium. Quart. J. Economics Economic Policy **16**(2), 413–428 (2021). https://doi.org/10.24136/eq.2021.015
14. Rigelsky, M., Gavurova, B., Nastisin, L.: Knowledge and technological innovations in the context of tourists' spending in OECD countries. J. Tourism Serv. **25**(13), 176–188 (2022). https://doi.org/10.29036/jots.v13i25.460
15. Nouel, G.L., A.A.R.P.I: Final Report – Study of the difficulties encountered by SMEs in Trade Defence Investigations and possible solutions (2010)
16. OECD: Promoting entrepreneurship and innovation in a global economy: Towards a more responsible and inclusive globalization. In Proceedings of the Second OECD Conference of Ministers Responsible for Small and Medium Sized Enterprises (SME). Istanbul, (2004).
17. Ortega-Argiles, R., Voigt, P.: Business R&D in SMEs. IPTS Working Paper On Corporate R&D And Innovation (2009). No. 07/2009. European Commission. Accessible at https://www.researchgate.net/publication/46464592_Business_RD_in_SMEs
18. Grant, R.M.: Toward a knowledge-based theory of the firm. Strateg. Manag. J. **17**(S2), 109–122 (1996). https://doi.org/10.1002/smj.4250171110
19. March, J.G.: Exploration and exploitation in organizational learning. Organ. Sci. **20**(1), 71–87 (1991). https://doi.org/10.1287/orsc.2.1.71
20. Levinthal, D.A., March, J.G.: The myopia of learning. Strat. Manag. J. **14**(S2), 95–112 (1993). https://doi.org/10.1002/smj.4250141009
21. Ganzaroli, A., Noni, I., Orsi, L., Belussi, F.: The combined effect of technological relatedness and knowledge utilization on explorative and exploitative invention performance post-M & A. European Journal of Innovation Management, 19(2), 167–188 (2016). /https://doi.org/10.1108/EJIM-08-2014-0092.
22. Baumol, W.J.: Entrepreneurship, Management and the Structure of Payoffs. MIT Press, Cambridge (1993)
23. Chen, J., Carlson, B.E., Del Genio, A.D.: Evidence for Strengthening of the tropical general circulation in the 1990s. Science **295**, 838–841 (2002). https://doi.org/10.1126/science.1065835
24. Metcalfe, S.: Entrepreneurship and Technological Change. Blackwell Publishing (2006)
25. Teece, D.J.: Dynamic capabilities: routines versus entrepreneurial action. J. Manag. Stud. **49**(8), 1395–1401 (2012)
26. Crawford, J.: Building and Effective Change Management Organisation, Second edition (2013)
27. Teece, D., Pisano, G., Shuen, A.: Dynamic capabilities and strategic management. Strategic Manag. J. **18**(7), 509–533 (1997)

28. Bannò, M., Piscitello, L., Amorim Varum, C.: The impact of public support on SMEs' outward FDI: evidence from Italy. J. Small Bus. Manag. **52**, 22–38 (2014). https://doi.org/10.1111/jsbm.12029

29. Kheradmand, Y., Honarbakhsh, A., Movahedifar, S.M., Afshari, A.R.: Development of a risk management model for using interpretive structural modeling. Int. J. Nonlinear Anal. Appl. **11**, 31–52 (2020)

30. Krüger, N.A.: A Risk Management Tool for SMMEs: The Case of Sedibeng District Municipality. Master's Thesis, North West University, Vanderbijlpark, South Africa (2020)

31. Hudáková, M., Buganová, K., Míka, V.T.: Masár, M. Integrovaný systém manažmentu rizík v podniku. 1. Vyvd. Žilina: EDIS ŽU, p. 375 (2021). ISBN 978-80-554-1759-2

32. Ritter, T., Wilkinson, I.F., Johnston, W.J.: Measuring network competence: some international evidence. J. Bus. Ind. Market. **17**(2/3), 119–38 (2002)

33. Walter, A., Auer, M., Ritter, T.: The impact of network capabilities and entrepreneurial orientation on university spin-off performance. J. Bus. Ventur. **21**(4), 541–67 (2006)

34. Mitręga, M., Zolkiewski, J.: Negative consequences of deep relationships with suppliers: An exploratory study in Poland', Industrial Marketing Management (2012)

35. Chrisman, J.J., McMullan, W.E.: Outsider assistance as a knowledge resource for new venture survival. J. Small Bus. Manage. **42**(3), 229–244 (2004)

36. Ramsden, M., Bennett, R.J.: The benefits of external support to SMEs: '"Hard"' versus '"soft"' outcomes and satisfaction levels. J. Small Bus. Enterp. Dev. **12**(2), 227–243 (2005)

37. Arendt, L.A., Priem, R.L., Ndofor, H.A.: A CEO-adviser model of strategic decision making. J. Manag. **31**(5), 680–699 (2005)

38. Johnson, S., Webber, D.J., Thomas, W.: Which SMEs use external business advice? a multivariate subregional study. Env. Plann. A **39**(8), 1981–1997 (2007)

39. Akhtar-Danesh, N.: A comparison between major factor extraction and factor rotation techniques in Q-methodology. Open J. Appl. Sci. **7**, 147–156 (2017)

40. Tang, S., Liao, S., Wang, L., Chen, W., Guo, Z.: A configurational analysis of small and medium-sized enterprises' radical innovations: the perspective of dynamic capabilities. Front. Psychol. **12**, 784738 (2022)

41. Tsai, F.-S., Cabrilo, S., Chou, H.-H., Hu, F., Tang, A.D.: Open innovation and SME performance: the roles of reverse knowledge sharing and stakeholder relationships. J. Bus. Res. **148**, 433–443 (2022)

42. Williams, B., Onsman, A., Brown, T.: Exploratory factor analysis: a five-step guide for novices. Australas. J. Paramedicine **8**, 1–13 (2010)

CyMed: A Framework for Testing Connected Medical Devices

Christopher Scherb$^{(\boxtimes)}$ ⓘ, Adrian Hadayah, Luc Bryan Heitz ⓘ,
Hermann Grieder, and Petra Maria Asprion ⓘ

University of Applied Sciences and Arts, Northwestern Switzerland,
Windisch, Switzerland
{christopher.scherb,luc.heitz,hermann.grieder,petra.asprion}@fhnw.ch,
ahadayah@sap-all.com

Abstract. Connected Medical Devices (CMDs) significantly benefit patients but are also vulnerable to malfunctions that can harm. Despite strict safety regulations for market entry, there's a notable shortage of specific cybersecurity frameworks for CMDs. Existing regulations on cybersecurity practices are often broad and lack detailed implementation steps. This paper introduces the CyMed framework, designed for vendors and end-users, offering explicit strategies to enhance the cybersecurity of CMDs. The effectiveness of CyMed is assessed through practical testing and expert interviews.

Keywords: Software Weaknesses · Fuzzing · Symbolic Execution · Medical Devices · Connected Medical Devices

1 Introduction

With the growing cyber threats, securing critical infrastructures, especially medical devices, is imperative for a digital and connected society. Due to regulatory constraints, patching Connected Medical Devices (CMDs) is slower than standard computers, necessitating alternative security measures. Network segmentation helps, yet it merely addresses symptoms, not the root cause. A holistic approach involves designing CMDs with minimal vulnerabilities, guided by European Medicines Agency (EMA) and Food and Drug Administration (FDA) regulations (EU 2017/745, EU 2017/746, 21 CFR 820, 21 CFR 11) and cybersecurity guidelines (MDCG 2019-16, Content of Premarket Submissions for Management of Cybersecurity in Medical Devices), focusing on risk management and security features. However, these guidelines lack specifics on technical implementation, a significant gap our CyMed framework aims to fill. CyMed enhances CMD cybersecurity through detailed measures, addressing Software in a Medical Device-software integral to CMD operation (e.g., in pacemakers, MRI machines) cited in [14], and Software as a Medical Device (SaMD)-independent software fulfilling medical functions (e.g., fitness apps, diagnostic software [8]). Our evaluation

© The Author(s), under exclusive license to Springer Nature Switzerland AG 2025
K. Hinkelmann and H. Smuts (Eds.): Society 5.0 2024, CCIS 2173, pp. 293–304, 2025.
https://doi.org/10.1007/978-3-031-71412-2_22

combines practical testing and expert feedback, leading to a comprehensive discussion on the CyMed framework's impact on CMD security in the following sections: In Sect. 2 we summarize our problem statement, in Sect. 3 we present related work and technologies as well as further background information, followed by the methodology in Sect. 4. In Sect. 5 we present our CyMed-framework for testing CMDs and afterwards we present our evaluation (Sect. 6), before we conclude our paper.

2   Problem Statement

Cybersecurity for CMDs is a critical topic, during the development phase and in operation. Generally, CMDs are strongly regulated devices, as described in Sect. 3, and there are a lot of guidelines and standards. Naturally, guidelines and standards are not designed to give detailed information about how a state-of-the-art security check is done but more abstract and guiding information which are more timeless. However, for manufacturers it is important to assess the state of the art possibilities for increasing the cybersecurity of their CMDs. We fill the gap by providing a framework giving tips and methods how to improve security of CMDs and how to protect them from cyber attacks. In this paper we answer the research questions:

– *How can the resistance of CMDs against cyber attacks be increased?*
– *Which concrete measure can be taken during and after the development process to improve the resistance against cyber attacks?*

3   Background and Related Work

In the following we will present details about existing guidance for cybersecurity of medical devices as well as methods we apply in our CyMed-framework.

3.1   Regulatory Guidance for Cybersecurity of Connected Medical Devices

The MDCG 2019-16[1], by the EU's Medical Device Coordination Group, offers detailed cybersecurity guidelines for CMDs, detailing stakeholder responsibilities and urging manufacturers to adopt comprehensive IT, operation, and information security practices. It advocates for secure design, lifecycle risk management, and defense against unauthorized access, while balancing cybersecurity with device safety to prevent functionality hindrance or manipulation risks. The document defines essential security capabilities for medical devices and addresses potential cyber threats, emphasizing the importance of continuous cybersecurity efforts across the device lifecycle [15] (Fig. 1).

---

[1] https://health.ec.europa.eu/system/files/2022-01/md_cybersecurity_en.pdf.

| Automatic Logoff |
| Audit Controls |
| Authorization |
| Configuration of Security Features |
| Cybersecurity Product Upgrades |
| Personal Data De-Identification |
| Data Backup and Disaster Recovery |
| Emergency Access |
| Personal Data Integrity and Authenticity |
| Malware Detection / Protection |
| Node Authentication |
| Person Authentication |
| Physical Locks |
| System and OS Hardening |
| Security and Privacy Guides |
| Personal Data Storage Confidentiality |
| Transmission Confidentiality |
| Transmission Integrity |

Fig. 1. Indicative List of security capabilities for CMDs

The FDA Guideline *Premarket Submissions for Management of Cybersecurity in Medical Devices*[2] defines a security strategy based on the NIST Cybersecurity Framework, with the strategy of identify, protect, detect, respond and recover [13]. A documentation about a hazard analysis and a trace matrix between cybersecurity controls risk is expected. The risk should be managed and controlled as shown in Fig. 2. Following a market release, the FDA has the *Postmarket Management of Cybersecurity in Medical Devices*, which describes postmarket measures, since cybersecurity is constantly evolving and it is not enough to only consider premarket. Postmarket measures can contain requirements for patching and updates.

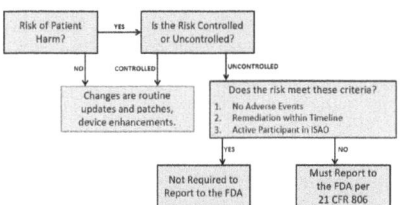

Fig. 2. FDA risk assessment

Besides the mentioned standards, others focus on risk and quality management without delving into cybersecurity specifics.

ISO 13485[3] outlines a quality management system for medical devices, covering expectations for quality management and various management responsibilities [17].

---

[2] https://www.fda.gov/regulatory-information/search-fda-guidance-documents/cybersecurity-medical-devices-quality-system-considerations-and-content-premarket-submissions.

[3] https://www.iso.org/standard/59752.html.

IEC 62304[4] categorizes medical devices into three classes based on the potential risk of injury or harm from malfunctions and standardizes software life cycle processes including development, maintenance, and risk management [18].

ISO 14971[5] emphasizes risk management for medical devices, guiding manufacturers on identifying hazards, evaluating and controlling risks, and monitoring risk management measures [28].

Summary: While there are guidelines for assessing and controlling cybersecurity risks, specific directives on designing and testing CMD software for cybersecurity are scarce, highlighting a gap in guidelines for secure CMD software development.

3.2   Methods for Testing Cybersecurity

For filling the gap in methods to check CMDs for cybersecurity, we will present existing background information how to detect vulnerabilities during the development and during the testing process. This includes methods to detect known vulnerabilities in libraries used by the CMDs as well as to detect unknown vulnerabilities which may be introduced during the development process.

CVE Search. CVE, standing for Common Vulnerability and Exposure, offers a standardized method to catalog information security vulnerabilities and exposures in a database managed by the Mitre Corporation. This database helps identify software weaknesses, prompting timely updates, particularly for products utilizing third-party libraries. Given the complexity of modern software with numerous dependencies, tracking and updating for security can be challenging. Automatic tools like the *cve_bin_tool*[6], designed to scan Unix-based firmware and software, alleviate this by detecting vulnerabilities in software libraries and programs, as exemplified in Fig. 3.

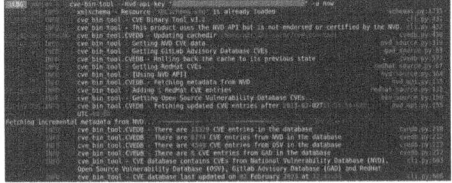

Fig. 3. Output of the cve_bin_tool

---

[4] https://www.iso.org/standard/38421.html.
[5] https://www.iso.org/standard/72704.html.
[6] https://github.com/intel/cve-bin-tool.

Firmware Analyzer. Firmware analyzers offer advanced vulnerability detection in CMDs and IoT devices beyond what *cve_bin_tool* can achieve, identifying issues like hard-coded credentials, malware, and weak permissions [26,30]. These tools facilitate early detection of potential security flaws, including common mistakes like default development passwords. They can also dissect and evaluate the firmware's file system, enabling both developers and end-users to assess security levels before deployment. EMBA stands out as a comprehensive Unix-based firmware analyzer, equipped with numerous modules for identifying security vulnerabilities[7], and produces detailed reports, as illustrated in Fig. 4.

Fig. 4. Output of EMBA

For non Unix based firmware, the analysis can be far more complicated. For statically linked firmware running directly on the hardware, e.g. insulin perfusors or pacemakers, with no or minimal operating system, reverse engineering is often the only way to understand which libraries are used, when no source code is available [31]. In the case where the source code is available, as it would be for manufacturers and developers, *cve-search*[8] can be used to automatically check the used library versions against the CVE database.

Fuzzing. Fuzzing is a potent method for uncovering unknown software vulnerabilities by sending generated inputs to trigger crashes or flaws [20]. It primarily targets APIs and interfaces prone to data input, crucial for cybersecurity. Fuzzing operates by either mutating existing inputs or creating new ones based on specified rules, monitoring the program's response to refine the input process. Inputs leading to unexplored code sections are prioritized for enhanced code coverage and flaw detection [11]. There are mutation-based, generation-based, and hybrid fuzzers, the latter combining fuzzing with techniques like concolic execution [23] [27].

Notable fuzzers include *AFL++* [11] and *hongfuzz*[9], with *LibAFL* providing customization for task-specific adaptations [12]. Fuzzing is also viable on

---

[7] https://github.com/e-m-b-a/emba.
[8] https://github.com/cve-search/cve-search.
[9] https://github.com/google/honggfuzz.

embedded devices through hardware in the loop testing [3,10], demonstrating its adaptability and effectiveness in various settings. Figure 5 shows AFL++ in operation.

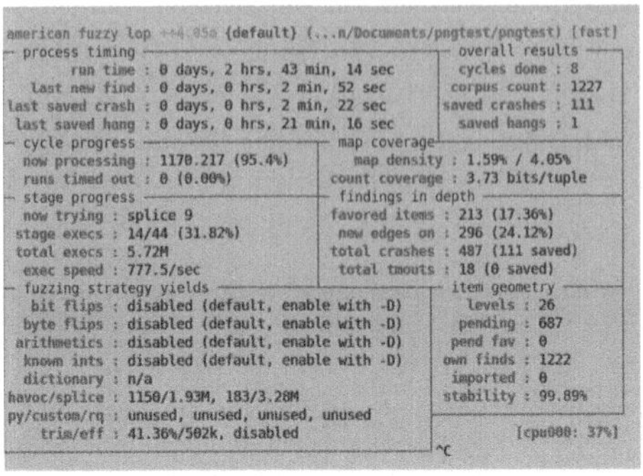

Fig. 5. Fuzzing with AFL++

Symbolic Execution. Symbolic Execution is a formal method to analyze the behavior of computer programs by executing them symbolically, considering any non determined input to be a symbolic variable which could have any possible value [4,19]. In symbolic execution, all reachable paths are executed and non-reachable paths are ruled out by solving the path constraints. While being very slow for larger program due to the high number of different paths and combinations of paths a computer program could go, when feasible symbolic execution can prove the absence of certain bugs. For example, Symbolic Execution can detect paths, where the Instruction Pointer of a computer program depends on input instead of the program flow, which clearly is a vulnerability. Moreover, Symbolic Execution can generate test cases which test all possible outcomes using the constraint solver.

Weak Functions. Vulnerable functions in standard libraries pose significant cybersecurity risks, especially in C/C++ used for developing CMDs, due to unsafe usage or inherent vulnerabilities [1,29]. Despite the availability of more secure languages like Rust and Ada [5,7], C/C++ remain prevalent. Functions such as *gets* are inherently unsafe, while *strcpy* and *sprintf* can be dangerous if misused. Even functions considered safer, like *strncpy* and *snprintf*, require careful use to prevent vulnerabilities, emphasizing the importance of avoiding or cautiously using these functions.

4 Methodology

We employed Design Science Research (DSR) as recommended by Hevner and Chatterjee [16] to develop our CyMed framework, suitable for crafting information system frameworks. Initially, we gathered cybersecurity testing methods and standards for medical devices from databases like Google Scholar and IEEE, focusing on "cybersecurity testing for medical devices" among other related terms. This phase aimed to pinpoint effective cybersecurity testing methods, as detailed in our literature review.

Testing identified methods on CMD-specific needs, evaluating their complexity and efficacy in security testing. We conducted practical tests with actual CMD firmware and operating systems[10] to select the best vulnerability detection tools for our framework. Following this, we consulted ten domain experts from various cybersecurity and medical fields through semi-structured interviews to refine CyMed, integrating their recommendations into the final framework design.

5 Framework for Testing CMDs

This section introduces the CyMed framework, designed to enhance CMDs' resilience against cyber threats. Targeting manufacturers and CMD developers, CyMed also guides operators and end-users on conducting cybersecurity tests without source code. Its primary goal is preventing cyber attacks on devices, indirectly bolstering patient data protection and integrity. An overview of the CyMed framework is provided in Fig. 6.

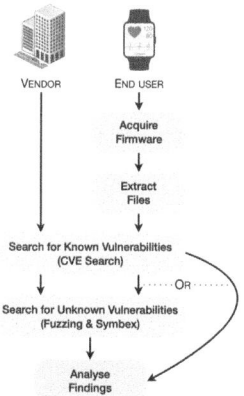

Fig. 6. The CyMed-framework to strengthen cybersecurity of CMDs

The CyMed framework begins differently based on source code access. Without it, acquiring and extracting firmware is necessary. Vendors or those with open-source CMD firmware skip this step. Next, CyMed searches for known vulnerabilities, particularly from third-party libraries, and checks CMD configurations for any development artifacts like default passwords. It then seeks

---

[10] https://resources.sw.siemens.com/en-US/white-paper-using-linux-in-a-medical-device.

previously unknown vulnerabilities within the code and third-party libraries. These steps provide an overview of potential security issues, offering manufacturers insights for improvements. The final phase involves deciding on fixes for identified bugs and vulnerabilities. Further details on each phase are provided subsequently.

5.1   Acquiring Firmware

Firmware analysis requires access, which is straightforward for vendors but challenging for operators aiming to evaluate CMD security. While direct acquisition from manufacturers is ideal, alternatives include sourcing from update sites or extracting directly from devices. However, these methods may be impractical for those without cybersecurity training, restricting firmware security assessments to specialists. Our findings indicate some CMD vendors restrict firmware analysis by mandating device returns for updates, complicating independent security evaluations.

5.2   Extracting the Firmware

If a firmware file could be obtained, the firmware needs to be extracted. Here are two cases. Many firmware are built on top of (real time) Linux or Unix systems. A Linux or Unix firmware can be extracted using tools like *binwalk* or *firmwalker*. *binwalk* analyzes a dumped firmware file and can extract the Unix file system.

5.3   Search for Known Vulnerabilities

After extracting firmware, the next step involves scanning for known vulnerabilities against a CVE database using tools like *cve-bin-tool* or *EMBA*. The *cve-bin-tool* accesses the National Vulnerability Database API to evaluate executables and libraries for known vulnerabilities, producing a dashboard of findings. *EMBA*, on the other hand, both extracts and analyzes firmware, offering a detailed report but requiring more time due to its thorough analysis.

5.4   Search for Unknown Vulnerabilities

This step, though optional, can significantly enhance CMD security and reliability. Vendors are encouraged to test their software for hidden vulnerabilities using dynamic analysis techniques like fuzzing and symbolic execution, which analyze software during execution for more accurate results than static analysis. The application of these techniques within CyMed by both vendors and end-users will be detailed further.

Fuzzing. Fuzzing has been a valuable method for uncovering vulnerabilities, though it cannot assure their complete absence. For vendors with source code access, tools like *AFL++* enhance fuzzing by tracking code coverage, aiding in software hardening pre-release [11]. This technique can also be adapted for firmware without source code access [33]. Fuzzing, inherently open-ended, rarely achieves full coverage, presenting a trade-off between time and thoroughness. Manufacturers are advised to integrate fuzzing into the development cycle, rejecting and refining code based on fuzzing outcomes, akin to unit testing practices. Priority targets for fuzzing include API functions, particularly those involving network communication, due to their vulnerability to attacks. Operators and testers may extend fuzzing indefinitely, ceasing only upon bug discovery or test termination.

Symbolic Execution. Similar to fuzzing, symbolic execution analyzes code by systematically executing all parts of a program, making it deterministic and thorough. Although slower, it serves as a formal method to verify the absence of specific bugs, making it unsuitable for continuous integration in the build pipeline. Instead, it's best utilized towards the end of the development process to ensure software resilience against cyber attacks. Setting up symbolic execution involves analyzing API functions and control flow to identify reachable program parts and potential vulnerabilities, akin to the initial steps in fuzzing.

5.5 Analyze Findings

In the final stages of CMD security assessments, it's crucial to analyze findings and take appropriate measures. Known vulnerabilities typically require vendor updates or adherence to vendor/regulatory guidelines for remediation. If a timely patch isn't feasible, especially for internet-connected devices, taking them offline or segregating them within the network may be necessary.

For new vulnerabilities, vendors should conduct their investigations, supported by tools like triage to efficiently assess crash exploitability and impact before manual debugging. CASR (see Fig. 7) is highlighted as an effective triage tool, helping prioritize fixes based on the potential for exploitation and the overall safety impact [24]. This ensures a focus on both device security and user safety.

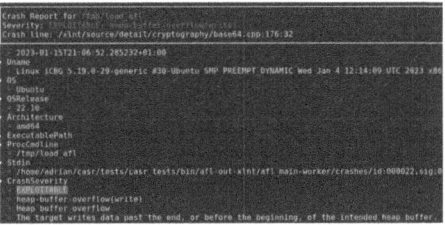

Fig. 7. A triage tool (here: CASR) to find the security relevant crashes

6   Evaluation

Our evaluation of the CyMed framework involved two phases: initial tool capability analysis based on a literature review and expert interviews to assess the framework's practicality.

In the first phase, we selected tools, such as *EMBA* and fuzzing, based on their proven effectiveness in identifying software vulnerabilities in medical devices. Our findings suggest these tools are not only potent in detecting bugs but also feasible to integrate into software development processes, with *EMBA* and *cve-bin-tool* being notably user-friendly even for those with limited technical knowledge.

The second phase, conducted through semi-structured interviews, focused on the applicability and relevance of the CyMed framework. Experts confirmed the framework's comprehensibility and its complex nature, especially for those without source code access. While acknowledging the necessity of cybersecurity expertise in such cases, they also recognized the framework's potential for enhancing vendor credibility. Discussions also emphasized the importance of complementing fuzzing with other techniques like manual code review, model checking for critical protocols, and unit testing that encompasses failure scenarios. A cybersecurity professor highlighted the cost and criticality of model checking for essential components, suggesting its selective application [21]; [9]. Additionally, a medical professional pointed out the growing digitalization in healthcare, like electronic patient records, and the lack of security training among medical staff.

Overall, experts agreed that the CyMed framework integrates state-of-the-art testing technologies, potentially boosting both the security and reliability of CMDs. They recommended regular updates to the framework to keep pace with technological advancements in software testing.

The responses are aligned with our expectations and prove the relevance of our cybersecurity framework CyMed to provide guidelines for better and more sustainable development of CMDs.

7   Conclusion and Future Work

In our study, we introduce and assess CyMed, a framework designed to enhance the cybersecurity of Connected Medical Devices (CMDs). Unlike existing frameworks that often lack specific actionable steps for vendors, CyMed provides a structured approach based on a thorough literature review and hands-on testing of various tools to identify and address cybersecurity vulnerabilities. Following its development, expert interviews confirmed the industry's demand for such a framework and validated the selected tools' effectiveness in securing CMDs against cyber threats. CyMed addresses critical research questions by offering practical tools and strategies for improving CMDs' cyber resilience, as detailed in Sect. 2. Beyond securing CMDs, safeguarding the broader organizational environment is essential, utilizing approaches like the NIST framework [2,6], and ensuring robust data protection protocols [22,32]. Additionally, educating users through modern training methods, including awareness campaigns and phishing simulations, is crucial [25]. While CyMed currently focuses on software security for CMDs, its future expansion could include broader security practices for healthcare organizations. Keeping CyMed updated with the latest in security testing tools and methodologies will be vital for its continued relevance and effectiveness.

References

1. Almansoori, M., Lam, J., Fang, E., Mulligan, K., Soosai Raj, A.G., Chatterjee, R.: How secure are our computer systems courses? In: Proceedings of the 2020 ACM Conference on International Computing Education Research, pp. 271–281 (2020)
2. Asprion, P., Giovanoli, C., Scherb, C., Bhat, S.: Agile management in cybersecurity. In: Gerber, A., Hinkelmann, K. (eds.) Proceedings of Society 5.0 Conference 2023. EPiC Series in Computing, vol. 93, pp. 21–32. EasyChair (2023). https://doi.org/10.29007/9fg8, https://easychair.org/publications/paper/1gvl
3. Bacic, M.: On hardware-in-the-loop simulation. In: Proceedings of the 44th IEEE Conference on Decision and Control, pp. 3194–3198. IEEE (2005)
4. Baldoni, R., Coppa, E., D'elia, D.C., Demetrescu, C., Finocchi, I.: A survey of symbolic execution techniques. ACM Comput. Surv. (CSUR) **51**(3), 1–39 (2018)
5. Barnes, J.: Ada 95 Rationale: The Language The Standard Libraries. Springer, Heidelberg (1995). https://doi.org/10.1007/BFb0051526
6. Barrett, M.: Framework for improving critical infrastructure cybersecurity version 1.1 (2018). https://doi.org/10.6028/NIST.CSWP.04162018
7. Boebert, W.E., Kaln, R., Young, W.D., Hansohn, S.: Secure ada target: issues, system design, and verification. In: 1985 IEEE Symposium on Security and Privacy, p. 176. IEEE (1985)
8. Carroll, N., Richardson, I.: Software-as-a-medical-device: demystifying connected health regulations. J. Syst. Inf. Technol. **18**(2), 186–215 (2016)
9. Cicotti, G., Coronato, A.: Towards a probabilistic model checking-based approach for medical device risk assessment. In: 2015 IEEE International Symposium on Medical Measurements and Applications (MeMeA) Proceedings, pp. 180–185. IEEE (2015)
10. Dunne, M., Fischmeister, S.: Powertrace-based fuzzing of can connected hardware. In: 2022 IEEE International Conference on Cyber Security and Resilience (CSR), pp. 239–244. IEEE (2022)
11. Fioraldi, A., Maier, D., Eißfeldt, H., Heuse, M.: AFL++ combining incremental steps of fuzzing research. In: Proceedings of the 14th USENIX Conference on Offensive Technologies, p. 10 (2020)
12. Fioraldi, A., Maier, D.C., Zhang, D., Balzarotti, D.: LibAFL: a framework to build modular and reusable fuzzers. In: Proceedings of the 022 ACM SIGSAC Conference on Computer and Communications Security, pp. 1051–1065 (2022)
13. Food, Administration, D., et al.: Cybersecurity in medical devices: quality system considerations and content of premarket submissions: draft guidance for industry and food and drug administration staff (2023)
14. Gordon, W.J., Stern, A.D.: Challenges and opportunities in software-driven medical devices. Nat. Biomed. Eng. **3**(7), 493–497 (2019)
15. Granlund, T., Vedenpää, J., Stirbu, V., Mikkonen, T.: On medical device cybersecurity compliance in EU. In: 2021 IEEE/ACM 3rd International Workshop on Software Engineering for Healthcare (SEH), pp. 20–23. IEEE (2021)

16. Hevner, A., Chatterjee, S., Hevner, A., Chatterjee, S.: Design science research in information systems. Design Res. Inf. Syst.: Theory Pract. 9–22 (2010)
17. ISO, I., CFR, A., CMDR, M., JPAL, T.: ISO 13485: 2016 (2016)
18. Jordan, P.: Standard IEC 62304-medical device software-software lifecycle processes (2006)
19. King, J.C.: Symbolic execution and program testing. Commun. ACM **19**(7), 385–394 (1976)
20. Li, J., Zhao, B., Zhang, C.: Fuzzing: a survey. Cybersecurity **1**(1), 1–13 (2018)
21. Li, T., Tan, F., Wang, Q., Bu, L., Cao, J.N., Liu, X.: From offline toward real time: a hybrid systems model checking and cps codesign approach for medical device plug-and-play collaborations. IEEE Trans. Parallel Distrib. Syst. **25**(3), 642–652 (2013)
22. Marxer, C., Scherb, C., Tschudin, C.: Access-controlled in-network processing of named data. In: Proceedings of the 3rd ACM Conference on Information-Centric Networking, ACM-ICN 2016, pp. 77–82. Association for Computing Machinery, New York (2016)https://doi.org/10.1145/2984356.2984366
23. Miller, C., Peterson, Z.N., et al.: Analysis of mutation and generation-based fuzzing. Independent Security Evaluators, Technical report, vol. 4 (2007)
24. Savidov, G., Fedotov, A.: Casr-Cluster: crash clustering for Linux applications. In: 2021 Ivannikov ISPRAS Open Conference (ISPRAS), pp. 47–51. IEEE (2021). https://doi.org/10.1109/ISPRAS53967.2021.00012
25. Scherb, C., Heitz, L.B., Grimberg, F., Grieder, H., Maurer, M.: A cyber attack simulation for teaching cybersecurity. EPiC Ser. Comput. **93**, 129–140 (2023)
26. Schulz, M., Wegemer, D., Hollick, M.: The Nexmon firmware analysis and modification framework: empowering researchers to enhance wi-fi devices. Comput. Commun. **129**, 269–285 (2018)
27. Stephens, N., et al.: Driller: augmenting fuzzing through selective symbolic execution. In: NDSS, vol. 16, pp. 1–16 (2016)
28. Teferra, M.N.: ISO 14971-medical device risk management standard. Int. J. Latest Res. Eng. Technol. (IJLRET) **3**(3), 83–87 (2017)
29. Yang, G., et al.: The source and exploitation of the program vulnerability. In: 2018 3rd Joint International Information Technology, Mechanical and Electronic Engineering Conference (JIMEC 2018), pp. 89–94. Atlantis Press (2018)
30. Zaddach, J., Bruno, L., Francillon, A., Balzarotti, D., et al.: AVATAR: a framework to support dynamic security analysis of embedded systems' firmwares. In: NDSS, vol. 23, pp. 1–16 (2014)
31. Zaddach, J., Costin, A.: Embedded devices security and firmware reverse engineering. Black-Hat USA (2013)
32. Zhang, H., et al.: Sharing mhealth data via named data networking. In: Proceedings of the 3rd ACM Conference on Information-Centric Networking, pp. 142–147 (2016)
33. Zheng, Y., Davanian, A., Yin, H., Song, C., Zhu, H., Sun, L.: FIRM-AFL: high-throughput greybox fuzzing of IoT firmware via augmented process emulation. In: USENIX Security Symposium, pp. 1099–1114 (2019)

Checklist for Effective Knowledge Visualization

Iddo-Imri Scholtz[(✉)] [iD] and Hanlie Smuts[iD]

Department of Informatics, University of Pretoria, Pretoria, South Africa
iddo.imri@gmail.com, hanlie.smuts@up.ac.za

Abstract. Rapid increase of data in the current digital age has led to an unprecedented rate of knowledge acquisition while the half-life of knowledge decreases.
Communication and transfer of knowledge is a challenging and time-consuming
task, especially when using the written word. Visual representation of knowledge
is superior to verbal and written communication but has a high level of difficulty
and cost regarding the maintenance of the visualizations, the reification of invalid
views and the possibility of misinterpretation that could mislead or manipulate
users. Therefore, the aim of this study is to provide a checklist of knowledge visualization success factors to guide designers in creating effective visualizations with
maximum communicative power. The checklist of knowledge visualization success factors was developed through a document analysis where 25 success factors
were identified. The 25 success factors were grouped according to the *why, what,
for whom,* and *how* of knowledge before a questionnaire was distributed to software engineering professionals to validate and triangulate the findings. The use
of the checklist provides designers with a list of knowledge visualization success
factors to be considered to improve the effectiveness of the visualization.

Keywords: Knowledge visualization · knowledge visualization success factors ·
knowledge management · knowledge transfer · knowledge communication

1 Introduction

The rapid increase of data in the current digital age leads to knowledge and state-of-the-art
technologies changing the way organizations manage, combine and distribute knowledge
and expertise, make calculated decisions, control business models, and manage value-
creation operations to satisfy different stakeholders' requirements and needs [1]. With
the rapid increase of data, global knowledge increases at an unprecedented rate while
the half-life of knowledge decreases, and time is a scarce resource yet essential in
communicating complex knowledge. Communicating and transferring knowledge is a
challenging task, especially when using the written word [2]. Primarily using only text
and numbers to transfer knowledge is no longer sufficient [3–6], and from a cognitive
perspective, presenting information and knowledge through visual means instead of text
appears to be advantageous [7, 8].

Visual representation of knowledge is superior to verbal and written communication
as it better illustrates relationships between objects, makes it easier to identify patterns,

© The Author(s), under exclusive license to Springer Nature Switzerland AG 2025
K. Hinkelmann and H. Smuts (Eds.): Society 5.0 2024, CCIS 2173, pp. 305–319, 2025.
https://doi.org/10.1007/978-3-031-71412-2_23

demonstrates both an overview and detail of the subject matter, supports problem-solving and is more effective in communicating different knowledge types [9–12]. Visualizations also provide the added benefits of enabling participants to externalize ideas and opinions and their relationships [13] by utilizing both verbal and visual means [14], consequently facilitating participants' ability to build on each other's thoughts [15] and increasing the memorability of the discussed concepts [16, 17].

Visualization can be an effective tool for representing knowledge but has a high level of difficulty and cost regarding the maintenance of the visualizations, the reification of invalid views and the possibility of misinterpretation that could mislead or manipulate users [1, 18]. According to Van Wijk [19], visualization can have an excessive initial cost to be understood when new processes are developed, is sometimes subjective, and can be inaccurate and misleading. Therefore, several different factors should be considered to design and create effective visualizations [3, 20] that can enrich the creation, transfer and sharing of knowledge. Hence, the aim of this research is to understand the key considerations for creating successful knowledge visualizations. Consequently, the research question that this paper aims to address is: *"What are the key success factors for effectively visualizing knowledge?"* By addressing this question, the paper intends to present a list of knowledge visualization success factors to aid in the creation of effective visualizations.

In Sect. 2 the background to the study is presented followed by the research approach in Sect. 3. Section 4 discusses the data analysis and findings, while Sect. 5 concludes the paper.

2   Background

Visualization can be considered a form of computing that aims to inspire consciousness and insight that transforms data into becoming easier to understand through the sense of sight. At its core, the visualization process consists of a series of steps, including gathering, processing, image rendering, analyzing and interpreting data [21]. From a scientific perspective, visualization is an advanced field that comprises a resource base of accepted methods and meticulous processes, which includes guidelines to assist with the development of data and information visualizations [20, 22–24]. Conversely, knowledge visualization is not as mature [5, 24–27] and, therefore, lacks a generic set of guidelines [4, 20, 24]. Information visualization is an interconnected field and predecessor of knowledge visualization, and both these fields utilize a human's natural abilities to successfully process visual representations [4, 10, 24, 27]. Despite these fields using natural visual abilities, how they utilize these abilities differs. Information visualization intends to examine a large amount of abstract data to amplify cognition [4, 10, 28], obtain new perceptions, or make the data more approachable [24]. Knowledge visualization intends to enhance the transfer and creation of knowledge among people by providing a richer approach to communicating what they know [10, 27]. While information visualization assists in improving the retrieval, access and presentation of information from large data sets, knowledge visualization is mainly concerned with increasing knowledge-intensive communication among people [18, 24].

Burkhard [10] first identified the need for a new discipline that utilizes visualizations to assist in the transfer of knowledge and introduced the term knowledge visualization

[4]. The seminal work by Eppler and Burkhard [18] shortly followed, which established the new discipline and defined it as "the use of visual representations to improve the creation and transfer of knowledge between at least two people". Based on this definition, Renaud and Van Biljon [20] extended the definition to "the use of graphical means to communicate experiences, insights and potentially complex knowledge in context, and to do so with integrity. Such means should be flexible enough to accommodate changing insights and facilitate conversations. Such representations facilitate and expedite the creation and transfer of knowledge between people by improving and promoting knowledge processing and comprehension, using familiar concepts where possible".

It is a long-standing goal of knowledge management to make knowledge visible so that it can be better discussed, communicated, valued, accessed and managed [6, 18, 20, 23, 24, 29–32]. Therefore, knowledge visualization is an essential part of knowledge management that aims to create, transfer and share knowledge through visualizations [3, 4, 6, 8, 33, 34] and is critical for comprehending and communicating phenomena and issues while also supporting strategic decision-making [1, 8, 35]. Knowledge visualization aims to use visualizations to promote effective and efficient knowledge transfer from one person to another [1, 4, 10, 25, 26, 33, 36]. Knowledge visualization goes beyond the basic transfer of facts to convey insights, experiences, points of view, values, assumptions, outlooks, beliefs and prognoses in such a manner that empowers someone to rebuild, recall and implement these insights accurately [1, 18, 24, 29]. Proper implementation of knowledge visualization can potentially utilize the key strengths of the human cognitive processing system to improve communication and the transfer and sharing of knowledge [18, 24, 37].

In the next section an overview of the research approach is presented.

3   Research Approach

The overall objective of this paper was to understand what constitutes the successful visualization of knowledge. Consequently, the paper identified and defined a list of success factors to serve as a checklist in the effective creation of knowledge visualizations. The checklist is intended to provide guidance in the creation of knowledge visualizations to improve the effectiveness of knowledge creation, transfer and sharing amongst individuals and groups by increasing the communicative power of the visual.

To achieve the aim of this paper, a document analysis was conducted to construct a list of success factors found in existing literature. According to Bowen [38], document analysis is typically used in collaboration with other qualitative research methods as a means of triangulations. Therefore, the paper also used the survey research approach and distributed a questionnaire targeted at software engineering professionals to determine the relevance for each of the identified knowledge visualization success factors. The questionnaire aimed to triangulate the findings of the document analysis and validate the relevance for each of the identified success factors while also allowing for the removal of irrelevant success factors or the addition of missing success factors.

During the document analysis of existing literature, a taxonomy of 25 success factors for the visualization of knowledge were identified as shown in Table 1 – summarizing the knowledge visualization success factors, a short description of the factor and the reference where the factor was extracted from.

Table 1. Overview of the knowledge visualization success factors from the literature

Knowledge visualization success factors	Description	Source
Accessibility	Ensure that the level of abstraction aligns with the audience's prior knowledge of the knowledge subject area	[5, 24, 36, 39–43]
Aesthetics	The visualization should be appealing to the observer without causing distractions. For example, make the visual as symmetrical as possible	[5, 27, 42, 44–48]
Audience Engagement	Enhance and facilitate communication and engagement among participants to elicit different insights and relate these ideas to others to promote learning through interaction and experience	[1, 3, 24, 26, 29, 33, 36, 49–51]
Audience Need	Consider for whom the visualization is intended, e.g., an individual, a class, a group, a community, etc. and ensure that the intended audience's needs are met	[3, 20, 24, 33, 36, 52–54]
Clear Boundaries	To help navigating and enclosing knowledge within a specific domain	[5, 36, 42, 55]
Clarity	Ensure that the visualization is not ambiguous and is easy to understand	[3, 5, 20, 24, 27, 36, 42, 52, 56–60]
Cohesion	Clearly show the relationships between knowledge concepts and how they work together	[5, 24, 36, 41, 42, 58, 60–63]

(continued)

Table 1. (*continued*)

Knowledge visualization success factors	Description	Source
Consistency	The use of visual elements such as color, symbols and shapes should be the same for the same kind of information	[3, 5, 20, 24, 27, 33, 36, 42, 56, 57, 64, 65]
Context	Present the overview and detail. An overview provides the context information of a field, while detail provides more information about a part of the overview. The boundaries around elements and the connections to other elements should be clear	[3, 5, 24, 33, 36, 39, 42, 54, 63, 65–67]
Dual Coding	Use both text and visuals	[3, 5, 16, 20, 26, 27, 36, 42, 54, 57, 59, 68]
Essence	Identify and utilize the essentials and their relationships from a body of knowledge	[3, 5, 20, 24, 26, 33, 36, 42, 67, 69–72]
Explanatory Power	Visualization must have explanatory power and not merely descriptive value. The knowledge visualization requirement must be considered in this instance, i.e., is it for recall, sharing new insights or elaborating existing knowledge?	[24, 26, 27, 33, 39, 73]
Familiarity Association	Utilization of recognizable and familiar visual images associated with real-world experiences, ensures that visualization elements are recognized rather than recalled	[3–5, 20, 24, 29, 36, 42, 59, 64, 74, 75]

(*continued*)

Table 1. (*continued*)

Knowledge visualization success factors	Description	Source
Flexibility	Must be revisable or flexible to accommodate changing insights as time passes	[1, 20, 26, 27, 50]
Graphical Excellence	Focus on the useability of the visualization and avoid irrelevant elements that might distract the audience from the content of the topic	[3, 5, 20, 24, 29, 36, 39, 40, 42, 56, 75]
Knowledge Transfer Cognitive Process	Process of transferring knowledge between people by organizing, creating, discovering, capturing or distributing knowledge and ensuring its availability for future users	[1, 24, 26, 33, 50, 62, 73, 76]
Know the Data	A designer must first understand and evaluate the content before creating relevant visualizations	[3, 36, 39, 65]
Legend	Provides the information required for clarifying and explaining the knowledge visualization meaning and interpretation	[5, 24, 36, 42, 67, 77–82]
Simplicity	Everything should be made as simple as possible but not simpler	[3, 5, 20, 24, 26, 33, 36, 42, 57–59, 80, 83]

(*continued*)

Table 1. (*continued*)

Knowledge visualization success factors	Description	Source
Use of Colors	The use of colors to specify a format that is applicable to a set of instances, to differentiate relationships, beautification, mapping, grouping and classifying visualizations	[5, 36, 42, 65, 84, 85]
Visual	The image/picture must be visual in the sense that the knowledge being portrayed is presented within a diagram, map, chart or any other KV format type or a combination thereof	[20, 26]
Visual Guidance	Should clearly indicate the flow of knowledge	[5, 26, 42, 86, 87]
Visual Integrity	The knowledge visualization should not distort the underlying knowledge or create a false impression or interpretation of that knowledge	[3, 20, 24, 39, 40, 54, 60]
Visual Playfulness	A visualization should incorporate playful components to present issues in a different light and guide participants towards a new mindset	[26, 86, 87]
Visual Variety	A single visualization consists of multiple visual formats like sketches and visual metaphors to express the elicited knowledge	[26, 88, 89]

The purpose of the 25 knowledge visualization success factors is to empower the designers of visualizations with a list of factors that serve as a checklist to produce effective visualizations with maximum communicative power [5]. Some of the factors are overarching and support one another as the implementation of one gives credit to the execution of another [36]. For example, the use of colors complements the aesthetic factor of the visualization while the dual coding factor increases the explanatory power and cognitive transfer of knowledge.

In the next section the checklist of knowledge visualizations success factors will be discussed in more detail.

4 Checklist for Effective Knowledge Visualization

The communication of knowledge includes the *how, why, what, where, when* and *who* perspectives of knowledge [20, 90] and failure to represent any of these adequately renders the communication process ineffective [91]. Secundo et al. [8] state that an effective knowledge visualization framework or checklist consists of four complementary perspectives: *why* should the knowledge be visualized (the aim), *what* type of knowledge should be visualized (the content), *who* is going to receive the message (the target group), and *which* approach should be used to visualize the knowledge (the medium). In the context of success factors, the authors agree that the *which* can be replaced with the *how* perspective of knowledge as the success factors complement the chosen medium by providing guidance on *how* to effectively visualize the content using the chosen medium. Furthermore, the remaining perspectives: *where* should the knowledge be visualized and *when* should the knowledge be visualized were considered and the authors decided to exclude these perspectives on the basis that they do not directly impact the effective visualization of knowledge. Therefore, the 25 knowledge visualization success factors have been categorized according to the *why, what, for whom,* and *how* perspectives of knowledge.

Requirement elicitation within the software engineering industry is plagued by inaccurate requirements primarily caused by ineffective communication and transfer of knowledge [92, 93]. Consequently, a growing trend to foster and promote the use of visualization within requirements engineering began in 2006 [94, 95]. Therefore, a questionnaire was developed and distributed to software engineering professionals which consisted of both the designers and interpreters of knowledge visualizations.

The questionnaire aimed to determine the relevance of each of the categorized knowledge visualization success factors. The questionnaire consisted of 1 open- and 25 close-ended questions where the close-ended questions presented each of the different success factors with a short description followed by a Likert scale ranging from *0 = Needs to be Removed* to *3 = Highly Relevant* requesting the participant to rate the relevance of the success factor. The open-ended question allowed participants to recommend the addition of any success factors not included in the initial list.

The questionnaire collected a total of 76 responses from a variety of different roles within the software engineering space with most participants being software engineers and business analysts. The participants ranged from novice to experienced software engineering professionals as shown in Table 2.

The analysis of the responses revealed that the initial list of the 25 knowledge visualization success factors is comprehensive and no new factors were discovered. It also

Table 2. Questionnaire participant's experience

Experience Range	Number of Participants
0 to 2 years	18 (24%)
3 to 5 years	17 (22%)
6 to 8 years	12 (16%)
9 to 12 years	4 (5%)
13 to 15 years	6 (8%)
16 and more years	19 (25%)

validated and confirmed the relevance of each of the success factors identified from literature with some of the factors having a higher relevance rating (calculated mean) than others as shown in Fig. 1.

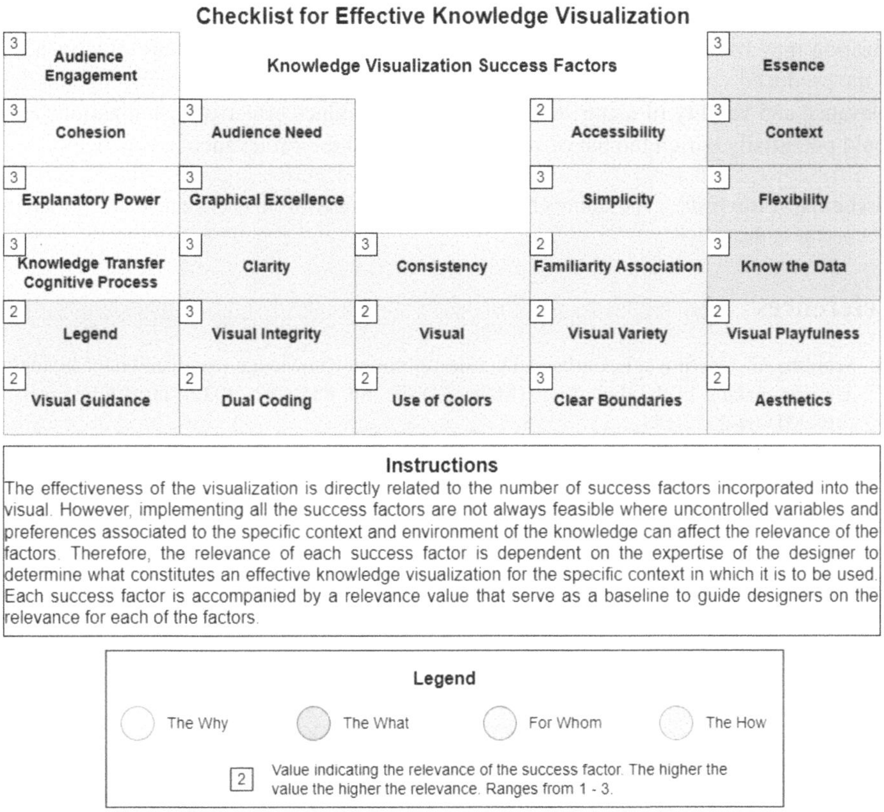

Fig. 1. Checklist for effective knowledge visualization

5 Conclusion

The use of visualizations to communicate and transfer knowledge has proven to be more effective than verbal and written communication. However, poorly constructed visualizations distort and dilute the essence of knowledge and limit the successful communication of knowledge. Therefore, to effectively utilize the full potential of knowledge visualization, it is essential to understand the key considerations for successful visualization with maximum communicative power that promotes and fosters the creation, transfer and sharing of knowledge. Consequently, the aim of the study was to identify a list of knowledge visualization success factors to serve as a checklist to guide designers in creating effective visualizations.

The proposed checklist consists of 25 success factors extracted from existing literature through a document analysis. The identified factors were grouped according to the *why, what, for whom* and *how* perspectives of knowledge before the findings were validated and triangulated with the aid of a questionnaire distributed to software engineering professionals. The success factors form the basis of the checklist that designers should consider to produce effective knowledge visualizations.

In terms of future research opportunity, the checklist for effective knowledge visualization may be tested in a real-world setting where the application and effectiveness of the produced visualization is measured. This may lead to valuable knowledge on the relevance and validity of using such a checklist to produce effective visualizations and could potentially enrich the list of success factors and their relevance in practice.

Disclosure of Interests. The authors have no competing interests to declare that are relevant to the content of this article.

References

1. Schiuma, G., Gavrilova, T., Carlucci, D.: Guest editorial: Knowledge visualisation for strategic decision-making in the digital age. Manag. Decis. **60**, 885–892 (2022). https://doi.org/10.1108/MD-04-2022-181
2. Crowley, B.: Tacit knowledge, tacit ignorance, and the future of academic librarianship. Coll. Res. Libr. **62**, 565–584 (2001). https://doi.org/10.5860/crl.62.6.565
3. Burkhard, R.A.: Knowledge Visualization: The Use of Complementary Visual Representations for the Transfer of Knowledge: a Model, a Framework, and Four New Approaches, (2005)
4. Meyer, R.: Knowledge visualization. In: Trends in Information Visualization, pp. 23–30. University of Munich, Munich, Germany (2010)
5. Van Biljon, J., Osei-Bryson, K.-M.: The communicative power of knowledge visualizations in mobilizing information and communication technology research. Inf. Technol. Dev. **26**, 637–652 (2020). https://doi.org/10.1080/02681102.2020.1821954
6. Vesperi, W., Ventura, M., Melina, A.M., Gentile, T.A.R.: Knowledge Visualisation as a Tool to Support Complex Organisations in a State of Emergency. In: European Conference on Knowledge Management. pp. 803–812. Academic Conferences International Limited, Kidmore End, United Kingdom (2021). https://doi.org/10.34190/EKM.21.117
7. Goransson, K., Fagerholm, A.-S.: Towards visual strategic communications: an innovative interdisciplinary perspective on visual dimensions within the strategic communications field. J. Commun. Manag. **22**, 46–66 (2018). https://doi.org/10.1108/JCOM-12-2016-0098

8. Secundo, G., Elia, G., Margherita, A., Leitner, K.-H.: Strategic decision making in project management: a knowledge visualization framework. Manag. Decis. **60**, 1159–1181 (2021). https://doi.org/10.1108/MD-02-2021-0196

9. Bauer, M.I., Johnson-Laird, P.N.: How diagrams can improve reasoning. Psychol. Sci. **4**, 372–378 (1993)

10. Burkhard, R.A.:Learning from architects: the difference between knowledge visualization and information visualization. In: Proceedings. Eighth International Conference on Information Visualisation, 2004. IV 2004. pp. 519–524 (2004). https://doi.org/10.1109/IV.2004.1320194

11. Glenberg, A.M., Langston, W.E.: Comprehension of illustrated text: pictures help to build mental models. J. Mem. Lang. **31**, 129–151 (1992). https://doi.org/10.1016/0749-596 X(92)90008-L

12. Larkin, J.H., Simon, H.A.: Why a diagram is (sometimes) worth ten thousand words. Cogn. Sci. **11**, 65–100 (1987). https://doi.org/10.1111/j.1551-6708.1987.tb00863.x

13. Kernbach, S.: The Facilitative Power of Visual Artifacts for Knowledge Sharing in Client-consultant Interactions. In: Academy of Management Proceedings, p. 14578 (2015). https://doi.org/10.5465/AMBPP.2015.14578abstract

14. Paivio, A.: A dual coding approach to perception and cognition. In: Modes of Perceiving and Processing Information. Psychology Press (1978)

15. Mengis, J., Eppler, M.J.: Understanding and managing conversations from a knowledge perspective: an analysis of the roles and rules of face-to-face conversations in organizations. Organ. Stud. **29**, 1287–1313 (2008). https://doi.org/10.1177/0170840607086553

16. Kernbach, S., Nabergoj, A.S.: Visual design thinking: understanding the role of knowledge visualization in the design thinking process. In: 2018 22nd International Conference Information Visualisation (IV), pp. 362–367. IEEE, Fisciano, Italy (2018). https://doi.org/10.1109/iV.2018.00068

17. Mengis, J., Eppler, M.J.: Seeing versus arguing the moderating role of collaborative visualization in team knowledge integration. J. Univ. Knowl. Manag. **1**, 151–162 (2006)

18. Eppler, M.J., Burkhard, R.A.: Knowledge Visualization: Towards a New Discipline and Its Fields of Application. Università della Svizzera italiana, Faculty of Communication Sciences, Institute for Corporate Communication, Lugano (2004)

19. Van Wijk, J.J.: Views on Visualization. IEEE Trans. Visual Comput. Graphics **12**, 421–432 (2006). https://doi.org/10.1109/TVCG.2006.80

20. Renaud, K., Van Biljon, J.: Charting the path towards effective knowledge visualisations. In: Proceedings of the South African Institute of Computer Scientists and Information Technologists on – SAICSIT'17, pp. 1–10. ACM Press, Thaba'Nchu, South Africa (2017)

21. Gotel, O.C.Z., Marchese, F.T., Morris, S.J.: On requirements visualization. In: Second International Workshop on Requirements Engineering Visualization, pp. 11–20. IEEE, New Delhi, India (2007)

22. Elmqvist, N., Fekete, J.-D.: Hierarchical aggregation for information visualization: overview, techniques, and design guidelines. IEEE Trans. Visual Comput. Graphics **16**, 439–454 (2010). https://doi.org/10.1109/TVCG.2009.84

23. Kelleher, C., Wagener, T.: Short communication: ten guidelines for effective data visualization in scientific publications. Environ Model Softw. **26**, 822–827 (2011)

24. Smuts, H., Scholtz, I.-I.: A conceptual knowledge visualisation framework for transfer of knowledge: an organisational context. In: Hattingh, M., Matthee, M., Smuts, H., Pappas, I., Dwivedi, Y.K., Mäntymäki, M. (eds.) Responsible Design, Implementation and Use of Information and Communication Technology, pp. 287–298. Springer International Publishing, Cham (2020). https://doi.org/10.1007/978-3-030-45002-1_24

25. Cañas, A.J., et al.: Concept maps: integrating knowledge and information visualization. In: Tergan, S.-O., Keller, T. (eds.) Knowledge and Information Visualization. LNCS, vol. 3426, pp. 205–219. Springer, Heidelberg (2005). https://doi.org/10.1007/11510154_11

26. Eppler, M.J.: What is an effective knowledge visualization? insights from a review of seminal concepts. In: 2011 15th International Conference on Information Visualisation. pp. 349–354 (2011). https://doi.org/10.1109/IV.2011.13

27. Renaud, K., Van Biljon, J.: A Framework to Maximise the Communicative Power of Knowledge Visualisations. Presented at the September 17 (2019). https://doi.org/10.1145/3351108.3351111

28. Card, S., Mackinlay, J., Shneiderman, B.: Readings in Information Visualization: Using Vision To Think (1999)

29. Eppler, M.J., Burkhard, R.A.: Visual representations in knowledge management: framework and cases. J. Knowl. Manag. **11**, 112–122 (2007)

30. Handzic, M.: Visualizations supporting knowledge-based decision making in cultural heritage management. Cult. Soc. Econ. Politics. **1**, 32–40 (2021). https://doi.org/10.2478/csep-2021-0009

31. Handzic, M., Dizdar, S.: Knowledge management meets humanities: a case study of diplomatic correspondence visualisation. In: 11th Forum on Knowledge Asset Dynamics – Towards a New Architecture of Knowledge: Big Data. Culture and Creativity (IFKAD 2016), pp. 1445–1457. Dresden, Germany (2016)

32. Sparrow, J.: Knowledge in Organizations: Access to Thinking at Work. SAGE Publications Ltd, London; Thousand Oaks, Calif (1998)

33. Burkhard, R.A.: Towards a framework and a model for knowledge visualization: synergies between information and knowledge visualization. In: Tergan, S.-O., Keller, T. (eds.) Knowledge and Information Visualization. LNCS, vol. 3426, pp. 238–255. Springer, Heidelberg (2005). https://doi.org/10.1007/11510154_13

34. Gavrilova, T., Alsufyev, A., Grinberg, E.: Knowledge visualization: critique of the St. Gallen School and an analysis of contemporary trends. Bus. Inform. **3**, 7–19 (2017). https://doi.org/10.17323/1998-0663.2017.3.7.19

35. Killen, C.P., Kjaer, C.: Understanding project interdependencies: the role of visual representation, culture and process. Int. J. Project Manage. **30**, 554–566 (2012). https://doi.org/10.1016/j.ijproman.2012.01.018

36. Fadiran, A., Van Biljon, J., Schoeman, M.: How can visualisation principles be used to support knowledge transfer in teaching and learning? Presented at the March 1 (2018). https://doi.org/10.1109/ICTAS.2018.8368739

37. Keller, T., Tergan, S.-O.: Visualizing knowledge and information: an introduction. In: Tergan, S.-O., Keller, T. (eds.) Knowledge and Information Visualization. LNCS, vol. 3426, pp. 1–23. Springer, Heidelberg (2005). https://doi.org/10.1007/11510154_1

38. Bowen, G.: Document analysis as a qualitative research method. Qual. Res. J. **9**, 27–40 (2009). https://doi.org/10.3316/QRJ0902027

39. Figueiras, A.: How to Tell Stories Using Visualization. Presented at the Proceedings of the International Conference on Information Visualisation (2014)

40. Mazumdar, S., Varga, A., Lanfranchi, V., Petrelli, D., Ciravegna, F.: A knowledge dashboard for manufacturing industries. In: García-Castro, R., Fensel, D., Antoniou, G. (eds.) The Semantic Web: ESWC 2011 Workshops, pp. 112–124. Springer, Berlin, Heidelberg (2012). https://doi.org/10.1007/978-3-642-25953-1_10

41. Seppänen, H., Virrantaus, K.: Shared situational awareness and information quality in disaster management. Saf. Sci. **77**, 112–122 (2015)

42. Van Biljon, J., Renaud, K.: Knowledge Visualisation Checklist, knowvizonline.com. Last accessed 29 Dec 2022

43. Yan, Z., Lei, W., Liqun, Y.: A research for the classification of knowledge visualization. Presented at the September 1 (2011). https://doi.org/10.1109/ICECENG.2011.6056928

44. Alexander, J., Zeibland, S.: The Web–bringing support and health information into the home: the communicative power of qualitative research. Int. J. Nurs. Stud. **43**, 389–391 (2006). https://doi.org/10.1016/j.ijnurstu.2005.10.012

45. Gavrilova, T., Kudryavtsev, D., Grinberg, E.: Aesthetic knowledge diagrams: bridging understanding and communication. In: Handzic, M., Carlucci, D. (eds.) Knowledge Management, Arts, and Humanities: Interdisciplinary Approaches and the Benefits of Collaboration, pp. 97–117. Springer International Publishing, Cham (2019). https://doi.org/10.1007/978-3-030-109 22-6_6

46. Korkmaz, O.: Primary perceptual field in visual materials. Soc. Sci. **4**, 525–533 (2009)

47. Newell, R., Dale, A., Winters, C.: A picture is worth a thousand data points: exploring visualizations as tools for connecting the public to climate change research. Cogent Soc. Sci. **2**, 1201885 (2016). https://doi.org/10.1080/23311886.2016.1201885

48. Todres, L.: The qualitative description of human experience: the aesthetic dimension. Qual. Health Res. **8**, 121–127 (1998). https://doi.org/10.1177/104973239800800109

49. Bai, X., White, D., Sundaram, D.: Contextual adaptive knowledge visualization environments. Electronic J. Know. Manag. **10**, 1–14 (2012)

50. Troise, C.: Exploring knowledge visualization in the digital age: an analysis of benefits and risks. Manag. Decis. **60**, 1116–1131 (2021). https://doi.org/10.1108/MD-01-2021-0086

51. Yusoff, Z., Katmon, S.A., Ahmad, M.N., Miswan, S.H.M.: Visual representation: enhancing students' learning engagement through knowledge visualization. In: 2013 International Conference on Informatics and Creative Multimedia, pp. 242–247 (2013). https://doi.org/10.1109/ICICM.2013.48

52. Lanfranchi, V., Carvalho, R.F., Gentile, A.L., Mazumdar, S., Ciravegna, F.: A semantic knowledge management framework for informal communication exchanges. Presented at the 10th International Semantic Web Conference (ISWC 2011), Bonn, Germany October 27 (2011)

53. Ma, K.-L., Liao, I., Frazier, J., Hauser, H., Kostis, H.-N.: Scientific storytelling using visualization. IEEE Comput. Graphics Appl. **32**, 12–19 (2012). https://doi.org/10.1109/MCG.201 2.24

54. Marchese, F.T., Bannisi, E. (eds.) Knowledge Visualization Currents: From Text to Art to Culture. Springer-Verlag, London (2013). https://doi.org/10.1007/978-1-4471-4303-1

55. Diakopoulos, N., Kivran-Swaine, F., Naaman, M.: Playable data: characterizing the design space of game-y infographics. In: Proceedings of the SIGCHI Conference on Human Factors in Computing Systems, pp. 1717–1726. Association for Computing Machinery, New York, NY, USA (2011). https://doi.org/10.1145/1978942.1979193

56. Bresciani, S., Eppler, M.J.: The pitfalls of visual representations: a review and classification of common errors made while designing and interpreting visualizations. SAGE Open **5**, 2158244015611451 (2015). https://doi.org/10.1177/2158244015611451

57. Bresciani, S., Eppler, M.J.: The risks of visualization: a classification of disadvantages associated with graphic representations of information. In: Schulz, P.J., Hartung, U., Keller, S. (eds.) Identität und Vielfalt der Kommunikations-wissenschaft. UVK Verlagsgesellschaft mbH, Konstanz, Germany (2009)

58. Gavrilova, T., Leshcheva, I., Strakhovich, E.: Gestalt principles of creating learning business ontologies for knowledge codification. Knowl. Manag. Res. Pract. **13**, 418–428 (2015). https://doi.org/10.1057/kmrp.2013.60

59. Moody, D.: The "Physics" of notations: toward a scientific basis for constructing visual notations in software engineering. IEEE Trans. Software Eng. **35**, 756–779 (2009). https://doi.org/10.1109/TSE.2009.67

60. Olshannikova, E., Ometov, A., Koucheryavy, Y., Olsson, T.: Visualizing Big Data with augmented and virtual reality: challenges and research agenda. J. Big Data. **2**, 1–26 (2015). https://doi.org/10.1186/s40537-015-0031-2

61. Green, R.C., Wang, L., Alam, M.: The impact of plug-in hybrid electric vehicles on distribution networks: a review and outlook. Renew. Sustain. Energy Rev. **15**, 544–553 (2011). https://doi.org/10.1016/j.rser.2010.08.015
62. Štorga, M., Mostashari, A., Stanković, T.: Visualisation of the organisation knowledge structure evolution. J. Know. Manag. **17**, 724–740 (2013)
63. Succar, B., Williams, A.S., Sher, W.D., Aranda-Mena, G.: A proposed framework to investigate building information modelling through knowledge elicitation and visual models. In: Conference of the Australasian Universities Building Education Association. pp. 308–325. Melbourne, Australia (2007)
64. Grainger, S., Mao, F., Buytaert, W.: Environmental data visualisation for non-scientific contexts: literature review and design framework. Environ. Model. Softw. **85**, 299–318 (2016)
65. Ware, C.: Information Visualization: Perception for Design. Morgan Kaufmann, Waltham, MA (2012)
66. Burigat, S., Chittaro, L.: On the effectiveness of Overview+Detail visualization on mobile devices. Personal Ubiquitous Comput. **17**, 371–385 (2013). https://doi.org/10.1007/s00779-011-0500-3
67. Heer, J., Shneiderman, B., Park, C.: A taxonomy of tools that support the fluent and flexible use of visualizations. Interact. Dyn. Vis. Anal. **10**, 1–26 (2012)
68. Bresciani, S., Ge, J., Niu, Y.: The effect of visual mapping on attitude toward organizational strategy: scale development and application in Europe and China. **2**, 19 (2014)
69. Aigner, W., Rind, A., Hoffmann, S.: Comparative evaluation of an interactive time-series visualization that combines quantitative data with qualitative abstractions. Comput. Graph. Forum – CGF 31 (2012). https://doi.org/10.1111/j.1467-8659.2012.03092.x
70. Joel-Edgar, S., Gopsill, J.: Understanding user requirements in context: a case study of developing a visualisation tool to map skills in an engineering organisation. In: 2018 International Conference on Information Management and Processing (ICIMP), pp. 6–10 (2018). https://doi.org/10.1109/ICIMP1.2018.8325832
71. Kumar, S.: A review of recent trends and issues in visualization. Int. J. Comput. Sci. Eng. **8**, 14 (2016)
72. Mengis, J., Eppler, M.J.: Visualizing Instead of Overloading: Exploring the Promise and Problems of Visual Communication to Reduce Information Overload. In: Information Overload: An International Challenge for Professional Engineers and Technical Communicators, pp. 203–229 (2012). https://doi.org/10.1002/9781118360491.ch10
73. Boehnert, J.: Knowledge visualization in environmental communication. In: Jones, P. (ed.) Proceedings of Relating Systems Thinking and Design (RSD5) 2016 Symposium, pp. 1–10. Systemic Design Research Network, Ontario College of Art and Design, Toronto, Ontario Canada (2016)
74. Borkin, M.A., et al.: Beyond memorability: visualization recognition and recall. IEEE Trans. Visual Comput. Graphics **22**, 519–528 (2016). https://doi.org/10.1109/TVCG.2015.2467732
75. Haroz, S., Kosara, R., Franconeri, S.L.: ISOTYPE visualization: working memory, performance, and engagement with pictographs. In: Proceedings of the 33rd Annual ACM Conference on Human Factors in Computing Systems, pp. 1191–1200. Association for Computing Machinery, New York, NY, USA (2015). https://doi.org/10.1145/2702123.2702275
76. Wiele, P.V., Ribière, V.: Using knowledge visualisation techniques to support the development of curriculum for employability: exploring the capability tree representation. Int. J. Know. Learn. **9**, 43–62 (2014)
77. Candello, H., Fernandes Cavalcante, V., Braz, A., De Paula, R.A.: A validation study of a visual analytics tool with end users. In: Marcus, A. (ed.) Design, User Experience, and Usability. User Experience Design Practice, pp. 381–391. Springer International Publishing, Cham (2014). https://doi.org/10.1007/978-3-319-07638-6_37

78. Hall, A., Virrantaus, K.: Visualizing the workings of agent-based models: diagrams as a tool for communication and knowledge acquisition. Comput. Environ. Urban Syst. **58**, 1–11 (2016). https://doi.org/10.1016/j.compenvurbsys.2016.03.002
79. Heer, J., Shneiderman, B.: Interactive dynamics for visual analysis. Commun. ACM **55**, 45–54 (2012)
80. Hu Jiawei, Bailey, A., Sutcliffe, A.: Visualisation design knowledge reuse. In: Proceedings. Eighth International Conference on Information Visualisation, 2004. IV 2004, pp. 745–751 (2004)
81. Jeong, D.H.: Knowledge Visualization: From Theory to Practice (2010)
82. Shamim, A., Balakrishnan, V., Tahir, M.: Evaluation of opinion visualization techniques. Inf. Vis. **14**, 339–358 (2015)
83. Yaacob, S., Ali, N.M., Liang, H.N., Rahim, N.Z.A., Maarop, N., Ali, R.: Giving the boss the big picture: demonstrating convergence visualization design principles using business intelligence and analytical tools. J. Fundam. Appl. Sci. **10**, 1328–1337 (2018)
84. Hullman, J., Diakopoulos, N.: Visualization rhetoric: framing effects in narrative visualization. IEEE Trans. Visual Comput. Graphics **17**, 2231–2240 (2011). https://doi.org/10.1109/TVCG. 2011.255
85. Zhi, Q., Su, M.: Enhance collaborative learning by visualizing process of knowledge building with Padlet. In: 2015 International Conference of Educational Innovation through Technology (EITT), pp. 221–225 (2015). https://doi.org/10.1109/EITT.2015.54
86. Eden, C., Ackermann, F.: Where next for problem structuring methods. J. Oper. Res. Soc. **57**, 766–768 (2006)
87. Suthers, D.D.: Towards a systematic study of representational guidance for collaborative learning discourse. J. UCS **7**, 254–277 (2001)
88. Elkins, J.: The Domain of Images. Cornell University Press, Ithaca (2018)
89. Tufte, E.R.: Visual explanations: images and quantities, evidence and narrative. Graphics Press, Cheshire, Conn (1997)
90. Huang, Y., Jiang, Z., Liu, L., Song, B., Han, L.: Building a knowledge map model situated in product design. Int. J. Inf. Technol. Manage. **14**, 76–94 (2015). https://doi.org/10.1504/ IJITM.2015.066059
91. Eppler, M.J.: Knowledge communication problems between experts and managers: an analysis of knowledge transfer in decision processes. Encyclopedia Knowl. Manag. (2005). https:// doi.org/10.4018/978-1-59140-573-3.ch042
92. Distanont, A., Haapasalo, H., Rassameethes, B., Lin, B.: Knowledge transfer pattern in collaborative product development. Int. J. Intercultural Inform. Manag. **3**, 59–81 (2012). https:// doi.org/10.1504/IJIIM.2012.044461
93. Ferrari, A., Spoletini, P., Gnesi, S.: Ambiguity and tacit knowledge in requirements elicitation interviews. Requirements Eng. **21**, 333–355 (2016)
94. Abad, Z.S.H., Noaeen, M., Ruhe, G.: Requirements engineering visualization: a systematic literature review. In: 2016 IEEE 24th International Requirements Engineering Conference (RE), pp. 6–15 (2016). https://doi.org/10.1109/RE.2016.61
95. Cooper, J.R., Lee, S.-W., Gandhi, R.A., Gotel, O.: Requirements engineering visualization: a survey on the state-of-the-art. In: 2009 Fourth International Workshop on Requirements Engineering Visualization, pp. 46–55 (2009). https://doi.org/10.1109/REV.2009.4

Business Agility to Cope with the Increasing National Minimum Wage After the Covid-19 Pandemic: A Case of SMEs in Mauritius

Trisheeta Sewdin$^{(\boxtimes)}$ (ID), Hemant B. Chittoo, and Needesh Ramphul

University of Technology, Port Louis, Mauritius
`trisheetasew1@yahoo.com`

Abstract. Traditional business planning may not be the optimal preference for various firms across the world due to the unpredictable and dynamic business environment. The current research is based on business agility which involves the adaptability of firms particularly the SME Sector in Mauritius to the internal and external changes. A National Minimum Wage (NMW) was introduced in Mauritius in 2018 to alleviate alleged exploitation of low wage workers. The study intends to examine how the SMEs in Mauritius adapted themselves to survive in the market after the lockdown because of Covid-19. There are various factors to be taken into consideration in this study in terms of innovation, adaptability, optimisation of use of resources and digital transformation or automation of job tasks. The study adopted a quantitative approach via a survey through a questionnaire as a research instrument. A relatively large sample of 393 participants from the SME Sector responded to this survey. Three hypotheses emerged from the literature review which has been tested using the data collected from the questionnaire. The study revealed that with an increase in NMW and the Covid-19 pandemic, the SMEs have had to adopt changes with the factors under study and adoption of automation to remain competitive in the market. The outcomes of this research represent empirical evidence in the field.

Keywords: Automation · Business Adaptation · Business Agility · Innovation · National Minimum Wage · SMEs in Mauritius

1 Introduction

The world has experienced a significant and swift transformation after the Covid-19 pandemic in the economic, political and social elements impacting market volatility in a highly competitive setting. According to Sampath & Krishnamooorthy [1], to promote flexibility and proactive planning for the business to foster economic growth, it is crucial to enhance competitiveness and sustainability of resources and service. Che Omar, Ishak & Jusoh [23] acknowledged that there is a current emphasis on the necessity of adaptability for business resilience, particularly post the Covid-19 pandemic.

The study investigated on two main factors, firstly the introduction of a NMW in Mauritius and secondly the effect of Covid-19 pandemic in the SME Sector. At first

© The Author(s), under exclusive license to Springer Nature Switzerland AG 2025

K. Hinkelmann and H. Smuts (Eds.): Society 5.0 2024, CCIS 2173, pp. 320–333, 2025.
https://doi.org/10.1007/978-3-031-71412-2_24

glance, these two topics may seem disconnected, however, there are several reasons for investigating them together which could bring valuable insights. A NMW was introduced in Mauritius on 1st January 2018 and the Covid-19 hit the world in the late 2019. Both have significant implications for the economic landscape, particularly for the SME Sector. The study can provide a comprehensive understanding of the challenges and opportunities emerging from these two events for SMEs in Mauritius. This study would shed light in the relationship between labour costs, profitability and investment in SMEs following the introduction of a NMW along with the adaptation and resilience of SMEs to navigate external shocks post the lockdown caused by Covid-19. While investigating both the NMW and Covid-19 impacts together, the study can identify common strategies or challenges faced by SMEs in responding to these events.

1.1 Introduction to Minimum Wage

Minimum Wage is a global policy aimed at reducing poverty and labour exploitation by ensuring fair wages for middle- and low-income workers. Implemented through collective bargaining, government-enforced laws, or national boards, it protects low-wage workers based on factors like cost of living, worker welfare, labour market conditions, and inflation rates. The IOE [2] report identified objectives for the increase or implementation of a minimum wage system:

1. To decrease fairness disparities;
2. To reduce poverty;
3. To address power imbalances in the employment relationship;
4. To encourage working incentive programs;

1.2 SMEs in Mauritius

The SME Sector has made significant contributions to the modern economy, contributing to technological advancement, innovative product and service development, job creation, and export promotion. The SMEDA Act of 2009 in Mauritius provided a comprehensive definition of an enterprise, encompassing various forms of trade or manufacture, manual craftsmanship, cultivation of fruits, vegetables, or flowers, livestock breeding, and any other activity that has received approval from the relevant Authority.

In Mauritius, the definition of SME has been refined based on the number of employees, with small businesses having no more than 50 employees with a turnover of less than Rs30M and medium-sized businesses having no more than 200 employees and a turnover not exceeding Rs100M.

1.3 Problem Statement

The NMW in Mauritius aims to meet the basic needs of low-wage workers and improve their quality of life. However, it may be unaffordable for small and medium-sized businesses, especially in the wake of the Covid-19 pandemic. Employers may reduce non-wage benefits to maintain profit margins. The introduction of a NMW may decrease employment rates, especially in the SME sector, but also raise concerns about labour replacement and price inflation. The World Bank Group's 2018 study found that an increase in minimum wage has a marginally positive impact on sectors covered by the NRB. Therefore, this study will shed light on the strategies adopted by the SME Sector to adapt to the economic downturns because of the pandemic together with the yearly rise in the NMW in Mauritius.

2 Literature Review

This Section will provide theoretical and empirical evidence on the factors that may impact the business agility of SMEs as a result of an increase in NMW.

2.1 Channels to Increase Business Agility

New study on minimum wage impact on SMEs reveals that labor cost effects on firms. And there are adjustment pathways for firms facing cost increases. However, limited evidence on developing economies is found [3].

2.2 Channels for Business Adjustment

One adjustment channel for SMEs is investing in physical capital like machinery, equipment, and technology to improve internal management and processes. This can help companies maximize resource utilization and quality of physical capital. [4].

Labor policies can drive the use of labor-saving tech like the Green Revolution, boosting productivity while cutting down on labor. However, tech can also replace workers, especially those with easily automated jobs, leading to unemployment for less-skilled workers. In construction, tech has replaced some workers but increased machine operators, changing the sector's workforce [5].

Technological progress can lead to job losses in lower-skilled sectors due to cost considerations. In New Zealand, young workers were replaced but technology was adjusted. In the US, a major fast-food chain cut labor costs by using automated technology [6].

2.3 Covid-19 Pandemic

Minimum wage increases have had a significant impact on SMEs, with some businesses adjusting to the cost and others experiencing job displacement due to technological substitution. The Covid-19 pandemic, which began in Wuhan, China, has disrupted socioeconomic activities globally, causing thousands of deaths and disproportionately affecting industries like tourism, airlines, and hotels [7].

The five phases of a crisis include identifying the critical situation, setting up crisis response groups, containing the damage, finding a path back to normalcy, and taking heed from the experience. SMEs are likely to be more vulnerable to crises, with both positive and negative outcomes identified [8, 9]. The ability of a small business to weather a storm indicated its entrepreneurial spirit more than anything else. SMEs are less inclined to take risks and innovate during economic downturns, and implementing macroeconomic stabilization policies can help restore the idea that an entrepreneur's activities can have a decisive impact on business success [10].

The pandemic effect has had a significant impact on the profitability and survival of SMEs in Mauritius. Many businesses have adopted digital business mediums to avoid complete shutdown and remain operational during the lockdown. These technologies, such as virtual meetings using Zoom, have enabled businesses to operate remotely and prevent the transmission of the pandemic. However, some companies operating in specific industries were granted permission to operate but were required to maintain certain distance between their workers [11].

2.4 Strategies for Survival in the Competitive Market

Innovation is crucial for SMEs in Mauritius. Companies like Conserverie Sarjua Internationale Ltée, Sotravic Ltee, and Beteltee show how creativity fuels economic growth. Financial resources and government support help SMEs innovate [12]. Technology, research tools, and HRM practices play key roles [13] [14] [15] [16]. Workplace efficiency, business models, and global rivalry drive innovation [21] [25]. Institutional cooperation and a culture of entrepreneurship enhance productivity [22]. Simplified bidding processes and reduced transaction costs aid SME growth [17] [26]. Internal and external obstacles to innovation exist. The Mauritius government funds initiatives to support SME development and creativity.

2.5 Dependent Variables in this Study

The dependent variables under this study are business profits after the implementation of a NMW and the profitability and survival of SMEs post the Covid-19 pandemic. These variables were measured according to the inflation and other contextual factors which are as follows:

Business Profits = f (Training opportunities, change in price, change in quality, review the production costs, invest in automation).

Profitability and Survival = f (Ability to adapt after the Covid-19 pandemic, strategies for survival).

1. Business Profits Function:

Training Opportunities: Investing in employee training can enhance productivity and efficiency, ultimately affecting profits positively.

Change in Price: Adjusting prices can directly impact revenue and thus influence overall profits.

Change in Quality: Improving the quality of products or services can lead to customer satisfaction and loyalty, increasing sales and profits.

Review of Production Costs: Analyzing and optimizing production costs can directly impact the profit margin.

Investment in Automation: Automating processes can reduce labour costs and increase efficiency, impacting profits.

2. Profitability and Survival Function:

    - Ability to Adapt after the Covid-19 Pandemic: Businesses that can pivot their strategies, operations, and offerings to align with post-pandemic market demands and consumer behaviour are more likely to remain profitable and survive.

    - Strategies for Survival: Implementing robust strategies such as diversification, cost-cutting measures, strengthening online presence, and fostering innovation can enhance profitability and ensure business survival in the aftermath of the pandemic.

By considering these measures, businesses can gain a more comprehensive understanding of their performance, profitability and potential for long-term survival beyond traditional financial metrics.

2.6 Lessons

The literature review analyzed the impact of raising the minimum wage on economic variables like inflation, unemployment, poverty, prices, and firm productivity. It highlighted the effects on employment rates, income inequality, consumer costs, and employee output. The study noted the Covid-19 pandemic's significant impact on small and medium-sized enterprises (SMEs) due to movement restrictions and lockdown.

3   Methodology

3.1   Introduction

Neuman [27] defined methodology as the comprehensive understanding of the research process, including social-organizational context, philosophical assumptions, ethical principles, and political implications. Research methods involved techniques for selecting cases, measuring social life, collecting data, analyzing it, and reporting results. Blumberg, Cooper, and Schindler [28] emphasized the importance of research methodology in solving problems and achieving research goals. This section highlights the chosen methodology's benefits, limitations, validity, reliability, and ethical considerations.

A quantitative research design was approached for this research. The survey encompasses the structure and content of the questionnaire used to gather data. It is crucial to ensure that the questions are clear, unbiased and relevant to the research objectives. The design includes survey methods (online, telephone, in-person) and the order of the questions. For this study, the questionnaire was built up in the google form format and on paper and submitted to the population of SMEs selected for the survey. Sampling method refers to how participants are selected from the population in interest. For this research, convenience sampling was adopted in which participants are chosen based on their availability and willingness to participate in the survey.

3.2   Quantitative Approach

This study used a quantitative approach to examine the impact of the National Min-imum Wage (NMW) on SMEs in Mauritius, particularly in the context of the Covid-19 pandemic. The research involved distributing a questionnaire to SME owners and managers to assess the survival of SMEs in Mauritius. The questionnaire was de-signed to ensure data reliability and validity and was chosen for its convenience, affordability, and quick administration. Respondents were given three weeks to com-plete the questionnaire at their convenience.

The study covered various sectors, including agriculture, construction, wholesale, retail, manufacturing, transportation, storage, food services, and educational institutions. A convenience sampling method was used to ensure the data collected was representative of the population under study.

3.3 Sampling

Study on SMEs in Mauritius, 6000 population. Used convenience sampling, quick basic info. Sample size 376 by Slovin's formula. Questionnaire given by hand, pilot-tested for flaws. 15 questionnaires for pilot test. Distributed on paper and Google form for high response rates and data quality.

3.4 Validity and Reliability

Validity is considered as the extent to which the collected data covers the actual research topic [29]. Carrying out a reliability test is essential for a study, as it refers to the uniformity of a measuring instrument's components [30]. The study uses SPSS software to calculate the dependability of the collected data. Ethical issues include avoiding harm to participants without their knowledge and consent, deceiving them about the study's purpose, and revealing only a portion of the facts. Researchers should assume responsibility for participant safety and adhere to accepted professional practices. The survey data was analyzed using SPSS, primarily using mean score, factor analysis, and correlation analysis.

3.5 Correlation Analysis

Correlation analysis is a statistical method used to evaluate the relationship between two continuous variables. It uses the correlation coefficient to measure the strength and direction of the association [31]. The symbol "r" represents the correlation, and the Kolmogorov-Smirnow and Shapiro-Wilk tests are used to determine if a variable's frequency distribution deviates from a normal distribution. If these tests are inconclusive ($p > 0.05$), it indicates that the sample distribution is not significantly different from a normal distribution [32].

3.6 Limitations of Methodology

All researchers must be aware of limitations to avoid a substantial impact on their findings [33]. This investigation, which is not an exception, encountered certain limitations. The study's quantitative method, questionnaires, has limitations such as fluctuating response rates, which can indicate unreliable information, and the use of closed-ended questions for data collection. The study also faced time constraints, which may prevent a larger sample size and more accurate data. The respondents' willingness and availability to complete the questionnaire also affects the study's effectiveness.

4 Data Analysis and Discussion

4.1 Introduction

This section presents the data analysis and results for the variables. The result is based on the 393 SMEs who responded to this study. A chi-square test has been carried out to get an insight about the strength of association of the variables followed by a normality test to perform parametric or non-parametric tests for the correlation of the variables. Since all the composite variables follow a non-normal distribution, for the correlation analysis, Spearman RHO has been used to test the hypotheses built.

4.2 Business Profits and Investment in Automation

Table 1. Chi Square Test for Business Profits and Investment in Automation

No. of valid cases = 393	Value	Df	Sig
Pearson Chi-Square	68.784[a]	12	0.000
Likelihood Ratio	47.115	12	0.000
Phi	0.418		0.000
Cramer's V	0.242		0.000

a.8 cells (40.0%) have expected count less than 5. The minimum expected count is 0.03.

The purpose of a Pearson Chi Square test is to be aware of the strength of association between Business profits and Investment in Automation. Table 1 above shows that 8 cells (40.0%) have expected count less than 5 which does not satisfy the expected cell count assumption (not exceeding 20%). Therefore, the Pearson chi-square is ignored and the likelihood ratio will be taken into consideration. The Likelihood ratio has a value of 47.115, df = 12 and significant value of 0.000. The Phi and Cramer's V values are 0.418 and 0.242 respectively, showing an association between the variables under study.

Table 2. Normality Test for Invest in Automation

	Kolmogorov-Smirnov[a]			Shapiro-Wilk		
	Statistic	Df	Sig	Statistic	Df	Sig
Automation composite	0.176	393	0.000	0.932	393	0.000

a. Lilliefors Significance Correction.

According to Table 2, the normality test shows a significance of 0.000 for both K-S and S-W test therefore the variables are not normally distributed. Table 3.

Table 3. Correlations

			Business profits composite	Automation composite
Spearman's rho	Business profits composite	Correlation Coefficient	1.000	0.146**
		Sig. (2-tailed)	0.0	0.004
		N	393	393
	Automation composite	Correlation Coefficient	0.146**	1.000
		Sig. (2-tailed)	0.004	0.0
		N	393	393

**. Correlation is significant at the 0.01 level (2-tailed).

With respect to the following Hypothesis:

H0: The implementation of a NMW did not cause the SMEs to invest in automation to increase business profits.

H1: The implementation of a NMW has caused the SMEs to invest in automation to increase business profits.

Since correlation is significant at the 0.01 level, the null hypothesis is dismissed as for both composite variables the significance is at 0.000. This means that the implementation of NMW has caused the SMEs to consider automation to increase their business profits.

The study found that with increase in NMW, the firms will ultimately consider adopting technological devices. However same was done, not to replace the existing labour force, but rather to enhance the work process and avoid expenses such as overtime and extra duty allowances.

According to empirical evidence, automation has been one of the dominant forces that threatened low-skilled jobs in the US [18]. The main causes are due to the availability of advanced technological gadgets in the market and also the reduced prices of the cost of technology that can substitute low-skilled workers, or the firms may re-organise the work within the existing labour force to adopt the technological gadgets.

4.3 Profitability and Survival and Covid-19 Pandemic Effect

a.6 cells (37.5%) have expected count less than 5. The minimum expected count is 0.15.

Table 4 above displays the statistics from a Pearson chi-square test to show the strength of association between the variables 'Profitability and Survival' and 'Covid-19 Pandemic Effect'. According to the table, 6 cells (37.5%) have an expected cell count less than 5, thus, the assumption of expected cell count not exceeding 20% is violated. The likelihood ratio has a value of 61.468, df $= 9$ and significant value is 0.000. The Phi and Cramer's V values are 0.579 and 0.335 respectively showing an association between the variables Profitability and Survival and Covid-19 Pandemic Effect.

a. Lilliefors Significance Correction.

Table 4. Chi square test for Profitability and Survival and Covid-19 Pandemic Effect

No. of valid cases = 393	Value	Df	Sig
Pearson Chi-Square	131.942a	9	0.000
Likelihood Ratio	61.468	9	0.000
Cramer's V	0.335		0.000
Phi	0.579		0.000

Table 5. Tests of Normality

	Kolmogorov-Smirnova			Shapiro-Wilk		
	Statistic	Df	Sig	Statistic	Df	Sig
Profitability and survival composite	0.131	393	0.000	0.946	393	0.000

According to Table 5, the normality test shows a significance of 0.000 for both K-S and S-W test, therefore the variables are not normally distributed.

Table 6. Normality test for the covid-19 pandemic effect

Tests of Normality						
	Kolmogorov-Smirnova			Shapiro-Wilk		
	Statistic	Df	Sig	Statistic	Df	Sig
Covid-19 effect composite	0.119	393	0.000	0.965	393	0.000

a. Lilliefors Significance Correction.

According to Table 6, the normality test shows a significance of 0.000 for both K-S and S-W test therefore the variables are not normally distributed. Table 7.

With respect to the hypothesis below:

H0: The Covid-19 pandemic did not affect the profitability and survival of the SMEs.

H1: The Covid-19 pandemic has affected the profitability and survival of the SMEs.

Since correlation is significant at the 0.01 level, the null hypothesis is dismissed as for both composite variables the significance is at 0.000. This means that the Covid-19 pandemic has affected the profitability and survival of the SMEs.

The study has analysed several factors such as how the pandemic affected the prices, quality and availability of products in the market. Upon analysing the core factors, it was found that Covid-19 pandemic did affect the profitability and survival of the SMEs.

Table 7. Correlations

			Covid-19 effect composite	Profitability and survival Composite
Spearman's rho	Covid-19 effect composite	Correlation Coefficient	1.000	0.369**
		Sig. (2-tailed)	0.0	0.000
		N	393	393
	Profitability and survival composite	Correlation Coefficient	0.369**	1.000
		Sig. (2-tailed)	0.000	0.0
		N	393	393

**. Correlation is significant at the 0.01 level (2-tailed).

Many studies of small businesses in the context of COVID-19 confirmed that small businesses have less resilience and flexibility to survive the crisis than larger firms do [34]. Table 8.

4.4 Profitability and Survival and Strategies

Table 8. Chi Square Test for Profitability and Survival and Strategies

No. of valid cases = 393	Value	Df	Sig
Pearson Chi-Square	182.128a	9	0.000
Likelihood Ratio	62.967	9	0.000
Phi	0.681		0.000
Cramer's V	.393		.000

a.7 cells (43.8%) have expected count less than 5. The minimum expected count is 0.10.

The table above shows a Pearson chi-square test conducted to determine the strength of association between the variables Profitability and Survival and Strategies for Survival. The Pearson chi square test showed 7 cells (43.8%) have expected count less than 5 and since it does not satisfy the expected cell count assumption which should not exceed 20%, the chi square test is rejected, and the likelihood ratio will be considered. The likelihood ratio has a value of 62.967, df = 9, significant value = 0.000. Phi and Cramer's V values are 0.681 and 0.393 respectively and shows that there is an association between the variables Profitability and Survival and Strategies for Survival.
a. Lilliefors Significance Correction.

Table 9. Normality Test for Strategies for Survival

	Kolmogorov-Smirnov[a]			Shapiro-Wilk		
	Statistic	Df	Sig	Statistic	Df	Sig
Strategies composite	0.170	393	0.000	0.951	393	0.000

According to Table 9, the normality test shows a significance of 0.000 for both K-S and S-W test therefore the variables are not normally distributed. Table 10.

Table 10. Correlations

			Profitability and survival composite	Strategies composite
Spearman's rho	Profitability and survival composite	Correlation Coefficient	1.000	0.313[**]
		Sig. (2-tailed)		0.000
		N	393	393
	Strategies composite	Correlation Coefficient	0.313[**]	1.000
		Sig. (2-tailed)	0.000	0.0
		N	393	393

[**]. Correlation is significant at the 0.01 level (2-tailed).

With respect to the hypothesis below:

H0: The SMEs did not change their strategies to ensure their profitability and survival.

H1: The SMEs has changed their strategies to ensure their profitability and survival.

Since significance level at 0.01, the null hypothesis is dismissed as for both composite variables the significance is at 0.000. This means that the SMEs did not change their strategies to ensure their profitability and survival.

The study found that the SMEs has to alter their strategies along with business models in order to adapt to the new requirements in the market after the Covid-19 pandemic. The NMW regulation cannot be overruled and therefore new measures were implemented to cope with the increase NMW and also the sanitary precautions.

5   Recommendations for SME Sector

1. Optimize workforce productivity
   Implement National Minimum Wage, invest in training for efficiency.

2. Flexible Work Arrangements
   Adapt to Covid-19 with remote work, reduce costs, boost satisfaction.
3. Leverage Technology
   Use tech to cut costs, automate tasks, improve efficiency.
4. Focus on Customer Experience
   Prioritize service, quality, and personalization for loyalty.
5. Diversify Revenue Streams
   Explore new markets, offer new products, pivot to online sales.
6. Collaborate with stakeholders
   Gain insights, support from partners for growth.
7. Monitor and adapt
   Stay agile, respond to market changes for success.

6   Conclusion

Statistical analysis of survey data from SMEs in Mauritius examined. Chi square tests were used to assess variable associations. Normality tests were conducted to check data distribution. Spearman's RHO test used for variable correlation. Analysis of effects of National Minimum Wage in Mauritius on business profitability and sustainability. The study highlights challenges and benefits, suggesting adaptation to changing market demands.

Acknowledgements. We would like to express our gratitude to the University of Technology, Mauritius for their contribution. Additionally, we are thankful for the insightful comments and suggestions from the management during the development of this research. Finally, we extend our appreciation to all the assistance provided throughout this project.

Disclosure of Interest.   The authors declare that they have no conflicts of interest related to this study.

References

1. Sampath, G., Krishnamoorthy, B.: Is strategic agility the new Holy Grail? Exploring the strategic agility construct. Int. J. Bus. Excell. **13**(2), 160 (2017)
2. Omar, A.R., Ishak, S., Jusoh, M.A.: The impact of Covid-19 movement control order on SMEs' businesses and survival strategies. Malays. J. Soc. Space (2020). https://doi.org/10.17576/geo-2020-1602-11
3. International Organisation of Employers. https://www.ioe emp.org /fileadmin/ioe_documents/publications/Policy%20Areas/employment/EN/_2014–04– 15__IOE_Guidance_Paper_on_the_Minimum_Wage__April_2014_.pdf
4. Hamermesh DS.: Do labor costs affect companies' demand for labor? IZA World of Labor. (2021). https://doi.org/10.15185/izawol.3.v2
5. Garber, L., Radelet, S.: Review of the great surge: the ascent of the developing world. RadeletSteven. PRISM. **6**(4), 141–146 (2017)

6. Stillman S., Le T., Gibson J., Hyslop D., Maré D.: The relationship between individual labour market outcomes, household income and expenditure, and inequality and poverty in New Zealand from 1983 to 2003. RePEc - Econpapers. Published February 1, 2012. https://econpa pers.repec.org/paper/mtuwpaper/12_5f02.htmAccessed 17 March 2024.
7. Kraus, S., Clauss, T., Breier, M., Gast, J., Zardini, A., Tiberius, V.: The economics of COVID-19: initial empirical evidence on how family firms in five European countries cope with the corona crisis. Int. J. Entrep. Behav. Res. (2020). https://doi.org/10.1108/ijebr-04-2020-0214
8. Webster, P.: Virtual health care in the era of COVID-19. The Lancet. **395**(10231), 1180–1181 (2020)
9. Ting, D.S.W., Carin, L., Dzau, V., Wong, T.Y.: Digital technology and COVID-19. Nat. Med. **26**(26), 1–3 (2020)
10. Bartz, W., Winkler, A.: Flexible or fragile? The growth performance of small and young businesses during the global financial crisis — evidence from Germany. J. Bus. Ventur. **31**(2), 196–215 (2016)
11. Puddister, K., Small, T.A.: Trial by zoom? The response to COVID-19 by Canada's Courts. Can. J. Political Sci. (2020). https://doi.org/10.1017/s0008423920000505
12. The Global SME Mindset.: Oxford Economics (2013).
13. Organisation for Economic Co-operation and Development. The Measurement of Scientific and Technological Activities, Frascati Manual 2002: Proposed Standard Practice for Surveys on Research and Experimental Development. Organisation for Economic Co-operation and Development (2003).
14. Organisation For Economic Co-Operation And Development, Statistical Office Of The European Communities, Luxembourg: Oslo Manual. Paris Oecd Publishing (2015)
15. Kline, S.J., Rosenberg, N.: An Overview of Innovation. Studies on Science and the Innovation Process. Published online August 2009:173–203. https://doi.org/10.1142/9789814273596_0009
16. Ngah, R., Ibrahim, A.R.: The relationship of Intellectual capital, innovation and organizational performance: a preliminary study in Malaysian SMEs. Int'l J. Manage. Innovat. Syst. (2009). https://doi.org/10.5296/ijmis.v1i1.15
17. Smith, K.: Measuring Innovation. Oxford University Press, London (2006)
18. Autor, D.H., Dorn, D., Hanson, G.H.: Untangling trade and technology: evidence from local labour markets. Econ. J. **125**(584), 621–646 (2015)
19. Fairlie, R.: The impact of COVID-19 on small business owners: evidence from the first 3 months after widespread social-distancing restrictions. J. Eco. Manage. Strategy (2020). https://doi.org/10.1111/jems.12400
20. Deepankar, B., Foley, D.: Dynamics of Output and Employment in the U.S Economy. (2011). https://doi.org/10.7275/3317864
21. Haitham F, Alahrh OA.: Explaining the Relationship between Creativity, Innovation and Entrepreneurship. Business Economics (2014).
22. Narula, Dunning. transpacific foreign direct investment and the investment development path: the record
23. Ishak, S., Che Omar, A.R., Abd. Manaf A.: Entrepreneurial Leadership in the micro and small enterprises (MSES) research context: a literature review. Int. J. Academic Res. Bus. Soc. Sci. (2021). https://doi.org/10.6007/ijarbss/v11-i5/9815
24. Basu, D., Vasudevan, R.: Technology, distribution and the rate of profit in the US economy: understanding the current crisis. Camb. J. Econ. **37**(1), 57–89 (2013)
25. Adelakun, K. H.: The role of business model innovation in the commercialization strategies in SMEs. Master thesis, Faculty of Economics and Business Administration, University of Oulu (2014).
26. Baloyi, J. K. (2010). An analysis of constraints facing smallholder farmers in the Agribusiness value chain. University of Pretoria

27. Neuman, W.: Social Research Methods: Qualitative and Quantitative Approaches. Pearson, Essex (2014)
28. Blumberg, Cooper and Schindler: Business Research Methods, p. 2008. McGraw-Hill Higher Education, cop, London (2008)
29. Ghauri, P.N., Gronhaug, K.: Research Methods in Business Studies: A Practical Guide. Pearson, London (2005)
30. Huck. The role of business model innovation in the commercialization strategies in SMEs (2007).
31. Tabachnick, B.G., Fidell, L.S.: Using Multivariate Statistics. Harper & Row, Publishers Inc, New York (1989)
32. Field, A.: Reliability analysis. In: Field, A. (ed.) Discovering Statistics Using spss, 2nd edn. Sage, London (2005)
33. Hair, Bush and Ortinau. Marketing Research: Within a Changing Information Environment (2003).
34. Fairlie, R.: The impact of COVID-19 on small business owners: evidence from the first 3 months after widespread social-distancing restrictions. J. Eco. Manage. Strategy (2020). https://doi.org/10.1111/jems.12400

Harnessing Technology for Mangrove Research in the Western Indian Ocean to Enhance Climate Change Resilience

Reshma Sunkur[1]([✉]), Komali Kantamaneni[2,3], Chandradeo Bokhoree[1], Upaka Rathnayake[4], and Michael Fernando[3]

[1] Doctoral School, University of Technology, Mauritius, La Tour Koenig, Pointe Aux Sables, Mauritius
sunkurr@umail.utm.ac.mu
[2] United Nations-SPIDER-UK Regional Support Office, University of Central Lancashire, Preston, UK
[3] School of Engineering and Computing, University of Central Lancashire, Preston, UK
[4] Department of Civil Engineering and Construction, Faculty of Engineering and Design, Atlantic, Technological University, Sligo 91 YW50, Ireland

Abstract. Mangroves in the Western Indian Ocean face increasing threats from climate change such as rising sea levels and storm surges. To increase mangrove resilience in the region, there is a need to leverage technological innovations for research, management and monitoring purposes. The aim of this paper was thus to review the role of technology in supporting mangrove research regionally. A bibliometric analysis was conducted using Google Scholar for the period 2004–2024. From 31, 934 articles retrieved, 160 records were selected for the assessment and keyword co-occurrence was conducted on VosViewer. Remote sensing, GIS and modeling techniques were highlighted as key tools for monitoring mangrove health, extent and change over time. Community engagement through participatory strategies such as PGIS was noted as effective mangrove conservation and resilience building efforts. The keyword co-occurrence analysis showed that there was a strong link between mangrove, climate change and sea level rise suggesting the importance of mangroves in coastal resilience. By embracing advancements in technology and fostering collaboration between researchers, local communities and practitioners, coastal nations' resilience to climate change impacts can be enhanced by better managing and monitoring mangroves.

Keywords: mangrove · coastal management · climate change

1 Introduction

Over the last few years, mangrove conservation has become a key environmental priority globally with many large international conservation initiatives such as the Blue Carbon Initiative recognizing mangroves as a high priority ecosystem [1]. Despite the harsh environment in which they survive, mangroves have colonized almost all of the

© The Author(s), under exclusive license to Springer Nature Switzerland AG 2025
K. Hinkelmann and H. Smuts (Eds.): Society 5.0 2024, CCIS 2173, pp. 334–347, 2025.
https://doi.org/10.1007/978-3-031-71412-2_25

global tropical intertidal habitats where local conditions would allow [2]. These unique ecosystems offer a wide range of benefits such as reducing the harmful impacts of coastal erosion, stabilizing the coast, cushioning storm surges and high swells, acting as nursery sites for a number of marine species, providing habitats to several species including endangered species like the Royal Bengal Tiger and estuarine crocodiles, filtering water by trapping pollutants and sediment, supporting nutrient recycling, regulating climate through carbon sequestration, contributing to livelihoods and food security of coastal communities, providing educational ecotourism activities while being an integral part of marine ecosystems working in tandem with other habitats like coral reefs and seagrass beds to ensure the health of coasts and oceans [3]. Today, mangroves are recognized as key nature based solution to address the climate crisis [4] and help achieve the Paris Agreement on limiting global warming [5]. However, as almost half of the global population now resides within 150 km of coastlines [6], mangroves face a number of pressures such as illegal logging, deforestation for more economically viable activities such as aquaculture, coastal development, overexploitation of resources, invasive alien species, land based pollution and degradation which is now exacerbated by the effects of climate change [7].

The Western Indian Ocean (WIO) hosts 25% of Africa's mangroves, or 5% of global coverage, over an area of approximately 1 million ha with 90% of mangroves distributed in four countries Mozambique, Madagascar, Tanzania and Kenya [8]. Ten true mangrove species have been identified in the region [9], and similar to mangroves elsewhere, several endangered species like the endemic Colobus monkey inhabit the WIO mangroves. Mangroves in this region are a valuable resource for sustaining fisheries, boat-making, fuel wood and medicine as well as providing ecological services such as cushioning storm surges [8, 9]. However, mangroves suffered a net loss of 30,156 ha during the period 1996-2020 representing an average decline of 3.9% [9]. Direct causes of mangrove loss include overexploitation for resources, conversion of mangroves to other land uses such as agriculture and aquaculture and pollution while indirect causes can be attributed to coastal development, damming of major rivers thus decreasing downstream water flow and increased sedimentation [8]. As Africa, including the WIO region, emerges as a significant economic hub with several large-scale developments, pressure on mangrove forests is likely to increase substantially in the coming years. In the same line Poti et al. [10] observe that substantial ecological and social changes have been taking place within the WIO compared to other regions of the world such as increased warming which could eventually have disastrous impacts on tropical islands. Consequently, there is a pressing need for state-of-the-art solutions to successfully mitigate these effects and adapt to a changing climate.

In today's 'Information age', the internet and associated communication technologies facilitate the seamless flow of vast amounts of data resulting in the emergence of novel business models, governance structures and communication strategies in various areas including the environmental field [11]. Lahoz-Monfort et al. [12] in fact contend from humble beginnings of handcrafted devices like radio tracking to more current modern tools, technology has been integral in studying habitats and species for decades now thus supporting conservation efforts and dealing with threats. Technology provides access to real-time information, expanded spatial and temporal coverage, innovative data sources and swift processing and analysing capacities which help to monitor and measure changes from the species to ecosystem level [13]. As monitoring is at the heart of many international agreements such as the Aichi Biodiversity Targets of the Convention of Biological Diversity, technological tools significantly support on the ground conservation actions such as wildlife tracking, fighting illegal activities like poaching and even reducing pollution. To be sure, conservation biology has undergone significant paradigm shifts in the last few decades resulting in an interdisciplinary approach. With ongoing climatic change and alarming species loss, technological tools which are now cheaper and more accessible have become an integral pillar of modern conservation work [13, 14].

Hence harnessing the power of technology, especially in today's digital age, is crucial in strengthening mangrove conservation and preservation efforts, while supporting climate action in general. An array of technological tools and techniques are now available that can enhance such conservation efforts and revolutionize our understanding of mangrove ecosystems such as remote sensing as reviewed by Cárdenas et al. [15], Geographic Information Systems (GIS) e.g. [16], big data e.g. [17] and cloud based monitoring using deep learning as per Lomeo and Singh's [18] study amongst others. The present study therefore aims to explore the intersection of technology and mangrove research with a focus on how technological advancements can be leveraged to enhance climate change resilience. Technology here is defined according to the Collins Dictionary as 'methods, systems and devices which are the result of scientific knowledge being used for practical purposes' [19]. By synthesizing existing literature based on a bibliometric analysis and analysing case studies, this study seeks to elucidate the potential benefits, challenges and best practices with harnessing technology for mangrove protection in the WIO for climate change resilience. As the WIO region is undergoing rapid warming compared to other oceans of the world with repercussions on ecosystems, livelihoods and food security, this work will thus contribute to the growing body of knowledge aimed at safeguarding mangroves under a changing climate. It will serve as baseline information for those entering the field of conservation such as researchers, students, decision makers, public and private organizations by providing an overview of available options for those seeking to apply a particular technological tool or even explore new avenues as well as support professionals working in other areas of ecology since many of these technologies are useful beyond conservation.

2 Methodology

The Preferred Reporting Items for Systematic Reviews and Meta-Analyses (PRISMA) guidelines were used to identity technological tools and techniques used in the WIO region to support mangrove studies [20]. Google Scholar was used for the analysis as it is a freely accessible online platform, provides a comprehensive and interdisciplinary coverage of academic literature and has advanced search functionalities [21]. A 20-year period (2004–2024) was deemed suitable for the present study to identify technological tools used to support climate change studies. The search was conducted for publications in the English language and sorted by relevance. Keywords used to retrieve relevant publications were 'technology' AND 'mangroves' AND 'monitoring' AND 'mapping' 'climate change' AND 'Western Indian Ocean' AND 'Comoros' AND 'Reunion' AND 'Mauritius' AND 'Seychelles' AND 'Kenya' AND 'Madagascar' AND 'Mozambique' AND 'Somalia' AND 'South Africa' AND 'Tanzania'. Articles retrieved were manually screened and articles meeting the inclusion criteria were saved for further analysis. The inclusion criteria were (i) records having selected keywords only (ii) records in WIO region only (iii) records which were accessible (iv) records in the context of climate change (v) records in English only. Double screening was then conducted to reduce bias in the analysis. The main author conducted the initial search according to the above mentioned criteria and one independent researcher reviewed a sample of the included and excluded records (n = 50). Data visualization was then conducted using the bibliometric software VOSviewer (version 1.6.20). Text mining was used to build networks of the co-occurrence of keywords and visualize important terms from the retrieved data. Out of 531 terms from the selected records' titles, a minimum occurrence of 4 keywords was set, number of terms to be selected set at 15 and the relevance score set at 60%. Technological tools used in the studies were manually extracted from the retrieved records and a keyword cloud was generated using a word cloud generator. Figure 1.

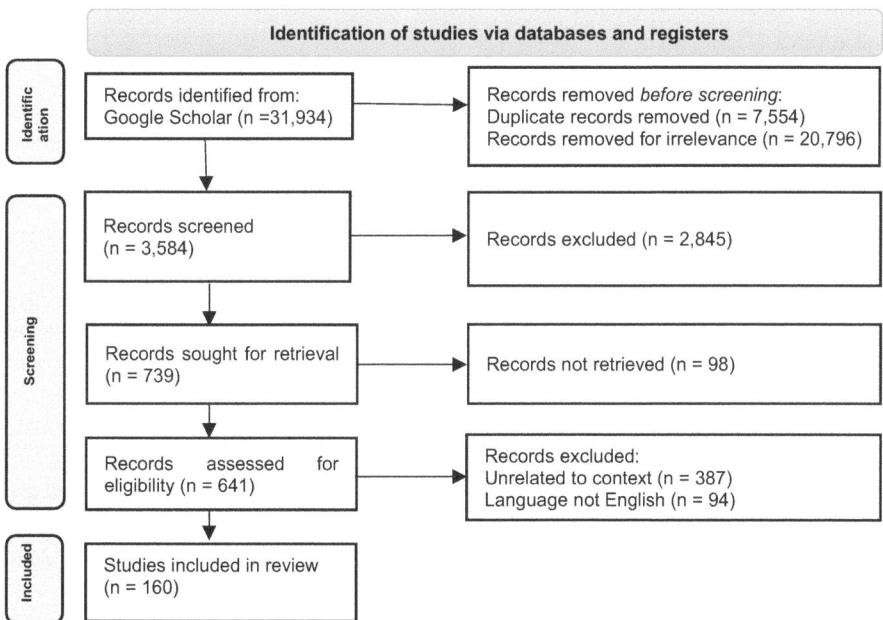

Fig. 1. PRISMA flowchart showing the selection process according to the criteria set, final records were n = 160

3   Results

From the selection and screening process mentioned above, 160 records were retrieved from Google Scholar in relation to technological tools and techniques used in mangrove studies for climate change resilience. Out of 31,934 records, 7,554 records were removed as they were duplicates and 20,796 were irrelevant. 3,584 records were then screened from which 2,845 were further excluded as they were not in the selected study site (WIO). 739 records were screened and 98 were excluded as they could not be retrieved due to expired web links. 641 records were assessed for eligibility and a further 387 were rejected as they were not in the context of climate change and 94 were not in English. Finally, 160 records met the criteria for the present assessment.

From VOSviewer, 15 items, 4 clusters, 25 links with 34 total link strengths were generated. Table 1 shows the 4 clusters and 15 items picked by the software's algorithm.

Table 1. Number of clusters generated by VOSviewer

Cluster 1	Cluster 2	Cluster 3	Cluster 4
Implication	Impact	Land cover	Climate change
Madagascar	Mapping	Land use	Mangrove
Mangrove forest	Mida Creek	LULC	Seal level rise
Remote sensing	Rufiji Delta		
South Africa			

The network visualization diagram linking the 15 terms is shown in Fig. 2. Climate change had the highest link strength at 9 connecting mangrove, sea level rise, impact, implication and South Africa. Mangrove followed at 8 connecting climate change, sea level rise, remote sensing, Madagascar and mapping. Remote sensing had a link strength of 7 linking mangrove, impact, land cover, Madagascar, South Africa and implication. At 5, land use was connected to Mida Creek, land cover and LULC and land cover also at 5 was linked to remote sensing, land use and LULC together with mapping at 5 linked to mangrove, Mida Creek and Rufiji Delta. At link strength of 4, LULC was connected to land use and land cover; Madagascar to mangrove, remote sensing, Mida Creek and implication; sea level rise to mangrove and climate change; South Africa to climate change, remote sensing and implication; impact to climate change, remote sensing and Mida Creek. Mida Creek had a link strength of 3 linked to mapping, impact and land use and mapping also at 3 was linked to mangrove, Mida Creek and Rufiji Delta. Mangrove forest at link strength 2 was connected to Madagascar and implication and Rufiji Delta at 1 was connected to mapping.

Fig. 2. Network visualization of selected terms

The overlay visualization of the interconnected nodes in relation to the year of publication is shown in Fig. 3. From the terms extracted, the majority of publications fall within the 2016 to 2020 period. Several studies on mangroves related to mapping, remote sensing, sea level rise and South Africa had been conducted during the 2016 period in the WIO region, with climate change studies related to land use, Madagascar and Rufiji Delta continuing in the 2017–2018 period. Studies on the implications of the collected keywords took place in 2019 with impacts and LULC studies in 2020.

Fig. 3. Keywords overlay visualization of interconnected nodes with year of publication

Figure 4 shows the density visualization of the connected nodes. Mangrove/climate change/sea level rise had the highest density suggesting a strongly interconnected network followed by mangrove forest, mapping, remote sensing, land use/land cover/LULC, impact, Mida Creek and South Africa.

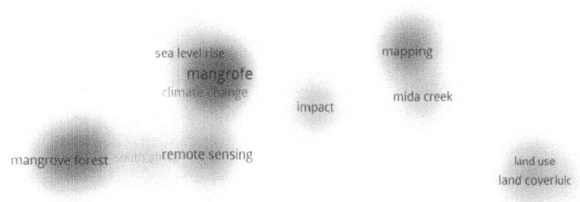

Fig. 4. Density visualization of keywords in interconnected nodes

Figure 5 shows the word cloud of technology used in mangrove studies to enhance climate change resilience in the WIO region. Remote sensing is observed to be the most common tool occurring 115 times followed by GIS (30), modeling (7), InVEST (5), aerial imagery (4), DSAS (2), deep learning (1) and big data (1).

Fig. 5. Keyword cloud of technology used in mangrove studies in the WIO region for climate change resilience

4 Discussion

4.1 Bibliometric Analysis

In the present study, it is observed that there is a strong connection (link strength 9) between mangrove and climate change, impacts and implications, sea level rise and South Africa. This suggests that mangroves play an important role in coastal protection but are also threatened by rising sea levels which could impact on coastal biodiversity and livelihoods such as South Africa's and how recognizing the link between climate change and mangroves underscores the importance of implementing adaptation strategies. Likewise, mangrove is strongly linked (link strength 8) to climate change, sea level rise, remote sensing, mapping and Madagascar. Here the implication could be that mangroves are vulnerable to climate change effects such as rising sea levels, and how mapping and monitoring mangroves with remote sensing techniques could support management efforts such as in Madagascar. Remote sensing was also strongly linked (link strength 7) to mangrove, impact, land cover, Madagascar, South Africa and implication. This could imply that remote sensing technology is used to study the impact of land cover changes especially relating to mangroves in regions like South Africa and Madagascar and how the implications of these findings could include environmental conservation efforts. At link strength of 5 were several keywords including land use, Mida Creek, land cover etc. as outlined above suggesting the interconnection between the different technologies and methodologies used such as remote sensing, mapping, land use/land cover/LULC analysis to assess and monitor mangroves particularly in Mida Creek and Rufiji Delta which are mangrove rich regions to support resilience in these coastal areas. The link strength of 4 for the terms LULC, land use, Madagascar as mentioned above suggests a moderate link between the various terms centred on the coastal ecosystem dynamics including climate change impacts, implication of land use and LULC changes, the application of remote sensing techniques to understand and manage these ecosystems especially in the region of South Africa and Madagascar. A slightly moderate link can be observed between keywords Mida Creek, mapping, LULC etc. suggesting that mapping studies are crucial in studying and monitoring coastal areas like in Mida Creek and Rufiji Delta which could provide critical data for informing conservation efforts in these regions. The weak link between mangrove and Madagascar could imply that Madagascar has significant mangroves with implications for biodiversity conservation and livelihood protection. The weakest link is between Rufiji Delta and mapping; this could suggest a potential connection between mapping activities at the delta such as mangrove distribution and LULC but this association is not very influential compared to the other connections made above.

4.2 Technology Supporting Mangrove Research in the WIO Region

Results from the present study shows that technology plays a critical role in supporting mangrove research in the WIO region. Most studies seem to focus on remote sensing techniques, which are often used with GIS tools as well as models such as InVEST. In terms of building resilience to climate change, such technology support mangrove research by allowing timely and accurate data collection, capturing data over large extent using remote sensing techniques, analysing spatial data with GIS, simulating mangrove dynamics with computational models and engaging local communities through visual datasets such as maps as discussed below.

4.2.1 Data Collection

Data collection is key to generate knowledge and understanding to make informed decisions about mangrove management efforts. Massive amounts of data are collected everyday by satellite imagery companies for people to access and retrieve useful information. Planet, one of the leaders in digital imagery, states that at least 20 terra bytes of satellite data are downloaded everyday including by mangrove researchers working on blue carbon, storm impacts and habitat mapping [22]. Based on such collected data, Tang et al. [23] compiled big geospatial data of 1512 SRTM (Shuttle Radar Topography Mission) tiles to estimate the biomass and carbon content of worldwide mangroves including in the WIO region. The role that mangroves play in sequestering and storing anthropogenic carbon is today of utmost importance to mitigate climate change effects and technology based estimates can be powerful tools to support such research [24].

4.2.2 Remote Sensing

Given the specific visible spatial and spectral signature of mangroves on satellite imagery, remote sensing is one of the most efficient ways to map and monitor mangroves [25]. Several types of low and medium resolution satellite images are now available for free for mangrove studies such as Sentinel, Landsat and Spot. High resolution satellite images are generally expensive in the range of 4.75 USD per sq km, but some are also available for free such as ICEYE, PlanetScope and Pléiades. Medium resolution remotely sensed data can be leveraged to extract useful data on mangrove distribution and spatio-temporal changes as illustrated in the WIO region through the studies of Zöckler et al. [26] on mangrove degradation in Madagascar, Hamza et al. [27] on mangrove cover change and exposure to coastal hazards in Kenya and Charrua's et al. [28] assessment of cyclone impact on land cover change including mangroves in Mozambique amongst others. Aerial imagery taken by manned aircraft have also been utilized such as Warui's et al. [29] study on mangrove status, utilization and succession in Kenya.

4.2.3 GIS

GIS are powerful decision support systems that have been used extensively in mangrove spatio-temporal analyses across the world for management purposes [30]. GIS helps visualize mangrove data within the spatial context, facilitate the integration of various types of data such as field surveys for monitoring mangrove health, enable habitat modeling to develop habitat suitability models and conduct risk assessments such as impacts of sea level rise [31]. Today, GIS together with remote sensing are the most convenient way to monitor mangrove ecosystems [31] as seen in the numerous studies conducted in the region such as Orimoloye's et al. [32] wetland shift monitoring in South Africa, Hickey's et al. [33] assessment of climate change induced migration of mangroves around the world including South Africa, Kairo's et al. [34] estimation of mangrove biophysical factors and carbon stock in Kenya to name a few. More recently, the integration of big data with GIS-based spatial analysis tools can support large scale studies such as Tang's et al. [23] analysis of global mangrove biomass and carbon stock estimation.

4.2.4 Modeling

Ecological models help us understand the importance of complex ecological processes such as in mangrove ecosystems at different scales and in simulating how systems will respond to rehabilitation efforts [35]. Rivera-Monroy et al. [36] report that despite the economic importance of mangroves globally, there is generally a lack of modeling tools in this field the most widely used one being spatial models like species distribution models (SDM). In the WIO context, some of the models used in mangrove studies include habitat suitability modeling to predict spatial distribution of mangroves using MaxEnt (Maximum Entropy) [37, 38], ecosystem services valuation with the model InVEST (Integrated Valuation of Ecosystem Services and Trade-Offs) [39, 40], coastline change and shoreline dynamics with using DSAS (Digital Shoreline Analysis System) [41, 42] and large scale mangrove mapping with deep learning models [43].

4.2.5 Community Engagement

Engaging local communities in mangrove management decisions creates solutions that work both for the environment and people to act as local environmental stewards [44]. When coupled to technological tools, community involvement can provide vital information on local ecological knowledge and practices related to mangrove ecosystems. PGIS (Participatory GIS) is one such method that allows the incorporation of a community's region specific knowledge into the planning process using GIS. In the WIO region, Käyhkö et al. [45] used a PGIS method to assess how local knowledge could support integrated spatial planning in Unguja Island, Tanzania and how this information when put in map form could support decision making.

4.3 Technology for Sustainable Development

Technological advancements today are revolutionizing mangrove research and conservation efforts by offering innovative solutions. Habitat fragmentation, estimates of forest loss and degradation and restoration potential of mangrove forests can now be conducted at very fine scale using big data from remote sensing [46]. The Commonwealth [22] in fact reports that earth observation technologies are supporting various nations such as Sri Lanka and Trinidad and Tobago in restoring and protecting mangrove forests while battling the impacts of climate change. Likewise, the African Union High Level Panel on Emerging Technologies [47] recognizes the importance of mangroves in addressing climate change issues and encourages African Union member states to adopt new technologies in mangrove restoration programmes (AUDA-NEPAD). Innovative technology can help with climate action as demonstrated by Ericsson's mangrove reforestation project in Malaysia where saplings were planted with sensors to monitor salinity, pH and soil conditions which substantially boosted monitoring activities the success of which led to additional monitoring of migratory birds in the Philippines using AI trained imagery [48]. Likewise, the ManglarIA (Spanish for AI for mangroves) project is being implemented along the coast of the Yucatan Peninsula and Naryarit along the Pacific coast to help mangroves adapt to a changing climate using a wide range of technologies including camera traps, drones and artificial intelligence [49].

However, it is worth to note that access to technologies is not equitable globally. There is a clear disparity between where adaptation technologies are being developed and where they are actually needed [50]. Looking at the results of the present study, it is evident that technology is being applied in mangrove research for climate change resilience in the WIO region, yet this application is limited to remote sensing analysis, GIS and freely available machine learning tools while a whole suite of technology is available for mangrove research like drones [49], field sensors [48], camera traps [51], radio telemetry [52] and numerical modelling [53]. While Kenya stands out in terms of technological innovation in the WIO region [50], the majority of coastal communities face several challenges such as limited access to technology, the high costs associated with acquiring and maintaining technology like drones, the lack of local data and technical capacity to implement and utilize technological tools, data security and fair and equitable use of data especially when it involves endangered species, legal implications of use of certain technologies such as permits for drone manipulation and social acceptance especially by local communities. Yet despite all these challenges it is also important to note that adaptation technologies need not be high-tech, shiny and expensive; they must be relevant to the local and/or regional context. Nations in the WIO can leverage funding from the private sector or regional or international organizations like the United Nations Development Programme to acquire appropriate technological tools and receive technical training and capacity building in the use and maintenance of these equipment; they can also import technologies from other countries through partnerships and technology transfer mechanisms. If nations are to meet the goals of the Paris Agreement while congruently striving to achieve the 2030 Agenda for Sustainable Development, it is critical to explore technologies that can reduce risks of coastal nations and livelihoods and support communities achieve their full socio-economic potential [54].

Limitations

One of the main limitations of the study was that only Google Scholar was used to retrieve data which limited the sources of data available such as national reports which are excluded from the portal. Likewise, as the WIO region is basically multi lingual, data published in other languages like French were excluded which could have biased the assessment. What's more, since conservation technology is an interdisciplinary field, it is possible that the method used (like the keywords) may not have captured all information relevant to the study.

5   Conclusion

Technological revolution has helped scientists and researchers make remarkable advances in the mangrove management and conservation programmes. The present study explored the different ways in which technological tools and techniques support mangrove studies in the WIO region to increase nations' resilience to climate change. A bibliometric analysis was conducted on Google Scholar and results were visualized on VosViewer. From 160 selected records, it was observed that there was a strong link between mangroves, climate change, its potential impacts such as sea level rise and South Africa, which could suggest how mangroves play a critical role in coastal protection but are also threatened by climate change induced impacts like sea level rise. The most common tool used in the region was observed to be remote sensing followed by GIS as well as models like InVEST. Through the integration of these tools, researchers gain valuable information on mangrove distribution, health and changes over time, facilitating the identification of vulnerable regions and informing adaptive management strategies especially by engaging communities. As the threat of climate change continues to loom over coastal communities, harnessing the power of technology in mangrove studies for fostering resilience, promoting sustainable management practices and guiding conservation efforts can safeguard these exceptional ecosystems ensuring their vital contributions to coastal resilience.

Funding. This work was supported by the RECOS project of the Indian Ocean Commission, funded by the French Development Agency (AFD) and the French Global Environment Facility (FFEM).

Disclosure of Interests. The authors declare no conflict of interest.

References

1. Friess, D.A., Yando, E.S., Abuchahla, G.M., Adams, J.B., Cannicci, S., Canty, S.W., Cavanaugh, K.C., Connolly, R.M., Cormier, N., Dahdouh-Guebas, F., Diele, K.: Mangroves give cause for conservation optimism, for now. Curr. Biol. (2020). https://doi.org/10.1016/j.cub.2019.12.054
2. Hamilton, S.E.: Mangroves and aquaculture: a five decade remote sensing analysis of Ecuador's estuarine environments. Vol. 33, pp. 1–40. Springer Cham (2020). https://doi.org/10.1007/978-3-030-22240-6
3. UNEP.   https://www.unep.org/news-and-stories/story/inside-look-beauty-and-benefits-man groves
4. Sunkur, R., Kantamaneni, K., Bokhoree, C., Ravan, S.: Mangroves' role in supporting ecosystem-based techniques to reduce disaster risk and adapt to climate change: a review. J. Sea Res. **196**, 102449 (2023). https://doi.org/10.1016/j.seares.2023.102449

5. World Economic Forum. https://www.weforum.org/agenda/2022/10/cop27-technology-man grove-reforestation-mitigate-climate-change/
6. Neumann, B., Vafeidis, A.T., Zimmermann, J., Nicholls, R.J.: Future coastal population growth and exposure to sea-level rise and coastal flooding–A global assessment. PLoS ONE **10**, e0118571 (2015). https://doi.org/10.1371/journal.pone.0131375
7. Gilman, E.L., Ellison, J., Duke, N.C., Field, C.: Threats to mangroves from climate change and adaptation options: a review. Aquat. Bot. **89**, 237–250 (2008). https://doi.org/10.1016/j. aquabot.2007.12.009
8. Bosire J. O., Mangora M. M., Bandeira S., Rajkaran A., Ratsimbazafy R., Appadoo C., Kairo J. G. (eds.): (2018). Mangroves of the Western Indian Ocean: Status and Management., pp.161. WIOMSA, Zanzibar Town. https://doi.org/10.4314/wiojms.v17i2.1
9. Erftemeijer, P., de Boer, M., Hilarides, L.: Status of Mangroves in the Western Indian Ocean Region. Wetlands International. (2022)
10. Poti, M., Hugé, J., Shanker, K., Koedam, N., Dahdouh-Guebas, F.: Learning from small islands in the Western Indian Ocean (WIO): a systematic review of responses to environmental change. Ocean Coast. Manag. **227**, 106268 (2022). https://doi.org/10.1016/j.ocecoaman.2022. 106268
11. Arts, K., Van der Wal, R., Adams, W.M.: Digital technology and the conservation of nature. Ambio **44**, 661–673 (2015). https://doi.org/10.1007/s13280-015-0705-1
12. Lahoz-Monfort, J.J., Magrath, M.J.: A comprehensive overview of technologies for species and habitat monitoring and conservation. BioSci. **71**, 1038–1062 (2021). https://doi.org/10. 1093/biosci/biab073
13. Pimm, S.L., et al.: Emerging technologies to conserve biodiversity. TREE. **30**, 685–696 (2015). https://doi.org/10.1016/j.tree.2015.08.008
14. Berger-Tal, O., Lahoz-Monfort, J.J.: Conservation technology: The next generation. Conserv. Lett. **11**, e12458 (2018). https://doi.org/10.1111/conl.12458
15. Cárdenas, N.Y., Joyce, K.E., Maier, S.W.: Monitoring mangrove forests: Are we taking full advantage of technology? Int. J. Appl. Earth Obs. Geoinf. **63**, 1–14 (2017). https://doi.org/ 10.1016/j.jag.2017.07.004
16. Jumawan, J.: Mangrove biodiversity, GIS weighted overlay analysis, and mapping of suitable areas in Alabel, Sarangani Province, Philippines. J. Ecosyst. Sci. Eco-Govern. **4**, 11–23 (2022). https://doi.org/10.54610/jeseg/4.1.2022.002
17. Worthington, T.A., et al.: Harnessing big data to support the conservation and rehabilitation of mangrove forests globally. OE. **2**, 429–443 (2020). https://doi.org/10.1016/j.oneear.2020. 04.018
18. Lomeo, D., Singh, M.: Cloud-based monitoring and evaluation of the spatial-temporal distribution of southeast asia's mangroves using deep learning. Remote Sens. **14**, 2291 (2022). https://doi.org/10.3390/rs14102291
19. Collins Dictionary. https://www.collinsdictionary.com/dictionary/english/technology
20. Page, M.J., Moher, D., Bossuyt, P.M., Boutron, I., Hoffmann, T.C., Mulrow, C.D., Shamseer, L., Tetzlaff, J.M., Akl, E.A., Brennan, S.E. and Chou, R.: PRISMA 2020 explanation and elaboration: updated guidance and exemplars for reporting systematic reviews. BMJ 372. (2022). https://doi.org/10.1136/bmj.n160
21. Jeyapragash., B., Muthuraj, A., Rajkumar, T.: Research Publications in Open Access with Special Reference to Directory of Open Access Journal an Analysis. Libr. Inf. Sci. **3**, 4–9. (2016)
22. The Commonwealth. https://thecommonwealth.org/news/how-space-tech-aiding-mangrove-conservation-commonwealth
23. Tang, W., Zheng, M., Zhao, X., Shi, J., Yang, J., Trettin, C.C.: Big geospatial data analytics for global mangrove biomass and carbon estimation. Sustain. **10**, 472 (2018). https://doi.org/ 10.3390/su10020472

24. Jones, A.R., Raja Segaran, R., Clarke, K.D., Waycott, M., Goh, W.S., Gillanders, B.M.: Estimating mangrove tree biomass and carbon content: a comparison of forest inventory techniques and drone imagery. Front. Mar. Sci. **6**, 784 (2020). https://doi.org/10.3389/fmars.2019.00784

25. Maurya, K., Mahajan, S., Chaube, N.: Remote sensing techniques: Mapping and monitoring of mangrove ecosystem—a review. Complex Intell. Syst. **7**, 2797–2818 (2021). https://doi.org/10.1007/s40747-021-00457-z

26. Zöckler, C., Wodehouse, D. and Markolf, M.: A visual assessment scale for rapid evaluation of mangrove degradation, using examples from myanmar and madagascar. In: Mangrove Ecosystem Restoration, p. 25. (2021). https://doi.org/10.5772/intechopen.95340

27. Hamza, A.J., Esteves, L.S., Cvitanović, M.: Changes in mangrove cover and exposure to coastal hazards in Kenya. Land **11**, 1714 (2022). https://doi.org/10.3390/land11101714

28. Charrua, A.B., Padmanaban, R., Cabral, P., Bandeira, S., Romeiras, M.M.: Impacts of the tropical cyclone idai in mozambique: a multi-temporal landsat satellite imagery analysis. Remote Sens. **13**, 201 (2021). https://doi.org/10.3390/rs13020201

29. Warui, M.W., Manohar, S., Obade, P.: Current status, utilization, succession and zonation of mangrove ecosystem along Mida Creek, Kenya. Int. J. Bonorowo Wetlands, **10**. (2020). https://doi.org/10.13057/bonorowo/w100103

30. Jumawan, J. and Macandog, D.: GIS weighted suitability analysis as decision support tool for mangrove rehabilitation in Oriental Mindoro, Philippines. J. Ecosyst. Sci. Eco-Govern. **3**, 1–13. (2021). https://journals.carsu.edu.ph/JESEG/article/view/35

31. Gnanappazham, L., Prasad, K.A., Dadhwal, V.K.: Geospatial tools for mapping and monitoring coastal mangroves. In: Mangroves: Ecology, Biodiversity and Management. 475–551. (2021). https://doi.org/10.1007/978-981-16-2494-0_21

32. Orimoloye, I.R., Mazinyo, S.P., Kalumba, A.M., Nel, W., Adigun, A.I., Ololade, O.O.: Wetland shift monitoring using remote sensing and GIS techniques: landscape dynamics and its implications on Isimangaliso Wetland Park. South Africa. Earth Sci. Inform. **12**, 553–563 (2019). https://doi.org/10.1007/s12145-019-00400-4

33. Hickey, S.M., Phinn, S.R., Callow, N.J., Van Niel, K.P., Hansen, J.E., Duarte, C.M.: Is climate change shifting the poleward limit of mangroves? ESCO. (2017). https://doi.org/10.1007/s12237-017-0211-8

34. Kairo, J., Mbatha, A., Murithi, M.M., Mungai, F.: Total ecosystem carbon stocks of mangroves in Lamu, Kenya; and their potential contributions to the climate change Agenda in the country. Front. For. Glob. Change. **4**, 709227 (2021). https://doi.org/10.3389/ffgc.2021.709227

35. Twilley, R.R., Rivera-Monroy, V.H., Chen, R., Botero, L.: Adapting an ecological mangrove model to simulate trajectories in restoration ecology. Mar. Pollut. Bull. (1999). https://doi.org/10.1016/S0025-326X(99)00137-X

36. Rivera-Monroy, V.H., Zhao, X., Wang, H., Xue, Z.G.: Are existing modeling tools useful to evaluate outcomes in mangrove restoration and rehabilitation projects? A Minireview Forests **13**, 1638 (2022). https://doi.org/10.3390/f13101638

37. Adams, J.B., Raw, J.L., Mbense, S.P., Bornman, T.G., Rajkaran, A., Van Niekerk, L.: Climate change and South Africa's blue carbon ecosystems. Water Res. Commission Rep. (2019). https://doi.org/10.1016/j.ecss.2020.106862

38. John, E., Bunting, P., Hardy, A., Roberts, O., Giliba, R., Silayo, D.S.: Modelling the impact of climate change on Tanzanian forests. Divers. Distrib. **26**, 1663–1686 (2020). https://doi.org/10.1111/ddi.13152

39. Niquisse, S., Cabral, P., Rodrigues, Â., Augusto, G.: Ecosystem services and biodiversity trends in Mozambique as a consequence of land cover change. Int. J. Biodivers. Sci. Ecosyst. Serv. Manag. (2017). https://doi.org/10.1080/21513732.2017.1349836

40. Hamza, A.: Understanding changes in mangrove forests and the implications to community livelihood and resource management in Kenya. Doctoral Thesis. Bournemouth University. (2022)

41. Mahamoud, A., Maher, G., Mohamed, N.A., Hamada, S.H., Montacer, M.: Monitoring shoreline change using remote sensing, GIS, and field surveys: a case study of the Ngazidja Island Coast Comoros. Arab. J. Geosci. (2023). https://doi.org/10.1007/s12517-023-11200-y

42. Ngowo, R.G., Ribeiro, M.C., Pereira, M.J.: Quantifying 28-year (1991–2019) shoreline change trends along the Mnazi Bay-Ruvuma Estuary Marine Park. RSASE, Tanzania (2021). https://doi.org/10.1016/j.rsase.2021.100607

43. Guo, Y., Liao, J., Shen, G.: Mapping large-scale mangroves along the maritime silk road from 1990 to 2015 using a novel deep learning model and landsat data. Remote Sens. **13**, 245 (2021). https://doi.org/10.3390/rs13020245

44. The Marine Diaries. https://www.themarinediaries.com/tmd-blog/conserving-mangroves-a-community-based-approach

45. Käyhkö, N., et al.: The role of place-based local knowledge in supporting integrated coastal and marine spatial planning in Zanzibar Tanzania. Ocean Coast. Manag. (2019). https://doi.org/10.1016/j.ocecoaman.2019.04.016

46. Global wetlands project. https://globalwetlandsproject.org/harnessing-big-data-to-support-mangrove-conservation-and-rehabilitation/

47. AUDA-NEPAD.https://www.nepad.org/blog/protecting-mozambican-mangroves-preservation-through-innovation-and-emerging-technologies#_ftn23

48. Ericsson. https://www.ericsson.com/en/blog/2022/10/connected-mangroves-and-climate-change-mitigation--ericsson

49. World Wildlife Foundation. https://www.worldwildlife.org/projects/manglaria-using-artificial-intelligence-to-save-mangroves-in-a-changing-climate

50. Medium. https://medium.com/we-the-peoples/can-technology-help-us-adapt-to-climate-change-ddd06264b07e

51. Rog, S.M., Clarke, R.H., Minnema, E., Cook, C.N.: Tackling the tide: A rapid assessment protocol to detect terrestrial vertebrates in mangrove forests. Biodivers. Conserv. **29**, 2839–2860 (2020). https://doi.org/10.1007/s10531-020-02001-w

52. Naha, D., Jhala, Y.V., Qureshi, Q., Roy, M., Sankar, K., Gopal, R.: Ranging, activity and habitat use by tigers in the mangrove forests of the Sundarban. PLoS ONE **11**, e0152119 (2016). https://doi.org/10.1371/journal.pone.0152119

53. Amma, P.K.G., Bhaskaran, P.K.: Role of mangroves in wind-wave climate modeling–A review. J. Coast. Conserv. **24**, 21 (2020). https://doi.org/10.1007/s11852-020-00740-0

54. UNFCCC. https://unfccc.int/ttclear/misc_/StaticFiles/gnwoerk_static/2020_coastalzones/b9e88f6fea374d8aa5cb44115d201160/3863c9fabdf74ea49710189acbf6907a.pdf

Unveiling the Power of Apomediation: Perspectives from Individuals Living with Autoimmune Disease

Eldridge van der Westhuizen[✉], Dalenca Pottas, and Sue Petratos

Nelson Mandela University, Port Elizabeth, South Africa
eldridge@mandela.ac.za

Abstract. The contemporary patient typically conducts online research prior to consulting a physician. They are no longer solely reliant on healthcare professionals for information, instead empowered to engage in independent research and collaborate with fellow individuals who possess first-hand experiences with their condition. In this digital age, social networking sites are progressively emerging as a popular resource for patients seeking information and support. This highlights the transformative potential of social networking platforms as channels for apomediation—where patients actively seek and share medical information and support, primarily through online platforms, beyond the confines of traditional healthcare channels. Ultimately, the modern patient plays an active and empowered role in their healthcare journey. Understanding their specific requirements becomes crucial in amplifying the value of tools such as social networking services. These platforms serve as vehicles to enhance apomediation, facilitating the exchange of health-related information and support among patients. The purpose of this study was to understand the requirements of individuals with autoimmune disease in respect of apomediation. By comprehensively examining these requirements, the study aimed to contribute to a better understanding of how the needs of individuals with autoimmune disease can best be served in a disintermediated setting using technology-based interactions.

Keywords: Apomediation · Disintermediation · Autoimmune · Trustworthiness · Credibility · Autonomy · Self-efficacy · Knowledgeable · Empowerment · Disempowerment · Interpretation · Misinterpretation · Salience · Accuracy · Self-management

1 Background

The ability to gain access, and make use of health information effectively, is critical to patient empowerment and allows them to feel in control of their health [1]. There has been a major, and positive, change in the information available to patients in the past couple of years, which has provided an increase in patient independence in medical care. With the rapid proliferation of health information on the internet, more patients are turning to online health as a first point of call versus the conventional manner of

© The Author(s), under exclusive license to Springer Nature Switzerland AG 2025
K. Hinkelmann and H. Smuts (Eds.): Society 5.0 2024, CCIS 2173, pp. 348–365, 2025.
https://doi.org/10.1007/978-3-031-71412-2_26

seeking a professional diagnosis by consulting a doctor [2]. The rise of health-related information available online has led to patients feeling more empowered and able to take control of their own health. The tendency of pursuing the input of others to enhance decision making does not necessarily mean that patients are now using online resources to replace the expert advice from their physicians [3]. Patients are using their newly found online knowledge to increase their understanding of their respective health problems to enable them to either acknowledge or question their doctor's diagnosis and treatment recommendations. In reality, patients might use both online information and doctors in a harmonising manner, or simply the easiest, or most appropriate information source, first [4]. Currently the easiest information source is the internet, and more specifically social networking sites focusing on health. These sites involve "the explicit modelling of connections between people, forming a complete network of relations, which in turn enables and facilitates collaboration and collaborative filtering processes" [5], p. [6]. The process of "cutting out the middleman" to go directly to the provider of a product or services is referred to as disintermediation. "As a result of this disintermediation, traditional intermediaries are being both complemented and replaced by apomediaries, who stand by consumers to guide them to trustworthy information, and/or provide credibility cues for information" [4, p. 144].

Apomediation is a term coined by Dr Gunther Eysenbach, who is a Health Policy and eHealth Professor at the University of Toronto. The term is best explained by Dr. Eysenbach himself, who states that apomediation is a new scholarly socio-technological term that characterises the process of disintermediation (intermediaries are middlemen or gatekeepers, e.g., health professionals giving relevant information to a patient, and disintermediation means to bypass them), whereby the former intermediaries are functionally replaced by apomediaries, i.e. network, group or collaborative filtering processes [4]. Eysenbach further states that "the difference between an intermediary and an apomediary is that an intermediary stands in between the consumer and information or service they are trying to obtain, i.e., is absolutely necessary to get a specific information or service. In contrast to this, apomediation means that there are people or tools available to direct a consumer to high quality information or services, without there being a requirement to obtain that information or service in the first place" [6]. Apomediation comprises the process of enriching health information of individuals with collaborative filtering and recommender systems like bookmarking, blogs, wikis and communication tools like social networking sites [5]. These systems enable their users to better understand and comprehend health information contained in prescriptions, notes written by a doctor and information contained in patient files. Some terminology and acronyms are worthless to a non-medical person, but having access to these wikis, blogs, and similar tools, it is possible to understand the health condition. It is the nature of social networking sites to provide peer support to individuals. It fosters communication, involvement, teamwork, and user-centeredness.

Most individuals that turn to the internet for help, have a desire to obtain more information to be sure that they have not missed anything important regarding their condition. Social networking sites have been widely used in the health context for individuals with health-related issues. It was the primary source of health information for many people during the COVID-19 pandemic [7]. Whether this online health information was factual or not is one of the reasons why apomediation is so vital concerning online health information, especially for social networking sites.

In an effort to increase the credibility of online health information, apomediaries can assist users to navigate through the onslaught of information provided by digital media, and provide credibility cues and additional metainformation to support the patient [4]. A renewed effort to provide grounded guidelines for consumers to determine quality health information is a research priority [8]. Many people searching for online health information trust the information and advice they find. However, this trust may be misplaced. The "degree to which apomediaries succeed in the same way as intermediaries in filtering and interpreting health information is largely unexplored" and that there is tremendous opportunity for research on this topic [4, p. 134].

In this study, we investigated how the needs of individuals with autoimmune disease can best be served in a disintermediated setting using a qualitative descriptive approach. An autoimmune disease is a disorder where the immune system is overactive, and the body begins to attack and damage its own tissue [9]. The immune system responds by producing antibodies that instead of fighting the infections, attack the body's own healthy tissue. Unfortunately, there is currently no cure for autoimmune disease, hence the importance to treat your specific condition correctly and receive the necessary support from your peers.

2   Methods

2.1   Literature Review

A literature review informed the conceptualization of the concept of "apomediation" as a starting point to determining the requirements of patients with autoimmune disease in respect of apomediation. The theories and models that informed the conceptualization are The Dynamic Intermediation/Disintermediation/Apomediation Model (DIDA) [4], The Disempowerment /Empowerment Model [10], Trust and Credibility Theories [11] and Information Seeking Behaviour [12]. Through a process of thematic analysis, 16 principal themes were identified from this literature review and these themes became the thematic framework used to capture the needs of individuals with autoimmune disease in respect of apomediation.

2.2   Questionnaire Design

This questionnaire was designed using a 4-point Likert scale, deliberately chosen for its capacity to distinctly capture participants' agreement or disagreement with statements, devoid of a neutral option. Employing this scale effectively facilitates the analysis of specific viewpoints and considerations held by study participants pertaining to the phenomenon under investigation [13]. Furthermore, the survey design fosters enriched responses by enabling participants to supplement their answers through open-ended questions, thus enhancing the depth of their input. A ranking query to assess the significance of various identified components highlighted in the study, is included. A succinct summary of the survey's content is presented in Table 1.

Table 1. Survey content

Nature of questions	Comment/example
Biographical data	Age (various age groupings provided)
	Number of years living with Autoimmune Disease(s)
Questions answered with 4-point Likert scale	16 Questions were based on the thematic framework
Questions answered through narrative	Participants were offered the opportunity to provide explanations of their choices in the 16 Likert-based questions to enhance the understanding of the participants' perspectives
Open-ended questions	Two questions inquired about participants' specific requirements regarding apomediation and invited them to share any additional information they deemed relevant
Ranking question	One question asked participants to rank in order of importance, the benefits received from apomediation

The researcher created the questionnaire using a software platform, QuestionPro[1], which allows online collection of data. Ethical clearance was obtained from the Faculty of Engineering, the Built Environment and Technology Research Ethics Committee (Human) at the Nelson Mandela University with reference number H21-ENG-ITE-005.

2.3 Sampling Procedures: Recruitment, Selection, and Sample Size

The researcher employed purposive sampling by approaching individuals affected by autoimmune disease through private Facebook groups. In addition, snowball sampling was employed, with invitations extended to individuals who had expressed interest [14]. Participants were required to meet two criteria for questionnaire completion: firstly, they had to be aged 18 years or above; secondly, they needed to be presently living with either an autoimmune disease or multiple autoimmune conditions. The questionnaire garnered a total of 473 views, resulting in 73 responses, with 31 of them being complete responses, thereby achieving a completion rate of 42.5%.

The predominant age of the participants was between 45 and 54, with the 35–44 age group also well represented, as depicted in Fig. 1.

---

[1] Https://www.questionpro.com/

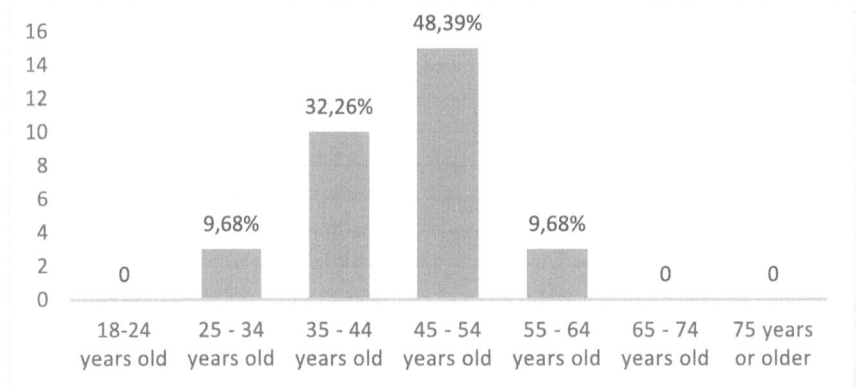

	Answer	Count	Percent
1.	18-24 years old	0	0.00%
2.	25 - 34 years old	3	9.68%
3.	35 - 44 years old	10	32.26%
4.	45 - 54 years old	15	48.39%
5.	55 - 64 years old	3	9.68%
6.	65 - 74 years old	0	0.00%
7.	75 years or older	0	0.00%
	Total	31	100%

Fig. 1. Survey age group classification.

There was also a good distribution between the participants based on the years they have been living with autoimmune disease(s). Some individuals were recently diagnosed (between 1–5 years), while others have had the disease for more than 20 years. This is depicted in Fig. 2.

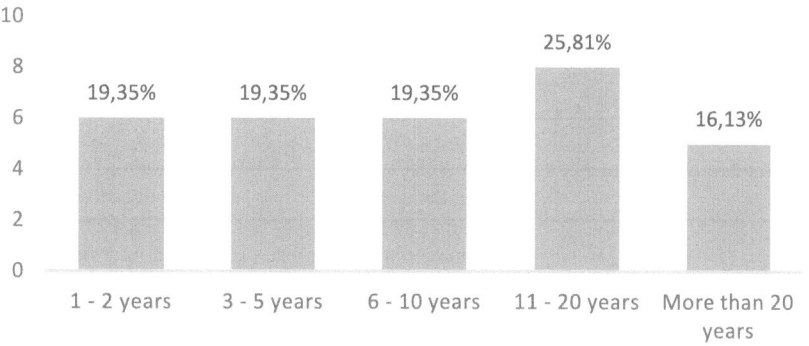

	Answer	Count	Percent
1.	1 - 2 years	6	19.35%
2.	3 - 5 years	6	19.35%
3.	6 - 10 years	6	19.35%
4.	11 - 20 years	8	25.81%
5.	More than 20 years	5	16.13%
	Total	31	100%

Fig. 2. Survey participants' years of living with autoimmune disease(s)

2.4   Data Collection and Analysis

A link to the questionnaire was posted within select private Facebook groups where membership comprises individuals affected by autoimmune disease. These individuals were encouraged to extend the invitation to participate to others among their acquaintances, who meet the requirements to participate.

The responses were captured using QuestionPro and quantitative results were summarised by the tool and availed to the researcher in numerical and visual formats. The questionnaire also enabled participants to supplement their answers through open-ended questions, thus enhancing the depth of their input. This qualitative data collected brings a deeper understanding to this research and was analysed using thematic analysis. The data was first arranged and collated, and the researcher could then identify keywords which lead to the generation of themes based on the reoccurrence of patterns or words.

3   Results

3.1   Thematic Framework

The outcome of a comprehensive literature review to determine patients' requirements in respect of apomediation is shown in Table 2. It is categorised into 16 identified components that formed the foundation of the statement questions in the survey.

Table 2. Components of apomediation – literature review

Component name [References used to identify components, descriptions, and requirements]	Description	Requirements
Intermediation/Disintermediation [15, 16]	Disintermediation is giving the user or the consumer direct access to information that otherwise would require a mediator. In contrast to this, intermediation is defined as the act of coming between	Patients want to make informed decisions and sometimes need to bypass the traditional intermediated model of the patient/doctor relationship
Trustworthiness [17, 18]	The ability to keep promises, to be honest, reliable and principled while never inappropriately betraying a confidence	The information provided on the apomediary platforms should be trustworthy
Credibility [17, 19]	The quality of being believed or trusted	The information provided on the apomediary platforms should be credible
Autonomy/Decision Making [20, 21]	A self-governing state	The patient should have a free choice to decide whether to make use of the proposed information apomediary platforms
Self-Efficacy [22, 23]	Refers to an individual's belief in his or her capacity to execute behaviours necessary to produce specific performance attainments	Helping a fellow patient with a similar condition to what you have creates a positive feedback loop where the individual's self-efficacy is boosted. This increased self-efficacy is a patient requirement of the apomediary platform
Knowledgeable [24, 25]	Possessing knowledge, insight and understanding	Patients, their insights, and rising knowledge are an essential part of this new world and a key requirement of an apomediary platform to distinguish between facts, truth and myths

(*continued*)

Table 2. (*continued*)

Component name [References used to identify components, descriptions, and requirements]	Description	Requirements
Empowerment/Disempowerment [26–28]	Empowering individuals means providing them with opportunities and the environment to develop skills, confidence, and knowledge to move from passive recipients to active partners in their journey. Disempowerment is most commonly an effect of discrimination, and a form of bullying	It is a requirement for the patient using these platforms to be more empowered and believe in their own abilities to control their own situation
Information Seeking [29, 30]	The process of attempting to obtain information in both human and technological contexts	The patient requires real-time interactions with fellow sufferers. This should reduce the information seeking barriers as the patient now has a wealth of tried and tested knowledge available from individuals on the same road
Patient/Doctor Relationship [31, 32]	A unique relationship between patient and doctor based on trust, honesty, respect and a mutual desire to improve health outcomes	Improved doctor/patient relationship as the patient has a wealth of information from fellow sufferers. The concept of Shared Decision Making requires the patient and doctor entering into a health journey partnership
Interpretation/Misinterpretation [24, 25]	It is either the correct or incorrect understanding of a matter	The patient should be fully aware that the apomediary platforms do not provide official medical advice by approved medical doctors and it is up to the patient to interpret this information as he/she pleases

(*continued*)

Table 2. (*continued*)

Component name [References used to identify components, descriptions, and requirements]	Description	Requirements
Health Literacy [33, 34]	The degree to which an individual has the capacity to obtain, process and understand basic health information in order to make appropriate health decisions	Apomediary platforms providing health information and support to patients should allow for simple, quick and inexpensive support from peers to assist fellow patients to understand certain health information better
Self-management [35, 36]	Ability to prioritise goals, decide what must be done and be accountable to complete the necessary actions	The use of the apomediary platforms should encourage the connection and facilitation of communication between individuals with similar conditions in a way previously not possible. Sometimes the patient just needs peers to listen and provide support
Access to Information [24, 37]	Critical for enabling individuals to exercise their voice and enter into informed dialogue about life altering decisions	Having a wealth of tried and tested information available from individuals on the same road as you via the apomediary platforms, is a requirement from patients
Accuracy and Completeness of Information [38, 39]	Accuracy is to ensure that information is correct and without any mistakes. Completeness refers to how comprehensive the information is, it would be unusable if the information is incomplete	The information provided by my peers and site administrators should be accurate and complete as there is a huge risk of inaccurate information with regards to content on some of the apomediary platforms

(*continued*)

Table 2. (*continued*)

Component name [References used to identify components, descriptions, and requirements]	Description	Requirements
Psychological adaptation [40]	Individuals' internal and cellular features enable them to survive in their environment	Health information seeking is a mechanism for dealing with uncertainties, crisis and gaining control of your life after stressful health situations. Therefore, the psychological adaption to the disease is faster due to the patient being more informed. There should be a feeling of hope and a brighter future due to peer support on the apomediary platforms
Salience [4, 40]	The information retrieved by the seeker satisfies their information needs and is applicable	Sometimes all an individual needs are their peers on these apomediary platforms to listen and provide support, which leads to a feeling of hope and a brighter future

3.2   Questionnaire Results

The requirements of individuals with autoimmune disease according to the questionnaire output supports the 16 components identified via literature study as identified in Table 2. Statements can be mapped to components identified in the literature review as indicated in Table 3. The results of the 16 statements are also included in Table 3. They are ranked according to most agreed to least agreed with the corresponding statement number in the survey in the first column. Take note that the disagree % column is a total of the strongly disagree and disagree outcome in the questionnaire, while the agree % column is a total of the strongly agree and agree outcome in the questionnaire.

Table 3. Statement survey results

Statement No	Statement	Mapping to component	Disagree	Agree
4	I have a free choice to decide whether to make use of the proposed information and guidance messages on the social networking support groups	Autonomy/Decision making	0%	100%
5	I am fully aware that these social networking support groups do not provide official medical advice by approved medical doctors	Interpretation	0%	100%
8	Social networking support groups allow for real-time interactions with fellow sufferers and reduces the information seeking barriers	Health literacy	0%	100%
9	Health information seeking is a mechanism for dealing with uncertainties, crisis and gaining control of your life after stressful health situations. Therefore, the psychological adaption to the disease is faster due to the patient being more informed	Psychological adaption	0%	100%

(*continued*)

Table 3. (*continued*)

Statement No	Statement	Mapping to component	Disagree	Agree
10	The use of social networking support groups encourages the connection and facilitation of communication between individuals with similar conditions in a way previously not possible	Intermediation/Disintermediation	0%	100%
7	Social networking support groups allow for simple, quick and inexpensive support from your peers	Health literacy	3,23%	96,77%
11	The use of social networking support groups gives you a sense of belonging	Self-management	3,23%	96,77%
14	As a fellow patient with a condition, I feel a sense of fulfilment helping my fellow patient by providing assistance on social networking support groups	Self-efficacy	3,23%	96,77%
12	Being part of social networking support groups make you now feel more empowered and have belief in your own abilities to be in control of your situation	Empowerment	6,45%	93,55%

(*continued*)

Table 3. (*continued*)

Statement No	Statement	Mapping to component	Disagree	Agree
13	The information received from these online support groups satisfy your needs and is it applicable to you	Salience	9,68%	90,32%
6	Online information is exchanged in real-time and in a way not possible in real life communities	Access to Information	12,91%	87,09%
16	The introduction of modern health technology aids like health sensors, wearable technology, mobile health apps and health symptom capturing tools like personal health records, has led to patient autonomy and supports the apomediation process	Autonomy/Decision Making, Knowledgeable	12,91%	87,09%
1	There is a risk of inaccurate information with regards to content on social networking support groups	Accuracy and completeness	19,36%	80,64%

(*continued*)

Table 3. (*continued*)

Statement No	Statement	Mapping to component	Disagree	Agree
15	The social networking support groups leads to improved doctor/patient relationships as the patient has a wealth of information available from fellow sufferers. This leads to shared decision making where the patient and doctor enters into a health journey partnership	Patient/Doctor relationship	29,04%	70,96%
2	The information provided on the social networking support groups, is trustworthy and credible	Trustworthiness, Credibility	32,26%	67,74%
3	The information provided by my peers and site administrators is accurate and complete	Accuracy and completeness	32,26%	67,74%

Looking at the results holistically, most participants agreed with the statements put to them obtained via the literature study. Some statements, however, received higher levels of disagreement than others, like statements 2,3 and 15. In contrast, statements 4,5, 8, 9 and 10 received no disagreement and show that the participants fully agreed with these statements. Based on the questionnaire results, three distinct groups of components can be identified that relates to the requirements of individuals with autoimmune disease in respect of apomediation. They are grouping of components that received 100% agreement, grouping of components that received less than 75% agreement (worst components based on survey), and the middle grouping of components that received between 99% and 75% agreement. This is indicated in Table 4.

Table 4. Component grouping

Strongest components (100%)	Middle (75 – 99%)	Weakest components (< 75%)
Autonomy/Decision Making	Health Literacy	Patient/Doctor relationship
Interpretation	Self-management	Trustworthiness
Information Seeking	Self-efficacy	Credibility
Psychological adaption	Empowerment	Accuracy and completeness
Intermediation/Disintermediation	Salience	
	Access to Information	
	Knowledgeable	

Key themes that could be highlighted from the open-ended questions in the questionnaire is the need to obtain more information about the participant's condition. The participants also valued the support of the community and the feeling of inclusiveness and belonging. The role of the doctor was also highlighted, and suggestions were given that the relationship between the doctor and the patient could potentially be strengthened by making doctors part of these online groups to enable them to better understand the patient's journey. A doctor's advice on these online support groups would also be valuable.

4   Conclusion

Requirements of individuals with autoimmune disease in respect of apomediation that were identified by literature study were confirmed by the results of this survey. Sixteen components were identified and ranked in three groupings according to their importance. Although some components were deemed as more important by the participants of the survey, all components are key for the successful usage of social networking sites by individuals with autoimmune disease in respect of apomediation. Future research can use these components to create a tool to determine the extent to which social networking sites support apomediation for individuals with autoimmune disease.

Acknowledgments. Financial assistance were received to conduct this study/analysis in the form of a Research Capacity Development grant as well as support for editorial work from the Nelson Mandela University.

Disclosure of Interests. The authors have no competing interests to declare that are relevant to the content of this article.

References

1. Patel, S., Dowse, R.: Understanding the medicines information-seeking behaviour and information needs of South African long-term patients with limited literacy skills. Health Expect. **18**(5), 1494–1507 (2015). https://doi.org/10.1111/hex.12131
2. Tan, S.S., Goonawardene, N.: Internet health information seeking and the patient-physician relationship: a systematic review. J. Med. Internet Res. **19**(1), e9 (2017). https://doi.org/10.2196/jmir.5729
3. Hesse BW., Connell, MO., Augustson EM., Sylvia W., Shaikh AR., Rutten LJF.: Realizing the Promise of Web 2.0: engaging community intelligence. Health (San Francisco) 16 (1), 1–20 (2012). https://doi.org/10.1080/10810730.2011.589882
4. Eysenbach G.: Credibility of health information and digital media: new perspectives and implications for youth. digital media, youth, and credibility. In: M. J. Metzger, A. J. Flanagin (Eds.), The John D and Catherine T MacArthur Foundation Series on Digital Media and Learning, pp. 123–154. Cambridge, MA: The MIT Press (2008).
5. Eysenbach, G.: Medicine 2.0: Social networking, collaboration, participation, apomediation, and openness. J. Med. Internet Res. 10 (3), 1–11 (2008) https://doi.org/10.2196/jmir.1030
6. Eysenbach G.: Apomediation (2010). https://wiki.p2pfoundation.net/Apomediation
7. Zhong, Y., Liu, W., Lee, T.Y., Zhao, H., Ji, J.: Risk perception, knowledge, information sources and emotional states among COVID-19 patients in Wuhan. China. Nursing Outlook **69**(1), 13–21 (2021). https://doi.org/10.1016/j.outlook.2020.08.005
8. Keselman, A., Logan, R., Arnott, S.C., Leroy, G., Zeng-Treitler, Q.: Developing informatics tools and strategies for consumer-centred health communication. J. Am. Med. Inform. Assoc. **15**(4), 473–483 (2008). https://doi.org/10.1197/jamia.M2744
9. Martins K.: What is an autoimmune disease?. WebMD. (2023). https://www.webmd.com/a-to-z-guides/autoimmune-diseases
10. Faulkner, M.: Empowerment and disempowerment: models of staff/patient interaction. NT Res. **6**(6), 936–948 (2001)
11. Metzger, M.J., Flanagin, A.J.: Credibility and trust of information in online environments: the use of cognitive heuristics. J. Pragmat. **59**(b), 210–220 (2013). https://doi.org/10.1016/j.pragma.2013.07.012
12. Zare-Farashbandi, F., Lalazaryan, A.: A review of models and theories of health information seeking behavior. Int. J. Health Syst. Disast. Manag. **2**(4), 193–203 (2014). https://doi.org/10.4103/2347-9019.144371
13. Leung, S.: A comparison of psychometric properties and normality in 4-, 5-, 6-, and 11-point Likert scales. J. Soc. Serv. Res. **37**(4), 412–421 (2011)
14. Naderifar, M., Goli, H., Ghaljaie, F.: Snowball sampling: a purposeful method of sampling in qualitative research. Strid. Dev. Med. Educ. (2017). https://doi.org/10.5812/sdme.67670
15. Boucher, J.L.: Technology and patient-provider interactions: improving quality of care, but is it improving communication and collaboration. Diabetes Spectr. **23**(3), 142–144 (2010). https://doi.org/10.2337/diaspect.23.3.142
16. Partridge, S.R., Gallagher, P., Freeman, B., Gallagher, R.: Facebook groups for the management of chronic diseases. J. Med. Internet Res. (2018). https://doi.org/10.2196/jmir.7558
17. Dalmer, N.K.: Questioning reliability assessments of health information on social media. J. Med. Libr. Assoc. **105**(1), 61–68 (2017). https://doi.org/10.5195/jmla.2017.108

18. Heath, S.: What drives patient trust in online medical info sources? Patient Engagement Hit (2017). https://patientengagementhit.com/news/what-drives-patient-trust-in-online-medical-info-sources
19. Un Kim, S., Yeon Syn, S.: Credibility and usefulness of health information on Facebook: A survey study with U.S. college students. Informat. Res. 21 (4) (2016).
20. Bernstein, C.A.: Take control of your health care (exert your patient autonomy). Harvard Health Blog - Harvard Health Publishing (2018). https://www.health.harvard.edu/blog/take-control-of-your-health-care-exert-your-patient-autonomy-2018050713784
21. Ringstad, Ø.: Patient autonomy in a digitalized world: supporting patients' autonomous choice. Croat. Med. J. **57**(1), 80–82 (2016). https://doi.org/10.3325/cmj.2016.57.80
22. Mental Health Foundation.: Peer Support (2021). https://www.mentalhealth.org.uk/a-to-z/p/peer-support
23. Prescott, J., Rathbone, A.L., Hanley, T.: Online mental health communities, self-efficacy and transition to further support. Ment. Health Rev. J. **25**(4), 329–344 (2020). https://doi.org/10.1108/MHRJ-12-2019-0048
24. Hodgkin P., Horsley L., Metz B.: The emerging world of online health communities. Stanford Soc. Innov. Rev. (2018). https://ssir.org/articles/entry/the_emerging_world_of_online_health_communities
25. Newberry C.: How to use social media in healthcare: a guide for health professionals. Hootsuite (2020). https://blog.hootsuite.com/social-media-health-care/
26. Benetoli, A., Chen, T.F., Aslani, P.: How patients' use of social media impacts their interactions with healthcare professionals. Patient Educ. Couns. **101**(3), 439–444 (2018). https://doi.org/10.1016/j.pec.2017.08.015
27. Househ, M., Borycki, E., Kushniruk, A.: Empowering patients through social media: the benefits and challenges. Health Inform. J. (2014). https://doi.org/10.1177/1460458213476969
28. Wong-Rieger D.: Patient empowerment – living with chronic disease. In: The 1st European Conference on Patient Empowerment, pp. 1–23 (2012)
29. Alwi, E., Murad, M.: Online information seeking: a review of the literature in the health domain. Int. J. Comput. Inform. Eng. **12**(12), 1025–1031 (2018)
30. Lee, K., Hoti, K., Hughes, J.D., Emmerton, L.: Dr google and the consumer: a qualitative study exploring the navigational needs and online health information-seeking behaviors of consumers with chronic health conditions. J. Med. Internet Res. **16**(12), 1–13 (2014). https://doi.org/10.2196/jmir.3706
31. da Mota, L.R.A., Ferreira, C.C.G., da Costa Neto, H.A.A., Falbo, A.R., de Barros Lorena, S.: Is doctor-patient relationship influenced by health online information? Rev. Assoc. Med. Bras. 64 (8), 692–699 (2018)
32. Ennis-O'Connor M.: What's the Influence of Patients' Internet Health Information-Seeking Behaviour on the Patient-Physician Relationship? Health Care Social Media (2019). https://hcsmmonitor.com/2019/10/08/whats-the-influence-of-patients-internet-health-information-seeking-behaviour-on-the-patient-physician-relationship/
33. Christmann S.: Health Literacy and Internet: Recommendations to promote Health Literacy by the means of the Internet. Health Care (April 2005)
34. Shiferaw, K.B., Tilahun, B.C., Endehabtu, B.F., Gullslett, M.K., Mengiste, S.A.: E-health literacy and associated factors among chronic patients in a low-income country: a cross-sectional survey. BMC Med. Inform. Decis. Mak. **20**(1), 1–9 (2020). https://doi.org/10.1186/s12911-020-01202-1
35. Celler, B.G., Lovell, N.H., Basilakis, J.: Using information technology to improve the management of chronic disease. Med. J. Aust. **179**(5), 242–246 (2003). https://doi.org/10.1111/j.1471-1842-2007.00758

36. Ure, C., Cooper-Ryan, A.M., Condie, J., Galpin, A.: Exploring strategies for using social media to self-manage health care when living with and beyond breast cancer: in-depth qualitative study. J. Med. Internet Res. (2020). https://doi.org/10.2196/16902
37. Korp, P.: Health on the Internet: implications for health promotion. Health Educ. Res. **21**(1), 78–86 (2006). https://doi.org/10.1093/her/cyh043
38. Basavakumar, D., Flegg, M., Eccles, J., Ghezzi, P.: Accuracy, completeness and accessibility of online information on fibromyalgia. Rheumatol. Int. **39**(4), 735–742 (2019). https://doi.org/10.1007/s00296-019-04265-0
39. Dutta-Bergman, M.J.: The impact of completeness and web use motivation on the credibility of e-health information. J. Commun. **54**(2), 253–269 (2004). https://doi.org/10.1111/j.1460-2466.2004.tb02627.x
40. Zare-Farashbandi, F., Lalazaryan, A.: A review of models and theories of health information seeking behavior. Int. J. Health Syst. Disaster Manag. **2**(4), 193 (2014)

A Conceptual Framework for Digitalized Payment Systems in South Africa

Mvelo Walaza$^{(\boxtimes)}$ (ID) and Sunet Eybers

University of South Africa, Pretoria, South Africa
53315804@mylife.unisa.ac.za

Abstract. South Africa is regarded as a dual economy in which a significant financial and digital gap exists between people who live in rural, underdeveloped areas and those who live in urban, developed areas. The people who live in rural areas are often referred to as financially excluded because they do not fully participate in the country's economy. In such environments, the financially excluded frequently travel long distances to access financial products and services. A payment system is any system used to settle financial transactions by transferring monetary value. The digitalization of payment systems, in the context of this study, refers to the modernization and enhancement of payment systems using innovation and technology. This paper explores digitalizing South African payment systems so that the financially excluded can access basic banking. Financial inclusion refers to people and businesses accessing good banking resources, financial products, and services – resulting in improved economic growth. The study is underpinned by the Technology-Organization-Environment (TOE) framework as a lens to understand TOE elements relevant to the digitalization (technology) assisting the South African banking industry (organization) in its attempt to foster financial inclusivity of those living in the rural areas (environment). This study used a systematic review of the literature to propose a conceptual research framework that could be used to investigate the digitalization of payment systems in the South African banking industry for financial inclusion.

Keywords: digitalized payment systems · financial inclusivity · Technology-Organization-Environment framework

1 Introduction

There's a movement worldwide to include marginalized groups and financially excluded people so that they can fully participate in the mainstream economy [32, 42]. In line with the movement, increased efforts focus on including the financially excluded groups in the banking system, such as those living in rural areas and other marginalized populations [1]. In many ways, technology helps close social and economic disparities, including the underprivileged and excluded in the financial sector, some of the most marginalized groups in society. The research question of this study is: *What focus areas should be considered when constructing a conceptual framework for digital payment systems to*

© The Author(s), under exclusive license to Springer Nature Switzerland AG 2025
K. Hinkelmann and H. Smuts (Eds.): Society 5.0 2024, CCIS 2173, pp. 366–377, 2025.
https://doi.org/10.1007/978-3-031-71412-2_27

achieve financial inclusion in South Africa? This paper explores the digitalization of South African payment systems so that the financially excluded can access basic banking systems.

Financial inclusion refers to people and businesses having access to good banking resources, financial products, and services [24]. It plays a vital role in inclusive economic growth and social development. According to the World Bank [43] financial inclusion helps countries boost shared prosperity through sustainable growth and end extreme poverty for the financially excluded population.

In many rural areas, no banking infrastructure is available for the financially excluded population. In some of these areas (small towns), there are often limited essential services and products such as debit and credit facilities (Automated Teller Machines (ATM) and Point of Sale devices), insurance, investment, and savings facilities [10]. For the financially excluded to get access to the banking system in the emerging era of digital payment systems, there needs to be a concerted effort from regulators and banking participants to improve Information and Communication Technology (ICT) infrastructure and resources in those areas [21].

The South African government, through its regulatory bodies in the field of banking, is aiming to move towards conducting financial transactions digitally [36], enabling banking access through digital payment systems. In this article, the researcher focuses on the financially excluded population in rural areas and attempts to align with the global movement of digitalizing payment systems for financial inclusion.

The remainder of the paper starts with a background section, providing valuable contextual information about the South African banking industry, financial exclusion and socio-economic conditions, and countries with digital payment systems. This is followed by a discussion of the benefits and challenges associated with digital payment systems. The underlying theoretical theory for the study is presented, followed by the methodological approach, data analysis, and conceptual framework presentation and discussion. A conclusion section completes the paper.

2 Background

The services offered by commercial banks in South Africa can be divided into four categories – namely, personal banking, investment banking, loans, and foreign exchange [7]. The banking industry in South Africa is highly regulated, with the central bank, known as the South African Reserve Bank (SARB), and its participants (banks) playing a pivotal role in their regulation. The SARB is the fourth oldest central bank established outside of Europe, followed by the Bank of Indonesia, the Bank of Japan, and the Federal Reserve. To keep up with changing times, the SARB periodically had to evolve in its quest to align with changing domestic and international developments and accommodate the socio-economic status of the people of South Africa [34].

Financial Exclusion: The financially excluded population comprises citizens living in underdeveloped rural areas [24], with no access to banking resources such as ATMs and other banking products and services. Many of these people are poor, unemployed, and illiterate and, therefore, only partially participate in the economy. This population is often dependent on government social grants for their daily needs. There has been a movement in countries like India, Brazil, and Kenya to ensure this population is included in the financial system [10].

According to Statista [37] any individual living in South Africa with less than R945 per month is considered poor – and those individuals who have less than R663 available for food per month live below the poverty line according to South African standards. In their report, BFAP [5] stated that low-income households spent around 13% of their income on food, whereas high-income households spent around 39%. This shows that there is a need to improve the socio-economic status of those who are considered poor in South Africa.

Countries with Digitalized Payment Systems: Many countries worldwide have dig-italized their payment systems to achieve economic growth, prosperity, and financial inclusion. For example, the Unified Payments Interface (UPI) was developed [38] in India, the PIX system was implemented in Brazil [3], the M-PESA in Kenya [29], the PayNow system was implemented in Singapore [39], the Troy system was developed in Turkey [33], and the PayNet system was developed in Malaysia [31]. These countries have digitalized their payment systems to implement platforms such as e-money, e-wallets, mobile payment platforms, real-time/instant payment platforms, and many more.

3 Benefits and Challenges of Digital Payment Systems

Countries that implemented digitalized payment systems have reaped significant benefits in recent years. Some of these benefits include financial inclusion, an increase in levels of cash displacement, interoperability in their domestic payment systems, and the ability to make interoperable cross-border payments [10, 24].

Financial Inclusion: Many South African citizens still need to participate fully in the economy. Because of many factors such as transport costs, banking fees, lack of banking resources, and many more, these individuals make use of banking services at very minimal levels [25]. One of the goals of the SARB's strategic vision of financial inclusion is to mitigate this scourge so that these people can be able to participate in the economy [35]. The participation of these individuals in the economy will stimulate and grow the economy.

Financial inclusion is one of the nine goals of the SARB's Vision 2025 strategy [35], and included to bridge the gap between the financially excluded population and those with full access to the South African banking system. In South Africa, the financially excluded population lives in under-resourced areas that do not have banking infrastructure and where many people are unemployed or have low income and are dependent on social grants [9]. Financial inclusion will help this population be included in the economy because being financially excluded often leads to poverty.

Cash Displacement: One of the driving forces of the digitalization of payment systems in the banking system across the world is the need to cut the costs of managing and processing physical cash. According to Mastercard [23], the management and processing of physical cash cost South Africa R23 billion in 2017. In a country with major socio-economic issues like South Africa, this amount could be channeled towards other avenues that could improve the economy. Another driving force is affordable, convenient, faster, and secure payments. According to Lee, Wewege, and Thomsett [29], digital banking systems are more convenient, are faster, and bring a personalized banking experience to customers.

Interoperability in Cross-Border Payments: One of the benefits of digital payments is the ability to make cross-border payments with other countries. The term cross-border payments refer to trade agreements between countries that are willing to trade in an efficient and interoperable manner. According to Mantyi [22] the interoperability of the payment systems between the countries often enables efficient trading, resulting in the growth of economies.

Inclusive Growth and Poverty Reduction: Introducing digital payment systems in rural areas will enable the financially excluded to access financial services such as loans, savings, insurance, and payments and remittance facilities. International organizations like the International Monetary Fund (IMF) and the World Bank are advocating for the swift implementation and development of digital payment systems that will improve the worldwide financial inclusion of the financially excluded population. This is because of the positive results of other developing countries like India and Brazil.

Challenges and Benefits of Digitalizing Payments: Some of the difficulties experienced by the countries that implemented digital payment systems included adopting digital payment systems, security concerns, banking fees and data costs, and digital and financial literacy.

Adoption of Digitalized Payment Systems: New technologies and innovations are usually met with some degree of reluctance from their intended recipients. This has also been the case in countries like India, Malaysia, China that have implemented digital payment systems [17]. According to Kajol et al. [17] many people in these countries preferred the usage of cash as opposed to digital payment systems, which initially resulted in the slow uptake of digital payment platforms being introduced.

Technology Security: One of the challenges for any payment system in existence is whether confidentiality, data integrity, authentication platforms, and non-repudiation [4]. Users of a payment system want to be assured that their transactions will not be compromised by unauthorized systems or individuals. To curb these technological security concerns, some countries that have implemented digital payment systems have used digital identification to curb the security challenges in their systems.

Banking Fees and Data Costs: In most developing countries, banking fees and data costs are still very high, which often causes financially excluded people not to have access to technology. When countries like India and Brazil implemented digital payments, their governments stepped in to subsidize technology providers to reduce data costs so that those who live in rural areas could be financially included through access to technology [15].

Digital and Financial Literacy: Lyons et al. [21] state that digital and financial literacy is pivotal in adopting digital payment systems for the financially excluded. A study conducted in South Asia and Sub-Saharan Africa found that many people need knowledge and adequate digital and financial skills to use digital payment system platforms effectively.

4 Theoretical Frameworks for Digitalized Payment Systems

Several theoretical frameworks were previously used to study and implement the digitalization of payment systems worldwide. This study explores the Technology Acceptance Model (TAM), the Unified Theory of Acceptance and Use of Technology (UTAUT), the Task-Technology Fit (TTF), the Innovation Diffusion Theory (IDT), and the Technology-Organization-Environment (TOE) based on their high citation rate.

TAM has been used to show how perceived usefulness and perceived use can influence the user's behavioral intention to adopt mobile payment systems. For instance, Dahlberg, Mallat, and Öörni [12] used TAM to explore the trust and acceptance of mobile payment solutions. Another study was done by Dlodlo and Mafini [12] who endeavored to establish a relationship between the acceptance and usage of e-commerce amongst South African and Kenya youth.

UTAUT was developed to clarify how the intention of the user may influence the usage behavior when using technology [40]. For instance, for a study in Uganda Mugambe [27] used UTAUT to explain the adoption of mobile services by customers of small and medium enterprises. It also played a significant role in identifying determinants of mobile money services by traders in Uganda [2].

The **TTF** model suggests that factors that influence the utilization of technology are based on the type of tasks performed by the users. In Kenya, it was used to investigate whether two mobile technologies meet the needs of the organizational structure. It was concluded that user acceptance and appropriateness were the determining factors in adopting electronic commerce that use mobile technologies [41]. In other studies, TTF was also used to assess the effectiveness of mobile business applications [14][44].

IDT explains how new ideas and innovations are adopted. It has also been used with other models to identify factors influencing the adoption of digital payments in developing countries. For example, in combination with TAM, IDT was used to determine the role of trust and risk in mobile commerce adoption within South Africa [16].

This study did not consider TAM due to its focus on users' behavioral intention to adopt technology. Subsequently, UTAUT was omitted because of the emphasis on user behavior while using technology, while TTF focused on user task types performed when using technology. IDT could have been used because of its reference to new ideas and innovations, but the study focused on more than just adoption.

The theoretical framework that underpins this study is the Technology-Organization-Environment (TOE) theoretical framework. This framework was chosen because it explains innovation adoption, according to Tornatsky and Fleischer [42]. It was selected because it advocates adopting and using digital payment systems in rural, underdeveloped areas. This study utilizes the TOE framework to construct and propose the envisaged conceptual framework that will be used to adopt innovation for the digitalization (through technology) of payment systems for financial inclusion. According to Modiba and Kekwaletswe [25], the three principles of the TOE govern an organization's process and implementation of technology and influence how an organization views, seeks and adopts the need for emerging technology. The technological context (also referred to as the technology group) relates to technologies used within an organization; the organizational context (also referred to as the organizational group) relates to the organization's resources that can either constrain or assist in adopting technologies. The environmental context (also referred to as the environmental group) relates to the environment in which the organization operates [28].

5 Research Approach

This study followed the Preferred Reporting Items for System Reviews and Meta-Analysis (PRISMA) as part of the systematic literature review process [26]. The PRISMA flowchart is a well-known method dictating structured tasks completed during the systematic literature review process. It includes the specification of inclusion criteria, search strategy, data collection and extraction, assessment of quality, and analysis.

Inclusion Criteria: Literature was included in studies on the socio-economic status and livelihoods of people living in rural areas. These people typically do not have full-time employment and depend primarily on government grants. The study excluded the literature and studies that focused on people with full-time jobs and those living in urban areas. It further included the literature related to the use of digital payment systems in developing countries.

Search Strategy: The study included academically published literature from peer-reviewed journals, conference papers, and theses published from 2018 to 2023. Google Scholar and the following research databases were consulted: Science Direct, Scopus, EBSCOhost, and IEEE Xplore. The literature search focused on digitalizing payment systems in rural areas for financial inclusion. It used the following search terms:- "digital transformation", "digitalization", "payment systems", "mobile money", "e-money", "e-payments", "rural areas", "financial inclusion", "South Africa," and "developing countries". Synonyms were also used in various search expressions to ensure that relevant papers were included in the research study. The following is one of search strings used: (("e-money" OR "electronic money" OR "e-wallet" OR "e-payments" OR "electronic money") AND ("digitalization" OR "digital transformation" OR "financial inclusion" OR "economic growth" OR "payments in developing countries" OR "e-payments in developing countries" OR "developing economy") AND (cash displacement OR digital payments OR security OR adoption) AND (discontinuing ATMs OR "cost of processing cash" OR financial literacy OR challenges OR banking fees OR data costs OR poverty reduction OR problems) AND (South Africa OR Africa OR "developing country")).

Data Collection and Extraction: As a first step, the researcher scrutinized the abstracts of each paper from the search results, considering the relevance to the research question. Secondly, the full texts of the relevant extracted papers were further analyzed to ensure inclusiveness. All fields were extracted and stored.

Assessment of Quality: An independent researcher evaluated the research article pool. They looked at the list of sources the researcher used, the search strategy, and the sources' relevance.

Screening: 224 applicable articles were identified, and 83 duplicate records were removed. The screening phase considered the titles and abstracts of the remaining 141 articles, whereas another 83 articles were excluded. The reasons for exclusion were irrelevant titles and keywords and inadequate research output. After further screening, 97 articles were excluded based on the following criteria: (a) some studies were conducted in both urban and rural areas, (b) the study was not related to the digitalization of payment systems, and (c) some studies were not related to the banking industry. The final research article pool consisted of 44 articles.

5.1 Data Analysis

Atlas.ti was used to determine the focus area of articles in the final research article pool. Word frequencies were used based on the title, abstract, and keywords, and lastly, its introduction and literature review sections to identify focus areas. These included: - Digitalization of Payment Systems, Technology Security, Banking Industry, Adoption, Cash Displacement, Banking Fees and Data Costs, Inclusive Growth and Poverty Reduction, South Africa, Rural Areas, Interoperability of Cross-border Payments, and Digital and Financial Literacy. These focus areas were further grouped into Technology, Organization, and Environment per the adopted TOE framework.

6 Discussion and Findings: Conceptual Research Framework

The conceptual framework in Fig. 1 depicts the focus areas identified during the data analysis and grouped according to the TOE framework.

The *Technology group* included technological aspects of the digitalization of payment systems and technology security considerations for those living in rural, underdeveloped areas. **Digitalization of Payment Systems**. As a result of the digitalization of the payment systems, many countries like Brazil, Kenya, Singapore, and Malaysia have seen significant economic growth and financial inclusions [3]. In these countries, significant economic growth and financial inclusion were achieved by the involvement of various governments and relevant regulatory bodies. For instance, in India, the government played a critical role by subsidizing data costs and banking fees for the financially excluded population [38]. **Technology Security**. The mechanism of digital identification has been used as a means to ensure that there is efficient authentication, confidentiality, and data integrity when using digital payment systems [15]. Digital identification is necessary for digital payments to link transactions to individuals or organizations and prevent crimes like money laundering. This assists regulators in tracing all transactions to individuals or organizations, allowing for the investigation into illegal activity. Some of the countries that initially implemented digital payments needed to have this functionality in place. For instance, India had to develop and implement the Aadhar ID to resolve this issue [38]. Other countries like Brazil and Singapore have also implemented their digital identification technologies to curb the technology security challenges of payment systems.

The *Organization group* depicts the role played by the banking industry in financial inclusion development. **Banking Industry**. The South African banking industry, through

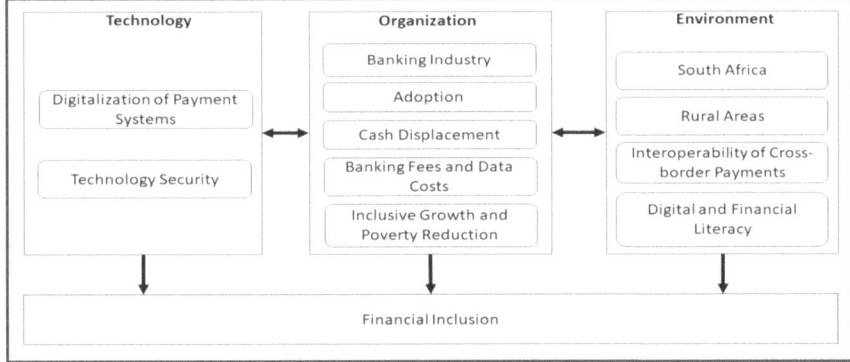

Fig. 1. Conceptual Framework for Digitalized Payment Systems

its regulatory body (the SARB), has a mission to include the financially excluded population in the mainstream economy [35]. **Adoption of Digital Payment Systems**. There was reluctance among older adults to adopt digital payment systems, mainly caused by a need to understand digital platforms. One of the reasons for this reluctance in developing or low-income areas is the lack of proper infrastructure and resources [19]. People and the businesses that operate in these areas are lagging in the digital race; many of them are still unbanked and are, therefore, financially excluded [32]. This further contributes to a need for more adoption of digital payment systems in these areas. **Cash Displacement**. Many countries are moving away from using physical cash and towards using digital payment systems because of the costs of managing and processing cash. According to Cnaan et al. [10] the Indian government aims to move away from physical cash and replace it with digital financial transactions. The United Kingdom is in the process of displacing ATMs, thereby encouraging the use of digital payments instead of physical cash [6]. The success of cash displacement in other countries – by saving cash processing costs – has enabled the regulators to invest and improve their payment systems. **Banking Fees and Data Costs**. As a result of the digitalization of payment systems, countries like India and Brazil subsidized banking fees and data costs [15]. This ensured that even those living in underdeveloped areas could participate in the economy and access digital payment systems. **Inclusive growth and poverty reduction**. Access to digital payment systems and other banking services has resulted in inclusive growth and poverty reduction in some areas of the world. This financial inclusion through digital banking has alleviated and reduced poverty and achieved some degree of inclusive growth in developing countries. Bourainy et al., [8] state that financial inclusion is achieved by improving citizens' well-being, providing more opportunities, and protecting against unexpected negative scenarios. The adoption and use of digital payment system platforms improve security, as people do not have to move with large amounts of cash [20].

The *Environment group* depicts the environment in which this digitalization will occur – the South African rural areas. **South Africa**. Through regulatory bodies like the SARB and the Payments Association of South Africa (PASA), the South African government is embarking on a journey to include the financially excluded populations in underdeveloped rural areas into the financial system [36], enabling banking access through digital payment systems. **Rural Areas**. To successfully include the financially excluded (people who live in rural areas) in the banking system in the emerging era of digital payment systems, research studies found that there needs to be a concerted effort from regulators and banking participants to improve ICT infrastructure and resources in those areas [21]. **Interoperability of Cross-border Payments**. Wewege, Lee, and Thomsett [29] state that FinTech's have developed digital payment platforms enabling users to make global payments. Therefore, because of digital payment systems, there has been interoperability in payment systems across different economies. Countries like India and Singapore could benefit from their digital payment systems because they are interoperable. This assisted in the growth of these economies because they could trade with each other faster, more securely, and efficiently. **Digital and financial literacy**. In their study, Aziz and Naima [1] found that in Bangladesh, financial literacy was one of the barriers to adopting digital payment systems in rural areas. They found that some consumers lacked the basic knowledge of digital technologies and, in some instances, basic financial knowledge. Financial literacy is an instrument for financial awareness, knowledge, and skills that can be used to access and utilize financial services effectively.

Lastly, the *Financial Inclusion* foundation represents the end goal of this study – the financial inclusion of the financially excluded population. **Financial inclusion** is one of the main reasons that digitalization of payment systems has been considered in many countries worldwide. It has been advocated by multilateral agencies such as the World Bank, International Monetary Fund (IMF), and the United Nations as a means to improve economic growth and social welfare across the world [18]. A large population of people residing in underdeveloped countries with no banking infrastructure are financially excluded. According to Dirir [11] the digital payment systems implemented in countries such as India, Singapore, and Brazil have positively impacted these people in the economy (financial inclusion). Digital payment systems have aided the financially excluded population in participating in the economies of these countries. This has resulted in considerable growth in these economies. All the groups in the conceptual framework contribute to the end goal of **financial inclusion**.

7   Conclusion

Using the TOE elements, this research identified the focus areas to be considered when working towards implementing the digitalization of payment systems for financial inclusion. The **Technology group** of the conceptual framework focused on technological aspects of achieving financial inclusion through digitized payment systems. One main concern was technology security [13]. Like other countries implementing digital payment systems, South Africa must consider stringent technology security mechanisms to gain users' trust.

Even though socio-economic issues like the lack of infrastructure in rural and remote areas can hamper digital payment systems, it remains essential as successful implementation can have an enormous impact on the growth of the South African economy [25], i.e., the bigger **Organizational group**. In their report, Mastercard [30] illustrated the high cost of managing and processing cash in South Africa. The cost-saving implication of digital payments can assist in redirecting the money spent on cash management to the development and growth of the economy. Countries like India and Singapore have reported positive growth in their economies as a result of efficient cross-border payments that emanated from efficient digital payment systems among them [30].

The South African **Environment** is often characterized as one of the most financially divided economies in the world. Digital payment systems are, therefore, an essential part of achieving financial inclusion. If the large, financially excluded population living in rural areas can be included financially, the local economy can grow substantially. In conclusion, this conceptual framework provides a good foundation, offering a structured approach for future studies focusing on adopting and implementing digital payment systems.

References

1. Aziz, A., Naima, U.: Rethinking digital financial inclusion: evidence from Bangladesh. Technol. Soc. (2021). https://doi.org/10.1016/j.techsoc.2020.101509
2. B, M.R., et al.: Determinants of mobile money services adoption by traders in Uganda. Int. J. Multidiscip. Res. Dev. **4**(8), 189–201 (2017)
3. Banco Central do Brasil: What is Pix?, https://www.bcb.gov.br/en/financialstability/pix_en. Accessed 29 Jul 2023
4. Bezhovski, Z.: The future of the mobile payment as electronic payment system. Eur. J. Bus. Manage. **8**(8), 127–132 (2016)
5. BFAP: How South Africans spend their food budgets (2020)
6. Blakey, D.: Cash displacement: 1 in 5 UK citizens still rely on cash, https://www.electronicpaymentsinternational.com/features/uk-cash-displacement-1-in-5-still-use-cash/. Accessed 21 Mar 2023
7. Botes, K.: An investigation into the service delivery by commercial banks in South Africa. Cent. Univ. Technol. (2008).
8. Bourainy, M.E., et al.: Assessing the impact of financial inclusion on inflation rate in developing countries. Open J. Soc. Sci. **09**(01), 397–424 (2021). https://doi.org/10.4236/jss.2021. 91030
9. Cicchiello, F.A.: Digital transformation in South Africa: opportunities and challenges during Covid-19 pandemic. Int. EFAL-IT BLOG. **1**(7), 2019–2021 (2020)
10. Cnaan, R.A., et al.: Financial inclusion in the digital banking age: lessons from rural India. J. Social Policy (2021). https://doi.org/10.1017/S0047279421000738
11. Dirir, S.A.: Performing a quantile regression to explore the financial inclusion in emerging countries and lessons African countries can learn from them. Eur. J. Dev. Stud. **2**(5), 1–9 (2022)
12. Dlodlo, N., Mafini, C.: The relationship between technology acceptance and frequency of mobile commerce use amongst Generation Y consumers. Acta Commer. **13**(1), 1–8 (2013). https://doi.org/10.4102/ac.v13i1.176
13. Van Dyk, R., Van Belle, J.P. Factors influencing the intended adoption of digital transformation: a South African case study. Proc. 2019 Fed. Conf. Comput. Sci. Inform. Syst. **18** 519–528 (2019).
14. Gebauer, J., Shaw, M.J.: Task−technology fit for mobile information systems. J. Inf. Technol. (2006). https://doi.org/10.1057/jit.2010.10
15. Haralayya, B.: How digital banking has brought innovative products and services to India. J. Adv. Res. Qual. Control Manage. **6**(1), 16–18 (2021)
16. Joubert, J., van Belle, J.-P.: The role of trust and risk in mobile commerce adoption within South Africa. Int. J. Bus. Humanit. Technol. **3**(2), 27–38 (2013)

17. Kajol, K., et al.: Adoption of digital financial transactions: a review of literature and future research agenda. Technol. Forecast. Soc. Change (2022). https://doi.org/10.1016/j.techfore.2022.121991
18. Kass-Hanna, J., et al.: Building financial resilience through financial and digital literacy in South Asia and Sub-Saharan Africa. Emerg. Mark. Rev. (2022). https://doi.org/10.1016/j.ememar.2021.100846
19. Legowo, M.B., et al.: A conceptual framework of technological innovation for the financial and banking industry in Indonesia. Int. J. Inf. Bus. Manage. **12**(4), 100–114 (2020)
20. Lochy, J.: Financial inclusion—a word with many meanings, https://www.finextra.com/blogposting/18441/financial-inclusion--a-word-with-manymeanings. Accessed 24 Jul 2023
21. Lyons, A.C., Kass-Hanna, J.: Financial inclusion, financial literacy and economically vulnerable populations in the Middle East and North Africa. Emerg. Mark. Financ. Trade **57**(9), 2699–2738 (2021). https://doi.org/10.1080/1540496X.2019.1598370
22. Mantyi, L.: An evaluation of the inhibitions caused by legacy systems on digital transformation in a South African Retail Bank. University of the Witwatersrand (2020)
23. Mastercard: Cash costs South African consumers R23 billion a year – Mastercard study, https://paymentsafrika.com/cash-costs-south-african-consumers-r23-billion-a-year-mastercard-study-2/#:~:text=Cash cost consumers R23 billion or 0.52 percent,serving as a major barrier to financial inclusion. Accessed 08 Jul 2023
24. Melubo, K.D., Musau, S.: Digital banking and financial inclusion of women enterprises in Narok County, Kenya. Int. J. Curr. Aspects Finan. Bank. Account. 2 (1) 28–41 (2020).
25. Modiba, M.M., Kekwaletswe, R.M.: Technological, organizational and environmental framework for digital transformation in South African financial service providers. Int. J. Innov. Sci. Res. Technol. **5**(5), 180–196 (2020)
26. Moher, D., et al.: Preferred reporting items for systematic reviews and meta-analyses: the PRISMA statement. Int. J. Surg. (2010). https://doi.org/10.1016/j.ijsu.2010.02.007
27. Mugambe, P.: UTAUT model in explaining the adoption of mobile money usage by MSMEs' customers in Uganda. Adv. Econ. Bus. (2018). https://doi.org/10.13189/aeb.2017.050302
28. Oliveira, T., Martins, M.F.: Understanding e-business adoption across industries in European countries. Ind. Manag. Data Syst. **110**(9), 1337–1354 (2010). https://doi.org/10.1108/02635571011087428
29. Owigar, J.: How M-Pesa is changing everyday life in Kenya, https://www.urbanet.info/mpesa-kenya-how-it-is-changing-everyday-life/. Accessed 30 Jul 2023
30. Pandey, S. et al.: Digital Public Infrastructure for Efficient Cross-Border Data Flow Abstract (2023)
31. Payments Network Malaysia: PayNet, https://paynet.my/about-paynet.html. Accessed 30 Jul 2023
32. Philip, L., Williams, F.: Remote rural home based businesses and digital inequalities: understanding needs and expectations in a digitally underserved community. J. Rural. Stud. (2019). https://doi.org/10.1016/j.jrurstud.2018.09.011
33. PPRO: Troy, https://www.ppro.com/payment-methods/troy/. Accessed 30 Jul 2023
34. Rossouw, J.: A selective reflection on the institutional development of the South African reserve bank since 1921. Econ. Hist. Dev. Reg. **26**(sup1), S3–S20 (2011). https://doi.org/10.1080/20780389.2011.586405
35. SARB: The South African Reserve Bank (SARB) has legal responsibility for the national payment system (NPS), which is the backbone of South Africa's financial system, https://www.resbank.co.za/en/home/what-we-do/payments-and-settlements. Accessed 15 Jul 2023
36. SARB Media Relations: South Africa clears the way for broader financial inclusion with the launch of a low-value, real-time digital payment service (2023)
37. Statista: National poverty line in South Africa as of, https://www.statista.com/statistics/1127838/national-poverty-line-in-south-africa/ (2022). Accessed 29 Jul 2023

38. Sujith, T.S., Julie, C.D.: Opportunities and challenges of e-payment system in India. Int. J. Sci. Res. Manage. (2017). https://doi.org/10.18535/ijsrm/v5i9.02
39. The Association of Banks Singapore: What is PayNow, https://www.abs.org.sg/consumer-banking/pay-now. Accessed 30 Jul 2023
40. Venkatesh, V., Zhang, X.: Unified theory of acceptance and use of technology: U.S. vs. China. Global Inf. Technol. Manage. (2010). https://doi.org/10.1080/1097198X.2010.10856507
41. Wamuyu, P., Maharaj, M.: Factors influencing successful use of mobile technologies to facilitate E-commerce in small enterprises the case of Kenya. Afr. J. Inf. Commun. (AJIC) 3(2), 2 (2011)
42. Winn, J.K.: Mobile Payments and Financial Inclusion: Kenya, Brazil, and India as Case Studies. (2016)
43. World Bank: Universal Financial Access 2020: Lessons for the Future (2021). https://doi.org/10.1596/39736
44. Zhou, T., et al.: Computers in human behavior integrating TTF and UTAUT to explain mobile banking user adoption. Comput. Hum. Behav. **26**(4), 760–767 (2010). https://doi.org/10.1016/j.chb.2010.01.013

Exploring the Innovation Capabilities of South African SMEs: A Principal Component Analysis Approach

Lizette Weilbach[1]([✉]) [iD], Hanlie Smuts[1] [iD], Aleesha Boolaky[2] [iD], Hemant Chittoo[2] [iD], Diroubinee Mauree-Narrainen[2] [iD], Kesseven Padachi[2] [iD], and Needesh Ramphul[2] [iD]

[1] University of Pretoria, Pretoria, South Africa
{lizette.weilbach,hanlie.smuts}@up.ac.za
[2] University of Technology Mauritius, Port Louis, Mauritius
{aboolaky,hchittoo,d.mnarrainen,kpadachi,needesh.r}@utm.ac.mu

Abstract. Small and Medium-sized Enterprises (SMEs) play a critical role in the economic growth and innovation of any nation. Despite their importance, SMEs often face significant challenges that hinder their innovation processes, including financial limitations and restricted access to information and technology. Additionally, understanding how open innovation practices can sustain competitive advantages in fast-evolving global markets is essential. This study investigates the innovation capabilities in South African SMEs, focusing on their relative importance in driving innovation, highlighting their multifaceted approach to drive innovation and remain competitive. A survey of 220 South African SMEs evaluated 19 innovation capabilities across 8 dimensions using a 5-point Likert scale. Principal component analysis identified five key factor groupings: risk management, customer acquisition, knowledge management, business networks, and innovation/product enhancement. The findings reveal that SMEs strategically manage risks, leverage customer insights, and cultivate networks to enhance their innovation capabilities, thereby positioning themselves as competitive players. By pinpointing the primary drivers of innovation, this study proposes strategies to strengthen these capabilities in the dynamic global economic landscape.

Keywords: SME · innovation · innovation capacity · innovation capabilities · principal component analysis

1 Introduction

Small and medium-sized enterprises (SMEs) occupy a pivotal position within the South African economy, contributing substantially to the national gross domestic product (GDP) and serving as engines of innovation, job creation, and economic expansion [1–4]. Beyond mere statistical figures, SMEs are instrumental in nurturing innovation and propelling socio-economic progress throughout the country [5]. Recognized as essential components in achieving national development objectives, they are uniquely poised to tackle socio-economic challenges such as unemployment and poverty alleviation [6].

© The Author(s), under exclusive license to Springer Nature Switzerland AG 2025
K. Hinkelmann and H. Smuts (Eds.): Society 5.0 2024, CCIS 2173, pp. 378–390, 2025.
https://doi.org/10.1007/978-3-031-71412-2_28

Innovation within SMEs emerges as a cornerstone for encouraging competitive advantage and ensuring sustainable growth [7]. The capacity for innovation, defined as the strategic utilization of resources to effectively meet customer needs [8], is a critical determinant of business success. It encompasses the dynamic processes of ideation, development, and implementation of novel solutions that not only add value but also foster enduring growth within diverse organizational contexts [9]. This aspect of business strategy has gained attention within academic and industrial spheres alike, particularly within the dynamic and challenging landscape of South Africa.

This paper aims to delve into the innovation capabilities of South African SMEs, with a specific focus on understanding their relative importance in driving innovation. The primary research question guiding this exploration is: *How do the innovation capabilities that enable South African SMEs to innovate compare in terms of relative importance?* By employing a principal component analysis approach, this study seeks to illuminate these critical aspects by systematically analyzing the relative importance of innovation capabilities within South African SMEs. Through this investigation, key drivers of innovation will be identified, and strategies will be proposed to safeguard these capabilities in the face of the dynamic global economic landscape.

The forthcoming sections present an overview of the literature in Sect. 2, followed by an exposition of our research approach in Sect. 3. Section 4 delves into the discussion of the data analysis and findings, while Sect. 5 elucidates the contribution of the study. Finally, Sect. 6 provides the concluding remarks for the paper.

2 Background

Given the foundational significance of SMEs in any country's economy and their role in driving innovation and economic development, it is imperative to explore the factors influencing their innovation capabilities comprehensively. Studies have pointed to diverse challenges hampering the innovation processes within this sector, ranging from financial constraints to inadequate access to information and technology [8]. Furthermore, the interplay between open innovation practices and the capacity for sustaining competitive advantages amidst rapidly evolving global markets presents an area ripe for exploration. This paper aims to shed light on these crucial aspects by systematically analyzing how the innovation capabilities enabling South African SMEs to innovate compare in terms of relative importance. Through this investigation, key drivers of innovation will be identified, and strategies proposed to safeguard these capabilities amidst the dynamic global economic landscape.

2.1 SMEs and Economic Development

Small and Medium-sized Enterprises (SMEs) play a pivotal role in economic development, making substantial contributions to the global economy. These contributions encompass income creation, employment generation, fostering competitive market dynamics, poverty reduction, promoting entrepreneurship, and driving technological innovation [10, 11]. They are recognized as crucial agents of economic growth, accounting for a substantial portion of enterprises worldwide [12]. Through capacity building and competitive innovation, SMEs drive not only their individual success but also the broader economic prosperity of their regions and countries [11].

2.2 SMEs and Innovation Capacity

Innovation holds significant importance for the competitiveness and sustainability of SMEs in today's dynamic business environment. However, SMEs often face unique challenges in developing and harnessing their innovation capabilities effectively.

Financial constraints are a significant barrier to innovation within SMEs, limiting their ability to invest in research and development (R&D) activities [13]. A lack of financial resources may hinder SMEs from exploring new technologies, developing innovative products or services, and adapting to changing market demands.

SMEs may also encounter difficulties in accessing external knowledge and resources necessary for innovation [14] and may struggle to establish and maintain collaborative relationships with external stakeholders, limiting their access to valuable information, expertise, and market opportunities [15, 16].

Furthermore, the ability of SMEs to recognize and capitalize on entrepreneurial opportunities is essential for fostering innovation [17]. These entrepreneurial skills are critical for SMEs to adapt to changing market conditions, navigate competitive challenges, and drive sustainable growth through innovation [16].

By enhancing their innovation capacity, SMEs can unlock new growth opportunities, improve their competitiveness, and contribute to the overall prosperity of the economy.

2.3 SMEs and Innovation Capabilities

This subsequent section delves into a comprehensive literature review focusing on the critical aspects of SMEs' innovation capabilities. The review encompasses 8 dimensions of capabilities: knowledge exploitation, entrepreneurial, risk management, networking, development, change management, external, as well as radical and incremental innovation capabilities. Each dimension plays a pivotal role in shaping SMEs' innovation strategies, enabling them to capitalize on new opportunities, respond to market dynamics, and leverage external knowledge for competitive edge. The significance of both radical and incremental innovations further highlights the multifaceted nature of innovation in SMEs, illustrating their collective importance in fostering sustained growth and adaptation [13].

Knowledge Exploitation Capabilities. Knowledge management and exploitation serve as pivotal innovation capabilities for SMEs, allowing them to leverage internal and external knowledge resources effectively [18]. By systematically managing and utilizing knowledge, SMEs can identify emerging trends, understand customer needs, and capitalize on market opportunities [19]. This capability enables SMEs to adapt quickly to changing market dynamics, develop innovative products or services, and stay ahead of competitors. Fostering a culture of continuous learning and knowledge sharing, SMEs can enhance their ability to innovate and drive sustainable growth in today's competitive business landscape [9].

Entrepreneurial Capabilities. Entrepreneurial capabilities and opportunity recognition are fundamental innovation capabilities for SMEs, playing a critical role in driving business growth and competitiveness [20]. SMEs with strong entrepreneurial skills possess the agility and vision to identify emerging market trends, consumer needs, and untapped opportunities [21]. By leveraging these capabilities, SMEs can seize new market niches, develop innovative products or services, and establish themselves as industry leaders. Entrepreneurial prowess enables SMEs to navigate through challenges, adapt to evolving market conditions, and capitalize on changes in consumer preferences, ultimately driving innovation and fostering sustainable business growth [16].

Risk Management Capabilities. Risk management capabilities enables SMEs to navigate uncertainties and mitigate potential threats associated with innovation endeavours [22]. Effective risk management strategies allow SMEs to assess and anticipate risks, make informed decisions, and allocate resources strategically to minimize adverse impacts on business operations. By proactively identifying and addressing risks, SMEs can enhance their resilience, safeguard against potential failures, and optimize the success rate of innovation initiatives [23]. A robust risk management framework fosters a culture of experimentation and learning within SMEs, encouraging innovation while simultaneously managing and mitigating associated risks [24].

Networking Capabilities. Networking capabilities are essential for innovation within SMEs, facilitating collaboration, knowledge exchange, and access to valuable resources and opportunities [25]. By fostering collaborative relationships with external stakeholders such as other businesses, industry experts, research institutions, and government agencies, SMEs can tap into a diverse pool of knowledge, expertise, and market insights [26]. Effective networking enables SMEs to stay abreast of industry trends, emerging technologies, and market developments, providing them with valuable information to drive innovation and adapt to changing market dynamics. Networking facilitates the formation of strategic partnerships and alliances, enabling SMEs to leverage complementary strengths, pool resources, and co-create innovative solutions [27].

Development Capabilities. Development capabilities encompass the ability of SMEs to generate new innovations [28], improve existing processes [29], products and services [30], and leverage external innovations effectively [31, 32]. SMEs need to continuously innovate to differentiate themselves from competitors, meet evolving customer needs, and stay ahead in the market. By creating novel solutions that offer unique value propositions, SMEs can carve out a niche for themselves and gain a competitive edge [28]. According to Branzei, et al. [33], the capacity to enhance existing products and services allows SMEs to stay relevant in the market by continuously refining and updating their offerings to meet changing customer preferences and technological advancements. SMEs can capitalize on external innovations by identifying and adopting promising ideas or technologies developed by others, thereby accelerating their innovation efforts and staying at the forefront of industry trends.

Change Management Capabilities. Change management or adaptive capabilities reflect SMEs' ability to adapt their business operations in response to market dynamics and evolving customer needs [34]. SMEs operate in dynamic environments where change is constant, necessitating agility and flexibility to stay competitive [35]. By effectively managing change, SMEs can anticipate shifts in the market landscape, identify emerging opportunities, and swiftly realign their strategies and resources to capitalize on these changes [36]. This proactive approach enables SMEs to stay ahead of the curve and maintain relevance in the marketplace. Change management capabilities empower SMEs to foster a culture of innovation within their organizations, encouraging experimentation, risk-taking, and continuous improvement [37].

External Input to Innovation. External input from outside sources is paramount in the innovation process for SMEs, facilitating access to diverse perspectives, expertise, and resources crucial for driving innovation [13]. By engaging with external stakeholders such as customers, suppliers, industry experts, and research institutions, SMEs can tap into valuable insights, trends, and best practices that may not be readily available within their own organizations [38]. This external input fosters a culture of collaboration and knowledge exchange, enabling SMEs to stay abreast of industry developments, emerging technologies, and market trends. External networks provide SMEs with access to potential partners for joint ventures, co-creation initiatives, and strategic alliances, thereby expanding their innovation ecosystem and enhancing their capacity to develop novel solutions and enter new markets [39].

Radical and Incremental Innovation Capabilities. Radical innovations, characterized by their novelty and departure from existing market offerings, enable SMEs to pioneer groundbreaking solutions that revolutionize industries and redefine market norms [31]. By daring to explore uncharted territories and challenge conventional wisdom, SMEs can disrupt markets, leapfrog competitors, and carve out unique value propositions that resonate with customers [40]. On the other hand, incremental innovation, while less disruptive, plays a crucial role in enhancing the competitiveness and relevance of SMEs. Through continuous improvement and refinement of existing products or services, SMEs can differentiate themselves in crowded markets, address evolving customer needs, and maintain a competitive edge over time [41].

3   Research Approach

This paper aims to investigate the innovation capabilities of South African SMEs, recognizing their vital role in enhancing competitiveness, sustainability, and growth in today's dynamic business environment. By fostering innovation, SMEs can differentiate themselves from competitors, navigate changing market dynamics, and seize emerging opportunities, thus driving business success. Innovation enables SMEs to develop sustainable business models, expand into new markets, and optimize operations, enhancing their long-term viability and adaptability [28]. Additionally, innovation enables SMEs to embrace technological advancements, regulatory changes, and evolving consumer demands, positioning them for sustained relevance and prosperity.

   To comprehensively understand these factors, it is essential to examine their relative importance and potential consolidation: Are all innovation capabilities equally crucial, and can they be streamlined into fewer core competencies?

The study employed survey research to collect data from South African SMEs. An online questionnaire, structured according to the literature on disruptive innovation capabilities within SMEs, was developed for this purpose. Following pilot testing to ensure clarity and relevance, respondents provided data on their SMEs' innovation capabilities. The questionnaire comprised of 20 questions addressing the 8 dimensions of innovation capabilities, outlined in Sect. 2.3. Convenience sampling targeted individuals from the South African SME population owning or working for an SME. A web link was shared on LinkedIn to invite participation, resulting in 220 respondents.

To address questions regarding the relative importance and potential consolidation of innovation capabilities, quantitative research, specifically principal component analysis (PCA), was utilized. PCA is a statistical technique that reduces the dimensionality of datasets while retaining variance, revealing linear combinations of original variables (principal components) that explain significant variation. This approach was selected to effectively identify underlying patterns among these innovation capabilities. The profile of the SME respondents is presented in Table 1.

The profile of the SMEs who participated in the questionnaire reveals a diverse range of characteristics and attributes. In terms of the size of their businesses, most respondents (67.3%) reported annual turnovers ranging from Rands 2 million to Rands 10 million, with a significant proportion (36.8%) employing between 5 and 19 permanent employees. However, there was also representation from larger enterprises, with 5.9% reporting 200 or more employees. Regarding the longevity of their businesses, a substantial portion (43.6%) had been in operation for more than 10 years, while 22.3% had a tenure of 6 to 10 years. Interestingly, the age distribution of respondents varied, with the majority falling within the 31 to 45 age bracket (43.2%), followed by those aged 46 to 55 (37.7%). Education levels were diverse, with a notable percentage (34.0%) holding a degree and a smaller percentage (9.5%) possessing a post-graduate degree. Concerning research and development (R&D) expenditure, the majority (68.6%) reported none, while a minority invested varying amounts, with 20.9% spending less than R50 000 and only 1.0% allocating R1 000 000 or more. This comprehensive profile sheds light on the demographic and operational characteristics of SMEs in the surveyed population, providing valuable insights for understanding their needs and behaviors in the business landscape.

The next section will delve into the quantitative analysis of the collected data, aiming to derive the capability groupings for innovation within South African SMEs.

4 Data Analysis and Findings

The relative importance of the 19 capabilities was explored by means of 5-point Likert rating scale questions in a questionnaire instrument. Statistical analysis undertaken with SPSS v29.0.0.0 included descriptive analysis, reliability tests using Cronbach's alpha, one-way analysis of variance and principal component analysis. The Cronbach's alpha reliability for the factors is 0.944 suggesting that the 19 capabilities have excellent internal reliability [42, 43]. This implies that the factors are closely correlated with each other.

Principal component analysis is used to identify a relatively small number of factor groupings that can be used to represent relationships among sets of many interrelated

Table 1. SA SME demographic profile

Number of permanent employees	% of respondents	How long in business?	% of respondents
1 - 4 employees	30.5%	Less than a year	4.1%
5 - 19 employees	36.8%	1 - 2 years	9.5%
20 - 49 employees	19.1%	3 -5 years	20.5%
50 - 199 employees	7.7%	6 - 10 years	22.3%
200 or more employees	5.9%	More than 10 years	43.6%
Annual turnover over the last financial year (Rands)	% of respondents	Age of respondent	% of respondents
Rands 2 million to Rands 10 million	67.3%	18 - 30 years	10.0%
Above Rands 10 million to Rands 20 million	18.7%	31 - 45 years	43.2%
Above Rands 20 million to Rands 30 million	13.2%	46 - 55 years	37.7%
Above Rands 30 million to Rands 100 million	0.8%	56 - 65 years	8.2%
		66 years or older	0.9%
Highest qualification	% of respondents	Amount spent on R&D (Rands)	% of respondents
Secondary/High School	5.0%	None	68.6%
Certificate	13.6%	Less than R50 000	20.9%
Training and Vocational	6.8%	R50 001 - R200 000	7.3%
Diploma	31.0%	R200 001 - R300 000	1.2%
Degree	34.0%	R300 001 - R1 000 000	1.0%
Post-graduate degree	9.5%	R1 000 000 or more	1.0%

variables [44, 45]. This technique was applied to the questionnaire data to explore the groupings that might exist among the capabilities enabling innovation in SMEs. Varimax rotation method was used to produce factor loading that minimizes the number of variables with high loadings, either positive or negative, for each factor [46]. For the capabilities analysed, the principal component analysis shows that 19 capabilities can be grouped into 5 principal factors depicted in Table 2 and interpreted as follows:

- Factor grouping 1 represents *risk management*.
- Factor grouping 2 represents *customer and market acquisition*.
- Factor grouping 3 represents *knowledge management*.
- Factor grouping 4 represents *business networks*.
- Factor grouping 5 represents *innovation and product enhancement*.

Table 2. Rotated component matrix of innovation capacity factors for SMEs (Authors' own analysis)

Factor components	Component (Factor grouping)				
	1	2	3	4	5
Willingness to take risks	0.894				
Capabilities for risk assessment	0.889				
Abilities to take risk	0.888				
Capabilities to recognize new opportunities	0.591				
Capabilities to generate new innovations which differ from competitors' offerings	0.560				
Capabilities to expand to new markets		0.828			
Capabilities to acquire new customers		0.782			
Capabilities to increase sales to existing customers		0.752			
Capabilities to exploit opportunities for generating new profitable business		0.634	0.482		
Capabilities to seize new opportunities for developing new solutions		0.489	0.461		
Capabilities to quickly implement change based on market and customer knowledge		0.472			
Capabilities to internalize new external knowledge			0.863		
Capabilities to recognize relevant external knowledge			0.851		
Capabilities to exploit new knowledge for innovation			0.650		
Capabilities to create collaborative relationships				0.837	
Following a networking orientation				0.733	
Capabilities to exploit networks in business				0.648	
Capabilities to exploit innovations developed by others					0.822
Capabilities to improve existing products and services					0.729

Note: Extraction Method: Principal Component Analysis; Rotation Method: Varimax with Kaiser Normalization; Rotation converged in 7 iterations

The eigenvalue refers to the total variance explained by each factor and the 5 factor groupings describe 78% of the total variances among SME innovation capabilities. After the Varimax rotation, factor grouping 1 (risk management) accounts for 21.59% of the total variances among SME innovation capabilities, while factor grouping 2 (customer and market acquisition) accounts for 19.53% of variances among SME innovation capabilities. Factor grouping 3 (knowledge management) accounts for 15.88%, factor grouping 4 (business networks) accounts for 11.31% and factor grouping 5 (innovation and product enhancement) accounts for 9.74% of the total variances among SME innovation capabilities.

5   Discussion of Findings

Each factor grouping identified through PCA represents a cluster of innovation capabilities crucial for SME success. Factor grouping 1, risk management, consists of 5 SME innovation capabilities all reflecting high factor loading [44]. The factors with the strongest association (0.894, 0.889 and 0.888 respectively), are willingness to take risks, capabilities for risk assessment and abilities to take risk. The next 2 SME innovation capabilities with a strong, yet lowest, association (0.591 and 0.560 respectively) call for the capability to recognize new opportunities and to differentiate the SME offering. Willingness to take risks influences an SMEs ability to assess risks and make informed decisions, which in turn affects their capacity to recognize new opportunities. Those who possess strong capabilities for risk assessment are better equipped to evaluate potential innovations, thus increasing their ability to generate unique offerings distinct from competitors. Ultimately, the interplay between risk-taking, risk assessment, opportunity recognition, and innovation capabilities shapes an SME's competitive advantage in the market.

Factor grouping 2, customer and market acquisition, consists of 6 SME innovation capabilities. The factors with the strongest association (0.828, 0.782 and 0.752 respectively), are capabilities required to expand to new markets, capabilities to acquire new customers and capabilities to increase sales to existing customers. The willingness to take risks and adept capabilities in assessing and seizing opportunities are vital for expanding into new markets, acquiring new customers, and increasing sales to existing ones, thus driving sustained business growth and competitive advantage. The capabilities to exploit opportunities for generating new profitable business, capabilities to seize new opportunities for developing new solutions and the capabilities to quickly implement change based on market and customer knowledge, have associations of 0.634, 0.489 and 0.472, while capabilities to exploit opportunities for generating new profitable business and seizing new opportunities for developing new solutions, also have cross-loading to factor grouping 3, knowledge management. Proficiency in exploiting opportunities for new profitable ventures aligns with the capacity to seize opportunities for developing innovative solutions that utilizes organizational knowledge effectively. These capabilities synergize to drive sustainable growth by leveraging both market potential and internal resources for competitive advantage.

Factor grouping 3, knowledge management, consists of 3 SME innovation capabilities. The factors with the strongest association of 0.863 and 0.851 respectively are the capability to internalize new external knowledge and the capability to recognize relevant external knowledge. The lowest association of 0.650 is the capability to exploit new knowledge for innovation. The ability to internalize and recognize relevant external knowledge enhances the capacity to exploit new insights for innovation within the organization, fostering dynamic adaptation and growth. These interconnected capabilities form a symbiotic relationship, facilitating the continuous infusion of fresh perspectives and ideas to drive sustainable innovation and competitive advantage.

Factor grouping 4, business networks, incorporates 3 SME innovation capabilities. Capabilities to create collaborative relationships with a strong association of 0.837, the capability to follow a networking orientation with a strong association of 0.733, and the capability to exploit networks in business with an association of 0.648, describe net-working proficiency and collaborative capabilities. The capabilities to create collaborative relationships complement a networking orientation, fostering a robust ecosystem conducive to leveraging networks for business advancement. These intertwined capabilities enable effective utilization of networks, augmenting opportunities for innovation, resource sharing, and market expansion, ultimately enhancing SME success and competitiveness.

Factor grouping 5, innovation and product enhancement, consists of 2 SME innovation capabilities, both with high loading. Capabilities to exploit innovations developed by others with an association of 0.822 and capabilities to improve existing products and services with an association of 0.729, points to SME capability for innovation absorption and product and service enhancement. These two capabilities foster a dynamic ecosystem of continual improvement and adaptation and enable SMEs to leverage external advancements while refining their internal offerings, enhancing competitiveness, and meeting evolving customer needs.

6   Conclusion

The paper aimed to explore the innovation capabilities of South African SMEs by collecting data from 220 SMEs through an online questionnaire. An analysis of literature on SMEs' innovation capacity identified eight dimensions of innovation capabilities, leading to the identification of nineteen specific capabilities. The significance of these capabilities was examined using a 5-point Likert scale questionnaire, with statistical analysis conducted using SPSS v29.0.0.0, encompassing descriptive analysis, reliability testing with Cronbach's alpha, one-way analysis of variance, and principal component analysis.

The research makes a significant contribution to the understanding of innovation capabilities within South African SMEs. Through systematic analysis via principal component analysis, valuable insights into the multifaceted nature of SME innovation are provided. The identification of five distinct factor groupings - risk management, customer and market acquisition, knowledge management, business networks, and innovation and product enhancement - highlights the comprehensive approach SMEs use to drive innovation and remain competitive in dynamic market environments. SMEs strategically manage risks (Factor Grouping 1) associated with innovation while leveraging their adeptness in customer and market acquisition (Factor Grouping 2) to drive forward-thinking solutions. Additionally, they harness knowledge management practices (Factor Grouping 3) and cultivate strong business networks (Factor Grouping 4) to continuously enhance innovation and product offerings (Factor Grouping 5), positioning themselves as agile and competitive players in their industries.

The results have actionable implications for SMEs seeking to boost innovation practices to sustain long-term growth. By analyzing the interplay of these innovation capabilities, the study offers valuable insights to support SME innovation efforts among policymakers, industry practitioners, and researchers. This emphasizes the crucial role of SMEs in driving innovation-led economic growth and sets the stage for future research and policy interventions to promote a dynamic innovation and entrepreneurship ecosystem. Future research could explore comparative analysis with SMEs from diverse countries to gain insights into the distinctive factors influencing their innovation capabilities. By comparing innovation ecosystems, regulatory frameworks, and resource limitations across various contexts, best practices can be identified and strategies customized to suit the requirements of South African SMEs.

References

1. SMEs need support to thrive. https://www.sun.ac.za/english/Lists/news/Disp Form.aspx?ID=10014#:~:text=They%20contribute%20roughly%2034%20percent,as%20drivers %20for%20reducing%20unemployment.Accessed 20 Feb 2024
2. Supporting digital transformation through South Africa's SMEs. https://blog.google/intl/ en-africa/company-news/supporting-digital-transformation-through-south-africas-smes/#:~: text=In%20South%20Africa%2C%20SMEs%20generate,%2C%20and%2080%25%20of% 20jobs. Accessed 20 Feb 2024
3. Tsatsenko, N.: (2020) SME development, economic growth and structural change: evidence from Ghana and South Africa. Journal of Agriculture and Environment 2(14), https://doi.org/ 10.34190/ecsm.10.1.1055
4. Rajagopaul, A., Magwentshu, N., Kalidas, S.: (2020) How South African SMEs can survive and thrive post COVID-19. Providing the right support to enable SME growth now and beyond the crisis
5. Van Staden, L.J.: The influence of certain factors on South African small and medium-sized enterprises towards export propensity. Dev. South. Afr. **39**, 457–469 (2022)
6. Makwara, T.: Taking on the challenge: small, micro and medium enterprises (SMMEs) and socioeconomic development in South Africa. African J. Hospitality Tourism Leisure **8**, 1–14 (2019)
7. Mogashoa, M.M., Selebi, O.: Innovation capacity: a perspective on innovation capabilities of consulting engineering firms. South. African J. Entrepreneurship Small Bus. Manage. **13**, 372 (2021)
8. Iddris, F.: Innovation capability: A systematic review and research agenda. Interdiscip. J. Inf. Knowl. Manag. **11**, 235–260 (2016)
9. Mendoza-Silva, A.: Innovation capability: a systematic literature review. Eur. J. Innov. Manag. **24**, 707–734 (2021)
10. Alaghbari, M.A.: (2022) Impact of SMEs on economic development: a systematic review of literature. Int. J. Green Manage. Bus. Stud. 1,
11. Yahaya, H.D., Nadarajah, G.: Determining key factors influencing SMEs' performance: a systematic literature review and experts' verification. Cogent Bus. Manage. **10**(3), 2251195 (2023)
12. Gherghina, ȘC., Botezatu, M.A., Hosszu, A., Simionescu, L.N.: Small and medium-sized enterprises (SMEs): the engine of economic growth through investments and innovation. Sustainability **12**, 347 (2020)
13. Saunila, M.: Innovation capability in SMEs: A systematic review of the literature. J. Innov. Knowl. **5**, 260–265 (2020)
14. Apa, R., De Marchi, V., Grandinetti, R., Sedita, S.R.: University-SME collaboration and innovation performance: the role of informal relationships and absorptive capacity. J. Technol. Transf. **46**, 961–988 (2021)

15. Laperche, B., Liu, Z.: SMEs and knowledge-capital formation in innovation networks: a review of literature. J. Innovat. Entrepreneurship **2**, 21 (2013)
16. Adam, N.A., Alarifi, G.: Innovation practices for survival of small and medium enterprises (SMEs) in the COVID-19 times: the role of external support. J. Innovat. Entrepreneurship **10**(1), 15 (2021)
17. Audretsch, D.B., Guenther, C.: SME research: SMEs' internationalization and collaborative innovation as two central topics in the field. J. Bus. Econ. **93**, 1213–1229 (2023)
18. Yu, C.-P., Zhang, Z.-G., Shen, H.: The effect of organizational learning and knowledge management innovation on SMEs' technological capability. Eurasia J. Math. Sci. Technol. Edu. **13**, 5475–5487 (2017)
19. Khraishi, A., Paulraj, A., Huq, F., Seepana, C.: Knowledge management in offshoring innovation by SMEs: role of internal knowledge creation capability, absorptive capacity and formal knowledge-sharing routines. Supply Chain Manage. Int. J. **28**, 405–422 (2023)
20. Miocevic, D., Morgan, R.E.: Operational capabilities and entrepreneurial opportunities in emerging market firms: explaining exporting SME growth. Int. Mark. Rev. **35**, 320–341 (2018)
21. Usman, M., Vanhaverbeke, W., Roijakkers, N.: How open innovation can help entrepreneurs in sensing and seizing entrepreneurial opportunities in SMEs. Int. J. Entrep. Behav. Res. **29**, 2065–2090 (2023)
22. Farjam, F., Shojaei, P., Askarifar, K.: A conceptual model for open innovation risk management based on the capabilities of SMEs: a multi-level fuzzy MADM approach. Technovation **127**, 102844 (2023)
23. Pulka, B.M., Ramli, A.B., Bakar, M.S.: Marketing capabilities, resources acquisition capabilities, risk management capabilities, opportunity recognition capabilities and SMEs performance: a proposed framework. Asian J. Multidiscip. Stud. **6**, 12–22 (2018)
24. Gao, S.S., Sung, M.C., Zhang, J.: Risk management capability building in SMEs: A social capital perspective. Int. Small Bus. J. **31**, 677–700 (2013)
25. Vrontis, D., Basile, G., Andreano, M.S., Mazzitelli, A., Papasolomou, I.: The profile of innovation driven Italian SMEs and the relationship between the firms' networking abilities and dynamic capabilities. J. Bus. Res. **114**, 313–324 (2020)
26. Aggarwal, V.A.: Resource congestion in alliance networks: How a firm's partners' partners influence the benefits of collaboration. Strateg. Manag. J. **41**, 627–655 (2020)
27. Hilmersson, F.P., Hilmersson, M.: Networking to accelerate the pace of SME innovations. J. Innov. Knowl. **6**, 43–49 (2021)
28. Ali, H., Hao, Y., Aijuan, C.: Innovation capabilities and small and medium enterprises' performance: an exploratory study. J. Asian Finance. Econ. Bus. **7**, 959–968 (2020)
29. Hervas-Oliver, J.L., Boronat-Moll, C., Sempere-Ripoll, F.: On process innovation capabilities in SMEs: a taxonomy of process-oriented innovative SMEs. J. Small Bus. Manage. **54**, 113–134 (2016)
30. Hanaysha, J.R., Al-Shaikh, M.E., Joghee, S., Alzoubi, H.M.: Impact of innovation capabilities on business sustainability in small and medium enterprises. FIIB Bus. Rev. **11**, 67–78 (2022)
31. Maes, J., Sels, L.: SMEs' radical product innovation: the role of internally and externally oriented knowledge capabilities. J. Small Bus. Manage. **52**, 141–163 (2014)
32. Rumanti, A.A., Rizana, A.F., Septiningrum, L., Reynaldo, R., Isnaini, M.M.R.: Innovation capability and open innovation for small and medium enterprises (SMEs) performance: response in dealing with the COVID-19 pandemic. Sustainability **14**, 5874 (2022)
33. Branzei, O., Vertinsky, I.: Strategic pathways to product innovation capabilities in SMEs. J. Bus. Ventur. **21**, 75–105 (2006)
34. McAdam, R., Stevenson, P., Armstrong, G.: Innovative change management in SMEs: beyond continuous improvement. Logist. Inf. Manag. **13**, 138–149 (2000)

35. Ates, A., Bititci, U.: Change process: a key enabler for building resilient SMEs. Int. J. Prod. Res. **49**, 5601–5618 (2011)
36. Ali, Z., Sun, H., Ali, M.: The impact of managerial and adaptive capabilities to stimulate organizational innovation in SMEs: a complementary PLS–SEM Approach. Sustainability **9**, 2157 (2017)
37. Abdul-Halim, H., Ahmad, N.H., Geare, A., Thurasamy, R.: (2019) Innovation Culture in SMEs: the Importance of Organizational Culture, Organizational Learning and Market Orientation. Entrepreneurship Res. J. https://doi.org/10.14707/ajbr.190059
38. Audretsch, D.B., Belitski, M., Caiazza, R., Phan, P.: Collaboration strategies and SME innovation performance. J. Bus. Res. **164**, 114018 (2023)
39. Tsai, F.-S., Cabrilo, S., Chou, H.-H., Hu, F., Tang, A.D.: Open innovation and SME performance: the roles of reverse knowledge sharing and stakeholder relationships. J. Bus. Res. **148**, 433–443 (2022)
40. Tang, S., Liao, S., Wang, L., Chen, W., Guo, Z.: A Config
41. urational Analysis of Small and Medium-Sized Enterprises' Radical Innovations: The Perspective of Dynamic Capabilities. Frontiers in Psychology 12, (2022)
42. Oduro, S., Nyarku, K.M.: Incremental innovations in Ghanaian SMEs: propensity, types, performance and management challenges. Asia-Pacific J. Manage. Res. Innovation **14**, 10–21 (2018)
43. Moring, B.: Research methods in psychology: Evaluating a world of information. WW Norton & Company (2014)
44. Yaraghi, N., Langhe, R.G.: Critical success factors for risk management systems. J. Risk Res. **14**, 551–581 (2011)
45. Williams, B., Onsman, A., Brown, T.: Exploratory factor analysis: A five-step guide for novices. Australasian J. Paramed. **8**, 1–13 (2010)
46. Zhao, X., Hwang, B.-G., Low, S.P.: Critical success factors for enterprise risk management in Chinese construction companies. Constr. Manag. Econ. **31**, 1199–1214 (2013)
47. Akhtar-Danesh, N.: A comparison between major factor extraction and factor rotation techniques in Q-methodology. Open J. Appl. Sci. **7**, 147–156 (2017)

Predictors of Workplace Satisfaction: Working Onsite Versus Working from Home

Xinhua Wittmann[1,2](✉) and Daria Klyushina[1](✉)

[1] School of Business, University of Applied Sciences and Arts, Northwestern Switzerland, Windisch, Switzerland
xinhua.wittmann@fhnw.ch, dklyushina@gmx.net
[2] Faculty of Economics, Business Administration, and Informatics, University of Zürich, Zürich, Switzerland

Abstract. The Covid-19 pandemic has not only taught us about viral infections, but also provided employers with unique opportunities to experiment with different work modes. What leads employees to be more satisfied: working onsite or working from home? The aim of this paper is to elucidate how the work environment impacts workplace satisfaction. In the framework of Herzberg's motivation theory, we define the physical, digital, and social environment as the most important hygiene factors. In our study, we investigate the relationship between these hygiene factors and workplace satisfaction. Based on the survey data from office workers in Switzerland, we identify the predictors of workplace satisfaction for working onsite and working from home respectively. Our statistical analysis shows that the three hygiene factors have a significant positive impact on workplace satisfaction both for working onsite and working from home. Specifically, the workplace design in the context of the physical environment stands out to have the strongest effect on the workplace satisfaction for onsite work. In contrast, for working from home, the software availability in the context of the digital environment exerts the greatest influence on workplace satisfaction. Thus, workplace satisfaction can be maximized by targeted optimization of specific aspects of the work environment depending on the work mode.

Keywords: Workplace satisfaction · Working onsite · Working from home · Workplace environment · Hygiene factors · Physical environment · Social environment · Digital environment

1 Introduction

Knowledge and human capital are the most important assets of any organization. Thus, attracting and retaining employees are a central concern for organizations [1, 2]. Flowers and Hughes [2] have identified that employee retention and turnover are related to two factors: employees' job satisfaction and workplace environment. Another study conducted by Cotton and Hart [3] found that employee turnover has a strong correlation with employees' well-being. This finding is particularly applicable to office workers as they spend a high percentage of time in their workplace environment, which has a

© The Author(s), under exclusive license to Springer Nature Switzerland AG 2025
K. Hinkelmann and H. Smuts (Eds.): Society 5.0 2024, CCIS 2173, pp. 391–402, 2025.
https://doi.org/10.1007/978-3-031-71412-2_29

significant impact on their well-being [4]. Previous research has found that a focus on employees' satisfaction and well-being in the workplace can influence their behaviour and therefore increase their create thinking, engagement, and productivity [5, 6]. Other studies found there is a strong influence of well-being on employee performance [7].

Since the publication of Herzberg's motivation-hygiene theory, numerous studies have identified different motivators that can lead to job satisfaction and well-being of employees. While organizations have become more knowledgeable about what motivates employees to work more effectively and efficiently, the relevance of hygiene factors such as working conditions and environments are often overlooked [8]. As the Covid-19 pandemic has largely affected daily life and work across the globe, how to enable employees to work from remote effectively has played a crucial role in the continuity of businesses. After the lifting restrictions on social distance, remote work mode in the form of working from home continues in the practice to varying extents as people expect to return to a different workplace [5]. According to recent studies, work mode is increasingly hybrid. A combination of working onsite and from home is creating completely different workplace experiences [9]. Consequently, organizations need to close the gap between working onsite and from home while providing employees with necessary working conditions and surroundings. Adapting to different workspaces while meeting employees' expectations and needs presents employers with new challenges [10]. This implies employers must consider various factors that contribute to the satisfaction and well-being of employees onsite as well as working from home [5]. Only then can the gap between onsite and remote work be managed [11]. Hitherto two questions unexplored in the literature are how the workplace environment influences employees' satisfaction and well-being, and what the differences of these relationships are in the context of working onsite versus from home.

The present paper tries to answer these two questions by means of developing two research models, namely workplace environment model and workplace satisfaction model. The correlations between workplace satisfaction and workplace environment underlined in our research model are illustrated on the basis of statistical analysis of empirical data. We conclude our research results by providing predictors of workplace satisfaction for working onsite and from home in the context of workplace environment and suggesting avenues for future research.

In the following sections we first review relevant literature and theories, and then introduce our research models and hypotheses followed with the presentation of empirical study and results. In the last section, we discuss the research findings and make some concluding remarks.

2   Theories and research models

2.1   Literature review

Two-factor motivational theory. Herzberg, et al. [12] developed the two-factor motivational model, which explains the variables that affect motivation in the workplace. Motivational factors aim to lead job satisfaction on a long-term basis, while hygiene factors, when positively expressed, prevent the development of dissatisfaction. Hence, if the hygiene factors are missing, employee satisfaction decreases. Hygiene factors are unrelated to the employment but to the work environment where the job is conducted, including interpersonal relations (employees and supervisors), safety and security, physical work conditions, and physical comfort [8]. Often, these factors are taken for granted by employers as most companies focus on motivational factors such as recognition or achievement. However, employees' expectations have changed. This has become very clear during the Covid-19 pandemic when office workers are forced to complete their jobs from remote, mostly in home-office. The hygiene factors, therefore, are increasing in importance [13].

Workplace environment. The workplace is a combination of different elements and is often regarded as the employees' surroundings when working. While several research papers have only focused on the physical environment [6], Srivastava [14] has defined the workplace as the "… physical and psychosocial work environment." According to Becker [15], the workplace can be seen as a combination of organizational and social factors. Joroff [16] has also referred to digital technologies that allow employees to change and redesign the workplace, opening new possibilities in terms of flexible working independent of the location.

Recent studies and literature have increasingly paid attention to workplace experience in the working environment. According to Gensler's research [5] on workplace experience, four main aspects were identified that could influence employees' effectiveness and engagement: space, which includes office functionality and aesthetics; culture, which comprises inspiration, creativity, and innovation; interaction, social connection, and technology; and behaviour, which consists of work modes and reflection.

Remote workplace environment. Several studies have shown that employees' productivity improved when working from home-office. Furthermore, remote work has enabled employees to be more flexible and efficient [17]. Despite these advantages, there are also several disadvantages to the physical environment at home. For instance, it is often difficult to separate work and private life, which negatively influences work-life balance [18], and distractions from children, family, or roommates can be a challenge [19]. Some workers also do not have an adequate workplace or necessary equipment available at home [9]. Hence, factors such as access to amenities and the possibility to focus entirely on work play an essential role in employee satisfaction for working from home [5], especially when remote workplaces are not designed for daily work like onsite offices [20].

In addition, remote workers may feel isolated and lonely due to a lack of social interaction. Research from three organizations—Deloitte, BCG and McKinsey [17, 21, 22] has found that a lot of the respondents cited the deficit of personal interaction with coworkers as one of the biggest disadvantages of working from home. Indeed, Gensler [5] argued the main reasons for employees to return to the office as the personal interaction with colleagues, the possibility of arranging meetings, face-to-face contact, and a sense of belonging as part of the team and community. Moreover, almost one-third of employees surveyed stated that their overall mental well-being and health were at risk as they often felt isolated in their home office [17, 21, 22].

A survey on workers' mental health conducted during lockdown found that employees struggled with negative emotions, lack of concentration, and lack of motivation [23]. Confronted with these new phenomena, improving social connectivity is one of the greatest challenges for organizations. The focal tasks should therefore be managing relationships and social cohesion, thereby promoting team spirit and a positive work atmosphere through team-building and other online activities [21].

2.2 Workplace Environment Model

Our literature review reviled the big gap in research and thus our understanding on how the hygiene factors for working onsite and from home differentiate and how relevant of each hygiene factor in terms of workplace environment to the satisfaction of employees. With the research framework illustrated in Fig. 1, we focus our research on the three hygiene factors in the workplace environment.

Fig. 1. Three-factor model of workplace environment (authors' conceptual model)

Physical environment. The physical environment relates to the physiological and safety requirements in Herzberg's' hygiene factors which involves different elements such as workspace design, equipment, and furniture as well as sensory inputs and amenities [24, 25]. Several studies have confirmed the influence of physical workplace environment on employees' satisfaction and well-being [26, 27].

Social environment. The social environment includes all human relations in the workplace, hence the interpersonal relationships between work colleagues and the general atmosphere of the workplace [28]. A study by Daniels et al. [29] has found that the social environment at work is influenced by shared activities, which leads to higher satisfaction and performance. Team-building activities create a bond between employees and thus also create a positive work environment and atmosphere, which helps to increase well-being and improve productivity [5, 30].

Digital environment. The digital workplace environment can be defined as an IT infrastructure that can be seen or experienced by the user. It is regarded as part of the organizational and procedural structure of a company that enables employees to conduct their work [31]. Schönefeld [32] has also defined the environment as a combination of platforms, applications, and devices needed for daily work in the office. According to Vuolle [33], the digital environment includes information and communication technologies needed for interaction with colleagues.

Different studies have confirmed that digitalization and technologies improve and increase employees' job satisfaction [34]. However, some researchers have also mentioned that technology can also have a negative effect on employees, especially when their control over technology is reduced or a digitalization process is too complex. Consequently, this effect has a negative influence on well-being [35].

Workplace satisfaction. According to Herzberg's theory, hygiene factors do not lead to positive satisfaction and higher motivation, though dissatisfaction results from their absence. Critics of this theory argued that hygiene factors can also have an influence on employees' satisfaction [36]. Because the relevance of hygiene factors is increasing [13], and the work conditions are linked to the workplace environment in companies, hygiene factors have a significant influence on employees' satisfaction and well-being [37]. In this study, we assume that hygiene factors have a direct impact on employee satisfaction and well-being.

Since our research is workplace environment focus, based on the Satisfaction With Life Scale (SWLS) definition [38], we adapt the measurement of SWLS to the workplace environment. This implies that, instead of overall life or job satisfaction, employees' perceptions of workplace satisfaction and well-being are examined [39].

2.3 Workplace Satisfaction Model and Research Hypotheses

Considering the theories and previous research discussed in the sections above, we construct the workplace satisfaction model, see Fig. 2, to underline the relationships to be investigated. Our research spans two time slots: before Covid-19 and during Covid-19; and two work environments: working onsite and working from home. In this model, the physical environment is divided into two aspects: the Equipment, particularly concerning its comfort and ergonomics, and the workplace design, which includes the space and its structure, including sensory inputs. The social environment includes interpersonal relationships and the offered/promoted team activities. The third variable is the digital environment which consists of software availability, such as digital tools and programs, as well as IT-support. To distinguish the independent variables in the two work environments, we denote 1 for the onsite work environment and 2 for the workfrom-home environment.

To examine the correlations established in the workplace satisfaction model shown in Fig. 2, we further develop four hypotheses about the effect of the three workplace environment factors, i.e. physical, social and digital environment in the workplace for working onsite and working from home respectively. The hypothetical statements for onsite work environment are presented Table 1 and for work-from-home environment in Table 2.

3 Empirical study and results

3.1 Descriptive analysis

To test our hypotheses related to the workplace environment for working onsite and working from home, we designed a questionnaire and conducted an online survey between end of March and middle of April 2021 to the employees residing in Switzerland. who need to be physically present onsite in normal times. After eliminating the invalid responses, we got a total of 112 valid samples. Of the 112 participants, 70 were male,

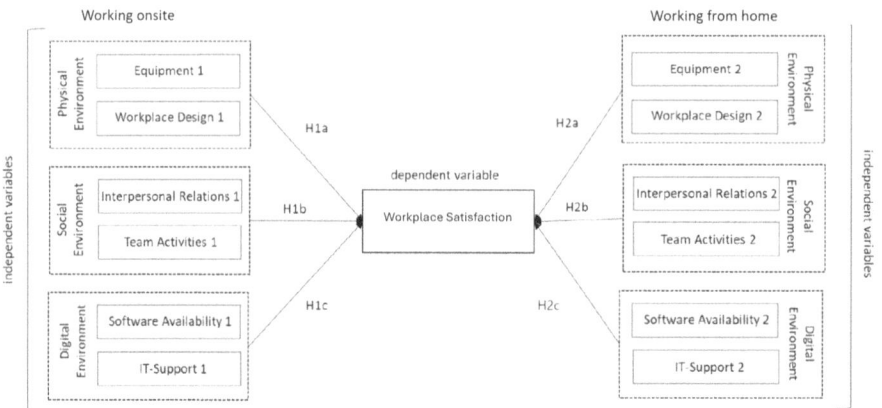

Fig. 2. Workplace satisfaction model (authors' research framework)

Table 1. Hypotheses on working onsite.

Symbol	Hypothesis statement on working onsite
H1	The onsite workplace environment has a significant influence on the workplace satisfaction
H1a	The two factors of physical environment in onsite workspace have a positive influence on the workplace satisfaction.
H1b	The two factors of social environment in onsite workspace have a positive influence on the workplace satisfaction
H1c	The two factors of digital environment in onsite workspace have a positive influence on the workplace satisfaction

Table 2. Hypotheses on working from home.

Symbol	Hypothesis statement on working from home
H2	The workplace environment at home has a significant influence on the workplace satisfaction
H2a	The two factors of physical environment in home workspace have a positive influence on the workplace satisfaction
H2b	The two factors of social environment in home workspace have a positive influence on the workplace satisfaction
H2c	The two factors of digital environment in home workspace have a positive influence on the workplace satisfaction

42.9% are employees in the banking sector, 28.6% in the insurance sector, and the rest respondents work in real estate, investments, or pension sectors. The dependent variable, namely workplace satisfaction is constructed based on three questions adapted from the model of Diener, et al. [40]. Informants were invited to rate their experiences with respect to work environment onsite before Covid-19 and from home during Covid-19 lockdown period in 7-likert-scale from 1 = strongly agree 1 to 7 = strongly disagree.

To ensure the consistency and reliability of our dataset, prior to examining the correlations and testing the hypotheses, we checked the normal distribution and the Cronbach's alpha of the variables. In addition, a factor analysis was conducted. Finally, multicollinearity was tested using Pearson's correlation.

3.2 Statistical Evaluation Results

To understand the influence of the independent variables on the dependent variables, a multiple regression analysis was performed. The stepwise forward method is used to confirm or reject the hypotheses stated Table 1 and 2. In the first step of regression analysis, only demographic factors as control variables (gender and age) are entered into calculation, while in step 2, the workplace environment factors are considered. For both work modes, gender and age do not show any significant influence on workplace satisfaction, therefore only the six workplace environment factors as independent variables are calculated by using the formular as shown in Question (1). We use the software SPSS 26 for the multiple linear regression analyses. The results of multiple regression analysis are shown in Fig. 3.

$$Workplace\ Satisfaction = \alpha + \beta_1\ Equipment + \beta_2\ WorkplaceDesign$$
$$+ \beta_3\ InterpersonRel. + \beta_4\ TeamAct. + \beta_5\ Software + \beta_6\ IT\text{-}Support \qquad (1)$$

Fig. 3. Multiple independent variables as predictors of workplace satisfaction

4 Discussion and conclusions

4.1 Predictors of workplace satisfaction for working onsite

To identify how hygiene factors in the context of workplace environment impact on workplace satisfaction, we test our hypotheses based on the workplace satisfaction model. For work mode onsite, multiple regression results reveal Equipment 1, Workplace Design 1, Interpersonal Relations 1, Team Activities 1, and Software Availability 1 have direct influence on the Workplace Satisfaction of the employees. This implies that Hypotheses H1, H1a, and H1b are fully supported while H1c is only partially confirmed because IT Support has no significant effect. From β-value and adjusted R^2 shown in Table 3, we can conclude that equipment, workplace design and interpersonal are the most important variables to workplace satisfaction. With $\beta = 0.289$ and $R^2 = 0.306$, which explains 30.6% of the variances, Equipment 1 has the strongest impact on workplace satisfaction. A plausible explanation for this result is that equipment plays an important role in the workplace onsite and has a strong positive effect if it meets the requirements of the employees. Hence, the satisfaction can be attributed to a good overall comfort and ergonomics of the workplace equipment as described in the literature [25].

Table 3. Predictors of workplace satisfaction for working onsite.

Independent Variable	Mean	β	Adj. R^2
Equipment 1	2.23	0.289***	0.306
Workplace Design 1	2.54	0.272***	0.187
Interpersonal Relations 1	2.30	0.246**	0.170
Team activities 1	3.21	0.189**	0.031
Software Availability 1	2.98	0.245***	0.041

4.2 Predictors of workplace satisfaction for working from home

In the case of work-from-home, multiple regression results show Workplace Design 2, Interpersonal Relations 2 and Software Availability 3 to have significant influence on workplace satisfaction, see Table 4. Equipment 2, Team Activities 2 and IT support 2 do not show significant influence on workplace satisfaction in home workspace, thus Hypotheses H2, H2a, H2b, and H2c are partially accepted. We notice Software Availability 2 with a β-value of 0.585 and $R^2 = 0.292$ demonstrates the strongest impact on workplace satisfaction. This finding is congruent with the study by Blok et al. [41], which identified that availability and good remote access to corporate networks have a positive effect on satisfaction with the digital environment.

4.3 Comparison of workplace environments onsite and at home

To verify how employees perceived workplace satisfaction with respect to the six factors of workplace environment for working onsite versus from home have changed, we

Table 4. Predictors of workplace satisfaction for working from home.

Independent Variable	Mean	β	Adj. R^2
Equipment 2	3.15	0.199**	0.180
Interpersonal Relations 2	3.69	0.173*	0.079
Software Availability 2	2.88	0.585***	0.292

perform t-Test by using the same data set. The measurement scale is 7-likert-scale from 1 = very satisfied to 7 = very dissatisfied. The paired t-Test exams whether the means of the dependent variables are significantly different. From Table 5 we observe that employee satisfaction decreases the most due to Interpersonal Relations, Team Activities, and Equipment. The explanation for the strong decrease (r = 0.67) in Interpersonal Relations 2 is that social contact for working from home is largely prevented, which is confirmed by the studies conducted by McKinsey, BCG, and Deloitte. Employees decried the lack of personal interaction with coworkers as they often felt isolated in their home office.

Table 5. Comparison of workplace satisfaction with workplace environment factors between working onsite and working from home*.

Independent Variable	M1	M2	T	df	r
Equipment	2.23	3.15	6.125***	111	0.50
Workplace Design	2.54	2.09	2.39*	111	0.22
Interpersonal Relations	2.30	3.69	9.501***	111	0.67
Team activities	3.21	4.34	7.304***	111	0.57
Software Availability	2.98	2.88	0.915	111	0.08
IT-Support	3.02	3.16	1.437	111	0.14

* M1 = mean value for workplace onsite; M2 = mean value for workplace at home

4.4 Concluding Remarks

Since the world experienced Covid-19 pandemic, our workplace has become more diverse. The most frequent work mode is either onsite where employees conduct daily businesses in the work environment created by the employers, or remote workplace, typically work-from-home, or a combination of both. The purpose of this paper is to investigate the relationships between workplace satisfaction and hygiene factors with respect to working conditions and environment in the context of working onsite and working from home. We analyse how the three aspects of the workplace environment, namely physical environment, social environment, and digital environment influence employees' satisfaction with workplace environment. By comparing the relative weight of each workplace environment factor in their respective workplace, we are able to identify what leads to employees' workplace satisfaction.

In the case of working onsite, Equipment, Workplace Design, Interpersonal Relations, Team Activities and Software Availability have direct influence on employees' satisfaction with the workplace. When working from home, Workplace Design and Team Activities are no longer relevant, instead Interpersonal Relations, and Software Availability become more important. It is worth noting that IT-Support for working onsite as well as work-from-home does not show any significant impact on workplace satisfaction. It is probably because professional IT-Support in most organizations has become routine and the advancement in IT technologies plays a critical role in ensuring the continuity of businesses independent of the workplace.

From theoretical perspectives, our research proves workplace environment factors, which are within the category of hygiene factors defined by Herzberg, do have significant direct influence on satisfaction. Additionally, our research findings have important practical implications in terms of indications of which workplace environment factors are more relevant for various work modes. Due to the quantitative limitations of our samples and our informants are from Switzerland where infrastructure and IT equipment are on an advanced level, the effects of the hygiene factors may not be applicable widely. We anticipate the correlations will turn out to be very different when hygiene factors together with motivators are taken into consideration simultaneously.

References

1. Memon, M.A., Mangi, R.A., Rohra, C.L.: Human capital a source of competitive advantage "ideas for strategic leadership." Aust. J. Basic Appl. Sci. 3(4), 4182–4189 (2009)
2. Flowers, V. S., Hughes, C. L.: Why employees stay. Competitive strategy. https://hbr.org/1973/07/why-employees-stay (1973)
3. Cotton, P., Hart, P.M.: Occupational wellbeing and performance a review of organisational health research. Aust. Psychol. 38(1), 118–127 (2003)
4. Hafeez, I., Yingjun, Z., Hafeez, S., MansoorKhaliq, R., Rehman, U.: Impact of workplace environment on employee performance: mediating role of employee health. Bus. Manage. Edu. (2019). https://doi.org/10.3846/bme.2019.10379
5. Gensler: U.S. Workplace survey 2019. Gensler Research Institute. https://www.gensler.com/uploads/document/614/file/Gensler-US-Workplace-Survey2019.pdf (2019)
6. Kamarulzaman, N., Saleh, A.A., Hashim, S.Z., Hashim, H., Abdul-Ghani, A.A.: An overview of the influence of physical office environments towards employee. Procedia Eng. 20(1), 262–268 (2011). https://doi.org/10.1016/j.proeng.2011.11.164
7. Haddon, J.: The impact of employees' well-being on performance in the workplace. Strateg. HR Rev. 17(2), 72–75 (2018). https://doi.org/10.1108/SHR-01-2018-0009
8. Herzberg, F.I.: Work and the Nature of Man. World Pub. Co., Cleveland, USA (1966)
9. Lund, S., Madgavkar, A., Manyika, J., Smit, S.: What's next for remote work: An analysis of 2,000 tasks, 800 jobs, and nine countries. https://www.mckinsey.com/featured-insights/future-of-work/whats-next-for-remote-work-an-analysis-of-2000-jobs-800-jobs-and-nine-Countries (2020)
10. Jarvis, J.: Remote vs. home working – do you know the difference? https://www.twinfm.com/article/remote-vs-home-working-do-you-know-the-difference (2020)

11. Wiles, J.: HR's role in the organization's return-to-workplace debate is to advocate for health and safety while deciding when and who to return, and what the experience will be like. https://www.gartner.com/smarterwithgartner/return-to-workplace-guide-for-hr-leaders/ (2020)

12. Herzberg, F., Mausner, B., Snyderman, B.: The Motivation to Work, 2nd edn. John Wiley, New York, USA (1959)

13. Bhavya, S.N.R., Satyavathi, R.: Employee job satisfaction. Int. J. Eng. Manag. Res. **7**(5), 85–94 (2017)

14. Srivastava, A.K.: Effect of perceived work environment on employees' job behaviour and organizational effectiveness. J. Indian Acad. Appl. Psychol. **34**(1), 47–55 (2008)

15. Becker, F.: Improving organisational performance by exploiting workplace flexibility. J. Facil. Manage. **1**(2), 154–162 (2002)

16. Joroff, M.: Workplace mind shifts. J Corporate Real Estate **4**(3), 266–274 (2002). https://doi.org/10.1108/14630010210811886

17. Melian, V., Zebib, A.: How Covid-19 contributes to a long-term boost in remote working. https://www2.deloitte.com/ch/en/pages/human-capital/articles/howcovid-19-contributes-to-a-long-term-boost-in-remote-working.html (2020)

18. Naughton, J.: Working from home was the dream but is it turning into a nightmare? https://www.theguardian.com/commentisfree/2020/aug/15/working-fromhome-was-the-dream-but-is-it-turning-into-a-nightmare (2020)

19. Prossack, A.: 6 Easy Ways to overcome work from home distractions. https://www.forbes.com/sites/ashiraprossack1/2020/04/29/overcome-work-from-home-distractions-with-these-easy-tips/?sh=6329dc504626 (2020)

20. Gaskell, A.: How to design the best workplace (even when it's at home). https://www.forbes.com/sites/adigaskell/2020/03/12/designing-the-best-workplaceeven-when-its-at-home/?sh=2a699c4d50b7 (2020)

21. Bailey, C., Dahik, A., Kennedy, D., Lovich, D., Kreafle, A., Kilmann, J., Roongta, P., Schuler, F., Tomlin, L., Wenstrup, J.: What 12,000 employees have to say about the future of remote Work. https://www.bcg.com/publications/2020/valuableproductivity-gains-covid-19 (2020)

22. Emmett, J., Schrah, G., Schrimper, M., Wood, A. COVID-19 and the employee experience: How leaders can seize the moment. https://www.mckinsey.com/business-functions/organization/our-insights/covid-19-and-the-employee-experience-howleaders-can-seize-the-moment (2020)

23. Meister, J.: Employee experience is more important than ever during the Covid-19 pandemic. Forbes. https://www.forbes.com/sites/jeannemeister/2020/06/08/employee-experience-is-more-important-than-ever-during-the-covid-19pandemic/?sh=5c1fe05034bc(2020)

24. Babak, G., Ebrahim, A., Lila, A.: The effect of empowerment, employee's working environment and perceived organizational support on loyalty and citizenship behaviour of employees (case study: social security organization of Khuzestan Province). Int. Bus. Manage. **10**(5), 6593–6600 (2016)

25. Anderson, J., French, M.: Sustainability as promoting well-being: psychological dimensions of thermal comfort. https://www.irbnet.de/daten/iconda/CIB20934.pdf (2010)

26. Parvin, M.M., Kabir, M.M.: Factors affecting employee job satisfaction of pharmaceutical sector. Aust. J. Bus. Manag. Res. **1**(1), 113–123 (2011)

27. Raziq, A., Maulabakhsh, R.: Impact of working environment on job satisfaction. Procedia Econ. Finan. **1**(23), 717–725 (2015)

28. Bosch-Sijtsema, P., Ruohomäki, V., Vartiainen, M.: Knowledge work productivity in distributed teams. J. Knowl. Manage. **13**(6), 533–546 (2009). https://doi.org/10.1108/13673270910997178

29. Daniels, K., Watson, D., Gedikli, C.: Well-Being and the Social Environment of Work: a systematic review of intervention studies. Int. J. Environ. Res. Public Health (2017). https://doi.org/10.3390/ijerph14080918

30. Scudamore, B.: Why team building is the most important investment you'll make. Forbes. https://www.forbes.com/sites/brianscudamore/2016/03/09/whyteam-building-is-the-most-important-investment-youll-make/?sh=3a7e59a7617f (2016)

31. Schmidt, C. F., Präg, C. P., Guenther, J.: (2018). Designing digital workplace environments. In: Conference: 2018 IEEE International Conference on Engineering, Technology and Innovation, Stuttgart, Germany https://doi.org/10.1109/ICE.2018.8436349

32. Schönefeld, F.: Social intranet —The new role of the intranet for the digital workplace. In: F. Wolf (Eds.), Social Intranet —Promoting Communication —Sharing Knowledge — Working Together Efficiently (pp. 14–40). München, Germany: Carl Hanser Verlag (2011)

33. Vuolle, M.: Productivity impacts of mobile office service. Int. J. Serv. Technol. Manage. **14**(4), 326–334 (2010)

34. Cijan, A., Jenič, L., Lamovšek, A., Stemberger, J.: How digitalization changes the workplace. Dyn. Relat. Manage. J. (1), 1 https://pdfs.semanticscholar.org/458b/f4371ab9c6a3eca4f3620 844e014a94537cd.pdf (2019)

35. Kraan, K.O., Dhondt, S., Houtman, I.L.D., Batenburg, R.S., Kompier, M.A.J., Taris, T.W.: Computers and types of control in relation to work stress and learning. Behav. Inf. Technol. **33**(10), 1013–1026 (2014). https://doi.org/10.1080/0144929X.2014.916351

36. Tomo, A., Simone, S.: Exploring factors that affect the well-being of healthcare workers. Int. J. Bus. Manage **12**(6), 49–61 (2017). https://doi.org/10.5539/ijbm.v12n6p49

37. Batenburg, R., Van der Voordt, D. J. M.: Do facilities matter? Effects of facility satisfaction on perceived productivity. European Facility Management Conference, Manchester, United Kingdom. https://www.cfpb.nl/media/uploads/publicaties/upload/Voordt_Batenburg_full_paper_Do_Facilities_matter_080326.pdf (2008)

38. Diener, E., Oishi, S., Tay, L.: Handbook of Well-being. Salt Lake City: DEF Publishers (2018). nobascholar.com. ISBN: http://www.nobascholar.com/books/1

39. Chandrasekar, K.: Workplace environment and its impact on organisational performance in public sector organizations. Int. J. Enterp. Comput. Bus. Syst. 1(1), 1–20 (2011). http://www.ijecbs.com/January2011/N4Jan2011.pdf

40. Diener, E., Emmons, R.A., Larsen, R.J., Griffin, S.: The satisfaction with life scale. J. Pers. Assess. **49**(1), 71–75 (1985)

41. Blok, M., Groenesteijn, L., Schelvis, R., Vink, P.: New ways of working: does flexibility in time and location of work change work behavior and effect business outcomes? IOS Press **41**(1), 5075–5080 (2012). https://doi.org/10.3233/WOR-2012-1028-2605

Author Index

A

Adebesin, Funmi   1, 14
Antulay, Nawaaz   14
Asprion, Petra Maria   293

B

Barjak, Franz   25
Bhundhoo, Sanjayduth   41
Bindah, Eric   173
Binswanger, Mathias   57
Bokhoree, Chandradeo   334
Boolaky, Aleesha   282, 378

C

Chittoo, Hemant B.   320
Chittoo, Hemant   282, 378
Coetzer, Adriaan   68
Coolen, Preeya Vijayalakshmee   41

D

Dall'Agnolo, Miriam Mei Yi   84

E

Emambocus, Nousrat Banu   173
Eybers, Sunet   98, 366

F

Fernando, Michael   334
Fouché, Rouxan Colin   111
Fraser, Roslyn S.   41
Frey, Alice   242
Fulena, Viraj   123

G

Geerawo, Thakoor Sharma   136
Goeldi, Susan   152
Grieder, Hermann   293
Gunnoo, Leenshya   173

H

Hadayah, Adrian   293
Hattingh, Marié   68
Heimsch, Fabian   25
Heitz, Luc Bryan   293

J

Jüngling, Stephan   84

K

Kantamaneni, Komali   334
Klyushina, Daria   391
Kodye-Domah, Dayalutchmee   187
Kroeze, Jan H.   98
Kruger, Sean   207

L

Langerman, Josef   254
Laurenzi, Emanuele   218
Lukea-Bhiwajee, Soolakshna Desai   187

M

Machikape, Keoitshepile   229
Mahadew, Bhavna   136
Mauree-Narrainen, Diroubinee   282, 378
Mawela, Tendani   269
Meyer, Dario   218, 242
Meyer, Rolf   242
Mhlanga, Sandile Thamie   254
Moesch, Patrick   218
Msweli, Nkosikhona Theoren   269

N

Nel, Wynand   111

O

Oluwadele, Deborah   1, 229

© The Editor(s) (if applicable) and The Author(s), under exclusive license
to Springer Nature Switzerland AG 2025
K. Hinkelmann and H. Smuts (Eds.): Society 5.0 2024, CCIS 2173, pp. 403–404, 2025.
https://doi.org/10.1007/978-3-031-71412-2

P
Padachi, Kesseven   282, 378
Panchoo, Shireen   68
Petratos, Sue   348
Pottas, Dalenca   348

R
Ramphul, Needesh   282, 320, 378
Rathnayake, Upaka   334

S
Scherb, Christopher   293
Scholtz, Iddo-Imri   305
Sewdin, Trisheeta   320
Smuts, Hanlie   84, 305, 378

Sobha, Leena Devi   187
Sunkur, Reshma   334

T
Thees, Oscar   152

V
van der Westhuizen, Eldridge   348
van Staden, Corne J.   98

W
Walaza, Mvelo   366
Weilbach, Lizette   68, 282, 378
Wittmann, Xinhua   391

SPRINGER NATURE

GPSR Compliance

The European Union's (EU) General Product Safety Regulation (GPSR) is a set of rules that requires consumer products to be safe and our obligations to ensure this.

If you have any concerns about our products, you can contact us on ProductSafety@springernature.com

In case Publisher is established outside the EU, the EU authorized representative is:

Springer Nature Customer Service Center GmbH
Europaplatz 3
69115 Heidelberg, Germany

The manufacturer's authorised representative in the EU is Springer
Nature Customer Service Centre GmbH, Europaplatz 3, 69115 Heidelberg,
Germany. If you have any concerns regarding our products, please
contact ProductSafety@springernature.com

Printed and bound by CPI Group (UK) Ltd, Croydon, CR0 4YY
29/04/2026
02099541-0003